Also by Jim Loewen

Lies Across America: What Our Historic Sites Get Wrong

Lies My Teacher Told Me:
Everything Your American History Textbook Got Wrong

The Mississippi Chinese: Between Black and White

Mississippi: Conflict and Change (with Charles Sallis, et al.)

Social Science in the Courtroom

The Truth About Columbus:
A Subversively True Poster Book for a Dubiously Celebratory Occasion

Sundown Towns

A Hidden Dimension of American Racism

James W. Loewen

THE
NEW
PRESS

NEW YORK
LONDON

© 2005, 2018 by James W. Loewen
Preface © 2018 by James W. Loewen
All rights reserved.
No part of this book may be reproduced, in any form, without written permission from
the publisher.

Requests for permission to reproduce selections from this book should be mailed to:
Permissions Department, The New Press, 120 Wall Street, 31st floor, New York, NY 10005.

Originally published in the United States by The New Press, New York, 2005
This edition published in the United States by The New Press, New York, 2018
Distributed by Two Rivers Distribution

ISBN 978-1-62097-468-1 (hc)
ISBN 978-1-62097-434-6 (pb)
ISBN 978-1-62097-454-4 (ebook)
CIP data is available

The New Press publishes books that promote and enrich public discussion and understanding
of the issues vital to our democracy and to a more equitable world. These books are made
possible by the enthusiasm of our readers; the support of a committed group of donors,
large and small; the collaboration of our many partners in the independent media and the
not-for-profit sector; booksellers, who often hand-sell New Press books; librarians; and above
all by our authors.

www.thenewpress.com

Printed in the United States of America

10 9 8 7 6

Contents

Preface to the 2018 Edition

For decades, sundown towns kept out African Americans. Some excluded other groups, such as Mexican Americans, Native Americans, or Asian Americans, Jews, even Catholics and Mormons. These places get called "sundown towns" because some, in past decades, placed signs at their city limits typically saying some version of "Nigger, Don't Let the Sun Go Down on You in [name of town]."

In 1999, when I started serious research on these communities, I expected to find perhaps ten in Illinois, my home state, and maybe fifty across the country. I had no idea how widespread the practice was. Neither did anyone else I talked with.

Today my estimate for the number of sundown towns in Illinois alone stands at 507. That is two-thirds of all the towns in the state! A similar proportion went sundown in Oregon, Indiana, and various other northern states.

This book, *Sundown Towns,* first came out in 2005. Since then, I have maintained an active research interest in the topic, including establishing a website with a map and database of all the sundown towns I have been able to document.[1] This new introduction reports on how sundown towns have changed in the years since the book first came out, describes what I call "second-generation sundown town issues," responds to criticisms of the book I've received, and suggests things readers can do to ameliorate the issues the book depicts.

Sundown Towns Are Declining

Sundown towns are now on the decline. Censuses since 1990 show that many towns in the East, Midwest, and Appalachia, and almost all in California and the Pacific Northwest, have given up their policies of exclusion.[2] (There never were many sundown towns in the classic South.) So we as a nation are slowly moving beyond this scourge.

One reason for the decline in sundown towns is a change in white ideology. A leading citizen of Carthage, a town in western Illinois, illustrated this change in 2001. I asked him if Carthage still kept out African Americans. "You can't do that so easily, nowadays," he replied. If enough people believe that, then it becomes true, a self-fulfilling prophecy. Conversely, if most whites felt they *could* still keep blacks out, it's possible that they would find a way. As attitudes have changed, however, fewer whites now think they *should* keep blacks out.[3]

America's increasingly multiracial makeup also undermines the exclusionary policies of sundown towns. This first happened on the West Coast. Towns that had kept out Mexican Americans and Asian Americans as well as African Americans relaxed their prohibitions against the first two groups early in the 1960s. A decade later, this led to a new openness to African Americans too, as Caucasians saw their world had not come to an end as a result of having Asian and Hispanic neighbors. In addition, the new Asian and Mexican residents were not as racist as whites and didn't endorse the exclusionary policies. Ten years later, this multiracial dynamic reached the Midwest. As of 1980, white residents of Cicero, for example, a suburb at the western edge of Chicago, were still adamant in their refusal to admit black families, but they were not so sure about Hispanics. Hispanics might be white, after all. So Hispanics moved in, and by 1990, 25,000 lived in Cicero, alongside 50,000 whites. In that year, almost 1,000 African Americans also lived in Cicero.

Sometimes the progress is appallingly slow. Pekin, a city of 33,000 in central Illinois, was the Ku Klux Klan capital of Illinois during the 1920s, the Klan's heyday. As late as 1970, not one African American lived in Pekin. In the words of a former resident, "There was a sign on the south side of Pekin, I used to drive by it every day, which read, 'Don't let the sun set on your black ass in Pekin, Illinois.'" Such signs still appeared sporadically during the 1970s. Even by 2000, Pekin had just five households with a black householder (the five households together had a total population of only sixteen, some of whom may have been white). So Pekin was still a sundown town. By 2010, Pekin's black population had edged up to sixteen households, 0.14 percent of all households, so we can say that between 2000 and 2010, Pekin took small but discernable steps toward residential integration.

In deepest Appalachia, too, counties that had historically kept out African Americans are now relenting. Forsyth County, Georgia, famously went sundown in 1912, driving out its African Americans in a fiery pogrom. (Less well known are the twelve additional counties to the northwest and northeast of Forsyth that also went sundown around that time.) By 2000, African Americans had returned to Forsyth, although their foothold was still tenuous in the northern half of the county. The other counties, including Dawson, Fannin, and Towns, remained almost all-white until after 2000. The 2010 census finally showed change. Fannin County, for example, which had just 5 black residents in 1990, now showed 75 or 0.3 percent.

The Ozarks likewise had developed an awesome reputation for racism on the black "grapevine." Between 1890 and 1940 most Ozark towns went sundown, including entire counties in southern Missouri, northwestern Arkansas, and eastern Oklahoma. As late as 2017, reporter Ed Pilkington found that African Americans were "apprehensive about what they might encounter" in the Ozarks as tourists, let alone as residents.[4] Between 2000 and 2010, many Ozark counties saw African American families move in, but a few counties remained so white that they must still be classed sundown.

Even though 0.14 percent and 0.3 percent black may be tiny steps forward, these incremental developments constitute an important stride forward for race relations in the United States. Now African Americans can travel fairly freely even in white suburbia, Appalachia, and places like Pekin. Moreover, as a few black families move into a sundown town, usually they wind up dispersed across the city as houses happen to sell. Rarely do they concentrate into just one neighborhood. So these towns may avoid the creation of ghettos that plagued so many cities when African Americans first moved north in large numbers a century ago.

Second-Generation Sundown Town Issues

Even after some African American families have moved in to a former sundown town, some "second-generation sundown town issues" usually remain. The city's workforce—police officers, teachers, trash collectors—may still be all or majority white. The school curriculum likely includes few black writers. The city's day-to-day practices, from how it hires new employees to what kind of jokes people tell at work, still linger from its white supremacist past.

As sundown towns give up their overt racism, many residents feel they should be able to do so in silence. After the first edition of this book came out in 2005, I met with some residents of Martinsville, notorious across Indiana for being a sundown town. In 1968, Carol Jenkins, a young African American woman from nearby Rushville who was selling encyclopedias in Martinsville, was stabbed to death on a main street because she was there after dark.

Although Martinsville had been no more (and no less) racist than hundreds of other sundown towns in Indiana to that point, afterward it seemed to take the heat for all of them.

The people I talked with made it clear that Martinsville's reputation mortified them. About half of the group wanted Martinsville to stop being a sundown town, while the other half just wanted it to stop *being known as* a sundown town. In 2011, the president of the Morgan County Historic Preservation Society and some other Martinsville residents manifested that second position in a session they titled "Victimized by Folklore" when the American Folklore Society met nearby at Indiana University. They claimed that theirs was *not* a racist community; the charge amounted to nothing but folklore, by which they meant falsehood. Of course, that is not an acceptable definition of "folklore." Unfortunately, not facing the past leaves many sundown town practices in place. Sundown town police forces, in addition to being all-white, may still be viewed by themselves and other residents as a city's first line of defense against black interlopers. As a result, they engage in DWB ("Driving While Black") policing, targeting black motorists for minor infractions like failing to signal turns. They then subject black drivers and their passengers to uncomfortable questions as to what they are doing in town. At least as late as 2006, police in Greensburg, Indiana, got complaints from white residents "every time a black person walks down a street," and used the term "B.I.G." for "Black In Greensburg," according to one resident.[5]

Another site of continuing conflict in former sundown towns is schools, which often suffer from overwhelmingly white teaching staffs and curricula. The lack of diversity contributes to an educational climate that invites African American students to drop out or leads them to get suspended disproportionately.

Sundown towns continue to discriminate in their hiring. That's because most job openings in small towns are advertised by word of mouth, coupled with notices in the local newspaper. In a sundown town, those methods reach only white people, of course. Affirmative action is needed simply to provide equal opportunity.

Finally, the racial rhetoric common in sundown towns does not ease simply because a few black families move in. Cruel jokes and routine use of the n-word endure. The thug minority—deviant young white men aged fifteen to thirty—still feel empowered to vandalize the houses of African American newcomers and beat up or freeze out the lone black kid in school. Meanwhile, many white residents continue to dread "the racial other" and avoid vacationing or attending college at places where nonwhites might be numerous.

This sign in front of a store in central Illinois in August 2016 provides an example of sundown town rhetoric. It mocks the character of Michael Brown, an unarmed black man killed by a white police officer in Ferguson, Missouri, a year earlier. We can infer that the owner feels sure that the residents of Farmer's City, a sundown town, will find it as humorous as he did.

In Martinsville, repeated incidents after 2000 showed that the city was still racist, absent any overt effort to deal with its past. Certainly its police seemed biased when its assistant chief, Dennis Nail, complained to the local newspaper about "Hadji Hindu," "Buddy Buddha," and "queers" like Ellen DeGeneres on TV. He then spoke to the local chapter of the Conservative Citizens Councils, successor to the notorious White Citizens Councils. After some outcry, the city held a public meeting that drew eighty people. Only one criticized Nail, and after Nail spoke at the end of the meeting, he got a standing ovation.[6] Residents I spoke with in 2007 were reluctant even to propose setting up a human relations council, to try to get Martinsville to admit it had been a sundown town, or to take any other meaningful action to get the town to recognize or transcend its past. Not only would the town never take such steps, residents agreed, some worried that they would be ostracized simply for suggesting them. The 2010 census showed only five households in Martinsville with a black householder, about 0.1 percent of the city's 4,610 households.[7]

On November 2, 2017, however, Martinsville took a step forward: its new mayor dedicated a memorial marker to Carol Jenkins, who had been murdered in 1968 because she was there after dark. Thus even Martinsville has agreed that silence is not a good way forward. "We tried not talking about it for all those years," Mayor Shannon Kohl said. "But we need to acknowledge it."[8]

Most former sundown towns have never admitted their racism. An example would be Ferguson, Missouri, which became nationally notorious for its "Driving While Black" policing in 2014. Ironically, from its early days and unlike most St. Louis suburbs, Ferguson had a small black neighborhood. In 1940, 38 African Americans called Ferguson home. Then, like suburbs across the United States, Ferguson moved toward becoming all white. Whites carved St. Louis County into dozens of small municipalities, reifying into law neighborhoods based on race and class. Ferguson put a chain across the main street connecting it with Kinloch, the tiny black enclave to its west. Ferguson realtors refused to show homes to black would-be buyers. Police followed motorists who "did not belong in Ferguson"; DWB became an offense; indeed, the U.S. Department of Justice found Ferguson's police still guilty of unreasonable searches and seizures in 2015.[9] The tactics worked. Between 1940 and 1960, Ferguson cut its black population in half, to just 15 persons or .07 percent.

In the 1960s, continued black migration into the St. Louis metropolitan area, combined with the 1968 "Fair Housing" law, finally broke the barrier. By 1970, 165 African Americans lived in Ferguson. At this point, having defined African Americans as inferior, problematic, to be kept out, whites had ideological reasons to leave once "they" had breached the city limits. Many white residents responded by moving to sundown exurbs farther out. By 2014, Ferguson was two-thirds black, yet it never addressed its racist past.

And vestiges of this past remained, creating a common second-generation sundown town issue, namely an overwhelmingly white police force. In 2014 the Ferguson force employed just 3 African Americans out of 53 officers, in a city two-thirds black. Such a proportion simply asks for trouble; I had learned that lesson in Mississippi way back in 1967 when I was researching Chinese Americans and how they fit into a social structure built for two races. Most ran grocery stores, usually serving the majority black population. A grocer in Vicksburg, whose store provided something of a social center for its biracial neighborhood, told me what happened when customers created disturbances that warranted calling the police. "They always ask about the race of the people. If it's white, they send a white officer; if it's black, they send black." This made sense to the grocer and to me as well. That way, issues with the police cannot escalate into *racial* conflict.

In August 2014, after a white police officer shot Michael Brown, a young black resident, Ferguson spiraled out of control. Brown had taken some cigarillos from a convenience store. Even though he was black and the clerk was Indian American, the police sent white officers to the store and to the scene of Brown's death and the initial unrest that ensued. To calm the continuing disturbances, the governor finally replaced the overwhelmingly white Ferguson and St. Louis County police officers with state police led by a black captain. It later developed that Ferguson's police force had not only continued its DWB policing from the sundown town era but was getting much of the town's budget from fines and penalties disproportionately assessed by white police officers upon black drivers. So even a majority-black town needs to deal with its white supremacist past.

Critical Reception for *Sundown Towns*

Although the book's findings were surprising to many, critical reaction to *Sundown Towns* was favorable. It won two awards. Unfortunately, it also attracted positive attention from the extreme white supremacists of the "alt-right," some of whom use it as a reverse *Negro Motorist Green Book*—a directory of overwhelmingly white communities where they might feel at home.

Some critics said the book relies too much on oral history, which they disparaged as unreliable. This assessment fails to recognize the degree to which written documents begin as oral history. Even the census, numbers on paper, began as oral history, when enumerators knocked on doors. While today the census depends on mailed-in forms, that change was not made to improve accuracy but to save money. Indeed, the census forms, first used in 1970, gave rise to more than forty lawsuits filed by cities charging undercount.[10] Likewise, most news articles begin as oral interviews. A reporter asks questions, confirms with others, and produces "the rough draft of history," as said by a leading South Carolina newspaper in 1905.[11] Voilà—a written source!

Now that my book has been out for more than a decade, the only error I know I made—the only town I wrongly identified as a sundown town—was Buffalo, a hamlet near Springfield, Illinois. Ironically, I relied on a newspaper article from the time to conclude that whites drove out its black population. The 1908 story in the *Chicago Tribune* was lurid:

> News came from Buffalo, fifteen miles from Springfield, today, saying that race hatred has reached a high pitch here. In front of the interurban station at Buffalo is a large sign:
>
> 'All niggers are warned out of town by Monday, 12 am., sharp.
> BUFFALO SHARP SHOOTERS'[12]

William English Walling quoted this passage in his article, "The Race War in the North," published the next month in *The Independent*. Since then at least five scholarly publications have reprinted it.[13] However, when I gave a talk on sundown towns in 2007 at Illinois State University, 60 miles northeast of Buffalo, Michelle Cook, an African American who grew up in Buffalo, attended. She told me her family had lived in Buffalo for generations, as had other black families. Later she guided me around the town, showing me where various black families had lived, where some still resided, and the church they attended. She knew that Dawson, another village three miles west of Buffalo on the same interurban line, had long been a sundown town, complete with a sign at the edge of town. She also told me that the "Buffalo Sharp Shooters" was a hunting club that existed at least as recently as 1963. In that year, some Dawson area whites, unaffiliated with the Sharp Shooters club, tried to run the Cooks out of Buffalo, and a Cook family member called the Sharp Shooters, with whom they now were friends as fellow hunters, for support. The Sharp Shooters came in force, and by the time the ruffians showed up, they found the house an armed camp and sped away.

As the *Tribune* story implied in its first sentence, the reporter had never left Springfield. As the news traveled from Dawson to Springfield to the reporter, somewhere along the way the town of Buffalo got conflated with the Buffalo Sharp Shooters, who were named for the animal, not the town.[14]

Even though admittedly only one anecdote, this mistake confirms a point Chapter 8 makes: well-done oral history can equal and often surpass written sources in accuracy. This is especially true for stigmatized subjects like severe racism. Face to face, most interviewees admit that their town indeed kept out African Americans, but when I have asked in writing or by e-mail, as Chapter 8 tells, usually I have received no reply or very misleading replies.

Historians claim to "interrogate the document," but documents don't actually reply. When a long-time resident told me her town kept out African Americans, I could always ask, "How do you know that?" which isn't an option with a newspaper article.

Of course, oral history has problems too. People misremember. I watched a brother and sister in Colp, a small interracial town in southern Illinois, talk about neighboring Carterville. Before my eyes (and ears), he, now in his fifties and moved to Chicago, convinced her, still living in Colp, that Carterville had displayed the traditional sundown town sign at its city limits when they were children. Although Carterville was a particularly vicious sundown town, other sources denied it ever boasted a sign, and the flow of the conversation in Colp that afternoon did not convince me otherwise. Oral history should be criticized if it seems vague, if the researcher has not asked, "How do you know that?" and if the source has reason to mislead the researcher. But then, so should written history.

Chapter 8 offers several reasons why residents of a sundown town might not acknowledge in writing or e-mail that their town kept out African Americans. I conclude that whites often "know and don't know" about their town's racial customs. Upper-class white families want to move into suburbs like Darien, Connecticut, and Kenilworth, Illinois, for example, whose whiteness (and richness) confers prestige, only so long as lack of racial diversity seems to have happened by accident. If a town is all-white on purpose, that connotes "lower-class" behavior and is not prestigious. Deniability is key. Similarly, when talking with a researcher, many people want to be helpful and appear unprejudiced, so they will speak openly about incidents they know about, but they too want deniability. They don't want their neighbors to know they ratted out the town. Replying in writing or e-mail eliminates the possibility of deniability. An untaped oral conversation does not.

Keeping Out the Messenger

Another response to the book was to try to bar me from speaking about it in public. In 2006, when it was locating a new $550 million car factory, Honda settled on Greensburg, Indiana, which had driven out most of its black population in 1907. Honda also decreed that prospective employees had to live within 35 miles of the plant. Indianapolis, with its black community—the only black population anywhere near Greensburg—happens to lie 50 miles away.[15]

This turns out to be habitual Honda behavior, according to James Treece, news editor at *Automotive News*. In 1988, Honda paid what was then the largest EEOC settlement ever—$6 million—owing to discriminatory hiring patterns at its Marysville, Ohio, factory. Honda had similarly red-lined Columbus, Ohio, and its black residents as too far away to work for Honda.[16]

I thought this behavior on the part of Honda was wrong, so I wrote an op-ed about it. The *Indianapolis Star* declined it, so I e-published it at *History News Network*.[17] "While Honda was choosing its site," I pointed out, "its executives had to have noticed the racial composition of Greensburg and Decatur County."

A reporter at the Bloomington, Indiana, *Herald-Times* noticed my article and cited it in a story he wrote about Greensburg. In the process of reporting the story, he asked Mayor Frank Manus whether Greensburg was a sundown town. Manus replied, "I think there might have been something way back when, but, hell, we don't have anything like that now. We have several colored people who live in the city." The mayor's antiquated terminology, typical of residents of sundown towns, caused the Bloomington paper to make his sentence a "quote of the week." Other newspapers picked up the story, and eventually Greensburg's newspaper published an editorial condemning the mayor's terminology. One resident defended the mayor:

> At least he didn't make the comment about what the signs on the outskirts of town said because I do believe the first word was the 'N' word. 'N, don't let the sun set on your back in Decatur County!' . . . I can remember seeing it with my own 2 eyes.[18]

This modest media tempest finally prompted the *Indianapolis Star* to do a story, which brought my work to the attention of Governor Mitch Daniels, now president of Purdue University. Daniels knew Honda executives personally, having met them in the process of persuading Honda to locate in Indiana. He should have responded by putting my questions to Honda himself. He might then have gone on to suggest that *all* sundown towns in Indiana need to take distinct steps to move beyond their white supremacist pasts.

Instead, the governor's office tried to keep me from speaking in Indiana. In *Sundown Towns,* I estimate that most incorporated communities, including 18 to 30 entire counties in the Hoosier state, kept out African Americans. Impressed by this information, in 2007 the Indiana Civil Rights Commission set up a modest speaking tour for me: a talk in their office about "sundown towns," coordinated with Indiana University-Purdue University of Indianapolis (IUPUI), and a talk and workshop at nearby Ball State University. I was already scheduled to speak at a regional conference of the National Association of Student Personnel Administrators in Indianapolis. Shortly before I was to leave, I got a distraught phone call from my contact at the Civil Rights Commission: they had had to cancel all three events. I asked why and got a confused answer. I managed to reach people at IUPUI and Ball State who re-established all three events without the participation of the commission. At the IUPUI event, law professor Florence Roisman introduced me with an eloquent disquisition on the First Amendment.

Afterward, I learned that the governor's office had intervened. Landing Honda had been Governor Daniels's biggest boast in his campaign to be recognized nationally as pro-business. Facilitating a speaker who might raise questions about the deal was not going to happen. Later my would-be host at the commission got fired for having invited me. I considered putting this story under the heading "Critical Reception," but I realized that Governor Daniels had not tried to stop me from speaking because I was wrong about sundown towns in Indiana but because I was right.

I must add, however, that Honda is in the minority. Most corporations prefer to locate in diverse communities. Then they don't have to worry when they place a new manager who might be nonwhite. Besides, diverse communities are more interesting to live in, more open to new ideas, and more welcoming of newcomers. In eastern Illinois, for example, not far from Greensburg, Quaker Oats would not locate a new plant in Danville unless Danville enacted an open-housing ordinance, and Danville was not even a sundown town.[19] White supremacists know this, which is why some sundown towns make little effort to attract new industries or new residents. These towns would rather stagnate than integrate.

What You Can Do About Sundown Towns: The Three-Step Program in Action

To help sundown towns transcend their pasts and end second-generation sundown town issues, I suggest a "Three-Step Program":

- Admit it: "We did this."
- Apologize: "It was wrong, and we apologize."
- Renounce: "And we don't do it anymore."

Some "recovering" sundown towns, no longer explicitly excluding blacks, but still overwhelmingly white, have taken these steps. On March 17, 2015, the mayor and city council of Goshen, Indiana, unanimously passed a resolution to "acknowledge the racist and exclusionary aspects of Goshen's 'sundown town' history, along with the pain and suffering that these practices caused." Since "healthy communities are able to recognize past mistakes," they went on to "pledge to work toward the common good in building a community where people of all races and cultural backgrounds are welcome to live and prosper." One concerned citizen, Dan Shenk, sparked the process that led to this day of truth and reconciliation.[20]

In La Crosse, an undergraduate at the University of Wisconsin–La Crosse sparked it. Jennifer DeRocher researched the town's past and proved it to have been sundown. As she graduated, she created a video from her findings and left behind a handful of people committed to moving La Crosse forward.

After a public discussion including an airing of the video on December 8, 2016, the mayor and former mayor signed a resolution influenced by the resolution passed in Goshen. It acknowledged the city's past as a sundown town and pledged:

> to work toward the common good in building a warm and welcoming community, where all people of goodwill—regardless of race, color, gender identity or expression, religion, sexual orientation, national origin or ancestry, age, disability, marital status, physical appearance, political activity and familial status—can live, be free, and pursue happiness.[21]

Once a town has taken such steps, its racist minority may still exist but can no longer assume it has license to target the "racial other." Neither can the police. Even the "harmless" racial joke may no longer seem suitable to say in public.

Of course, towns can choose other ways to acknowledge and move beyond their sundown pasts. Murray Bishoff of Pierce City, Missouri, put up an exhibit in the town's historical museum about its 1901 riot that drove out the town's African Americans. On the centennial of the riot in 2001, he dedicated a memorial in the cemetery commemorating those who died. Three years later, an African American moved into Pierce City; two years after that, he was elected to the city council.[22]

In 2005, the National League of Cities developed an "Inclusive Communities" program. Most of the cities that joined had never been sundown towns, however, and most sundown towns have not joined. One, Bluffton, Indiana, signed on literally—displaying its new welcoming signs at its city limits, where its sundown town signs had been in the past.

My hope is that this preface will inspire readers to act. First, you can use the strategies outlined in Appendix B, "How to Confirm Sundown Towns," to help in the ongoing effort to identify every sundown town, past and current, in America.[23] When you confirm one, please send me the results for the interactive map at the Sundown Towns website.[24]

Next, use your results to get the towns you identify talking about race relations. In my experience, few people these days defend sundown town policies in public. Enlist allies—individuals, church groups, maybe the Chamber of Commerce—and mount a campaign to get your town to take actions to acknowledge its past—which you have confirmed—and put it to rest.

Finally, use the progress depicted in this preface to help all Americans conclude that racism is no longer "cool." It used to be, and in some ways and in some places, such as elite white suburbs, it may still be. Those places manage to use their resources to avoid the kinds of overt violence that working-class suburbs often employ to try to stay sundown. Those exclusive suburbs, however, are the fount of the problem, by seeming to equate whiteness with status. Elite white suburbs make it hard for interracial suburbs to stay interracial, because too many white Americans, as they become richer, express their wealth by moving to whiter, "more prestigious" locales. Consider Kenilworth, Chicago's richest and most prestigious suburb. Formed with an ordinance forbidding blacks and Jews, in 2010 Kenilworth had not a single black household. Tuxedo Park, outside New York City, may have exactly one. We must peel the prestige off the Kenilworths and Tuxedo Parks of America. If someone you know tells of living in a suburb or neighborhood you know to be "exclusive," don't say, "Oh, what a pretty area!" Rather respond, "Oh, I'm sorry to hear that." If they are a family: "You're not raising children there, are you?"

All-white neighborhoods still plague our nation. With your research and encouragement, we can end them.

Note to the Reader

Readers may need to brace themselves to deal with the language they will meet in this book. I shall not soften it by using *n-word* or other euphemisms. People said what they said and wrote what they wrote; their language is part of the story. Indeed, this language is part of what makes sundown towns distinctive, so I could not tell their story honestly while expurgating the language.

Younger readers need to understand that *Negro* was the standard term used to refer to African Americans before about 1972, by blacks as well as whites, and connoted no disrespect. Before about 1950, writers did not always capitalize *Negro,* although since it was parallel to *Caucasian,* they should have. I have taken the liberty of capitalizing *negro* in quoted sources from these earlier years. When writers used *negro* even after 1972—long after most authors had converted to *black* or *African American*—I have left *negro* uncapitalized. After 1972, writers who persist in using *negro* demonstrate either a deliberate refusal to use *black* or to capitalize *Negro* or an appalling ignorance of correct usage, which I would not want to mask from my readers. Such writing would be uncommon in a multiracial town by 1974.

Occasionally I place quotation marks around a name at first occurrence, indicating that the name is fictitious. Some other names have been omitted or disguised, to avoid any repercussion to people who kindly shared information with me, because the informant asked not to be identified, or because I did not know them.

Notes placed in the midst of paragraphs are content footnotes. Reference footnotes come at the end of paragraphs. In the references, web sites are listed without http:// or www. and are followed by the date accessed. Names followed by dates—Jane Doe, 9/2002—refer to interviews in person or by phone.

I don't footnote the U.S. census; finding population figures there is not hard and not eased much by citations. In the 2000 census I used the single-race counts, because it is not clear how an individual who states two or three races on the census form identifies in society, because the census uses single-race data for important tables such as "households," and because only 2.4% of census respondents chose more than one race.

Often I quote from e-mails. Unfortunately, not to bother to write e-mails in correct English has become conventional, perhaps because this ephemeral electronic form is viewed as intermediate between talking and writing. Since quoting changes the form to traditional written, I have usually taken the liberty of correcting minor lapses in spelling and grammar in e-mails.

PART I

Introduction

1

The Importance of Sundown Towns

"Is it true that 'Anna' stands for 'Ain't No Niggers Allowed'?" I asked at the convenience store in Anna, Illinois, where I had stopped to buy coffee.

"Yes," the clerk replied. "That's sad, isn't it," she added, distancing herself from the policy. And she went on to assure me, "That all happened a long time ago."

"I understand [racial exclusion] is still going on?" I asked.

"Yes," she replied. "That's sad."

—conversation with clerk, Anna, Illinois, October 2001

ANNA IS A TOWN of about 7,000 people, including adjoining Jonesboro. The twin towns lie about 35 miles north of Cairo, in southern Illinois. In 1909, in the aftermath of a horrific nearby "spectacle lynching," Anna and Jonesboro expelled their African Americans. Both cities have been all-white ever since.[1] Nearly a century later, "Anna" is still considered by its residents and by citizens of nearby towns to mean "Ain't No Niggers Allowed," the acronym the convenience store clerk confirmed in 2001.

It is common knowledge that African Americans are not allowed to live in Anna, except for residents of the state mental hospital and transients at its two motels. African Americans who find themselves in Anna and Jonesboro after dark—the majority-black basketball team from Cairo, for example—have sometimes been treated badly by residents of the towns, and by fans and students of Anna-Jonesboro High School. Towns such as Anna and Jonesboro are often called "sundown towns," owing to the signs that many of them formerly sported at their corporate limits—signs that usually said "Nigger, Don't Let the Sun Go Down on You in __." Anna-Jonesboro had such signs on Highway 127 as recently as the 1970s. These communities were also known as "sunset towns" or, in the Ozarks, "gray towns." In the East, although many communities excluded African Americans, the term "sundown town" itself was rarely used. Residents of all-white suburbs also usually avoided the term, though not the policy.

Sundown Towns Are Almost Everywhere

A sundown town is any organized jurisdiction that for decades kept African Americans or other groups from living in it and was thus "all-white" on purpose.[2] There is a reason for the quotation marks around "all-white": requiring towns to be literally all-white in the census—no African Americans at all—is inappropriate, because many towns clearly and explicitly defined themselves as sundown towns but allowed one black household as an exception.[3] Thus an all-white town may include nonblack minorities and even a tiny number of African Americans.

It turns out that Anna and Jonesboro are not unique or even unusual. Beginning in about 1890 and continuing until 1968, white Americans established thousands of towns across the United States for whites only. Many towns drove out their black populations, then posted sundown signs. (Portfolio 7 shows an example.) Other towns passed ordinances barring African Americans after dark or prohibiting them from owning or renting property; still others established such policies by informal means, harassing and even killing those who violated the rule. Some sundown towns similarly kept out Jews, Chinese, Mexicans, Native Americans, or other groups.

Independent sundown towns range from tiny hamlets such as De Land, Illinois (population 500), to substantial cities such as Appleton, Wisconsin (57,000 in 1970).[4] Sometimes entire counties went sundown, usually when their county seat did. Independent sundown towns were soon joined by "sundown suburbs," which could be even larger: Levittown, on Long Island, had 82,000 residents in 1970, while Livonia, Michigan, and Parma, Ohio, had more than 100,000. Warren, a suburb of Detroit, had a population of 180,000 including just 28 minority families, most of whom lived on a U.S. Army facility.[5]

Outside the traditional South—states historically dominated by slavery, where sundown towns are rare—*probably a majority of all incorporated places kept out African Americans.* If that sentence startles, please suspend disbelief until Chapter 3, which will show that Illinois, for example, had 671 towns and cities with more than 1,000 people in 1970, of which 475—71%—were all-white in census after census.[6] Chapter 3 will prove that almost all of these 475 were sundown towns. There is reason to believe that more than half of all towns in Oregon, Indiana, Ohio, the Cumberlands, the Ozarks, and diverse other areas were also all-white on purpose. Sundown *suburbs* are found from Darien, Connecticut, to La Jolla, California, and are even more prevalent; indeed, most suburbs began life as sundown towns.

Sundown towns also range across the income spectrum. In 1990, the median owner-occupied house in Tuxedo Park, perhaps the wealthiest suburb of New York City, was worth more than $500,000 (the highest category in the census). So was the median house in Kenilworth, the richest suburb of Chicago. The median house in Pierce City, in southwestern Missouri, on the other hand, was worth just $29,800 and in Zeigler, in southern Illinois, just $21,900. All four towns kept out African Americans for decades.

This History Has Been Hidden

Even though sundown towns were everywhere, almost no literature exists on the topic.[7] No book has ever been written about the making of all-white towns in America.[8] Indeed, this story is so unknown as to deserve the term *hidden*. Most Americans have no idea such towns or counties exist, or they think such things happened mainly in the Deep South. Ironically, the traditional South has almost no sundown towns. Mississippi, for instance, has no more than 6, mostly mere hamlets, while Illinois has no fewer than 456, as Chapter 3 will show.

Even book-length studies of individual sundown towns rarely mention their exclusionary policies. Local historians omit the fact intentionally, knowing that it would reflect badly on their communities if publicized abroad. I read at least 300 local histories—some of them elaborate coffee-table books—about towns whose sundown histories I had confirmed via detailed oral histories, but only about 1 percent of these mentioned their town's racial policies. In conversation, however, the authors of these commemorative histories were often more forthcoming, showing that they knew about the policy but didn't care to disclose it in print.

Social scientists and professional historians often have done no better in their books. During the Depression, for instance, Malcolm Brown and John Webb wrote *Seven Stranded Coal Towns,* a report for the federal government about towns in southern Illinois. All seven were sundown towns—most still are—yet the authors never mention that fact. In 1986, anthropologist John Coggeshall wrote about thirteen southern Illinois communities; most were probably sundown towns when he wrote; I have confirmed at least five. Yet he never mentions the topic. In *Toward New Towns for America,* C. S. Stein treats Radburn, New Jersey; "the Greens"—Greenbelt, Maryland, near Washington, DC; Greenhills, Ohio, near Cincinnati; and Greendale, Wisconsin, southwest of Milwaukee—planned towns built by the FDR administration; and several other planned communities, all sundown towns, without ever mentioning race. This takes some doing; about Radburn, for example, Stein details the first residents' occupations, religious denominational member- ships, educational backgrounds, and incomes, without once mentioning that all of them were white—and were required to be. Lewis Atherton's *Main Street on the Middle Border* treats small towns across the Midwest but makes no mention of sundown towns or indeed of African Americans or race rela- tions in any context.[9]

Historians and sociologists may have omitted the fact because they sim- ply did not know about sundown towns. For example, several historians as- sured me that no town in Wisconsin ever kept out or drove out African Americans. James Danky, librarian at the Wisconsin Historical Society, whose book on the black press in America is the standard reference, wrote:

> I have checked with three of my most knowledgeable colleagues and there is consensus, we do not know of any such towns in Wisconsin. Clearly the Badger State has a full supply of racism, just no such towns or counties. I believe you have found such entities elsewhere, it is just that I think that it is a small category, at least in terms of being formally established.

Later, Danky was intrigued to learn I had confirmed 9 sundown towns in Wisconsin and 194—no "small category"—in neighboring Illinois. Now I count 20 confirmed sundown towns in Wisconsin and perhaps as many as 200, as well as 506 in Illinois. Across the North, social scientists and historians have gone slack-jawed when hearing details of community-wide exclusion from towns and counties in their state, lasting at least into the late twentieth century.[10]

Overlooking sundown towns stands in sharp contrast to the attention be- stowed upon that other violent and extralegal race relations practice: lynch- ing. The literature on lynching is vast, encompassing at least 500 and perhaps thousands of volumes; at this point we have at least one book for every ten confirmed lynchings. Still the books keep coming; Amazon.com listed 209 for sale in 2005. Yet lynchings have ceased in America.[11] Sundown towns, on the other hand, continue to this day.

Sundown towns arose during a crucial era of American history, 1890–1940, when, after the gains of the Civil War and Reconstruction eras, race relations systematically grew worse. Since the 1955 publication of

C. Vann Woodward's famous book, *The Strange Career of Jim Crow,* historians of the South have recognized that segregation became much stricter after 1890. No longer could African Americans vote; no longer could they use the restaurants and public parks that whites used; even streetcars and railroad waiting rooms now put up screens or signs to isolate blacks in separate sections. African Americans were also beset by violence, as lynchings rose to their highest point.[12] However, most Americans have no idea that race relations *worsened* between 1890 and the 1930s. As Edwin Yoder Jr. wrote in 2003 in the *Washington Post,* "Notwithstanding the brilliant revisionist works of the late C. Vann Woodward, few Americans even remotely grasp the earthquake of 1890–1901 that overthrew biracial voting in the South."[13]

This backlash against African Americans was not limited to the South but was national. Neither the public nor most historians realize that the same earthquake struck the North, too. Woodward actually did; he wrote in the preface to the second edition of his classic that the only reason he did not treat the worsening of race relations in the North was because "my own competence does not extend that far." Unfortunately, except for a handful of important monographs on individual states and locales, few historians have tried to fill the gap in the half century since.[14] Thus they missed one of the most appalling and widespread racial practices of them all: sundown towns. While African Americans never lost the right to vote in the North (although there were gestures in that direction), they did lose the right to live in town after town, county after county.[15]

My Own Ignorance

Initially, I too thought sundown towns, being so extreme, must be extremely rare. Having learned of perhaps a dozen sundown towns and counties—Anna and Edina; Cicero and Berwyn, suburbs of Chicago; Darien, Connecticut, a suburb of New York City; Cedar Key, Florida; Forsyth County, Georgia; Alba and Vidor, Texas; and two or three others—I imagined there might be 50 such towns in the United States. I thought a book about them would be easy to research and write. I was wrong.

I began my on-site research in Illinois, for the simple reason that I grew up there, in Decatur, in the center of the state. Coming of age in central Illinois, however, I never asked why the little towns clustered about my home city had no black residents. After all, I reasoned, some communities are not on major highways, rivers, or rail lines; are not near African American population concentrations; and have not offered much in the way of employment. Probably they never attracted African American residents. I had no idea that *almost all* all-white towns and counties in Illinois were all-white on purpose.

The idea that intentional sundown towns were everywhere in America, or at least everywhere in the Midwest, hit me between the eyes two years into this research—on October 12, 2001. That evening I was the headliner at the Decatur Writers Conference. It was an interesting homecoming, because at the end of my address, I mentioned my ongoing research on sundown towns and invited those who knew something about the subject to come forward and talk with me. In response, a throng of people streamed to the front to tell me about sundown towns they knew of in central Illinois. Moweaqua (2000 population 1,923, 0 African Americans) was all-white on purpose, two people said. Nearby Assumption (1,261, 0 African Americans) was also a sundown town, except for its orphanage, Kemmerer Village, and the few African American children there often had a hard time in the Assumption school because of their color. An Illinoisian who "grew up on a farm just west of Decatur and attended high school in Niantic," a hamlet just west of Decatur (738, 0 African Americans), wrote later, "I had always heard that it was against the law for blacks to stay in Niantic overnight. Supposedly, when the railroad section crew was in the area, they would have to pull the work train, with its sleeping quarters for the section hands, out on the main track for the night." Another person confirmed the railroad story, and two others agreed separately that Niantic kept out black people, so I had to conclude that Niantic's population was all-white not because it was so small, but because African Americans were not permitted. Still others came down with information about De Land, Maroa, Mt. Zion, Pana, Villa Grove, and a dozen other nearby towns.

That evening in Decatur revolutionized my thinking. I now perceived that in the normal course of human events, most and perhaps all towns would *not* be all-white. Racial exclusion was required. "If they did not have such a policy," observed an African American resident of Du Quoin, Illinois, about the all-white towns around Du Quoin, "surely blacks would be *in* them." I came to understand that he was right. "If people of color aren't around," writes commentator Tim Wise, "there's a reason, having something to do with history, and exclusion. . . ."[16]

Though mind-boggling to me, this insight proved hardly new. As early as 1858, before the dispersal of African Americans throughout the North prompted by the Civil War, the *Wyandotte Herald* in Wyandotte, in southeastern Michigan, stated, "Wyandotte is again without a single colored inhabitant, something remarkable for a city of over 6,000 people." Even then, the *Herald* understood that a city of over 6,000 people was "remarkable" for being all-white. We shall see that a series of riots and threats was required to keep Wyandotte white over the years.[17]

Later, after slavery ended, African Americans moved throughout America, making it "remarkable" even for smaller towns to be all-white. The anonymous author of *History of Lower Scioto Valley,* south of Columbus, Ohio, writing in 1884, recognized this in discussing Waverly, a sundown town since before the Civil War:

> In 1875 a local census showed Waverly to have 1,279 inhabitants. . . . It will be seen that the fact of Waverly's not having a single colored resident is a rare mark of distinction for a town of its size. And what makes the fact more remarkable, there never has been a Negro or mulatto resident of the place.[18]

Sundown Towns Are Recent

In 1884, it was "a rare mark of distinction" for a town the size of Waverly to be all-white. A few years later, however, beginning around 1890 and lasting until at least 1968, towns throughout Ohio and most other states began to emulate the racial policy of places like Wyandotte and Waverly. Most independent sundown towns expelled their black residents, or agreed not to admit any, between 1890 and 1940. Sundown suburbs arose still later, between 1900 and 1968. By the middle of the twentieth century, it was no longer rare for towns the size of Waverly to be all-white. It was common, and usually it was on purpose.

So sundown towns are not only widespread, but also relatively recent. Except for a handful of places such as Wyandotte and Waverly, most towns did not go sundown during slavery, before the Civil War, or during Reconstruction. On the contrary, blacks moved everywhere in America between 1865 and 1890. African Americans reached every county of Montana. More than 400 lived in Michigan's Upper Peninsula. City neighborhoods across the country were fairly integrated, too, even if black inhabitants were often servants or gardeners for their white neighbors.

Between 1890 and the 1930s, however, all this changed. By 1930, although its white population had increased by 75%, the Upper Peninsula was home to only 331 African Americans, and 180 of them were inmates of the Marquette State Prison. Eleven Montana counties had no blacks at all. Across the country, city neighborhoods grew more and more segregated. Most astonishing, from California to Minnesota to Long Island to Florida, whites mounted little race riots against African Americans, expelling entire black communities or intimidating and keeping out would-be newcomers.

The Role of Violence

Whenever a town had African American residents and no longer does, we should seek to learn how and why they left. Expulsions and prohibitions often lurk behind the census statistics. Vienna, a town in southern Illinois, provides a rather recent example. In 1950, Vienna had 1,085 people, including a black community of long standing, dating to the Civil War. In the 1950 census, African Americans numbered 34; additional black families lived just outside - Vienna's city limits. Then in the summer of 1954, two black men beat up a white grandmother and allegedly tried to rape her teenage granddaughter. The grandmother eventually died, and "every [white] man in town was deputized" to find the culprits, according to a Vienna resident in 2004. The two men were apprehended; in the aftermath, whites sacked the entire black community. "They burned the houses," my informant said. "The blacks literally ran for their lives." The *Vienna Times* put it more sedately: "The three remaining buildings on the South hill in the south city limits of Vienna were destroyed by fire about 4:30 o'clock Monday afternoon." The report went on to tell that the state's attorney and circuit judge later addressed a joint meeting of the Vienna city council and Johnson County commissioners, "telling them of the loss sustained by the colored people." Both bodies "passed a resolution condemning the acts of vandalism" and promised to pay restitution to those who lost their homes and belongings. Neither body invited the black community to return, and no one was ever convicted of the crime of driving them out. In the 2000 census, Vienna's population of 1,234 included just 1 African American.[19]

Violence also lay beneath the surface of towns that showed no sudden decline in black residents, never having had any. In 1951, for example, a Chicago bus driver, Harvey Clark, a veteran, tried to move into an apartment in suburban Cicero. First, the police stopped him by force, according to a report by social scientist William Gremley:

> As he arrived at the building with the moving van, local police officials, including the Cicero police chief, stopped him from entering. When he protested, they informed him he could not move in without a "permit." Clark argued in vain against this edict and finally telephoned his solicitor, who assured him that

there was no provision in local, state, or federal laws for any such "permit." The police officials then bluntly ordered him and the van away, threatening him with arrest if he failed to comply with their demand. Clark then left, after being man-handled and struck.

Two weeks later, with help from the NAACP, Clark got an injunction barring the Cicero police from interfering with his moving in and ordering them "to afford him full protection from any attempt to so restrain him." As he moved in, a month after his first attempt, whites stood across the street and shouted racial epithets. That evening, a large crowd gathered, shouting and throwing stones to break the windows in the apartment Clark had just rented. Pru-dently, the Clark family did not occupy the apartment. The next night, the mob attacked the building, looted the Clarks' apartment as well as some adjoining flats, threw the Clarks' furniture and other belongings out the win-dow, and set them afire in the courtyard below. Local police stood by and watched.[20]

The following night, a mob of 3,500 gathered and rioted. According to a summary by Peter and Mort Bergman, "Gov. Adlai Stevenson called out the National Guard, and 450 guardsmen and 200 Cicero and Cook County po-lice quelled the disorder; 72 persons were arrested, 60 were charged, 17 peo-ple were hospitalized." Violence like this happened repeatedly in Cicero and adjacent Berwyn. In the 1960s, a white mob stoned members of the Congress of Racial Equality (CORE) marching through Cicero supporting open hous-ing. Whites in Cicero beat seventeen-year-old African American Jerome Huey to death in the summer of 1966. In 1987, Norbert Blei, a Cicero resi-dent, wrote *Neighborhood*, a warm memoir about the city. He told how an African American family

> "almost" moved into Cicero on West 12th Place last spring. But they didn't make it. The black family said that they didn't know the home they bought was in Cicero. They thought it was in Chicago. But Cicero reminded them with gas-filled bottles and shots in the dark. "The area is well-secured," said Cicero's council president, John Karner, after the incendiary incident.

So far as I know, no one was ever convicted in Cicero or Vienna.[21]

This is not ancient history. Many victims of Vienna's ethnic cleansing are still alive; some even return to Vienna from time to time to obtain birth certifi-cates or transact other business.[22] The perpetrators and the victims of the

1987 Cicero incident still live. Moreover, African Americans who tried to move into other sundown suburbs and towns have had trouble as recently as 2004, as later chapters will tell.

Across America, at least 50 towns, and probably many more than that, drove out their African American populations violently. At least 16 did so in Illinois alone. In the West, another 50 or more towns drove out their Chinese American populations.[23] Many other sundown towns and suburbs used violence to keep out blacks or, sometimes, other minorities.

Sundown Nation

Sundown towns are no minor matter. To this day, African Americans who know about sundown towns concoct various rules to predict and avoid them. In Florida, for instance, any town or city with "Palm" in its name was thought to be especially likely to keep out African Americans. In Indiana, it was any jurisdiction with a color in its name, such as Brownsburg, Brownstown, Brown County, Greenfield, Greenwood, or Vermillion County—and indeed, all were sundown locales. Across the United States, African Americans are still understandably wary of towns with "white" in their name, such as Whitesboro, Texas; White City, Kansas; White Hall, Arkansas; Whitefish Bay, Wisconsin; and Whiteland, Whitestown, and White County, Indiana—and again, all the foregoing communities probably kept out African Americans. So have a number of towns named for idealistic concepts—Equality, Illinois; New Harmony, Indiana; Liberty, Tennessee, and the like. Actually, most places with "white" in their name were named after someone (or some fish) named "White"; these sundry rules "work" only because *most* communities were sundown towns.

Millions of Americans—including many of our country's leaders—live in or grew up in sundown towns and suburbs. An interesting way to see the ubiquity of these towns is to examine the backgrounds of all northern candidates for president nominated by the two major parties since the twentieth century began and sundown towns became common.[24] Of the 27 candidates for whom I could readily distinguish the racial policies of their hometowns, one-third were identified with sundown towns. Starting at the beginning of the century, these include Republican William McKinley, who grew up in Niles, Ohio, where "a sign near the Erie Depot," according to historian William Jenkins, "warned 'niggers' that they had better not 'let the sun set on their heads.' " McKinley defeated Democrat William Jennings Bryan, who grew up in Salem, Illinois, which for decades "had signs on each main road going into town, telling the blacks, that they were not allowed in town after sundown," according to Ed Hayes, who graduated from Salem High School in 1969. Teddy Roosevelt was most identified with Cove Neck, a tiny upper-class peninsula on Long Island that incorporated partly to keep out undesir-ables, including African Americans, requiring large building lots. As late as 1990, its small black population consisted overwhelmingly of live-in maids. In 1920, Warren G. Harding ran his famous "front porch campaign" from his family home in Marion, Ohio; a few months before, Marion was the scene of an ethnic cleansing as whites drove out virtually every African American. Ac-cording to Harding scholar Phillip Payne, "As a consequence, Marion is an overwhelming[ly] white town to this date [2002]." Herbert Hoover grew up in a part of Iowa that may have gotten rid of its blacks around that time, but I cannot confirm his hometown as a sundown town.[25] Wendell Willkie's father was mayor of Elwood, Indiana, a sundown town that is still all-white today; Willkie went to Elwood in 1940 to deliver his speech accepting the Republi-can nomination. Owosso, Michigan, briefly became mildly notorious as a sun-down town in 1944 and 1948 because Thomas Dewey, Republican candidate for president, grew up there. But Democrats couldn't make too much of that fact, especially in 1948, because their own candidate, Harry Truman, also grew up in a sundown town, Lamar, Missouri. Reporter Morris Milgram pointed out that Lamar "was a Jim Crow town of 3,000, without a single Negro family. When I had spoken about this with leading citizens of Lamar . . . they told me, all using the word 'n——r,' that colored people weren't wanted in Lamar." Another Democrat, Lyndon Johnson, grew up in Johnson City, Texas, probably a sundown town.[26] The trend continues to the present: George W. Bush lived for years in Highland Park, a sundown suburb of Dal-las; so did his vice president, Dick Cheney, from 1995 until he moved to Washington to take office.[27] The first African American to buy a home in Highland Park did so only in June 2003. In all, nine of America's presidential candidates since 1900 grew up in probable sundown towns and suburbs, eighteen came from towns where blacks could live, and five from towns[28] whose policies I haven't been able to identify.[29]

Besides presidents, such famous Americans as public speaker Dale Carnegie (Maryville, Missouri), folksinger Woody Guthrie (Okemah, Okla-homa), Senator Joe McCarthy (Appleton, Wisconsin), etiquette czar Emily Post (Tuxedo Park, New York), and architect Frank Lloyd Wright (Oak Park, Illinois) grew up in towns that kept out African Americans. So did novelists Ernest Hemingway (Oak Park), Edna Ferber (Appleton), and James Jones (Robinson, Illinois), although as far as I can tell, they never mentioned the matter in their writing. I do not know if apple pie was invented in a sundown town, but Spam (Austin, Minnesota), Kentucky Fried Chicken (Corbin, Kentucky), and Heath Bars (Robinson) were. Other signature American edibles such as Krispy Kreme doughnuts (Effingham, Illinois[30]) and Tootsie Rolls (West Lawn, Chicago) also come from sundown communities. Tarzan may have lived in "darkest Africa," but he was born in one sundown town (Oak Park, home of Edgar Rice Burroughs), and the proceeds from his wildly successful novels and movies underwrote Burroughs's creation of another (Tarzana, California).[31] The highest-grossing movie of all time (in constant dollars), *Gone with the Wind,* was made in a sundown town, Culver City, California, from which vantage point producer David Selznick was baffled by petitions from African Americans concerned about the racism in its screenplay.[32] *Gentleman's Agreement,* on the other hand, the only feature film to treat sundown towns seriously, was made in Los Angeles.[33]

Chapter 3, "The Great Retreat," will show that large cities like Los Angeles could not exclude blacks completely—the task was simply too daunting—although residents of New York City, Fort Wayne, Tulsa, and several other cities tried. Nevertheless, whole sections of cities did keep out African Americans and sometimes other groups. Although this book doesn't usually treat "mere" neighborhoods, some sundown neighborhoods are huge. West Lawn in Chicago, for instance, has its own Chamber of Commerce, whose executive director brags that it is "a small town in a big city." It is also the birthplace of the Dove ice cream bar and the Tucker automobile. According to reporter Steve Bogira, in 1980 West Lawn had 113,000 whites and just 111 African Americans. Every large city in the United States has its all-white neighborhoods, all-white by design; certainly the West End of Decatur, where I grew up, was that way. All too many small towns, meanwhile, if they are interracial at all, still consist of sundown neighborhoods on one side, overwhelmingly black neighborhoods on the other, and the business district or a railroad in between. So sundown neighborhoods form another major part of the problem.[34]

Why Dwell On It Now?

Since 1969, I have been studying how Americans remember their past, especially their racial past. Sometimes audiences or readers ask, "Why do you insist on dredging up the abominations in our past?" About sundown towns in particular, some people have suggested that we might all be happier and better off *not* knowing about them. "Why focus on that?" asked an old African American man in Colp, in southern Illinois, in 2001, when he learned I was studying the sundown towns that surrounded Colp in every direction. "That's done with." [35]

I thought about his suggestion seriously. After all, during the 1980s and 1990s, many communities relaxed their prohibitions and accepted at least one or two black families, sometimes many more. But I concluded there were several reasons why the sad story of sundown towns should not be kept out of view.

First—and most basically—it happened. Our country *did* do that. Surely the fact that since about 1890, thousands of towns across the United States kept out African Americans, while others excluded Jewish, Chinese, Japanese, Native, or Mexican Americans, is worth knowing. So is the panoply of methods whites employed to accomplish this end. I hope this book prompts readers to question all-white communities everywhere, rather than take them for granted. Whenever the census shows that a town or county has been all-white or overwhelmingly white for decades, we do well to investigate further, since across the nation, most all-white towns were that way intentionally. Telling the truth about them is the right thing to do.

It is also true that the powers that be don't want us to learn about their policy of exclusion and have sometimes tried to suppress the knowledge. The truth about sundown towns implicates the powers that be. The role played by governments regarding race relations can hardly be characterized as benign or even race-neutral. From the towns that passed sundown ordinances, to the county sheriffs who escorted black would-be residents back across the county line, to the states that passed laws enabling municipalities to zone out "undesirables," to the federal government—whose lending and insuring policies from the 1930s to the 1960s *required* sundown neighborhoods and suburbs—our governments openly favored white supremacy and helped to create and maintain all-white communities. So did most of our banks, realtors, and police chiefs. If public relations offices, Chambers of Commerce, and local historical societies don't want us to know something, perhaps that something is worth learning. After all, how can we deal with something if we cannot even face it?

There are other reasons to incorporate sundown towns into our accounts of our nation's past. "I am anxious for this book," a high school history teacher in Pennsylvania wrote.

> I tend to collect evidence for my students that racism and discrimination still exist. Many like to pass it off as a part of the distant (before they were born) past, thus no further energy or thought need be expended on the issue!

Chronicling the sundown town movement teaches us that something significant has been left out of the broad history of race in America as it is usually taught. It opens a door into an entire era that America has kept locked away in a closet. I hope that *Sundown Towns* will transform Americans' understanding of race relations in the North during the first two-thirds of the twentieth century. Realizing that blatant racial exclusion increased during the first half of the twentieth century and in many places continues into the twenty-first can help mobilize Americans today to expend energy to end these practices.[36]

Many people wonder why African Americans have made so little progress, given that 140 years have passed since slavery ended. They do not understand that in some ways, African Americans lived in better and more integrated conditions in the 1870s and 1880s, that residential segregation then grew worse until about 1968, and that it did not start to decrease again until the 1970s and 1980s, well after the Civil Rights Movement ended. Recovering the memory of the *increasing* oppression of African Americans during the first half of the twentieth century can deepen our understanding of the role racism has played in our society and continues to play today.

Sundown Towns Persist

In other spheres of race relations, America has made great strides. The attention given to southern segregation—not just by historians but, more importantly, by the Civil Rights Movement and the courts, beginning in 1954—ended its more appalling practices. Whites, blacks, and other races ride the same subways, buses, trains, and planes. Americans of all backgrounds work together in offices, restaurants, factories, and the military. Universities, north and south, now enroll African American undergraduates; some even compete for them. Republican as well as Democratic administrations include African Americans in important positions as a matter of course. We have made far less progress, however, regarding where we live. Aided by neglect, the number of sundown towns and suburbs continued to grow after 1954, peaking around 1968. Many sundown towns had not a single black household as late as the 2000 census, and some still openly exclude to this day.

Many whites still feel threatened at the prospect of African American neighbors—maybe not just one, but of any appreciable number. Residential segregation persists at high levels. "What is more," wrote Stephen Meyer in his 2000 book, *As Long as They Don't Move Next Door*, "many Americans of both races have come to accept racial separation as appropriate." Indeed, many whites see residential segregation as *desirable*. Across America, such elite sundown suburbs[37] as Darien, Connecticut; Naperville, Illinois; and Edina, Minnesota, are sought-after addresses, partly owing to, rather than despite, their racial makeup.[38]

Therefore this book has important implications for current racial policies. Most attempts to understand or ameliorate America's astounding residential concentrations of African Americans and Latinos have focused on the ghetto, barrio, or "changing neighborhood." We shall see, however, that these problem areas result primarily from exclusion elsewhere in the social system—from sundown towns and suburbs. But despite their causal importance, these white "ghettoes" have been dramatically underresearched. As a result, few Americans realize that metropolitan areas are not "naturally" segregated and that suburban whiteness has been produced by unsavory policies that continue in part to this day. If Americans understood the origins of overwhelmingly white communities, they might see that such neighborhoods are nothing to be proud of.

On the contrary, all this residential exclusion is bad for our nation. In fact, residential segregation is one reason race continues to be such a problem in America. But race really isn't the problem. Exclusion is the problem. The ghetto—with all its pathologies—isn't the problem; the elite sundown suburb—seemingly devoid of social difficulties—is the problem. As soon as we realize that the problem in America is white supremacy, rather than black existence or black inferiority, then it becomes clear that sundown towns and suburbs are an intensification of the problem, not a solution to it. So long as racial inequality is encoded in the most basic single fact in our society—where one can live—the United States will face continuing racial tension, if not overt conflict.

Thus the continued existence of overwhelmingly white communities is terribly important. Moreover, residential segregation exacerbates all other forms of racial discrimination. Segregated neighborhoods make it easier to discriminate against African Americans in schooling, housing, and city services, for instance. We shall see that residential segregation also causes employment inequalities by isolating African Americans from the social networks where job openings are discussed. Thus some of the inadequacies for which white Americans blame black Americans are products of, rather than excuses for, residential segregation.

All-white communities also make it easier for their residents to think badly of nonwhites. Because so many whites live in sundown neighborhoods, their stereotypes about how African Americans live remain intact, unchallenged by contact with actual black families living day-to-day lives. In fact, these stereotypes get intensified because they help rationalize living in sundown neighborhoods in the first place. Black stereotypes about whites also go unchallenged by experience. Trying to teach second-graders not to be prejudiced is an uphill battle in an all-white primary school in a culture that values all-white communities. Among adults, living in overwhelmingly white neighborhoods and suburbs ties in with opposing policies that might decrease the sharp differences between the life chances of blacks and whites in our society.

The Plan of the Book

This book is divided into six parts. Part I, "Introduction," consists of this chapter, "The Importance of Sundown Towns," and Chapter 2, "The Nadir: Incubator of Sundown Towns." Chapter 2 begins with the "springtime of race relations" following the Civil War, when blacks moved everywhere in America. Then it tells of the time when race relations actually moved backward—the era that not only gave rise to sundown towns, but made them seem necessary, at least to some white Americans. Today's overwhelmingly white towns, suburbs, and neighborhoods linger as living legacies from that tragic period when race relations grew harsher.

Part II, "The History of Sundown Towns," includes three chapters. Chapter 3, "The Great Retreat," suggests a term for the massive strategic withdrawal that African Americans—and Chinese Americans before them—were forced to make from northern and western towns and rural areas to our large cities. Until now, historians have largely overlooked the forced departure of minorities, the Nadir period in the North that gave rise to the Great Retreat, and the "springtime of race relations" in the North that preceded the Nadir. "The Great Retreat" also shows statistically how widespread the sundown town movement was. Chapter 4, "How Sundown Towns Were Created," explains the mechanisms underlying these statistics. It supplies examples of the use of violence, threats, law, and official policy; informal means such as freezeouts and buyouts; and suburban methods including zoning and public planning, all in the service of creating all-white communities. Chapter 5, "Sundown Suburbs," notes that the rush to the suburbs wasn't originally racial but became racially tagged after about 1900. Sundown suburbs then grew even more widespread than independent sundown towns and persisted in forming into the late 1960s. By the time the federal government finally switched sides and tried to undo the resulting segregation, great damage had been done to our metropolitan areas.

Part III, "The Sociology of Sundown Towns," also contains three chapters. Often a sundown town is located near an interracial town. What explains why the first went sundown while the second did not? What explains Anna-Jonesboro, for example, when five miles north, Cobden, Illinois, always allowed African Americans to live in it? Chapter 6, "Underlying Causes," suggests several basic conditions that underlie and predict sundown towns; unaware of these factors, many residents believe nonsensical or tautological "reasons." Chapter 7, "Catalysts and Origin Myths," deconstructs the triggering incidents that residents often invoke to justify their town's policy and shows how these stories function as origin myths. Chapter 8, "Hidden in Plain View: Knowing and Not Knowing About Sundown Towns," tells why most Americans have no idea that sundown towns exist. This chapter also sets forth the methods and evidence underlying the claims made throughout the book. Some readers suggested relegating this material to an appendix, but I need you to read the book actively, assessing my claims as you go along. I invite skeptics (which I hope includes all readers) to turn to this chapter at any point, and also to the "Portfolio" in the center of the book—photographs and newspaper headlines that introduce visually some of the evidence for these claims.

The two chapters of Part IV, "Sundown Towns in Operation," explain how, once they made their decision to go all-white, sundown communities managed to stay so white for so long. Chapter 9, "Enforcement," tells the sometimes heartbreaking consequences inflicted upon casual and even inadvertent visitors caught after dark in sundown towns, and the still worse repercussions that awaited persons of color who tried to move in permanently. Chapter 10, "Exceptions to the Sundown Rule," explains that many all-white towns allowed an exceptional African American or Chinese American or two to stay, even as they defined their communities as sundown towns. Usually these exceptions reinforced the sundown rule by making it all the more obvious.

Part V, "Effects of Sundown Towns" answers the question, what difference do these towns make? Its three chapters show that they have bad effects "On Whites" (Chapter 11), "On Blacks" (Chapter 12), and "On the Social System" (Chapter 13). The resulting pattern of "chocolate cites and vanilla suburbs" has damaged everything from Republican Party platforms to black employability and morale.

Part VI, "The Present and Future of Sundown Towns," contains two chapters. Chapter 14, "Sundown Towns Today," tells that many communities relaxed their prohibitions since about 1980, while others did not. This recent improvement has made choosing the appropriate verb tense difficult. Putting a practice in the past—"Fans in many sundown towns seemed affronted that African Americans dared to play in their town"—would mislead, because fans in many sundown towns continue to taunt visiting interracial athletic teams. At the same time, writing "such elite sundown suburbs as Darien, Connecticut" might imply that Darien still keeps blacks out today—which I don't know and even doubt. I resolved my verb tense dilemma as best I could, usually using the continuing past ("has excluded") or the present tense ("keeps out") if a town kept out African Americans (or other groups) for decades, regardless of whether it does so now.[39] *Such statements do not necessarily mean that the town is sundown to this day.* Please do not assume that a town still keeps out African Americans without checking it out yourself. Meanwhile, concurrent with this improvement, Americans have also been developing new forms of exclusion, based no longer on race—at least not explicitly—but on differences in social class that then get reified on the landscape in the form of gated communities.

The final chapter is titled "The Remedy: Integrated Neighborhoods and Towns." It suggests tactics for everyone from members of Congress to individual homeowners who want to end sundown towns—surely a national disgrace.

The Penultimate Denial of Human Rights

How could America do these things? How could white Americans drive Chinese Americans and African Americans and sometimes other groups from hundreds of towns? How could thousands of other towns and suburbs flatly prevent African Americans, Jewish Americans, or others from living in them? After all, after life itself, allowing someone to live in a place is perhaps the most basic human right of all. If people cannot live in a town, they cannot attend school in it, vote, or participate in any other form of civic life or human interaction.

In the 1857 *Dred Scott* decision, that most racist of all Supreme Court decrees, Chief Justice Roger B. Taney held that African Americans "had for more than a century before been regarded as beings of an inferior order, and altogether unfit to associate with the white race, either in social or political relations, and so far inferior, that they had no rights which the white man was bound to respect." Between 1890 and the 1930s—and continuing to the present in some places—many white Americans actually tried to put his words into practice, in the form of sundown towns and suburbs. "After all," they reasoned, "if the founding fathers and their successors, including Taney, thought

African Americans were 'altogether unfit to associate with the white race,' then let's stop associating with them. And let's do this, not by altering *our* behavior, but by limiting *their* choices—by excluding *them*."

Of course, other countries have flatly denied the rights of an entire race of people to live in a town or wider area. In Germany, beginning in 1934, according to historian James Pool, local Nazis began to put up signs "outside many German towns and villages: JEWS NOT WANTED HERE." Pool goes on:

> Before long the signs outside some towns were worded in more threatening terms: JEWS ENTER THIS TOWN AT YOUR OWN RISK. At this point the Nazi government in Berlin reluctantly intervened. . . . Although Berlin ordered all threatening signs removed, most of them stayed up.

Two years later, most German sundown signs actually came down at Berlin's insistence as Germany prepared for the 1936 Olympic Games. During this period, hundreds and perhaps thousands of towns in America already displayed signs like the ones the Germans were putting up, directed against African Americans, but our government in Washington never ordered any of them removed, not even those on California highways as America prepared for the 1932 Los Angeles Olympics. To be sure, beginning in 1938, Germany's "Final Solution" made communities free of Jews in a much more vicious way than anything the United States ever achieved. Still, it is sobering to realize that many jurisdictions in America had accomplished by 1934–36 what Nazis in those years could only envy.[40]

Residential Segregation Lives On

Germany reversed course in 1945. The Allies forced it to. The sundown town movement in the United States did not begin to slow until 1968, however, even cresting in about 1970, and we cannot yet consign sundown towns to the past. More than half a century after the U.S. Supreme Court decreed in *Brown v. Board of Education* that whites cannot keep blacks out of white schools, and more than forty years after the 1964 Civil Rights Act made it illegal to keep them out of a restaurant, hundreds of towns and suburbs still keep African Americans out of entire municipalities.

Several towns near Colp, Illinois, for example, are *not* done with being sundown towns. Consider the town with which we began this chapter, Anna, some 30 miles southwest. In September 2002, to the best knowledge of

Anna's reference librarian and newspaper editor, neither Anna nor its companion city of Jonesboro had a single African American household within their corporate limits. In 2004, a rural resident of the Anna-Jonesboro School District confirmed, "Oh no, there are no black people in Anna today." Do these towns still actively keep out African Americans, or is their all-white nature merely the result of inertia and reputation? At the very least, Anna and Jonesboro—like most other sundown towns—have taken no public steps to announce any change in policy.[41]

Anna is only an example, of course. Hundreds of other towns and suburbs across the United States have kept out African Americans even longer than Anna and are equally white today. Unfortunately for our country, America has not reached the point where all-white towns and suburbs are seen as anachronisms. Indeed, in a way, sundown towns are still being created. White families are still moving to overwhelmingly if not formally all-white exurbs distant from inner suburbs that have now gone interracial. And Americans of all races are moving to gated communities, segregated on income lines and sometimes informally segregated on racial grounds as well.

Not only our sundown past but also our sundown present affronts me. I believe that Americans who understand that all-white towns still exist—partly owing to past government actions and inactions—will share my anger and will support government and private actions in the opposite direction, to open them to everyone. I hope also that lifting the veil of secrecy that conceals the overt and often violent cleansings that produced sundown towns and suburbs will prompt Americans to see these "racially pure" communities as places to be avoided rather than desired.

Where we live does affect how we think, and eliminating all-white towns and neighborhoods will decrease racial prejudice and misunderstanding. Social psychologists have long found that a good way to reduce prejudice is for different people to live together and interact on an equal footing. We will see in "The Remedy" that racial integration usually does work. It helps to humanize most individuals who live in interracial communities, and the existence of such communities helps to humanize our culture as a whole. As sociologist Robert Park wrote decades ago, "Most if not all cultural changes in society will be correlated with changes in territorial organization, and every change in the territorial and occupational distribution of the population will effect changes in the existing culture." So if we want American culture to be nonracist, Park would tell us, we have to eradicate our racially exclusive communities.[42]

"The Remedy" will challenge you to do something about the history it presents. I am optimistic: at last, many people seem ready to talk about sundown towns, ready even to change them. Americans have come to decry overt racism, after all, and the task could hardly be more important. Indeed, integrating sundown towns and suburbs becomes, ultimately, a battle for our nation's soul, and for its future.

To summarize, waves of ethnic cleansing swept across the United States between about 1890 and 1940, leaving thousands of sundown towns in their wake. Thousands of sundown suburbs formed even later, some as late as the 1960s. As recently as the 1970s, elite suburbs like Edina, Minnesota, would openly turn away Jewish and black would-be home buyers. Some towns and suburbs were still sundown when this book went to press in 2005.

At this point you may be shocked: how could it happen that in 1909 whites in Anna, Illinois, might run every African American resident out of their community, never to return? That many other towns across the United States could take similar actions as late as 1954? That Hawthorne, California, had a sign at its city limits in the 1930s that said, "Nigger, Don't Let The Sun Set On YOU In Hawthorne"? Or that Minden and Gardnerville, Nevada, sounded a whistle at 6 PM to tell all American Indians to get out of town before sundown?[43]

To understand how so many sundown towns formed in the United States, we must examine the era—1890 to 1940—that gave rise to them.

2

The Nadir: Incubator of Sundown Towns

The elevation of the Negro race from slavery to the full rights of citizenship is the most important political change we have known since the adoption of the Constitution of 1787. No thoughtful man can fail to appreciate its beneficent effect upon our institutions and people. . . . The influence of this force will grow greater and bear richer fruit with the coming years. . . .

The emancipated race has already made remarkable progress. . . . So far as my authority can lawfully extend they shall enjoy the full and equal protection of the Constitution and the laws.

—President James A. Garfield, Inaugural Address, 1881

In the half decade of the 1860s following the Civil War and during the 1870s, the organized activities and individual happenings within the Negro group still found a place in the newspapers, but as the emotions of the Civil War era cooled and Negroes gradually took their place in the everyday life of Northern communities, the special interest and the ready sympathy of earlier days waned.

—Leola Bergmann, after analyzing Iowa newspapers[1]

THE FACTS ABOUT SUNDOWN TOWNS prove hard for many people to believe, partly because high school textbooks in American history present a nation that has always been getting better, in everything from methods of transportation to race relations. We used to have slavery; now we don't. We used to have lynchings; now we don't. Baseball used to be all-white; now it isn't. Step by step, race relations have somehow improved on their own, according to the textbooks' archetypal story line of constant progress, and the whole problem has now been fixed or is on the way to being fixed. "The U.S. has done more than any other nation in history to provide equal rights for all," *The American Tradition,* a representative textbook, blandly assures us, as if its authors have examined race relations in Andorra, Botswana, Canada, or any other country.[2]

The assumption of progress has blinded us to the possibility that sometimes things grew worse. As a result, most Americans have no idea that race relations *deteriorated* in the 1890s and in the first third of the twentieth century. Sundown towns cannot be understood outside of the historical period that spawned them. This era, from 1890 to the 1930s, when African Americans were forced back into noncitizenship, is called the Nadir of race relations in the United States.

Unfortunately, most Americans do not even know the term. Instead, the period has been broken up into several eras, most of them inaccurate as well as inconsequential, such as "Gay Nineties" or "Roaring Twenties." During the Gay Nineties, for example, the United States suffered its second-worst depression ever, as well as the Pullman and Homestead strikes and other major labor disputes. Thus "Gay Nineties" hardly signifies more than the decade itself and leads logically to the query, "Gay for whom?"

Historian Rayford Logan began to establish "Nadir of race relations" as a term in his 1954 book, *The Negro in American Life and Thought: The Nadir*. Since then, the idea that race relations actually grew worse has become well accepted in American history, but the deterioration has hitherto mainly been identified only in the South.[3]

Impact of the Civil War

To be sure, the idea of keeping out African Americans was not born in this period. It first occurred to northern whites during the slavery period. Before the Civil War, several entire states passed laws to accomplish this end. The 1848 Illinois state constitution provided:

> The General Assembly shall at its first session under the amended constitution pass such laws as will effectually prohibit free persons of color from immigrating to and settling in this state, and to effectually prevent the owners of slaves from bringing them into this state, for the purpose of setting them free.

Ohio, Michigan, Indiana, California, and Oregon passed similar laws, thus becoming "sundown states" so far as any new African Americans were concerned, although only Oregon's law saw much enforcement. No state made a serious effort to expel African Americans[4] already residing within its borders.

Until at least 1861, North and South, most white Americans defined "black inferiority" as the problem, to which slavery was the solution. The Civil War changed all that, at least for a time. As the war continued, on the United States side it became not just a struggle to maintain national unity, but also a war to end slavery. As early as 1862, U.S. soldiers were marching to songs such as George Root's "Battle Cry of Freedom":

> We will welcome to our numbers the loyal true and brave,
> Shouting the battle cry of freedom.
> And although he may be poor, not a man shall be a slave,
> Shouting the battle cry of freedom.[5]

During the war, many white U.S. soldiers met and came to know African Americans for the first time. The actions of these African Americans played a big role in challenging white racism. Slaves fled to Union lines to be free, to get married and launch normal family lives, to make a living, and to help the United States win the war. The contributions of black soldiers and sailors to the war effort made it harder for whites to deny that African Americans were fully human, since they were acting it. Real friendships formed—between white officers of United States Colored Troops and their men, between white officers in white units and their black orderlies, and between escaped Union POWs and the African Americans who sheltered them behind enemy lines. Ordinary enlisted men, white and black, came increasingly to rely on each other, albeit in separate units, for the mutual support necessary for survival on the battlefield.

Anti-racist Idealism During and After the Civil War

Thus it came to pass that during the Civil War and Reconstruction, especially in the North, most whites defined slavery as the problem, to which fuller civil rights for African Americans, exemplified in the Thirteenth, Fourteenth, and Fifteenth Amendments, would be the answer. As a result, for a time right after the war, anti-racist idealism played a dominant role in American political life. During this time, northern Republicans reinterpreted the Declaration of Independence to include African Americans among the "all men created equal," a process begun by Lincoln at Gettysburg. According to historians Shepherd McKinley and Heather Richardson, "Northern Republicans in 1865 had little doubt that upon setting the slaves free in southern society, they would overcome all temporary barriers, . . . accumulate capital, and achieve self-sufficiency." Congress passed important civil rights acts protecting black rights, and especially during U.S. Grant's first term (1869–73), the federal government even tried to enforce them. Consequently, African Americans lived under *better* conditions between 1865 and 1890—and not just in the South—than they would in the sad decades after 1890.[6]

After the Civil War, it was in Republicans' political interest to demand the right to vote for African American men, and the GOP led the nation to pass the Fifteenth Amendment to the Constitution, granting African Americans this vital prerogative of citizenship. Suffrage without regard to race was not just in Republicans' interest, however, but also in the national interest: black votes were needed in southern states to elect public officials who would support the United States rather than try to revive secession. Moreover, Republicans did not support rights for African Americans solely to advance their party. They also did so because they believed it was just. In Iowa, for example, before the Fifteenth Amendment passed nationally, Republicans thrice brought before the people a proposal to allow African Americans to vote. Although it took three tries, it finally passed. Republicans hardly did this for political gain; it enfranchised fewer than a thousand African Americans. They did it not to garner those few votes, but because it was the right thing to do.[7]

The Fourteenth Amendment, passed in 1868, also shows this anti-racist idealism. Often called the "equal rights amendment," this shining jewel of our Constitution conferred citizenship on all Americans, including state citizenship, and guaranteed every person, including African Americans, "due process" and "the equal protection of the laws."[8] Although the Thirteenth, Fourteenth, and Fifteenth amendments are called the "Reconstruction amendments," they also had important implications for the North, which, not having seceded, never underwent political reconstruction. The Fourteenth Amendment made moot the prewar state laws keeping out African Americans. The Fifteenth enfranchised African Americans, which only a handful of northern states had done prior to its passage.

In 1866 and 1868, white voters returned "radical" Republicans to Congress in landslides across the North that signaled their satisfaction with this anti-racist national policy. Republicans also won control of most northern state governments, even briefly of Maryland, formerly a slave state.

Welcoming African Americans, 1862–1890

Many towns and counties throughout the North reflected this anti-racism by welcoming African American immigrants during and after the Civil War. Often veterans played a direct role. For example, the Reverend J. B. Rogers from Fond du Lac, Wisconsin, chaplain of the 14th Wisconsin Volunteers, got reassigned to Cairo, Illinois, which had become a place of refuge for hundreds of African Americans dispossessed by the fighting farther south along the Mississippi River. Rogers set up a school and taught more than 400 ex-slaves. He then helped bring a group of his students, all former slaves, to Wisconsin. Sally Albertz, Fond du Lac historian, pictures the scene that October day in 1862:

> As a great crowd of people congregated at the train depot, a "car-load" of ex-slaves arrived at the Fond du Lac depot, chaperoned by Rev. Rogers. Word had spread throughout the area that anyone who wanted to "engage a contra-band" or to help in any way should be at the depot. After the excitement had died down, local women served the weary travelers a welcome meal. They were then given rooms at the American Hotel until they could be hired out.

Whites in most Republican areas showed similar anti-racist behavior, and re-turning veterans brought African Americans whom they had met during the war home with them to many parts of the North.[9]

To be sure, anti-racism was hardly the sole response to the Civil War. Be-fore the war, Democratic Party rhetoric had already been overtly racist to jus-tify slavery. After the rise of the Republicans in the late 1850s, Democrats turned on the Republicans as the "party of miscegenation," a term for interra-cial sexual relations coined by Democrats in 1863. As the war continued, an-tiwar Democrats increasingly blamed "the Negro" for the conflict. Some Democratic towns in the North responded to their party's rhetoric, and to the frustrations generated by the long and bloody conflict, with a wave of forced expulsions of African Americans. Chesterton, Indiana, near Lake Michigan, drove out its African Americans in about 1863. That same year, a mob of twenty-five men led by an Anna, Illinois, doctor forced forty African Ameri-can Civil War refugees, employed as farmworkers, to flee Union County. Also in 1863, white residents of Mason County forced out five African American residents; the county remained forcibly all-white for more than a century. The next chapter tells of an incident in 1864 in which LaSalle residents drove out a group of African Americans passing through that town en route to enlisting in the army. Since LaSalle lies in northern Illinois, Mason County in central Illinois, and Union County in southern Illinois, expelling African Americans during the Civil War was obviously widespread,[10] albeit mostly in Democratic areas.[11]

Nevertheless, in Republican communities, in the period 1865–90, letting in African Americans was seen to be the appropriate, even patriotic thing to do. It was in tune with the times. Many Americans really were trying to give our nation "a new birth of freedom"—freedom for African Americans—for which, as Lincoln had suggested, Union soldiers had died at Gettysburg.[12] Opening one's community to black families after the Civil War seemed right— like opening one's college campus to black students after the Civil Rights Movement a century later. Congress said so: the 1866 Civil Rights Act declared that "citizens of every race and color . . . shall have the same right . . . to inherit, purchase, lease, sell, hold, and convey real and personal property." Presidents said so—James A. Garfield at his inauguration in 1881, quoted at the head of the chapter, clearly stated that the nation had granted equal rights to African Americans and that this was fitting and proper. Quakers in particular, abolitionists before the war, now made it their business to welcome African Americans to their communities, hire them as farmworkers, blacksmiths, or domestics, and help them get a start. So did Unitarians, Congregationalists, and some Methodists and Presbyterians. We can see the result in census figures, summarized in Table 1 in the next chapter (page 56): African Americans went everywhere after the Civil War. By 1890, all across the North—in northeast Pennsylvania river valleys, in every Indiana county save one, deep in the north woods of Wisconsin, in every county of Montana and California—African Americans were living and working.

Historians have long recognized the importance of this era called Reconstruction, but they have usually confined their analysis of it to the South. Legally, Reconstruction did apply only to the South. But Reconstruction was also an ideological movement, and the ideological currents that motivated Reconstruction not only touched but emanated from the North. Historian Lerone Bennett called it "the first and, in many ways, the last real attempt to establish an interracial democracy in America." But most historians have not included the increased acceptance of African Americans across the towns and counties of the North as part of our national narrative. Reconstruction was a period of possibility for African Americans in the North, as in the South.[13]

Northern communities, especially where Republicans were in the majority, enjoyed something of a "springtime of race relations" between 1865 and 1890. During those years, African Americans voted, served in Congress, received some spoils from the Republican Party, worked as barbers, railroad firemen, midwives, mail carriers, and landowning farmers, and played other fully human roles in American society. Their new rights made African Americans optimistic, even buoyant. "Tell them we is risin'!" one ex-slave said to a northern writer, come to see for himself how the races were getting along in

the postwar South. The same confidence fueled the black dispersal throughout the postwar North.

The "Fusion" Period, 1877–1890

Supporters of white supremacy did not fold their tents and depart, however.
With increasing tenacity and Ku Klux Klan violence, Democrats fought the
interracial Republican coalitions for control of each southern state.[14] In
Louisiana, for example, in the summer and fall of 1868, white Democrats
killed more than a thousand people, mostly African Americans and white Republicans. The intimidation continued for eight more years, until by the beginning of 1877, the Democrats had more or less won control across the
South. But their victory was incomplete. African Americans still voted—
though not freely. Democrats set up "Fusion" tickets, giving blacks some
minor offices while Democrats won the governorships and dominated state
legislatures. But Democrats were never sure they could keep control of southern state governments against possible coalitions of African American voters
and white Republicans, Readjusters (William Mahone's party in Virginia),
and Populists. In Virginia, North Carolina, and Alabama, interracial coalitions briefly won statewide and would have won more often had elections
been fair. African Americans still had the rights of citizenship—at least formally—until the 1890s.

In the North, the impulse to grant blacks rights and welcome them did
not die with the end of Reconstruction either. Ironically, this is demonstrated
by Waverly, Ohio, noted in Chapter 1 as one of the few towns in America to be
sundown from its inception, before the Civil War. Waverly's treatment in the
massive 1884 *History of Lower Scioto Valley* includes this optimistic prediction:

> Although the traditions of hostility toward his race keeps alive the fears of the
> black man, yet with the new order of things the people here, as elsewhere, have
> changed in their prejudices and it is altogether probable that now a Negro could
> take up his residence here in perfect freedom.[15]

Unfortunately, "the new order of things" was destined to last only six
more years. In 1890, trying to get the federal government to intervene against
violence and fraud in southern elections, the Republican senator from Massachusetts, Henry Cabot Lodge, introduced his Federal Elections Bill. It lost by
just one vote in the Senate. After its defeat, when Democrats again tarred Re-

publicans as "nigger lovers," now the Republicans replied in a new way. Instead of assailing Democrats for denying equal rights to African Americans,
they backed away from the subject. The Democrats had worn them down.
Thus the springtime of race relations during Reconstruction was short, and it
was followed not by summer blooms but by the Nadir winter, and not just in
the South but throughout the country. In Ohio, Waverly remained all-white
for another century and boasted a sundown sign until after World War II.[16]

The "Three *I*'s"

What caused this collapse? From the formation of the Republican Party in the
mid-1850s through 1890, anti-racism had constituted its clearest point of difference vis-à-vis the Democrats. Now this contrast faded. The idealism
spawned by the Civil War was fading too, as memories of the war dimmed. By
1890, only one American in three was old enough to have been alive when it
ended; a still smaller proportion was old enough to have any memory of the
war.[17] Millions more immigrated to the United States long after the war's end
and played no role in it.

The ideology of anti-racism was further strained by three developments—"the three *i*'s"—having nothing directly to do with black rights. The
first was Indian wars. Although the federal government had guaranteed the
Plains Indians their land "forever," after whites discovered gold in Colorado,
the Dakotas, and elsewhere, they took it anyway. In 1890, the army destroyed
the last important vestige of Native American independence in the massacre
at Wounded Knee, South Dakota. If it was OK to take Indians' land because
they weren't white, wasn't it OK to deny rights to African Americans, who
weren't white either?[18]

Second, immigrants remained a problem for Republicans. Irish, Italian,
and Polish Americans persisted in voting Democratic, no matter how Republicans tried to win them over. Republican intolerance of alcohol and of
Catholicism played a role. On the Democratic side, the new hyphenated
Americans immediately learned that it was in their interest to be considered
"whites," differentiated from "blacks," who were still at the bottom of the social hierarchy. In the West, white miners and fishermen were competing with
Chinese immigrants and hating them for it, and Democratic politicians
shouted, "The Chinese must go!" In the East, the Democrats' continued
white racism appealed to new European immigrants in competition with
African Americans for jobs at the wharves, in the kitchens, on the railroads,
and in the mines. Perhaps Republicans converted to a more racist position to

win white ethnic votes. Or perhaps their anti-immigrant thinking, manifesting itself in jokes, slurs, and anti-immigrant cartoons, spilled over into increased racism vis-à-vis African Americans. Senator Lodge, who had pushed for black rights in 1890, helped found the Immigration Restriction League a few years later, to keep out "inferior" racial strains. How can a party claim to be basically superior to immigrants and still maintain "that all men are created equal"?[19]

Imperialism was the third *i*. The growing clamor to annex Hawaii included the claim that we could govern those brown people better than they could govern themselves. After winning the Spanish-American War, the McKinley administration used the same rationale to defend making war upon our allies, the Filipinos. Imperialism as an ideological fad was sweeping the West, and it both depended upon and in turn reinforced the ideology of white supremacy. After 1890, imperialism led the United States successively to dominate Hawaii, Puerto Rico, Cuba, the Philippines, Nicaragua, Haiti, the Dominican Republic, the Virgin Islands, and several other Caribbean and Central American nations. Democrats pointed out the inconsistency of denying real self-government to Hawaiians, Filipinos, Haitians, and others, partly on the basis of their alleged racial inferiority, while insisting on equal rights for African Americans. The Republicans had no real answer.

There were still other causes of the decline of Republican anti-racism. During what some historians call the Gilded Age, some capitalists amassed huge fortunes. Doing likewise became the dream of many Republicans, a goal that was hard to reconcile with the party's former talk of social justice.[20] This increasing stratification sapped America's historic belief that "all men are created equal." To justify the quest for wealth, a substitute ideology was created, Social Darwinism—the notion that the fittest rise to the top in society. It provided a potent rationale not only for class privilege, but for racial superiority as well.

The worsening of race relations cannot be explained by downturns such as the Panic of 1893, for the Nadir began before 1893 and persisted through economic ups and downs. To be sure, economic determinism and racial competition, usually exploited by the Democrats, played a part, as we have seen. But the deepening racism of the Nadir was first and foremost a cultural movement, stemming from the decay of Civil War idealism, the evolution of ideas such as imperialism and eugenics, changes in the Republican Party, and other historical developments. Therefore it was historically contingent, not preordained. *If* President Grant and his successors had achieved a fairer Indian policy, *if* the Senate had passed the Federal Elections Bill, *if* Republicans had not caved in on race after the bill's defeat, *if* McKinley had not attacked the

Philippines and taken us down the road to imperialism, *if* the national government had put down the white violence that ended the last interracial southern political movements between 1890 and 1898, *if* affluent WASPs had rejected instead of embraced the anti-Semitism that flourished around 1900—if any of these had happened, then the Nadir might never have occurred. Then if a town or suburb had tried to drive out or keep out African Americans in 1895 or 1909 or 1954, the federal government under the Fourteenth Amendment might have intervened. So might state governments have done.

Of course, ultimately racial superiority as an ideology derives from slavery. An Arkansas librarian whom I interviewed while doing research for this book put this as succinctly as I've heard it: "African Americans were the people enslaved. So whites had to make them intellectually inferior to justify enslaving them." Because there was slavery, blacks were stigmatized as a race and black skin became a badge of slavery. Because there was slavery, whites made African Americans a pariah people whose avoidance—except on unequal terms—conferred status upon whites. Thus because there was slavery, there was segregation. Ultimately, racism is a vestige of "slavery unwilling to die," as Supreme Court Justice William O. Douglas famously put it in 1968. In the final analysis, the Nadir period, as well as the sundown towns and suburbs it spawned, are relics of slavery. Like the Civil War itself, neither the Nadir nor sundown towns would have occurred absent slavery.[21]

The Nadir of Race Relations Sets In

We have seen that the Republicans removed themselves as an effective anti-racist force after about 1891. The Democrats already called themselves "the white man's party." It followed that African Americans played no significant role in either political party from 1892 on. Now, regardless of which party controlled it, the federal government stood by idly as white southerners used terror, fraud, and "legal" means to eliminate African American voters. Mississippi pioneered the "legal" means in 1890 when it passed a new state constitution that made it impossible for most black Mississippians to vote or hold public office. All other southern and border states emulated Mississippi by 1907.

In 1894, Democrats in Congress repealed the remaining federal election statutes. Now the Fifteenth Amendment was lifeless, for it had no extant laws to enforce it. In 1896, in *Plessy v. Ferguson,* the United States Supreme Court declared de jure (by law) racial segregation legal, which caused it to spread in at least twelve northern states.[22] In 1898, Democrats rioted in Wilmington,

North Carolina, driving out the mayor and all other Republican officeholders and killing at least twelve African Americans. The McKinley administration did nothing, allowing this coup d'état to stand. Congress became resegregated in 1901 when Congressman George H. White of North Carolina failed to win reelection owing to the disfranchisement of black voters in his state. No African American served in Congress again until 1929, and none from the South until 1973.

Southern whites, at least Confederate and neo-Confederate whites, were delighted. Indeed, in about 1890, the South, or rather the white neo-Confederate South, finally won the Civil War. That is, the Confederacy's "great truth"—quoting Alexander Stephens, vice president of the Confederacy, speaking on March 21, 1861: "Our new government's foundations are laid, its cornerstone rests, upon the great truth that the Negro is not equal to the white man"—became national policy. States as far north as North Dakota passed new laws outlawing interracial marriage. Lynchings rose to their all-time peak, and not just in the South. A lynching is a public murder, not necessarily of an African American, although four of every five lynching victims have been nonwhites. The public nature of a lynching signaled that the dominant forces in the community were in league with the perpetrators. Portfolio 5 shows the further development of the "spectacle lynching," publicized ahead of time, that drew crowds in the hundreds, even thousands. White Americans, north and south, joined hands to restrict African Americans' civil and economic rights.[23]

After 1890, as in the South, Jim Crow practices tightened throughout the North. The so-called Progressive movement was for whites only; often its "reforms" removed the last local black leaders from northern city councils in favor of commissioners elected citywide. Northern whites attacked African Americans, verbally and often literally. Segregation swept through public accommodations. In 1908, the famous reporter Roy Stannard Baker toured the North for an article, "The Color Line in the North." He noted the deterioration even in Boston, the old citadel of abolitionism: "A few years ago no hotel or restaurant in Boston refused Negro guests; now several hotels, restaurants, and especially confectionery stores, will not serve Negroes, even the best of them." Writing of the day-to-day interactions of whites and blacks in the Midwest, Frank Quillen observed in 1913 that race prejudice "is increasing steadily, especially during the last twenty years." In the 1920s, Harvard barred an African American student from the very dormitory where his father had lived decades earlier when attending the university. *Like Reconstruction, the Nadir of race relations was national.*[24]

A 1912 referendum across President Garfield's home state of Ohio exemplified most dramatically America's grievous retraction of "the full rights of citizenship" for African Americans, about which he had rightly bragged in 1881. In 1912, even blacks' right to vote was questioned in Ohio, when voters rejected an amendment to the state constitution removing "white" from the clause defining eligibility for the franchise. In 1870, Ohio had ratified the Fifteenth Amendment, which granted African Americans the right to vote. Ever since the amendment became law in that year, black men had been voting in Ohio. Because federal law superseded state law, the 1912 action was only cosmetic, to bring the state constitution in line with the federal one. Yet by rejecting the change, white Ohioans in 1912 made clear that they wanted black voting to stop.[25]

Leola Bergmann carefully analyzed Iowa newspapers and found a shocking decrease in sympathy and increase in antipathy among whites in that state, which President Grant had called "bright radical star" after it granted African Americans the right to vote. In the quote at the head of the chapter, she tells of the inclusion of "the organized activities and individual happenings within the Negro group" in newspapers up to about 1880. Then such stories gradually stopped appearing. Worse, she noted, "in the kind of news that was reported one can detect the opposition that slowly accumulated in the public mind." Nearly all the stories about African Americans that newspapers printed in the late 1880s and throughout the 1890s concerned crime. "If colored groups engaged in worthwhile educative or social projects—and certainly they did—newspaper readers were not often apprised of it." Bergmann supplies an example—a black Iowan was named ambassador to Liberia in 1890—that went wholly unreported in the Iowa press.[26]

Occupationally, blacks fared even worse. Before the Nadir, African Americans worked as carpenters, masons, foundry and factory workers, postal carriers, and so on. After 1890, in both the North and the South, whites expelled them from these occupations. The expulsions were most glaring in sport, supposedly a meritocracy that rewards superior performance no matter who exhibits it. African Americans had played baseball in the major leagues in the 1880s. Whites forced out the last black at the beginning of the Nadir, in 1889; the last African Americans left the minor leagues in the 1890s. In 1911, the Kentucky Derby eliminated black jockeys. Only boxing offered a relief, but Jack Johnson's 1910 victory over Jim Jeffries, the Great White Hope, just confirmed whites' stereotype of African Americans as dangerous fighters.[27]

The *Chicago Defender*, a nationally important black newspaper, was full of articles between 1910 and 1925 chronicling the erosion of black employment. In 1911, an article headlined "The Passing of Colored Firemen in Chicago" lamented that only seven black firefighters were left, whites having forced out all the rest. Indeed, in some ways the North proceeded to treat African Americans *worse* than the South did. Ironically, segregation, which grew more entrenched in the South than in the North after the end of Reconstruction in 1877, created some limited opportunities for African American workers in Dixie. If the job was clearly defined as inferior, southern whites were happy to hire African Americans to cook their food, drive their coaches and later their cars, be their "yard boy," even nurse their babies. (The term *boy*, applied to adult male African Americans, itself implies less than a man.) Thus traditional white southerners rarely drove all African Americans out of their communities. Who would then do the dirty work? During and after slavery this pattern spread to the North, but only to a limited degree. Around 1900, many white Americans, especially outside the traditional South, grew so racist that they came to abhor contact with African Americans even when that contact expressed white supremacy. If African Americans were inferior, they reasoned, then why employ them? Why tolerate them at all?[28]

How the Nadir Gave Birth to a Sundown Town

Harrison, Arkansas, had been a reasonably peaceful interracial town in the early 1890s. "The town had its colored section in those days," in the words of Boone County historian Ralph Rea. "There was never a large Negro population in Harrison, probably never more than three or four hundred, but they had their church, their social life, and in the main there was little friction between them and the whites." Rea goes on to tell how whites and African Americans patronized a black barbecue to help fund a school for African American children. While the whites already *had* a school, of course, funded by public tax monies, nevertheless the barbecue shows cordial social intercourse between the races. Then, throughout Arkansas as elsewhere, race relations worsened around the turn of the twentieth century. Democrat Jeff Davis (no relation to the Confederate president) successfully ran for governor in 1900, 1902, and 1904, and then for the U.S. Senate in 1906. His language grew more Negrophobic with each campaign. "We have come to a parting of the way with the Negro," he shouted. "If the brutal criminals of that race . . . lay unholy hands upon our fair daughters, nature is so riven and shocked that the dire compact produces a social cataclysm."[29]

    Another factor was the bankruptcy on July 1, 1905, of the Missouri and North Arkansas Railroad, intended to connect Harrison with Eureka

Springs and ultimately St. Louis and the world. This put unemployed rail-road track layers, some of them African American, on the streets of Harrison and was also an economic hardship for townspeople who had invested in the scheme. Then, according to Arkansas researchers Jacqueline Froelich and David Zimmermann, on Saturday night, September 30, 1905, "a black man, identified only as Dan, reportedly seeking shelter from the cold, was arrested for breaking into the Harrison residence of Dr. John J. Johnson and was jailed with another African-American prisoner, called Rabbit." Two days later, whites in Harrison took Davis's campaign rhetoric to heart. In Zimmermann's words:

> A white mob stormed the building and took these two Negroes from jail along with several others, to the country, where they were whipped and ordered to leave. The rioters swept through Harrison's black neighborhood with terrible intent. The mob of 20 or 30 men, armed with guns and clubs, reportedly tied men to trees and whipped them, tied men and women together and threw them in a 4-foot hole in Crooked Creek, burned several homes, and warned all Ne-groes to leave town that night, which most of them did without taking any of their belongings.

"From house to house in the colored section they went," conclude Froelich and Zimmermann, "sometimes threatening, sometimes using the lash, always issuing the order that hereafter, 'no Nigger had better let the sun go down on 'em.' "[30]

Three or four wealthy families sheltered their African American servants, who stayed on for a few more years. Then in 1909, another African American was charged with a crime—armed robbery, possibly also including rape—and had to be spirited out of town to avoid a lynch mob. "This mob proved the last straw for even the most resilient of the 1905 survivors," in Zimmermann's words. "Fearing for their lives, most of Harrison's [remaining] black residents fled town the night of January 28." Harrison remained a sundown town at least until 2002.[31]

African Americans, Not Racism, Become "the Problem"

Harrison exemplifies how the increasing racism of the Nadir led to the expul-sion of African Americans. How were northern whites to explain to them-selves their acquiescence in the white South's obliteration of the political and civil rights of African Americans in places such as Harrison? How could they defend their own increasing occupational and social discrimination against African Americans?

The easiest way would be to declare that African Americans had never deserved equal rights in the first place. After all, went this line of thought, conditions had significantly improved for African Americans. Slavery was over. Now a new generation of African Americans had come of age, never tainted by the "peculiar institution." Why were they still at the bottom? African Americans themselves must be the problem. *They* must not work hard enough, think as well, or have as much drive, compared to whites.[32] The Reconstruction amendments (Thirteenth, Fourteenth, and Fifteenth) provided African Americans with a roughly equal footing in America, most whites felt. If they were still at the bottom, it must be their own fault.[33]

Ironically, the worse the Nadir got, the more whites blamed blacks for it. The increasing segregation and exclusion led whites to demonize African Americans and their segregated enclaves. African Americans earned less money than whites, had lower standing in society, and no longer held public office or even voted in much of the nation. Again, no longer could this obvious inequality be laid at slavery's doorstep, for slavery had ended around 1865. Now "white Northerners came to view blacks as disaffected, lazy, and dangerous rabble," according to Heather Richardson. "By the 1890s, white Americans in the North concurred that not only was disfranchisement justified for the 'Un-American Negro,' but that he was by nature confined to a state of 'permanent semi-barbarism.' "[34]

To this day, public opinion polls show that many nonblack Americans—especially those who live in towns that have few African Americans whom they might get to know as individuals—still believe these generalizations, at least when they are phrased more politely. To be sure, the theme of African Americans as problems doesn't stand up to scrutiny. Whites forced out African American from major league baseball not because they couldn't play well, but because they could. Whites expelled black jockeys from the Kentucky Derby not because they were incompetent, but because they won 15 of the first 28 derbies. They drove blacks out of the job of postal carrier so they could do it themselves, not because blacks couldn't do it. The foregoing seems obvious, but when it comes to housing, even today, deep inside white culture as a legacy from the Nadir is the sneaking suspicion that African Americans *are* a problem, so it *is* best to keep them out.[35]

History, Popular Culture, and Science Legitimize the Nadir

During the Nadir, America took a wrong turn, North as well as South. In fact, we took perhaps the wrongest turn we have ever taken as a nation, a turn so wrong that we have not yet been able to comprehend all that it has done to us. In these years white Americans who never met an African American became racist anyway, because stereotypes of white superiority resonated throughout American culture. Historians played a major role. After the final overthrow of Reconstruction in 1890, historians converted the era into a tale of oppressed whites, beset by violence and corruption. As Harvard's Albert Bushnell Hart put it in 1905:

> Every [southern] legislature had Negro members, and some of them a Negro majority.[36] Most of these Negroes were ignorant men who were controlled by two classes of whites, called "scalawags" (southern Republicans) and "carpet-baggers" (northern men who had gone down South to get into politics). Taxes were increased, debts run up, and the extravagance and corruption of some of the legislatures surpass belief.

Such interpretations so distorted the historical record that by 1935 black scholar W. E. B. DuBois lamented, "We have got to the place where we cannot use our experiences during and after the Civil War for the uplift and enlightenment of mankind."[37] Even today, these interpretations from the Nadir still distort high school American history textbooks, including their portrayal of such men as John Brown and Ulysses Grant.[38]

During the Nadir, minstrel shows came to dominate our popular culture. They had been invented before the Civil War but flourished after 1890. In our electronic age, it is hard to imagine how prevalent minstrel shows became. "By the turn of the century," in the words of historian Joseph Boskin, "practically every city, town, and rural community had amateur minstrel groups." Minstrel shows both caused and reflected the Nadir. As black poet James Weldon Johnson put it, minstrel shows "fixed the tradition of the Negro as only an irresponsible, happy-go-lucky, wide-grinning, loud-laughing, shuffling, banjo-playing, singing, dancing sort of being." James De Vries, who studied Monroe, Michigan, in this era, wrote that minstrel shows portrayed African Americans as "the complete antithesis of all those qualities of character valued as important and worthwhile by white Americans." In small towns across the North, where few blacks existed to correct this impression, these stereotypes provided the bulk of white "knowledge" about what African Americans were like.[39]

In the twentieth century, movies gradually replaced minstrelsy and its off-spring, vaudeville. Unfortunately for race relations, the first grand epic, *The Birth of a Nation,* released by D. W. Griffith in 1915, right in the heart of the Nadir, was perhaps the most racist major movie ever made. It lionized the first Ku Klux Klan (1865–75) as the savior of white southern civilization and fueled a nationwide Klan revival. Near the end of the Nadir, in 1936, *Gone with the Wind* sold a million hardbound books in its first month; the book and the resulting film, the highest-grossing movie of all time, further convinced whites that noncitizenship was appropriate for African Americans.[40]

Also in the new century, Social Darwinism morphed into eugenics, which provides the ultimate rationale for blaming the victim. Not only are the poor at the bottom owing to their own fault, they cannot even be helped, eugenics tells us, because the fault lies in their genes. Anthropologists measured average brain sizes of people around the world and concluded that whites' brains were larger. According to historian Richard Weiss, "Organized eugenics got its immediate impetus at a meeting of the American Breeders Association in 1904"—and we are not talking about dogs. In 1909, Harvard's president Charles W. Eliot, denounced "any mixture of racial stocks." He and Madison Grant agreed that white Anglo-Saxons deserved to be on top, but both worried that they might not stay there unless they took steps to keep other races out, which is why Grant wrote *The Passing of the Great Race* in 1916. Margaret Sanger, patron saint of birth control, was another stalwart believer in eugenics who admitted, "We do not want word to get out that we want to exterminate the Negro population." In the 1920s, the *Saturday Evening Post* began to quote and commend Grant's ideas. Grant, a stalwart in the American Breeders Association and trustee of the American Museum of Natural History, framed a bill restricting immigration that reached Congress in 1924.[41]

Anti-Semitism increased as well. During World War I, the U.S. Army for the first time considered Jews "a special problem whose loyalty to the US was open to question." Along with other government agencies (and the Ku Klux Klan), the Military Intelligence Department mounted a campaign against Jewish immigrants that helped convince Congress to pass Grant's restrictive immigration bill in 1924. In the 1920s and '30s, many state legislatures passed sterilization laws for people of "dubious stock." These people included isolated rural folk, interracial people, the poor, and those with low IQ test scores.[42]

IQ tests and the Scholastic Aptitude Test (SAT) came to the fore at this time, as the handmaidens of eugenic theory. In 1910, Henry Goddard began administering intelligence tests as indicators of fitness for citizenship to would-be immigrants at Ellis Island. Around that time Louis Terman modified Alfred Binet's IQ test into the Stanford-Binet IQ Test. Robert Yerkes developed the U.S. Army's "alpha test" and used it during World War I. Carl Brigham produced the SAT in the early 1920s. Each of these psychometricians believed that intelligence was innate, some races had more than others, and white Anglo-Saxons came out on top. Their tests "proved" as much—blacks, Jews, Slavs, and Italians did poorly. Brigham later underwent a dramatic but little-publicized change of heart, concluding that test scores mostly reflected social background and experience, but the damage had been done.

Other branches of social and biological science chimed in. E. A. Ross, president of the American Sociological Association, Henry F. Osborn, the paleontologist who named *Tyrannosaurus rex,* and zoologist Louis Agassiz claimed that their respective sciences proved that blacks were inferior. Physical anthropologists who believed that the "black race" evolved earlier than the "white race" concluded that blacks were therefore more primitive, while those who believed that blacks developed later than whites also concluded that blacks were more primitive, being "closer to the ape." [43]

The Nadir Continued to About 1940

From 1913 to 1921, Woodrow Wilson was president; he was surely the most racist president since Andrew Johnson. A southerner, Wilson was an outspoken white supremacist who used his power as chief executive to segregate the federal government. If blacks were doing the same tasks as whites, such as typing letters or sorting mail, they had to be fired or placed in separate rooms or at least behind screens. Wilson segregated the U.S. Navy, which had not previously been segregated; now blacks could only be cooks, firemen, and dishwashers at sea. He appointed southern whites to political offices previously held by African Americans. His legacy was extensive: he effectively closed the Democratic Party to African Americans for another two decades, and parts of the federal government stayed segregated into the 1950s and beyond. [44]

Triggered by the astounding success of *The Birth of a Nation,* the Ku Klux Klan rose again after 1915, only this time the Klan was national, not southern. It dominated state politics for a time in the 1920s in Oregon, Colorado, Oklahoma, Indiana, Georgia, and Maine, and had great influence throughout rural and small-town America. In some communities, especially towns that had already driven out their African Americans, the KKK targeted white ethnics, such as (Catholic) Italians, Poles, or Jews. Klan support was another reason why Congress passed and President Coolidge signed the 1924 immigration act to restrict newcomers from just about everywhere except northern and western Europe.

It's hard to date the end of this terrible era precisely. According to W. E. B. DuBois, "The election of 1928 probably represented the lowest point to which the influence of the Negro in politics ever fell in the United States since enfranchisement." He thus implies that politically at least, things got better after about 1930. The idea that whites had every right to bar nonwhites from "white" occupations and communities hardly died in 1930, however, and the Nadir hardly ended in that year.[45]

On the contrary, another group faced its own crisis in the 1930s, as the 1930 census reclassified Mexican Americans from white to nonwhite. This helped make the 1930s a mini-nadir for Chicano-Anglo relations. Several California towns followed up on the census reclassification by segregating Chicanos from Anglos in their public schools. During the Depression, the United States by official policy deported thousands of Mexican workers and their families, including many Mexican Americans, to Mexico. According to a survey of race relations across Colorado published by the University of Colorado Latino/a Research and Policy Center in 1999, "In 1936, a huge banner flew in [Greeley]: 'All Mexican and other aliens to leave the State of Colorado at once by order of Colorado State vigilantes.' "[46]

The Great Depression also intensified the pressure on African Americans. "Menial public service jobs such as street-cleaning and garbage collection, to which 'no self-respecting white man' would stoop a decade or so ago, are rapidly becoming exclusively white men's jobs," wrote sociologists Willis Weatherford and Charles S. Johnson in 1934. In some towns whites now drove blacks from the position of hotel waiter and porter. Black barbers (for whites) had been under attack for decades, and more barbers were forced out as the Depression set in. In 1929, white elevator operators replaced blacks in Jefferson City, Missouri, a setback that symbolized the difficulties African Americans faced throughout the country. After all, the position of elevator operator, while it has its ups and downs, is hardly a skilled or prestigious job. If whites could now deem blacks unfit for *that* job, what might be left for them? Certainly not the National Football League: the NFL, which had allowed black players and even a black coach in the 1920s, banned African Americans in 1933.[47]

The leadership of the new Congress of Industrial Organizations (CIO) unions in the 1930s did campaign against the exclusion of African Americans in the auto industry and some other manufacturing areas. Otherwise, as labor unions gained in power during the 1930s and into the '40s, the position of African Americans grew worse. In Missouri, according to *Missouri's Black Heritage,* "white labor unions, traditionally hostile to black workers, became even more so during the 1930s." Railroads had been the largest single employer of African Americans. To be sure, they had never hired blacks as locomotive engineers (by definition a "white job" requiring intelligence) but they had in some states as firemen (a "black job" involving shoveling coal into a hot firebox). Now unemployed whites shot at and killed black railroad firemen, making that a "white job" in many states. In 1932, white workers on just one railroad, the Illinois Central, killed ten African American trainmen in a campaign to drive them out of railroad jobs. By 1940, white unions had mostly thrown blacks out of all railroad work, except for Pullman porters, who supplied personal service to sleeping-car passengers.[48]

The administration of Franklin D. Roosevelt was largely under the thumb of white southerners so far as race relations was concerned, at least to 1938.[49] The president never pushed for an anti-lynching bill, even though such a bill would merely have criminalized a crime and although Republicans did try to pass it. Housing the government built or subsidized for defense workers during World War II was deliberately more segregated even than the housing in surrounding communities. Indeed, under FDR the federal government built seven new towns that explicitly kept out African Americans. The armed forces also maintained rigid segregation throughout the war.

FDR's economic programs were legally open to all Americans without regard to race, however, and they spoke to the poverty many African Americans endured during the Depression, even if they were not administered fairly. In 1941, Roosevelt also did set up the Fair Employment Practices Committee, which opened some defense plants to black workers. These policies, along with the symbolic gestures of Eleanor Roosevelt, the rise of the CIO, and processes set in motion by Adolf Hitler and his demise, led to some improvement in race relations beginning around 1940. That's why I now date the Nadir as 1890–1940.

Setting the Stage for the Great Retreat

Thus the textbook archetype of uninterrupted progress falsifies the history of race relations between 1890 and the 1930s. It is almost unimaginable how racist the United States became during the Nadir. If African Americans in those years had experienced only white indifference, rather than overt opposition—often legal and sometimes violent—they could have continued to win the Kentucky Derby, deliver mail, and buy homes in "white" towns and neighborhoods. The ideology of white supremacy increasingly pervaded American culture during this era, more even than during slavery. Convinced by this ideology that African Americans were inferior, whites all across America asked, "Why even let them live in our community?"

The next chapter tells the result: the "Great Retreat" of African Americans from towns and rural areas across the North to black ghettoes in large northern cities. We live with the results—sundown towns and suburbs—to this day. They form the most visible residue on the American landscape of the nightmare called the Nadir.

PART II

The History of
Sundown Towns

3

The Great Retreat

In spite of the fact that the total Negro population of Indiana showed a fivefold increase between 1860 and 1900, some parts of the state showed little or no increase, while there was actually a decline in some places. In some instances this was due to a deliberate anti-Negro policy. . . . Some communities gained a reputation for being so hostile that no Negro dared stay overnight in them.
—Emma Lou Thornbrough, *The Negro in Indiana*, 1957[1]

DURING THE NADIR, deliberate policies, formal and informal, created America's most complete form of residential segregation: the complete exclusion of African Americans—and sometimes other groups—from entire communities. As part of the deepening racism that swept through the United States after 1890, town after town outside the traditional South[2] became intentionally all-white.

This happened in two waves. First, an epidemic of attacks against Chinese Americans across the West prompted what I call the "Chinese Retreat," resulting in the concentration of that minority in Chinatowns in Seattle, San Francisco, Los Angeles, and a few other cities.[3] Then whites began forcing African Americans out of towns and rural areas across the North. This resulted in what I hope becomes generally recognized as the "Great Retreat"— the withdrawal of African Americans from towns and counties across the United States to black ghettoes in large northern cities.

Aching to Be All-White

How a problem is formulated influences how it gets thought about and what qualifies as a solution. After 1890, as we have seen, most whites no longer viewed slavery and racism as the problem—slavery was over, after all, and racial discrimination had been made illegal under the Fourteenth and Fifteenth Amendments. Now African Americans themselves were seen as the problem, by white northerners as well as southerners. Outside the traditional South, few whites now argued that their town *should* be interracial, as Republicans had done during Reconstruction. Whites now ached to be rid of their African Americans. The editor of the *Cairo Bulletin* summarized the feelings of white residents of Cairo, at the southern tip of Illinois, in 1920:

"CAIRO DISAPPOINTED"

Cairo's population on January 1, 1920, was 15,203, a gain of 655, or 4.5 per cent. This announcement was made by the Census bureau at Washington yesterday morning and transmitted to the *Bulletin* by Associated Press.

The Population in 1910 was 14,548.

Disappointment was expressed by some that the figure was not larger but those who knew how the population was made up were gratified at the showing. It is estimated that more than 2,000 Negroes have left Cairo since the last census, making the increase in the white population nearly 2,700 people.

Although "disappointed" that Cairo's overall population had gained only 4.5%, white residents were "gratified"[4] at its now whiter makeup.[5]

This line of thought was hardly unique to Cairo. During the first half of the twentieth century, towns competed by advertising how white they were; several Portfolio items show examples. In its *1907 Guide and Directory*, Rogers, Arkansas, bragged about what it had, including "seven churches, two public schools, one Academy, one sanitorium, ice plant and cold storage, etc.," and also what it did not have: "Rogers has no Negroes or saloons." Not to be outdone, nearby Siloam Springs claimed "Healing Waters, Beautiful Parks, Many Springs, Public Library," alongside "No Malaria, No Mosquitoes, and No Negroes." Whites in Cumberland County, Tennessee, forced out African Americans around 1900; in the 1920s, its main newspaper, the *Crossville Chronicle,* boasted, "No Mosquitoes, No Malaria, and No Niggers."

White residents of much of Oklahoma and the "non-southern" parts of Texas adopted this rhetoric. Land owners and developers who were trying to entice whites to central and western Texas in the 1910s exhorted them to "leave the niggers, chiggers, and gravediggers behind you!" Terry County, Texas, advertised itself in 1908 as a sundown county:

Terry County is thirty miles square, situated eighty miles north from Stanton, on the T & P railroad, and about eighty southwest from Plainview, terminus of

the Santa Fe; was organized in 1904, and has about 2,000 population. ALL
WHITE, about 400 homes . . .

Comanche County, Texas, drove out its African Americans in 1886. It was delighted also to have no Jews, almost no Mexicans, and few immigrants from
southern and eastern Europe. After the 1940 U.S. Census, Representative Bill
Chambers announced that according to a congressional report, "Comanche
County, long famous for many unique advantages, has gained national distinction, for being the home of the purest Anglo-Saxon population of any county
in the United States." Among its 19,245 residents, just 28 were born in countries other than the United States, including only 2 from Mexico, both listed
as white.[6]

Many towns in the Midwest were likewise thrilled to be all-white. After
bragging about high literacy and home ownership rates, the 1936 *Owosso and
Shiawassee County Directory* in Owosso, Michigan, declared, "There is not a
Negro living in the limits of Owosso's incorporated territory." Mentone, Indiana, bragged, "With a population of 1,100, Mentone has not a Catholic, for-
eigner, Negro, nor Jew living in the city." In its 1954 pamphlet titled "Royal
Oak: Michigan's Most Promising Community," the Detroit suburb's Chamber of Commerce proudly proclaimed, "The population is virtually 100%
white."[7]

The Far West was equally smitten with the idea. Fliers for Maywood
Colony, a huge development entirely surrounding the town of Corning, California, trumpeted:

GOOD PEOPLE

In most communities in California you'll find Chinese, Japs, Dagoes, Mexicans, and Negroes mixing up and working in competition with the white folks.
Not so at Maywood Colony. Employment is not given to this element.[8]

Thus except in the traditional South, driving African Americans out and
keeping them out became the proper civic-minded thing to do, in the thinking
of many whites of all social strata between about 1890 and 1940, lasting until
at least 1968. Doing so seemed a perfectly reasonable solution once African
Americans were defined as "the problem." Spurred by the ideological developments of the Nadir, towns with no black residents—including some with little prospect of attracting any—now passed ordinances or informally agreed
that African Americans were not to be allowed after sundown. Where blacks
did live, whites now forced them to flee from town after town, county after

county, even entire regions—the Great Retreat. Threat of mob attack dangled over every black neighborhood in the nation (as it had earlier over most Chinese neighborhoods) as an ever-present menace. In short, an epidemic of sundown towns and counties swept America between 1890 and about 1940.

The Chinese Retreat

Before African Americans made their Great Retreat, the Chinese provided something of a dress rehearsal. Until about 1884, Chinese Americans lived in virtually every town in the West.[9] They were farmers and domestic servants, played a major role in the California fishing industry, and mined gold along streams in countryside newly wrested from the Indians. Hundreds of Chinese Americans mined coal in Wyoming in the 1870s. Their role in building the railroad and many other construction projects is well known. Republicans usually defended their right to immigrate to America and compete for employment.

Capitalists benefited from the competition, of course, but white workers did not, frequently resulting in sundown towns. Between 1885 and about 1920, dozens of communities in the West, including towns and counties as far inland as Wyoming and Colorado and cities as large as Seattle and Tacoma, drove out their entire Chinese American populations—some briefly, some for decades.

Rock Springs, Wyoming, built at a coal mine owned by the Union Pacific that was the biggest single source of coal for its locomotives, was the site of one of the earliest expulsions. The railroad had hired hundreds of Chinese American miners, most of whom lived in a separate neighborhood, "Chinatown." On September 2, 1885, led by the Knights of Labor, at least 150 white miners and railroad workers, most of them armed, gave the Chinese "one hour to pack their belongings and leave town," according to historian Craig Storti. Then they attacked. "The Chinamen were fleeing like a herd of hunted antelope, making no resistance. Volley upon volley was fired after the fugitives," Storti tells. It was chaotic: "Most carried nothing at all, not even their money." Many hid in their homes, but the rioters then burned Chinatown, incinerating those who were hiding there. Storti quotes an eyewitness:

> The stench of burning human flesh was sickening and almost unendurable, and was plainly discernible for more than a mile along the railroad both east and west. . . . Not a living Chinaman—man, woman, or child—was left in the town where 700 to 900 had lived the day before, and not a single house, shanty, or

structure of any kind that had ever been inhabited by a Chinaman was left unburned.

Those who fled were hardly better off, because the temperature dropped below freezing that night, so scores died from exposure. According to Bill Bryson, this persecution in Rock Springs led to the expression "He doesn't have a Chinaman's chance." Copycat riots and expulsions then swept the West, including almost every town in Wyoming; Cripple Creek and later Silverton, Colorado; Hells Canyon, Oregon; Grass Creek and Corinne, Utah; and communities in most other western states.[10]

The retreat of Chinese residents from Idaho was especially striking. In 1870, Chinese made up one-third of the population of Idaho. By 1910, almost none remained. In the 1880s, assaults and murder became common practice. In 1886, white Idahoans held an anti-Chinese convention in Boise, and a mass movement against the Chinese spread throughout the state, growing even worse after statehood in 1890. Historian Priscilla Wegars tells that in 1891, "all 22 Chinese in Clark Fork were run out of town," followed by Hoodoo the same year, Bonners Ferry in 1892, Coeur d'Alene in 1894, and Moscow in 1909. Chinese returned to some towns within a year or two but stayed out of Moscow until the mid-1920s and Coeur d'Alene until at least 1931.[11]

Around this time, Chinese in California also came under attack. Democrats supported white workers' attempts to exclude them. In May 1876, whites drove out Chinese from Antioch, California, one of the early expulsions, and in Rocklin the next year, they burned Chinatown to the ground. Expulsions and anti-Chinese ordinances peaked in the 1880s but continued for decades. In the 1890s whites violently expelled Chinese people from the fishing industry in most parts of the state. In all, between about 1884 and 1900, according to Jean Pfaelzer's careful research, more than 40 California towns drove all their Chinese residents out of town and kept them out. Around 1905 came Visalia's turn: whites "burned down the whole Chinatown," according to a man born there in 1900 who remembered that it happened when he was small. In June 1906, the city council of Santa Ana, California, passed a resolution that called for "the fire department to burn each and every one of the said buildings known as Chinatown"; on June 26 a crowd of more than a thousand watched it burn. Many of these towns enacted policies excluding Chinese Americans and remained "Chinese-free" for decades.[12]

One of the better-studied expulsions was from Eureka, in Humboldt County in northern California. On February 6, 1885, a city councilman was killed by a stray bullet fired by one of two quarreling Chinese men. White workers had already been clamoring, "The Chinese must go." That night, some 600 whites met to demand that all Chinese leave Humboldt County within 24 hours. Some white citizens defended the Chinese and tried to keep their own domestic servants but were forced to give them up. The next morning, some 480 Chinese and whatever belongings they could carry were aboard two steamships that then sailed for San Francisco. A week later, "a large crowd assembled at Centennial Hall to hear the report of the citizens' committee," according to Lynwood Carranco, who wrote a detailed account of the incident. They adopted several resolutions:

1) That all Chinamen be expelled from the city and that none be allowed to return.
2) That a committee be appointed to act for one year, whose duty shall be to warn all Chinamen who may attempt to come to this place to live, and to use all reasonable means to prevent their remaining. If the warning is disregarded, to call mass meetings of citizens to whom the case will be referred for proper action.
3 That a notice be issued to all property owners through the daily papers, requesting them not to lease or rent property to Chinese.[13]

Copycat expulsions followed from Arcata, Ferndale, and Crescent City (Portfolio 1 shows a broadside advocating "ridding Crescent City of Chinese"). By October 1906, some 23 Chinese workers had returned to work in a cannery in Humboldt County; they lasted less than a month before whites again drove them out. (Portfolio 2 shows this expulsion.) In 1937 the *Humboldt Times* published a souvenir edition on its 85th anniversary that bragged about its Chinese-free status:

Humboldt County has the unique distinction of being the only community in which there are no Oriental colonies. . . . [14] Although 52 years have passed since the Chinese were driven from the county, none have ever returned. On one or two occasions offshore vessels with Chinese crews have stopped at this port, but the Chinamen as a rule stayed aboard their vessels, choosing not to take a chance on being ordered out. Chinese everywhere have always looked upon this section of the state as "bad medicine" for the Chinamen.[15]

The attacks on Chinese in the West grew so bad that Mark Twain famously said, "A Chinaman had no rights that any man was bound to respect," deliberately echoing Roger Taney's words in *Dred Scott*. Whites even tried to drive out Chinese from large cities such as San Francisco and Seattle but failed, owing to the enormity of the task.[16]

The Chinese Retreat and the Great Retreat

From 1890 to the 1930s, whites across the North (and the nontraditional South) began to do to African Americans what westerners had done to Chinese Americans.[17] The Chinese retreat can be dated from the mid-1870s to about 1910, antedating the Great Retreat by fifteen to twenty years. There were other differences. Because Chinese Americans were not citizens, and because they had played no role in the Civil War, it was much harder for antiracists to mobilize sentiment on their behalf. In 1879, only 900 California voters supported continued Chinese immigration, while 150,000 favored keeping them out. Also, municipal policies to keep out Chinese Americans mostly relaxed in the 1970s or even earlier, while sundown towns vis-à-vis African Americans lasted much longer.

However, there are at least seven close parallels between the two movements. First, Democrats led the attacks on both groups, in line with their position as the party of white supremacy. Second, there was some safety in numbers; ironically, some of the largest and most vicious race riots proved that. Although they tried, whites could not drive all Chinese Americans from Seattle, San Francisco, or Los Angeles. They succeeded in smaller places such as Rock Springs and Humboldt County. Similarly, blacks did find some refuge in majority-black neighborhoods in the inner city. Whites usually proved reluctant to venture far into alien territory to terrorize residents. Although whites attacked black neighborhoods in Chicago; East St. Louis, Illinois; Washington, D.C.; Tulsa; and other cities between 1917 and 1924, they were unable to destroy them for good.

Third, whites sometimes allowed one or two members of the despised race to stay, even as they forced out all others, especially if a rich white family protected them. Fourth, both groups often resisted being expelled or violated the bans. The 1906 return by Chinese Americans to Humboldt County offers a case in point; African Americans also returned repeatedly to towns that had driven them out. Fifth, after one town drove out or kept out Chinese Americans, whites in nearby towns often asked, "Why haven't *we* done that?" so an epidemic of expulsions resulted. Expulsions or prohibitions of African Americans likewise proved contagious, sweeping through whole regions. Sixth, once a community defined itself as a sundown town—vis-à-vis Chinese or

African Americans—typically it stayed that way for decades and celebrated its all-white status openly. Eureka did not repeal its anti-Chinese ordinance until 1959. Some sundown towns vis-à-vis African Americans *still* maintain their all-white status, although less openly than in the past.

Finally, and most important for our purposes, Chinatowns became the norm for Chinese American life only *after* the Chinese Retreat—about 1884 to 1910. Likewise, only after the Great Retreat did big-city ghettoes become the dwelling places of most northern blacks. African Americans were a *rural* people in the nineteenth century, and not just in the South, from which they moved, but also in the North, to which they came. In 1890 the proportion of black Illinoisans living in Chicago, for example (25%), was less than that for whites (29%). Nevertheless, by 1940 amnesia set in, and Americans forgot completely that in the nineteenth century, Chinese had lived in towns and hamlets throughout the West, while blacks had moved to little towns and rural areas across the North. Americans also repressed the memory of the expulsions and ordinances that created sundown towns. Now Americans typecast African Americans as residents of places such as Harlem and the South Side of Chicago, and Chinese Americans as Chinatown dwellers.[18]

In reality, white evictions and prohibitions provided the most important single reason for these retreats to large cities. In places where no such pressures existed, such as Mississippi, Chinese Americans continued to live throughout the Nadir period, sprinkled about in tiny rural towns such as Merigold and Louise; few lived in the metropolitan areas of Jackson or the Gulf Coast.[19]

The Great Retreat Was National

What happened next was national, not regional, and affected America's largest minority, far more than the 100,000 Chinese Americans then in the country. From town after town, county after county—even from whole regions—African Americans were driven by white opposition, winding up in huge northern ghettoes.

Sometimes this was accomplished by violence, sometimes by subtler means; the next chapter tells how sundown towns were created. Here it is important to understand that we are not talking about a handful of sundown towns sprinkled across America. The Great Retreat left in its wake a new geography of race in the United States. From Myakka City, Florida, to Kennewick, Washington, the nation is dotted with thousands of all-white towns that are (or were until recently) all white on purpose. Sundown towns can be found in almost every state.[20] This chapter takes us on a whirlwind journey around the United States, exploring sundown towns and counties in every region. Independent sundown towns are fairly common in the East, frighteningly so in the Midwest, nontraditional South, and Far West, but rare in the traditional South. Sundown suburbs are common everywhere, although they are now disappearing in the South and Far West. Indeed, because sundown towns proved to be so numerous, this chapter proved the hardest to write. If it described or even merely listed sundown towns by state, the chapter would become impossibly long, but if it only generalized about the extent of the problem, it would be unconvincing. I tried to find a middle path, a mix of examples and generalities, and set up a web site, uvm.edu/~jloewen/sundown, giving many more examples.

County Populations Show the Great Retreat

One way to show the Great Retreat is by examining the population of African Americans by county. Between 1890 and 1930 or 1940, the absolute number of African Americans in many northern counties and towns plummeted.[21] Table 1, "Counties with No or Few African Americans' in 1890 and 1930," shows this phenomenon in several ways. The "total" row at the bottom of the table shows that, as a result of the relatively welcoming atmosphere of the 1860s–80s, only 119 counties in the United States (excluding the traditional South) had no African American residents in 1890. *But by 1930, the number of counties with not a single African American had nearly doubled, to 235.* Counties with just a handful of African Americans (fewer than 10) also increased, from 452 in 1890 to 694 by 1930.[22] Many entire counties that had African Americans in 1890 had none by 1930. Other counties with sizable black populations in 1890 had only a handful of African Americans by 1930.

These findings fly in the face of normal population diffusion, which would predict continued dispersal over time. Thus the number of counties with no members of a group would normally decrease, even if no new members of the group entered the overall system, just from the ordinary haphazard moves of individuals and families from place to place. That the opposite happened is quite surprising and indicates the withdrawal of African Americans from many counties across the Northern states. Table 1 excludes the traditional South;[23] we shall see why shortly.

Table 1. Counties with No or Few (< 10) African Americans, 1890 and 1930

STATE	1890 0 BLACKS	1890 <10 BLACKS	1930 0 BLACKS	1930 <10 BLACKS
Arizona	0	1	1	1
Arkansas	0	1	3	8
California	0	4	0	8
Colorado	5	19	8	28
Connecticut	0	0	0	0
Delaware	0	0	0	0
Idaho	1	9	14	33
Illinois	0	6	6	17
Indiana	1	14	6	20
Iowa	13	28	12	38
Kansas	6	20	6	23
Kentucky	0	0	0	4
Maine	0	2	0	5
Maryland	0	0	0	0
Massachusetts	0	0	0	0
Michigan	4	23	7	26
Minnesota	22	57	16	61
Missouri	0	8	12	28
Montana	0	2	11	41
Nebraska	9	41	28	64
Nevada	1	6	1	8
New Hampshire	0	0	0	2
New Jersey	0	0	0	0
New Mexico	0	9	3	11
New York	0	0	0	1
North Dakota	13	26	20	42
Ohio	0	1	1	2
Oklahoma	2	10	4	11
Oregon	1	16	4	24
Pennsylvania	0	3	1	4
Rhode Island	0	0	0	0
South Dakota	19	37	23	52
Texas	3	20	8	29
Utah	5	16	15	22
Vermont	0	3	1	4
Washington	5	16	6	20
West Virginia	1	3	1	4
Wisconsin	8	27	16	42
Wyoming	0	5	1	11
Total	119	456	235	694

Boldface indicates states with more counties with 0 or few blacks in 1930 than in 1890.

The striking uniformity in Table 1 also reveals the startling extent of the Great Retreat. Beginning at the top, we note that every Arizona county had at least one African American in 1910, the first year for which data exist. But by 1930, one Arizona county has no African Americans at all. One county is not worth reporting, but the trend grows more pronounced in Arkansas, which also had no county without African Americans in 1890 but had three by 1930, as well as five more with just a handful. The pattern then holds with remarkable consistency in California, Colorado, and all the rest. Of the 39 states in the table, *not one showed greater dispersion of African Americans in 1930 than in 1890. In 31 of 39 states, African Americans lived in a narrower range of counties in 1930 than they did in 1890.* Minnesota showed a mixed result,[24] and seven states—Connecticut, Delaware, Maryland, Massachusetts, New Jersey, New York, and Rhode Island—had virtually no counties in either year with fewer than ten blacks, so they could show no trend in Table 1. However, the Appendix provides a closer look at those eight states and reveals that there, too, African Americans concentrated in just a few counties in 1930, to a far greater extent than did whites.[25] *Thus those states also fit the pattern; hence every state in Table 1 shows some confirmation of the Great Retreat.*

Some of the statewide retreats indicated in Table 1 are dramatic. For example, African Americans lived in every Indiana county but one in 1890. By 1930, six counties had none and another fourteen had fewer than ten African American residents, even though many more African Americans now lived in the state. I have confirmed eighteen Indiana counties as sundown throughout or in substantial part. Moreover, even when Table 1 does not show a dramatic decline, looking at the actual number of African Americans in each county does. For example, in 1890, every county in the state of Maine had at least eighteen African Americans, except one with just two and another with nine. By 1930, Maine looked very different. Now five counties had eight or fewer African Americans. Several showed striking drops in their black populations: Lincoln County from 26 to 5, for example, and Piscataquis from 19 to just 1. Hancock County dropped from 56 in 1890 to just 3, yet Hancock had more than 30,000 people in 1930. Geography does not seem to account for these declines; the counties with fewer than eight African Americans were sprinkled about, not concentrated in Maine's isolated rural north.

The Great Retreat and the Great Migration

These decreases to no or only a few African Americans by 1930 came in the teeth of huge increases in the black population nationally and in many northern states. Nationally, the number of African Americans went up by nearly 60%, from 7,388,000 in 1890 to 11,759,000 in 1930. Moreover, beginning about 1915, African Americans from Dixie started moving north in large numbers, a movement now known as the "Great Migration," in response to the impact of World War I, which simultaneously increased the demand for American products abroad and interfered with European migration to northern cities.[26] More than 1,000,000 African Americans moved north between 1915 and 1930. Thus the absolute declines in black population by 1930 in many northern counties are all the more staggering. Without a retreat to the cities, these increases in overall black populations would have caused the number of counties with zero or few blacks to plummet.

Coming in the middle of the deepening racism of the Nadir, this Great Migration prompted even more white northerners to view African Americans as a threat. A 1916 editorial from Beloit, Wisconsin, exemplifies the "Negro as problem" rhetoric:

> The Negro problem has moved north. Rather, the Negro problem has spread from south to north. . . . Within a few years, experts predict the Negro population of the North will be tripled. It's your problem, or it will be when the Negro moves next door. . . . With the black tide setting north, the southern Negro, formerly a docile tool, is demanding better pay, better food, and better treatment. . . . It's a national problem now, instead of a sectional problem. And it has got to be solved.[27]

Historians and sociologists took note of the growing urban concentration of African Americans between 1890 and 1930, continuing to about 1960. One of the foremost writers on race relations of the era, T. J. Woofter Jr., put it this way: "It is remarkable that Negro city population should have increased by a million and a half between 1900 and 1920; but it is astounding that a million of this increase should have been concentrated in the metropolitan centers of the East and the Middle West." More than half of this increase was absorbed by just 24 cities, each having black populations of more than 25,000, he observed. "This emphasizes the astonishing degree of concentration that has taken place."[28]

But neither Woofter nor other commentators noted the *decreases* in black populations—often to zero or to a single household—in smaller cities and towns across the North. The Great Migration seems to have masked the Great Retreat. Scores of books discuss the Great Migration; none tells of the Great Retreat (by this or any other name). The increased black population in, say,

Chicago got ascribed to migration from Mississippi, which was largely true; hence the internal migration of African Americans from small towns in Illinois to Chicago went unnoticed. Not grasping the extent of anti-black sentiment in smaller northern towns during the Nadir, social scientists somehow found it "natural" for people from tiny Glen Allan, Mississippi, to wind up in Chicago; for those from Brownsville, Tennessee, to move to Decatur, Illinois; and for inhabitants of Ninety Six, South Carolina, to move to Washington, D.C. This is not how other migrations to the North worked. People from small villages in Italy often wound up in places such as Barre, Vermont, or West Frankfort, Illinois, as well as St. Louis. Norwegians went to Mount Horeb, Wisconsin, not just Minneapolis. But this was not true of African Americans—not after the 1890s, anyway.

Indeed, historians and social scientists have used the Great Migration to "explain" the increased racism in the North. That is, they used documents such as the Beloit editorial to explain the increased segregation African Americans experienced: the masses of newcomers strained the system, threatened whites' jobs, upset existing equilibriums, and the like. But the Great Migration did not cause the Great Retreat. Whites were already driving African Americans from small towns across the Midwest *before* those towns experienced any substantial migration from the South. They continued to drive out blacks from towns that never saw any sizable influx after 1915. The Great Retreat started in 1890, a product of the increasing white racism of the Nadir. It cannot be understood as a reaction to a migration that started in 1915.

Now let us tour the country, seeing the profusion of sundown towns almost everywhere, beginning in the Midwest. In the process, we shall visit towns that excluded not only African Americans, but also Chinese, Jewish, Native, and Mexican Americans—and in a few cases Catholics, labor union members, homosexuals, and some others. We shall see that prime real estate—elite suburbs, beach resorts, mountain vacation spots, and islands—has typically been off-limits. And we shall encounter whole subregions where African Americans are generally not allowed, even in unincorporated rural areas.

The Great Retreat in the Heartland

I did more research in Illinois than in any other single state. Table 1 shows that African Americans lived in every Illinois county in 1890. By 1930, six counties had none, while another eleven had fewer than ten African American residents. Without a doubt, exclusion underlies these numbers. In Illinois and elsewhere, entire counties developed and enforced the policy of keeping out

African Americans. Many of the towns confirmed as sundown towns in my research are county seats, and when they went sundown, often—not always—the rest of the county followed suit. I have confirmed that ten of these seventeen counties had gone sundown by 1930 and suspect all seventeen[29] did.

Various written and oral sources tell of Illinois counties that kept out African Americans as a matter of county policy. Malcolm Ross of the Fair Employment Practices Commission wrote about Calhoun County, for example, "Calhoun County is recorded in the 1940 census as '8,207 whites; no Negroes; no other races.' This is not by accident. Calhoun people see to it that no Negroes settle there." According to an 83-year-old lifelong resident of Mason County, north of Springfield, the sheriff "would meet [blacks] at the county line and tell them not to come in."[30] Mason County has remained all white for many decades, despite its location between Springfield and Peoria, both with large African American populations, and on the Illinois River, an important trade route.[31]

Table 1 is a useful way to summarize the entire northern United States, but county data can only hint at the extent of the problem, because county is such a broad unit of analysis. Illinois may have had seventeen sundown counties in 1930, but it had far more sundown towns than that. Several entire counties in Illinois allowed no African Americans except in one or two isolated locations, for example, but that one place sufficed to remove such a county from Table 1. Town is a more useful jurisdiction to examine. Most sundown towns in Illinois lie in counties that never appear in Table 1. In 1970, when sundown towns were probably at their maximum, Illinois had 621 towns larger than 1,000 people, ranging from Wyanet, with 1,005, to Chicago.[32] Of these, 424 or almost 70% were "all-white" (as defined in Chapter 1) in census after census. In addition, my universe of towns must include 50 hamlets smaller than 1,000 that came to my attention because of evidence confirming them as sundown towns. Therefore my list of Illinois towns totaled 671, ranging from tiny hamlets to Chicago. Of these 671 towns, 474 or 71% were all-white,[33] while 197 had African Americans.

Of course, the mere fact that they were all-white does not confirm the 474 as sundown towns. That requires information as to their racial policies in the past. I was able to get such material on 146 of the 424 all-white towns larger than 1,000. Of these 146, I have confirmed 145 as sundown towns or suburbs, or 99.5%.[34] In addition, the 50 hamlets smaller than 1,000 in population were confirmed as sundown towns. Confirmed Illinois sundown towns range in size from communities of just a few hundred people to Cicero, which in 1970[35] had 67,058 residents, and Pekin, which in 1970 had 31,375 and another 3,500 in its suburbs.

If 145 of the 146 suspected sundown towns larger than 1,000 on which we have information indeed turned out to be confirmed, what can we predict about the remaining 278 towns, on which we have no historical information beyond census data? Our best estimate would be that 99.5%—the same proportion as among the towns we have checked out—or about 277 of them would be sundown towns. There is no good reason to suppose the next towns will be different from those we know.[36] When we add to that estimate of 277 the 145 towns that I have confirmed, plus the 50 hamlets, *our best single estimate is that 472 of the 474 all-white towns and hamlets were all-white on purpose.*

Of course, we would not be surprised if "only" 465 (98%) of the 474 towns turned out to be sundown, or if 473 were sundown. Applying the principles of inferential statistics, we can calculate a range within which we can be confident the true number of sundown towns will fall. Statisticians call this the "confidence limits" for our best estimate of 472 or 99.5%.[37] They find these limits by computing the statistical formula known as the standard error of the difference of two percentages. Here this standard error equals .0205 or 2.05%.[38] The more rigorous confidence band used by statisticians is the 99% limit, the range that is large enough that we can be 99% sure that it includes the true proportion of sundown towns among the unknown towns. Here that range is 5.3%.[39] Accordingly, our estimate for the correct proportion of sundown towns among the unexamined towns would be .995 ± .053 or 94.2% to 104.8%. Of course, numbers above 100% are impossible; we can be 99% confident that the number of sundown towns among the unknown towns is roughly 94% to 100%, or 261 to 278 of the 278 towns.[40] Adding the 195 known sundown towns yields an overall estimate that the number of sundown towns among all 474 overwhelmingly white towns in Illinois lies between 456 (96%) and 473 (99.8%). We can say with a 99% level of confidence that between 96% and 99.8% of all the all-white towns in Illinois were sundown towns.[41] Our best single estimate remains 472, or 99.5%.

Even this total, 472, is not the full number of sundown towns in Illinois. I included communities smaller than 1,000 inhabitants only when informants or written sources brought them to my attention. These 50 confirmed sundown hamlets persuaded me to be suspicious of even very small all-white communities; many other hamlets no doubt kept out blacks.[42] Also, various sundown towns larger than 1,000 in population missed getting on my radar in the first place,[43] owing to nonhousehold African Americans such as prisoners.

These sundown towns are spread out throughout the state. Southern Illinois had many more even than Map 1 shows. Central Illinois has just as many: oral history confirmed some three dozen communities as sundown towns just within a 60-mile radius of Decatur, and written documentation confirmed another dozen. Northern Illinois has even more, owing to the sundown suburbs ringing Chicago. As a correspondent suggested about Ohio, instead of studying sundown towns, perhaps I should have researched the exceptions—towns that never excluded blacks—since that would be a more manageable number.

Similar maps could be drawn, showing most towns in boldface, in most other states in the Midwest, the Ozarks, the Cumberlands, the suburbs of any city from Boston to Los Angeles, and many other areas of the United States. But before we leave Illinois, this statistic of 472 probable sundown towns might come alive if I supply examples. I have chosen three, one from each section of the state.

LaSalle and Peru in northern Illinois are separate towns, each with its own library, city hall, etc., but they share a high school and a common boundary, and most people consider them really one entity. I don't know when they first became sundown towns. Not one African American lived in the towns on the eve of the Civil War, when their combined population was 8,279. Even back then, the absence of blacks was surprising, since both towns lie on the Illinois River, a major artery, and on the Illinois-Michigan Canal, connecting Lake Michigan to the river at Peru, which opened up a water route from New Orleans to the Great Lakes. By 1860, when railroads became dominant, LaSalle-Peru found itself equally favored, being on a main line of the Illinois Central as well as the Rock Island Line, a major east-west railroad from Chicago. These trade routes surely would have brought African Americans to LaSalle-Peru had they been allowed. In 1864, seven African Americans from nearby Mendota signed up for the army and traveled with their recruiting officer to LaSalle to go up the canal to Joliet to be mustered in. In LaSalle a gang of "Copperheads" attacked them and drove them out of the city.[44] Census takers in 1870 found only one African American in Peru, none in LaSalle. Yet the war had caused many African Americans to wind up in Cairo, whence they diffused through the Midwest, and the Illinois Central directly connects Mississippi, Cairo, and LaSalle-Peru. In 1880, LaSalle was the only city in Illinois (defined as larger than 4,000 in that year) with no African Americans, and Peru was one of only two cities that had just one. An 1889 article in the

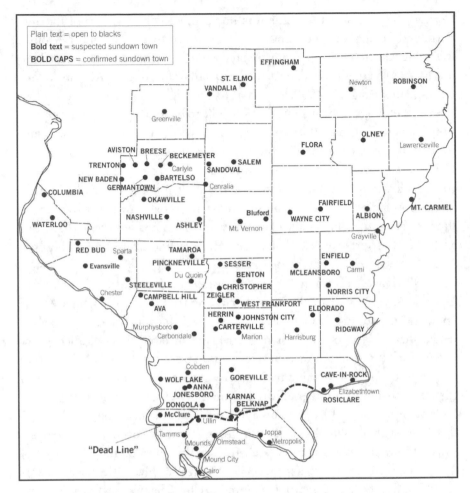

Map 1. Centers of Manufacturing in Southern Illinois

In 1952 Charles Colby mapped 80 communities in southern Illinois—including every larger city, many towns, and some hamlets—all chosen because they had factories. Identifying their racial policies shows how widespread sundown towns were, at least in this subregion. Of his 80 towns, 55 or 69% are suspected sundown towns, "all-white" for decades. Among these 55, I confirmed the racial policies of 52, and of those 52, 51 (all but Newton) were sundown towns.

The dotted line at the bottom is the "dead line," north of which African Americans were not allowed to live (except in the unbolded towns). South of this line, cotton was the major crop; white landowners employed black labor, following the southern tradition of hierarchical race relations rather than northern sundown policies. All 8 towns below this line allowed African Americans to live in them. Among the 72 towns above the line, only 18—a quarter—did so to my knowledge.

Chicago Tribune noted that this was no accident: "The miners of LaSalle, Peru, and Spring Valley do not allow a Negro in their city limits." Around this time, the towns apparently posted sundown signs, which stayed up until after World War II. The cities clearly still refused to let African Americans spend the night in 1952, for in that year its high school band director had to skirt the policy to host an integrated college band. By 1970, their populations had grown to 22,508, of whom just five were African American. Again, these numbers are shockingly low, since the cities were now also served by U.S. 6, a major east-west highway from Atlantic to Pacific, and U.S. 51, which runs all the way to New Orleans and was the most important single highway in Mississippi before the advent of the interstate system. An undergraduate at the University of Illinois-Chicago who grew up in LaSalle-Peru in the 1980s and 1990s reported that LaSalle-Peru High School stayed all-white until 1998.[45]

Villa Grove, a central Illinois town seventeen miles south of Champaign-Urbana, is newer and smaller than LaSalle-Peru, but equally white. After I spoke in Decatur in October 2001, two people came forward to say they had heard that Villa Grove had or has a whistle or siren that sounded every evening at 6 PM to tell all African Americans to be out of town. I filed the story under "urban legends," thinking it absurd that anyone could possibly worry that any substantial number of African Americans were clamoring to get *into* Villa Grove, a town of 2,553 people located on no major highway. The story did suggest that Villa Grove is a sundown town, however, so I visited the town. To my surprise, interview after interview confirmed the whistle story. Today Villa Grove is both a local service center supplying the needs of surrounding farmers and a bedroom community for Champaign-Urbana. Some Champaign-Urbana residents moved to Villa Grove and now commute to work to minimize their contact with African Americans in Champaign-Urbana. One African American woman at the University of Illinois told of conversations with a white colleague at her former job. He was a native of Villa Grove, as was his wife, from whom he had separated. As he recounted it, his wife insisted that he wash his hands at her home before picking up their daughters for weekend visitation, because she knew an African American was employed at his workplace and they might have touched common objects.[46]

In July 1899, striking white miners drove a group of African American strikebreakers down the railroad tracks out of Carterville, a town of 3,600 in southern Illinois. In the process, they shot five of them dead. Eventually the whites were all acquitted, the strikers won, and all African Americans were forced to leave. Carterville had already pushed the sundown town concept to a new level before 1899, not permitting African Americans to set foot inside the city limits, even during the day. This policy remained in force for decades. Even Dr. Andrew Springs, the black physician serving Dewmaine, a small black community about a mile north of Carterville, had to wait at the edge of town in the 1930s for drugs he had ordered from Carterville's pharmacy to be delivered to him. In the late 1970s, the first black family moved in. According to Carl Planinc, who has lived in Carterville for several decades, "ironically, their first night, there was a fire, and their house burned down." [47]

Stories such as these exist for each town that I list as confirmed, and I believe similar information, differing only in detail, remains to be harvested from almost every one of Illinois's 474 all-white towns. What about other states? Roberta Senechal, one of the handful of authors who have mentioned sundown towns, noted that "such banning of blacks by custom and unwritten law from rural and small-town communities was not a phenomenon limited to Illinois." She is right, of course, so I widened my circle, turning first to Indiana, next door. [48]

Indiana showed a similar pattern. Of course, of all states, Indiana is most like Illinois and borders it for 300 miles. In 1964, in an affectionate memoir, *My Indiana,* Irving Leibowitz wrote, "Intolerance was everywhere. 'NIGGER, DON'T LET THE SUN SET ON YOU HERE,' was a sign posted in most every small town in Indiana." As in Illinois, whole Indiana counties kept out African Americans entirely or restricted them to one or two small hamlets. [49] Map 2 shows eighteen confirmed sundown counties and fifteen suspects in 1970. In addition, many confirmed sundown towns lie sprinkled across Indiana's unshaded counties. [50]

Some Indiana sundown towns were famous for their policy. Elwood's moment of notoriety as a sundown town came in 1940 when native son Wendell Willkie was nominated for president there. Its population was then 11,000; as many as 150,000 people crowded in for the rally. Frances Peacock wrote a memoir about two black Republicans who never made it, George Sawyer and his father:

> In 1940 George and his father, an active Republican, were on their way to Elwood, Indiana, to attend a rally for Wendell Willkie, the Republican presidential candidate. When they arrived at Elwood that morning before the convention, they saw two road signs posted at the city limits: "Niggers, read this and run. If you can't read, run anyhow," and "Nigger, don't let the sun set on you in Elwood."

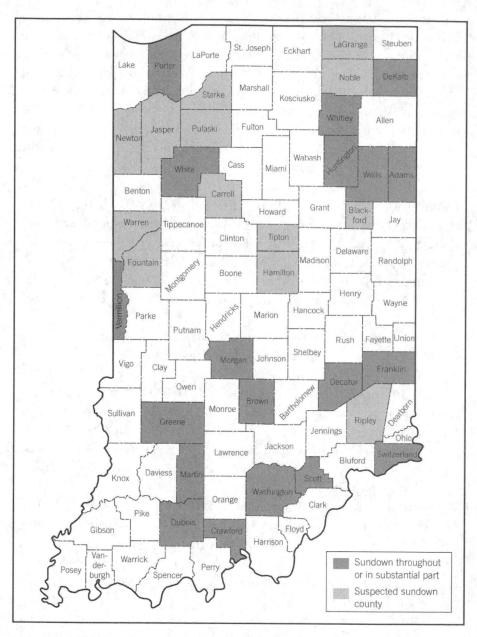

Map 2. Sundown Counties in Indiana

Indiana had only 1 black-free county in 1890, but 6 by 1930, as well as 27 others with a handful of African Americans. All 33 were probably sundown counties; I have confirmed 18.

George's father turned the car around and drove back to Anderson. And from then on, he was a Democrat.[51]

I identified a total of 231 Indiana towns as all-white.[52] I was able to get information as to the racial policies of 95, and of those, I confirmed all 95 as sundown towns.[53] In Indiana, I have yet to uncover *any* overwhelmingly white town that on-site research failed to confirm as a sundown town. Ninety-five out of 95 is an astounding proportion; statistical analysis shows that it is quite likely that 90 to 100% of all 231 were sundown towns. They ranged from tiny hamlets to cities in the 10,000–50,000 population range, including Huntington (former vice president Dan Quayle's hometown) and Valparaiso (home of Valparaiso University).

Portfolio 25 shows the last page from the 1970 census for Indiana towns with 1,000 to 2,499 residents.[54] Note the striking number of dashes in the "Negro" column—towns that had not a single African American. Surely Leibowitz was right. Indeed, almost four decades after Leibowitz wrote, my research uncovered oral or written history, usually from more than one source, of actual sundown signs posted in at least 21 Indiana communities.[55] Most had come down by the end of World War II, but according to Mike Haas, signs in the little town of Sunman said "NIGGER! BETTER NOT BE SEEN HERE AFTER SUNDOWN!" until well into the 1980s. The most recent sign was spotted in White County in 1998.[56]

Intentionally all-white communities dot the rest of the Midwest. In Ohio, independent sundown towns are found from Niles in the north to Syracuse on the Ohio River, and sundown suburbs proliferate around Cincinnati and Cleveland. Missouri has an extraordinary number of sundown towns, at least 200. Many are in the Ozarks and will be treated later in this chapter, but the more midwestern parts of Missouri have dozens of sundown towns and counties as well. In sum, by 1930 probably a majority of all towns in the heartland kept out African Americans. No wonder blacks moved to Chicago and St. Louis.

Sundown Towns in the Far North

Clearly sundown towns were a phenomenon throughout the lower Midwest. But what about states farther north? Ohio, Indiana, and Illinois border former slave states, after all, and Missouri was a slave state, so they were near black populations. Initially I did not expect to find sundown towns in far northern states such as Maine, Michigan, Wisconsin, Idaho, or Oregon. I labored under the misapprehension that all-white towns so far north were unlikely to be purposeful. I thought that because these states were so distant from African American population centers, it may be unreasonable to expect their towns to have black residents in the first place. Also I imagined that whites so far north, faced with no possible "threat" from any large number of African Americans, would be unlikely to adopt exclusionary policies. I was wrong on both counts.

Take Wisconsin, for example, not usually considered a place where African Americans concentrated, except perhaps Milwaukee. In 1890, the state was indeed only 0.15% black. Nevertheless, before 1890, black people hardly limited themselves to Milwaukee. Table 1 shows that only 8 of Wisconsin's 68 counties held no African Americans in 1890; another 27 counties had fewer than 10. Twenty-six counties had at least twenty African Americans, and these were sprinkled about the state. Four counties around Lake Winnebago—Calumet, Fond du Lac, Outagamie, and Winnebago—boasted 389 African Americans among them, almost as many as Milwaukee. In all, 1,986 African Americans lived outside of Milwaukee, along with 458 black Milwaukeeans.

By 1930, the number of African Americans living in Milwaukee had swelled almost tenfold to 4,188, while outside Milwaukee lived fewer blacks—just 1,623—than in 1890. In 1890, less than 20% of Wisconsin's African Americans lived in Milwaukee; by 1930, 72% did. The most dramatic declines came in the counties around Lake Winnebago, by 1930 home to just 86 African Americans, most of them in Winnebago County. Fond du Lac's 178 African Americans in 1880 dwindled to just 22 in 1930 and 5 by 1940. Statewide, 16 counties had no African Americans at all by 1930, and another 42 had fewer than ten.

Among its 144 cities of more than 2,500 population in 1970, Wisconsin had 126 all-white communities (as defined in Chapter 1). No prior published histories treat the phenomenon of sundown towns in Wisconsin, so far as I know, and I could not spend nearly as much time doing oral history in Wisconsin as in Illinois and Indiana. Nevertheless, I confirmed nine as sundown towns; for ten others, including several towns near Lake Winnebago, I have some evidence.[57] I am sure that many additional Wisconsin towns, including several Milwaukee suburbs, also excluded African Americans, but have not done on-site research to prove it.

Some Wisconsin sundown towns were tiny hamlets; even some unincorporated rural locales kept out African Americans by refusing to sell them land or hire them as farm labor. Some were startlingly large cities, such as Appleton, population 60,000, and Sheboygan, 45,000.[58] Sheboygan, for example, acted as if it had passed a sundown ordinance: it had a police officer meet trains at the railroad station to warn African Americans not to stay there, according to a resident there in the early 1960s. At least one town, Manitowoc, posted signs. Grey Gundaker, now a professor at the College of William and Mary, saw them when he lived there from 1962 to 1964: "The signs were worded approximately 'NIGGER: Don't let the sun go down on you in our town!' " he recalls. "I think the words were in italics and painted across a picture of a green hill with the sun setting halfway behind it." [59]

Beaver Dam, 60 miles northwest of Milwaukee, grew steadily from 4,222 people in 1890 to 10,356 in 1940 and 14,265 in 1970. Despite this growth, its black population fell from eight in 1890 to just one a decade later, then stayed at one or two until after 1970.[60] A 1969 report at Wayland Academy, a prep school located in Beaver Dam, evaluated "the feasibility of admitting Negroes to Wayland"; its authors interviewed townspeople "to determine problems which might face a Negro as he lives in this presently nonintegrated community." Several older inhabitants of Beaver Dam "all said the same thing in the same words" to Moira Meltzer-Cohen, Beaver Dam resident and resourceful researcher: " 'A couple of black families tried to move in during the '60s and '70s and they were run right out.' " [61]

Wisconsin exemplifies findings from other far north states. Oregon had just one county with no African Americans at all in 1890, although it had sixteen more with fewer than ten. By 1930, however, Oregon had four counties with no African Americans and twenty more with fewer than ten. Exclusion was responsible. Correspondents have sent me evidence confirming that a string of towns along what is now Interstate 5 in western Oregon, for instance, including Eugene, Umpqua, Grants Pass, Eagle Point, Medford, and others, kept out African Americans until the recent past. Other examples across the far north from west to east include Kennewick and Richland in Washington; Ashton and Wallace in Idaho, and probably all of Lemhi County; Austin, Minnesota; many towns in Michigan; and Tonawanda and North Tonawanda in New York, almost on the Canadian border. Wallace, for example, expelled its Chinese in the nineteenth century; in the twentieth it put up a sign at the edge of town that said "Nigger, Read This Sign and Run"; and in the 2000 census it still had no African Americans and just one Asian American. So even in the Idaho panhandle up by Canada, towns felt the need to keep out people of color.[62]

The Great Retreat Did Not Strike the "Traditional South"

Very different race relations evolved in what I call the "traditional South"— Virginia, North Carolina, South Carolina, Georgia, Florida, Alabama, Tennessee, Mississippi, and Louisiana, all states historically dominated by slavery.[63] There, in contrast to the North, slavery grew more entrenched after the American Revolution. Some whites grew wealthy from the unpaid labor, and most others yearned to emulate them. After slavery ended, the tradition continued in the form of sharecropping, which kept many blacks in peonage, unable to pay the perpetual debt by which white landowners bound them to the land. In towns, blacks continued to do the domestic chores, janitoring, and backbreaking work that whites avoided—now in exchange for inadequate wages. To hire blacks, whom they could pay less than whites, was in the interest of plantation owners, railroads, and other employers.

County populations in the traditional South do not show the Great Retreat. Indeed, during the Nadir, when sundown towns were most in vogue, whites from the traditional South expressed astonishment at the practice. Why expel your maid, your agricultural workforce, your school janitor, your railroad track layers? Writing about Washington County, Indiana, Emma Lou Thornbrough noted that African Americans "were not allowed to come in even as servants, a fact which occasioned surprise among visitors from the South." Traditional white southerners saw African Americans as workers to be exploited and sometimes as problems to be controlled but not expelled.[64]

Therefore the traditional South has almost no independent sundown towns, and never did. This does not make whites in the traditional South less racist than in other parts of the South or other regions of the country. Racist they were—indeed, racism arose in Western cultures primarily as a rationale for racial slavery—but the tradition entailed controlling and exploiting blacks, not getting rid of them. Indeed, the original sundown rule was a curfew at dusk during slavery times; to be out after dark, slaves had to have written passes from their owners. After slavery ended in the traditional South, whites often lynched African Americans to keep them down; elsewhere in the United States, whites sometimes lynched them, we will see, to drive them out.

Thus Mississippi, for example, has just two all-white towns with a population over 1,000, Belmont and Burnsville, and they lie barely in the state, in the northeast corner near the Alabama line, in Appalachia.[65] It also had three suburbs that excluded African Americans between 1945 and 1975. Alabama has two sundown counties and a handful of sundown towns, but all except one are in far north Alabama—in Appalachia, not in the traditional South—and the exception is a sundown suburb of Mobile.[66] Louisiana has a few, but they are tiny. The cotton culture part of Arkansas boasts not a single sundown town. California has more sundown towns than all parts of the traditional South put together. Illinois has many times more.

The Great Retreat from the Rest of the South

More like the Midwest and West is the "nontraditional South"—Appalachia, the Cumberlands, the Ozarks, much of Florida, and north and west Texas. There, huge swaths of counties, as well as many individual towns, drove out their African Americans beginning in about 1890.[67] Follansbee, West Virginia, for example, kept out African Americans "for years" before the early 1920s. Then some mills brought in African Americans as employees. In October 1923, the Ku Klux Klan burned two fiery crosses and painted a threat on the fence facing "the colored section," warning all blacks to leave immediately, according to the *Pittsburgh Courier*. They fled, and the sundown policy apparently remained in force, for in 2000, Follansbee had 3,115 people, but not a single African American household.[68]

Table 1 shows that much of the nontraditional South did expel its African Americans during the Nadir. Arkansas shows the difference dramatically. In 1890, it had no county without African Americans and only one with fewer than ten; by 1930, three counties had none and another eight had fewer than ten, all in the Arkansas Ozarks. I suspect all eleven were sundown counties and have confirmed six. If we draw a line from the southwest corner of Arkansas northeast to the Missouri Bootheel, the resulting triangle bordering Oklahoma and Missouri includes all 11 counties and all 74 suspected sundown towns in Arkansas. The southeastern part of the state, in contrast, where cotton culture dominated and secession sentiment was strongest, includes not a single sundown town or county.

Similarly, most sundown towns and counties in Texas are in north Texas or southwest of Fort Worth, rather than in the traditionally southern areas of East Texas. Maryland, Kentucky, and Missouri also show this pattern: their sundown towns are in the hills and mountains or are suburbs. Maryland's one sundown county, Garrett, is its farthest west, in Appalachia. Garrett County doesn't show in Table 1 but had become overwhelmingly white by 1940. At least two far west counties in Virginia and two in North Carolina, along with two counties and several towns in east Tennessee, also went sundown after 1890. So did six counties in north Georgia—including Forsyth—and most of Winston County in northern Alabama. Indeed, the Great Retreat was particularly pronounced from the nontraditional South. Map 3 shows some of the areas in the nontraditional South where many counties and towns went sundown, almost all after about 1890.

In the first two decades of the twentieth century, whites expelled African Americans from almost the entire Cumberland Plateau, a huge area extending from the Ohio River near Huntington, West Virginia, southwest through Corbin, Kentucky, crossing into Tennessee, where it marks the division between east and middle Tennessee, and finally ending in northern Alabama. In most parts of the plateau throughout most of the twentieth century, when night came to the Cumberlands, African Americans had better be absent.[69] The twenty Cumberland counties in eastern Kentucky had 3,482 African Americans in 1890, or 2% of the region's 175,631 people. By 1930, although their overall population had increased by more than 50%, these counties had only 1,387 black residents. The decline continued: by 1960 the African American population of these counties had declined to just 531, or 0.2%, one-tenth the 1890 proportion.

Throughout the plateau, this decline was forced. Picking a few examples from north to south, Rockcastle County, Kentucky, had a sundown sign up as late as the mid-1990s, according to George Brosi, editor of *Appalachian Heritage*. In the 1990 census, Rockcastle had no African Americans among its 14,743 people. Esther Sanderson, historian of Scott County, Tennessee, made clear her county's policy:

> There was a big sign on the road at the Kentucky state line and at the entrance at Morgan County [the next county south]: "Nigger, don't let the sun set on your head." The Negroes rarely ever passed through; if they did, they made haste to get through.

Farther south, the sundown policy of Grundy County, Tennessee, garnered national attention in the 1950s when Myles Horton defied it and located his Highlander Folk School, famed for training civil rights leaders, there.[70] Highlander's interracial policy was unpalatable to the county, so in 1959 they got the Tennessee legislature to investigate the school. Eventually Grundy County took Highlander to court and forced the institution to leave, charging Horton with beer sales on its property. Did race have anything to do with it? Paul Cook, Grundy County resident and a member of the jury that found Highlander guilty, assures us it did not:

> That integration business, that didn't have anything to do with it. Lots of folks around here resent the colored, and we still don't have any in this county—but they'd have been in trouble without the niggers.

The Cumberland band of sundown towns and counties then continues across the Alabama line into the Sand Mountains, notorious in the 1930s and '40s

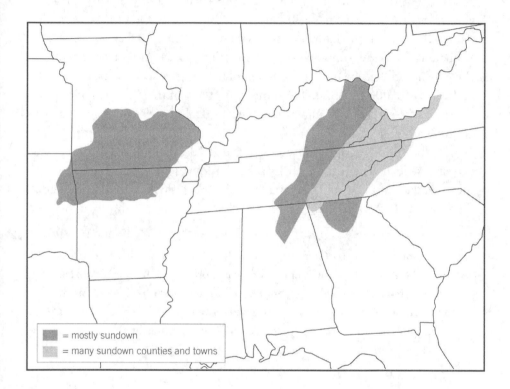

Map 3. Sundown Areas in the Nontraditional South

The lightly-shaded area denotes parts of Appalachia where some counties and towns went sundown, mostly after 1890. Heavily-shaded areas include a V-shaped region in north Georgia, the Cumberlands, and the Ozarks, where *most* counties and towns went sundown, again mainly after 1890.

for their sundown signs. Portfolio 15 shows a representation of such a sign from the 1930s. Historian Charles Martin told of an "old-timer," interviewed by one of his students, who used the usual sundown "problem" rhetoric: "We didn't have any racial problems back then. As long as they were off the mountain by sundown, there weren't any problems."[71]

The Ozarks also went sundown after 1890. No county in Missouri had zero African Americans in 1890, but by 1930, most of the Ozarks were lily white. The same thing happened across the state line in Arkansas. In 1923, William Pickens saw sundown signs across the Ozarks. And in 2001, Milton Rafferty noted that the black population of the Ozarks declined from 62,000 in 1860 to 31,000 by 1930. The sundown policy of the Arkansas and Missouri Ozarks spilled over into northeastern Oklahoma, leaving most of two counties all-white there.[72]

Noting sundown signs still extant in the 1970s, sociologist Gordon Morgan said African Americans in the Ozarks had coined a new term for the towns they marked: "gray towns." So far as I know, this term was not used outside the Ozarks. Morgan goes on:

> In the not too distant past some vigilante whites thought their duty was to police the towns and, with the tacit support of the law, proceeded to harass any black people who might pass through. Some cars carrying blacks have been stoned, and weapons have been brandished by whites. Even today some blacks will not stop in these gray towns for gas or food even though discrimination in the public places is forbidden.

In 2002, some African Americans who live near the Ozarks said they still avoid the region.[73]

The Great Retreat in the West

Table 1 points to the Great Retreat from every state in the Great Plains and Rocky Mountains. African Americans left most rural areas and retreated to a handful of cities with black population concentrations. Every state in the Great Plains and Rocky Mountains also saw a decline in overall black population percentages. States that had no centers of black population for African Americans to retreat to even saw declines in their absolute numbers of African Americans. The black population of North Dakota, for example, slid from

372 in 1890 to 243 in 1930. As a proportion of the population, blacks dropped from 0.2% in 1890 to a minuscule 0.03% by 1930. In South Dakota the decline was from 0.16% to 0.09%, in Montana from 1.13% to 0.23%. Six counties in Nebraska that had 20 to 50 African Americans each in 1890 had just 1 to 8 by 1930; at the same time, Omaha and Lincoln doubled in black population. Wyoming, the "equality state," had the largest proportion of African Americans in any of these states—1.52% in 1890, its year of statehood—but by 1930, blacks were only 0.55% of its population. Utah's blacks likewise decreased as a proportion of the population, and those who remained beat a retreat to Salt Lake and Weber (Ogden) Counties; by 1930, 88% of the state's African Americans lived in those two counties.

Again, these declines were hardly voluntary. We have already seen how, especially in the West, expulsions and prohibitions have been directed not only at African Americans, but also at Chinese Americans and sometimes others. Indeed, western locales established a bewildering variety of rules. Some towns in the West excluded Native Americans but not Chinese Americans. Minden and Gardnerville are adjoining towns south of Carson City, Nevada. In the 1950s, and probably for many years prior, a whistle sounded at 6 p.m., audible in both towns, to warn American Indians to be gone by sundown. William Jacobsen Jr., an anthropologist who lived in Gardnerville in 1955, says it worked: "Indians made themselves scarce." A Chinese American family didn't have to leave. On the other hand, Esmeralda County, two counties to the southeast, allowed black residents but not Chinese. Meanwhile Fallon, Nevada, had a big sign at the railroad depot that said "No Niggers or Japs allowed," and the newspaper in Rawhide, Nevada, bragged in 1908 that "Dagoes" from southern Europe, as well as African Americans, "have been kindly but friendly [*sic*] informed to move on." [74]

South Pasadena, a sundown suburb of Los Angeles, let in Native Americans while keeping out Mexican and Asian Americans. Historian Fred Rolater relates how Professor Manuel Servin at the University of Southern California became the first Mexican American to break the taboo, in about 1964. Servin bought the Loomis House, a historic mansion. South Pasadena thought he was Native American, which was OK; "what the city did not know," Rolater went on to point out, was that his family was from Mexico and had come to the United States in the 1920s. "Thus the anti-Mexican restrictive covenant was broken by a Ph.D. American Indian who happened to be Mexican." [75]

Other California towns also kept out Mexican Americans, including

Chester, a lumber mill town north of Sacramento, and Palos Verdes Estates, an elite oceanfront suburb of Los Angeles. Historian Margaret Marsh points to the irony of its sundown policy: "Palos Verdes excluded Mexican-Americans . . . from living in the estates, yet Mexican-inspired architecture was mandated in most of the area." According to the University of Colorado Latino/a Research and Policy Center, in the late 1930s Longmont, Colorado, sported signs saying "No Mexicans After Night."[76]

In 1907, whites in Bellingham, Washington, drove out its entire "Hindu" population—Sikhs, actually, numbering between 200 and 300—during three days of lawlessness. The chief of police, according to a pro-police account written years later, "recognized the universal demand of the whites that the brown men be expelled," so he had his men stand by while a mob did the work. "Like the Chinamen, who have never returned to Tacoma," the account concludes, "the Hindu has given Bellingham a wide berth since." The Bellingham newspaper editorialized against "the means employed," but expressed "general and intense satisfaction" with the results. "There can be no two sides to such a question," the editor concluded. "The Hindu is a detriment to the town, while the white man is a distinct advantage."[77]

Despite the West's patchwork policies—barring Native Americans but not Chinese here, Chinese Americans but not blacks there, Jews somewhere else—for the most part, as in other regions, racism has long been strongest toward African Americans. The West is dotted with independent sundown towns that kept out blacks—places such as Duncan and Scottsdale, Arizona; Murray, Utah; and Astoria, Oregon. California had just eight potential sundown counties but scores of confirmed or likely sundown towns and suburbs. Most suburbs of Los Angeles and San Francisco and most communities in Orange County were established as white-only.

Sundown Subregions and "Dead Lines"

We have seen that entire subregions of the United States, such as the Cumberlands, the Ozarks, and the suburbs of Los Angeles, went sundown—not every suburb of Los Angeles, not every county in the Ozarks or the Cumberlands, but enough to warrant the generalization. In several subregions of the United States, signs in rural areas, usually on major highways, announced "dead lines" beyond which blacks were not to go except at risk of life itself. In Mississippi County, Arkansas, for example, according to historian Michael Dougan, a "red line" that was originally a road surveyor's mark defined where blacks might not trespass beyond to the west. That line probably continued north into the Missouri Bootheel and west beyond Paragould, encompassing more than 2,000 square miles. In southern Illinois, African Americans were not permitted "to settle north of the Mobile & Ohio switch track. This has been a settled feeling for years," according to a 1924 newspaper report that described a series of attacks—arson, attempted murder, and dynamite—against blacks who tried to move north of that line and against a white farmer in Elco who hired them. Unconfirmed oral history in east Wisconsin holds that there was a sign outside Fond du Lac along Highway 41 warning that blacks were not welcome north of there. This sign sighting needs corroboration but is credible, because in addition to Fond du Lac itself and confirmed sundown towns Appleton and Oshkosh, all towns north of that point were overwhelmingly white.[78] The Arkansas and Illinois dead lines may still be in effect; as recently as 1992, a black friend said, "I can't go into that town," to reporter Jack Tichenor when he proposed buying a bag of charcoal after dark in Karnak, just north of the Illinois dead line. However, African Americans do live north of the Wisconsin line without difficulty today.[79]

From west to east, other confirmed sundown subregions—not just individual counties or towns—include:

- A 4,000-square-mile area southwest of Fort Worth, Texas, including Comanche, Hamilton, and Mills counties, where whites drove out African Americans in 1886
- A thick band of sundown counties and towns on both sides of the Iowa-Missouri border
- Virtually every town and city along the Illinois River, from its mouth at the Mississippi northeast almost to Chicago, except Peoria

Still other subregions need confirmation. More research is needed, everywhere.

The Great Retreat from Prime Real Estate

Another way of characterizing the distribution of intentionally white communities in the United States is by type rather than location. From the Great

Lakes, moving east to New England, then south to Florida, and then again in California and Oregon, we see the practice of keeping African Americans (and often Jews) off prime beauty spots such as islands, beaches, and coasts, and outside the city limits of oceanside towns. In mountain areas in the East, beginning in the late 1880s, many vacation destinations and retirement communities sprouted "Restricted" signs, meaning "white Gentiles only." Elegant seaside suburbs such as Manchester-by-the-Sea, Massachusetts, kept out all Jews and all African Americans except servants living in white residences. Long Island exemplified the process in microcosm: most of its beach communities kept blacks out, while the inside, the potato farm area, was interracial.[80]

Famous tourist spots such as Seaside Park, New Jersey, and Rehoboth Beach, Delaware, were for whites only. African Americans and "Moors," a local mixed-race people, worked in Rehoboth Beach but could not live there, according to Elizabeth Baxter, who resided in Rehoboth in the late 1930s; this was confirmed by an 84-year-old lifelong resident. Nor could Jews. Islands and beaches in the Carolinas and Georgia, including Wrightsville Beach, North Carolina, and Isle of Palms, South Carolina, were all-white into the 1990s. Florida is rimmed with sundown communities on both coasts. California had even more, especially clustered around Los Angeles and San Francisco. Some of these towns are elite, some multiclass, some working-class.[81]

Several Florida beach towns, such as Delray Beach, between Fort Lauderdale and West Palm Beach, kept out Jews but not African Americans. In 1959, the Anti-Defamation League of B'nai B'rith described Delray Beach as "one of the nation's most completely anti-Semitic communities." It quoted a leading Delray Beach realtor who proudly called it "the only city on the East Coast [of Florida] fully restricted to Gentiles both in buying and selling."[82] A longtime resident told me, "Mostly northerners lived there, not southerners, but they were just as prejudiced. They didn't want Delray Beach to become majority Jewish and garish like Miami Beach." At the time Delray Beach had 5,363 African Americans in its population of 12,230; in the North, rarely did a place keep out Jews while admitting African Americans. On the Pacific coast, La Jolla, California, legally part of San Diego but often thought of as an independent community with its own zip code, long kept out Jews, African Americans, and Mexican Americans. In 1925, the Parent-Teacher Associations asked the La Jolla Civic League to prevent "a Mexican Squatter" from occupying land he had leased in La Jolla. According to Leonard Valdez of Sacramento, La Jolla was still keeping out Mexican Americans in the 1960s.

Of course, Valdez noted, many retired naval officers lived in La Jolla, and "there were no Mexican naval officers."[83]

Almost All Suburbs Were Sundown Towns

Residential areas near cities are also valuable real estate, of course, owing to their proximity to jobs, cultural venues, up-to-date health care, and other big-city amenities. To a still greater extent than vacation areas, suburbs went all-white, beginning in about 1900. The so-called Progressive movement, beginning shortly thereafter, was for whites only. Among its tenets was the notion that the big city and its ward politics—dominated by immigrants and "the machine"—were "dirty." The answer was to move to the suburbs, leaving the dirt, vice, pollution—and African Americans—behind.

Across the United States, most suburbs came into existence well after the sundown town movement was already under way. In suburbia, excluding African Americans (and often Jews) became the rule, not the exception. As we saw in Mississippi and Alabama, even the traditional South was not exempt, developing its share of sundown suburbs, mostly after World War II.

Like beaches and resort towns, suburbs added another ground for exclusion—religion—that most independent towns ignored. Many and perhaps most suburbs of Boston, New York, Philadelphia, Chicago, Minneapolis, and Los Angeles, as well as smaller cities such as Harrisburg, Pennsylvania, kept out Jews for decades. Long Island was especially vicious. Some suburbs kept out Catholics.

Sundown suburbs continued to be developed rather recently, many between 1946 and 1968. The peak for independent sundown towns was probably reached around 1940. Between 1940 and 1968, a handful of independent towns went sundown, such as Vienna, Illinois, which burned out its black community in 1954, but African Americans successfully moved into a larger handful of sundown towns, such Portales, New Mexico, in about the same year. Thus the overall number of independent sundown towns dropped a bit after 1940. Not so for sundown suburbs. Until 1968, new all-white suburbs were forming much more rapidly than old sundown towns and suburbs were caving in. Thus 1968 might be the peak year for independent sundown towns and sundown suburbs combined.[84]

To supply an exact number of sundown towns in the United States is hard, partly because it depends on the definition of "town," but in many states outside the South, a majority of all towns[85] can probably be confirmed as sundown in 1968.[86] In all, I believe at least 3,000 and perhaps as many as 15,000

independent towns went sundown in the United States, mostly between 1890
and about 1930. Another 2,000 to 10,000 sundown suburbs formed a little
later, between 1900 and 1968.[87] The range is broad because I could not and
did not locate every sundown town in America; there are far too many. I have
confirmed about 1,000 sundown towns and suburbs across the United States
but have left many more unconfirmed.

Sundown Neighborhoods

White America's new craze for all-white residential areas extended also into
central cities and inner suburbs. As we have seen, African American were too
numerous to be driven from larger cities such as Chicago and Washington,
D.C., or medium-sized ones such as Omaha or Tulsa, but after 1890, neighborhoods within cities and inner suburbs increasingly went all-white.

As a rule, American cities had not been very racially segregated in the
nineteenth century. During the Nadir, that began to change. Cities and towns
that did not expel their African Americans after 1890 concentrated them into
a few neighborhoods. Residential segregation increased dramatically within
northern cities between 1900 and 1960. Even in places far removed not only
from the South but also from any large population of African Americans,
blacks now found themselves unwelcome. Historian Howard Chudacoff describes the increasing residential segregation in Omaha:

> During the last decades of the 19th century Omaha housing was available to all
> who could meet the price, blacks included. . . . Beginning in 1902, however,
> the newspapers printed increasing numbers of housing advertisements specify-
> ing "for colored families." For other groups, more freedom of choice prevailed.

Roy Stannard Baker found residential segregation growing everywhere, including once-liberal Boston: "A strong prejudice exists against renting flats
and houses in many white neighborhoods to colored people. The Negro in
Boston, as in other cities, is building up 'quarters,' which he occupies to the
increasing exclusion of other classes[88] of people."[89]

The Index of Dissimilarity (D) provides a common measure of the degree
of residential segregation within a metropolitan area.[90] When D = 0, integration is perfect: every census tract has exactly the same racial composition as
every other census tract. 100 represents complete apartheid: not one black in

any white area, not one white in any black area. For values between 0 and 100, D tells the percentage of the smaller group—usually African Americans—that would have to move from disproportionately black areas to white areas to achieve a completely neutral distribution of both races. In 1860, the average northern city had a D of 45.7—only moderately segregated. If 45.7% of the blacks in an average city moved to predominantly white neighborhoods, the city would be perfectly integrated. Reynolds Farley and William Frey, premier researchers on residential segregation, point out that until about 1900, "in northern cities, some blacks shared neighborhoods with poor immigrants from Europe." Even middle-class areas were interracial: "Tiny cadres of highly educated blacks lived among whites in prosperous neighborhoods." Southern cities were even less segregated spatially, with an average D of 29.0. To some degree, especially in the South, these low D's reflected the age-old pattern of servant housing near upper-class white housing. Even so, the low indexes reflected a lack of residential racial segregation, especially in working-class areas.[91]

After 1900, hostility ranging from shunning to violence forced the involuntary retrenchment of African Americans from dispersed housing in many parts of the city to concentration in inner-city ghettoes—an intracity manifestation of the Great Retreat. By 1910, northern cities averaged 59.2 and southern cities 38.3 on the Index of Dissimilarity. Even larger increases characterized the next few decades. By 1920, D was above 80 in most northern U.S. cities, and the South was catching up. Northern cities averaged 89.2 in 1940, southern cities 81.0. By 1960, the average northern city held at 85.6, while the average southern city rose to 91.9.[92] These are astonishing levels, considering that the end of the scale, 100, means not one black in any white neighborhood and not one white in any black neighborhood.

Creating All-Black Towns

During the Nadir, African Americans were hardly passive victims. They thrashed about, trying tactic after tactic to deal with America's increasing racism. One was the development of all-black towns. It is a matter of semantics, I suppose, whether these towns were an alternative to the Great Retreat or part of it. Certainly they were founded at precisely the same time.

Some commentators have interpreted the black-town movement as a giving up on white America. On the contrary, black towns such as Nicodemus, Kansas; Boley, Oklahoma; and Mound Bayou, Mississippi, emulated white towns. Indeed, their initial development was marked by a sense of self-respect and competition: they wanted to outdo white towns. They also hoped to provide employment and political opportunities not available elsewhere. Black towns ran their own post offices, which therefore hired African Americans, even when the Woodrow Wilson administration was shutting blacks out of this work. Black towns ran their own precincts, which therefore let African Americans vote, even as the outside society was shutting blacks out of politics.

To be sure, black towns were founded in a difficult, even dangerous period. The movement began in reply to the end of Reconstruction in the South, when African Americans were no longer voting freely and lynchings were increasing. In 1879, African Americans began an exodus from Mississippi and Louisiana to Indian Territory and Kansas, trying to find freedom and peace. In 1887, hoping to avoid the worst of the racist storm, African Americans founded Mound Bayou in former swampland in the Mississippi Delta. In 1904, African Americans in Indian Territory founded Boley. Both towns grew rapidly, fueled by a wave of optimism similar to that at the end of the Civil War, tinged this time with desperation. By 1908, Boley had 2,500 residents, two banks, two cotton gins, a newspaper, a hotel, and a college, the Creek-Seminole College and Agriculture Institute. Briefly Boley competed with Okemah, Weleetka, and Henryetta, nearby white-majority towns, for economic and political influence in the area.[93]

Unfortunately, the history of Boley and its neighboring towns shows that black towns offered no real solution to the increasing racism of the Nadir. Gradually Boley's residents themselves realized they were to have no real chance at social, economic, or political rights, owing to forces outside their town and beyond their control. In 1907, whites merged Indian Territory into the new state of Oklahoma. Democrats took over the state and passed vicious segregation laws modeled on Mississippi's 1890 constitution. Although the research has yet to be done by historians and sociologists in Oklahoma, I believe it will show that a wave of small expulsions swept through many Oklahoma towns shortly after statehood, as white Democrats reveled in their newly realized power over African and Native Americans.

Boley is located in Okfuskee County. Okemah, the county seat, had been founded as a sundown town in 1902. From time to time African Americans moved in, only to face violent opposition. In January 1907, for example, whites dynamited the homes of the only two black families in town.[94] Later that year, Okemah businessmen leased a building and set up a hotel for African Americans who traded with the local merchants or had to attend court and could not always get back to Boley by sundown. By April 1908 it was doing a brisk business, which ended when other whites placed a heavy charge of dynamite under the front wall of the hotel. "The building was badly damaged," wrote Okemah resident W. L. Payne. "Farmers living eight miles from Okemah were aroused by the terrific blast. This brought about a quick reduction in the Negro population of Okemah." [95]

Henryetta, the next town to the east, went sundown in December 1907. According to the *History of Okmulgee County,* "A number of black families— perhaps as many as 200 people—lived in one area of Henryetta"; just south of town lived another 30 or 40 black miners and their families. On Christmas Eve, James Gordon, African American, tried to rent a rig from Albert Bates, white, who owned a livery stable. Bates refused, an altercation followed, and Gordon shot him. A posse soon caught Gordon a mile east of town and brought him to the jail. Whites "were incensed. They surrounded the jail, battered down the door, smashed the jail lock with a sledge hammer, and dragged Gordon across the street to a telephone pole," where they "hanged him and riddled his body with bullets." All the next day, Christmas Day, "there were rumors of black uprisings," according to the county history:

> The talk on the street was that "no more negroes will be allowed to domicile in Henryetta." . . . Within a day or two, the whites rallied together with guns, rocks, bricks, "anything and everything" and ran the other black families out of town. "We didn't care where they went and don't know," said one irate resident. From then on, Henryetta was off-limits to blacks except for business during the day. [96]

Then Democrats eliminated Boley as a voting precinct and forced citizens of Boley to vote in a smaller town twelve miles away. Boley voters turned out in droves and compelled the whites running that precinct to let them cast ballots, which Democrats then didn't include in countywide tallies anyway. In 1910, Democrats amended the Oklahoma constitution with a "grandfather clause" that set up literacy requirements to keep African Americans from voting; whites were exempt so long as their ancestors could vote in 1861. Blacks' grandfathers, being slaves then, could not vote, so the combination took away the ballot from African Americans while granting it to European Americans. [97]

Residents of Boley still hoped they could just mind their own business and run their own affairs, but whites weren't satisfied with merely excluding African Americans from voting. In Bittle and Geis's words, "Not only would all avenues of political expression be cut off, but all avenues of social and economic expression as well." White neighbors set up Farmers' Commercial Clubs,

> the express purpose of which was to drive the Negro farmers from the area and to replace them with white farmers. Pacts were drawn up between whites in which each agreed to withhold employment from Negroes. . . . With each dreadful development, the Negroes attempted to reorganize their ethic for yet another time. But this reorientation became patently vapid, and the Negro community simply relented in the face of white hostility.

In 1911, Okemah residents lynched a mother and son who lived in the black community outside Boley (Portfolio 11), showing that a black town provided no safe harbor from white vigilante "justice." The drop in cotton prices in 1913 finished the job. Now Boley started to lose population. "The economic and political setbacks added up to almost total disillusionment on the part of the Okfuskee County Negroes. . . . There would be no growing respect and admiration from white neighbors and no industrial and agricultural prosperity." Boley still holds its annual celebration, but it became a shell of its former self. Its pariah status, conferred by the all-white towns nearby, sapped its morale.[98]

Black Townships

Sprinkled about the United States, often located at the edge of sundown towns or a few miles away, are other, smaller black communities, most of which never incorporated, many with dirt roads, off the beaten path. They are the flip side of sundown towns—places to which the excluded have retreated to live, yet close enough to nearby white towns to work. I call them "townships" because some of them resemble South Africa's black townships, those gatherings of shacks built by squatters that supply maids for Johannesburg's white households and janitors for its industries. Like Thokoza and Soweto, in America often these were haphazard gatherings of ramshackle houses, many of which were not, until recently, served by amenities such as city water.[99] Some still are not.

If even independent black towns succumbed to the demoralizing effect the increased racism of the Nadir had on African Americans nationally, townships showed much less heritage of black pride. They too offered some refuge from the racist storm, but they never made any pretense of providing a solution to America's racial inequality. The little area that housed African American adjoining Eugene, Oregon, during World War II was dubbed "Tent City" because its "houses" consisted of tents pitched over wooden frameworks on wooden floors.[100] To some degree, these communities resemble reservations—places to which whites restricted African Americans, whose labor they desired but whose presence they did not want. Their residents knew it.

Chevy Chase Heights was an unincorporated community located just north of the town of Indiana in western Pennsylvania. In 1960, when college student Ralph Stone studied Chevy Chase Heights, he elicited only scorn when he asked a clerk at the Indiana Chamber of Commerce for information on the community. "Who in the world would want to know that?" she replied. Asked if she at least had population figures for the community, she replied, "Nobody knows. If you want to know, go out and count them." Chevy Chase residents repeatedly petitioned Indiana for annexation so that they could have street lights, paved streets, and city sewage lines, and the settlement, "for geographical reasons, should be part of the borough," according to Stone. But Indiana "wants nothing to do with Chevy Chase," he concluded. Indeed, Indiana made this clear long before 1960: local historian Clarence Stephenson quotes a Works Progress Administration source telling that "the [black] families that formerly lived in the borough of Indiana were asked by the borough council to locate in Chevy Chase." By 1960, according to Stone, 20 African Americans remained in Indiana and about 577 lived in Chevy Chase Heights.[101]

Even their names sometimes imply the racism that was their reason for being. For years "The Colony" was the name used by blacks as well as whites for the mostly African American community south of Cullman, Alabama. A librarian in Cullman explained, "The only full-time African American residents of the entire county through most of its history have lived in a tiny community called 'The Colony' which is roughly twenty miles south of the city. . . . 'The Colony' was incorporated as 'Colony' in 1980." African Americans who worked as maids and handymen commuted into Cullman in the mid-1950s by carpools. The Colony had an elementary school, but before Cullman's schools desegregated in 1970, African Americans who wanted to go to high school had go to another county. Colp, Illinois, a majority-black hamlet 1 mile west of Herrin and 3 miles north of Carterville, began as #9 Mine, a coal mine that employed African American miners. White miners called it "Nigger Nine." Understandably taking offense, citizens of #9 Mine incorporated in 1915 as Colp, named for John Colp, the mine owner who employed them. But Herrin residents think Colp is short for "colored people" and thus mounts no challenge to white sensibilities. Now that mining has wound down, Colp residents work in Herrin, but for years Herrin residents informally threatened them with death if they remained overnight, and they could not set foot in nearby Carterville even during the daytime. Residents of Stump Town, a small African American community in western Illinois, worked in Warsaw but had to be out of there by nightfall. Residents of other sundown towns across the Midwest and border states simply called the little black townships near them "Niggertown," while its African American residents struggled to have them known by more specific and less demeaning terms, including "Little Africa" in southern Illinois.[102]

Metropolitan areas, too, have their black townships. Suburban Long Island alone has thirteen.[103] For that matter, many residents of sundown suburbs have long relied on maids and gardeners who commute from inner-city ghettoes, which are analogous to black townships. Some suburban black settlements date back to the nineteenth century.[104] Others grew after World War II, when white suburbs likewise exploded. Typically black townships supplied workers for nearby suburbs that wanted maids and gardeners but didn't want African Americans to spend the night. Often they were located in floodplains or next to railroad tracks just outside the city limits of the nearest suburb. In 1966, sociologists Leonard Blumberg and Michael Lalli identified sixty of these communities, which they called "little ghettoes . . . in the suburbs." Most of these communities were unincorporated or did not enforce their zoning ordinances and building codes, which allowed African Americans to build their own homes, keep chickens and even pigs, and thus create rural pockets in urban areas. Over time, however, as blacks were not allowed to live in incorporated suburbs, the stigmatized nature of the townships as "permitted locations for a negatively valued population," to use Blumberg and Lalli's formulation, became apparent to all. Geographer Harold Rose calls them "black colonies in the metropolitan ring."[105]

Not only African Americans but also other "deviants" were often confined to these black townships. In the 1950s and '60s, Colp had a regionally famous house of prostitution; it still has a thriving bar.[106] As early as the 1970s, the Chevy Chase Heights Community Center hosted monthly gay dances. In the 1960s, the Elks Club and Sadler's Bar in Chevy Chase Heights were perhaps the only places in Indiana County where whites and blacks might socialize and even dance together. Indeed, *within* black towns and townships, race relations were often good. "In Chevy Chase a man is treated as a man regardless of color," said Fred Johnson, black Elks Club member in 1960. "In Indiana a white man is treated as a man, but a colored man is treated as an animal." Residents of sundown towns usually put down whites who socialized or lived in nearby "black" townships as "white trash." At the same time, whites in sundown towns often drove to nearby black townships to buy alcohol during Prohibition.[107] For decades Locke, a Chinese township in California founded in 1915, supplied gambling, prostitution, and opium to residents of Sacramento. Today, locations in black inner-city neighborhoods play the same role for whites from sundown suburbs seeking illegal drugs.[108]

Unincorporated townships such as Stump Town and Chevy Chase Heights—and black ghettoes, for that matter—have no police forces of their own. White sheriffs and police chiefs often wink at deviant or illegal behavior in black townships, as it fulfills three functions at once in the white community. It relieves the demand for the deviance, which usually involves victimless "crimes" like drinking, gambling, buying drugs, and buying sex. It avoids arousing the forces of priggery because the behavior does not take place in neighborhoods they care about, hence is not salient. And it further stigmatizes both the black township and African Americans in general.

Alternatives to the Great Retreat

The Great Retreat to the larger cities of the North and West and to black towns and townships was not African Americans' only response to the wave of increasing white hostility they met during the Nadir—but there was no good answer. Following Booker T. Washington's advice to "cast down your buckets where you are" and seek only economic advancement, forgoing political and social rights, didn't work; white southerners sometimes lynched successful black businessmen and farmers simply because they were successful. Following the counsel of W. E. B. DuBois and pursuing voting rights and full citizenship led to such fiascoes as the Ocoee, Florida, riot, described in Chapter 7, in which whites drove out the entire black population and converted Ocoee to a sundown town.

We have seen that moving to small towns in the North became difficult as more and more of them went sundown. Emigrating to Indian Territory, which at first promised a more tolerant multiracial milieu, led to the overt racism of

Oklahoma after 1907, including sundown towns such as Okemah and Hen-ryetta. Going farther west didn't work either; an African American in Denver lamented in 1910 that what he called "the onslaught" against the race had reached Colorado, even though "the Mexican, Japanese, Chinese, and all other races are given a chance." Giving up hope for America, the author wrote, "We are leaving in great numbers to the far northwest, taking up claims in Canada." But Canada offered no real refuge; Portfolio 17 shows that it consid-ered closing its doors to blacks entirely. African Americans in Boley and in many interracial towns joined the back-to-Africa movements organized by Chief Sam and Marcus Garvey. The popularity of these movements did not derive from any developments in Africa but was another aspect of the Great Retreat, prompted by the white racism exemplified in the sundown town cru-sade. The movements organized by both Sam and Garvey ended in disarray, partly because they expressed pride and despair more than actual intentions to emigrate.[109]

The Great Retreat Was No Solution

We have seen that forming black towns and townships offered only partial relief. So did moving to large cities, which increasingly segregated their African American residents into constricted ghettos and marginal occupa-tions. Despair seemed to be the only answer to the hatred of the Nadir. Still relevant were the old slave spirituals such as "Nobody Knows the Trouble I've Seen."

Certainly the Great Retreat did not improve race relations. Regardless of how sundown towns were created, the whites within them only became more racist. They almost had to, to rationalize having forced or kept nonwhites out. Writing about Omaha, Howard Chudacoff points out another reason: be-cause African Americans increasingly lived in separate neighborhoods, whites no longer had the benefit of knowing them individually, so they fell back on thinking stereotypically about them as a group. "The lack of familiar-ity bred suspicion and resentment which burst during the riot of 1919."[110]

Chudacoff concludes, "Clearly, the experience of Negroes resembled those of no other ethnic group." Every white ethnic group experienced and even chose residential concentration during their initial immigration to the United States. Thereafter, as the years passed and they became more Ameri-canized, their residential concentration decreased—precisely when it was ris-ing for African Americans. As the years passed, African Americans found themselves more and more isolated—increasingly barred from towns, suburbs, and neighborhoods.[111]

How did this happen? How were sundown towns (and counties and neighborhoods) created? What were the mechanisms by which so many towns became all-white or, in the case of suburbs, created themselves that way? The next chapter tries to answer these questions.

4

How Sundown Towns Were Created

Negro Driven Away
The Last One Leaves Decatur, Ind., Owing to Threats Made

The last Negro has left Decatur, Ind. His departure was caused by the anti-Negro feeling. About a month ago a mob of 50 men drove out all the Negroes who were then making that city their home. Since that time the feeling against the Negro race has been intense, so much so that an Anti-Negro Society was organized.

The colored man who has just left came about three weeks ago, and since that time received many threatening letters. When he appeared on the streets he was insulted and jeered at. An attack was threatened. . . .

The anti-negroites declare that as Decatur is now cleared of Negroes they will keep it so, and the importation of any more will undoubtedly result in serious trouble.

—*New York Times,* July 14, 1902[1]

A FINE HISTORY by Jean Swaim of Cedar County, Missouri, provides a detailed example of the process that took place in many of the counties summarized in Table 1 of the previous chapter. Cedar County is located between Kansas City and Springfield, Missouri. African Americans had lived in the county since before the Civil War, originally as slaves. In the 1870s, a black community grew up within Stockton, the county seat, including a school, candy store, and "a park with a popular croquet court, where white Stockton men often spent their Sunday afternoons competing in tournaments." Some African Americans worked as domestic help, others at a local brickyard. By 1875, whites and blacks had organized the Stockton Colored School, which eventually had as many as 43 students. A newspaper account from August 1899 shows interracial cooperation: "About 1,500 attended colored people's picnic here. Order was good except for a few drunken whites. Stockton won the ball game from Greenfield, 20–1. Greenfield's colored band was a big attraction." African Americans also lived elsewhere in the county, including "Little Africa" near Humansville in the northeastern corner. Forty families lived there, with a church, school, and store. They held an annual picnic on the Fourth of July to which whites were invited and had a baseball team with a white coach.[2]

Then something bad happened, something that the local histories don't identify and that has been lost even to oral history. As another local historian, born in the county in the 1920s, put it, "It's just a dark history that nobody talks about," speaking of the event or chain of events that ended Cedar - County's racial harmony.[3] Around 1900, the county's black population declined precipitously, from 127 (in 1890) to 45. Whatever prompted the initial decline, we do know why it continued: Cedar County was becoming a sundown county. By 1910, only thirteen African Americans lived in the county, and by 1930, just one. Swaim refers to "many shameful incidents" in which "visiting ball teams, travelers, and even laborers were . . . told to be out of town by night. Blacks could find haven in Greenfield," the seat of the next county to the south. She tells of a black bricklayer whose work attracted admiring crowds: "Not only was he paving El Dorado Springs's Main Street in perfect herringbone pattern as fast as an assistant could toss him bricks, but he sang as he worked and moved in rhythm to his song." Nevertheless, he "had to find a place out of town at night." "In Stockton, prejudice was still rampant in the late 1960s," Swaim continues, "as black workmen constructing the Stockton Dam were provided segregated and inferior housing west of town. Their visiting wives cooked for them." Is Cedar County still sundown today? Swaim writes, "In the 1990s few blacks are seen in Cedar County." But the 2000 census counted 44 African Americans. One black couple lives in El Dorado Springs and seems to get along all right. Nevertheless, Cedar County in 2005 has yet to reach the level of black population and interracial cooperation that it showed in the 1890s.[4]

Swaim's fine account, summarized above, provides the texture of the Great Retreat from one Missouri county, but neither Swaim nor the other historian quite say how it all began. The initial "how" in Cedar County may be lost to history by this point. But in many other places, we do know how counties and towns went sundown, or how they were created that way in the first place. This chapter examines the variety of methods by which town after town across America excluded African Americans, mostly after 1890. We begin with violence because it was the most important. Moreover, threat of violent force underlies many of the "softer" methods: ordinance, informal actions by police and public officials, freezing out blacks from social interaction and from institutions such as schools and churches, buying them out, and other forms of bad behavior by white residents of the town. By dint of these methods, independent sundown towns were created, mostly between 1890 and 1930. Sundown suburbs were created a little later, mostly between 1900 and 1968, by a panoply of methods, among which violence and intimidation were also prominent.

Creating Sundown Towns by Violence

Often white residents achieved their goal abruptly, even in the middle of the night. *In town after town in the United States, especially between 1890 and the 1930s, whites forced out their African American neighbors violently, as they had the Chinese in the West.* Decatur, in northeastern Indiana, went sundown in 1902, as told in the excerpt above from the *New York Times.* Adams County, of which Decatur is the county seat, wound up without a single black household; a century later, it still had only five. Decatur exemplifies a widespread phenomenon: little riots, most of which have never been written about, even by local historians. These are cases of what Donald Horowitz calls "the deadly ethnic riot." He cites examples from India, Kyrgyztan, Malaysia, Nigeria, and other countries, and defines the form as:

> an intense, sudden, though not necessarily wholly unplanned, lethal attack by civilian members of one ethnic group on civilian members of another ethnic group, the victims chosen because of their group membership. . . . Members of one ethnic group search out members of another. The search is conducted with considerable care, for this is violence directed against an identifiable target group.[5]

Towns with successful riots wound up all-white, of course, or almost so, and therefore had an ideological interest in suppressing any memory of a black population in the first place, let alone of an unseemly riot that drove them out.[6]

Whites also tried to "cleanse" at least fifteen larger cities of their more substantial nonwhite populations: Denver (of Chinese) in 1880; Seattle (of Chinese) in 1886; Akron in 1900; Evansville, Indiana, and Joplin, Missouri, in 1903; Springfield, Ohio, in 1904, 1906, and again in 1908; Springfield, Missouri, in 1906; Springfield, Illinois, in 1908; Youngstown, Ohio, and East St. Louis, Illinois, in 1917; Omaha and Knoxville in 1919; Tulsa in 1921; Johnstown, Pennsylvania, in 1923; and Lincoln, Nebraska, in 1929. (Portfolio

10 shows the attempt in Tulsa.) They failed, mainly because the task would have taken three or four days, giving their governors time not only to call out their state's national guard but also to realize they would get considerable criticism—and so would their state—if they failed to act.

Some of these larger riots have received some attention, including books and historical markers. Since they were unsuccessful—in that they failed to drive out all African Americans—they have left fuller records of the process, because interracial communities have no need to deny that they had once had a black population. As well, they have black populations with their own collective memories. Indeed, in Tulsa, an ongoing controversy concerns reparations. But most of the little riots have gone entirely overlooked, and as a result, the pattern of widespread "ethnic cleansings," of which these failed large attempts represent the tip of the iceberg, is not generally understood. Moreover, even when the cleansings were incomplete, they made a profound impact upon surrounding towns, often inspiring satellite riots.

Consider the 1903 attack on the black community in Joplin. As was often the case, it started with an act of violence against one white person, in this case the murder of a police officer. There was little doubt that the assailant was a black tramp named Thomas Gilyard, who was quickly taken into custody. Several hundred white people then gathered outside the jail, broke through the wall, and lynched him, after a tug-of-war with other whites who tried to stop it. Then the mob went through black neighborhoods, attacking African Americans, burning their homes, and cutting firemen's hoses so they couldn't intervene. Half of Joplin's 770 African American residents fled for their lives. Joplin was large enough that the mob could not drive all African Americans from the city, but the results are still plain: in 2000 Joplin had a lower African American population proportion—just 2.7%—than it did in 1902. Moreover, this riot, along with several others in Missouri and Arkansas, helped foment an ideology of ethnic cleansing that made most of the Ozark Plateau a sundown region by 1920.[7]

Another unsuccessful cleansing—in Springfield, Illinois—had a still greater impact. In 1908, residents of Springfield acted on their desire to have an all-white city. A white woman, Mabel Hallam, claimed George Richardson, an African American, had raped her. Police jailed him, whereupon a mob gathered at the county jail to lynch him, along with another black prisoner accused of murder. The sheriff borrowed an automobile from businessman Harry Loper, however, and managed to get both prisoners safely out of town. Angry at being foiled, the mob destroyed Loper's restaurant and then turned its rage on the African American community in general. According to Roberta

Senechal, whose book is the standard source on the riot, "During two days of violence, white rioters gutted the capitol's black business district, left blocks of black homes in smoldering ruins, and lynched two innocent black men," Scott Burton and William Donnegan. "The rioters' ultimate goal seemingly was to drive away all of Springfield's blacks," Senechal concluded. The task was simply too large, however, since Springfield in 1908 had about 3,100 African Americans in a total population of 48,000.[8] Nevertheless, some 2,000 did flee the city. Only the belated arrival of the Illinois state militia kept the mob from finishing the job. Springfield being the capital, the state government simply could not ignore this riot.[9]

The Springfield riot was famous briefly throughout the world, not because it was unusual, which it was not, but because it happened in Abraham Lincoln's hometown.[10] Springfield's history encapsulates America's downward course in race relations from the Civil War to the Nadir. When Lincoln's funeral train brought his body back to Springfield for burial in 1865, a regiment of black troops led the procession to the state capitol. Thousands of African Americans "had journeyed for days in order to be in Springfield at the funeral," according to an officer in the military escort for Lincoln's body. Afterward, some of them stayed on to live in the city. Now the townspeople of the Great Emancipator were trying to expel them all. "Abe Lincoln brought them to Springfield and we will drive them out!" shouted members of the mob.[11]

After the riot, Hallam admitted she made up the story about being raped, to cover up an affair she was having. Nevertheless, most Springfield residents showed no regret, except about failing to drive every last black person from the city. The tree from which the mob hanged Scott Burton, a black barber, was hacked to pieces to make souvenirs of the occasion. After the riot, some employers fired their black employees, and many local shopkeepers now refused to serve African Americans. Later, 107 people were charged with crimes, but the only person sentenced was a man convicted of petty theft for stealing a sword from a National Guardsman. No one was ever convicted for murder, arson, or any other crime against an African American.[12]

The Springfield riot stands as a prototype for the many smaller riots that left communities all-white between 1890 and 1940, most of which have never been written about by any historian. Indeed, the Springfield riot itself spawned a host of imitators: whites shouted "Give 'em Springfield!" during attacks on African Americans as far away as Alton, Illinois; Evansville, Indiana; St. Louis, Missouri; and the Cumberland Plateau in Kentucky and Tennessee. Closer to home, the *Illinois State Register* reported, "At Auburn, Thayer, Virden, Girard, Pawnee, Spaulding, Buffalo, Riverton, Pana, Edinburg, Taylorville, Pleasant Plains, and a score of other places in central Illinois a Negro is an unwelcome visitor and is soon informed he must not remain in the town." [13] Some of these towns, such as Virden and Pana, were sundown towns before the Springfield riot; their exclusion policies had merely Dawson newsworthy owing to the riot. Others, such as Dawson and Pleasant Plains, excluded African Americans in its aftermath. Neither the local, county, state, or federal governments ever brought anyone to justice for any of these expulsions from smaller towns. Dawson, a little town nine miles east of Springfield, became all-white on August 17, 1908, two days after the National Guard ended the Springfield riot. Not to be outdone by Springfield, whites in Dawson posted the following ultimatum at the train station:

> All niggers are warned out of town by Monday, 12 m. sharp.
> Buffalo Sharp Shooters

Its black population fled, and since then Dawson has been all-white. Today some whites commute from Dawson to Springfield, because they feel Springfield is too black. Springfield was 15% African American in 2000. [14]

In addition to the small-town disturbances around Springfield in 1908, at least a score of other towns in Illinois alone became sundown through violence. Whites in Romeoville, in northeastern Illinois, expelled all the town's African Americans in June 1893 in a pitched battle in which eight people were killed. Other violent expulsions include Beardstown at an unknown date, East Alton and Spring Valley in 1895, [15] Virden in 1898, Pana in 1899, Carterville in 1901, [16] Eldorado in 1902, Anna-Jonesboro in 1909, West Frankfort in 1920, probably Pinckneyville in 1927 or 1928, and Vienna in 1954. Additional possible violent expulsions in Illinois that I have not confirmed include Newman back around 1879, Lacon and Toluca between 1898 and 1910, Granite City in 1903, Coal City at some undetermined date, and Zeigler by mine explosion in 1905. [17]

A series of at least six race riots in the Ozarks, along with smaller undocumented expulsions, led to the almost total whiteness of most Ozark counties, which continues to this day. In 1894, Monett, Missouri, started the chain of racial violence. As happened so often, it began with a lynching. Ulysses Hayden, an African American, was taken from police custody and hanged from a telephone pole, although Murray Bishoff, an authority on Monett, believes him innocent of the murder of the young white man for which he was hanged. After the lynching, whites forced all African Americans to leave Monett. Pierce City, just six miles west, followed suit in 1901. Again, a crime of violence had been perpetrated upon a white person, and again, after lynching the alleged perpetrator, the mob then turned on the black community, about 10% of the town's population, and drove them out.[18] In the process, members of the mob set fire to several homes, incinerating at least two African Americans inside. Portfolio 3 shows one of the destroyed residences. Some African Americans fled to Joplin, the nearest city, but in 1903 whites rioted there. Three years later, whites in Harrison, Arkansas, expelled most of their African Americans, and in 1909, they finished the job. In 1906, whites in Springfield, Missouri, staged a triple lynching they called an "Easter Offering."[19]

No one was ever convicted in any of these riots, which sent a message that violence against African Americans would not be punished in the Ozarks. On the contrary, it was celebrated. In Springfield, for example,

> souvenir hunters sifted through the smoldering ashes looking for bits of bone, charred flesh, and buttons to carry away with them in order to commemorate the event. Local drugstores and soda parlors sold postcards containing photographs of the lynching, and one enterprising businessman . . . [had] medals struck commemorating the lynching. One side of the medal read "Easter Offering," and the other side, "Souvenir of the hanging of 3 niggers, Springfield, Missouri, April 15, 1906."[20]

The immediate effect was a contagion of ethnic cleansing that drove African Americans from nearby towns such as Cotter, Arkansas. Sociologist Gordon Morgan wrote, "It is entirely possible that the trouble that was experienced in Boone County [Harrison] affected the black populations in surrounding counties. The census shows precipitous drops in black numbers in the 1900–1910 decade in Carroll and Madison counties, both of which adjoin Boone."[21]

Elsewhere in the United States, I have been able to confirm mini-riots that forced out the black populations from at least 30 other towns, including Myakka City, Florida; Spruce Pine, North Carolina; Wehrum, Pennsylvania; Ravenna, Kentucky; Greensburg, Indiana; St. Genevieve, Missouri; and North Platte, Nebraska.[22] Many of these mini-riots in turn spurred whites in nearby towns to have their own, thus provoking small waves of expulsions.

Creating Sundown Towns by Threat

Sometimes just the threat of violence sufficed, especially where whites were many and blacks few, as in Dawson. For that matter, because the historical record is incomplete, we cannot always know when violence or "mere" threat of violence forced a town's African Americans to leave. Most mass departures were probably forced by at least the threat of violence—why else would everyone leave at once?[23] Sometimes expulsions were more gradual, taking several years and requiring repeated threats or acts of violence.

When one member of the black community was lynched, all African Americans took that as a threat to their continued well-being. Often they were right. Frank Quillen, whose 1913 book *The Color Line in Ohio* stands as an oasis of honest scholarship during the arid Nadir period, observed that after a lynching, such as in Akron, Galion, and Urbana, Ohio, "I found the prejudice much stronger than it was before the lynching, and the Negroes fewer in number." A lynching by definition is a public murder. Those who carry it out do not bother to act in private, since they believe the community will support them. Thus a lynching becomes a community event in which all whites participate, at least vicariously, because the entire white community decides not to punish the perpetrators. After such an event, whites grew more likely to engage in such everyday practices as forcing African Americans from jobs like postal carrier or locomotive fireman, as well as from entire communities.[24]

The increasing frequency of mass "spectacle lynchings," in particular, played a major role in the spread of sundown towns. These events, often announced in advance, drew hundreds and even thousands of onlookers. Typically in their aftermath, not only was no one brought to justice, but also whites reveled in the brutality, selling fingers and bits of the victim's flesh as souvenirs and making postcards of photos of the event to send to friends across the country. Such events, reasonably enough, convinced African Americans in many towns that they were no longer safe. Chapter 7 tells how a spectacle lynching in Maryville, Missouri, not only caused African Americans to flee that town in 1931, but also led to their departure from neighboring counties.[25]

Mena, Arkansas, had a small African American population until February 20, 1901, when "Nigger Pete" was lynched. Pete was "considered by many locals to be insane," according to a 1986 article based on newspaper accounts of the time. He had gotten into "a fracas" with a twelve-year-old white girl, "knocking her down, and injuring her quite badly. Later in the evening Pete was arrested and placed in jail 'as has often been done before in similar offenses.' The episode flashed across town and it soon created strong feelings against the Negro." Whites then lynched him: they shot him, fractured his skull, and cut his throat. No one was ever apprehended for his death. According to an article written in 1980, "The black folks began to leave Polk County after the 'Nigger Pete' lynching." The county's African American population,

172 at one point, dropped to 12 in the aftermath, then slowly dwindled to zero as the remaining few died or moved away. Does this qualify as a violent expulsion? The African Americans obviously felt threatened. They also knew that two years earlier whites had posted notices around Mena warning blacks to leave. On that occasion other whites, including the mayor and newspaper editor, denounced the threat, but it had to have been unsettling nonetheless. Moreover, the editor had said then, "The number of Negro citizens in Mena is very small and as a whole exceeding well behaved. As long as these facts remain true they have their rights as citizens and the city officials will take any necessary steps to protect them." Pete's action, given whites' penchant for holding the entire African American community responsible for the misstep of any individual, threatened the premise undergirding white forbearance and prompted the expulsion. According to Shirley Manning, Mena historian:

> My father said he was only a boy of 5–7 (born in 1897) when the people of Polk County ran all the blacks out of town, and as they left from the race track, . . . white people set the wagons on fire. My dad died when I was 10, but I remember the story, and my much older brother has told it to me, also.

So in Mena, at least, threat of violence crossed over into actual attack.[26]

Many other towns saw their African American populations leave suddenly after one member of the group was lynched. On February 10, 1918, for example, whites in Estill Springs, Tennessee, lynched G. W. Lych, an African American minister. Two days later, in a spectacle lynching, they burned another African American alive before 1,500 spectators; "black residents of the community were forced to watch," according to Stewart Tolnay and E. M. Beck. "After the incident the black population of Estill Spring[s] quickly disappeared." The lynching of an African American by whites from Toluca and Lacon, north of Peoria, Illinois, in 1898 probably led to the exodus of African Americans from those towns.[27]

The Role of the Ku Klux Klan

The rise of the KKK after 1915—the so-called second Klan—often amounted to an implicit threat to blacks in largely white communities. In many towns across the North, from Maine to Illinois to Oregon, Klan rallies in the 1920s drew more people than any assemblages before or since. (See Portfolio 21 and 22.) On August 20, 1923, for example, 8,500 members of the Ku Klux Klan met two miles east of West Frankfort, Illinois—a gathering equal to the town's entire population at the time—and inducted 400 new members. A 1925 Klan rally near Montpelier, Vermont, drew nearly 10,000, almost twice that city's population. Such huge gatherings gave whites a sense of power, a feeling that they could do whatever they wanted to African Americans, and sometimes to Jews and Catholics as well. West Frankfort was already a sundown town, but in towns with black residents, these monster demonstrations had a chilling impact on the few and scattered African Americans, who knew their safety depended upon white goodwill.[28]

In Fond du Lac, Wisconsin, for instance, local historian Sally Albertz believes "the KKK was instrumental in driving the blacks away." In the early 1920s the Klan held a "Klanvocation" at the Fond du Lac fairgrounds; newspapers claimed that 5,000 people marched in the parade. Subsequently, several crosses were burned in the areas where the blacks lived in the city. The earlier sense of possibility for African Americans in Fond du Lac—the welcome meal, the rooms at the hotel described in the previous chapter—had been replaced by a sense of terror.[29]

Sometimes this implicit threat became explicit. The Klan played a direct role in making some Oregon towns all-white in the 1920s. In Medford, Klansmen took George Burr, a bootblack, to the mountains, placed a noose around his neck, hung him from a branch, then cut him down and ordered him to leave town. He did. In Oregon City, six masked Klansmen confronted car wash owner Perry Ellis, the only black man in town, accused him of sleeping with a white woman, and nearly lynched him. Ellis moved to Tacoma, Washington, and Oregon City had no black household thereafter until the 1980s.[30]

Creating Sundown Towns by Ordinance

Under the thrall of the white supremacist rhetoric of the Nadir, many towns passed ordinances to prohibit African Americans from being within the corporate limits of the town after sundown or forbade selling or renting property to them. As with sundown towns themselves, actions against Chinese Americans led the way. Several authors tell of ordinances in the West banning them. Eureka, in northern California, passed its ordinance informally, at a large civic meeting on February 14, 1885, the day it expelled its large Chinese population, nicely showing the link between violence and ordinance, and did not repeal it until 1959.[31]

Reports of ordinances against African Americans began to surface after about 1900. I collected oral and written history from 25 towns in Illinois that have a tradition of such ordinances. In 1965, Donald Royer did a small study for the Indiana Civil Rights Commission, checking out nineteen Indiana towns with oral traditions of having passed sundown ordinances. He could not find any on paper. Between 2000 and 2004, I collected oral and written history from some of the same towns, finding the tradition still vibrant, and added another town. I also found evidence of sundown ordinances in 22 other towns in California, Arizona, Oklahoma, Kansas, Nebraska, Iowa, Missouri, Wisconsin, Tennessee, Ohio, and Maryland.[32] In California, for example, historian Olen Cole Jr. tells how the Civilian Conservation Corps in the 1930s tried to locate a company of African American workers in a large park that bordered Burbank and Glendale. Both cities refused; "the reason given was an 'old ordinance of the cities of Burbank and Glendale which prohibited Negroes from remaining inside municipal limits after sun down.' "[33]

Most of these towns, especially in the Midwest, were not close to any black population concentration and would not have confronted any inundation by African Americans had they failed to pass an ordinance. Consider De Land, for instance, a small village in central Illinois, population 475 in 2000. Present and former members of the De Land board of trustees agreed in 2002 that it had passed such an ordinance decades ago. De Land never had more than a few hundred inhabitants and is not located on any major railroad or highway, so it never faced an influx of nonwhites. Why, then, did it enact such a law? Since by the 1890s African Americans were defined in American culture as the problem, passing such an ordinance seemed prudent—the progressive thing to do. Towns that took similar actions were "up to date." De Land is in Piatt County, whose county seat, Monticello, was also a sundown town and also has a tradition of having enacted an ordinance. I suspect De Land followed Monticello's lead, and I believe that a wave of these ordinances swept the Midwest somewhere between 1900 and 1930. I have yet to find the text of a single midwestern ordinance, however,[34] so I cannot follow their spread via a written and dated record.[35]

Ordinances, Legal or Illegal?

It turns out that these ordinances were all illegal. Again, action against Chinese Americans in the West led the way, in this case in a positive direction. In 1890, Chinese Americans challenged in court a San Francisco ordinance that required them to move outside the city entirely or live in "an area set aside for slaughterhouses and other businesses thought prejudicial to public health or comfort," in the words of John Noonan, summarizing *In re Lee Sing.* The plaintiffs won; the ordinance was declared unconstitutional.[36]

In 1910, Baltimore passed a residential segregation ordinance. Quickly this was seen as the thing to do, and similar ordinances followed in Winston-Salem, Birmingham, Atlanta, Richmond, Norfolk, Louisville, New Orleans, St. Louis, Dallas, and other southern and border cities and towns. The Louisville ordinance became a test case. It designated city blocks with a majority of African Americans "black blocks" and those with a majority of whites "white blocks." Blacks were not allowed to move into white blocks and vice versa. These ordinances were drafted to look equal so they could pass muster under the Fourteenth Amendment, as historian T. J. Woofter Jr. explained:

> Although theoretically the law is supposed to apply to white and colored alike, in practice it never does. The colored people do not protest against white invasion, while the white people in mixed blocks do not hesitate to protest. Altogether about 50 cases have been made against Negroes under the New Orleans ordinance, and there has not been a single case against a white person.

In 1917, in *Buchanan v. Warley,* the U.S. Supreme Court held the Louisville ordinance unconstitutional. White civil rights lawyer Moorfield Story argued the case for the NAACP. In 1917, no plea for black rights would have been likely to prevail. Story won because a *white* right was at stake: the right of a white seller to sell his house to the highest bidder, even if that person happened to be black. The court held that the ordinance "destroyed the right of the individual to acquire, enjoy, and dispose of his property," in violation of the due process clause of the Fourteenth Amendment.[37] Although *Buchanan* ruled unconstitutional a law intended to create sundown neighborhoods, there can be no doubt that as a precedent, it would also invalidate ordinances intended to create sundown towns, which did not hide their explicit anti-black intentions behind even a gloss of fairness.[38]

In November 1915, Mayor J. R. Voigt introduced a segregation ordinance to the North Chattanooga City Council in Tennessee. Mayor Voigt was aware of the ongoing constitutional challenges to such a bill, similar ordinances having already been declared illegal in Winston, North Carolina, and Richmond, Virginia. He phrased the measure evenhandedly:

> Section 1: It shall be unlawful for any colored person to move into and occupy as a residence, place of abode, or to establish and maintain as a place of public assembly, any house upon any block upon which a greater number of houses are occupied as residences, places of abode, or places of public assembly by white people than are occupied as residences, places of abode or places of public assembly by colored people.

Section 2 then repeated this language but with the races reversed, so it appeared to be in line with the "separate but equal" ruling in *Plessy v. Ferguson* two decades earlier. However, everyone knew that North Chattanooga had only two black families living in it. Therefore it had no block "upon which a greater number of houses are occupied . . . by black people." As the *Chattanooga Daily Times* put it, "The passage of this ordinance will consequently make the town practically of an exclusively white population." In short, it was a sundown ordinance.

To avoid legal challenge, Mayor Voigt also built in provisions so that the two black families then living in North Chattanooga would not be forced to leave. They got the message anyway, for by the time the ordinance passed, on December 22, 1915, the *Daily Times* was able to headline its story, "North Chattanooga Is Exclusively White Now." The newspaper was proud to report, "As there are now no Negroes in North Chattanooga, it might be called the only town of its size in the country where the population is exclusively white."[39] "Mayor Voigt has received many compliments on his segregation ordinance," the story concluded.[40]

Despite *Buchanan v. Warley,* many cities and towns seem simply to have ignored the constitutional issue. Cities kept right on passing them,[41] and as the authors of the *Encyclopedia of Black America* noted in 1981, "A number of these ordinances were maintained long after 1917. . . . Legal attempts to enforce them in the courts were still being made in the 1950s." There is a scholarly tradition in American legal history that questions whether the U.S. Supreme Court can cause or has ever caused significant social change. The history of *Buchanan v. Warley* makes a good case for this theory.[42]

Brea, California, offers an example of an ordinance, known to be illegal, yet still in force decades after *Buchanan.* Vincent Jaster, retired school superintendent of Brea, was an educated man who knew sundown ordinances were unconstitutional. He also knew their power, as can be seen in his answer when asked in 1982, "Why would you prefer to live in Brea rather than Yorba Linda, Fullerton, or elsewhere?"

> Lower taxes, for one thing, better climate, nice people, and good schools. I maybe shouldn't say this, but this was an item some years ago in the 1940s and is not going to trouble me at all. Brea used to have a law that no black person could live in town here after six o'clock. See, Fullerton had its colored section; Placentia at that time was predominantly a Mexican town. But for years there were no black people in Brea at all. The shoeshine man was black, but he had to

leave town by six o'clock. It was an illegal law, of course, if you'd gone to the Supreme Court.

No one took Brea to the Supreme Court, so its unconstitutional law was legal, so far as its effect in Brea was concerned. The same point held in countless other towns.[43]

Why shouldn't towns ignore the constitutional question? After all, during the Depression the federal government acted as if *Buchanan* did not exist when it set up at least seven towns—Richland, Washington; Boulder City, Nevada; Norris, Tennessee; Greendale, Wisconsin; Greenhills, Ohio; Arthurdale, West Virginia; and Greenbelt, Maryland—that explicitly kept out African Americans.[44] At the same time, and for three more decades, the Federal Housing Administration—a government agency—*required* restrictive covenants before insuring housing loans. If the United States government, charged with enforcing *Buchanan,* could exclude African Americans, obviously any community could.

Attempts to enforce illegal sundown ordinances in the streets were still being made in the 1990s. In 2001, a central Illinoisan related that when she and her husband were about to buy a house in Maroa a few years earlier, the realtor "told us we wouldn't have any problems with black neighbors because Maroa had an ordinance and they weren't allowed." Indeed, if a seller, agent, and black would-be buyer in Maroa all believe today that the ordinance is legal, in a very real sense it remains in effect, even though it *is* illegal. Residents will think that selling to an African American violates the law; some will conclude that it is also wrong. They will not sell to a black and may take steps to keep others from so doing. As an attorney who grew up in Martinsville, Illinois, a sundown town, put it, "If you say there's an ordinance, then whether there was or not, that gives it the color of law." Even an unconstitutional ordinance connotes to the residents of the sundown town that the black would-be newcomer is not *supposed* to be here—especially if those residents don't know that the law is illegal. Whether legal or not, and even whether actually passed or not, *belief in the ordinance puts it in force.* Indeed, residents in some midwestern towns think their sundown ordinances are *still* in effect.[45]

Creating Sundown Towns by Official Governmental Action

Even without enabling legislation, many municipal and county officials drove out or kept out African Americans by formal policy. Discussing Crawford

County, Indiana, historian Emma Lou Thornbrough tells of "a contractor for the Louisville, New Albany, and St. Louis Railroad who had hired a gang of colored construction workers." White residents warned him that they would not be allowed to work. "When he sought protection from the county officials, they confirmed that it was an unwritten law that Negroes were not permitted in the county." A resident of Crawford County in the 1960s told a similar story about contractors building a different railroad in a later decade who also hired blacks: the sheriff warned African Americans about the law, but this time he allowed them to remain in the county, so long as they stayed on railroad property. Accordingly, they lived in tents near the work site. An "unwritten law" enforced by county officials including the sheriff *is* a law, to all intents and purposes.[46]

For that matter, an unwritten law enforced by a police chief or sheriff can be even more serious than a written law. Consider this conversation real estate developer Hank Roth had with the sheriff of Graham County in western North Carolina in about 1969: "He wanted me to know they didn't have any blacks in Robbinsville. He said the last 'nigger' who came to town 'hung under that tree over there.' " Thus no bright line can be drawn between unwritten understandings backed by official actions and formal ordinances.[47]

Towns that posted sundown signs implied they were all-white by municipal action. I have confirmed 184 towns in 32 states that displayed sundown signs.[48] Consider the Connecticut town whose sign is: "Whites Only Within City Limits After Dark (Portfolio 7)." To the passerby, that certainly *looks* official, and year after year, no one took it down, after all. Willie Harlen, president of the Washington County (Indiana) Historical Society, made this point when he wrote, "It is said there was a sundown sign east of Salem near Canton. Our Historical Society Treasurer was born in 1928. She remembers her parents telling about the sign . . . I don't know whether there was an ordinance posted or blacks were made to believe there was." Of course, whites too were made to believe there was. Towns that sounded whistles or sirens to warn blacks to get out of town at 6 PM also implied they were sundown by official action. Historian David Roediger grew up in Columbia, Illinois, a sundown town near St. Louis. Like Villa Grove, Columbia had a 6 PM whistle. Roediger reported that his mother moved to Columbia from Cairo in 1941 to teach elementary school. The police chief "almost immediately took her aside to say that she should feel secure, unlike in Cairo, because Columbia had a 6 PM whistle to warn blacks out of town." Coming from the chief of police, that is official policy.[49]

Jim Clayton, a retired *Washington Post* reporter who grew up in Johnston

City, a sundown town in southern Illinois, wrote, "Although there never was an anti-black ordinance, it was well understood that blacks were not permitted to stay in [Johnston City] over night." An ordinance would be superfluous, he suggested: everyone already knew no African Americans were allowed in town, so why bother saying so? If a black person tried to move into Johnston City in the 1940s, according to Clayton, "the Chief of Police would have told them to leave, and that would have been all it would take." The police chief also played a key role in Batesville, Indiana. According to Judy Tonges of the Batesville Historical Society,

> From what I can piece together, there was never an ordinance or law in Batesville prohibiting blacks. However, the knowledge was there. I talked with our police chief who grew up next to a lumber yard. He would visit the black truckers who were delivering lumber. He said they always rushed to get unloaded and out of town before dark.

Of course they did, after the police chief "visited" them.[50]

Like Johnston City's, many towns' sundown reputations were so well known that the municipalities felt no need to pass an ordinance. According to a longtime resident of Niles, Ohio, Niles qualifies: "I would be surprised if there were official ordinances prohibiting African-Americans from settling here. Things operate here much more informally. . . . Laws and ordinances are irrelevant and unnecessary." Many other sundown town residents made this point about their home communities, large and small. African Americans, or in some cases Jews or Chinese Americans, were not to live there, period. It was, and in some communities remains, as simple as that—written or not, legal or not. In many sundown towns and suburbs, law enforcement officials follow and stop African American motorists to this day as a matter of departmental policy. Thus we cannot assume that towns with ordinances were more racist, more rigid, or more notorious as sundown towns than communities whose officials kept out African Americans without such laws.[51]

Creating Sundown Towns by Freeze-out

Sometimes no specific act of violence or formal policy was required to turn a town or county all-white. As the Nadir deepened, white churches, schools, and even stores across the North often made African Americans unwelcome. In 1887 in Grundy County, Missouri, for example, a white school that previously had admitted black children now barred them. Their parents sued under the Fourteenth Amendment, but in 1890 the Missouri Supreme Court denied their appeal. Yet fifteen black children were required before a county had to have a "colored" high school. So African American children in Grundy County simply had no high school. It comes as no surprise that the black population of Grundy County fell from 254 in 1890 to just 85 by 1930, 35 in 1950, and 18 by 1960.[52]

Historian Robert Nesbit documented what happened to Pleasant Ridge, a small black community that grew up in Grant County, Wisconsin, after the Civil War. The neighboring white school agreed to take in their children, and in the years after the Civil War, Pleasant Ridge hosted an annual picnic that "featured an agreeable mixing of the neighbors." But by the late 1880s, its white neighbors had rechristened it "Nigger Ridge" and no longer deigned to attend community events such as the picnic. Residents continued the picnic for a few years, "as a mostly Negro affair" in Nesbit's words, but Pleasant Ridge "went into decline."[53] No specific event forced African Americans out, but Grant County's black population fell from 98 in 1870 to 68 in 1890, 43 in 1920, and just 7, all males, by 1960. To be black in Pleasant Ridge in 1870 when there were 97 other African Americans in the county was all right, because one also had white friends and neighbors. By 1920, being one of 43 African Americans meant living in a sea of Caucasians who ranged from indifferent to actively hostile.[54]

In some towns, whites who still wanted to befriend their black neighbors now felt compelled to do so surreptitiously, lest they too be ostracized by the larger white community. The one black student in the Wyandotte (Michigan) public schools in the 1910s had white school "friends" who were pleased that he did not embarrass them by recognizing that he knew them when their paths chanced to cross away from school. A woman in southern Illinois told me she played with the children of the black family that lived near them, but only under cover of darkness. Faced with such discouragements, especially in towns and counties where they were few, African Americans could no longer struggle on. So they pulled back into larger cities. At least there one's pariah status wasn't always right in front of one's face, and one might have friends.[55]

No bright-line boundary can be drawn between public prohibition and private freeze-out. A "Mass Meeting" in Bell City, Missouri, 110 miles south of St. Louis, on December 20, 1939, exemplifies this blurring. Citizens passed eight "Resolutions," all dealing with forcing out every African American from Bell City and northeastern Stoddard County and keeping any new blacks from moving in. The first "resolved that all land and property owners . . . be invited, urged, and requested not to permit or allow any Negro or Mexican families or single person or persons to move and reside upon their lands or property in the above described territory for any purpose whatsoever." Another warned "that the moral standard of living conditions will be greatly lowered if Negroes or Mexicans are allowed to inhabit this territory." Resolution 7 was the most ominous:

> That every Negro family or individual which numbers some six or eight now residing in said district be invited to move out of said territory in a reasonable length of time and that the landowners where said Negroes now dwell be invited to rid their premises of said Negro in a reasonable time.

The final resolution invoked officers of the law:

> Further resolved that all citizens and peace officers in this and adjoining counties are asked to cooperate with this convention and its committees in carrying out these resolutions in a peaceful and lawful manner.

Clearly "John Wright, Ben Oakley, Rev. Jones, and Committee," who affixed their names to the resolutions and had flyers printed up—official-looking, suitable for posting—thought they would have the law on their side. Apparently they did, for by 2000, Bell City still had only 5 African Americans among its 461 residents. Yet just to the southeast lies one of Missouri's blackest areas.[56]

Communities that froze out their African Americans might seem at first glance to be "kinder" than those that forced them out violently or as a matter of law. But as Wyandotte historian Edwina DeWindt points out, for such a crusade to succeed requires "a general unity of action of all Wyandotte citizens in not renting or selling property to Negroes, refusing to serve them in stores and restaurants, and not hiring Negroes in places of employment." Such unanimity over time might require more widespread anti-black feeling—which Wyandotte had in abundance—and more systematic discrimination than is manifested in a town where a mob suddenly erupts to force out African Americans overnight. Moreover, some campaigns to force African Americans out by firing them were mounted in the 1920s by the KKK or labor unions that also threatened violence, so the intimidation level may have been no lower than in Fond du Lac. Whites who wanted to retain their black employees often found themselves violently intimidated and forced to let them go—so freezing out proves no kinder on close inspection.[57]

Creating Sundown Towns and Suburbs by Buyout

Some independent sundown towns bought out their African Americans to achieve all-white status. Especially in suburbia, buyouts were also often used to get rid of black would-be residents. I have collected examples of buyouts to keep blacks from completing purchases in Somerset, New Jersey; Astoria, Oregon; and many points in between. Indeed, buying out the lone African American family that dared to buy in a sundown suburb was so common that Lorraine Hansberry made such an offer the central plot element in her play *A Raisin in the Sun*.[58]

Buying out was not always kinder and gentler, because usually the offer was not to be refused, accompanied by a clear threat. In 1922, residents of Liberty Township in northern Indiana "have been worked up to a frenzy regarding the removal of a colored family, consisting of six persons into that vicinity," as reported in the *Chesterton Tribune*. "The race problem, as far as Liberty township is concerned," was "amicably settled" when the black would-be resident sold the property to a trustee of the township and returned to Gary "with his wife and four children." Now "Liberty township is at peace with the world again," the newspaper concluded. "Amicably settled" may be a euphemism for the resale process, however, given that all of Porter County was sundown at the time and for five decades thereafter. Perhaps the "frenzy" played some role in inducing the black family to sell.

Often, as in Porter County, the offer came from the local government. In that case, the black family usually had no choice; if they refused to sell, the jurisdiction then claimed that the land was required for a park or other public purpose, condemned it, and bought it.

Chapter 7 tells how Sheridan, Arkansas, induced its black population to leave in 1954 in response to *Brown v. Board of Education*. One man, Jack Williams, owner of the local sawmill and the sawmill workers' homes, was principally responsible. He made his African American employees an extraordinary buyout offer: he would *give* them their homes and move them to Malvern, 25 miles west, at no cost to them. This turned out to be a proposition they couldn't refuse, according to my source, who lived in Sheridan at the time, for if a family refused to move, he would evict them and burn down their home. Another longtime resident corroborated this account: "He wouldn't have them in school here. He had little shacks for them. He told them they could have the shacks and move them out, or he would burn them down." Not unreasonably, blacks "chose" to accept the buyout and move to Malvern in response to this ultimatum. A few other African Americans lived in Sheridan—

not in Williams's employ—but what could they do? The preacher, the beautician, and the cafe owner suddenly found themselves without a clientele. They left too.

Creating Sundown Suburbs

Suburbs used the largest array of different weapons for becoming and staying all-white, beginning around 1900, although ultimately they too relied on violence. It is important to understand that the whiteness of America's suburbs was no accident. On the contrary, all-white suburbs were *achieved*. As Dorothy Newman wrote in 1978, "Residential separation rests on a system of formal rules (though no longer worded in racial terms—the words are illegal) and informal but carefully adhered-to practices which no amount of legislation has been able yet to penetrate."

Moreover, the suburbs weren't always so white. Between 1870 and 1900, African Americans lived more widely scattered across metropolitan areas than they did by 1930 or later, just as African Americans lived more scattered across northern states in 1890 than they did by 1930 or later. When suburbanization set in, African American families already resided on the fringes of many cities. In many places—across the South, of course, but even as far north as Dearborn, Michigan, and Edina, Minnesota—developers had to get rid of African Americans, who already lived where the suburbs were being formed, to create the white suburbs we now take for granted. In 1870, before Dearborn township incorporated, among its 2,300 people lived 30 black residents, but by 1920, incorporated Dearborn's 2,470 residents included just one African American.[59]

When they sought to establish the town of Edina, for example—now the richest suburb of Minneapolis–St. Paul—developers faced the problem that a Quaker village already existed in Richfield Township where the new suburb was to be built. Throughout the North, Quakers had welcomed African Americans after the Civil War. Many black families now lived in the western half of Richfield Township. "Over the ensuing decades," according to Deborah Morse-Kahn, whose history of Edina is exceptional for its willingness to discuss the community's racial past, African Americans "became very involved in community life—very often as leaders." Indeed, "Edina Mills was a fully integrated and color-blind community well before the turn of the century." Whites attended black weddings. An African American woman founded the first PTA in Edina in the late 1880s and served as its first vice president. B. C. Yancey was a justice of the peace and village recorder.[60]

Then, just after World War I, Samuel Thorpe developed "the elegant Edina Country Club residential district," as Morse-Kahn correctly describes it, "with restrictive deed covenants in place." Now Edina's African American community "would feel estranged. Thorpe Brothers' building restrictions guaranteed to any buyer, in an era when municipal zoning was nonexistent, that their property would be 'safe' from devaluating circumstances, stating that blacks were explicitly ineligible to buy in the district." According to Joyce Repya, associate planner for Edina, deeds carried various restrictions such as "No fuel storage tanks above ground," "No shedding poplars, box elders, or other objectionable trees," and, most important, the racial exclusionary clause quoted at the head of the next chapter. And unlike all other restrictions, which phased out in 1964, the restriction to "the white or Caucasian race" continued in force forever. "By the late 1930s," in Morse-Kahn's words, "virtually all of Edina's black families had moved into Minneapolis and an historic era had ended for the village." At that point, Morse-Kahn goes on, anti-Semitism, which had been "virtually unheard-of in Edina before the First World War, became a haunting hallmark of Edina life. As late as the end of the 1950s, potential buyers known to be Jewish were often openly turned away by realtors and requested to look for residential property elsewhere."[61]

Other suburbs across America had to force out already existing pockets of African American residents to achieve all-white status. Especially across the South, African Americans have long lived in rural areas. For all-white suburbs to be built, those residents must be cleared out. And although the traditional South had few independent sundown towns, after the 1930s it developed its share of sundown suburbs. By that time some white Southerners were beginning to abandon their traditional view of African Americans as subjects for exploitation in favor of the northern view of them as nuisances to be rid of. And of course, African Americans were not as essential to the southern suburban economy as they had been to its plantation economy.

Chamblee, Georgia, began as a small town outside Atlanta. In 1940, Chamblee had 1,081 residents including 222 African Americans. After World War II, Chamblee became a suburb of Atlanta. By 1950, its population soared to 3,445, while its black population shrank to 92. Ten years later, Chamblee had 6,635 people, including just 2 African Americans. And by 1970, it had 9,127, including just 1 black woman, probably a maid. Developers built brand-new all-white subdivisions in the 1950s, according to a woman who grew up in two of them. I could not locate anyone in Chamblee who knew why its African Americans departed. Schooling provides one possible reason. Until massive school desegregation, which took place around

1970, African American families in suburbs throughout the South found living there hugely inconvenient. Most suburbs with small black populations had no black schools; instead they paid tuition for their black children to attend black schools in the inner city. This policy motivated many African American families to move to that city rather than impose long commutes on their children, often with no school buses. African Americans in Chamblee had no school, according to a former mayor, and had to attend the nearest black school in Atlanta. After 1970, Chamblee desegregated all over again, a story we will pick up in a later chapter, but in the 1940s and '50s, it seems to have embodied a "push-out" or "buyout" of its black population.[62]

The same thing happened outside Washington, D.C.; Gainesville, Florida; Memphis; New York City; and other expanding metropolises. Although southern white developers showed no more hesitation than northerners about removing black residents for new sundown suburbs, they usually respected black burial grounds. The result, found as far north as Maryland, is an occasional black church and cemetery standing isolated in an otherwise all-white suburb. Sometimes African Americans then abandoned their church and cemetery because they could not cope with repeated vandalism by white suburban teenagers.

Across the nation, according to a 1981 government report, "although white migration flows favored the suburbs throughout, until the late 1960s more blacks were moving to the city from the much smaller suburban base than were suburbanizing in the majority of the [metropolitan areas]." In other words, until about 1968, African Americans were getting displaced *from* still-whitening suburbs at a faster rate than they were moving *to* suburbia.[63]

Even maids and servants came to be seen as an unwanted presence after dark if they lived in independent households. In 1910, a committee of residents of Wilmette, an elite North Shore suburb of Chicago, asked all families unable to house their maids and gardeners on their own premises to fire them, especially if they lived in Wilmette, claiming that their presence had "depressed real estate values" in the village. According to Chicago historian Thomas Philpott, it worked: "Few blacks who did not have quarters in their white employers' homes remained in Wilmette." Even by 1970, Wilmette's 32,134 residents included just 81 African Americans, and most of them were live-in maids.[64]

All Planned Suburbs Were Intentionally Created All-White

Elite suburbs that were built by a single developer were especially likely to begin life as all-white on purpose. Tuxedo Park, New York, perhaps the richest of them all, may have gone sundown first, even before 1890. Affluent whites founded it "as a club community and maintained that discipline for nearly 50 years," as Albert Winslow put it in the town's official history, published in 1992. "Anybody seeking to buy property in the Park would by necessity be required to be a member of the Club. The association also maintained a police department and six gate houses." The gate houses were connected by barbed wire, according to historian Patrick McMullen, who credits Tuxedo Park with thus inventing the gated community in 1881. "Tuxedo Park also heralded the creation of a new entity, the homeowner's association, meant to influence the appearance, population, and social character of the community."

Just in case anyone tried to move in without being a member, Tuxedo Park developed additional methods for keeping out undesirables, primarily Jews and African Americans but also others who "did not enjoy the attributes for membership in the Club," as Winslow put it. He goes on to tell of a wealthy buyer who purchased a large house in Tuxedo Park in the late 1920s and tried to move in. "He was told his membership in the Club was out of the question. He persevered and then had to be told that if he did indeed buy he would be denied access to water and sewer lines, which were owned by the Tuxedo Park Association. . . . He did not buy!"[65]

As the twentieth century wore on, Americans continued to build planned communities. Every planned town that I know of—indeed, *every community in America founded after 1890 and before 1960 by a single developer or owner—kept out African Americans from its beginnings.* Chronologically, these include Highland Park near Dallas in 1907–13 and Mariemont near Cincinnati in 1914, both of which won fame for their innovative shopping centers. Shaker Heights, east of Cleveland, was designed to be "utopian" and excluded blacks, Jews, and Catholics from its inception. Near Los Angeles, planned all-white suburbs set up around this time include Beverly Hills, Culver City, Palos Verdes Estates, Tarzana (developed by Edgar Rice Burroughs from the proceeds of his *Tarzan* novels), and several others. Ebenezer Howard's "garden city" concept, imported from England, influenced at least seven suburbs or exurbs built around World War II: Radburn, New Jersey, in 1929; Greenbelt, Maryland, near Washington, D.C., Greenhills, Ohio, near Cincinnati, Greendale, Wisconsin, near Milwaukee, and Norris, Tennessee, in the 1930s; Richland, Washington, in 1942; and Park Forest, near Chicago, in the 1950s. All of these planned communities were developed as sundown towns.[66] The Franklin Roosevelt administration built the "Greens"— Greenbelt, Greenhills, and Greendale—to create jobs and supply needed housing during the Great Depression; all three remained all-white for decades. So did Norris, built by the Tennessee Valley Authority to house workers on nearby Norris Dam, Richland, put up to house workers at the Hanford atomic plant, and Boulder City, Nevada, built for workers on Boulder Dam.[67]

Most "Unplanned" Suburbs Were Also Created All-White

When a suburb expanded without a plan or single developer, African Americans had more opportunity to move in. Still, the overwhelming majority of unplanned suburbs were created all-white from their inception. Most kept out African Americans (and often Jews) openly and "legally," as Portfolio 28, an ad for a suburban development in Salt Lake City, exemplifies. Their most straightforward method was to pass a formal ordinance, like some of their country cousins, the independent sundown towns. Many suburbs never passed a formal ordinance but, like Batesville, Indiana, or Johnston City, Illinois, acted as if they had.

Most suburbs incorporated between 1900 and 1968. Often they formed in the first place to become sundown towns. According to John Denton, who studied housing in the San Francisco Bay area, "One of the principal purposes (if not the entire purpose) of suburban incorporations is to give their populations control of the racial composition of their communities." When they incorporated, suburbs typically drew their boundaries to exclude African American neighborhoods. In 1912, white voters in Brentwood, Maryland, rejected incorporation with tiny adjoining North Brentwood, majority black, so in 1924, North Brentwood incorporated separately. Two Texas sundown suburbs—Highland Park and University Park—are entirely surrounded by Dallas, which tried to annex them repeatedly between 1919 and 1945. The "Park Cities," as they call themselves, repeatedly rebuffed Dallas. Under Texas law, if one municipality entirely surrounds another, the larger can absorb the smaller. Although Dallas encircles the Park Cities, it can annex neither, because on one side each borders "another" city—the other Park City. I put quotation marks around "another" because the Park Cities are alike and even form one school system.[68]

In 1960, white city officials of Phoenix, Illinois, another south suburb of Chicago, pulled off what suburban expert Larry McClellan calls "a stunning

114   SUNDOWN TOWNS

example of racial politics." Instead of using municipal boundaries to keep African Americans out, they redrew the city limits to create white flight without ever moving! In the 1950s, Phoenix was going black, so in 1960, its white city officials "de-annexed" the part of the city where most whites lived, ceding themselves to Harvey, the next suburb west, and leaving Phoenix to the African Americans. It didn't work: Harvey also proceeded to go majority-black.[69]

Regardless of the Creation, the Result Was the Same

How a town went sundown—owing to a violent expulsion, a quiet ordinance, or a more subtle freeze-out or buyout—made no consistent difference over time. Either way, African Americans lost their homes and jobs, or their chance for homes and jobs. Either way, the town defined itself as sundown for many decades, and that decision had to be defended.

The white townspeople of Sheridan, Arkansas, for instance, were probably no more racist than residents of many other Arkansas towns until 1954. Indeed, they may have been *less* racist than many: as Chapter 7 tells, they almost chose to desegregate their schools in response to *Brown,* a step taken by only two towns in Arkansas. After the 1954 buyout, however, Sheridan's notoriety grew. As a lifelong resident said in 2001, the town "developed a reputation that was perhaps more aggressive than it really deserved. For years, black people wouldn't even stop in Sheridan for gas." In fact, Sheridan probably deserved its new reputation. Although originally prompted by a single individual, no Sheridan resident lifted a voice to protest the forced buyout of its black community. On the contrary, two different Sheridan residents said in separate conversations in 2001, "You know, that solved the problem!" Implicitly they defined "the problem" as school desegregation, or more accurately, the existence of African American children. With a definition like that, inducing blacks to leave indeed "solved the problem." Having accepted that "solution," whites in Sheridan were left predisposed to further racism. According to reports, they posted signs, "Nigger, Don't Let the Sun Set On You Here." Long after non-sundown towns in Arkansas desegregated their schools, Sheridan fans developed a reputation for bigotry when their high school played interracial teams in athletic contests. This reputation grew in the late 1980s and early 1990s, when Sheridan played rival Searcy, a majority-white town, but not a sundown town. Searcy had a talented African American on its roster, and when he got the ball in games played in Sheridan, white parents and Sheridan students would yell "Get the nigger" and similar phrases.[70]

The methods blur into each other on a continuum. Towns that went all-white nonviolently frequently employed violence to stay that way. A city official in tiny De Land remembers as a child in about 1960 overhearing an adult conversation to the effect that a black family recently moved into De Land, but there was a mysterious fire in their house and they left. "De Land had a sundown rule," the adults went on, "so what did they expect?" In this case, the passage of an ordinance probably contributed to private violence by heightening white outrage at the violation of community mores. Whether a given town became all-white violently or nonviolently, formally or informally, does not predict how it will behave later.[71]

Because suburbs got organized later than most independent towns, after the Nadir was well under way, a much higher proportion of them were created as sundown towns from the beginning, as the next chapter shows.

5

Sundown Suburbs

No lot shall ever be sold, conveyed, leased, or rented to any person other than one of the white or Caucasian race, nor shall any lot ever be used or occupied by any person other than one of the white or Caucasian race, except such as may be serving as domestics for the owner or tenant of said lot, while said owner or tenant is residing thereon. All restrictions, except those in paragraph 8 (racial exclusion), shall terminate on January 1, 1964.

—Typical restrictive covenant for property in Edina, Minnesota, sundown suburb of Minneapolis[1]

ACROSS AMERICA, most suburbs, and in some metropolitan areas almost all of them, excluded African Americans (and often Jews). This pattern of suburban exclusion became so thorough, even in the traditional South, and especially in the older metropolitan areas of the Northeast and Midwest, that Americans today express no surprise when inner cities are mostly black while suburbs are overwhelmingly white.

After 1900, precisely as the suburbs unfolded, African Americans were moving to northern metropolitan areas as part of the Great Retreat and, beginning around 1915, as part of the Great Migration. But the suburbs kept them out. Detroit, for example, slowly became overwhelmingly black, even though it touches at least four sundown suburbs—Dearborn, Grosse Pointe, Melvindale, and Warren. Map 4 shows these contiguous sundown suburbs and many others. Some black families from Detroit would have moved to these suburbs the way whites did, had they been allowed. Indeed, Inkster, a majority-black suburb founded in 1921, lies just beyond Dearborn, farther from Detroit. Yet while Inkster to the west and Detroit to the north and east grew in black population, Dearborn, between them, grew even whiter. Many of its residents took pride in the saying, "The sun never set on a Negro in Dearborn," according to historians August Meier and Elliott Rudwick. Dear-

Map 4. Detroit Suburbs

At least 47 of 59 suburbs outside Detroit were overwhelmingly white, decade after decade. Eleven were interracial and one requires more census study. I have confirmed only 15 of the 47 as sundown suburbs, but further research would surely confirm most of the rest. In 1960, for example, Garden City, which abuts interracial Inkster, had just two African Americans, both women, probably both live-in maids, among its nearly 40,000 residents. Twenty years later, large suburbs like Berkley, Clawson, Farmington, and Harper Woods had not one black inhabitant. Such numbers imply exclusion.

Moreover, of the 11 interracial suburbs, several were not meaningfully integrated; the black/white border merely happened to run through the suburb. In 1940, for example, 1,800 African Americans lived in Ecorse, but not one east of the tracks, where the whites lived. In 1970, whites in River Rouge could recall only one black family, "the first in 50 years," that lived on the east side, and they were intimidated into leaving.*

* Andrew Wiese, *Places of Their Own* (Chicago: University of Chicago Press, 2004), 49.

born's longtime mayor Orville Hubbard, who held office from 1942 to 1978, told a reporter that "as far as he was concerned, it was against the law for Negroes to live in his suburb." Dearborn was an extraordinary case because Hubbard was so outspoken, but David Good, Hubbard's biographer, cautions us not to see him as unique: "In a sense, Orville Hubbard's view was no different from that in any of a dozen or more other segregated suburbs that ringed the city of Detroit—or in hundreds of other such communities scattered across the country." [2]

The Importance of Suburbs

In time, suburbs came to dominate our nation. Between 1950 and 1970, the suburban population doubled from 36 million to 74 million as 83% of the nation's population growth took place in the suburbs. By 1970, for the first time, more people lived in suburbs than in central cities or rural areas. Thirty years later, more lived in suburbs than in cities and rural areas combined. [3] Since suburbanites vote at higher rates than anyone else, they are now by far the dominant political force in the United States. Thomas and Mary Edsall provide these statistics: during the twenty years from 1968 to 1988, the percentage of the presidential vote cast in suburbs grew from 36% to 48%. The rural vote declined from 35% to 22% while central cities stayed constant at about 29.5%. "What all this suggests," they conclude, "is that a politics of suburban hegemony will come to characterize presidential elections." [4]

Not only in politics do suburbs rule. In his 1995 primer *The Suburbs,* John Palen notes the increasing influence of suburbs in economic and cultural spheres:

> Suburbs have gone from being fringe commuter areas to being the modal locations for American living and working. There has been a suburban revolution that has changed suburbs from being places on the periphery of the urban cores to being the economic and commercial centers of a new metropolitan area form. Increasingly, it is the suburbs that are central with the cities being peripheral.

As early as 1978, a *New York Times* survey of suburban New Yorkers found that more than half did not feel they belonged to the New York metropolitan area at all, and a fourth never went to the city even once in the previous year. By 1987, suburban shopping malls accounted for 54% of all sales of personal and household items. Suburbs now contain two-thirds of our office space. Palen notes that "more than ¾ of the job growth during the 1980s in

America's twenty largest metropolitan areas occurred in the suburbs." He claims that the suburbs are also becoming dominant culturally. Many of the sporting and cultural events that used to take place downtown now play in suburban arenas and concert halls. In short, "although it somewhat twists the language, suburbs are more and more frequently the center of the metropolitan area."[5]

The Good Life

Why did this happen? The American rush to the suburbs wasn't just to avoid African Americans. Indeed, it wasn't *primarily* to avoid African Americans. It took place in metropolitan areas with few African Americans as well as areas such as Detroit whose core cities became majority-black. Families moved to the suburbs for two principal reasons: first, it seemed the proper way to bring up children, and second, it both showed and secured social status. That is, Americans saw suburbs as the solution to two problems: having a family and having prestige. Suburban dwellers wanted to raise their children to be safe, happy, and well educated in metropolitan areas. They also wanted to be upwardly mobile and to display their upward mobility.

The two functions were closely related, since "living well" begets status. As the twentieth century wore on, Americans told themselves increasingly that children need their own grass to play on and their own trees to play under, and families need their own plots of earth in which to put down roots. Today this idea is so firmly embedded in our national culture, at least that of our lower-upper and middle classes, as to seem "natural."[6] Of course, by "natural" we really mean so deep in our culture that we do not—perhaps cannot—question it. And of course, communities that embody such "obvious" values are by definition better—hence more prestigious—places to live.

Not all suburbs fit the same mold, of course. Some are centered around industry, such as Dearborn, Michigan, around Ford, and Granite City, Illinois, around the graniteware plant and several steel mills. Some of these working-class suburbs were founded as white enclaves; some, like Dearborn and Granite City, became sundown suburbs by forcing out their African Americans; still others remained interracial, especially if they had begun as interracial independent cities, as did Pontiac, Michigan. Among the benefits that sundown suburbs confer is participation in what political scientist Larry Peterson calls a "type of Americanization"—leaving the old Polish, Greek, or Italian city neighborhood for a new, ethnically mixed, but all-white neighborhood in the suburbs.[7]

Suburbs also offer other very real amenities. People move to them to get good schools, nice parks, good city services, and safety, as well as status and aesthetics. Children in elite suburbs have a leg up, because these communities concentrate opportunity. An elite suburban child is far more likely to know what the world has to offer and how to take advantage of it—from computers to summer jobs to coaching classes for the SAT. As a former school administrator in Stamford, Connecticut, said, "the keys to the kingdom" lie in these suburbs. And those keys are in addition to suburban tax base advantages that make possible much better public schools.

Avoiding the Problems of the City

"The city is doomed," announced Henry Ford. "We shall solve the city problem by leaving the city." And he moved Ford's headquarters and largest manufacturing unit to the sundown suburb of Dearborn. Suburbs took steps to define themselves as different from cities. The promoters of Highland Park, Texas, used the slogan "Beyond the City's Dust and Smoke" to distance their suburb from Dallas, even though Dallas eventually encompassed Highland Park. Upper-middle-class Americans were revolted by the dirt of the cities, not only from their factories and railroads, but also from their politics. If their political machines could not be reformed, then the "progressive" thing to do would be to form one's own government in the suburbs under the control of the "better element." In 1874, Brookline, Massachusetts, voted to reject union with Boston. By 1920, suburbs had rejected mergers with central cities across the United States, from Rochester to Pittsburgh to Chicago to Oakland.[8]

This withdrawal from the city is evident in suburban names. Earlier suburbs of Chicago were named, inter alia, North Chicago, East Chicago, South Chicago, and, yes, West Chicago. Later suburbs used *park* and *forest* to death. Chicago alone is surrounded by Bedford Park, Calumet Park, Deer Park, Edison Park, Elmwood Park, Evergreen Park, Forest Lake, Forest View, Franklin Park, Hanover Park, Highland Park, Ingalls Park, Jefferson Park, LaGrange Park, Lake Forest, Liberty Park, Melrose Park, Merrionette Park, Norwood Park, Oak Forest, Oak Park, Orland Park, Palos Park, Park City, Park Ridge, Richton Park, River Forest, Round Lake Park, Schiller Park, Stone Park, University Park, and Villa Park, not to mention Forest Park and Park Forest. The process continues: in 1973, East Paterson, New Jersey, changed its name to Elmwood Park. East Detroit became Erin Heights in 1984; eight years later, it changed to Eastpointe, trying desperately to grasp some of the prestige of Grosse Pointe, Grosse Pointe Woods, Grosse Pointe Farms, and Grosse Pointe Park, sundown suburbs to its south.[9]

Moving to the suburbs to escape the disamenities of the city—everything from industrial sectors and delivery trucks to crime and prostitution—not only makes aesthetic sense and provides a more pleasant lifestyle; it also makes for a better investment. A real estate agent put it this way, advising potential home buyers in 2001 in the *Chicago Tribune*:

> You should nearly always avoid buying in a "marginal neighborhood," such as one that is seriously flawed by commercial blight, heavy traffic congestion, loud environmental noise, pollution, or foul smells.
>
> "I would only do it if I'd been renting for years and years and absolutely could not afford to buy anywhere else," he says.

His advice makes sense and does not mention race, but like everything said about suburbs thus far, it has racial implications. Marginal people make for a marginal neighborhood, and no people have been more marginalized than African Americans.[10]

Blacks as a Key Problem to Be Avoided

African Americans' low prestige has long posed a danger to white status. Andrew Hacker, author of *Two Nations*, identified the status threat in 1961:

> If there is one sword which hangs over the heads of untold millions of white— and Northern—Americans it is that they cannot afford to live in close proximity to Negroes. The single social fact which can destroy the whole image of middle class respectability is to be known to reside in a neighborhood which has Negroes nearby.

In the early 1970s, among many items inquiring about relationships with African Americans, "'Having a Negro family as next door neighbors' was one of the most objected to," reported social psychologist Thomas Pettigrew. Writing in 2000, historian Stephen Meyer pointed out that race still plays the key role: "Many whites remain reluctant to accept African Americans as social equals. They refuse to accept African Americans as neighbors."[11]

In addition to their status concerns, white suburbanites also worry that African Americans are less intelligent, more prone to crime, and a threat to property values. That last concern—property values—rephrases the status issue as a very real pocketbook problem: whites feel an African American next door may make their own home less desirable when they go to sell it. The solution to this familiar blacks-as-problem thinking proves the same in the suburbs as in independent towns: keep them out.

Suburbs Start to Go Sundown

Most of America's first suburbs, built along railroad and streetcar lines, were not all white. Even elegant suburbs—"places like Greenwich, Connecticut; Englewood, New Jersey; Evanston, Illinois; and Chestnut Hill, Massachusetts," in urban historian Kenneth Jackson's words—made room for servants and workers, including independent African American households (in addition to those who lived in).[12] "The barons of Chestnut Hill regarded the close proximity of a poor servant class as an advantage." To commute all the way from the inner city was too expensive, and it was too hard to arrive in time to warm the house and fix breakfast. Some of these early suburbs grew up around stops on the new suburban rail lines. They replicated "the class-related spatial patterns of the core cities," writes Jackson, "with the poorest inhabitants living closest to the tiny business districts and the more affluent residents living in commodious homes on landscaped grounds." Thus Stamford, Connecticut, outside New York City, has its poorer section near what is now the Amtrak station, and Lower Merion, outside Philadelphia, includes Ardmore, near the SEPTA station, where its maids, chauffeurs, and gardeners lived.[13]

Gradually, such a hierarchy no longer seemed good enough. A black family living in Stamford or Evanston might become wealthy, after all, and might want to move into a more elite neighborhood. Already their children were in the public schools with the children of the elite, at least by high school. Affluent whites now declared their upward mobility by moving outward geographically, to all-white suburbs. They expressed their social distance from nonwhites and working-class whites by increasing the physical distance between them. Geographically and chronologically, Kenilworth was the next suburb north of Evanston. Chapter 8 notes that Joseph Sears, developer of Kenilworth, incorporated the restriction "Sales to *Caucasians only*" into his village's founding documents, according to Kenilworth's official historian. We have seen that independent sundown towns often allowed African Americans as live-in servants. Sears had forgotten to make this concession. Therefore, according to his daughter Dorothy: "When in 1903 he would have our colored coachman and his family move into the remodeled farmhouse, he sent a note to each resident, and none objected." Of course they didn't, for the coachman's family was hardly an independent household; moreover, Sears still controlled Kenilworth. Soon Kenilworth became the most elite suburb of Chicago.[14]

This was a national pattern. Like Kenilworth, Darien, the next suburb beyond Stamford, Connecticut, kept out African Americans. So did Palos Verdes Estates, outside of Los Angeles. Increasingly as the twentieth century wore on, white breadwinners chose to make burdensome commutes from ever more distant sundown suburbs. Elite sundown suburbs such as Kenilworth, Darien, and Palos Verdes Estates also differed from older suburbs in being exclusive by social class. The suburbanization of America and the segregation of our metropolitan areas went hand in hand, and the automobile—the same technological innovation that made mass suburbanization possible—facilitated this new separation by race and class. Today elite suburbs no longer need to include working-class homes. Even their teachers and police officers commute from housing they can afford, often two suburbs away. We have seen that some independent sundown towns had black communities nearby to supply workers, like the townships outside Johannesburg, South Africa. So do some sundown suburbs, in a way: "maid buses," sometimes subsidized by residents of the town, bring domestic workers from the nearest inner city every morning and return them home before sundown.

On the ground in Chevy Chase, Maryland, stands a tangible symbol of this difference between old and newer suburbs: the Saks Fifth Avenue store, looking like a bank surrounded by the green lawns of well-kept suburbia. In 1903, Francis Newlands, who set up the Chevy Chase Land Company to build an elite suburb just northwest of Washington, D.C., sold some land to developers to build a subdivision called Belmont to provide affordable housing for domestics and other workers. Shortly thereafter, according to *Washington Post* reporter Marc Fisher, "rumors swept the area that Belmont was to be a community for the suburb's black servants." Newlands claimed he had no such intent, and in 1909 his company filed suit, claiming that the developer was committing fraud "by offering to sell lots . . . to Negroes."[15] In the end, the Chevy Chase Company reacquired the land, and Chevy Chase became one of our first sundown suburbs. The Belmont property then lay vacant for decades, perhaps tainted by its past. That's why it was available for the Saks Fifth Avenue store and parking lot. Today Chevy Chase remains an enclave for rich whites. In 2000, its 6,183 residents included just 18 people[16] living in families with at least one African American householder.[17]

Nearby on the landscape is a reminder that throughout the decades when suburban America was being constructed—and constructed *white*—the federal government abetted the process. Newlands got the United States to create Rock Creek Park as our third national park and the largest urban park in the National Park System. At once the park increased the value of the land Newlands and his associates had bought by removing 2,000 acres from the market, created a beautiful amenity adjoining Chevy Chase, and interposed a green swath of forest to define the new suburb as "rural." Most important, Rock Creek Park buffered Chevy Chase from the increasingly black neighborhoods on what Chevy Chase residents came to call "the wrong side of the park." It still plays this role today.[18]

Sundown Cemeteries

Cemeteries had gone suburban even before the Nadir. According to the cemetery's web site, the founders of Mount Auburn Cemetery outside Boston, established in 1831, "believed that burying and commemorating the dead was best done in a tranquil and beautiful natural setting set apart from urban life." Mount Auburn's park-like imitators around the country actually helped inspire the suburban movement. If the suburbs embodied the good life, avoiding "the problems of the city," then the new cemeteries, complete with lakes, hills, and trees, represented the good death. Quiet and exclusive, they were very different from the burying grounds adjoining urban churches, where one might rub elbows in death with persons very different in race and social class. And during the Nadir, like their suburban environs, the new cemeteries too went sundown, leaving a vivid record of the process on the landscape in granite.[19]

In New Jersey in 1884, a cemetery refused burial to an African American sexton, which led to indignant criticism from the governor as well as the *New York Times*. The Nadir had not yet set in. By World War I, segregation was common practice in cemeteries and no longer aroused any protest, save from African Americans. In 1907, for example, the Forest Home Cemetery near Chicago adopted a resolution that only the remains of white persons would be buried in that cemetery from then on, "except that in cases where colored persons already owned lots in the cemetery, the remains of such colored persons and their direct heirs could be interred there."[20] Before this change, John Gaskill, African American, had buried four of his children in his lot in that cemetery. When his wife died, in 1912, he tried to bury her near them but was refused, because she was not his heir. He filed suit and took his case to the Illinois Supreme Court, which found against him, so his wife could not be buried near her children, or, if he followed through with his plans, near her husband. By 1930, most cemeteries had exclusionary clauses.[21]

Cemetery exclusion was not challenged in the courts until well after World War II. White Chapel Memory Gardens, a sundown cemetery in Syracuse, New York, did not allow a black body within its gates until 1981. Some cemeteries still maintain sundown policies.[22]

Keeping Out Jews

When Joseph Sears proclaimed Kenilworth open to *"Caucasians only,"* the phrase also meant no Jews. Lena and Modie Spiegel, of Spiegel Catalog fame, soon broke this barrier when they "rented Lawyer Merritt Star's large house at 40 Melrose for eight years," according to Colleen Kilner, Kenilworth historian. "How could there be objection when they purchased," she added, "especially after having proved themselves?" Kilner went on to note that their son was president of his eighth-grade class in 1925, but historian Michael Ebner says she painted far too rosy a portrait:

> In the years before World War I, Lena and Modie remained outsiders. Nor did their circumstances improve as perhaps they hoped they would, when the Spiegels became ardent practitioners of Christian Science in an effort to diminish their Jewish identity.

Kenilworth residents subsequently closed ranks against other Jews, according to Ebner: "It is generally thought that one outcome [of the Spiegels] was to buttress the practice of enforcing restrictive covenants," covenants that read "white Protestants only." Labor historian Harry Rubenstein says Kenilworth and nearby Lake Forest started letting Italians in after World War II. Not Jews, though: in 1959, the Anti-Defamation League reported, "The North Shore suburbs of Kenilworth, Lake Forest, Barrington, and Palatine are almost completely closed to Jews. Kenilworth's hostility is so well known that the community is bypassed by real estate agents when serving prospective Jewish purchasers." Finally in the 1970s, according to Rubenstein, Kenilworth admitted Jews.[23]

Kenilworth exemplified a national pattern. As the United States went more racist, it also went more anti-Semitic. After 1900, most elite suburbs quickly moved beyond barring blacks to bar Jews, and a few banned Catholics, especially if they were from southern or eastern Europe and looked "swarthy." Here sundown suburbs parted company with independent sundown towns, few of which made a big deal out of religion.[24] Chapter 9 shows how Grosse Pointe, Michigan, also made it difficult or impossible for Jewish families to move in.[25] Some suburbs limited sales to "members of the Aryan branch of the Caucasian race," thereby excluding "Mediterraneans" as well as Jews.

Imagining Jews as a problem pushes this line of thought to the breaking point, because Jews are *not* thought of as problems today, at least not as problems having to do with crime or poor school performance, but during the heyday of eugenics, Jews, like blacks, were thought to be stupid. On the standardized tests that came into vogue during and after World War I—the U.S. Army alpha test, the Stanford-Binet IQ test, and the SAT—Jews from Russia and Eastern Europe did perform poorly compared to WASPs.[26]

Affluent WASP families increasingly viewed living near Jews as a threat to their own social status. Residents of several Boston suburbs reported that their communities formerly kept out Jews. Laura Hobson's bestselling novel, *Gentleman's Agreement,* made Darien, Connecticut, a sundown suburb of New York City, briefly notorious in 1947 when it publicized the town's practice of not letting Jews spend the night. In 1959, the Anti-Defamation League commented on Bronxville, another suburb of New York City:

> The Incorporated Village of Bronxville in Westchester County has earned a reputation for admitting to its precincts as home-owners or -renters only those who profess to be Christians. According to informed observers, this mile-square village, with a population of 6500, does not have any known Jewish families residing within its boundaries. . . . Even in the apartment buildings located in Bronxville there are no known Jewish tenants.

A report on the Midwest by British economist Graham Hutton tells of Jews' precarious situation in that region just after World War II:

> With exceptions in the Midwest today that could almost be named and counted on the fingers of two hands, the Jewish families—at least, those known to be Jews—settled in defined districts and were "restricted" from refined ones. They are still kept out of the select residential districts and clubs and have therefore established their own.

The same pattern held in suburb after suburb, as far west as La Jolla, California. Most upper- and upper-middle-class suburbs kept out Jews, often until well after World War II.[27] Until the 1980s, Jewish Americans were typically confined to just a handful of suburbs. A resident who favored barring Jews gave one reason: "Where [Jews] come in, the niggers follow and knock the property [values] down."[28] Another reason was sheer status: a town or neighborhood was thought to be higher-class if it kept out Jews. This is still true in some parts of the upper class.[29]

Sundown Suburbs Explode After World War II

By the end of World War II, the housing pressure in African American neighborhoods in inner cities was enormous, greater even than the pent-up postwar demand among white families. A 1943 memo of the Illinois Interracial Commission pointed out that 80% of the black population of Chicago was packed into less than 5 square miles, making dwelling units "unbelievably crowded." Paradoxically, while World War II had a salutary effect on race relations in the United States, it also contributed to an explosion in the development of sundown suburbs. Between 1947 and 1967, more towns were established on a whites-only basis than ever before. Almost every suburb that sprang up or expanded after World War II was whites-only. Among the largest were the three Levittowns, in New Jersey, New York, and Pennsylvania, begun in the 1950s. In fact, Levitt & Sons was by far the largest home builder in America after World War II. By one estimate, the firm built 8% of all postwar suburban housing—all of it sundown. As Kenneth Jackson notes, "The Levitt organization . . . publicly and officially refused to sell to blacks for two decades after the war. Nor did resellers deal with minorities." The result—"not surprisingly," in Jackson's words—was that "in 1960 not a single one of the Long Island Levittown's 82,000 residents was black." William Levitt claimed, "Our housing policy has been to abide by local law or custom" when he built his sundown suburbs, but this was not true. The African American family that finally desegregated Levittown, Pennsylvania, moved in from an integrated town only a mile away. Even more disgraceful was his performance in Manhasset, on Long Island: according to journalist Geoffrey Mohan, Levitt used "restrictive covenants to ban Jews from his early Manhasset developments. It was strictly business." Levitt himself not only was Jewish but lived in Manhasset![30]

Even some suburbs now famous for their racial tolerance were all-white by policy at first. Oak Park, which abuts the western edge of Chicago, is now nationally renowned as an integrated community, but it was a sundown suburb in 1950, when the Percy Julian family tried to move in. The Julians could hardly have been more deserving candidates: Dr. Julian earned a doctorate in chemistry from the University of Vienna and synthesized cortisone in 1949; his wife was the first African American woman ever to earn a doctorate in sociology. Recognized for his scientific eminence, Percy Julian had been named Chicagoan of the Year in 1949. None of that helped when the Julians tried to become the first African American family to move into Oak Park. James Hecht, who worked for open housing in Buffalo and Richmond, tells what happened:

> When Dr. Percy L. Julian bought an expensive fifteen-room house in Oak Park in 1950, the color of his skin was more important to many people . . . than the fact that he was one of the nation's leading chemists. The water commissioner refused to turn on the water until the Julians threatened to go to court. There were threats by anonymous telephone callers, and an attempt was made to burn the house down. But Dr. Julian—then the chief of soybean research for the Glidden Company . . . a man known throughout the scientific world for his synthesis of hormones and development of processes for their manufacture—hired private guards and moved into the house.

Thus Oak Park, like Tuxedo Park, not only did not try to enforce fair housing but tried to use its control over access to water to stay all-white.[31]

The degree to which African Americans were simply shut out of the suburban explosion is astonishing. Historian Thomas Sugrue tells that in Detroit, "a mere 1,500 of the 186,000 single-family houses constructed in the metropolitan Detroit area in the 1940s were open to blacks. As late as 1951, only 1.15% of the new homes constructed in the metropolitan Detroit area were available to blacks." Just four African American families entered any of the white suburbs of Chicago in 1961–62 combined. By 1970, exclusion was so complete that fewer than 500 black families lived in white suburban neighborhoods in the entire Chicago metropolitan area, and most of those were in just five or six suburbs. Sociologist Troy Duster cites an even more amazing yet representative statistic: "Of 350,000 new homes built in northern California between 1946 and 1960 with FHA [Federal Housing Administration] support, *fewer than 100 went to blacks.* That same pattern holds for the whole state, and for the nation as well." Just as Palos Verdes Estates had been more segregated than the suburbs closer to Los Angeles, in the late 1950s and early 1960s the suburbs beyond Palos Verdes Estates took the phenomenon one step further, turning the entire Palos Verdes peninsula "into a congerie of walled, privatized residential 'cities,' " in the words of Mike Davis. "Rolling Hills did it, and Rancho Palos Verdes, and then Rolling Hills Estate." Orange

County, the next county out, was worse yet. Statewide, after the legislature passed a fair housing law in 1963, Californians repealed it by voting overwhelmingly for Proposition 14, but the California Supreme Court found this unconstitutional in 1966.[32]

The FHA Helped Create Our Sundown Suburbs

The Federal Housing Administration, set up during the Depression to make it easier for Americans to buy homes, was a large part of the problem. In fact, Charles Abrams, an early proponent of integrated housing, saw the FHA as the most important single cause of residential segregation. He wrote in 1955:

> From its inception the FHA set itself up as the protector of the all white neighborhood. It sent its agents into the field to keep Negroes and other minorities from buying houses in white neighborhoods. It exerted pressure against builders who dared to build for minorities, and against lenders willing to lend on mortgages.

In 1938, the FHA held, "If a neighborhood is to retain stability, it is necessary that its properties shall continue to be occupied by the same social and racial classes." The FHA advocated restrictive covenants, "since these provide the surest protection against undesirable encroachment," and its *Manual* contained a model restrictive covenant until 1948. In that year, assistant FHA commissioner W. J. Lockwood boasted, "The FHA has never insured a housing project of mixed occupancy."[33]

The FHA even engaged in such absurdities as requiring the developer of Mayfair Park, a postwar residential subdivision in South Burlington, Vermont, to include its model racially restrictive covenant in each deed before it would guarantee loans in the development. Scarcely a hundred black families lived in the entire state, so the covenants did not stop any mass influx of African Americans into the suburb. They did, however, make salient to white purchasers that their government believed black families were a danger from which whites required protection, even that far north. Portfolio 29 shows a physical legacy of the FHA's policy, still on the ground in Detroit.[34]

FHA publications repeatedly listed "inharmonious racial or nationality groups" alongside such noxious disamenities as "smoke, odors, and fog." Again, this was the familiar "blacks as the problem" ideology, and the FHA's solution was identical to that employed by independent sundown towns: keep "the problem" out. Palen states that loan guarantees by the FHA and Veterans

Administration (VA) were the most important single cause of postwar suburbanization, and more than 98% of the millions of home loans guaranteed by the FHA and VA after World War II were available only to whites. This was the money that funded the Levittowns and most other postwar sundown suburbs. America became a nation of homeowners largely *after* World War II, in the suburbs. Indeed, more Americans bought single-family homes in the decade after the war than in the previous 150 years, according to historian Lizabeth Cohen. African Americans were thus not only shut out of the suburbs but also kept from participating in Americans' surest route to wealth accumulation, federally subsidized home ownership. Federal support for home ownership not only included the FHA and VA programs but also the mortgage interest tax deduction, which made home ownership in the suburbs cheaper than apartment rental in the cities—for whites. Housing prices then skyrocketed, tripling in the 1970s alone; this appreciation laid the groundwork for the astonishing 1-to-11 black-to-white wealth ratio that now afflicts African American families.[35]

When the federal government did spend money on black housing, it funded the opposite of suburbia: huge federally assisted high-rise "projects" concentrated in the inner city. We are familiar with the result, which now seems natural to us, market-driven: African Americans living near the central business district and whites living out in the suburbs. Actually, locating low-income housing on cheaper, already vacant land in the suburbs would have been more natural, more market-driven. One of Chicago's most notorious housing projects, Cabrini Green, lies just a stone's throw west of an expensive and desirable lakefront neighborhood north of the Loop, separated by the elevated railroad tracks. This is costly land. To justify its price, the Chicago Housing Authority had to pile hundreds of units onto the tract, building poorly devised physical structures that bred a festering, unsafe social structure. The steps taken by suburban developers and governments to be all-white were interferences in the housing market that kept African Americans from buying homes and locked them in overwhelmingly black tracts inside the city.

Too Little, Too Late

In 1968, the federal government finally switched sides. Sympathetic reaction to the assassination of Dr. Martin Luther King Jr. gave Congress the political will to pass Title VIII of the Civil Rights Act of 1968. Often called the Fair Housing Act, this law prohibits racial discrimination in the sale, rental, and financing of housing. Also in 1968, the Supreme Court in *Jones v. Mayer* required "all housing, with no exception, open without regard to race, at least as a matter of legal right," in the words of W. A. Low and V. A. Clift. However, enforcement was left up "to litigation by persons discriminated against." The 1968 act also did not make the profound difference that its supporters expected, again owing to problems with enforcement. It was left to the victims, or perhaps the Department of Justice on their behalf, to enforce the law by litigation; the department that was supposed to enforce it, Housing and Urban Development (HUD), had no enforcement powers.[36]

Sociologist Douglas Massey tells the result very simply: "Discrimination went underground." In suburbs across the nation, gentlemen's agreements now came to the fore. It was "understood," there was a "gentleman's agreement," so no one had to say a word. Steering, lying, stalling, special requirements imposed on blacks, missed appointments, wrong addresses—all were used to shut out African American would-be home buyers.[37] Michael Danielson quoted a study of racial exclusion in the San Francisco Bay Area: "Every routine act [in buying a home], every bit of ritual in the sale or rental of a dwelling unit can be performed in a way calculated to make it either difficult or impossible to consummate a deal." For example, according to David Freund, "the courts did not ban the use of race-specific language in appraisal manuals until the late 1970s."[38]

The 1968 act and *Jones v. Mayer* did prompt some residential integration, at least by the 1990s. Unfortunately, open housing came too late, after suburbia was largely built. Across the United States, whites had kept African Americans out of most suburbs throughout most of the twentieth century. By 1968, suburbs were labeled racially. Once in place, these reputations were self-sustaining. Desegregating them was an uphill struggle, a mountain that we are still climbing. Like anyone else, African Americans don't want to live in a place where they aren't wanted, and one way to deduce that they aren't wanted is to note that no African Americans live there. Today, just a little steering by realtors suffices to keep sundown suburbs nearly all-white. Here is an example from Pennsylvania. Whites and blacks refer to the suburbs across the Susquehanna River from Harrisburg as "the white shore." A man who grew up there wrote me:

> I can tell you that there were (are?) sundown towns in Central Pennsylvania. You were right about the "white shore." I have no objective proof at all. However my mother grew up in Enola, and my uncle lived in Camp Hill. It was common knowledge that African-Americans would not be sold a house in those towns and those that surrounded them. It was indeed a "white shore."

By August 2002, when a new black employee moved to Harrisburg to take up her new job with the State of Pennsylvania, the pattern was in place. "The realtor told me I could live on the west shore, but it's really called 'the *white* shore,' so I'd probably be happier somewhere else." She bought in Harrisburg. Such steering is illegal, but it goes on every day.[39]

African Americans still have trouble getting equal treatment at each step of the home-buying process, according to speakers at a 2003 conference in Washington, D.C., subtitled "New Evidence on Housing Discrimination." Speakers presented data to show that in most suburbs of all social classes, realtors, lenders, and other parties to housing sales continue to discriminate covertly against African Americans, although the differences in treatment were not dramatic. In 2003, Shanna Smith, head of the National Fair Housing Alliance, summed up the problem: "The government is not serious about fair housing enforcement. If they were, they would fund it."[40]

As a result, African Americans remain markedly underrepresented in suburbs, and to the degree they do live in suburbia, they are overconcentrated in just a few suburbs. Nationally, in 1950, African Americans occupied 4.6% of all housing units outside central cities but still within metropolitan areas. By 1970, that proportion had actually dropped to 4.2%. Baltimore County, for example, a suburban jurisdiction to the east, north, and west of Baltimore, doubled in population during that interval. Meanwhile, the number of African Americans never budged, so the proportion of African Americans in the Baltimore suburbs fell from 7% to 3%.[41]

Even those small percentages were artificially inflated. Geographer Harold Rose points out that most "suburban" African Americans live in three types of towns:

- Historically black towns and townships[42]
- Independent industrial towns that then became part of a metropolitan area, such as Chester, Pennsylvania, or Pontiac, Michigan
- Older inner suburbs, contiguous to the city itself, that had become majority-black as early as 1970, such as East Orange, New Jersey (Newark); Seat Pleasant, Maryland (Washington); East Cleveland, Ohio (Cleveland); Hamtramck, Michigan (Detroit); University City, Missouri (St. Louis); and Inglewood, California (Los Angeles)

The first two categories have little in common with what most Americans mean by "suburbia" but account for many "black suburbanites."[43]

The concentration of African Americans into a handful of suburbs is striking in many metropolitan areas. "Long Island has the most racially isolated and segregated suburbs in the nation," according to reporter Michael Powell, writing in 2002. About 10% of Long Island's population is African American, but "almost all black residents are bunched into a dozen or so towns, from Roosevelt to Hempstead, Wyandanch, and Uniondale." Meanwhile, two-thirds of Long Island's municipalities remained less than 1% black, and half of those had no black residents at all. In northern New Jersey in 1970, 89% of Essex County's 72,000 African Americans lived in three towns—East Orange, Orange, and Montclair. Meanwhile, only 7 African Americans lived in Roseland and 8 in Fairfield. By 2000, 327,000 African Americans lived in Essex County; East Orange and Orange had gone majority-black; but just 65 African Americans lived in Roseland and Fairfield combined. Similarly, 80% of the African Americans in Oakland County, north of Detroit, lived in just three cities.[44]

Chicago follows the same pattern. In the 1960s, all of the African Americans who moved to the suburbs, 51,000 people, went to just 15 of 237 suburbs, according to Danielson. These 15 suburbs had 83% of Chicago's 128,300 suburban African Americans. Three of these—Harvey, Ford Heights, and Robbins—were overwhelmingly black and ranked among the poorest suburbs in the nation. Meanwhile, all other Chicago suburbs remained overwhelmingly white. By 1980, of Chicago's 285 suburbs, 9 had populations 30 to 50% black, while 117 were less than 1% black. "It is evident that those racial housing patterns didn't develop by accident," wrote Arthur Hayes in *Black Enterprise*. A study of suburban Chicago in 1993 demonstrated what Meyer called "the tenacity of segregation." Only 423 African Americans were among the 183,000 denizens of McHenry County, about 0.2% African Americans made up more than 10% of the population of Will County, but three-fourths of them lived in just three communities. Kane County was 5.8% African American in 2000, but nearly 96% of those black residents lived in just two towns, Aurora and Elgin.[45]

Sundown suburbs are the key reason why geographer Jeff Crump was able to maintain that "cities in the United States are the most racially segregated urban areas in the world." The normal processes of the marketplace would result in a sprinkling of African Americans everywhere, albeit with some areas of greater concentration, like the distribution of, say, Italian Americans.[46]

The next chapter explores the underlying reasons why towns and suburbs went sundown in the first place.

PART III

The Sociology of Sundown Towns

6

Underlying Causes

One of the most striking aspects of racial segregation in 1993 is the national sense that it is inescapable.
　　　—John C. Boger, "Toward Ending Residential Segregation," 1993[1]

THIS CHAPTER SEEKS ANSWERS to important "why" questions, the most basic of which is: Why have African Americans been particularly targeted for exclusion? Other key questions are: Why did thousands of towns and counties across America go sundown? What caused a town to expel its African Americans or resolve never to let any in? Why did another town, a few miles down the road, always allow African Americans to live in it? What predicts which suburbs opened to African Americans when most remained closed?

Why African Americans?

We have seen that sundown towns did not always direct their exclusionary policies against African Americans but sometimes drove out or prohibited Chinese, Japanese, Jewish, Native, or Mexican Americans. For shorter periods, a few towns kept out Greeks, Sicilians, or other European ethnic minorities. Still other towns drove out or excluded Mormons, homosexuals, labor union members, and perhaps Seventh Day Adventists.[2] Nevertheless, African Americans have been excluded much more universally than any other group.[3] Although a few Western counties did exclude Chinese Americans, none did so after 1970. I know of no county that ever prohibited any other group countywide. Indeed, after about 1970, few sundown towns or suburbs kept out any minority other than African Americans.

Why?

The answer to this last question *seems* to be that African Americans differ more from whites physically: in color, features, and general appearance. On reflection, however, this is not so obvious. Neither skin color in itself, nor aesthetics, nor physical characteristics explain racism. History does. Events and processes in American history from the time of slavery to the present explain why we think it "natural" to differentiate based on skin color. In his important book *Minority Education and Caste,* anthropologist John Ogbu observed that historically, European Americans systematically subjugated three groups: Native Americans, Mexican Americans, and African Americans, taking the land of the first two and the labor of the third. As part of the process of justifying American history, European Americans have therefore systematically stigmatized these groups as inferior. That's why Ogbu called Native Americans, Mexican Americans, and African Americans our "caste minorities," which he differentiated from other "voluntary minorities." [4]

Among these three caste minorities, whites encountered African Americans *primarily* as slaves for almost 250 years—from 1619 through at least 1863. To be sure, whites enslaved some Native Americans, but the most common encounters between European Americans and Native Americans were not master-to-slave. Even less was this true between Anglos and Mexicans. White racism therefore became first and foremost a rationale for African slavery. That is why America's *"real* non-whites," if you will, have for centuries been its African Americans. Ultimately, then, even after it ended, slavery was responsible for the continuing stigmatizing of African Americans, expressed in their exclusion from sundown towns, among other ways. Even today, whites feel most strongly about differentiating themselves from African Americans, not Jewish, Mexican,[5] Native, or Asian Americans.

The Nadir Made Sundown Towns Possible

Answering the other questions—why did so many towns go sundown? what caused one town to do so but not another?—is not so easy. It is always hard to assign causes for large-scale historical movements, and all the more so when the movement entails attitudes and actions that are embarrassing or repugnant in retrospect. I suggest two kinds of underlying factors were at work. First, the spirit of the times—the zeitgeist—changed. I am referring to the deepening racism known as the Nadir of race relations, of course, between 1890 and 1940. This change in our national culture affected towns all across America. But it did not affect them equally. The second type of underlying social and cultural causes predisposed some towns—but not others—to go sundown. These factors included a Democratic voting majority, mono-ethnic makeup, and strong labor movement. Such characteristics did not determine that a town would go sundown, but as the Nadir deepened, African Americans in these towns lived on the knife edge. The actions of a few individuals on one side or the other often swayed the outcome. Even chance played a role.

Chapter 2 analyzed how and why racism intensified after 1890 across the United States. Lynchings rose to their all-time high, the Ku Klux Klan was reborn as a national institution, and whites drove blacks from occupation after occupation. Causal factors underlying the Nadir included the three *i*'s— Indian wars, increasing opposition to immigrants, and imperialism—as well as the rise of Social Darwinism to justify the opulence of the Gilded Age. Of course, the racism that had arisen earlier in our culture as a rationale for slavery was always a key underlying ingredient.

If not for this intensification of white supremacy between 1890 and 1940, towns and suburbs across the North would never have been allowed to expel and exclude African Americans and others. The most obvious way that the Nadir of race relations gave birth to sundown towns was in the changed response of governments when whites drove out African Americans. Two incidents in Anna, in southern Illinois, one before the Nadir and one during it, highlight its impact. This book began with a mention of the 1909 lynching that led to the expulsion of African Americans from Anna; Chapter 7 tells that story in detail. But 1909 was not the first expulsion of African Americans from Anna-Jonesboro, which had long been anti-black. In 1862, citizens of Union County had supported a new state constitutional provision, "No Negro or Mulatto shall migrate or settle in this state," by a vote of 1,583 to 98. Complaining because ex-slaves passed through the county going north on the Illinois Central Rail Road, the Anna newspaper editor wrote, "We have laws prohibiting their settlement here." During the Civil War, Cairo was a place of refuge for African Americans from the Lower Mississippi Valley. United States Army officers struggled to cope with the flood of refugees. In 1863, residents in and around Cobden, six miles north of Anna, agreed to take some of these men and women as workers in their apple orchards. Benjamin Fenton brought in about 40 African American refugees to work on his farm. Whites from the Anna-Jonesboro area charged the orchard owners with "unlawfully and willfully bringing [slaves] into the State of Illinois . . . in order to free them," a violation of the old statewide racial exclusion law passed before the Civil War. Then a mob of about 25 men led by an Anna doctor visited Fenton and forced him to return his workers to Cairo.[6]

After the Anna mob drove the African American farmworkers from Union County in 1863, the army commander at Cairo who had let them go there in the first place was outraged. He wrote that he would have sent armed troops to protect them if the farmer who employed them had requested it. The military later arrested the mob leaders and imprisoned them for most of the rest of the war.

But when Anna whites again drove out their black population in 1909, no one was ever arrested. The federal government did nothing; neither did the state. Indeed, the times had shifted so much that there was no thought that either government *might* intervene. Although the increasing racism of the Nadir was a necessary characteristic underlying the outbreak of sundown towns, it cannot explain why one town went sundown while another did not. In Union County, for instance, the Nadir cannot explain why Anna drove out its African Americans in 1909 and has kept them out ever since, while Cobden, five miles north, has African American households to this day.[7]

Tautological "Causes"

Most residents of sundown towns and counties are of little help when asked why their town has been all-white for so long. They don't know about the Nadir, and few ever think about the underlying causes of their town's racial policy. Instead, local historians often offer tautological or nonsensical "explanations" for their town's absence of African Americans. Typically these alleged factors have nothing to do with race. Before planting the seedlings of the real causes, I need to clear out the underbrush of erroneous reasons that many people give to explain all-white communities.

The spokesman for a historical society in a Pennsylvania county "explained" its all-white demography with this sentence: "Most or all of our towns were white because the area attracted few blacks." The argument is airtight, of course, but circular. "There's never been much need for them" is another favorite—but how an area's "need" for new settlers comes with a racial label goes unexplained. "There wasn't work for what skills they had," said a local history expert from another Pennsylvania county whose white population between 1900 and 1940 was mostly farmers and miners. But mining and farming were precisely the occupations engaged in by most African American men.

The flip side of the "lack of jobs" theory is the notion that African Americans went to big cities because that's where the jobs were. "There were more jobs in Milwaukee," said several Wisconsin residents, trying to explain the increasing whiteness of midsized Wisconsin towns during the first half of the twentieth century. But "jobs in the cities" likewise fails as a cause of sundown towns. Of course, Milwaukee *does* have more jobs than any other Wisconsin city, but there were jobs aplenty in smaller Wisconsin cities such as Appleton, Fond du Lac, and Oshkosh, in the four counties surrounding Lake Winnebago. Indeed, those counties were urbanizing between 1890 and 1930. Precisely as their black population declined by 78%, their white population increased by 45%, from 149,514 to 216,143. Similarly, from 1900 to 1970, Granite City, Illinois, zoomed in population from 3,122 to 40,440, owing to skyrocketing employment, while its black population fell from 154 to 6. Obviously these growing cities had an abundance of new jobs—for whites.

As well, it is important to understand that most jobs in big cities were flatly closed to African Americans throughout the Nadir. Breweries in Milwaukee started to hire African Americans only in 1950, the city did not employ a single black teacher until 1951, and its first major department store to hire an African American as a full-time sales clerk did not do so until 1952. In northern cities, most jobs in construction were reserved for whites until the 1970s. So big-city jobs weren't much of a draw, except in a few cities such as Detroit and Pittsburgh, where a sizable fraction of industrial jobs were open to African Americans.[8]

The claim that lack of jobs caused towns to go all-white is rendered preposterous by those sundown towns where African Americans have been allowed to work but not to live. African Americans helped build Hoover Dam but had to commute from Las Vegas to do it, while white workers and their families lived in Boulder City, a sundown town built just for them. African Americans helped build Kentucky Dam, but after they finished, their housing—"Negro Village"—was razed, they were booted out, and Marshall County, Kentucky, resumed being a sundown county. Today African Americans commute from Hayti Heights, Missouri, to work in Paragould, Arkansas; from Peoria, Illinois, to Pekin; and from Mattoon, Illinois, to Effingham. African Americans care for patients at the Illinois State [Mental] Hospital in Anna but live in Cairo and Cobden. Sundown towns such as Cullman, Alabama, and Herrin, Illinois, have long been serviced during the day by domestics from nearby African American "townships." Ford Motor Company located its largest single plant in Dearborn, Michigan, a sundown suburb; thousands of African American car builders commuted to it every day from Detroit. In 1956, *U.S. News and World Report* estimated that "at least 15,000 Negroes" worked in Dearborn but were "barred, completely and semiofficially," from living there. More thousands commuted to a huge General Motors plant in neighboring Warren but had to return home to Detroit when night fell. In 1972, 4,353 African Americans worked in Livonia, another sundown suburb of Detroit, but could not live there. "Lack of jobs" can hardly explain the absence of African Americans from any independent town such as Paragould or multiclass suburb such as Dearborn in which they work but do not live, because these towns house *white* workers who do the same jobs.[9]

Even more blatant have been those sundown towns that allowed African American laborers to sojourn in temporary housing on construction sites for the summer construction season but would not let them stay once the season was over. In fact, using lack of jobs to explain black absence often gets the causation directly backward. In 1943, the chairman of Illinois's Inter-Racial Commission noted, "Many plants in towns where Negroes are not permitted to reside, give that as an excuse for not hiring Negroes."[10]

Some theories emphasize social isolation: why *should* African Americans move into out-of-the-way hamlets distant from centers of African American population? In short, the lack of blacks was just "natural," or resulted from historical coincidence. I began my research with this hypothesis—that most all-white towns never *happened* to draw any black residents—but it didn't hold up. Another near-tautology lurks: African Americans didn't move in because few African Americans lived there to attract them. Before 1890, however, African Americans moved to counties and towns throughout America, as Table 1 showed (page 56)—even to isolated places such as northern Maine, northern Wisconsin, and Idaho north of the Snake River Valley. Then during the Great Retreat, they withdrew to the larger cities and a mere handful of small towns. Distance from the South, from African American population centers, or from major trade routes cannot explain this pattern, because towns in Maine, Wisconsin, Idaho, and elsewhere were at least as isolated socially between 1865 and 1890, when African Americans were moving into them, as they were between 1890 and 1930, when African Americans were fleeing them.[11] In other words, because social isolation cannot explain the *increases* in black population in northern counties before 1890, it cannot explain why those increases reversed after that date. Something different went on after 1890.

Sundown Suburbs Are Not "Natural" and Not Due to Class

Social isolation has even been used to explain overwhelmingly white suburbs: whites have imagined that African Americans prefer the excitement of the big city to such suburban values as home ownership, peace and quiet, tree-lined streets, and good school systems. This notion is absurd, as historian Andrew

Wiese showed in 2004. Wiese summarized survey research as far back as the 1940s, finding no support for this stereotype. Among a sample of six hundred middle-income black families in New York City in 1948, for example, nine out of ten wanted to buy their own homes, and three in four wanted to move to suburbia. Many African American families have the same fervent desire for a patch of ground that white suburbanites manifest.[12]

Other whites seem to think it's somehow "natural" for blacks to live in the inner city, whites in the outer suburbs. This idea is a component of what law professor John Boger calls "the national sense that [residential segregation] is inescapable." Most African Americans arrived by train, goes this line of thought, and they're just taking a long time to move out from the vicinity of the train station; as soon as they make enough money, they too will move to the suburbs. But the whiteness of our suburbs is not "natural."[13]

Over and over, white academics as well as residents of sundown suburbs suggest that social class explained sundown suburbs, if not independent sundown towns. "*I* couldn't live in Grosse Pointe either," one professor put it in 2002, referring to one of Detroit's richest suburbs, also one of its whitest. For all-white suburbs to result from classism is seen as defensible, because classism is OK, since we all presumably have a reasonable if not equal chance to get into the upper class. This ideology is a form of Social Darwinism: the best people wind up on top, and whites are smarter, better students, work harder at their jobs, etc. People who think like this don't see Grosse Pointe's whiteness as a white problem but as a black problem. "They" haven't worked hard enough, etc., so they haven't accumulated enough wealth—and perhaps enough social connections and knowledge—to crack these suburbs.

This line of thought seems plausible. Segregation by class *is* an important component of suburbanization, and increasingly so. Residents of elite suburbs such as Grosse Pointe segregate on the basis of both race and class, and for the same reason: being distant from African Americans and from lower-class people conveys status.[14] Nevertheless, the reasoning does not hold up, for two reasons. First, it ignores history. People who think like this have no idea that as recently as the 1960s and 1970s, when today's mature adults were starting their careers, whites in much of the country flatly banned African Americans as a group from many occupations—not just professions but also jobs like construction work, department store clerk, flight attendant, and railroad engineer.

Second, sundown suburbs simply do not result from class. Research by Michael Danielson points to a key flaw in the argument: the proportion of a metropolitan area's blacks in a suburb, *controlling for income,* is less than half the proportion of whites in that suburb, except for the handful of interracial suburbs. That is, if we tried to guess the number of African Americans in a suburb just using income, we would always predict more than twice as many black people as actually lived there. Something has been keeping them out in addition to their class status. Conversely, a much higher proportion of poor white families live in suburbs, compared to poor black families. If income were the crucial factor, then there would be little difference by race in the distribution of the poor.[15]

Continuing with our Grosse Pointe example, in the Detroit metropolitan area, class has mattered even less, race even more, than elsewhere in the nation, according to research by Karl Taeuber. "More than half of the white families in each income level, from very poor to very rich, lived in the suburbs," he found. "Among blacks, only one-tenth of the families at each income level (including very rich) lived in the suburbs." In short, *social class, at least as measured by income, made little difference in the level of suburbanization.* Rich whites have been much more suburban than rich blacks; poor whites have been much more suburban than poor blacks.[16]

Sundown suburbs with an industrial base—such as Dearborn, Warren, and Livonia, around Detroit—have long employed African Americans, at least as janitors, but they could not spend the night. Some of these suburbs—like Livonia and Warren—are working-class. Other sundown suburbs, like independent sundown towns, are multiclass: houses in Dearborn, in 1997, ranged from starter homes around $45,000 to executive homes for $800,000 and up. Social class simply cannot explain the absence of African Americans from multiclass or working-class communities. Nor can it explain the absence of Jews from such elite suburbs as Kenilworth and Flossmoor, Illinois, and Darien, Connecticut.[17]

Sociologist Reynolds Farley and his associates used our old friend D, the Index of Dissimilarity, to compare the power of race to that of class. Specifically regarding Detroit, they observed, "If household income alone determined where people lived, the Index of Dissimilarity would be 15 [almost completely integrated] instead of 88 [almost completely segregated]." Instead,

> Economic criteria account for little of the observed concentration of blacks in central cities and their relative absence from the suburbs. The current level of residential segregation must be attributed largely to action and attitudes, past and present, which have restricted the entry of blacks into predominately white neighborhoods.[18]

Indeed, blaming the whiteness of elite sundown suburbs on their wealth actually reverses the causality of caste and class. It is mostly the other way around: racial and religious exclusion came first, not class. Suburbs that kept out blacks and Jews became more prestigious, so they attracted the very rich. The absence of African Americans itself became a selling point, which in turn helped these suburbs become so affluent because houses there commanded higher prices. To this day, all-white suburbs attract the very rich. Twelve of the communities on *Worth* magazine's list of 50 richest towns were all-white in 2000 or had just one or two African American families. Typically they were all-white first and became rich only when affluent families moved in. After 1959, for example, when Jews were let into La Jolla, California, a number of WASP families fled from La Jolla to Rancho Santa Fe, fifteen miles north and inland from the beach. Now Rancho Santa Fe is #16 on *Worth*'s list, well above La Jolla at #85,[19] based on median home price.[20]

In yet another way, blaming blacks for being poor, as a cause of segregation, reverses cause and effect. As Chapter 12 shows, residential segregation itself constrains and diminishes the cultural capital and social connections of African Americans, thus artificially decreasing their income and wealth. It won't do to then use blacks' lower income and wealth to explain residential segregation.

Other Nonsensical "Causes"

Related to the isolation hypothesis is climate. A historical society leader in western Maryland explained why Garrett County had only a handful of African Americans when all other Maryland counties had at least a thousand: "It's too cold here." Whites "know" that African Americans don't like cold weather, which "explains" why they didn't move to a given northern town or county. Persons making this claim have obviously never been to Detroit, where African Americans outnumber European Americans three to one, yet winter punishes anyone not prepared for its rigors. Garrett County is hardly colder than Detroit—hardly colder in 2002, for that matter, when I had the conversation, than it had been in 1890, when it had 185 African Americans. The fact that the very next county to the east had more than 1,000 African Americans, while Garrett County had at most one black household, is a dead giveaway. Such abrupt disparities can only result from different racial policies, not from factors such as climate.[21]

Counties in Maine or Wisconsin were also no warmer in 1865–90, when African Americans were moving into them, than in 1890–1940, when they were moving out. Moreover, African Americans returned to most Wisconsin all-white towns between 1970 and 1990. Manitowoc, a sundown town that had just 2 African Americans in 1970, had 71 by 1990, and Oshkosh had a whopping 435 (approaching 1% of its total population). The migration of African Americans to towns throughout Wisconsin after 1970, like their earlier arrival before 1890, underscores that something other than isolation or climate was required to force their departure between 1890 and 1940. Global warming to the contrary, Wisconsin winters did not turn noticeably warmer after 1970, when blacks were again moving into formerly all-white counties and towns across the state.

Also related to isolation is the claim that independent sundown towns are miserable backwaters. "Who would *want* to live there?" a white professor at Texas A & M University in Commerce suggested in 1999, referring to Cumby, a small nearby sundown town. "What a dump!" A white woman from Buffalo said, "There's nothing there!" referring to nearby Tonawanda and North Tonawanda. To be sure, some sundown towns *are* small, isolated, and backward—hardly the stars to which rational Americans of any race would hitch their wagons. Cumby, for example, *is* a dump. Moreover, during the twentieth century Americans of all races did migrate to cities, which they believed offered cultural as well as educational and economic opportunities lacking in small towns. Nevertheless, even to explain why towns as small, isolated, and backward as Cumby have *no* African Americans, "small, isolated, and backward" won't do, because humans are unpredictable. People are always moving into and out of small towns in America, even into dying towns, for all kinds of reasons. So would African Americans if given a chance. Indeed, so *did* African Americans between 1865 and 1890 and, in those places whose exclusionary policies have cracked, between 1980 or 1990 and 2005. The "backwater" explanation is rarely offered by residents of a town itself, because it puts down their town and because they know that it isn't so bad that a family has to be irrational to move into it.[22]

Amazingly, I have heard this explanation given for whole regions—the Ozarks, straddling the Missouri-Arkansas line for nearly 300 miles; the Cumberland Plateau in eastern Tennessee and Kentucky; the Texas and Oklahoma panhandles; large swaths of southern Illinois and southern Indiana; the Upper Peninsula of Michigan; and parts of Appalachia. "Who would want to live there, anyway?" But implying that African Americans have been making rational unconstrained choices to avoid such towns won't do, because they haven't been.[23] Their choices have been constrained. Indeed, many of the people who supply these explanations do know that the place under discussion has kept out African Americans by policy. They put down the town or even the region not really to explain its whiteness but merely to make it seem a problem not worth fixing.

Moreover, backwater isolation certainly wasn't judged adequate by whites who lived in such isolated little towns as Cumby, or De Land or Villa Grove, Illinois. They never relied on their towns' smallness, backwardness, or remoteness from black population centers to "protect" themselves from African Americans, instead taking care to pass ordinances, blow whistles, or engage in other acts, formal or informal, to keep them out. Furthermore, many all-white towns are not isolated. Some are on important transportation routes, including Effingham, Illinois, or Tonawanda, New York. Some are themselves important manufacturing or educational centers, such as Appleton, Wisconsin; Niles, Ohio; or Norman, Oklahoma. Isolation and happenstance make even less sense as explanations for sundown suburbs, because some of America's whitest suburbs grew up right next to some of our blackest cities.

All of these tautological and nonsensical "causes"—lack of skills, lack of jobs, social isolation, "natural," social class, climate, avoidance of backwaters— share two characteristics. First, they minimize the problem. Second, they let white society off the hook for it, relying instead on individual choices by African Americans. In recent years, some social scientists, such as Abigail and Stephan Thernstrom, have increasingly relied upon individual decisions by African American families to explain America's intractable residential segregation. Blacks don't want to live in an ocean of white faces, goes the reasoning. If we stop to think, however, sundown towns and suburbs cannot possibly result from decisions by people of color who happily choose to live in black neighborhoods. For there would always be at least *a few* African Americans who would choose to live in majority-white neighborhoods, for some of the same reasons whites do: better schooling, nicer parks, investment value, and social status, in the case of elite suburbs. Others would move for convenience—some African Americans who care for patients in the mental hospital in Anna, Illinois, for example, might choose to live there. Still others would wind up in formerly white towns owing simply to the vagaries of fortune. Voluntary choice simply *cannot* explain what kept sundown towns and suburbs *so* white for so many decades. Some underlying historical and sociological causes do. We will explore three: political ideology, white ethnic solidarity, and labor strife.[24]

Political Ideology as a Cause of Sundown Towns

From its inception, the Democratic Party was "the White Man's Party." Today it is hard for Americans to understand how racist the Democrats became during the Nadir, especially since the two parties flipflopped on this issue beginning in 1964. Historian Nicole Etcheson writes that midwestern Democrats supported what Chief Justice Taney said about black rights in *Dred Scott*: "that they had no rights which the white man was bound to respect." Some Republicans believed African Americans should have all the rights of citizenship, while others, including Abraham Lincoln, were "not, nor ever have been in favor of making voters or jurors of Negroes," as Lincoln put it in Charleston, Illinois, in 1858. As the Civil War progressed, Republican thinking about African Americans moved toward full equality. Democrats underwent no such ideological advance.[25]

In the Midwest I found a striking correlation between counties or towns voting Democratic in the 1850s and driving out their African Americans half a century later. Almost every town on the Illinois River, for example, which stretches diagonally across Illinois from the Mississippi near St. Louis northeast toward Chicago, voted for the Democratic candidate for president in 1868, except for Peoria. The same voting pattern held from at least 1856 to 1892. Between 1890 and 1930, almost every town along the river went sundown, except for Peoria. Why? The Illinois River valley was settled mostly by Democrats from Kentucky and Tennessee. Many of them were exceptionally racist to begin with, having left Kentucky and Tennessee to avoid both slavery and black people. Being a Democrat played a still greater role, owing to the continuing racism expressed by candidates of the Democratic Party.

We can see this same pattern of white supremacy in county histories. In every county along the Illinois River from the Mississippi River to LaSalle-Peru except one, local histories tell of substantial pro-Confederate sentiment during the Civil War. Moreover, treatments of the Civil War in these county histories, whether written in the late nineteenth century or as late as the 1980s, display a white perspective: they rarely mention slavery and say nothing about African Americans. Peoria, the largest city on the Illinois River, is the exception. The rhetoric in its late-nineteenth-century histories is profoundly different, even abolitionist. An 1880 Peoria history tells how midwestern farmers ignored slavery in the 1850s: "Immediately surrounded with peace and tranquility, they paid but little attention to the rumored plots and plans of those who lived and grew rich from the sweat and toil, and blood and flesh of others—aye, even trafficked in the offspring of their own loins." Histories in Democratic counties would never use such language.[26]

Public history as displayed on the landscape shows the same pattern. Peoria dedicated a large Civil War monument shortly after the war ended. Thirty thousand people attended, and the 1880 account of the monument tells how it "would commemorate for all time the names of . . . the men who gave their lives in defense of the Union and of human rights." In Democratic counties, "defense of the Union" would rarely be conjoined with "human rights." Peorians put up another Civil War monument a few years later in Springdale Cemetery, proclaiming "Liberty / Justice / Equality / Pro Patria." Equality would never secure a place on the landscape in a Democratic county.

So it should come as no surprise that during the Nadir, every town on the river *except Peoria,*[27] from the hamlets of Calhoun County all the way up to LaSalle-Peru, drove out or kept out African Americans.

Towns in other parts of Illinois show the same relationship. When Anna-Jonesboro expelled its black population in 1909, political background played a key role. Anna and Jonesboro were overwhelmingly Democratic, while Cobden was partly Republican. During the Civil War, Union County Democrats meeting in Jonesboro adopted a resolution protesting "the introduction of the Negro into our midst" and citing "with apprehension the dangers of robber and violence" to be expected from such an addition to the community. So the 1909 expulsion of African Americans from Anna-Jonesboro was neither novel nor surprising. Nor was Cobden's relative tolerance.

In central Illinois, Mattoon was Republican, in contrast to the next town to the northwest, Sullivan, seat of Moultrie County, highly Democratic. That political difference in 1860 translated to a high level of anti-black sentiment many decades later. Moultrie County had "a few families of the colored race" in 1880, according to an 1881 history, but only one African American was left by 1920. In the 1920s, the KKK burned crosses in Sullivan. Later, according to one oral history report, Sullivan wound up with a sign that read "Nigger, Don't Let The Sun Set On Your Ass." Mattoon, while no race relations haven, has had a stable African American community for many decades.[28]

This pattern—Republican areas in the 1850s remaining interracial in the Nadir, Democratic areas going all white—was not just true for Illinois. It held throughout the North, including California and Oregon.

To be sure, since Democrats called themselves "the White Man's Party," it is somewhat tautological to cite Democratic voting majorities as a cause of white supremacy, rather than as simply another manifestation of it. But not wholly. Americans were Democrats for many reasons, not just the party's racism, just as today Americans are Republicans for many reasons, not just the party's racism. Once an individual became a Democrat, however, perhaps owing to such nonracist reasons as attractive local leaders, one's ethnic group membership, or the Republicans' increasing support for Prohibition, it was hard not to become more racist. After all, the party's songs, speeches, and platform positions usually included attacks on African Americans, along with charges that Republicans favored black rights up to and including "miscegenation," a word coined by Democratic politicos in 1863.

A Different Pattern in the Upland South: Many Unionist Areas Later Expelled African Americans

Political ideology played quite a different role in the South. Politically, the traditional South had been split between Democrats and Whigs in 1850, but with the disintegration of the Whig Party, it became more Democratic, and overwhelmingly so as the South seceded. But Democrats in the traditional South, where slavery had been strong, did not try to drive African Americans out. Instead, they made money off their labor.[29]

The South also had areas, large and small—especially in the hills and mountains, where slaves were few—that tried to stay with the Union.[30] After the war, many of these Unionist areas voted Republican. Until the 1890s, they maintained fairly good relations with their small African American populations, partly because African Americans and white Republicans were political allies. In states where the Republican Party collapsed after the end of Reconstruction, some of these whites then supported third-party movements such as the Readjusters in Virginia, the Union Labor Party in Arkansas, and the Populist Party across all the southern and border states, again usually allied with black voters. After 1890 however, the nationwide tide of increasing white supremacy lapped at the valleys and mountains of the upland South. Like African Americans in Democratic towns in the Midwest and West, African Americans in these formerly Unionist or Republican areas now lived on a knife edge. Their town or county might go either way. Many went sundown.

What happened to cause this shift? Between 1890 and 1910, it became increasingly clear that interracial political coalitions would no longer be viable in the South. Since neither the federal executive nor the Supreme Court did anything to interfere with the "Mississippi Plan" for disfranchising African Americans "legally," other states passed new constitutions emulating Mississippi's between 1890 and 1907. Now white Republicans, Readjusters, Populists, or other anti-Democratic factions had no black counterparts with whom to ally. Democrats also used violence to demonstrate that they would no longer permit blacks or Republicans to hold political office; the coup d'état in Wilmington, North Carolina, in 1898 provided final proof. Now no politics was possible in the South outside the Democratic Party. The "solid South" would not really break until after the 1965 Voting Rights Act undid the disfranchisement of the Nadir period.

What were whites in the nontraditional South to do? In the newly solid South it would not pay to be anything but a Democrat. Allied with this Democratic resurgence, a wave of Confederate nationalism swept the southern and border states beginning shortly before 1890. No longer were Confederate leaders such as Jefferson Davis viewed with ambivalence, having led the South to defeat. Now they were seen as heroes. Now, indeed, the Confederate South had won—if not on the issue of secession, then on the matter of white supremacy. Now Confederate memorials went up across the South, even in counties in the nontraditional South that had not supported secession in 1860. In western Virginia and North Carolina, east Tennessee, northern Georgia and Alabama, north Texas, and much of Arkansas and Missouri, many formerly pro-Unionist whites changed their ideology to join this wave, now the winning side, often becoming hyper-Confederate and anti-black in the process.

At the same time, a new type of Democratic politician arose who professed to be pro-worker and pro-farmer, seemed not to be a tool of the aristocracy, and was rabidly anti-black. Jeff Davis in Arkansas (no relation to Jefferson Davis) was one example, as was James K. Vardaman in Mississippi and Benjamin "Pitchfork Ben" Tillman in South Carolina. Now African Americans were stigmatized, apparently for good, and so were whites identified with them. Now more than ever it was in whites' interest to distance themselves from blacks. So we find that precisely in counties where residents had questioned slavery before the Civil War and had been Unionists during the conflict, whites now often seemed impelled to prove themselves ultra-Confederate and manifested the most robust anti-black fervor.

Map 3 (page 73) shows places in the nontraditional South that went sundown as a result. Scott County, Tennessee, for example, had been overwhelmingly Unionist, sending 541 men to the United States army and just 19 to the Confederate army. According to county historian Esther Sanderson, "It was their strong nationalism, and not their love of the Negro that led them to fight desperately for the Union. They despised the [slave] system that had relegated them to the status of 'poor mountain whites.' " I believe Sanderson is right: most Appalachian whites were anti-slavery, not pro-black. But Sanderson then goes on to suggest, "An aversion to the Negroes was an aftermath of the war, for many Union men considered slavery the main cause of the war." Here I part company with her, because postwar population statistics in Scott County showed no evidence of "an aversion to the Negroes": 157 African Americans called Scott County home in 1880, and 366 in 1890. Moreover, Scott County voted overwhelmingly (95%) for U.S. Grant for president in 1868, who explicitly favored full rights for African Americans. Scott County did not drive out its African Americans until around 1910, well into the Nadir. By that time, interracial politics were over in Tennessee, at least on the statewide level.[31]

What happened in northwest Alabama is still more graphic. During the Civil War, Winston County famously seceded from the Confederacy and declared itself the "Free State of Winston," whereupon the Confederacy occupied the county by force. Many soldiers from the area deserted from the Confederate Army; some even took the next step and enlisted in the Union Army. After the war, many whites joined the Union League, an organization formed to support the Republican Party and black rights, because former Confederate leaders were still persecuting them. During the Nadir, however, Winston County found it expedient to lose the memory of its anti-slavery past, and while it didn't quite forget that many residents had supported the United States, its contemporary allegiance switched from blue to gray. Steve Suitts grew up in Winston County in the 1950s. On a class visit to Shiloh Battlefield in Tennessee, he bought a blue Civil War cap; his classmates all bought gray, called him a "damned Yankee," and meant it. As part of this switch, most of the county got rid of its African Americans in the 1890s. As late as 2002, except for Haleyville on its western edge, it was not clear that a black family could live peacefully in Winston County.[32]

Many other towns and counties in the nontraditional South that had been Unionist in the 1860s turned Confederate and went sundown at some point after 1890. Myakka City, Florida, for example, inland from Sarasota, had many Union sympathizers during the Civil War, some of whom joined the United States Army, according to local historian Melissa Sue Brewer. After 1890, neo-Confederates seized control and substituted a wholly Confederate past, and in the 1930s, Myakka City banished its African Americans. Although many counties in the Arkansas Ozarks opposed secession and harbored Unionists during the Civil War, every local history I read from Ozark counties, all written around 1890 or thereafter, tells of the war exclusively from the Confederate point of view. Most of these counties expelled their African Americans in the first two decades of the twentieth century. Although not in the Ozarks, Grant County in central Arkansas also had many Unionists during the Civil War; during Reconstruction it was named for one Union general, while Sheridan, its county seat, was named for another. Nevertheless, the Grant County Museum in Sheridan in 2002 had four different Confederate flags for sale and no U.S. flag. Sheridan got rid of its African Americans in 1954. Many counties in north Texas similarly opposed the Confederacy during the Civil War but lost that heritage and drove out their African Americans in the twentieth century.[33]

Hermann, Missouri, on the Missouri River 70 miles west of St. Louis, showed perhaps the most striking transformation in racial ideology of any town in America. Mark Lause, who grew up nearby, notes that Hermann "started as a radical German colony and was an antislavery center in the heart of a slave state." It became the most important Republican stronghold in the state outside of St. Louis. In 1860, Gasconade County, of which Hermann is the seat, cast 52% of its votes for Lincoln, 23% for northern Democrat Stephen A. Douglas, 19% for John Bell, the Constitutional Union candidate, and just 6% for John Breckenridge, the southern pro-slavery candidate, an astonishing proportion for Lincoln in a slave state. After the Civil War, "blacks in the general area used Hermann as the site for celebration of Emancipation Day for a number of years," according to Art Draper of the Gasconade County Historical Society. But, Draper wrote, early in the twentieth century "the German School constituents voted not to integrate the schools," by a margin of just one vote. After that, Hermann's anti-racist idealism collapsed, and the county slid into exclusion. In Draper's words, "The dominant conventional wisdom is that Hermann was a sundown town: 'didn't allow them to stay over night; could come and shop, OK, but don't stay.' " Lause calls this slide "unforgivably pathetic." Gasconade County teaches an important lesson about the power of the anti-black ideology of the Nadir period: if racism could grow to dominate Hermann, with its strong anti-slavery beginnings, it could dominate almost anywhere.[34]

Not every Unionist area in the southern and border states drove out its African Americans. Jones County, Mississippi, had been a center of Unionist activity; as with Winston, Confederates had to occupy it during the war. Jones County did not exclude African Americans. Neither did most counties in West Virginia. We shall see in the next chapter that such intangibles as historical contingency and local leadership made a difference. But even in these areas whites became far more racist during the Nadir than they had been during the Civil War and Reconstruction.

White Ethnic Solidarity

White ethnic group membership also helps to predict which towns would expel their African Americans. Of course, ethnic group membership often went hand in hand with politics, because the Democratic Party appealed more to most white immigrants. But ethnic group membership also made an independent difference, in three ways.

First, ethnic solidarity often led to sundown towns. When ethnic groups came to this country, first-generation immigrants from a country often lived together and worked together. They spoke the same language, shared the same culture, and planned to marry within the group. Often they came from one village in Italy to a village in, say, Vermont, where they quarried granite together, or from one county in Wales to a particular town in Wisconsin. They also banded together for protection from more-established Americans, who often put them down and tried to take advantage of them. Whole towns became overwhelmingly Czech, or German Mennonite, or Italian, sometimes because the town's primary employer—perhaps a coal mine or factory—had recruited its entire labor force from one place in Europe. It was only a short step from this kind of in-group to a town that looked upon any newcomer of a different heritage as an outsider. Such towns were more likely to keep out or drive out African Americans, since they already formed a tight monoethnic in-group. To explain the startling paucity of African Americans in Cedar Falls, Iowa, for example, compared to neighboring Waterloo, historian Robert Neymeyer suggested that Cedar Falls was overwhelmingly Danish, while nearby Waterloo "had a variety of ethnic groups (Germans, Danes, Norwegians, Irish, Italians) with no single dominant force. It was easier for them to accept Croatians, Greeks, Bulgarians, Polish and Russian Jews, and ultimately blacks." My impressionistic comparison of mono- versus multiethnic communities in Texas, Illinois, and elsewhere persuades me that Neymeyer is right: towns with more than one ethnic group were less likely to exclude African Americans than were mono-ethnic towns. Another predictor related to ethnic composition was the sheer size of the black community: African Americans did find some security in numbers.[35]

Second, some white ethnic groups wound up much more anti-black than others. Among mono-ethnic towns, WASP towns—especially elite suburbs—

seem most likely to exclude, particularly after their residual Republican anti-racism wore off in the 1890s. German socialist towns such as Hermann, Missouri, and perhaps Scandinavian and Finnish socialist areas such as Michigan's Upper Peninsula, may also have excluded after their ideological anti-racism wore off. German Lutheran and Catholic towns, Irish towns, Polish towns, and Dutch and German Reformed towns also seem to have gone sundown frequently.

Jews, Italians, and Mexicans were more open, in suburbs and also in neighborhoods within cities. After studying northern cities in the 1920s, T.J. Woofter wrote, "Almost without exception the groups which are most heavily mixed with Negroes in the North are Jewish and Italian. . . . Those least mixed are the Irish and native white people." Even after World War II, according to a long-term black resident of Lancaster, Pennsylvania, police cars served informally as taxis "to take us away from Cabbage Hill, the German neighborhood, when the sun went down," back to the Jewish-Italian-Greek-African American neighborhood that was home.[36]

Across the nation, when African Americans did move to previously white suburbs, often it was to majority Jewish neighborhoods. Unlike WASPs, Jewish Americans lacked the social power to keep blacks out, as Hillel Levine and Lawrence Harmon showed in the Boston area. So when brokers agreed to sell and bankers agreed to make loans to African Americans seeking homes in Jewish neighborhoods, Jews couldn't stop them. Many metropolitan associations of realtors kept out Jewish as well as black agents, making it more likely that Jews and blacks would deal with each other. Also, Jews were not as unified in opposition to blacks as some other ethnic groups. Having faced discrimination based on race themselves, some Jews refused to discriminate. In Detroit, for example, Jews were suspicious of racial covenants, concerned that such provisions might be turned against them. Not only did this make houses available to African Americans, it also undercut public support in Jewish neighborhoods for the kind of violent response that sealed off many other ethnic communities against black would-be pioneers.[37] Consequently, according to historian Charles Bright, "blacks have historically followed the lines of Jewish settlement." The process left most WASP, Irish, and Polish suburbs all-white for decades and helps explain the concentration of African Americans into just a handful of suburbs in each metropolitan area. Ironically, it also confirmed elite WASP suburbs in their anti-Semitism, one reason for which was their fear that "Jews will let blacks in." Evidence in Chapter 14 will suggest that more recently, Mexicans have also been both less willing and less able to keep blacks out. Both of these groups absorbed less of a "white privilege" viewpoint, which came all too easily to other immigrants after they had been in the United States for a decade or two.[38]

The case of Irish Americans merits further discussion. Certainly the Irish faced discrimination throughout the nineteenth century. Often they shared slum neighborhoods and lowly occupations with African Americans. Why, then, did they wind up, in Woofter's words, "least mixed" with blacks, along with WASPs? Writing in 1843, John Finch noted the Irish animosity toward African Americans:

> It is a curious fact that the Democratic Party, and particularly the poorer class of Irish immigrants in America, are greater enemies to the Negro population, and greater advocates for the continuance of Negro slavery, than any portion of the population in the free States.

Finch correctly ascribed Irish racism to *successful* competition. They drove African Americans from occupation after occupation in eastern cities. Then, in the words of Noel Ignatiev, author of *How the Irish Became White,* "To avoid the taint of blackness it was necessary that no Negro be allowed to work in occupations where Irish were to be found. Still better was to erase the memory that Afro-Americans had ever done those jobs."[39]

The third and final point about ethnic group membership is that white ethnic Americans rapidly became "regular" Americans, while African Americans were not allowed to. Even when the Swedish, Italian, Polish, or Greek American newcomers entered as strikebreakers, in competition with older groups, eventually the American part of their identity became more important than the foreign part. Owing to the restrictive 1924 immigration act, new white ethnics grew less common, so the communities of Swedish Americans, Italian Americans, Polish Americans, and Greek Americans grew less Swedish, Italian, Polish, or Greek. White ethnics lost their accents and changed their names. Anders Andersson, prototypical Swedish quarrier, became Michael Anderson, less Swedish and more American. His son in turn never went into the quarry but learned to fix those new horseless carriages and soon ran an automobile dealership. *His* son went to college and became an engineer. Indeed, by the end of the Nadir, around 1940, whites had coalesced as an in-group, except possibly Jews and Mexicans.[40] Soon enough, the only place it mattered that anyone was Swedish American was on public radio's *Prairie Home Companion.*[41] By 2004, an Eastern European name was a source of mild amusement if it was somewhat long, like Brzezinski, but was otherwise regarded as American. So was its bearer—as *white* American.

Even in multiethnic towns, African Americans increasingly served the function of America's primary outgroup, spurring in-group solidarity among whites. Their very presence—or, even better, their mandated absence—by definition grouped all European ethnics as "white." White ethnic groups more and more distanced themselves from African Americans during the Nadir, and even some multiethnic towns went sundown. The history of Granite City, Illinois, across the Mississippi from St. Louis, illustrates the process. Between 1900 and 1910, hundreds of new immigrants, mostly from Macedonia and Bulgaria, poured into Granite City. "Poorly paid, they lived in pathetic squalor, ignorant of American institutions," according to a book published in 1971, Granite City's 75th birthday. Nevertheless, Granite City at least tolerated and sometimes even welcomed these white ethnic group members. They were nonblack, which was more important than being non-American. Precisely at this time, Granite City expelled its African Americans. The white ethnics had started at the bottom, in competition with African Americans, but driving the blacks from Granite City erased that memory over the years. Moreover, when WASP, Irish, Polish, Greek, Italian, and now Macedonian and Bulgarian Americans joined to expel or keep out African Americans around 1903, the whites were now united. No longer could Poles be used against Germans, or Italians against Poles. And no longer could African Americans even live in the community. By 1971, Macedonian American and Bulgarian American children were fully accepted, while African Americans were still totally excluded. Historian Matthew Jacobson showed how whites nationally unified racially during the same period.[42]

Labor Strife

Our discussion of ethnic groups as strikebreakers has brought us to labor strife as an underlying historical and sociological reason for sundown towns. American labor history is replete with the use of outsiders as strikebreakers. Capitalists often used white ethnic groups different from (and lower in status than) their workers who were on strike, because these newer immigrants had little solidarity with the workers whose jobs they were taking. Coal mine owners especially, and on occasion quarry and factory owners, used each successive ethnic group as strikebreakers against the last. In Portland, Connecticut, in the 1870s, for example, Swedes broke into quarrying when Irish and German workers were on strike. Twenty-five years later, Italians did the same thing to the Swedes. Over and over, all across the country, each new group came in as strikebreakers vis-à-vis the former group. Always this generated interethnic animosity.[43]

But when African Americans were the strikebreakers, a special hostility came into play. Having first gotten their toehold in America by being strikebreakers in many cases, white ethnics now reacted venomously to *black* strikebreakers. As historian Ronald Lewis put it, writing about Virden and Pana, Illinois, "Not only were the imports scabs, they were *black* scabs, and the white miners displayed at least as much hostility to their color as to their status as strikebreakers."[44]

Only rarely did the more established group try to expel a white ethnic group en masse. "Whites" in West Frankfort, Illinois, did riot against "Sicilians" in 1920. Historian John Higham describes the scene:

> During the night of August 5, 1920, and all through the following day hundreds of people laden with clothing and household goods filled the roads leading out of West Frankfort, a mining town in southern Illinois. Back in town their homes were burning. Mobs bent on driving every foreigner from the area surged through the streets. Foreigners of all descriptions were beaten on sight, although the Italian population was the chief objective. Time and again the crowds burst into the Italian district, dragged cowering residents from their homes, clubbed and stoned them, and set fire to their dwellings. The havoc went on for three days, although five hundred state troops were rushed to the scene.

Terrible as it was, that scene was less vicious and less permanent than most expulsions of African Americans. Some of the "Sicilians" were willing "to sacrifice their property interests for anything they can get," according to a report in the nearby *Marion Daily Republican.* "Business men are discouraging that practice, assuring all the uneasy that everything will come out all right and they can live here in peace and quiet so long as they are good and loyal citizens." Many returned as soon as the violence died. In the same riot, however, whites forced out all African Americans from West Frankfort. No one made *them* any assurances, and they "went to stay," as a Franklin County history put it succinctly in 1942. In the 2000 census, West Frankfort had not one African American household among its 8,196 people. Similarly, miners in Zeigler drove all Greek Americans out of town at gunpoint and kept them out, but only for two days.[45] Residents of Zeigler told me that African Americans, on the other hand, were still unwelcome as of 2002.[46]

When African Americans were used as strikebreakers, if the strikers won, they typically drove all the black strikebreakers out of town.[47] Often, all other African Americans became fair game at that point—as they sometimes did after a lynching—and the workers simply drove them all out, thus creating a sundown town. In Spring Valley, in northern Illinois, the Italians had come in between 1886 and 1893, recruited by mine owners to depress the wages paid to the French and Belgians who had preceded them. In 1895, the owners used African Americans to threaten the Italian Americans. Late in the evening of August 4, 1895, a mob of more than 800 Italian American miners marched from Spring Valley to the settlement of African American miners two miles west of town, led by the Italian American band as a sort of disguise. "The residents, therefore, remained in their homes and did not react to the oncoming mob," writes historian Felix Armfield, who then quotes the account in the *New York Times*:

> Italians fell upon them like a lot of Apache Indians. Men were dragged from their homes, clubbed, trampled upon, and made targets for the shotguns, rifles, and small arms that the mob had brought with them. The women were insulted, slapped, and two of them, while begging for mercy, were shot down and fatally injured. No one was safe from the mob. Men, women, children, infants, the elderly, and even invalids were attacked.

The rioting continued, and on the second day the Italian miners announced, "The Black Men Must Go." Writing in 1945, historians Arna Bontemps and Jack Conroy summarized, "Nobody knows exactly how many Negroes died before the tumult subsided, but as years went by colored folks, at least, referred to the incident as the 'Spring Valley Massacre.' " The result was the expulsion not only of strikebreakers but of all African Americans in Spring Valley. However, Spring Valley apparently remained sundown only briefly, because African Americans protested statewide and the mine manager insisted on his right to hire black miners.[48]

Similar expulsions took place in Pana and Virden, in central Illinois, in 1898. Miners at four coal mines in Pana had been promised the "Springfield scale," 40 cents per ton, won by miners in nearby Springfield, to take effect April 1, 1898. They had been earning 33 cents. On April 1, the owners reneged, so the workers struck. On May 25, after negotiations, the owners offered 30 cents a ton. So at the next meeting, May 30, the workers demanded 35 cents. On June 29, mine owners announced they would bring in strikebreakers from Alabama. Union miners then surrounded the coal mines with mass picket lines, which kept the mines from opening. Eventually, with the

help of police and many ordinary citizens deputized into the police, the owners reopened the mines, using African American labor. On September 28, in
the words of Pana historian Millie Meyerholtz, "striking union coal miners
and imported Negroes engaged in a pitched battle on the main street. One
hundred shots were exchanged." Five blacks and one bystander were hurt; no
one was wounded in the union ranks. Both sides then raised the ante. Miners
from nearby towns—"heavily armed," according to Meyerholtz—poured into
Pana. Hundreds went east, to intercept a train carrying 60 black miners from
Indiana.

> The train was flagged down two miles west of Tower Hill by a large company of
> armed men whose faces were covered by handkerchiefs. The masked men
> boarded the train and at point of gun, forced men, women, and children to un-
> load. They marched them along the track to Tower Hill. The purpose was to
> place them on another train and send them back south.

Meanwhile, state militia arrived in Pana on a train with two Gatling guns. September was marked by daily incidents. African Americans were never safe outside of the mine compound. Whites with clubs chased blacks down alleys and
through yards and threw rocks at them. Some blacks went back south on
trains. "There was a daily passage of insults, slights, and shoves which led to
street brawls and secret means of revenge," according to Eleanor Burhorn,
who wrote a master's thesis on the event. "Each side antagonized the other."
On October 12, whites rioted at the mine in Virden, 40 miles west, where
African Americans were also working as strikebreakers. The union had been
tipped off that additional black strikebreakers were on their way. When the
four-coach train came through Virden, 600 miners lined the tracks and
opened a deadly crossfire killing eleven men, including three St. Louis detec-
tives.[49]

On November 15, the Virden owners capitulated to the white miners.
Virden has kept out African Americans ever since, although in 2000, it had
one black household. On November 25, 1898, Adjutant Gene Reece of the
state militia made the wisest analysis of the Pana situation.

> To unionize the blacks is most reasonable to establish the [wage] scale. But the
> probabilities of its being carried out are few. The bitterness that has been en-
> gendered by the union's fight on the Alabama blacks is such, that it is not prob-
> able that the blacks would listen to a union man under any circumstances.

Then, too, the race question has entered into the fight to such an extent that it is
not likely a movement to get these blacks into the union would meet with favor.

Racism had poisoned the well, making it impossible for black and white miners to drink from any cup of solidarity. On April 10, 1899, a shootout between
blacks and whites killed seven people, including a union miner, three black
men, a black woman, and a bystander, and wounding fifteen. In June the Pana
mine owners admitted defeat too. They closed their mines, stranding their
black miners without even train fare to get out of Pana. Eventually 211 African
Americans left to go west, perhaps to Kansas and Indian Territory, and 63
went back to Birmingham. Pana also drove out its other blacks, excepting one
or two families, as we have seen, and became a sundown town, complete with
signs at the edge of town.[50]

Besides Pana and Virden, many other communities trace their origins as
sundown towns to a successful strike. Something darker may have happened
in Mindenmines, Missouri, where mine operators brought African American
strikebreakers to their coal mine in about 1900. Marvin Van Gilder, author of
a 1972 history of Barton County, recounts blandly, "Many of them died during their relatively brief residence at the mining camps . . . and a cemetery for
the Negro community was established northwest of Mindenmines near the
state line." Van Gilder does not explain why or how "many of them died," but
Mindenmines became a sundown town upon their demise and probably remains so to this day. According to a staff member at Missouri Southern State
College who grew up in the town, a black family moved in for a week in about
1987 and left under pressure; another lived there for about six weeks in about
1990 and left after someone fired a gun at their home. In 2000, Mindenmines
was still all-white.[51]

Most shocking of all may be what happened in Zeigler, which has been a
sundown town since a series of coal mine explosions between 1905 and 1909
killed dozens of black strikebreakers. Zeigler is a fascinating town, built in
concentric circles by its founder, Joseph Leiter, in 1903, who owned its mine.
In July 1904, 268 United Mine Workers (UMW) members walked out of the
mine on strike. Leiter ordered them out of Zeigler, which he owned, and proceeded to fortify the town. He had an 8-foot-high wooden stockade built, 800
feet long and 400 feet wide, with a live wire on top, enclosing the mine and adjacent territory. Gun turrets were built at each corner of the stockade, and another adorned the roof of the mine office, located in the center of town. Each
had a machine gun, and a searchlight mounted on the mine tipple swept the

town at night. Strikebreakers came in by train, but the union was often tipped off and opened fire on the trains before they got inside the fortified area. Most strikebreakers quit as soon as they saw the dangerous conditions facing them. Leiter hired more—Italians and others from Europe and African Americans from Kentucky. The strike continued into the winter of 1904–05. "Night after night guns blazed," in the words of Zeigler historian Allan Patton, "bullets ricocheted off of buildings, and dynamite blasts rocked the city." Leiter's fortress held, however, and by spring, many of the striking miners were seeking employment at other mines.[52]

Then on April 3, 1905, the Zeigler mine blew up. Fifty bodies were eventually retrieved, but the remains of some miners were never recovered. The Zeigler mine endured at least three more catastrophes. On November 4, 1908, it had a fire; on January 10, 1909, 26 miners were killed in another explosion; and a third explosion a month later killed three more. Finally Leiter gave up and sold the mine to another owner, who signed with the UMW.

What caused the disasters? The most intriguing account was written in 1953 by Ruby Goodwin, a major figure in neighboring Du Quoin's black community. In her memoir, *It's Good to Be Black,* she tells in detail how a black miner "walked boldly up to the office and applied for a job." He turned out to be "an expert shot firer from upstate" and a union stalwart. "If anyone had been watching they would have seen him climb up the ladder and get into a waiting surrey just a few minutes before the explosion." Goodwin's account intrigues because she is both African American and a devotee of the UMW—for decades the only major union that recruited black members—so she is sympathetic to the murder of 50 to 100 African American miners because it preserved an interracial union. Also, no argument can be made with one statement she makes: "The miners knew that the explosion was not untimely. It was timed to perfection." Unfortunately, neither Patton nor historian Paul Angle, who also treated Zeigler, discuss Goodwin's account.[53] Oral tradition today in the white community in Zeigler and in the black community in Du Quoin agrees with her, holding that the dead miners were mostly black and that one explosion—the first?—was set by union miners.[54] It is this story that Zeigler residents still told me, in 2002, to explain its all-white tradition.[55]

As with ethnicity, labor strife as an underlying cause of sundown towns shares some overlap with politics. Workers—especially union members—were more likely to be Democrats, an alliance that helped make some of them more racist, just as capitalists' alliance with the Republican Party helped make some of them less racist for a time.[56] Indeed, I would argue that racism as a cultural element in the labor movement was more important in causing a town to go sundown than the presence or absence of black strikebreakers as a specific causal variable. Political scientist John Peterson agrees, pointing out that "African American workers joined unions in large numbers whenever they were treated equally." Thus union exclusion usually preceded and facilitated the use of black strikebreakers. In 1894, American Federation of Labor (AFL) head Samuel Gompers allowed unions to join his organization that were white-only, and most AFL unions proceeded to go all-white. As they achieved power during the next 30 years, unions shut blacks out of railroad employment, from construction, and in some places from meatpacking, lumber, and mining as well.[57] After 1900, Gompers repeatedly made racist speeches attacking African Americans, and union workers responded. Often sundown towns resulted.[58]

Of course, not every union town went sundown. Neither did every Democratic or monoethnic town. Not only did the actions taken by local leaders of both races come into play, but so did happenstance—whether something occurred in a given locale to induce white residents to question the right of African Americans (or another minority) to exist in "their" town. The next chapter will explore these immediate "triggers"—catalyzing incidents, usually of real or alleged black misbehavior, sometimes as inoffensive as a black boxing victory a thousand miles away—that prompted whites in a given community to expel its entire black population.

7

Catalysts and Origin Myths

About forty years ago Negroes began to settle in this township in numbers, and it was not long before they became a nuisance. Stealing was rife and all kinds of depredations were going on. Ned Harrigan, who lived here at the time, says that the whites met at the . . . school building, and decided to clear the country of the blacks. A notice was served on the offenders giving them 24 hours to get out of town, and by noon the next day every Negro shanty was empty, and that was the last that was ever heard of them.

—*Chesterton Tribune*, 1903, explaining why and how
that northern Indiana town went all-white[1]

MOST RESIDENTS of the typical sundown town are not good sociologists and never invoke factors such as those given in the previous chapter—political ideology, ethnic makeup, and the like—to explain their town's racial policy. For that matter, the underlying sociological causes do not flatly determine the outcome in a given community. Not every Democratic town expelled its African Americans, although Democratic towns did so far more often than Republican towns. Not every monoethnic town kept blacks out, although monoethnic towns did so more often than multiethnic towns. Not every town with strong white supremacist labor unions drove out *all* its African Americans, although many did. However, as racism intensified during the Nadir, the position of African Americans in towns marked by any or all of these three factors grew so tenuous that the least disturbance—an incendiary remark by a demagogic white politician, news of the next town getting rid of its blacks, a criminal act by a black resident—might set off an expulsion.

What residents of a sundown town often *do* recall is the immediate "reason" why its African Americans were expelled—the trigger. These events play the role of catalysts. If the underlying conditions are right, just as a catalyst in a chemical reaction provides a surface or "hook" enabling the reaction to proceed more rapidly, so the triggering incident provides an excuse or justification for the expulsion or prohibition of African Americans.

In most towns that had African Americans and then had none, some account of this triggering event persists in the local culture to explain their absence. This story then gets raised to the level of myth and becomes used not only as the sole reason for the original expulsion but also to justify the town's continuing exclusion of African Americans.

Labor Strife as Excuse

One underlying cause—organized labor and racialized labor strife—is often cited by residents as the cause of their town's sundown policy. In some towns, however, black strikebreakers were not the real reason for a town going sundown, but only the pretext. This may have been true in Linton, Indiana, for example, which barred all African Americans after a coal company attempted to use black strikebreakers. In the summer of 1903, union miners made a "riotous attack upon the colored waiters at Linton," according to a newspaper account. Linton put up a sundown sign, and all of Greene County, of which Linton is the largest city, went sundown, according to a history teacher who grew up in nearby Vincennes. A black family tried to move into the county in the late 1940s, she said, and "was burned out. No one black would ever *dare* live in Linton," she told me in 2002, and as of the 2000 census, 5,774 people lived in Linton, but there was not one black household.[2] "The colored waiters" had nothing to do with any strikebreakers, however—indeed, nothing to do with mining. White coal miners in Linton were hardly in competition with waiters, so the motivation for the 1903 "riotous attack" wasn't economic. The mining strike seems just an excuse for a more general policy.[3]

As in Linton, workers in Austin, Minnesota, expelled not only black strikebreakers, but all African Americans. In Oshkosh, Wisconsin, according to Andrew Kirchmeier, professor at nearby Ripon College, unions had an agreement with the city, not the employers, to keep African Americans out of town as a matter of municipal policy. Perhaps unions in each city felt that the easiest way to guarantee that black strikebreakers would never trouble them again would be to give their town a reputation for being inhospitable to all African Americans. Or perhaps workers were simply acting on their racist beliefs, shared by their political and labor leaders.[4]

Moreover, unions did not have to be racist to succeed, so it is fallacious to "credit" black strikebreakers with causing a town to go sundown. Labor had examples of nonracist practice, such as Du Quoin, Illinois, where the United

Mine Workers organized an interracial union. There, when managers tried to engage blacks as strikebreakers, unionized African Americans were on hand to dissuade them. The town stayed interracial, the mines stayed organized, and Du Quoin has long been an oasis of racial tolerance compared to its neighboring communities, most of which are sundown towns. It even elected a black alderman in 1918. Thus racism did not flow automatically as a result of social class or union membership.[5]

Some sundown towns invoked labor disputes long after the fact, as an excuse. Miners in Carterville, Illinois, 130 miles south of Pana, faced African American strikebreakers in 1898. Like the mine owners in Pana, Samuel Brush, who operated the biggest mine in Williamson County, just north of Carterville, refused to pay the Springfield scale agreed to by other mine owners with the United Mine Workers. Four-fifths of his workers struck. Brush replaced them with 178 African American miners from Tennessee. Two years of intermittent labor disputes, often marked by violence, followed. On September 17, 1899, some 25 or 30 whites confronted about 15 African Americans at the Illinois Central railroad station and ordered them to get out of town. The blacks started walking up the railroad tracks, with the whites following at a distance. According to historian Paul Angle:

> Suddenly one of the Negroes drew a pistol and fired at the group of pursuers. The miners answered with a volley. Several of the Negroes fell; the others ran for their lives. The whites followed, firing at the fugitives. In a few minutes, not a black man could be seen. Five lay dead; the others, some of them wounded, escaped to the safety of the mining camp.

To this day, some residents of Carterville explain the town's sundown policy by referring to the "black scabs." Historian Herbert Gutman took this position in "The Negro and the UMW." It turns out, however, that Carterville already was a sundown town *before* the importation of the strikebreakers. As Angle noted, Carterville "had long imposed on the Negro a subhuman status. No colored person was permitted even to enter the town."[6]

On the Knife Edge

While black strikebreakers have been wrongly invoked to excuse sundown policies—their actions can never logically justify expelling African Americans who were *not* strikebreakers—nevertheless labor strife does qualify as a catalyst. Often whether a town went sundown came down to such small moments in time as whether a strike was won or lost. If the strikers lost, some striking miners came back to work, joining some of the African American strikebreakers. In the few Pennsylvania towns where African Americans do reside today, "in most cases they are the descendants of strikebreakers," according to Philip Jenkins, author of a study of the Ku Klux Klan in Pennsylvania. Other interracial towns resulting from strikebreakers include Coal Creek, Indiana; Braidwood and Danville, Illinois; Waterloo, Iowa; and Weir City, Kansas. If the union was smart, which the United Mine Workers of America often was, it then organized white and black workers so as not to be undercut by black strikebreakers in the future.[7]

Sometimes a truly insignificant incident made the difference. Mine owner Joseph Leiter was about to sign with the United Mine Workers in a meeting with UMW leaders in Zeigler, Illinois, in June 1904, a month before the strike. Then, in Allan Patton's words:

> According to local legend, John Wesley Shadowen, one of the local [UMW] union officials, made a loud boast of the union conquest of Leiter.[8] Immediately Leiter threw the pen that he held to sign the agreement into the wall and [threw] the contract at Shadowen. In a loud voice Leiter stated that, "Zeigler will run scab forever!"

What if Shadowen had not made his intemperate remark? Then Leiter would have signed with the interracial UMW, and Zeigler might not be a sundown town today.[9]

Other events showed how tenuous was the position of African Americans in towns poised on the knife edge owing to the towns' underlying characteristics. On July 4, 1910, for example, black heavyweight Jack Johnson defeated Jim Jeffries, the "Great White Hope," in Reno, Nevada. African Americans rejoiced in the victory of one of their own, until they came up against the response of white Americans to Jeffries's defeat. Whites attacked African Americans in at least 30 American cities. In Slocum, Texas, they killed 20; all others fled. So Slocum became a sundown town in response to a boxing match more than a thousand miles away. This is what historians call "historical contingency": if Johnson had lost, blacks might have survived in Slocum.[10]

Claims to Equality Led to Sundown Towns

The real reason that Jack Johnson's victory led to at least one sundown town and to many attacks on African American neighborhoods was that he demonstrated that blacks could be the equal of whites, at least in the boxing ring. During the Nadir, that was a dangerous claim for an African American to make. Indeed, Johnson boldly maintained that he was socially equal to whites as well, openly dating and marrying white women. Whites have often been unwilling to concede that African Americans might be their equal in wealth, social status, or even more minor skills such as boxing or poker, and their anger at the possibility often triggered sundown towns.

Whites might claim to be upset by problematic African Americans—criminals and ne'er-do-wells—but more frequently they lashed out at those who were industrious and successful, for it was these families whose existence set up a claim to social and economic equality. Such claims underlay the expulsion by white Democrats of about 200 African Americans from Washington County, Indiana, shortly after the Civil War. The earliest victim of the violence was John Williams, "who had acquired a farm and an unusual amount of wealth for a Negro," in the words of historian Emma Lou Thornbrough. "In December, 1864, he was shot to death in his own dooryard. In 1867 there was another murder, the victim being an inoffensive old man who had aroused the ire of some of his white neighbors by persisting in attending their church, even after he had been warned to stay away." These and other terrorist actions led to an exodus, and Washington County remained all-white until 1990. To achieve wealth or attend church implied that African Americans were the social equals of whites, which these Indiana whites would not tolerate.[11]

In the larger riots for which we have more information, such as the 1908 attempt in Springfield, Illinois, and the 1921 attempt in Tulsa, Oklahoma, to cleanse these cities of African Americans, we can see the same dynamic at work. Margaret Ferguson, an African American trying to avoid the mob in Springfield, pointed out, "There was a great deal of animosity toward any well-established Negro who owned his own house and had a good job." Rioters there specifically targeted William Donnegan, an elderly African American who had been Abraham Lincoln's cobbler. His sin, besides his race itself, was that he was prosperous, and also that he had been married to a white woman for over 30 years. The mob cut his throat and hanged him. "They were very busy hurting the prominent," Ferguson wrote later, "and so of course we were frightened, you see, because we, also, were affluent." In Tulsa, too, whites particularly targeted successful middle-class families.[12]

Sometimes the affront may seem trivial until we recognize that a claim for equality was involved. In Owosso, in central Michigan, on October 4, 1871, African American residents held a party, complete with an Italian band. Some white residents apparently tried to crash it, and the African Americans said they were not welcome, since blacks had been ejected from a white masquerade ball some months earlier.[13] An argument ensued; the blacks ousted the whites and beat them on the street. The white community returned en masse and forced all African Americans[14] out of town.[15]

Sometimes direct economic competition between small-business owners engaged in the same trade played a role. In 1892, when whites in Norman, Oklahoma, first drove out their black residents, an African American named Doll Smith, a barber, received a note of warning:

> You are hereby notified to leave this town in the next ten days. We are determined that no "niggers" shall live in this town. We give you timely warning to get your things and "git" or you must stand the consequences.

Smith did leave, and nine months later, when whites forced the black residents of nearby Lexington to flee, a white barber, George Elkins, played a leading role. In Lexington, according to the *Guthrie [Oklahoma] News,* "Negro men were tied up and beaten, and Negro women outraged." Federal District Court indicted twenty whites, but the cases were continued for a year and finally dismissed.[16]

In November 1920, African Americans in Ocoee, Florida, west of Orlando, made a still more serious claim to equality: they tried to vote. A Republican judge, John Cheney, facilitated their registration, which outraged white Democrats, who dominated much of Orange County. The "Grand Master Florida Ku Klucks" sent the following notice to Judge Cheney:

> If you are familiar with the history of the days of Reconstruction which followed in the wake of the Civil War, you will recall that the "Scallawags" [*sic*] of the North, and the Republicans of the South proceeded very much the same as you are proceeding, to instill into the Negro the idea of social equality. You will also remember that these things forced the loyal citizens of the South to organize clans of determined men, who pledged themselves to maintain white supremacy and to safeguard our women and children.
>
> And now if you are a scholar, you know that history repeats its self, and that he who resorts to your kind of a game is handling edged tools. We shall always enjoy WHITE SUPREMACY in this country and he who interferes must face the consequences.

On election day, two prosperous African American landowners in Ocoee, Mose Norman and Julius Perry, went to the polls. Democratic officials turned them away. Norman returned later with a shotgun, insisting that he be allowed to vote. "An altercation ensues," in the words of Bianca White, co-director of a documentary film on the incident, "and Mose Norman is pistol whipped and sent away a second time. Mose Norman is never heard from again." Colonel Sam Salisbury then organized a lynch mob to punish Norman and Perry for trying to vote. By nightfall, white residents of Ocoee, joined by more than 250 Klansmen from around the state, collected in the town and attacked its black neighborhoods. More than 300 African Americans fled for their lives "into the orange groves, swamps, and neighboring towns." Many were burned in their homes or shot as they fled them. Twenty-five homes, two churches, and a Masonic lodge were incinerated; the death toll was between 8 and 60. Perry's body was found hanging from a light pole the next morning. For nearly a week deputized Klansmen held the city. They divvied up the land owned by African Americans and sold it for $1.50 an acre. Ocoee stayed all-white until 1981.[17]

Until 1921, residents of Montlake, then a small coal mining town, now a suburban area near Soddy-Daisy in East Tennessee, drew their water from a centrally located spring, "the only one available for general use," according to an article in the *Chicago Defender,* the nation's premier black newspaper. As segregation drew stricter during the Nadir, whites grew less willing to countenance the equality of status implied by sharing a spring. "The prejudice of the whites had made them try to keep any one but themselves from using the spring," in the *Defender*'s words. "On several occasions individuals have had fights over the water, and, in a number of instances, the whites have been worsted. It is felt that this condition led to the circulation of reports that if anything should happen again the whites were going to band together to force the other residents from their homes." At this point a black girl, eight-year-old Jewel Flipper, went to the spring for water. Four white girls apparently stopped her. An altercation ensued, and in the aftermath, whites drove out the entire African American population—some 60 miners and their families. "After driving them out the whites guarded the streets, went into the cabins and took all of value, and kept any one from entering the town by way of the roads." Decades later, according to oral history, Soddy-Daisy sported a sign that said "Niggers' Fun, Look and Run." [18]

Threat of School Desegregation Led to Sundown Towns

School desegregation presented a similar claim of equality. We saw that school desegregation was involved in Hermann, Missouri, which proved unable to find a stable equilibrium between the equality implied by common schooling and the stigma of total exclusion. Segregation embodies the idea that African Americans are an inferior people with whom whites must never have equal social contact. For that reason among others, in 1954 the United States Supreme Court struck down the system of racial segregation in American education. *Brown v. Board of Education* ordered schools to desegregate, clearly as a first step toward ending segregation in all aspects of public life. Towns as far north as Topeka, Kansas; Washington, D.C.; and southern Illinois struggled to comply, while whites in Deep South towns struggled *not* to comply.

Sheridan, Arkansas, coped with *Brown* by getting rid of all its African Americans. Shortly after the 1954 edict came down from the Supreme Court, the all-white Sheridan school board voted to comply, a constructive step taken by only two other towns in Arkansas. Sheridan had been operating an elementary school for African Americans but was busing its black high school students to adjacent counties. The decision to desegregate led to a "firestorm of protest" in the white community, in the words of a Sheridan native, which led to a new meeting the next night at which the school board unanimously reversed itself. Thereafter, as told in Chapter 4, Sheridan's entire black community was induced to leave town, leaving Sheridan all-white on purpose. Thus Sheridan, which would have been one of the most racially progressive towns in Arkansas if its initial school board decision had stood, instead became one of the most backward.[19]

Like Sheridan, Highland Park and University Park, Texas, contiguous "suburbs" entirely surrounded by Dallas, got rid of their black children after 1954. The "Park Cities" already were sundown suburbs allowing no independent African American households, but some of their affluent white families had live-in maids and gardeners. Before the 1954 Supreme Court decision, children of these adults were quietly allowed to attend black schools in Dallas, with tuition paid by Highland Park and University Park. After *Brown,* Park Cities officials realized they would be vulnerable to a desegregation lawsuit. Alderman C. K. Bullard suggested that Park Cities residents who employed African Americans with children be asked to fire them "so that Park Cities would not be confronted with white and Negro children attending classes together." Most African American families moved out by the late 1950s. Dallas didn't actually stop accepting black students from the suburbs until 1961. At least one African American servant with children still lived in Highland Park at that point, so her employer, a rich white family, paid rent on a Dallas address for her so that her children could stay in school in Dallas while living with her at their house in the Park Cities.[20]

Even before *Brown,* whites in many locales were upset with having to pay taxes to support *separate* schools for African American children. Sometimes they responded by driving black families from their communities. In Case Township, north of Norman, Oklahoma, for example, residents grew alarmed because two white landowners hired three or four black families to farm their land. One resident who signed himself "A Hoodlum" wrote to the Norman newspapers: "Farmers of Case township are as just [*sic*] much against mixing up with niggers as the good people of Norman are and what is more they don't intend to have their farms taxed to put up Negro school houses." Eventually the whites burned down one black family's house but may not have succeeded in driving all the African Americans away. I suspect similar reasoning led to anti-black actions in Arkansas, Kentucky, Missouri, and Tennessee.[21]

Around the time of the *Brown* decision, the African American population of at least five counties in Kentucky and Tennessee fell precipitously.[22] Perhaps the black families in these counties moved away voluntarily, but the example of Sheridan raises suspicion. Historian Mary Waalkes has done research on one of the five, Polk County, Tennessee, which abuts North Carolina in the Appalachian Mountains. According to one account, she writes, *Brown* prompted whites there to force black families to sell their farms, "in an effort to rid the county of school children who would have to be integrated into the Polk County system."[23] The number of African Americans in Polk County—which had been 566 in 1890—fell from 75 in 1950 to just 28 ten years later, and only 4 of school age, among 12,160 inhabitants. Across America, many whites in sundown counties felt blessed to have no black children in 1954; as Esther Sanderson put it in 1974, "Scott County [Tennessee] definitely has no segregation problem for there is not a single negro [*sic*] living in the entire county." Some other communities in Arkansas, Kentucky, Missouri, and Tennessee may also have gotten rid of their African Americans after *Brown,* as white families reacted to the possibility that unless the few black families in town could be induced to leave, their children might wind up in "our school."[24]

Other Catalysts

Every sundown town, especially those that expelled their African Americans violently, has its own answer as to why it went all-white. Residents of sundown towns and suburbs rarely refer to the increased racism of the Nadir or to such social and cultural factors as politics, ethnic composition, or labor history. Instead, residents "explain" their town's policy by telling about the incident that triggered it. We must not accept these trigger stories at face value: sometimes there are competing accounts, and often they are after-the-fact rationalizations detailing acts that may or may not have taken place. Even where an account of the beginning of a town's sundown policies is accurate, leaving it as the actual cause of its continuing exclusion is far too simple.

The events that triggered mass expulsions were often instances of black misbehavior. Some African American did something wrong, and whites responded by taking it out on the entire group. Such was the case in Anna, Illinois, in 1909. The convenience store clerk quoted at the beginning of this book who confirmed in 2001 the continuing nickname for Anna, "Ain't No Niggers Allowed," also related Anna's explanation for its policy: "My girlfriend told me how that all got started. A black man raped a white girl, and she's buried up in the cemetery with a memorial stone, and they hung him." Her girlfriend is right: residents of Anna do date its sundown status to 1909. On November 8 of that year, Anna Pelley, a 24-year-old white woman, was murdered in Cairo, some 30 miles south. She was found in an alley near her home the next morning, gagged and strangled, her clothing ripped off. Bloodhounds led police to a black-owned house where they later arrested Will James, a deliveryman for the Cairo Coal & Ice Co. That evening a lynch mob gathered in Cairo, but the police chief quieted them by pointing out that the police weren't sure they had the right man. After all, the evidence against James consisted mostly of the fact that "bloodhounds had sniffed their way to his house," as a contemporary newspaper account put it. The following Friday, November 11, rumors that James had confessed caused whites again to threaten a lynch mob. The sheriff, Frank Davis, decided to get his prisoner out of Cairo. That evening the sheriff, a deputy, and James "boarded the northbound Illinois Central train to escape the lynch mob." But whites in Cairo telephoned news of Davis's flight to Anna, 30 miles north—Anna Pelley's hometown—where another mob assembled to await his arrival.[25]

"It would not do to stay on the train and try to get through Anna with him," the sheriff later explained. "That was the former home of the girl he was accused of killing, and I knew that the news that we were coming would be telephoned and telegraphed to Anna in time for her friends to collect a mob at the depot that would take him from me. So I had the train stopped at Dongola [ten miles south], and we struck out in the darkness across the country eastward." The mob now combed the woods around Dongola. Eventually, walking through the night, the prisoner and his guards reached the little town of Karnak, where Sheriff Davis bought sardines, crackers, and soft drinks for the three of them. They didn't dare stay in Karnak, however, lest they be recognized, so they walked on toward Belknap. There they hoped to catch a 5 PM northbound train on a different railroad and evade Anna and the mob altogether. Unfortunately, a train crew at Karnak had recognized them and relayed their whereabouts back to Cairo. "When we discovered late in the afternoon that a mob was tailing us," in the sheriff's words, "we traveled as fast as we could, in the hope of keeping ahead until dark. . . . But the pursuers closed in on us, and when we found that we were in greater danger of being seen if we kept on than if we hid where we were, we concealed ourselves in the bushes and waited, hoping that they would pass us by, but they found us." [26]

The mob overpowered the prisoner and his guards and forced them onto a southbound train at Karnak. Word of the capture preceded them. When they reached Cairo, thousands of people, many from Anna and other nearby towns, gathered to watch at the main downtown intersection, spanned by a double ornamental steel arch festooned with hundreds of bright lights. (See Portfolio 5.) A reporter described the scene:

> The mob that hanged James was led by women, many of them the wives of influential residents of Cairo. The rope was pulled taut by female relatives of Miss Pelley, aided by several score of their sex. As the Negro was pulled up into the air, these same women sang and screamed in delight.
>
> The men were for the most part spectators until the rope that was strangling the Negro broke and his dying body fell to the ground. Then hundreds of revolvers flashed and 500 bullets crashed into the quivery form of the Negro. The riddled dead man was then dragged through the principal streets of the city to the spot where the Pelley girl was assaulted and slain.
>
> Women applied the torch to the bonfire that had been prepared and into which the body of James was thrown. Ten thousand cheered and danced at the scene.

Interestingly, this became an "equal-opportunity lynching," for the crowd later grabbed another prisoner from the jail, a white photographer accused of killing his wife the previous summer, and hanged him from a telegraph pole at a different downtown location. [27]

When the mob members from Anna returned home on a later Illinois Central train, they decided to drive all African Americans from the town—primarily some 30 or 40 men who worked at a local quarry, along with their families. To the best of my knowledge, Anna has been all-white ever since. So has its twin city, Jonesboro. According to oral tradition, "one old lady who had been a slave" was allowed to stay when the other blacks were driven out. [28]

Few whites displayed any remorse or even embarrassment at the expulsion of African Americans from Anna-Jonesboro. Most residents of Anna felt they had improved their town by the act; some residents of surrounding towns were jealous. For that matter, most whites were not appalled even by the lynchings. Before burning the body of Will James, members of the mob cut out his heart; then they cut it up and carried the pieces away for souvenirs. Afterward, James's half-burned head was displayed on top of a pole in a Cairo park, and photographers sold postcards of his hanging. Ministers justified both lynchings from the pulpit. The *Carbondale Free Press* reprinted with approval an editorial in the *Cairo Bulletin*, "In Memory of Miss Pelley," suggesting

> that on November 10 of each year every Cairo man wear a small knot of rope in the lapel of his coat "as a quiet and dignified manifestation of the end of evil doers of any and all races, who outrage or insult pure womanhood. Every white and colored man of the city can thus place himself on record for law and order for a day each year."

Neither editor saw any irony in using a symbol of a lynching rope as a celebration of "law and order." A public subscription was taken up to purchase an extraordinary tombstone for Pelley (Portfolio 6).[29]

Interracial Rape as Catalyst

Anna is hardly the only community to use rape or murder as an excuse to drive out or keep out all African Americans. Residents of many sundown towns explain their communities' all-white status by invoking incidents that embody the familiar "African American as problem" ideology, but with specific local details about what blacks did wrong *here*. Ever since, to justify the continued vigilance and sometimes brutal actions required to maintain a town or suburb as an all-white community, whites summon up the long-ago alleged misbehavior of the victim class. Interracial rape was the excuse for the 1912 expulsion of African Americans from Forsyth County, Georgia, for example. On September 10 of that year, alleged rapist Edward Collins, an African American, was shot in the Forsyth County jail by a lynch mob. Several other African Americans, allegedly his accomplices, were threatened with lynching, but officers spirited them to Atlanta for safety.[30] The mob then turned upon the African American community. Between September 10 and the end of that year, according to the Forsyth county historian, notices were given to all the Negro population to leave the county. . . . A few persisted in staying and were promised protection by their landlords. A few houses were dynamited and burned and then the whites were notified to get rid of their Negro tenants or have their houses and barns likewise burned. This accomplished the removal of the rest of the blacks.

The African American population in Forsyth County plummeted from 1,100 in 1910 to 30 in 1920 and 17 in 1930.[31]

Many other expulsions and attempted expulsions followed allegations of interracial rape. The 1908 riot that swept Springfield, Illinois, for example, began after Mabel Hallam, a white woman, claimed that George Robinson, a black man, had raped her. The black community was driven out of Pinckneyville, Illinois, in about 1928; one explanation extant in Pinckneyville today states that a black man raped a white woman, so the whites got a bus, loaded all the blacks on it, and took them to East St. Louis. Unconfirmed oral history in LaSalle-Peru, twin cities in northeastern Illinois, holds that they have been all-white since the lynching of a black man who raped an Irish American woman.[32]

Black "Crime Waves" as Catalyst

If not rape, often sundown towns and counties invented black crime waves by African Americans to "explain" why they drove out their black populations. When Green Saunders referred to "the second killing of white people by Negroes" as the reason for driving all African Americans from Comanche County, Texas, he was conflating two very different African American criminals, eight years apart, to create a menace. In about 1878, Mose Jones, an old ex-slave, had been living with his wife, child, and stepdaughter on the T. J. Nabers farm. According to Eulalia Wells, "Mose did the morning chores about the kitchen" and also worked at the stable. "Mose was apparently one of the most humble of Negroes in town. It was characteristic of him that when he met white people he at once held his hat against his breast and bowed and spoke with deep humility." But after his wife died, "Old Mose" snapped. First he tried to marry his fourteen-year-old stepdaughter. He then killed the stepdaughter, his own daughter, the Nabers' two young boys, "and but for Mrs. Nabers being a light sleeper would have murdered her and her husband." He set fire to the house and fled. "By daybreak about 200 men were searching for Mose," Wells goes on. "He was found about six miles east of town on the other side of Indian Creek—and was shot." Wells then writes a telling paragraph:

Everyone thought that Old Mose was the only mean Negro in town—so the others were allowed to remain. The Negroes kept coming into the county during the next few years and soon a large settlement of them located in the northeastern part of the county.

To her, writing in 1942, it is natural that whites would have the right to decide whether African Americans as a group will be "allowed to remain" after this one event by an obviously deranged man. And after one more interracial crime—eight years later—Comanche County whites snapped.[33]

To garner support for the 1895 Spring Valley, Illinois, massacre described in the previous chapter, Italian American miners blamed African Americans "for every crime committed in the area," in Felix Armfield's words. "Euramerican whites in the town soon sided with the Italian cause." A Tennessee county historian tells of a similar expulsion based on a wave of thefts and arson but admits that the crimes continued after the African Americans had been driven out. Whites in Wyandotte, Michigan, drove out their African American residents repeatedly, most prominently in 1916. Wyandotte residents treating the 1916 expulsion in the 1940s tried to blame the victims: "Negroes in 1916 era were very low type, ran houses of ill repute, attacked Wyandotte women and children, a real threat to law abiding citizens." But according to Edwina DeWindt, compiler of "Wyandotte History; Negro," African Americans posed no threat; city records from the time show no record of white protests about their behavior. Surely the vaguest crime wave of all took place in Chesterton, Indiana, described by the newspaper editor at the head of this chapter: "All kinds of depredations were going on."[34]

Catalysts Do Not Explain

"Explanations" that blame the origin of sundown policies on criminal characteristics of the excluded group contain two obvious fallacies: collective guilt and circular reasoning. The events described in the Chesterton newspaper neatly exemplify both. When one or more African Americans commit crimes, the entire group is considered responsible and should be punished. And once blacks were gone, since Chesterton subsequently had no major crimes, the paper's editor knows that the town's policy "saved this county many a tragedy," so the townspeople were right to have gotten rid of them. Similarly, once Anna expelled its blacks, it had no more black murderers—even though it never had any to start with, the murder having taken place elsewhere. The "explanation" thus provides continuing justification for a town's continuing policy of excluding African Americans.

I place quotation markes around "explanation" because these crimes or alleged crimes do not really reveal why a town or county drove out its black population, partly because when a European American committed a similar crime, whites as a group faced no similar repercussions. Moreover, often the catalysts do not hold up even as triggers. The attempted rape and murder of Anna Pelley, followed by the lynching of Will James, do not really explain why Anna-Jonesboro went sundown, for example. For one thing, James may have been innocent. Sheriff Davis thought so: "I questioned him a great deal while we were in the woods together and he insisted all the time that he was innocent. I am very much in doubt whether he is the guilty man or not." Moreover, both the murder and the lynching took place 30 miles away, not even in the same county.

In Forsyth County, the mob did apparently get the right person, for the white victim identified three African Americans as the perpetrators, one of whom was lynched, the other two convicted. Even so, interracial rape cannot have been the real cause for the subsequent eviction of the entire black population of the county, because Forsyth was one of six adjacent counties in north Georgia that expelled their African Americans at about this time. Indeed, Forsyth was probably the third to do so, after Towns and Union Counties, and I know no claims of black rape or murder as the catalyst for those expulsions. Whites in Dawson County, between Forsyth and Union, expelled their African Americans about when Forsyth did; all were gone by 1920. Parts of Fannin and Gilmer Counties, just west of Union, also went sundown at this time. No claims of rape were ever made, so far as I know, to justify the expulsions of African Americans from Dawson, Fannin, and Gilmer Counties. Surely contagious rioting in the white communities—"Towns County did it; why haven't we?"—is more likely than any undocumented epidemic of African Americans raping whites in county after contiguous county.[35]

We cannot conclude that interracial rape was really the cause of the attempted expulsion of African Americans from Springfield either, because it turns out there had been no rape. Mabel Hallam dropped all charges against George Robinson; eventually she confessed that she had had sex with her white lover and had invented the black rapist story to escape blame from her husband and friends. The Pinckneyville rape story is thoroughly vague and conflicts with accounts offered by others in town. The alleged rape in LaSalle-Peru is even vaguer, including no date or names, and implies the towns *had* a black population that whites then drove off in the aftermath of a crime. Either the crime took place before the Civil War or the rise and fall of such a population would have to have been rapid and intercensal, since LaSalle and Peru have been all-white in every census from 1860 to the recent past. I suspect both of these sketchy anecdotes are attempts by whites years later to ascribe the sundown policies to origins that seem plausible but in fact did not take place.

Various catalyst stories were reported to explain and justify the 1907 expulsion of Sikhs from Bellingham, Washington. According to one account, the riot may have started "when a gang of young rowdies who were collected on a corner decided to have some fun with the Hindus." Another version held that "the Hindus agreed to pay the landlord of a shack in Old Town $15 a month for the place and as a result a white woman who was living there was forced to move. It is reported that she is the one who incited the trouble." However, underlying conflict between European American and Sikh workers at lumber mills in the city had been festering for some time and was surely more important than any trigger.[36]

Vague or Mislaid Catalyst Stories

If catalysts do not provide satisfying explanations of why towns keep African Americans from living in them, some accounts of the original expulsion or prohibition have grown so vague over time that they can barely function even as catalysts. Tonawanda and North Tonawanda are located at the western end of the Erie Canal. Many African Americans have lived in the area, especially in Buffalo to the south and Niagara Falls to the north, and blacks always worked on the canal boats; such centrally located towns could not have been all-white for decades by accident. As late as 1990, Tonawanda had just 28 African Americans among 17,284 people, while North Tonawanda had 56 among 35,000. It turns out that both were sundown towns. Law professor Bill Kaplin grew up there in the 1940s and '50s and learned only that "some black man allegedly did something bad" long ago; whites then drove out all African Americans and forbade them to live there after that. Kathy Spillman, who grew up in North Tonawanda two decades later, could not recall even that much, although she knew the towns kept out African Americans. Some old-timers in the Tonawandas may remember when and how African Americans were forced out, but it's not a living memory shared by the community as a whole.[37]

Sometimes alternative catalyst stories compete. On Halloween night, 1919, whites in Corbin, Kentucky, a railroad town of about 3,400, forced their African Americans out of town after two white switchmen lost all their money in a poker game with black track layers. To cover their losses, the switchmen said African Americans had robbed them. A mob formed "and searched the city for Negroes," according to the account in the *Lexington Herald*.

> The Negroes who felt the fury of the mob in the greatest degree were a gang of about 200 Negroes working on the Louisville and Nashville grade for ten months at South Corbin, where the railroad company is making big improvements. Crowds went to restaurants and other public places, caught all the Negro employees they could, and drove them singly or in gangs at the point of guns to the depot. Many Negroes were beaten, and 200 were driven out of town.

At gunpoint whites then forced almost the entire African American population onto railroad cars and shipped them to Knoxville, Tennessee. But residents of Corbin haven't found this origin story satisfying over the years, so they make up new ones. One woman volunteered that four black men were lynched for attacking a white woman. One man, interviewed for Robby Heason's gripping 1990 documentary about Corbin as a sundown town, said that he really didn't know what to believe for sure, because "I have heard that story a hundred times since I've been in Corbin, and it's been told to me about a hundred different ways."[38]

Usually even such vague or conflicting accounts still suffice as catalyst stories, because they make reference to black misbehavior. Implicitly, most African Americans are thought to share this characteristic, which is why "we" must exclude them. However, residents of some sundown towns have completely forgotten why they ever expelled African Americans. In 2002, residents of Crossville, Tennessee, knew theirs was a sundown county and had had a black population until about 1905, but they had lost any oral tradition to explain exactly how and why their African Americans were forced out. Other communities have even forgotten that they ever had any African Americans, let alone that they expelled them. Many suburbs display this amnesia, especially those that reopened to blacks more than a decade ago. Chamblee, Georgia, for example, has experienced such international and diverse immigration as a booming suburb of Atlanta that only one-third of its residents in 2000 were born in the United States; still fewer were born in Georgia, and only a handful in Chamblee. The result is that today's residents have no memory that Chamblee became a sundown town after World War II and was all-white in 1970—let alone why. For at least two decades, Chamblee has been thoroughly multiracial and multiethnic, so the town has no reason to maintain an account of why it is or was all-white.

Contagion as Catalyst

Some towns went sundown simply because a neighboring town did so. The neighboring event served as a catalyst of sorts, but actually it shows the absence of a catalyst. The only cause required to set off an expulsion seemed to be envy of a neighboring town that had already driven out its African Americans. In southwestern Missouri, for instance, newspaper editor Murray Bishoff believes that Monett's prosperity after it threw out all its African Americans in 1894 likely contributed to Pierce City's copycat riot seven years later. Bishoff thinks Pierce City in turn became a model for other nearby towns in Missouri and Arkansas. After whites expelled African Americans from Corbin, Kentucky, in 1919, a copycat mob rioted a few months later in Ravenna, 70 miles north, and forced Ravenna's black railroad workers out; Ravenna remained all-white into the 1990s.[39]

As we saw with Anna, a lynching in one town might trigger an expulsion in another. Lynchings typically inflamed white opinion, not against the crime but against the victim class, and often this animus crossed state lines. After the 1931 lynching of Raymond Gunn in Maryville, in northwest Missouri, white passions were inflamed in small towns in northeastern Kansas more than 50 miles distant. In 1920, a huge mob hanged three African American circus workers in Duluth, Minnesota, believing they had raped Irene Tusken, a white woman. In reality, whether she was raped by anyone is doubtful. Nevertheless, in the aftermath, the acting chief of police of neighboring Superior, Wisconsin, declared, "We are going to run all idle Negroes out of Superior and they're going to stay out." His decree was hardly limited to "idle Negroes"; all African Americans employed by a carnival in Superior were fired and told to leave the city, even though they were working, and the overall black population of Superior tumbled from 169 in 1920 to just 51 ten years later. Such edicts again show black communities balanced on a knife edge, for no one even bothered to claim that its members did anything to provoke retribution *here*.[40]

Sometimes epidemics of expulsions or sundown ordinances washed like a wave across entire subregions. In 1886, for example, after whites rioted and drove out African Americans from Comanche County, Texas, nearby residents picked up on the idea, so a broad area of about 3,000 square miles in north-central Texas drove out their African Americans at this time, including all or part of at least four counties. No grievous crime of rape or murder was alleged in those counties to provide a catalyst or excuse; the expulsions were merely copycat actions. We have seen that whites rioted and drove out African Americans from county after county in northern Arkansas and southwestern

Missouri around 1900, and in northern Georgia around 1910. Portfolio 13 tells of an outbreak of expulsions in southern Indiana. I suggest that future investigations may unearth similar epidemics wherever a chain of all-white towns or counties nestles nearby.[41]

If rioting was contagious, so too were quieter methods of achieving sundown status, I believe. These days, municipalities deliberately copy each other's ordinances on many topics, rather than inventing them from scratch. I suspect municipalities copied each other's ordinances in the past as well. If Monticello, the seat of Piatt County, Illinois, passed a sundown ordinance, which an attorney there says it did, then trustees of De Land, a smaller town in Piatt County, would want to keep up with the times, and did, according to its officials—and so on, across the Midwest and the nation. I must admit, however, that while the foregoing seems logical to me,[42] it is entirely speculative.

The contagion of exclusion was even more pronounced in the suburbs. When one suburb, deemed to be prestigious, was all white on purpose, it became the thing to do, and other suburbs hastened to emulate the leader. Soon, almost all of the suburbs around a major city kept out African Americans.

Catalyst Stories as Origin Myths

Although catalysts don't really explain much, they remain important stories nevertheless. Even today, residents of Anna, for instance, cite the story of Anna Pelley's death to explain why their town has no African American residents. Many residents of sundown towns give similar explanations: they admit openly that their town excludes African Americans and proceed to tell why, relying on the catalyzing incident to justify the practice. Thus the story of the initial incident gets elevated into an origin myth.

Origin myths tell us why we are here as a people or why we are the way we are. Often they tell us how to be, how to behave, and that we are right, even "God's chosen people." The Anna myth still functions in these ways, thus helping to keep its sundown policy alive. As late as the 1970s, signs on Route 127 warned, "Nigger, Don't Let the Sun Go Down on You in Anna-Jonesboro," and Anna and Jonesboro still appear to have no black households.

The memory of the rape that triggered the 1912 expulsion from Forsyth County was similarly functioning as an origin myth at least as late as 1987. On January 17 of that year, civil rights leaders from Atlanta marched in the county seat of Forsyth to prove that African Americans had a right to be in the county. They failed: a crowd of more than 500, vastly outnumbering the police officers on hand, pelted the marchers with rocks and bottles. A week later, the civil rights forces numbered 20,000, the counterdemonstrators 1,000, 3,000 police and National Guard members maintained order, and the marchers finished their route. Oprah Winfrey broadcast a live TV show from Forsyth County later in the year. She found the origin myth still very much alive in the minds of some of the residents who attended. One woman said,

> I've been here all my life. I have—my family goes back four generations. . . . And I have a fear of black—I did have a fear of black people. And the only reason was because the girl that got killed back in 1912 is related to me.

The incident was still current, still troubling this woman 75 years later. Another member of the audience brought the fear of African Americans to the present in a more general form: "If niggers come in here, it's going to be like Decatur [Georgia], DeKalb County, Fulton County, Atlanta. It's going to be nothing but a slum area."[43]

In some sundown towns, the origin myth has become coupled with an object or location that keeps it salient today. To this day, adolescents in Anna go in groups to pay their respects to Anna Pelley's tombstone (Portfolio 6)— sort of a rite of passage that keeps vivid and justifies Anna's all-white nature to the next generation. Other towns have "hanging trees" that remind residents what happened to the last African American who wandered within the city limits. Smokey Crabtree, a longtime resident of Fouke, a sundown town in western Arkansas, used a lighthearted tone in 2001 to convey his amusement at Fouke's sundown policy and the symbol that helps to maintain it:

> As far back as the late twenties colored people weren't welcome in Fouke, Arkansas to live, or to work in town. The city put up an almost life sized chalk statue of a colored man at the city limit line, he had an iron bar in one hand and was pointing out of town with the other hand. The city kept the statue painted and dressed, really taking good care of it. Back in those days colored people were run out of Fouke, one was even hung from a large oak tree, and there's a tree that is still referred to as the hanging tree. The man was hung with a necktie and a red handkerchief; a five-dollar bill was sticking out of his pocket for any person wanting to bury the man. The story was that the man had come into Fouke, committed rape among other things, was apprehended and hung. Justice was served. The original "hanging tree" died of natural causes back in the mid sixties. The story has been passed on to another tree that could easily be mistaken for the original tree. My guess is that Fouke will always have a "hang-

ing tree," the name being passed down from one tree to another, keeping the story alive.

Similar stories about hanging trees are in the folklore in Fairfield, Illinois; Crossville, Tennessee; Robbinsville, North Carolina; and other towns. Just as the trees become mythical, so perhaps have the crimes. And just as the trees keep the stories alive, so the stories keep the policy alive.[44]

Towns with strong and extant origin myths seem harder to "crack" than towns that "merely" passed an ordinance or expelled their African Americans as part of a wave of such actions or that have lost their memory of when and why they went sundown. Origin myths that locate a town's anti-black policy in labor conflict seem particularly long-lived. While the punishment—total banning of the race from then on—may be severe, at least a substantial part of the out-group committed the strikebreaking offense, and committed it against "us," the white community, or at least a sizable proportion of it. This may explain why residents of towns with such origin myths seem uncommonly forthcoming about their policy. Origin myths about "black scabs" may also encourage residents to be especially racist toward the next African American who ventures in. Certainly some towns whose origin myths involve black strikebreakers have been particularly vicious toward African Americans for decades afterward. For example, both Pana and Carterville, Illinois, went beyond becoming sundown towns[45] to prohibit blacks from shopping during the daytime as well.

Historical Contingency: The Influence of a Single Individual

Although the underlying factors discussed in the previous chapter—political history, ethnic makeup, and labor relations—helped to explain which communities went sundown, they did not determine the outcome. Neither did the catalysts described in this chapter. Individuals also made a difference. Thus historical contingency inevitably came into play.

Even after an interracial rape, an interracial claim for equality, or another form of catalyst, the actions of one person who tries to start—or sometimes stop—a mob can make all the difference. Sociologists who study mass behavior know that crowds go through a period of indecision while they test their own willingness to go further and become a purposeful mob. Then there is usually a further testing process: members mill about, individuals shout out suggestions, and would-be leaders take tentative steps and gauge the reaction of the rest. Comanche County, Texas, embodied the process in the 1880s. It had 8,600 people, including 79 African Americans. Unfortunately for all of the latter, on July 24, 1886, an African American named Tom McNeal allegedly killed a white farm woman, Sallie Stephens.[46] He was captured the next day, and taken to the farm and hanged by a lynch mob the day after. Comanche County historian Eulalia Wells describes how one man influenced what happened next:

> While he dangled, a certain man climbed upon a large stump and spoke: "Boys, this is the second killing of white people by Negroes and it's more than the people will put up with. I propose we give the Negroes a reasonable time to get out of the county—never allow them to return, and never allow one of color to settle here."

According to Billy Bob Lightfoot, a Comanche County native who wrote a master's thesis on its history, that "certain man" was Green Saunders, who proceeded to denounce African Americans as "by nature evil." Following his suggestion, the mob then rounded up the African American community in nearby De Leon and ordered them "to come out and bury the corpse," in Lightfoot's words. The crowd then gave the blacks who were burying McNeal's body "the warning to pack up and get out within ten days or be killed. Take what they could, leave what could not be sold or carried, but be across the county line by sunset on August 6, 1886." That evening the mob visited every black resident in Comanche County with the same message. Whites posted a sign at the train station in De Leon: "Nigger, Don't Let the Sun Set on Your Head in This Town." Armed white vigilantes then went door-to-door throughout Comanche County. The expulsion was followed by "a lucrative business in souvenirs carried on by an itinerant peddler who sold 'authentic remains of the last Negro buried in Comanche County and pieces of the rope used to hang him with!' through the county as late as 1889," according to Lightfoot. Comanche County then kept out African Americans— and possibly Mexican Americans—for more than a century, but had Saunders not spoken, or had he been a force for tolerance, another outcome might have ensued.[47]

What if just one person had voted differently in Hermann, Missouri? Then Hermann would have admitted black children to its school, which would have put it on a trajectory toward equal rights for African Americans rather than a descent into policies of racial exclusion. Similarly, we have seen that Sheridan, Arkansas, was poised to make the progressive decision to desegregate its schools. Then, owing to the energy, wealth, and racism of one man, it flipflopped and got rid of its entire African American population.

One individual cannot carry the issue without at least some support from a larger public, however. Having it both ways, the same whites in Wyandotte who blamed the bad behavior of African Americans for their 1916 expulsion also condemned the leader of the riot, one Carl Juchartz, "a town character of irresponsible actions and mental capacity unable to even formulate good speaking English." Certainly some individuals are more racist than others, and I'm sure Juchartz led the way. No other whites stopped him, however, and many joined in. The key question is, do those whites willing to keep out African Americans sense that they have at least tacit backing from the police and public? If they do, it only takes a few of them, unfettered by others, to create or maintain a town's racist reputation.[48]

Contingency Again: The Positive Influence of an Individual

Two adjacent articles in the June 17, 1902, *New York Times* show how individuals can cause similar events to lead to very different outcomes, outcomes that then persist for decades. The first is headlined "Bitter Race War Threatened":

> French Lick and West Baden and the valley in which the two famous Indiana health resorts are located bid fair to furnish the next scene of Indiana lawlessness. Both places and the entire length of the valley are threatened with a race war more vicious and more bitter than any that has occurred in the State within the last ten or fifteen years.
>
> Already, reports from the two resorts state, whites have posted notices ordering the Negroes to make a hasty evacuation. The notices, tacked to trees and placed in conspicuous places about the grounds of the two prominent hotels, are adorned with skull and crossbone decorations, underneath which is written the ultimatum. All the waiters at the hostelries have received letters, some signed by the words "White Cap," . . . declaring that if they do not take their departure at once they will be horsewhipped. Some, in fact, were threatened with death. The Negroes are terror-stricken, and many have already obeyed the injunction. Many others, however, having been assured protection, are remaining at their posts.

Immediately below this story, another dispatch, "Race War in Illinois," tells of a similar event 125 miles west, in southeastern Illinois:

> Another attack was made last night on the home of the Rev. Peter Green, pastor of the African Methodist Church at Eldorado. The crowd told Mr. Green to leave town in 24 hours, under penalty of death. He defied the mob and stood at his gate with a shotgun, threatening to shoot the first man who molested him.
>
> The anti-Negro crusade has at last aroused the respectable white element, and an effort will be made to induce the colored people to reopen the Normal and Industrial School.[49]

Eldorado did force out its black preacher and all his congregation, and the school never reopened, "the respectable white element" to the contrary. No governing official, from the town through the county to the state, took any action. According to Robyn Williams, a nearby teacher, Eldorado sported a sundown sign until the 1980s. In about 1990, according to someone who was then a resident, a white couple in Eldorado who adopted a biracial child "had sewage thrown on their lawn" and other problems and left town shortly thereafter.[50]

The next paragraph in the French Lick article, in contrast, tells that the governor has instructed his secretary "to notify him immediately upon receipt of any startling information from the valley." Perhaps for that reason, forced eviction of African Americans from the French Lick area did not take place, and French Lick and West Baden Springs have African American populations to this day.[51]

Another public official who did the right thing was Governor Arthur Weaver of Nebraska. In Lincoln in 1929, a mob of whites drove 200 African Americans from the city after a white policeman was shot. Weaver ordered "that those persons driven out must be permitted to return, and that if any further difficulties ensued, martial law would be instituted." Lincoln stayed interracial.[52]

Business leaders could also make a difference. Bronson, in east Texas, expelled its blacks in 1914; only recently, according to Thad Sitton and James H. Conrad, authors of a fine 1998 study of Texas sawmill towns, were African Americans even allowed to *work* at the Bronson sawmill. In Diboll, on the other hand, 40 miles west, the mill owner, T.L.L. Temple, did not want the word *nigger* spoken, and it wasn't; Diboll remained an interracial town. In Call, Texas, the Ku Klux Klan sent notices to the African American barber and the black dance hall operator in the 1920s telling them to leave town. The management of the local sawmill responded by firing some Klansmen, and Call never drove out its African Americans.[53]

Somewhere between 1870 and 1890, John Hay, Abraham Lincoln's secretary during the Civil War, wrote a poem whose full title is "Banty Tim (Remarks of Sergeant Tilmon Joy to the White Man's Committee of Spunky Point, Illinois)." In it, Hay imagines a meeting of Democrats proposing to expel Spunky Point's sole African American, Banty Tim, to create a sundown town. One white man, Tilmon Joy, faces them down, preventing a mob from forming and preserving Spunky Point as interracial. Excerpts follow:

> I reckon I git your drift, gents—
> You 'low the boy sha'n't stay;
> This is a white man's country;
> You're Dimocrats, you say . . .
>
> Why, blame your hearts, jest hear me!
> You know that ungodly day
> When our left struck Vicksburg Heights, how ripped
> And torn and tattered we lay . . .
>
> Till along toward dusk I seen a thing
> I couldn't believe for a spell:
> That nigger—that Tim—was a crawlin' to me
> Through that fireproof, gild-edged hell!
>
> The Rebels seen him as quick as me,
> And the bullets buzzed like bees;
> But he jumped for me, and shouldered me,
> Though a shot brought him once to his knees;
>
> But he staggered up, and packed me off,
> With a dozen stumbles and falls,
> Till safe in our lines he drapped us both,
> His black hide riddled with balls.
>
> So, my gentle gazelles, that's my answer,
> And here stays Banty Tim:
> He trumped Death's ace for me that day,
> And I'm not goin' back on him!

Hay got several things right, including the white supremacy of the Democrats and the anti-racist idealism stemming from shared experience in the Civil War.[54]

After World War II, a latter-day Tilmon Joy popped up in New York City in the form of ex-GI Leo Miller. On the East Side, Metropolitan Life had just opened Stuyvesant Town, a huge housing project for returning veterans. Miller was outraged that Met Life excluded black veterans. "The courage and sharp shooting of a Negro machine-gunner saved my life with a dozen other white GIs" in the Battle of the Bulge, he pointed out. "Can any one of us who live in Stuyvesant Town say he may not be my neighbor? I can't." Met Life threatened to evict Miller and other white residents who protested its policy, and even after New York City passed a law in 1951 forbidding racial discrimination in "publicly assisted private housing" such as Stuyvesant Town, the company refused to accept applications from blacks, but eventually Miller and his allies won.[55]

One man also stood up to the Roosevelt administration in Boulder City, Nevada, one of the eight sundown towns built by the federal government during the Depression. Clarence Newland, owner of the Green Hut restaurant, hired McKinley Sayles, African American, whose pies were "the best you could buy anywhere in the state of Nevada," in the estimation of Boulder City resident Robert Parker. Townspeople complained to Sims Ely, the czar of the town under the Roosevelt administration, and Ely told Newland to get rid of Sayles.[56] According to Parker, Newland replied, "As long as that Green Hut belongs to me, you're not telling me who to hire and fire around here."[57]

Maybe behind many an interracial town lies a white person—or several—who stopped a threatened eviction, which, because it did not happen, is now lost to history. I know no way to recover the memory of such events and no way to predict where and when such leaders will occur. We have gone about as far as we can in explaining why certain towns across America went sundown, while others did not.

In some towns, whites failed to stop wholesale evictions but did intercede on behalf of an individual person of color. When white residents of Eureka, California, evicted their Chinese population in 1885, eventually only one Chinese American man, Charley Moon, was left in Humboldt County.[58] When a group of Eureka residents came to Tom Bair's Redwood Creek Ranch to take his ranch hand, Bair reportedly stood in the road with a gun and told them that they would have to take him first; the men turned around and left. Moon then worked on the Bair ranch for years and "was well liked and respected"; according to historian Lynwood Carranco, "nobody molested him." James Wilson likewise protected Alecta Smith when whites drove all other African Americans from Harrison, Arkansas, in 1905 and 1909. According to oral history summarized by David Zimmermann, "Wilson met the mob at his door with a shotgun and told them no one in his home was going to be hurt." Another white man in Harrison, George Cotton, didn't go that far, but he did help his black porter escape to safety during the riot, according to - Cotton's grandson. Cotton put "Nigger George" in his buggy at midnight and took him to Eureka Springs—a twelve-hour buggy ride.[59]

One man also helped to soften the 1918 expulsion of African Americans from Unicoi County, Tennessee, on the North Carolina line. Like so many other expulsions, this one began with an interracial assault. African American Tom Devert allegedly grabbed a white teenage girl a mile and a half from Erwin, the county seat.[60] Four nearby whites interceded, shooting Devert as he tried to swim across the Nolichucky River with the girl. Whites then tied Devert's body to a locomotive and dragged it back to Erwin. A large mob gathered, and the entire black population, between 60 and 70 people, was forced to watch as his body was burned. A reporter for the *Bristol Herald* paints a dramatic scene:

> Men with pistols, shotguns, and clubs stood before the lined up Negroes to prevent their running away, and as the last cross tie and the last dash of oil was thrown on the heap one of the men is reported to have turned to the cowering crowd and said, "Watch what we are going to do here. If any of you are left in town by tomorrow night, you will meet the same fate."

Whites would have burned down the black part of Erwin that night "but were dissuaded by General Manager L. H. Phettaplace of the C. C. & O. Railway," according to the account published in the nearby *Johnson City Daily*. Erwin and Unicoi County went all-white the next day, but Phettaplace may have saved some lives that riotous night. Jon Voight's character in John Singleton's film *Rosewood*, who helps several African Americans escape from the white riot that destroyed the black community of Rosewood, Florida, is based on a similar person who in fact existed.[61]

"A movie should be made of the experience of the Braden and Wade families in 1954. Carl and Anne Braden bought a house in Shively, a sundown suburb of Louisville, Kentucky, and resold it to Andrew and Charlotte Wade, a black couple. Just past midnight on June 27, a dynamite blast wrecked half of the Wade's house. Although the police had a confession, no one was ever charged with the crime. Instead, the prosecutor arrested the Bradens and claimed the bombing was Communist plot! Carl Braden was found guilty of sedition, sentenced to fifteen years, and served seven months in jail before his conviction was overturned on appeal."[62]

This chapter and its precedessor, on sociological causation, are first attempts to address why sundown towns came into being. No one has ever tried to answer such questions before. Everything about sundown towns—that the absence of African Americans was involuntary, how widespread they have been, even the origin myths their residents told themselves—has been mystified and left out of history books over the years. The next chapter tells of that mystification. It explains how most Americans came to be ignorant about even the sheer fact of their existence. It also summarizes the methods I used, so you can assess my claims to have proven that these towns do exist and were all-white on purpose.

8

Hidden in Plain View: Knowing and Not Knowing About Sundown Towns

Local persons giving quotes to the newspaper should be more careful in the wording of such statements to prevent misinterpretation. . . . The Chamber, through this committee, [shall] keep a close watch on future news reporting and take any appropriate action should further detriment to the City of Rogers be detected.

—Report of Rogers, Arkansas, Chamber of Commerce after the Rogers
newspaper stated in 1962 that Rogers was a sundown town[1]

BARRING AN OCCASIONAL NEWS STORY about an individual all-white town—typically treated as an anomaly—America's independent sundown towns, numbering in the thousands, have mostly escaped notice until now. Even the origin myths that whites used to explain such towns' racial policies rarely got written down. Sundown suburbs, equally plentiful and concentrated around major cities, could not escape notice, but their whiteness was often dismissed as "natural," resulting from market forces. As I tell audiences how sundown towns and suburbs were created, sometimes they gasp audibly, astonished to learn that there are so many sundown towns and suburbs, that these towns were created intentionally, often by violent means, and sometimes that they themselves live in one.

White residents do know the racial composition of their town, of course; it may even be a reason why they chose to move there. But most haven't thought about *how* it came to be so white; it just seemed natural. Afterward, audience members often come up to tell me that their town or suburb is all-white or was until recently. Now they are curious: could it be that way on purpose? As one person from a sundown town near Champaign, Illinois, put it: "How naive I was growing up! I was in a sundown town and had no clue until now. Sad!"[2]

Knowing and Not Knowing About Sundown Towns

White Americans encounter sundown towns every day but rarely think about them or even realize that they're in one. They look like other towns, especially to most non-black people, who often don't notice the difference between 95% white and 100% white. Motorists driving through Anna, Illinois, might stop to see its famous library, designed in 1913 by Walter Burley Griffith, the Prairie School architect who went on to design Canberra, Australia. Or they might be visiting a mentally ill relative in the Illinois State Hospital. They don't notice that Anna is a sundown town unless they know to ask. Most sundown towns and suburbs are like that: invisible, until a black wayfarer appears and the townspeople do something about it.

At the same time, whites have nicknames for many overwhelmingly white towns: "Colonial Whites" for Colonial Heights, near Richmond, Virginia; "the White Shore" across the Susquehanna River from Harrisburg, Pennsylvania, instead of the West Shore; "Caucasian Falls" for Cuyahoga Falls near Akron, Ohio; "Whiteface Bay" for Whitefish Bay, north of Milwaukee; and so forth across the country to "Lily White Lynwood" outside Los Angeles. Whites make up jokes about the consequences of an African American being found after dark in many sundown towns and suburbs. "Even the squirrels are white in Olney" is a quip about a sundown town in southeastern Illinois known also for its albino squirrels.[3] Such nicknames and jokes show that the whiteness of these towns has registered; whites do understand that the absence of blacks is no accident. Residents of a metropolitan area also know which suburbs are said to be the whitest and which police departments have a reputation for racial profiling. The practice of stopping and questioning African Americans in Darien, Connecticut, for example, was "an open secret in town," according to Gregory Dorr, who grew up there. Nevertheless, when told that many American towns and suburbs kept out African Americans for decades and some still do, often these same individuals claim to be shocked.[4]

Perhaps it is more accurate to say that white Americans know and don't know about sundown towns. This curious combination of knowing and not knowing seems eerily reminiscent of Europe, 1938–45: surely Germans (and Poles, French, Dutch, etc.) knew that Jewish and Romany people were being done away with—their houses and apartments were becoming vacant and available before their very eyes, after all. Yet many professed shock when told about it afterward. I do not claim that America's rash of sundown towns is a Holocaust. The murdered probably total fewer than 2,000 and the refugees fewer than 100,000, nothing like the fury the Nazis unleashed upon Jewish and Rom people. Yet there is a parallel question: why have so few white Americans ever heard of sundown towns, even when they live in one?

The preface tells of my reception in Indiana after my 2006 article about Greensburg's sundown town history. In 2013 to 2015, that issue still reverberated, prompting rebuttals by Pat Smith, columnist in the *Greensburg Daily News*. I had written, "In 1906 [sic], Greensburg's white residents drove out most of its black population." Smith replied, "That did not happen. Why do a few people want to believe the worst about us?" She emphasized that the 1907 stories about Greensburg's riot appeared in "non-local" newspapers. What would we make of a German who wrote today about Kristallnacht, "Why do a few people want to believe the worst about us?" Let me add quickly that the *Daily News* printed a rebuttal to Smith by resident John Vanderbur, including a detailed account of the riot. Other Greensburg natives detailed more recent practices and comments, including "Mayor Ryle," mayor in the late 1970s: "I always instructed the officers to send them out of town, it has been the last several mayors who have allowed them to stay."[5]

The Unsuspecting Researcher

It is all too easy to overlook the sundown nature of an all-white town. I know, because I too was oblivious. Until doing the research for this book, I never noticed most sundown towns. Being white myself and having grown up in an all-white neighborhood, I took most all-white neighborhoods, towns, and even counties for granted, assuming that African Americans simply happened not to live in them. Indeed, the biggest mistake I have ever made in print was about sundown towns, and I made it in my most recent book, *Lies Across America*. In an essay comparing three Arkansas counties, I commended Grant County for being "most hospitable of the three for African Americans." *I did not notice that Sheridan, seat of Grant County, was a sundown town!* When I was there (too briefly!) in 1996,[6] about 400 African Americans lived in the county, but whites did not allow them to spend the night in the county seat.[7]

Having learned during *this* research that Sheridan was a sundown town during my previous visit, having confirmed that more than 30 other towns and counties in Arkansas excluded African Americans, having identified 50 more as likely suspects, and having found some 472 probable all-white towns in Illinois alone, I now see how naive *I* was.

American Culture Typically Locates Racism in the South

How could we Americans have been so ignorant of sundown towns for so long? Even if we grew up in a place with few sundown towns nearby—Mississippi, for example—how could we not have known that so many thousands of sundown towns formed elsewhere in the United States? After all, students in New Hampshire know about slavery. Why isn't knowledge of sundown towns part of our living historical tradition?

Our culture teaches us to locate overt racism long ago (in the nineteenth century) or far away (in the South) or to marginalize it as the work of a few crazed deviants who carried out their violent works under cover of darkness. Most high school American history textbooks downplay slavery in the North, so from the start race relations seems to be a sectional rather than national problem. Research shows that white eleventh graders before *and after* taking U.S. history viewed only white southerners as the dominant actors in U.S. racial oppression. American literature likewise puts most overt racism in the South, not the North. In her memoir *I Know Why the Caged Bird Sings,* Maya Angelou characterizes Mississippi with the phrase "Don't Let the Sun Set on You Here, nigger, Mississippi." Tennessee Williams has the sheriff in *Orpheus Descending,* also set in Mississippi, make a similar reference. But Angelou and Williams would have been more accurate had they used the phrase to characterize California or Ohio. William Burroughs makes the same blunder of locating his sundown town in the South in *Naked Lunch.* Malcolm Ross, a member of the Fair Employment Practices Commission during World War II, recognized Calhoun County, Illinois, as a sundown county in his memoir, *All Manner of Men;* astonishingly, Ross then went on to talk about "the white boys from Calhoun County, and a hundred other counties of the South." Calhoun County is just 65 miles southwest of Springfield, the capital; it's not even in southern Illinois. As recently as 2002, Jerrold Packard repeats this stereotype: in *American Nightmare: The History of Jim Crow,* he writes, "Some all-white *Southern* towns" placed sundown signs at their city limits.[8] Actually, among the 184 towns that had sundown signs to my knowledge, only 7 were in the traditional South, along with another 52 in places like the Cumberlands and the Ozarks; 125 were northern and western.

Hollywood perpetuates this stereotype. In *The Fugitive Kind,* the sheriff in a small southern town tells Marlon Brando about a nearby town with a sign saying, "Nigger, Don't Let the Sun Go Down on You in This County." He goes on to say, "Now this ain't that town, and you ain't that nigger, but imagine a sign saying, 'Boy, Don't Let the Sun Rise on You in This County!' "[9] *Sudie and Simpson,* a 1984 film starring Louis Gosset Jr., is set in 1940s Georgia. The local town, Linlow, is shown to have a sign: "Nigger!! Don't Let the Sun Set on You in Linlow." Actually, the sundown syndrome does afflict six counties in Appalachian north Georgia, but otherwise Georgia is almost free of the phenomenon. Danny Glover's 2000 made-for-TV film *Freedom Song,* an otherwise accurate portrayal of the Mississippi Civil Rights Movement, shows a sign saying, "Nigger, Read and Run / If You Can't Read, Run Anyway." Signs with that wording indeed (dis)graced many sundown towns, but none in Mississippi. Meanwhile, in northern locations where black exclusion actually happened, Hollywood covers it up. Take *Grosse Pointe Blank,* for example, a 1997 John Cusack vehicle. This film not only fails to tell that Grosse Pointe was all-white on purpose throughout the era it depicts, it inserts a black alumnus or two into the major character's high school reunion. *Hoosiers,* a 1986 basketball movie starring Gene Hackman, similarly obfuscates the racial reality of 1950s small-town Indiana. As one Indiana resident wrote in 2002, "All southern Hoosiers laughed at the movie called *Hoosiers* because the movie depicts blacks playing basketball and sitting in the stands at games in Jasper. We all agreed no blacks were permitted until probably the '60s and do not feel welcome today." A cheerleader for a predominantly white but interracial Evansville high school tells of having rocks thrown at their school bus as they sped out of Jasper after a basketball game in about 1975, more than twenty years after the events depicted so inaccurately in *Hoosiers.* I know of only one film treatment of residential exclusion[10] and no image of a sundown sign in any movie set in a northern locale.[11]

Placing a sundown sign in fictional Linlow is one of the ways Hollywood connotes southernness, and Tennessee Williams, Danny Glover, and Maya Angelou may have followed the same convention. It's too easy, though, and it's inaccurate. Placing sundown towns in Dixie where they don't occur only encourages Americans to overlook them in the North where they do. In the North, whites don't expect to see such overt racism, so they don't. In her autobiography *My Lord, What a Morning,* Marian Anderson goes along with this convention. She tells of staying in some hotels that made an exception for her, since she was performing in the town's fine-arts series, but would not house any other African Americans. But she speaks only on the South in this regard. This simply does not describe the facts of her accommodations. On many occasions she could not stay the night in white hotels in the North. In northern sundown towns, she could not stay anywhere, even in private homes. Anderson's autobiography never hints at any problem in the North, however. She even tells how Albert Einstein put her up in Princeton without ever mentioning that he volunteered to do so after the only hotel in town said no. Perhaps she didn't want to alienate white northerners who might be potential allies to change southern segregation. The Civil Rights Movement also picked on the "legally" segregated South for the same reason, as Scott Malcomson points out: it made a better target. Ironically, although the NAACP itself was born in the aftermath of the 1908 attempt by white residents to drive all African Americans from Springfield, Illinois, it rarely attacked sundown towns in the North or even acknowledged that they existed.[12]

Even within northern states, whites assume the southern or backward sections have the sundown towns. Literally scores of Illinois residents have said, "Oh, yes, in *southern* Illinois," when they learn what I am studying. "Yes," I reply, "and central Illinois, and northern Illinois, and especially the Chicago and Peoria suburbs." They are shocked. The guidebook to a 1995–97 exhibit at the Indiana State Historical Museum, *Indiana in the Civil War,* came to the same easy conclusion for that state: "Some small towns and rural areas, especially in southern Indiana, developed reputations for hostility and intimidation, causing blacks residing there to leave and discouraging newcomers." Certainly that happened in southern Indiana, but similar intimidation and hostility were also visited upon African Americans in small towns and rural areas around Indianapolis, in the northeast quarter of the state, and just south of Lake Michigan, resulting in sundown towns just about everywhere. Pennsylvania residents aren't surprised to learn that very rural areas such as Warren and Potter Counties are all-white, perhaps on purpose, but are shocked to see the number of all-white towns in the densely settled river valleys of eastern Pennsylvania.[13]

The lack of concern our society pays to racism in the North can also be seen in our culture's stress on lynching as a topic of study, rather than sundown towns, and its particular attention to Southern lynchings. Most studies of lynchings focus solely on the South. The databases themselves show this bias: the principal list, from Tuskegee Institute, includes only nine Southern states (those that seceded, minus Virginia and Texas) plus Kentucky, and Project HAL (Historic American Lynchings), whose list of lynchings some consider the most complete, also includes only the same ten states. Yet controlling for the smaller size of the black population outside the South, lynchings were recorded about as often in Ohio, Kentucky, Indiana, Illinois, and California as in Southern states. Indeed, we simply have no idea how many lynchings occurred in the Midwest or Northeast because of scholars' concentration on the South. Certainly three of the most famous lynching photographs come from the Midwest—Omaha in 1919, the triple hanging in

Duluth in 1919, and the twin hangings in Marion, Indiana, in 1930. The result of this overemphasis is an inability of Northern scholars to perceive the racism in their own communities, at least before African Americans moved north in the Great Migration that began around 1915. Even as late as the Civil Rights Movement in the 1960s, the South has simply been viewed as the venue where race relations played out in America.[14]

Inadvertently, I generate this same mistake in conversation: over and over I tell historians and social scientists about my research, and they assume I'm studying the Deep South. Even when I correct them, the correction often fails to register. I tell a sociologist friend that I've just spent months researching sundown towns in the Midwest. Ten minutes later he has forgotten and again assumes I have been traveling through the South.

A Conspiracy of Silence

Deliberate suppression has also played a role in keeping sundown towns hidden. This seems to be true in Myakka City, Florida, a small town twenty miles inland from Sarasota. By 1920, African Americans had built two churches and made up more than a third of the town's population. "But just 20 years later," according to *Tampa Tribune* reporter Roberta Nelson, writing in 2001, "blacks had vanished from Myakka City." Myakka resident Melissa Sue Brewer wrote, "Myakka City 'historians' have erased all mention of African-Americans." Suppressing the memory was hard because the expulsion apparently took place in the late 1930s, recent enough that oral history can still be done. Nelson interviewed one white woman, Marilyn Coker, who moved to Myakka City when she was eight; her late husband, a Myakka native,

> remembered when the Negroes left, and how upset everyone was about it. The [white] people were upset that they were made to leave town. It was a vigilante kind of thing. Most of the people who lived here were not a part of it. But, all of a sudden, one day they were all gone.

Of course, not all white people were upset; some were the "vigilantes." Other Myakka City old-timers remembered specific African American individuals, such as "Preacher Harper, who was ordered to leave on short notice and denied time to sell off his hogs and chickens." Oral history on the disappeared black community may yet bring the full story to light.[15]

"It just breaks my heart to see my town appear in your book," said a librarian in West Frankfort, Illinois, in 2002, a feeling I heard repeated in many other sundown towns. This sentiment causes many residents who are ashamed to be living in all-white communities to hide the nature of their community from outsiders. Residents of sundown towns who are pleased to be living in all-white communities may not want to talk openly about it either, lest their open racism become the target of legal action or scorn. Either way, residents usually cover up, especially in print. Commemorative histories, in particular, rarely treat embarrassing facts or controversial topics. People don't want to publish anything negative about their own town, especially in the coffee table book that marks its centennial. Consider *One Hundred Years of Progress,* published in 1954 in Anna, Illinois. You will recall that whites in Anna drove out all African Americans in the city in 1909, and the town has been sundown ever since. This 446-page book provides a history of every organization in town, down to the local Dairy Queen. Yet it contains no mention of African Americans, the murder and lynching that led to their banishment, the expulsion itself, their continuing exclusion, or the nickname that confirms Anna's notoriety. These facts are hardly obscure; everyone in town knows them; I confirmed the nickname in my first conversation in the city. Published in the year when the U.S. Supreme Court had just declared segregation illegal, the book can hardly have omitted these facts by accident. The anonymous authors had to have known that to say openly that Anna was now known as "Ain't No Niggers Allowed" would no longer reflect credit on their town.[16]

Only a handful of local histories treat the exclusion of African Americans (or Chinese or Jewish Americans) from their community or county forthrightly. Most—like Anna's—do not. The overt racism that led to sundown suburbs has been especially mystified. In 1961, for example, on the occasion of its 35th anniversary, *Life Newspapers,* serving the west Chicago suburbs, published a 150-page special issue, featuring an article, "Cicero . . . the Best Town in America," that contained not a word about the 1951 race riot that made Cicero nationally notorious. This is all too typical of the publications put out by local newspapers and historical societies. The result is not happy for today's researcher.[17]

One might imagine that priests and preachers might chide their congregations about their un-Christian attitude toward people of color, but clergy, like local historians, avoid controversy by not saying anything bad about their town. In 1960, a Baptist minister in Vandalia, Illinois, told of a nearby town: "When I was pastor in Pinckneyville, they had an unwritten rule that no Negroes should be in town after sundown. No Negro could live in the community." The minister was right about Pinckneyville but ignored the same rule in

Vandalia, where he was living. A still more heroic omission comes in the *Proceedings* produced by the annual Valparaiso University Institute on Human Relations from 1950 to 1968, an interracial Lutheran group that often focused on concerns of race relations—but never in Valparaiso. Valparaiso was a sundown town from at least 1890 until the early 1970s. The 1951 conference passed a resolution about the Cicero, Illinois, riot of that year, condemning Cicero's all-white policy. In later years, the conference printed articles favoring integrated housing, discussed black-white issues in Chicago, Cleveland, and other American cities, and passed resolutions against apartheid in South Africa—but never said a thing about Valparaiso. Even the 1966 conference, "Where You Live," never once mentioned that they were meeting in a sundown town. Yet many speeches and papers were by faculty members and the president of Valparaiso University, who had to know this. For that matter, all participants of color had to be housed on campus because they could not spend the night elsewhere in the city. If the conference and the college had taken a stand *in Valparaiso,* they might have accomplished something. It is not clear that their resolutions had any impact on Cicero, South Africa, or Cleveland. Such studied ignorance has a payoff: one need not do anything. If forced to recognize that they speak in sundown towns, the Pinckneyville minister and Valparaiso professors might feel the need to criticize and try to change their communities. This could be risky: even tenured professors can be let go, and Baptist churches can hire or fire their ministers at any time.[18]

Often residents of sundown towns have gone beyond merely covering up their communities' exclusionary policy to laud their towns as particularly democratic. The centennial history of Pekin, Illinois, published in 1949 by the Pekin Chamber of Commerce, contains this paragraph:

> Pekin has no social divisions. There are no special neighborhoods in Pekin, either social, economic, religious, or racial. It is this Democracy or Near-Equality which frequently first impresses strangers in our city.

Yet Pekin has been notorious as a Klan center ever since the 1920s. It has also long been one of the larger sundown cities in the United States. African Americans across the United States remain in awe of its fearsome reputation even today. In a certain ghoulish sense, the book is accurate, of course. Just as various German cities can boast today that they have no Jewish ghetto, Pekin can brag that it has no black neighborhood. Likewise, in 1942, writing the history of his hometown, Libertyville, an all-white and probably sundown town northwest of Chicago, Lowell Nye said,

> Perhaps the one factor most evident to the newcomer who observes Liber-
> tyville's population is its unusually pure American quality. . . . It is an Ameri-
> can town that is genuinely American; its basic stock can be identified with no
> one nationality. Taken as a whole, it is a happy tolerant society.

In her 1938 autobiography, *A Peculiar Treasure,* novelist Edna Ferber made a similar assertion about Appleton, Wisconsin: "a lovely little town of 16,000 people; tree shaded, prosperous, civilized. Creed, color, race, money—these mattered less in this civilized, prosperous community than in any town I've ever encountered." This is an extraordinary claim about a sundown town. Ferber, who was Jewish, may not have encountered anti-Semitism in Apple-ton, but she could not have failed to notice its complete absence of African Americans, and she had to know that their absence was by design. As histo-rian James Cornelius put it, "When I went to Lawrence University [in 1978], that's one of the first things I learned, that Appleton was a sundown town." "Color, race" made the *key* difference in this "civilized, prosperous commu-nity," and in Pekin, and probably in Libertyville. Surely these authors protest too much.[19]

These exuberant proclamations of equalitarianism in sundown towns ex-emplify not only base hypocrisy but also what sociologists call "herrenvolk democracy"—democracy for the master race. White Americans' verbal com-mitment to nondiscrimination forms one horn of what Swedish economist Gunnar Myrdal famously called "The American Dilemma." Blatant racism forms the other horn. In elite sundown suburbs, this dilemma underlies what we shall later term the "paradox of exclusivity."

Silence on the Landscape

Having written a book on how America's historic sites and historical mark-ers mostly omit or distort embarrassing facts in our past, I was eager to see what the historical markers in sundown towns say about their racial poli-cies. Most say nothing. From west to east: Tacoma, Washington, expelled its Chinese population on November 5, 1883, but the landscape is silent on the matter. Richland, Washington, created by the U.S. government to house workers producing our atomic bombs, was established as a sun-down town and enforced that policy for years, but its landscape is equally silent. Whites drove Chinese Americans from all except a single town in Wyoming, but one cannot learn this on the Wyoming landscape. The ex-tensive state marker for Ste. Genevieve, Missouri, totals more than 300 words, yet never mentions the town's 1930 expulsion of almost all its African Americans. The historical marker for Mariemont, Ohio, a sundown suburb adjoining Cincinnati, states:

> Ground was broken for Mariemont by Mary M. Emery, the village's founder, on April 25, 1923. This planned community was designed by eminent town planner John Nolen and twenty five of America's leading architects. As part of the "garden city movement," Mariemont was influenced by English models. . . .

but contains not a word on Mariemont's policy of exclusion, started by Emery. A Pennsylvania state marker tells of the town of Wehrum, now abandoned, but fails to tell how its white residents forced out all African Americans on a cold February day in 1903; "the Negroes had to find shelter wherever they could," according to a newspaper account. And so it goes, across the nation to Darien, Connecticut, whose glaring lack of candor I critiqued in *Lies Across America*.[20]

I know just four exceptions.[21] Nevada City, California, recently erected a memorial telling of their expulsion of Chinese Americans. An Idaho state historical marker tells of the lynching of five Chinese men in Pierce in 1885 and the expulsion of all other Chinese from that area. A monument in the cemetery of Pierce City, Missouri, commemorates the 200 African Americans killed or driven from that town by white residents in 1901. An indoor exhibit in the museum in Greenbelt, Maryland, admits that Greenbelt was founded during the Depression for whites only, although the town's lengthy historical marker says nothing on the matter.[22] Otherwise, the sundown towns of America, hundreds of which used to boast of their policy with signs and billboards at their corporate limits, now hide that fact on their landscape.[23]

Local Newspapers Don't Say a Thing and Vanish if They Do

Like centennial histories and historical markers, small-town and suburban newspapers like to present only the sunny side of their community to outsiders. Early in the sundown town movement, many communities were so racist that their newspapers happily published full accounts of the actions their white citizens were taking against their African American neighbors, sometimes even including editorial exhortations before the events. Later, after civic leaders realized that these acts might strike outsiders as reprehensible, the accounts sometimes vanished. Harrison, Arkansas, for example, drove out its African Americans in 1905 and 1909. This was no trivial event, according to Jacqueline Froelich and David Zimmermann, whose article is the definitive treatment of these riots:

> The ethnic cleansing of Harrison . . . is arguably the most important event in the town's social history—devastating the lives of those African American citizens for whom Harrison had been home, encouraging the use of violence to force social change and protect local interests, and petrifying the town's approach to race for many years to come.

Nevertheless, despite their importance, or rather because of it, the riots were never talked about in Harrison. "Conspicuously missing from the files of the *Harrison Times* newspaper were issues that were printed near the time of the two events," according to David Zimmermann, who had to reconstruct them from other sources. The same thing happened in Tulsa. During that city's now-notorious 1921 race riot, whites attacked Tulsa's African American community on the ground and from the air: six airplanes dropped dynamite bombs to flatten homes and businesses. As Portfolio 10 shows, rioters made a concerted attempt to drive all African Americans out of Tulsa. Although they failed, they did pull off the largest race riot in American history. Later, the newspapers for the period mysteriously (and now famously) disappeared. The riot became, said one resident, "something everybody knew about but nobody wanted to discuss."[24]

Sometimes coverage was stifled from the start. Jim Woodruff, a resident of Springfield, Illinois, and a student of its 1908 race riot, tells how Springfield's newspapers downplayed the riot in anticipation of the celebration of the one hundredth anniversary of Lincoln's birthday the next year. According to historian Arnold Hirsch, major white riots in Chicago after World War II got very little coverage in that city's newspapers, partly at the behest of the Chicago Commission on Human Relations, which was trying to prevent whites in other neighborhoods from engaging in copycat riots of their own. The riot in suburban Cicero, July 10–12, 1951, did get covered, but not for the first two days. Only after the National Guard was called out on July 12 and after the story made the local TV news did the *Tribune* and *Sun-Times* publish anything about that now infamous event. The advent of television did not end the suppression everywhere, however. In 1972, a realtor who wanted to expose the anti-Semitism of La Jolla, California, had to go to Tijuana, Mexico, to be interviewed, because no San Diego television station would touch the story.[25]

Since then, sundown towns have become still more secretive, as most public officials and newspaper editors have come to realize that a town cannot legally keep out would-be residents on account of race. The newspaper editor of Anna, Illinois, said he had considered doing a story or series of stories on Anna's racial makeup and its history several years ago but had been warned off the topic by local businessmen. Not just omission but denial sometimes results. In 2002, I elicited an apparent example of attempted containment by a small-town paper. I spent a day in Villa Grove, Illinois, south of Champaign-Urbana. As we saw, until recent years Villa Grove had sounded a whistle at 6 PM every evening to warn African Americans to get out of town. My last interview of the day was with the editor of Villa Grove's weekly newspaper. By then, eleven of eleven interviewees had verified that Villa Grove is or at least was a sundown town.[26] Therefore I was blunt:

> "Hello, I'm Jim Loewen. I grew up over in Decatur, and now I'm doing research on all-white towns that are all-white on purpose, including this one."
>
> The editor nodded.
>
> "I understand you have, or used to have until recently, a whistle on your water tower that went off every evening at 6 PM"
>
> "Yes," he agreed.
>
> "Tell me the story about that whistle," I asked.
>
> "I don't know any story about that whistle," he replied.
>
> "OK," I said, and started to make my farewell. Nine of eleven interviewees had already confirmed the story, and I saw no reason to question him further.
>
> As I turned to leave, his secretary asked me, "You mean the story that that was the signal for blacks to be out of town?"
>
> I nodded and replied, "Yes, that story."
>
> "I never heard that story!" she said.[27]

Chambers of Commerce Stifle Coverage

Suppression was general in northern Arkansas. "There is almost a total absence of available written material on the black communities," complained sociologist Gordon Morgan in 1973, trying to write the history of African Americans in the Ozarks. "Some white towns have deliberately destroyed reminders of the blacks who lived there years ago." In Rogers, in northwest Arkansas, the foresighted staff of the Rogers Historical Museum saved evidence of the process of historical repression at work. After the 1962 Fats Domino concerts in Rogers, the *Rogers Daily News* noted this progress in a front-page editorial:

> The city which once had signs posted at the city limits and at the bus and rail terminals boasting "Nigger, You Better Not Let the Sun Set on You in Rogers," was hosting its first top name entertainer—a Negro—at night!

The *Daily News* also ran a front-page news story on the event. The next day, the Rogers Chamber of Commerce called a special meeting of its Publicity and Public Relations Committee. The Chamber called in the reporter and editor of the *Daily News,* the manager of the Victory Theatre, where the concert had taken place, and the chief of police, Hugh Basse, who had been quoted in the news story. The purpose of the meeting was to challenge the newspaper coverage. Singled out for attention was the statement about the signs. The newspaper defended its statement as historically accurate and necessary background for the editorial. The committee contended that the statement was "unnecessary even if a substantiated fact in view of the possible repercussions it might have in the future." [28]

The Rogers Historical Museum obtained and saved the formal two-page "Committee Report" resulting from this meeting. Among its seven conclusions:

- Local persons giving quotes to the newspaper should be more careful in the wording of such statements to prevent misinterpretation.

- The conference with the newspaper representatives was fruitful in that the committee feels a better job of reporting the news will be done.

- A written report [will] be filed with the Board of Directors requesting official Chamber action to bring this matter to the attention of supervisory personnel of the Reynolds chain.

- The Chamber, through this committee, [will] keep a close watch on future news reporting and take any appropriate action should further detriment to the City of Rogers be detected.

The chilling intent is obvious. [29]

Chambers of Commerce still spread disinformation about their towns' sundown policies. A Chamber official in Corbin, Kentucky, a town that drove out its black population in 1919, pretended to be mystified by Corbin's whiteness in the 1991 documentary *Trouble Behind*: "The [African Americans] have chosen to live in either Barbourville, Williamsburg, or north of Clarenton-Corbin . . . but their reasons for that decision—I have no knowledge of that." Certainly Corbin cannot be at fault: "I don't feel there is any more prejudice in Corbin, Kentucky, than you'll find in any other community in the country." This man is intelligent enough to know that other Corbin residents will tell the filmmaker that no African American should move into Corbin, thus exposing the falseness of his statement; in fact, some young white males did just that in other footage in the film. Nevertheless, he thinks it best to dissimulate about Corbin's racism, undoubtedly because it's not good for Corbin's image.[30]

Historical Societies Help to Suppress the Truth

The Rogers Historical Museum is unusual among local historical societies and museums in telling the truth about its community's racist past and saving material that documents that past. The usual response I got when I asked at local libraries, historical societies, and museums if they saved the sundown sign from their community or a photo of it was "Why would we do that?" while they laughed out loud.

Writing historical societies proved particularly useless for most towns. Since I could hardly visit all the probable sundown towns and counties in the United States, I wrote or e-mailed the historical societies in many of them. Unfortunately, like the Chamber of Commerce in Corbin, historical societies don't like to say anything bad about their towns or counties. For example, Shirley De Young, director of the Mower County Historical Society in southern Minnesota, said she had no information confirming Austin and Mower County as sundown communities. Actually, it is common knowledge in Austin that it was sundown from at least 1922 to the 1980s. In 1890, Mower County, of which Austin is the seat, had 36 African Americans, a number surpassed by only six counties in the state. The county then witnessed probably four expulsions of its African Americans: in the late 1890s, shortly before 1920, in 1922 (prompted by a railroad strike, described below), and between 1924 and 1933 (described below). Much later, historian Peter Rachleff studied the famous Hormel strike of 1985–86 in Austin. He wrote:

> It was noticeable that there were exactly two Black workers among the workforce, both of whom were young Africans who had come to the U.S. to attend college and had run out of money. This seemed rather stunning, given the high percentage of African American workers in the meat-packing industry in Omaha, Chicago, KC [Kansas City], etc. When some of us asked about this, union members and retirees recounted a local tale—that in 1922, during the railroad shopmen's strike, a number of African American strikebreakers had

been brought in by rail and housed inside the RR roundhouse. A crowd of strikers, family members, and local supporters laid siege to the roundhouse and the strikebreakers fled for their lives, many of them jumping into the Cedar River and swimming to safety . . . or drowning. No African American had lived in Austin since 1922, we were told.[31]

Thanks to historian Roger Horowitz, who did oral history in Austin, we have a detailed account of Austin's last two expulsions. He taped John Winkols, a veteran labor leader, in 1990.

One time Hormel hired 40 niggers . . . and they put 'em all in the plant at one time.

And at that time, you know, they used to scab, you know. Really not their fault, but the companies that hired them scabbed them. Well, first of all, they hired them when the roundhouses were on strike, they hired a boxcar full of 'em . . .

My cousin was up here, and we went to a dance in town. . . . And so my cousin says, "You want to go over to the roundhouse? We're gonna chase the niggers out of town."

I said, "What'd *they* do?" . . .

And he said, "They're scabbing on the workers in the roundhouse, because they're on strike."

"OK, let's go!" [I] had a piece of shovel handle; we went. . . . We surrounded them at the roundhouse and broke it in and went in to the roundhouse. The sheriff or the cops couldn't do nothing because hell, they were the same as the workers. We went in there and run the niggers out. Hit 'em over the head, you know, and tell them to "get goin"! . . . Albert's Creek runs through there, and some of them run that way, and we was after 'em, chased them, and one of them fell in the creek. He got up on his feet and he says, "Lordy mercy, if I ever gets on my feet again, I'll *never* come in this town again!"

Then Hormel hired them forty. We run *them* out of town . . . somewhere between '24 and '33. . . . After supper we got clubs and went down there and we run *them* out. After that they didn't come in no more, because they knew they couldn't hire them.

After the last expulsion, as his last sentence implied, Austin stayed sundown.[32]

De Young's professed ignorance of what was commonly known in Austin is typical of historical society officials. A high school history teacher in northern Indiana wrote that Hobart, Indiana, still had a sundown sign in the 1970s; three other longtime Hobart residents corroborated that Hobart was a sundown town. One Hobart native told of hearing "of a black family attempting to move in and their car being firebombed" in 1980 or 1981. Nevertheless, Elin Christianson, president of the Hobart Historical Society, wrote, "We have received your letter about your research into 'sundown towns.' We have no documentation that Hobart fits the parameters you describe." The careful reader will note that his statement, the native's, and Norwine's may all be correct—but I had asked Christianson about oral history as well as documents. Moira Meltzer-Cohen, then a resident of Beaver Dam, Wisconsin, did extensive research to confirm Beaver Dam as a sundown town, findings summarized in Chapter 3. She got no help from the historical society: "Unfortunately, when I have approached the historical society and the library about verifying this, they have become defensive and showered me with information about Frederick Douglass" (who once visited Beaver Dam in 1856).[33]

In 2002, Patrick Clark, curator at the Andrew County Museum in northwest Missouri, wrote:

> Fortunately for our county, we should not be listed as a "Sundown Town" for your project. Also, we are not aware of communities in adjacent counties that would be designated as such.

Apparently Clark did not know that Missouri's last spectacle lynching occurred in Maryville, seat of the next county north of Andrew, in 1931. A mob of almost 3,000 whites marched Raymond Gunn, a black man accused of murdering a white schoolteacher, from Maryville to the scene of the crime, 3 miles away. Then they watched as ringleaders chained him "to the ridgepole and burned [him] to death as the schoolhouse itself was consumed," in the words of Arthur Raper's famous book, *The Tragedy of Lynching*. The sheriff permitted the lynching and never arrested anyone. In the aftermath, the huge crowd searched the ashes for teeth and bone fragments and pieces of charred flesh as souvenirs. Then white paranoia set in: rumors swept the town that "a large band of Negroes was moving on Maryville to wreak vengeance for the lynching," in the words of the nearby *St. Joseph Gazette*.[34] This fanciful news "sent Maryville citizens and farmers of the vicinity heavily armed upon the streets . . . late Saturday night." "There was almost a complete exodus of colored people from town following the lynching, and for most of the week they remained away," according to Raper. Whites gave a list of ten African Americans to the black minister "that were branded as undesirable, and he was requested to ask these never to return. This he did." Some whites tried to run all blacks out, but several businessmen refused their demand to fire their janitors, so not all African Americans left immediately. Most did, however, and the black population of Nodaway County, of which Maryville is county seat, fell from 95 in 1930 to 33 ten years later and still fewer thereafter. In 1958, the Maryville Industrial Development Corporation advertised this accomplishment to seek new industries:

> This 8,600 population town and surrounding community possesses an abundant number [*sic*] native born, nigger-free, non-union workers who believe in giving an honest day's work for a day's pay.

"We cannot offer any tax inducements," said Joe Jackson Jr., chair of the corporation, but

> we can offer them all-white contented labor. We don't have any niggers here in Maryville. There may be three or four left in Nodaway County, but all of them are in their 70s and wouldn't be seeking any jobs in the plants. We had to lynch one nigger back in 1931 . . . and the rest of them just up and left. So we've got an all-white town and all-white labor to offer anybody who brings new industry here.

Many members of the crowd of spectators came from surrounding counties, including Andrew County. Andrew County itself then showed a parallel decline in black population, from 42 in 1930 to 33 in 1940 and 5 by 1960. Moreover, Albany, seat of Gentry County, which adjoins Andrew County to the northeast, "maintained as part of the city code a rule that said blacks couldn't spend the evening in the town," according to a native of Albany. As far as I can ascertain, Gentry County has not had a single black household since at least 1930 and still doesn't. Yet Patrick Clark of the Andrew County Museum is "not aware of communities in adjacent counties" that kept out African Americans. Surely he is in denial.[35]

A recent published example of the problem comes from Chittenden County, Vermont. In 2003, Sylvia Smith wrote an entire article on Mayfair Park, a residential subdivision of South Burlington, Vermont, for the *Chitten-*

den County Historical Society Bulletin. In it she treats at length "protective covenants, which met required objectives of the Federal Housing Administration for the protection of the subdivision." She tells how they "established strict limits on sizes of lots, buildings, and setbacks." She goes on to quote "covenants pertaining to 'quality of life' concerns," which she believes are "of interest in present times," such as:

> No noxious or offensive trade or activity shall be carried on upon any lot nor should anything be done thereon which may become an annoyance or nuisance to the neighborhood. . . . No dwelling costing less than $3,500 shall be permitted on any lot in the tract. These covenants shall run with the land.

The ellipsis in the above quotation indicates a passage left out, of course. That passage was, in substantial part:

> No persons of any race other than the white race shall use or occupy any building or any lot, except that this covenant shall not prevent occupancy by domestic servants of a different race domiciled with an owner or tenant.

Precisely this missing sentence makes the covenant "restrictive" rather than merely "protective." Smith later tells that in 1951 a "vote was taken to eliminate and revoke the restrictive covenants," but she never mentions what these were. Only those few readers who already know that Mayfair Park was all-white on purpose can possibly understand what was undone in 1951.[36]

Absent from the History Books

Academic historians have long put down what they call "local history," deploring its shallow boosterism. But silence about sundown towns is hardly confined to local historians; professional historians and social scientists have also failed to notice them. Most Americans—historians and social scientists included—like to dwell on good things. Speaking to a conference of social studies teachers in Indiana, Tim Long, an Indiana teacher, noted how this characteristic can mislead:

> Today if you ask Hoosiers, "How many of you know of an Underground Railroad site in Indiana?" everyone raises their hands. "How many of you know of a Ku Klux Klan member in Indiana?" Few raise their hands. Yet Indiana had a million KKK members and few abolitionists.

The same holds for sundown towns: Indiana had many more sundown towns after 1890 than it had towns that helped escaping slaves before 1860. Furthermore, Indiana's sundown towns kept out African Americans throughout most of the twentieth century, some of them to this day, while its towns that aided slaves did so for about ten years a century and a half ago. Nevertheless, historians, popular writers, and local historical societies in Indiana have spent far more time researching and writing about Underground Railroad sites than sundown towns. The Underground Railroad shows us at our best. Sundown towns show us at our worst.[37]

Authors have written entire books on sundown towns without ever mentioning their racial policies.[38] I am reminded of the Hindi scene of the elephant in the living room: everyone in the room is too polite to mention the elephant, but nevertheless, it dominates the living room. Some city planners seem particularly oblivious to race. Karl Lohmann wrote *Cities and Towns of Illinois* in 1951, when most of them were all-white on purpose, but never mentioned a word about race. Instead, he made various uninteresting generalizations, such as that several towns had lakes. Gregory Randall wrote an entire monograph on one sundown suburb of Chicago, Park Forest, which later famously desegregated, but although he grew up in the suburb and also was conversant with research that candidly stated its sundown policy, he claims not to know for sure that Park Forest was all-white by design.[39] Long before he wrote in 2000, Park Forest had desegregated successfully, but Randall cannot tell that story, having never let on that it had been sundown. Randall also treats at length "the Greens"—Greenbelt, Maryland; Greenhills, Ohio; and Greendale, Wisconsin—yet never mentions that all three were founded as sundown towns. In *Toward New Towns for America,* C. S. Stein similarly whitewashes the Greens; Radburn, New Jersey; and several other planned communities.[40]

Two anthropologists, Carl Withers and Art Gallaher, each wrote an entire book on Wheatland, Missouri, a sundown town in a sundown county. Gallaher never mentioned race, and Withers's entire treatment is one sentence in a footnote, "However, no Negroes live now in the county." Penologist James Jacobs wrote "The Politics of Corrections" about the correctional center in Vienna, Illinois, but even though its subtitle focused upon "Town/Prison Relations," he never mentioned that Vienna was a sundown town, while most of the prisoners were black and Latino. This pattern of evasion continues: most entries on sundown suburbs in the *Encyclopedia of Chicago,* for instance, published in 2004, do not mention their striking racial composition, let alone explain how it was achieved. Romeoville, Illinois, for example, went sundown after a deadly battle between black and white workers on June 8,

1893, and stayed that way until the 1970s, but the entry on Romeoville is silent on the matter. Worse yet, the entry on Berwyn blandly says, "While Berwyn's Czech heritage retained its importance, increasing ethnic diversity further tested the city." Considering that Berwyn famously kept African Americans out as recently as 1992, this is another whitewash.[41]

Journalists, too, have dropped the ball. We have seen how business interests sometimes stop local newspapers from saying anything bad about a town. Propensities within journalism also minimize coverage of racial exclusion. Occasionally a race riot or a heinous crime relates to sundown towns and has caused the topic to become newsworthy. The 1908 race riot in Springfield, Illinois, prompted newspapers to note the sundown nature of nearby towns because African Americans driven from Springfield found no refuge in them. A murder brought media attention to Vidor, an east Texas sundown town with a long history of Klan activity and sundown signs. Under court order, Vidor had admitted four black households to its public housing units in 1992, but by 1993, Ku Klux Klan demonstrations and other threats forced out the last African American, William Simpson. When he was gunned down in nearby Beaumont by a young black man on the night after he moved out of Vidor, the irony prompted several news stories about Vidor. But attention waned after the murder; seven years later, Vidor had just a single black household, made up of two persons, among its 11,440 inhabitants in the 2000 census. Reporters for the *New Yorker* and *People* covered the 2002 arrest of the man who killed African American Carol Jenkins for being in Martinsville, Indiana, after dark, but the result was to demonize Martinsville as distinctive. As a result, I could not get an official of the Indiana Historical Bureau to address how general sundown towns might be in Indiana; instead, she repeated, "Martinsville is an entity unto itself—a real redneck town." But Martinsville is not unusual. For the most part, precisely what is so alarming about sundown towns—their astonishing prevalence across the country—is what has made them *not* newsworthy, except on special occasions. Murders sell newspapers. Chronic social pathology does not.[42]

Journalism has been called the "first draft of history," and the lack of coverage of sundown towns in the press, along with the reluctance of local historians to write anything revealing about their towns, has made it easy for professional historians and social scientists to overlook racial exclusion when they write about sundown communities. Most white writers of fiction similarly leave out race. In *White Diaspora,* Catherine Jurca notes that suburban novelists find the racial composition of their communities "so unremarkable" that they never think about it.[43]

So far as I can tell, only a handful of books on individual sundown towns has ever seen print, and this is the first general treatment of the topic.[44] That is an astounding statement, given the number of sundown towns across the United States and across the decades. Social scientists and historians may also have failed to write about sundown towns because they have trouble thinking to include those who aren't there. "People find it very difficult to learn that the absence of a feature is informative," note psychologists Frank Kardes and David Sanbonmatsu. Writers who don't notice the absence of people of color see nothing to explain and pay the topic no attention at all. Where does the subject even fit? Is this book African American history? Assuredly not—most of the towns it describes have not had even one African American resident for decades. It is *white* history . . . but "white history" is not a subject heading in college course lists, the Library of Congress catalog, or most people's minds. Perhaps the new but growing field of "whiteness studies" will provide a home for sundown town research.[45]

I don't mean to excuse these omissions. The absence of prior work on sundown towns is troubling. Omitted events usually signify hidden fault lines in our culture. If a given community has not admitted on its landscape to having been a sundown town in the past, that may be partly because it has not yet developed good race relations in the present. It follows that America may not have admitted to having sundown towns in its history books because it has not yet developed good race relations as a society. Optimistically, ending this cover-up now may be both symptom and cause of better race relations.

To be sure, all-white communities are about much more than race. Tuxedo Park, New York, was noted for its role in the invention of radar. Mariemont, Ohio; Park Forest, Illinois; Highland Park, Texas; and the Greens offer interesting examples of innovative urban design. Edina, Minnesota, boasted the nation's first totally enclosed shopping mall, by the renowned architect Victor Gruen. Arcola, Illinois, is famous for its annual Broom Corn Festival. The Winnetka Plan, named after a Chicago sundown suburb, is a progressive method of teaching taught in most graduate schools of education.

At the same time, however, sundown towns *are* about race. Speaking of the dozen or so race riots that led to all-white towns in Missouri and Arkansas around 1910, historian Patrick Huber calls them "defining events in the history of their communities." Even without a riot—so far as I know, none of the towns listed in the foregoing paragraph experienced such an event—eternal vigilance toward the occasional person of color is the price for maintaining racial purity. Thus to a degree sundown towns are *always* about race.[46]

There is no excuse for being oblivious to that fact. Not to treat the sundown nature of sundown towns—often not even to *see* that nature—points to a weakness in white social science and history. If this seems harsh, well, I too was oblivious for most of my life.

Defining "Sundown Town"

Given that so little historical work existed to be examined and summarized, I was reduced to discovering the facts about sundown towns myself. How should I proceed?

Chapter 1 defined "sundown town" as any organized jurisdiction that for decades kept out African Americans (or others). It also noted that towns could have a black household or two as explicit exceptions. Here we shall see that some additional nuances must be considered. To locate sundown towns, I began with the United States Census, looking for cities with 2,500 or more residents that had no or fewer than 10 African Americans. I usually left towns of fewer than 2,500 residents off my "suspect" list if they had 2–9 blacks in repeated censuses.[47] For cities larger than 10,000, I changed my definition for "all-white town" to "less than 0.1% black," decade after decade.

The census can mislead, however. It includes as part of a town's population African Americans who live in institutions—such as the residents of Anna's mental hospital—in many sundown towns that maintained a taboo against independent black households.[48] Thus only late in my research did I learn that Dwight, in northern Illinois, and Vienna, in southern Illinois, were sundown towns; African Americans in their prisons, included in their census populations, had caused me not to put them on my list of suspected towns. I cannot know how many other sundown towns I have missed by beginning with the census.

The census can also mislead by counting African Americans in white households: live-in maids and gardeners and in later decades black or biracial adopted children. "I cannot account for the 17 and 21 African Americans you list as having lived in Cullman [Alabama] in 1950 and 1960," John Paul Myrick, Cullman County librarian, wrote in 2002. "To my knowledge, there were none that lived here, other than maybe a few domestic workers who lived with their employers and/or perhaps students at the then operating St. Bernard and Sacred Heart colleges." Writing in 1986 about Darien, Connecticut, whose restrictive covenants and "gentleman's agreements" had been the subject of Laura Hobson's bestselling 1947 novel, *Gentleman's Agreement*, Richard Todd noted, "The overwhelming absence in Darien is the absence of black faces. If there was ever a time when a black householder lived here, no one seems to remember it. No black families at all live in Darien now. In the past there were a few black live-in servants, but there appear to be none today." Historian Gregory Dorr, who grew up in Darien, wrote that during his childhood (1968–1990), "no African American families lived in town, and rumor was that only one black family ever attempted (unsuccessfully) to move into town." Yet the census found 58 African Americans in 1990. The solution to this puzzle, as Myrick hints, may be live-in servants who rarely venture out. Certainly that was the case in wealthy Darien.[49]

Inner suburbs present a different census anomaly. These cities typically contain large apartment houses located on major arteries in very urban sectors of the larger metropolitan area—what sociologists call "gesellschaft," the opposite of "gemeinschaft" or community. Since there is little gemeinschaft in such an area, there is no one to feel offended that blacks have moved into "his" or "her" neighborhood—*there is no neighborhood*. With all the shoppers, janitors, deliveries, and other miscellaneous tradespeople of all races, few residents may even realize that a black renter has moved in. Even if they do, being transient themselves, they may not feel a need to protest or realize that their suburb's sundown tradition confers upon them a "right" to protest. The 1990 census showed 54 African Americans in Berwyn, an inner suburb of Chicago, "most, if not all, in apartments," according to Alex Kotlowitz. Two years later, he described how threats, arson, and other bad behavior drove out Clifton and Dolcy Campbell and their three children after they bought a home in a Berwyn neighborhood and moved in. Some neighbors befriended the black family, but city officials did little. As he departed, Clifton Campbell explained, "When we realized that we had no official support for being in Berwyn, we felt like outside intruders." Thus Berwyn still acted as a sundown suburb in 1992.[50]

Sometimes the census "finds" African Americans where they flatly don't exist. It listed 1 African American in Searcy County in the Arkansas Ozarks in 1930, 1940, and 1950, and none in 1960, but found 22 in 1970. Gordon Morgan, who was doing research for his book *Black Hillbillies of the Arkansas Ozarks* around that time, noted, "The later figure is highly questionable and such people cannot be found in the county." Pranksters may be responsible. Jim Clayton wrote that the census for Johnston City, Illinois, showed one African American resident in 1960. This so upset the mayor that he "staged an all-out search to try to find out who that was." The mayor never found out, and Clayton suspects it was a joke by a local. In recent years, when most people fill out their own forms and return them by mail, respondents may also simply check the wrong box by accident.[51]

All-White on Purpose?

Even granted the foregoing issues, the census remains our best starting point, and classifying a community "all-white" based on census data proved doable. In 1970, using the above definition of "all-white town," Illinois had about 424 such towns with more than 1,000 people, as Chapter 3 told. But just because a town or suburb is all-white doesn't make it a place in which African Americans are not *allowed* to live. Were they all white on purpose? What defines "on purpose"?

In a sense, sundown towns self-define: if residents of a town *say* they keep out African Americans, or used to, most likely they do, or did. If African Americans have moved in and quickly out, perhaps reporting unwelcoming behavior, that would be still better evidence. I never assumed that a given town or suburb was all-white on purpose. Only when credible sources, oral or written, confirm that a community expelled its African Americans (or other minority) or took steps to keep them from moving in do I list that community as a sundown town. The rest of this chapter describes the methods and information I used to determine whether a given all-white town was a sundown town and talks about some of the issues involved in making that decision.

Oral History

This chapter has noted the difficulty of relying on written history when doing research on sundown towns. Documents are important to historians and social scientists, of course. Given the widespread suppression of material on *this* topic, however, for historians and social scientists to conclude in their absence that a town did not have sundown policies would be a gross error. Indeed, doing so would allow those community leaders who deliberately left no documentary trail to succeed in bewildering those who would understand their policies. Even in towns where no deliberate suppression was involved, primary written sources are often scarce because small towns often did not keep even such basic records as minutes of city council meetings. Furthermore, the sundown policy in many towns was informal, so nothing was written down in the first place.

Instead, we must talk with longtime residents. Some historians disparage oral history, but about sundown towns, oral history is usually more accurate than written history. The oral histories I have collected typically include revealing details about how and when a town kept out African Americans, details unlikely to have been invented. A key question to put to any historical source is: Is this person in a position to know? One must ask interviewees who say theirs was a sundown town *how* they know what they claim to know. "Where did you learn that?" "Who told you?" "When?" My sources gave persuasive replies, or I didn't rely on them.

I suggest that when it is off the mark, oral history often *understates* the degree to which a town excluded blacks. Although local historians have told me things about their communities that they would never commit to print, what they tell is still often softened by their desire to say only nice things about their hometown. Also, some interviewees may not be in a position to know. Moreover, fear can affect what people will tell. Some African Americans, like some white Americans, fear offending what might be called "the powers that be." Michelle Tate elicited this fear from two of her best interviewees, an elderly African American couple in Mattoon, Illinois: "The saddest part of all was when the woman looked at me and made sure I would not use their names in my paper. I assured her I would not." I elicited the same reluctance from several white interviewees and made the same promises. Fearful interviewees may not divulge all that they know.[52]

Notwithstanding the foregoing cautions, I have found that most respondents are much more open in oral interview than when writing. They do want to help the person who is asking them questions. It is hard not to, after all, when they are in the midst of a conversation, especially when their relative expertise on the history of the locale has been acknowledged. Even pillars of the community, such as officials of the local historical society, are usually much more forthcoming in conversation than in print. A final reason why oral history often works is this: sundown towns were not usually created by far-out racists throwing bombs in the night. Unfortunately, most white residents of sundown towns and suburbs either approved of their policy of exclusion or said nothing to stop its enforcement. The whiteness of all-white towns is therefore the consensual product of entire communities—made tangible in sundown ordinances, in the blanket adoption of restrictive covenants, or by widespread acts of public or private harassment that townspeople commended, participated in, or at least allowed to go unpunished. Therefore knowledge of towns' sundown practices was equally widespread. In town after town, when one asks the right people, one learns how their community went sundown, why, and sometimes when, and who did it.

Of course, it is always best to corroborate white oral history with testimony from African American residents of the nearest interracial town. It is also important to triangulate oral history with census data and written sources.

Ordinances, Written or Oral?

One way that cities and towns went all-white or stayed all-white was by passing an ordinance forbidding African Americans from being within their corporate limits after sundown or prohibiting them from owning or renting property in the town. Or at least they *say* they did. Whether such ordinances ever existed has become controversial. My web site, uvm.edu/~jloewen/, tells of the controversy and lists towns with oral history of an ordinance. I have put considerable effort into finding such ordinances and have found only one, in East Tennessee, reported in Chapter 4. The difficulty in finding ordinances provides a special case of the issues of written versus oral sources when it comes to sundown towns, so it is appropriate to treat those difficulties here.

Diverse written sources tell of sundown ordinances banning African Americans. In Illinois, written references describe sundown ordinances in East Alton, Fairfield, Granite City, Herrin, and Kenilworth. *The Negroes of Nebraska,* a product of the Nebraska Writers' Project during the Depression, tells that Plattsmouth and other cities in Kansas and Nebraska passed sundown ordinances. Documents also tell of other enactments by local governments. The "Inventory of the County Archives" of Pike County, Ohio, for example, prepared by the WPA in 1942, tells how "the Downing family, original proprietors" of Waverly, the county seat, gave to the county its central square, for a courthouse site, in 1861.

> The Downings caused to be written into the agreement accepting the donation of the public square a provision that if any Negroes ever should be permitted to settle within the corporation limits, the square should be sold and the proceeds revert to the down heirs. Present-day Waverly has no Negro residents. The Downings said that the "correct way to treat a Negro was to kill him."[53]

Despite these sources and many other written and oral reports of ordinances, finding such laws has proven difficult. Many—indeed, perhaps most—towns have lost their records. Consider the case of Kenilworth. That affluent Chicago suburb was the creation of its developer, Joseph Sears; widespread oral and written tradition holds that he made it a sundown town in its founding documents. The town's official history, *Joseph Sears and His Kenilworth,* by Colleen Kilner, hired by the Kenilworth Historical Society for the task, begins by designating Kenilworth "Number One on the Suburban Totem Pole" according to "the press," and it is an understatement to call her

account of Kenilworth sympathetic. Kilner uses italics to emphasize the four
principles that guided Sears:

> These restrictions were incorporated in the village ordinance:
> 1. *Large lots . . .*
> 2. *High standards of construction . . .*
> 3. *No alleys.*
> 4. Sales to *Caucasians only.*

When I visited the Kenilworth Historical Society in 2002, however, my request for Kenilworth's ordinances or incorporation documents baffled them.
Helpful staff members provided boxes of papers, including scattered minutes
of meetings of the board Sears created to govern Kenilworth in its early days,
but no ordinances. Surely Kenilworth had ordinances—one prohibiting alleys, for example. It cannot be found either, but Kenilworth has no alleys, just
as it has no blacks. Moreover, the local acclaim that met Kilner's 1969 book,
and its reprinting without change in 1990, suggest that Kenilworth residents
had no quarrel with its statement about the restrictive ordinance because it
was accurate. Even some recent towns have lost their records. Rolling Hills
Estates, for example, founded probably as a sundown suburb of Los Angeles
in 1958, can find no ordinances before 1975, according to a municipal clerk
there.[54]

Even when records exist, finding these ordinances proves next to impossible because they never got codified—that is, listed in a book, organized by
topic or even by year. Attorney Armand Derfner explains, "A lot of ordinances
never got codified. They only put in the things they were going to need all the
time."[55] And some small towns have never codified their ordinances at all.[56]

Ordinances Are Real, Written or Not

Some white Americans have told me that without a written ordinance, there
is little evidence that a town kept out African Americans. This is absurd.
Major league baseball, which kept out African Americans from 1890 to
1947, never had a formal prohibition. In fact, Kenesaw Mountain Landis,
commissioner of baseball from 1921 through 1944, stated, "There is no rule,
formal or informal . . . against the hiring of Negroes in organized baseball."
Nevertheless, everyone knew blacks were not allowed, and when the Pittsburgh Pirates sought to hire Josh Gibson from the Negro Leagues in 1943,
Landis wouldn't let them. It is the same with sundown towns. Laws about

daily practice are rarely read anyway. When newcomers move to a town, they learn the rules from those already there. If people say that it is illegal to park facing south on the east side of a north-south street, newcomers park "correctly," facing north. Oral tradition is crucial because people live in the oral tradition. They don't go to city hall and look up ordinances.[57]

If the written ordinance cannot now be located, so what? If whites have *not* had the power, legally, to keep African Americans out of town since 1917, so what? Tell that to the three African American families in Saline County, Illinois, whose homes whites dynamited in 1923. To Harvey Clark, whose furnishings were destroyed in the 1951 Cicero riot. To the engineers on the Wabash Railroad, who took care to pull their work trains east beyond the Niantic, Illinois, village limits when a black work crew was on board, because it was "against the law" for African Americans to stay in Niantic overnight. Or to black would-be home buyers in Maroa today, who are not shown houses because a realtor doesn't think she should sell to them, because of an ordinance.[58]

Historian Clayton Cramer grasps this point:

> When I lived in La Crescenta, just north of Glendale [California] in the 1970s, locals told me that Glendale had maintained a "no blacks allowed after sundown" ordinance on the books until the end of World War II. I'm not sure that I believe that an actual ordinance to that effect was still on the books that late. Of course, just because it isn't in writing doesn't mean it doesn't get enforced.[59]

Ordinances are passed orally first, after all, by voice vote of the body passing them. Whether they get written down depends on several factors, including the level of record keeping in the town. Here are two examples of ordinances passed orally in rather recent years. New England towns transact some of their important business by town meeting, and in 1973 the annual meeting of Ashby, Massachusetts, voted 148 to 79 *against* inviting people of color into town. Sure enough, the 1980 census showed Ashby with 2,311 people including no African Americans. New Market, in southwestern Iowa, re-passed its sundown ordinance even later, in the 1980s. African American John Baskerville, now a historian at the University of Northern Iowa, tells the story:

> I played in a band called Westwind, from Tarkio, Missouri, in the northwest corner of the state of Missouri. . . . In the summer of 1984 or 1985, we had a chance to play a street dance in New Market for a guy who owned a car dealer-

ship and a restaurant . . . [and] was also a member of the New Market city council. We had been playing for a couple of hours and it was starting to get dark, when during one of our breaks between sets, he came over and said exactly, "Hey, we almost had an incident here. The sheriff reminded me that it was against city ordinance for a 'colored' person to be in town after dark and that we were about to break the law. So, since most of the members of the city council are here [it was the only happening party in town that night], we held a special meeting of the council and voted to suspend the law for the night." I mind you, for the NIGHT! He went on to inform me that to his knowledge, all of those little towns in southwest Iowa (Gravity, Bedford, Villisca, most of Taylor county) all had laws prohibiting African-Americans in town after dark and that if we were going to continue to play in the area, we'd better check first before booking any gigs in the area.

So New Market's sundown ordinance went right back into effect the following night. Twenty years after the 1964 Civil Rights Act made it illegal for a bar owner to keep African Americans out of his or her tavern, the city officials of New Market thought they had the power to keep them out of an entire town, at least after dark. Apparently they still do, for the 2000 census showed no African Americans in New Market, and none in Gravity, Bedford, or Villisca. Indeed, neither Taylor County nor adjoining Adams County had a single black household.[60]

Errors of Inclusion and Exclusion

In the end, I did my damnedest to find the data. But all the deception and omissions, especially in the written record, make sundown towns hard to research. Therefore I cannot be sure of all the claims made about sundown towns in this book. Some towns I list as sundown may not be. Some may merely have happened to have no African Americans, decade after decade. There is also the question of change. A town may have been sundown for decades but may not be sundown today. Chapter 14, "Sundown Towns Today," describes the relaxation of sundown policies in many towns and suburbs since about 1980. I certainly do not claim that all the towns that I describe as confirmed are all-white on purpose to this day.

When deliberating whether to list a town as sundown based on sometimes scanty information, I tried to minimize errors of inclusion and exclusion. An error of inclusion would be falsely classing a town as sundown when it was not. Such a mistake could upset townspeople who might protest that they are *not* racist and the town never had a sundown policy. Uncorrected, the inaccuracy might also deter black families from moving to the town. I don't mean to cause these problems, and I apologize for any such errors. All readers should check out the history of a given town for themselves, rather than taking my word for its policies. Please give me feedback (jloewen@zoo.uvm.edu) if you learn that I have wrongly listed a town as sundown when it was not; I will make a correction on my web site and if possible in future editions of this book. In practical terms, however, I doubt that any notoriety a town mistakenly receives from its listing in my book will make a significant difference to its future. Moreover, if a town protests that it *is* welcoming, such an objection itself ends the harm by countering the notoriety and increasing the likelihood that African American families will test its waters and experience that welcome[61]—a happy result.

An error of exclusion would be missing a town that kept out African Americans. Such a mistake might encourage the town to stay sundown and to continue to cover up its policy. People of goodwill in the community might imagine no problem exists, while my erroneous omission would hardly bother those in the town who want to maintain its sundown character. Such an error might also mislead a black family to move in without fully understanding the risk. Nationally, such errors might convince readers that sundown towns have been less common than is really the case, thus lessening readers' motivation to eliminate sundown policies and draining our nation's reservoir of some of the goodwill needed to effect change.

Some towns I have confirmed as sundown through a single specific written source, often by a forthright local historian, or a single oral statement with convincing details. For example, the following anecdote, told to me by a Pinckneyville native then in graduate school, would by itself have convinced me that Pinckneyville, Illinois, was a sundown town and displayed a sign:

> Pinckneyville was indeed a sundown town. I grew up three miles east of town, and I can vividly recall—though my mom and aunts vehemently deny it—seeing a sign under the city limits sign, saying "No Coloreds After Dark." I don't know when they came down; I'd presume late '60s/early '70s, because I don't recall them when I was of junior-high age. However, I am sure they did exist, because one of my most vivid memories is of being four or five years old and driving to town with my dad. I was becoming a voracious reader, and I read the sign and said, "But that's wrong, Daddy. They're 'colors' (our local word for 'Crayolas'), not 'coloreds.'" He laughed and laughed at me, finally saying, "No, baby,

not 'colors,' 'coloreds'—you know, darkies. It's just a nicer way of saying 'niggers.' " [62]

In fact, many other sources, written and oral, confirm Pinckneyville. For other towns the evidence is considerably weaker, not always yielding a definite yes-or-no answer.[63] I believe my responsibility is to state the most likely conclusion based on the preponderance of the evidence I have, even though often that conclusion may not be proven beyond the shadow of a doubt. To be too insistent on solid proof before listing a town as sundown risks an error of exclusion. To list a town as sundown with inadequate evidence risks an error of inclusion. It is a balancing act.

We have seen that evidence of a town's sundown practices can come from oral history, newspapers of the time, local histories, newspaper articles written today based on some of the above, and various other sources, confirmed with census data. Getting such evidence usually requires on-site research, contact with current or former residents, and/or published secondary sources in a library. For most towns, this research is doable and not too difficult: most on-site inquiries quickly reveal whether an all-white town is intentional. My biggest problem was that I soon discovered that most of the thousands of all-white towns in the North had not always been all-white and probably became all-white on purpose. I therefore had far more towns to check out than I could possibly manage.

How have sundown towns managed to stay so white for so long? Their whiteness was enforced, and the next chapter tells how.

MASS MEETING.

A Mass Meeting of the citizens of this place and vicinity will be held at Darby's Hall, on Sunday, Jan. 31, at 2 o'clock P. M., to devise some lawful means of ridding Crescent City of Chinese.

R. W. Miller, R. G. Knox, L. F. Coburn and others will address the meeting.

All are invited to attend.

[1] Chinese Americans had lived in Crescent City, California, near the Oregon line, since at least the 1870s. The meeting advertised on this broadside was the first of a series lasting until mid-March, 1886. Eventually "lawful" was dropped and a mob forced the Chinese to depart on three sailing vessels bound for San Francisco. Whites in Humboldt County, the next county south, had already expelled 320 Chinese Americans from Eureka in 1885. In 1886 they drove Chinese from Arcata, Ferndale, Fortuna, Rohnerville, and Trinidad. [2] In 1906 they finished the job, loading these cannery workers onto boxcars, leaving their belongings behind. No Chinese returned to Humboldt Bay until the 1950s. *(Notes for this Portfolio section begin on page 523; photography credits begin on page 525.)*

In an all-night riot in August, 1901, white residents of Pierce City, Missouri, hanged a young black man alleged to have murdered a white woman, killed his grandfather, looted the armory, and used its Springfield rifles to attack the black community. African Americans fired back but were outgunned. [3] The mob then burned several homes including this one, Emma Carter's, incinerating at least two African Americans inside. At 2 A.M., Pierce City's 200 black residents ran for their lives. They found no refuge in the nearest town, Monett, because in 1894 it had expelled its blacks in a similar frenzy and hung a sign, "Nigger, Don't Let The Sun Go Down." [4] The house below stands in the "Black Hills," home to African Americans in Pinckneyville, Illinois, until they were driven out around 1928. A woman born across the street in 1947 recalls being teased in school "for living in niggertown." This house was formerly the black school.

[5] Will James, who had been arrested for the murder of Anna Pelley, has just been hanged under this brilliantly illuminated double arch that was the pride of downtown Cairo, Illinois, on November 11, 1909. Among the thousands of spectators were some from Anna, 30 miles north, where Pelley had grown up. Afterward, they returned home and drove all African Americans out of Anna. [6] Public subscription then paid for this striking granite tombstone commemorating Pelley. Adolescents in Anna still pay their respects at this site, a rite that helps maintain Anna as a sundown town.

Eyewitnesses tell of sundown signs in more than 150 communities in 31 states. Most read, "Nigger, Don't Let The Sun Go Down On You In ___." Some came in series, like the old Burma-Shave signs: "Nigger, If You Can Read," "You'd Better Run," "If You Can't Read," "You'd Better Run Anyway." Despite considerable legwork, I have not located a single photo of such a sign. Local librarians laugh when I ask if they saved theirs or a photo of it: "Why would we do that?" [7] James Allen, who assembled a famous exhibit of lynching postcards, bought this sign around 1985; its only provenance is "from Connecticut." [8] At left is a sign still extant, a black mule, used by residents of sundown towns in Arkansas, Kentucky, Missouri, and Tennessee to warn African Americans to "get their black ass" outside the city limits by sundown. Margaret Alam photographed this example just west of Liberty, Tennessee, in 2003. However, some evidence indicates that this mule's origin was not racial. Other towns used sirens. [9] In 1914, Villa Grove, Illinois, put up this water tower. Sometime thereafter, the town mounted a siren on it that sounded at 6 P.M. to warn African Americans to get beyond the city limits, until about 1998.

[10] On June 1, 1921, whites tried to make Tulsa, Oklahoma, a sundown town. As part of the attack, deputized white men raided a munitions dump, commandeered five airplanes, and dropped dynamite onto the black community, making it the only place in the contiguous United States ever to undergo aerial bombardment. Like efforts to expel blacks from other large cities, the Tulsa mob failed; the job was simply too large.

Earlier, in May, 1911, the teenage son of Laura Nelson, who lived near Boley, Oklahoma, a black town, killed a deputy who was searching their cabin for stolen meat. His mother, trying to protect him, claimed she did it. [11] "Her innocence was determined weeks before the lynching," according to James Allen, who collected this postcard of the lynching. Nevertheless, a white mob from Okemah, a sundown town ten miles east of Boley, hanged Nelson and her son from this bridge spanning the North Canadian River. Residents then stayed up all night to fend off an imagined mob, said to be coming from Boley to sack Okemah. Similar fears prompted similar mobilizations in sundown suburbs during urban ghetto riots in the 1960s.

DON'T LET THE SUN SET ON YOU HERE, UNDERSTAND?

Norman, Okla., Feb. 10.—Agitation involving Race musicians has become quite widespread since the beating up of Howard's orchestra in Miami, Fla., some weeks ago. The latest instance of intimidation occurred in this city.

An orchestra composed of Race men had been sent for to come from Fort Worth, Texas, to play at a dance given for students of the University of Oklahoma. When it was discovered that the musicians were in town a free-for-all fight was only narrowly averted. Like many Southern towns there is a disposition here to make this a lily-white community and keep out from it certain citizens of the republic.

Thus, soon after the dance started a mob gathered outside the hall and began throwing stones and bricks through the windows. An investigation revealed the cause or motive for the mob action. Calls were immediately made for the police, who came in time to save the musicians from further mistreatment. Several score students surrounded the orchestra and escorted it to an interurban station, where it entrained for Fort Worth.

ANTI-NEGRO CRUSADE

Indiana River Towns Are Taking Drastic Measures

TO RID THEMSELVES OF THE OBNOXIOUS

Scores Indicted for Selling Their Votes—In Many Places No Negroes Are Allowed to Live.

Evansville, Ind., Jan. 28.—Cities and towns along the Ohio river have begun a crusade against the negroes. The entire trouble dates back to the lynching of the negroes at Rockport and Boonville for the murder of the white barber, Simmons, at Rockport one night last month. The board of safety of this

University of Oklahoma students invited a black orchestra to play for their dance, but citizens of Norman intervened because the musicians violated Norman's sundown rule. [12] This 1922 story in the *Chicago Defender* uses "Race" where we would use "black." [13] At right, datelined Evansville, a report tells of a wave of anti-black actions in southwestern Indiana in 1901, triggered by "the lynching of the Negroes at Rockport and Boonville for the murder of the white barber." Only contagion can explain how the murder of one barber could prompt three lynchings in Rockport, one in Boonville, and "vigilance committees" to drive African Americans from at least five other towns. [14] The full headline below is "White Men Shoot Up Church Excursioners." Black motorists stranded in sundown towns have always been in danger, no matter their circumstances. In August 1940, a church group in Charleston, South Carolina, hired a bus to attend an event. On their way home, it broke down in the little town of Bonneau. While they were waiting for a replacement bus, sixteen white men came on the scene and ordered them to "get out [of] here right quick. We don't allow no d—n n—rs 'round here after sundown." They then opened fire on the parishioners with shotguns, causing them to flee into nearby woods.

WHITE MEN SHOOT UP CHURCH

| EAST AND WEST WAIT AT GATE |

GROUP IS TOLD "NO N----RS ALLOWED AFTER SUNDOWN"

MONCKS CORNER, S. C., Aug. 15—(ANP)—Five persons returning from a church excursion at Eutawville Sunday night were wounded by shotgun blasts when they were fired upon at a filling station in Bonneau, near here, by unidentified white men. Francis

Greene was admitted to Dorchester and was driven into a filling station County Hospital in Summerton at Bonneau and left by the ville suffering from gunshot wounds driver with consent of the opera

5,384 GALL STONES TAKEN FROM WOMAN

WILSON, N. C., Aug 15—The largest number of gall stones ever recorded in the medical history of this section, 5,384, were taken from a 50-year-old woman at Wilson hospital recently. Physicians said, however, that she would recover.

n----rs 'round here after sundown." The excursioners, the white driver and the station operator tried to explain the emergency to no avail. A second car drove up with eight more white men who began firing on the group with shotguns. Having no weapon, the excursioners fled into nearby woods. Many were still missing when the bus left at 1:30 Monday

Gua In C

CH AG geated action to the transp las, ated Univ he ordinance cials are consid the street cars b ways and the r unified city cant ownership. Negr ated against in ployment.

[15] This 1935 linoleum cut by Lin Shi Khan is part of a collection titled *Scottsboro Alabama*. Scottsboro was not a sundown town, but most towns in the nearby Sand Mountains were. [16] For his 1973 novel *Breakfast of Champions*, Kurt Vonnegut drew this Indiana sundown sign. A character relates that when a black family got off a boxcar in "Shepherdstown" during the Depression, perhaps not seeing the sign, and sought shelter in an empty shack for the night, a mob got the man and "sawed him in two on the top strand of a barbed-wire fence." Vonnegut grew up in Indianapolis, surrounded by sundown towns. His is the only visual representation I have found of a sundown sign in the Midwest or West, even though I have evidence of such signs in more than 100 towns in those regions and suspect they stood in more than 1000.

The Nadir reached Canada, too. Canada had welcomed fugitive slaves, but by 1910, whites in Canada's western provinces, facing a trickle of African Americans fleeing racism in the Plains states, protested to Ottawa. [17] In 1911, the government replied by prohibiting "any immigrants belonging to the Negro race." The prohibition was repealed two months later, but Canada did send agents to Oklahoma to discourage black immigrants. [18] Some riots that drove African Americans from small towns left documentary hints, such as the telegram below. In Missouri, a black Civilian Conservation Corps unit was scheduled to work in Lawrence County in 1935, prompting this telegram to Gov. Guy Park. I think the "riot and blood shed several years ago" alludes to a riot in Mt. Vernon, Missouri, in 1906, but it may refer to a more recent event. The telegram worked: the camp was moved; and Lawrence County's black population declined to just 21 by 1950.

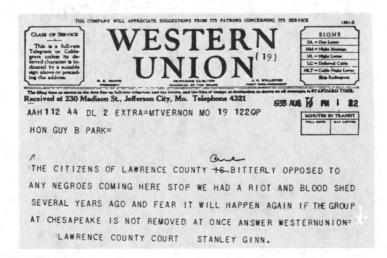

WESTERN UNION (19)

Received at 230 Madison St., Jefferson City, Mo. Telephone 4321

AAH112 44 DL 2 EXTRA=MTVERNON MO 19 1220P

HON GUY B PARK=

THE CITIZENS OF LAWRENCE COUNTY IS BITTERLY OPPOSED TO
ANY NEGROES COMING HERE STOP WE HAD A RIOT AND BLOOD SHED
SEVERAL YEARS AGO AND FEAR IT WILL HAPPEN AGAIN IF THE GROUP
AT CHESAPEAKE IS NOT REMOVED AT ONCE ANSWER WESTERNUNION=
LAWRENCE COUNTY COURT   STANLEY GINN.

[19] After Comanche and Hamilton counties in Texas drove out their African Americans in 1886, Alec and Mourn Gentry were the only two who "have been permitted to reside in this section," in the words of the 1958 Hamilton County centennial history. " 'Uncle Alec' and 'Aunt Mourn' lived to a ripe old age. . . . They were Gentry Negroes, and former slaves of Capt. F. B. Gentry. . . ." They were no one's uncle or aunt in Hamilton County, of course; these are terms of quasi-respect whites used during the Nadir for older African Americans to avoid "Mr." or "Mrs." (Aunt Jemima Syrup and Uncle Ben's Rice linger as vestiges of this practice.) Gentry's pose shows that he knows his place, essential to his well-being in a sundown county.

"UNCLE ALEC" GENTRY

[20] Elizabeth Davis and her son were the only exceptions allowed in Casey, Illinois, until well after her death in 1963 at 76. She was a nurse-midwife, and this 1952 newspaper photo was accompanied by a poem, "A Tribute to Miss Davis," showing Casey's respect for her. At the same time, Davis was known everywhere as "Nigger Liz," and Casey at one time boasted a sundown sign at the west edge of town.

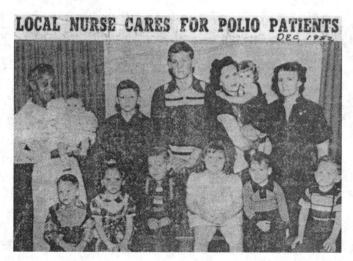

LOCAL NURSE CARES FOR POLIO PATIENTS
DEC 1952

Between 1920 and 1928, KKK rallies were so huge that they remain the biggest single meetings many towns have ever seen. [21] This lecture in Westfield, Illinois, in 1924 was an example; a later article told of a "Big Demonstration" planned for "Klan Day" at the Clark County
Fair in neighboring Martinsville. Predicted the newspaper, "As we know that a Klan gathering
draws spectators like jam draws flies, we can expect that Martinsville on that date will witness
the largest gathering of people ever assembled in Clark County." Yet many of these towns—
including Martinsville and Westfield—were sundown towns that had already gotten rid of
their African Americans and had no Jews and few Catholics, so in a sense there was nothing
left for the Klan to do. [22] Similarly, African Americans hardly existed in most of Maine in the
1920s—sometimes owing to sundown policies—yet Milo boasted the "first daylight [Klan]
parade in U.S.A." In the 2000 census, Milo finally showed its first African American household. Martinsville and Westfield still have none.

FIRST PARADE IN N.E. STATES
OF KU KLUX KLAN AND FIRST
DAYLIGHT PARADE IN U.S.A.
AT MILO. MAINE 9/3/23.

PHOTO BY
THE CLEMENT STUDIO
MILO. ME.

[23] Audiences cackle at the last line on this bust of Christopher Columbus. They "know" Italians are not a race. It seems obvious now that there are only three races (Caucasoid, Mongoloid, Negroid), or four (Australoid), or five (American Indian). This was not Hitler's understanding, who "knew" Jews to be a race; nor was it Italian Americans' in 1920 when they erected this bust at the Indiana State Capitol. At that time eugenicists ranked Greeks, Italians, and Slavs *racially* inferior and aimed the 1924 immigration restrictions largely at them. By 1940, however, these races became one—"white." Jews, Armenians, and Turks took just a little longer. Now "white" seems to incorporate Latin and Asian Americans, which most sundown towns have long admitted. In 1960, Dearborn, Michigan, called Arabs "white population born in Asia" and Mexicans "white population born in Mexico" in official documents, thus remaining "all white" as a city. Sundown town policy now seems to be: all groups are fine except blacks.

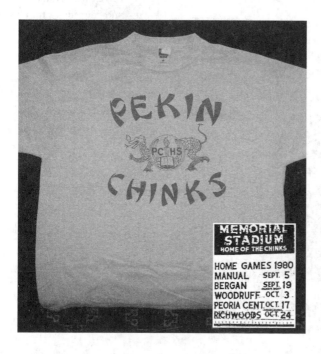

[24] Although Pekin, Illinois, called its high school athletic teams "Chinks," referencing Peking (now Beijing) China, it insisted this was a compliment and allowed Chinese as residents. The name changed in 1980, but even today many graduates defend the old name. "I can't wait to get Chinks memorabilia, and my kids would love to see it too," stated one alum in 2000. I bought this new T-shirt in Pekin in 2002. It shows visually the bluntly racist rhetoric many residents of sundown towns routinely employ.

Table 32. **General Characteristics for Places of 1,000 to 2,500: 1970**

[For minimum base for derived figures (percent, median, etc.) and meaning of symbols, see text]

Places	Population					
		Sex		Race		
	Total	Male	Female	White	Negro	Other
Rome City	1 354	674	680	1 353	-	1
St. John	1 757	885	872	1 753	-	4
Seelyville	1 195	571	624	1 185	-	10
Shelburn	1 281	623	658	1 280	-	1
Sheridan	2 137	999	1 138	2 133	2	2
Shoals	1 039	489	550	1 039	-	-
Smith Valley (U)	1 679	831	848	1 678	-	1
South Whitley	1 362	639	723	1 360	-	2
Spencer	2 423	1 114	1 309	2 418	3	2
Summitville	1 104	531	573	1 104	-	-
Swayzee	1 073	521	552	1 071	-	2
Sweetser	1 076	520	556	1 075	-	1
Syracuse	1 546	758	788	1 546	-	-
Thorntown	1 399	671	728	1 394	-	5
Town of Pines	1 007	509	498	1 001	-	6
Tri Lakes (U)	1 193	610	583	1 189	1	3
Van Buren	1 057	496	561	1 052	-	5
Veedersburg	1 837	872	965	1 835	1	1
Versailles	1 020	480	540	1 012	-	8
Vevay	1 463	665	798	1 460	-	3
Wakarusa	1 160	558	602	1 153	-	7
Walkerton	2 006	983	1 023	1 996	2	8
Walton	1 054	479	575	1 053	-	1
Warren	1 229	562	667	1 229	-	-
Waterloo	1 876	894	982	1 876	-	-
Westfield	1 837	877	960	1 833	3	1
Westport	1 170	552	618	1 170	-	-
Whiteland	1 492	732	760	1 492	-	-
Williamsport	1 661	810	851	1 659	-	2
Winamac	2 341	1 079	1 262	2 335	2	4
Winslow	1 030	469	561	1 029	-	1
Worthington	1 691	788	903	1 688	-	3
Yorktown	1 673	823	850	1 673	-	-
Zionsville	1 857	853	1 004	1 844	1	12

[25] This page from the 1970 census shows how widespread all-white towns—probably sundown towns—have been in Indiana. Twenty-six of these 34 had not a single black resident, and bearing in mind that sundown towns often allowed an exception for one black family, we cannot be sure that *any* of the 34 admitted African Americans. Indiana had twenty times as many African Americans as "Others" in 1970, yet Others lived much more widely. [26] To avoid sundown towns and negotiate travel without danger or embarrassment, African Americans produced guidebooks such as *Travelguide: Vacation and Recreation Without Humiliation* and this *Negro Motorist Green Book*. They listed hotels, restaurants, auto repair shops, etc., that would serve black travelers.

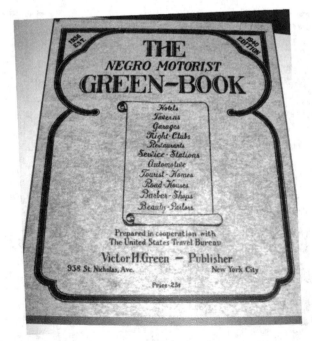

[27] In the mid-1920s, Mena, county seat of Polk County, Arkansas, competed for white residents and tourists by advertising what it had and what it did *not* have. The sentiment hardly died in the 1920s. A 1980 article, "The Real Polk County," began, "It is not an uncommon experience in Polk County to hear a newcomer remark that he chose to move here because of 'low taxes and no niggers.' " [28] Suburbs followed suit. In 1914, developers of Highland Park near Salt Lake City appealed to would-be homebuyers to leave behind the problems of the city, like its smoke. By 1919, the appeal had become racial. Even today, the most prestigious suburbs are often those with the lowest proportions of African Americans.

In 1948, a Federal Housing Administration commissioner boasted that "the FHA has never insured a housing project of mixed occupancy." **[29]** This six-foot concrete block wall was built to separate a white neighborhood from an interracial one in northwestern Detroit so homes on the white side could qualify for FHA loan guarantees. It runs for half a mile, from the city limits to a park. Today African Americans live on both sides, but the wall still divides the neighborhood in two and serves as a reminder on the landscape that federal policies explicitly favored segregated neighborhoods until 1968. **[30]** A street barrier marks the border between North Brentwood, a black community, and Brentwood, Maryland, a sundown suburb into the 1960s. Struck by the absence of any social class difference between homes on both sides of the barrier, I asked Denise Thomas, who grew up in North Brentwood in the 1950s, "What kept people from North Brentwood from crossing that line?" "KKK!" was her heartfelt answer. By that she meant not only the Klan, which burned crosses in North Brentwood, but also many other instances of harassment. "They threw things at us, called us 'nigger,' 'spook,' all kind of things." "The white children?" I asked. "Uh-huh," she affirmed, "and the adults."

"YE OLDE LEVITTOWNE"

"No FENCES, EITHER FABRI-CATED OR GROWING, MAY BE PUT UP WITHOUT THE WRITTEN CONSENT OF COUNTY COMMU-NITY CORP."

"Only PORTABLE, REVOLVING DRYERS ARE PERMITTED THEY MUST BE USED ONLY IN THE REAR YARD--NOT ON SATUR-DAYS, SUNDAYS OR HOLIDAYS."

"LAWNS MUST BE CUT AND TALL WEEDS REMOVED AT LEAST ONCE A WEEK BE-TWEEN APRIL 15TH AND NOVEMBER 15TH."

"THE TENANT AGREES NOT TO PERMIT THE PREM-ISES TO BE USED OR OCCUPIED BY ANY PERSON OTHER THAN MEMBERS OF THE CAUCASIAN RACE."

www.zippythepinhead.com

COVENANT & RESTRICTIONS, LEVITT & SONS, 1949

[31] In 2002, Bill Griffith's comic strip "Zippy the Pinhead" quoted the regulations set up by Levitt & Sons for the first Levittown. No one made light of them in the 1950s when the three Levittowns were going up. It would not have been cause for amusement or concern then, just everyday life, for Levitt & Sons was by far the largest single homebuilder in post-World War II America. If regulations didn't work, violence usually did. [32] In July, 1951, a mob rioted for three days to keep a black bus driver, Harvey Clark, and his family from occupying an apartment in this building in Cicero, a sundown suburb of Chicago. In this photo, whites have thrown the Clarks' furniture and other possessions into the courtyard of the complex and set it on fire. Eventually a grand jury indicted the owner, Camille DeRose, not the mob! Cicero remained all white until the 1990s.

[33] According to historian Kenneth Jackson, "the most conspicuous city-suburban contrast in the U.S. runs along Detroit's Alter Road" separating Detroit from Grosse Pointe. Just across the line is this park, but Detroit children cannot play on its playground equipment. "It's not fair," observed Reginald Pickins, who grew up less than 50 feet from the border. "Why should we have to have passes to go into their parks? They don't need passes for ours."

[34] Tarzan, the white man who mastered the African jungle, was born in one sundown suburb, Oak Park, Illinois, where his creator, Edgar Rice Burroughs, wrote the first Tarzan books, and gave birth to another sundown town when Burroughs used the proceeds from his novels, movies, and long-running comic strip to create Tarzana, California. In this 1934 strip "the island savages" flee "in terror" from jungle creatures, "believing the beasts were demons conjured up by Tarzan." The strip literally shows white supremacy: Tarzan is more intelligent, courageous, and moral than the black "savages," whom he literally walks all over.

PART IV

Sundown Towns in Operation

9

Enforcement

It was well known any black people arriving in town were not to venture beyond the block the bus stop or train station were in. My father even remembers a group of three teenage boys bragging that they had seen the "niggers" from the bus stop walking down the street and stopped them and told them they were not allowed to leave the bus stop. Another individual who is slightly older than my parents and lived in Effingham said the police would patrol the train station and bus stop to ensure black people did not leave them. She stated that she was unsure whether this was due to prejudice on the part of police, or to protect the black people from the individuals residing in Effingham.

> —Michelle Tate, summarizing oral history collected
> in and around Effingham, Illinois, fall 2002[1]

A STRIKING CHARACTERISTIC of sundown towns is their durability. Once a town or suburb defines itself "white," it usually stays white for decades. Yet all-white towns are inherently unstable. Americans are always on the move, going to new places, and so are African Americans. Remaining white in census after census is not achieved easily. How is this whiteness maintained?

Residents have used a variety of invisible enforcement mechanisms that become visible whenever an African American comes to town or "threatens" to come to town. The *Illinois State Register* stated the basic method of enforcement in 1908 in the aftermath of the Springfield riot: "A Negro is an unwelcome visitor and is soon informed he must not remain in the town."[2] But there are many variations in how this message has been delivered. We shall begin with the cruder methods relied upon by independent sundown towns, then "progress" to the more sophisticated and subtler measures that sundown suburbs have taken to remain overwhelmingly white—but we must note that even elite sundown suburbs have resorted to violence on occasion.

The Inadvertent Visitor

From time to time, an African American person or family have found themselves in a sundown town completely by accident. Immediately they were suspect, and usually they were in danger. Sundown towns rarely tolerated African American visitors who happened within their gates when night fell. Even if they were there inadvertently—even if they had no knowledge of the town's tradition beforehand—whites viewed them as having no right to be in "our town" after dark and often replied with behavior that was truly vile, yet in the service of "good" as defined by the community.

Hiking from town to town was a common mode of travel before the 1920s and grew common again during the Great Depression. Walking was the most exposed form of transit through a sundown town. As we saw previously, whites in Comanche County, Texas, drove out their African Americans in 1886. Local historian Billy Bob Lightfoot tells of an African American who made a bet some years later that he could walk across the county, but "was never seen again after he stopped at a farm near De Leon for a drink of water." He made less than eight miles before whites killed him.[3]

Walking could be just as dangerous in the Midwest. A 1905 article in the Fairmont, West Virginia, *Free Press* provides a glimpse of the process by which residents maintained Syracuse, Ohio, as a sundown community:

> In Syracuse, Ohio, on the Ohio river, a town of about 2,000 inhabitants, no Negro is permitted to live, not even to stay overnight under any consideration. This is an absolute rule in this year 1905, and has existed for several generations. The enforcement of this unwritten law is in the hands of the boys from 8 to 20 years of age . . .
>
> When a Negro is seen in town during the day he is generally told of these traditions . . . and is warned to leave before sundown. If he fails to take heed, he is surrounded at about the time darkness begins, and is addressed by the leader of the gang in about this language: "No nigger is allowed to stay in this town over night. Get out of here now, and get out quick."
>
> He sees from 25 to 30 boys around him talking in subdued voices and waiting to see whether he obeys. If he hesitates, little stones begin to reach him from unseen quarters and soon persuade him to begin his hegira. He is not allowed to walk, but is told to "Get on his little dog trot." The command is always effective, for it is backed by stones in the ready hands of boys none too friendly.
>
> So long as he keeps up a good gait, the crowd, which follows just at his

heels, and which keeps growing until it sometimes numbers 75 to 100 boys, is good-natured and contents itself with yelling, laughing, and hurling gibes at its victim. But let him stop his "trot" for one moment, from any cause whatever, and the stones immediately take effect as their chief persuader. Thus they follow him to the farthest limits of the town, where they send him on, while they return to the city with triumph and tell their fathers all about the function, how fast the victim ran, how scared he was, how he pleaded and promised that he would go and never return if they would only leave him alone.

Then the fathers tell how they used to do the same thing, and thus the heroes of two wars spend the rest of the evening by the old campfire, recounting their several campaigns.[4]

Anywhere that a black man might be unexpected, walking was hazardous. In Sullivan's Hollow, one of the few sundown communities in Mississippi, white farmers caught an African American on foot early in the twentieth century, tied a bundle of barbed wire to his back, and made him crawl a mile on all fours before letting him leave the Hollow. In Ralls County, Missouri, just south of Hannibal, "even the mere sight of a black man at times could throw Ralls County white women into a panic," writes historian Gregg Andrews. "Ilasco judge John Northcutt bound over John Griggsby, an African American, to a grand jury in July, 1906, after Etta Hays accused Griggsby of attempted criminal assault." All Griggsby had done was to step off a train at Salt River and walk in the direction of her house. "Although she admitted that Griggsby never came within fifty yards of her, the judge still held him for the grand jury." Eventually he was released. Griggsby got off easy: I have other stories of black men being convicted or shot on the spot for the same offense.[5]

After a race riot, African American refugees usually faced particular hostility when they fled on foot to other towns, because the rioting was contagious and traveled ahead of them. Roberta Senechal, whose book on the Springfield, Illinois, riot of 1908 is the standard account, writes:

When a lone Springfield refugee appeared on the streets of the village of Spaulding eight miles from the city, he was greeted by a menacing mob of nearly 100 whites. Deputy sheriffs arrived before any harm was done and saw to it that the man moved on. Black refugees sparked hostility outside of Sangamon County, too. . . . When a small band of Springfield blacks appeared in the village of Greenridge in Macoupin County to beg for food, the residents of the place denied them anything and stoned them out of town.[6]

Public Transportation Through Sundown Towns

After 1940, walking from town to town became uncommon, as most Americans had enough money for public transportation or automobiles. But trains and buses posed hazards too when they stopped in sundown towns, and sometimes merely while passing through. Even Pullman porters, just doing their jobs on trains stopped in stations, were threatened in some towns. According to a leader of the Comanche County Historical Museum, "Whites in De Leon would rope black porters and drag 'em through the streets and put them back on the train, just for meanness." Porters took to hiding in the baggage car during the time the train was in Comanche County. Eventually the Houston & Texas Central Rail Road asked De Leon to move the town's sundown sign from the train station, because white residents were using it as a pretext, so De Leon relocated it to the town well. Immediately after the 1899 riot that expelled all African Americans from Pana, Illinois, a traveler passing through observed, "The men have the Afrophobia so badly that the colored porters on the trains crawl under the seats" when they go through Pana. After whites drove African Americans from Pierce City, Missouri, in 1901, according to a reporter,

> citizens declare no Negro porters will be allowed to run through here in trains, and it is probable the 'Frisco line will have to change porters at Springfield hereafter. Today a shot was fired into a train, and it is supposed to have been aimed at the porter.[7]

William Pickens, writing in 1923, told of harassment in the Ozarks: "When trainloads of colored people recently passed through bound from the east to some great convention in Muskogee, Oklahoma, they had to shut the windows and pull down the shades to avoid the murderous missiles that are sometimes hurled especially at 'a nigger in a Pullman' "—by definition "uppity." In Wheeler County, Texas, in the 1920s, according to Arthur Raper, "as one man put it, Negroes were not even permitted 'to stick their heads out of the train coaches.' "[8]

All kinds of dangers might beset the unwary traveler who actually got off at a sundown town. In 1921, an African American had been working in Ballinger, Texas, and took the train home to Teague, in central Texas. "By mistake he took the wrong train and was put off at Comanche in the middle of the night," according to the *Chicago Defender*.

He entered the waiting room of the railroad station, where he was found asleep the next morning by a local police officer. It soon became known that he was in town—the first one to have been seen here for 35 years. Crowds of townspeople gathered around him and among them were many young men and women who never before had seen a man of our Race. For his own safety the man was taken to the county jail and locked up, pending the arrival of the next outgoing train. He was escorted to the station by an armed guard and placed aboard the train.

In Oneida, Tennessee, in about 1940, the police were not so helpful, according to local historian Esther Sanderson, writing in 1958:

One Negro hobo got off a freight train in Oneida; police and civilians started toward him and he started running. His bullet-riddled body was brought back out of the woods in about an hour. One young pilot from Scott County in World War II who saw the Negro after he was killed remarked on his return from the War, "You know, as I watched the blood flow from the wounds of the dead and dying Negroes on our transport planes, I thought of that old Negro who was killed in Oneida."[9]

Some sundown towns allowed African Americans traveling by train or bus to wait in the stations but venture no farther, even during the day. So far these examples have antedated World War II, but some towns, including Effingham, Illinois, as noted at the head of the chapter, continued to enforce this practice much more recently. David Blair reported that this rule worked a special hardship on black Greyhound bus drivers in Effingham in the mid-1960s. His father worked in the bus station cafeteria.

He would sometimes give black bus drivers a two block ride to the Brentwood Hotel. . . . White bus drivers could just walk over to it from the station, but black drivers had to call a cab and then wait longer for the cab to show than the walk would have been. My father would offer to give them a lift since he was white. To my knowledge he was never hassled because of it but the black drivers would ask if he was aware that there could be problems just in giving them a two block lift.

Effingham and a few other towns enforced this policy even during the daytime. Many towns did after dark.[10]

Taxis are another form of public transportation, but until recently, taxi drivers in sundown towns simply refused to pick up black would-be fares.

The same refusals still affect taxi service in many urban all-white neighbor-hoods today. One exception was Ray Pettit, who ran the Liberty Cab Company in Waverly, a sundown town in southern Ohio, until his death in the 1960s. His granddaughter, Jeanne Blackburn, remembers her mother's stories "about how my grandfather would transport blacks out of the city limits, should they be in town too late to make it on their own, so they would not be punished." Of course, his assistance, while kind and even possibly lifesaving, did not challenge the sundown law but enforced it.[11]

Automobile Travel Through Sundown Towns

The advent of private automobiles made life a little safer for African American travelers, but not much. Often, bad things have happened to motorists of color whose vehicles broke down. In Memphis, Missouri, near the Iowa line, around 1960, according to a librarian who grew up there,

> a black family stopped on the edge of town with car trouble. Some local men gathered quickly to "stop the agitators from wrecking the town." Even though they found an innocent family instead, they saw fit to "scare them out of town." It was a "get your car fixed and go" confrontation. I heard that one of the white men even shot a "warning shot" over the car just to make his point clear.

She went on to emphasize that many whites in Memphis, including her family, "found their behavior to be mean, ridiculous and embarrassing," "especially considering that the black family members did not seek to stop in Memphis but were there because their car broke down." But no one stood up for the black family at the side of the road at the time.[12]

Unlike Missouri, whites in Bonneau, South Carolina, didn't miss when they used a shotgun to warn African Americans to clear out fast. A black church group had rented a bus and driver from a white-owned company. As told in the August 17, 1940, *Pittsburgh Courier,* a national African American newspaper:

> According to the Rev. Mr. [Robert] Mack, the bus developed motor trouble and was driven into a filling station at Bonneau and left by the driver with consent of the operator while another bus was being secured from North Charleston. Leaving Bonneau at 10 o'clock for the second bus, the driver returned at midnight.

As passengers were transferring to the second bus eight white men drove up and ordered the excursioners to "get out here [*sic*] right quick. We don't allow no d——n n————rs 'round here after sundown." The excursioners, the white driver, and the station operator tried to explain the emergency to no avail. A second car drove up with eight more white men who began firing on the group with shotguns. Having no weapons, the excursioners fled into nearby woods. Many were still missing when the bus left at one Monday morning.

Four church members and the white driver were wounded by the shotgun blasts.[13]

In Owosso, Michigan, an ultimatum from an officer of the law terrified a stranded motorist: local historian Helen Harrelson recalls overhearing him frantically phoning relatives in Flint, 25 miles to the east, and saying, " 'The police have given me half an hour to get out of town.' " But sometimes police intervention in sundown towns, while fearful, ironically resulted in better service. Residents of Pinckneyville, Illinois, and Harrison, Arkansas, tell how police helped to get parts or have a car towed to the nearest interracial town. "The blacks were very grateful," my Harrison informants concluded, for the sundown violation was thus avoided. In Arcola, Illinois, according to a then-resident, service was even better: when a black family's bus broke down there on a Sunday, police got a mechanic to open his garage and fix the problem that day, so they could leave Arcola.[14] And in Martinsville, Indiana, located on the highway between Indiana University and Indianapolis, police until recently would carry African American student hitchhikers to the other side of town, thus preserving the racial purity of the town as well as the welfare of the hitch-hiker.[15]

"Keep moving" was the refrain, no matter why African Americans stopped. Local historian Jean Swaim tells of a shameful incident in Cedar County, Missouri: "Even a busload of black choir members who saved the lives of four El Dorado Springs teenagers by pulling them from a burning car were then turned away." In Mena, Arkansas, African Americans did not even have to stop to get in trouble. Shirley Manning, a high school student there in 1960–61, describes the scene:

The local boys would threaten with words and knives Negroes who would come through town, and follow them to the outskirts of town shouting "better not let the sun set on your black ass in Mena, Arkansas," and they often "bumped" the car with their bumper from behind. I was along in a car which did this, once, and saw it done more than once.

Moving vehicles were also targeted in Benton, in southern Illinois, in the mid-1980s: white teenagers threw eggs and shouted "nigger" at African Americans who drove through town after dark.[16]

Another way to vex African American motorists was to refuse to sell them fuel. Whites in Slocum, Texas, wouldn't sell gas to African Americans until 1929. In Mt. Olive and Gillespie, Illinois, this policy was in effect at least through the 1950s. According to historian John Keiser, who grew up in Mt. Olive, African American motorists routinely carried an extra ten gallon tank in their trunk when traveling from St. Louis to Chicago "because no one would sell them gas en route." A former resident of Pana, Illinois, reported that filling station attendants in that central Illinois town would not pump gas for African American customers as recently as the 1960s. Back then, stations were not self-serve, so "they had to go on to Vandalia or Kinkaid." To this day, many African Americans still take care to drive through Pana without stopping. Gas stations in Martinsville, Indiana, refused to sell to African American motorists as recently as the early 1990s. As racist as Mississippi was during the civil rights struggle, I lived there for eight years and never heard of a town or even an individual gas station that would not sell gasoline to African Americans. It seems irrational to refuse to sell fuel to a person whom you want out of town, when fuel is precisely what they need to *get* out of town. In the case of Pana, moreover, at least fifteen other nearby towns in all directions were also sundown towns, including Vandalia and probably Kinkaid. If they all similarly refused to sell gas to African Americans, central Illinois would wind up with hundreds of stranded black motorists, hardly the outcome whites intended.[17]

"Driving While Black"

Harassment has not stopped; on the contrary, it has become official. In many communities police follow and stop African Americans and search their cars when they drive in or out, making it hard for African Americans to work, shop, or live there. The practice has been going on for decades. Jim Clayton, who grew up in Johnston City, Illinois, writes, "In the late 1940s, the police often followed any car containing blacks that turned off Route 37 into town. And there were many such cars on that route because it was a main line from the South to Chicago." Route 37 is now Interstate 57, but black motorists who stray are still in trouble: 60 miles north, a recent graduate of Salem High School reports that police officers there say on their radio, "Carload of coal coming down X street," to alert other officers to the presence of African Americans. In Dwight, in northern Illinois on the other interstate highway going to Chicago, police used "NCIC" as shorthand for "New Coon In County," whom they then harassed out of town, according to an ambulance volunteer there in the 1980s. Florida resident Melissa Sue Brewer wrote about a related alphabetical expression used by police in that state, "NBD," meaning "Nigger on the Beach after Dark." [18]

Only a few sundown suburbs resorted to the brazen city-limits signs used by some independent sundown towns. Instead, police often provide the first "defense" against African Americans in sundown suburbs. Police harassment, including racial profiling, can be even scarier than private violence, because one can hardly turn to the police for protection. Sundown suburbs near cities with sizable African American populations are especially likely to rely on their police—and the notoriety in the black community they earn—to stay white. Mary Pat Baumgartner pointed this out about "Hampton," her pseudonym for a New York City suburb: "Since [residents] cannot do away with [arterial] streets altogether, however, they turn to the police to scrutinize those who use them." Residents of sundown suburbs expect and applaud police harassment of outsiders. As Gary Kennedy, state representative from Dallas, wrote, "Blacks, Chicanos, and even poor whites with older automobiles avoid Highland Park for fear of being hassled by the police." [19]

Gregory Dorr, now a professor of history at the University of Alabama, spent the first 22 years of his life in Darien, Connecticut, a sundown suburb of New York City. He reports,

> Darien's Explorer Post 53 is one of the only volunteer adult-student run ambulance corps in the nation. Well, the "Posties" (as we called them) all had belt-worn pagers that could also double as police scanners. They (and those of us with them) often monitored the police, for giggles and grins and to give friends a warning if cops were called to break up a party. Whenever an African American was spotted in town, most frequently walking or hitching along Route 1 or I-95, the cops were called to check them out. They often stopped these folks, questioned them, etc. About the only black folk not harassed were those who were obviously domestics waiting at the few bus stops along Route 1. [20]

Recently such racial profiling has become newsworthy, leading to the term "DWB," "Driving While Black." Lawsuits or public protests have been lodged against the practice in suburbs in Maryland, New Jersey, Illinois, California, and several other states. White Americans sometimes get a sense of the adventure DWB entails when they are passengers in black-driven cars in sundown towns. Consider this account from Vandalia, Illinois, in about 1998:

When I was in high school in the late '90s, a (white) friend from my high school and I were back seat passengers in a car driven by a friend from a neighboring town, who was black. One of his friends, who was also black, sat in the passenger seat. We ended up driving on the town's main road, and the two guys got extremely nervous, claiming that every time they drove through Vandalia, they got pulled over by the police for no good reason. One of them said a police officer pulled him over to simply ask, "What's your business here?" Sure enough, an officer pulled us over and forcefully asked for all of our licenses. He claimed that the driver had taken too long to turn on his headlights, which I didn't think was the case. As soon as the officer saw our licenses, he got a very embarrassed look on his face, said he was sorry to bother us, and left. He spoke directly to my girl friend and me. Our parents were fairly prominent figures in the town, and as soon as the officer saw our last names on our licenses, he felt embarrassed for stopping us for no real reason. Who knows how the scenario would have played out had those two guys not had the two of us with them.[21]

In an ironic sense, the police are not to blame, for in a way, they're only doing good police work! As a Glendale, California, police officer explained to resident Lois Johnson, officers stopped any African American person after dark "because they did not live there." The police never could have stopped white motorists because *they* did not live there—the officers would find that out only *after* they stopped them. In sundown towns African Americans by definition "should not be there," hence are suspicious.[22]

Sometimes these practices die hard. A communications company in Carmel, Indiana, a suburb of Indianapolis that had been all-white until the 1980s, employed a number of African Americans in the mid-1990s. By this point, Carmel had about 250 black residents in a total population of some 30,000. After DWB complaints, including a successful lawsuit against the city's police department, Carmel created special tags for black employees of the company, visible to police officers, to identify those black drivers as acceptable. Thus *they*—unlike all other African American motorists—would be safe from unprovoked stops. Carmel was no longer all-white, but apparently its police had not gotten the message.[23]

Sundown During the Daytime

A few towns, including Effingham; Owosso; Buchanan County, Virginia; Burnside, Kentucky, according to oral history; Pollock, Louisiana; Arab, Alabama; Carterville, Gillespie, and East Alton, Illinois; and in some years Syra-

cuse, Ohio, did not allow African Americans within their city limits even during the day. During World War II, historian Herbert Aptheker saw a sign at the
edge of Pollock, "Nigger Stay Out of Pollock." Aptheker characterized Pollock as "somewhat unusual for it forbade black people into the town—
period." Michelle Tate, who interviewed residents of several Illinois sundown
towns, reports that Gillespie, a city of about 4,000 near St. Louis, had a similar sign at the edge of town into the early 1960s. "Even after the sign was removed, it was still an unwritten rule that black people entering this town
would not be tolerated, day or night." The signs at the edge of Buchanan
County, in western Virginia, said the usual—"Nigger, Don't Let the Sun Set
on You in This County"—as remembered by a white man who grew up
nearby, but "blacks were afraid to go to Grundy," the county seat, day or night,
according to an African American who grew up not far away in West Virginia
in the 1940s. He worked for an upholstery shop in Bluefield, and "when we
went to Grundy, I had to get out of the cab and get in the back under a tarp
with the furniture until we got to the house." Then he got out and helped deliver the furniture. "Then I had to get back in the back under the tarp until we
got back to Tazewell [County], and then I could get back in the cab."[24]

Towns such as Martinsville and Pana that would not let African Americans buy gas thus intimidated them from further shopping, even during the
day. In sundown suburbs, black shoppers have long been a concern. In 1956,
Dearborn resident George Washabaugh wrote his mayor to complain, "More
and more niggers are beginning to shop in our shopping centers, and I wish
there was some way we could stop this." In 2005, shopping is still an issue in
some majority-white suburbs. Mall managers don't want their shopping centers to get identified as "too black," which can prompt whites to shop elsewhere. Malls have died in response to the presence of young African
Americans—even in solidly white middle-class areas—because white shoppers flee black youth. Also, a mall can easily lose its cachet; then cutting-edge
retailers move to trendier locations. Suburban city officials also know that
shopping malls often desegregate first, leading to white uneasiness that can
fuel white residential flight. Today some suburbs do what they can to discourage African Americans from visiting their malls: persuading public transportation agencies not to service the malls with bus routes from black
neighborhoods, surveiling African American shoppers and making them uneasy, and having police follow black motorists.[25]

Many towns that might tolerate an occasional African American during
the day, shopping or buying gas, drew the line at full-time workers. This was
especially true if they had to stay the night, even if it was known to be for a

short period of time. A white man named J. J. Wallace invited a black carpenter into Norman, Oklahoma, in 1898 to do construction work. The mayor and other whites beat up Wallace because of it and ran the African American out of town. Wallace sued the government, arguing lack of protection, but the court concluded that neither it nor the state could be expected to do anything about local sentiment—even though the mayor helped lead the attack. Unfortunately, this case set an important precedent that shielded sundown town governments from legal consequences when they failed to stop whites who attacked African American workers and their white employers, according to law professor Al Brophy.[26]

The following clipping shows an example of the kind of terror that African American workers often encountered in sundown towns. It is from Rogers, Arkansas, probably between 1910 and 1920.

> A Bentonville contractor was building one of the first brick business houses here and he brought with him a colored man to carry the mortar hod, figuring that no white man would want to do such heavy, menial labor. A group of young men were gathered in the Blue saloon when the Negro entered, probably looking for his employer. The group seized the Negro and began telling what they were going to do with him. A well had been started at the rear of a business house but after going down some feet, the work was halted and the hole covered with planks.
>
> It was suggested they drop the Negro in the old well after they had hanged him but others objected on the ground that the odor from the ones already planted there was becoming objectional to the neighborhood. As some of the men pulled aside the planks to investigate, the ones holding the trembling Negro loosened their grip on their victim.
>
> It was the chance for escape he had been seeking, and in a matter of seconds he was just a blur on the horizon—and he never did return to Rogers. It was just another of the incidents that gave all colored people good excuses for not stopping here.

The incident was meant to be funny, for had the men been serious, they could easily have apprehended the runaway via auto or horse. Yet the prank was not entirely in jest, for it accomplished the disemployment of the man, surely one of its aims.[27]

An attorney not only is a hired worker but is necessary for court to proceed. Nevertheless, in Platte City, Missouri, north of Kansas City, a black attorney defending two clients "was met at the front door [of the courthouse] by a mob of white men" in December 1921, according to a report in the *Chicago Defender*. "The leader of the mob had a handkerchief bound around his mouth. Pointing an automatic revolver at [W. F.] Miles's head, he ordered him to turn around and leave town. Miles, his life in danger, did as he was bid." The sheriff and a deputy overtook him and brought him back to the court. The attorney then

> explained to the judge that he was being threatened in connection with the defense of the McDaniels and asked the court that note of the matter be made in the court record. The judge upbraided him for making any such charge before the jury. . . . Following this the court admonished Miles to have his clients change their pleas from not guilty to guilty. Miles did so and they were immediately sentenced to three years in the penitentiary. Miles persuaded the sheriff to protect him until he should reach Kansas City.[28]

As the attorney's saga implies, even when African Americans were admitted, their daytime position in many sundown towns could be quite tenuous. In 1923, Benton, Illinois, flirted with barring African Americans during the day. Whites threw a threatening note into the Franklin Hotel, "giving the colored help warning to leave town within a certain length of time," according to the *Benton Republican*. "The darkies left at once, with the result that the hotel was helpless and Mr. Ross was forced to close down his dining rooms Monday." The report went on to note, "Benton has never been very friendly to colored people making their homes here, but have never been partial before as to where they would permit them to work and where they would not be permitted to work." Apparently the movement did not become general, however, and African Americans were able to continue working elsewhere in Benton, so long as they did not stay after dark.[29]

During the Depression, the Civilian Conservation Corps (CCC) set up work camps in various locales to house formerly unemployed young men who worked on projects to better the community, such as sewage systems, state parks, and soil erosion barriers. The projects benefited the community, but sundown towns nevertheless often did not want them if it meant putting up with African American workers. In Richmond, California, just north of Berkeley, whites objected continuously to an interracial CCC camp in 1935; finally the company was replaced with one that was all-white. Yet Richmond was not even all-white, although most of its 270 African Americans in 1940 had to live in North Richmond, an unincorporated area outside the Richmond city limits. In Burbank, a suburb of Los Angeles, the CCC tried to locate an African American company in Griffith Park, but park commissioners refused to let them, citing an "old ordinance of the cities of Burbank and Glendale which prohibited Negroes from remaining inside municipal limits after sun down." Portfolio 18 shows how residents of Mt. Vernon, a sundown town in southwestern Missouri, threatened bloodshed to keep out a proposed black CCC camp.[30]

Wyandotte, Michigan, went a step beyond Mt. Vernon: it would not accept African American workers even during the daytime, commuting from Detroit. In December 1935, 55 Works Progress Administration men were sent to Wyandotte to build new sewers; 40 were African American. According to the *Wyandotte Daily News*:

> F. W. Liddle, director of the work projects in this city, refused to allow the men to go to work on the projects and so informed the director in Detroit. He stated as his reason for refusing to allow the men to work, the feeling in Wyandotte on the part of many against Negroes. . . . All projects were halted in the city for today.

The city's other newspaper, the *Herald,* claimed that Liddle's action "was based more on a desire to protect the colored workers than any racial prejudice. Wyandotte has never been a pleasant place for Negroes. In years gone by, colored people who tried to effect a residence here were either compelled or induced to leave town."[31]

During World War II, the War Department grew concerned because a huge defense contractor in East Alton could not hire African Americans. Truman K. Gibson Jr., aide to the secretary of war, reported:

> East Alton does not allow any Negroes to come into town. They can't ride on the public transportation system. The Mayor has said that if they come in, he will not be responsible for their protection. No Negroes live or work in East Alton. I am not entirely unacquainted with the attitude of many downstate cities toward Negroes.[32]

Even after World War II, many sundown towns and counties continued to exclude black workers. In Grundy County, Tennessee, Dr. Oscar Clements hired four African American bricklayers from Chattanooga. Whites drove them off, saying, "We won't even allow Negroes to come into Grundy County, much less work here." A better outcome occurred in Aurora, Indiana, near Cincinnati on the Ohio River. A contractor brought in four African American workers, whereupon "a crowd attacked them and tried to drive them away," according to historian Emma Lou Thornbrough, "while a citizens' committee warned the employer to get rid of them. This he refused to do, and the Negroes finished the job for which they were employed, but under police protection." Unfortunately, this set no precedent: Aurora displayed a sundown sign as recently as the 1960s, and a student at nearby Northern Kentucky University reported that Aurora was still a sundown town as of November 2002.[33]

Also after World War II, residents of Greenbelt, Maryland, a sundown suburb outside Washington built by the FDR administration during the Depression, shunned African Americans doing daytime janitorial work, denying them even customary salutations. Some residents tried to keep the local store from selling them food for lunch, but the Greenbelt council dismissed the objections. Whites in Neoga, in central Illinois, tried to keep out black workers even later. Michelle Tate interviewed an elderly African American couple in Mattoon, Illinois; the husband had worked on railroad tracks in various towns in central Illinois.

> The woman repeatedly spoke of her fear when he was working in Neoga. The railroad crew traveled places on an old school bus. This is where the men slept at night when they had finished working for the day. He talked of people meeting the bus on the way into [Neoga] and yelling to keep the "niggers" out of their town. He even stated that one time, when they were working in Neoga, a group of white men from Neoga came to Mattoon and broke out all the windows in the bus and tore up the inside, including leaving feces inside.

Thus residents expressed their outrage that blacks would be working in Neoga day or night.[34]

Night Work in Sundown Towns

Night work has long posed special problems for African Americans in sundown towns. A former worker at the Oregon Shakespeare Festival in Ashland wrote, "Most think that Ashland was such a town," and noted that theater almost always involves night work. In the 1950s, the Shakespeare Festival "hired their first black actress, and she had to be escorted as she traveled to and from the theatre for safety." Commonwealth Edison in the sundown town of Pekin, Illinois, was employing African Americans by the mid-1980s, but these workers drew unwanted police attention at least until the mid-1990s, according to an African American in nearby Peoria: "Those who worked the third shift, police would follow you in and follow you out, until they got a sense of where you were going." Similar harassment was visited upon African Americans working the third shift in the huge Ford plant in Dearborn.[35]

Two librarians in Oak Lawn, a sundown suburb southwest of Chicago, told me proudly in 1997, "We had a black woman working here in the library for almost two years, on the front desk, and no one was ever prejudiced to her." But they agreed it was not prudent for her to work the evening shift. Similarly, an African American college student from the Cleveland area said, "My mom worked in Parma, and they never encouraged her to stay late to get overtime. It was always, 'Why don't you come in early. . . . ' They didn't want her in Parma after dark." Door-to-door selling is especially problematic. An African American woman hired to sell vacuum cleaners door-to-door in Mahomet, Illinois, a sundown town just west of Champaign-Urbana, told me, "The company warned me not to be there after dark." Many African Americans would never consider taking jobs requiring them to be outdoors alone in sundown towns, even in daylight.[36]

Economic and Social Ostracism

Ford, the Oak Lawn library, and Commonwealth Edison were demonstrating some boldness merely by hiring African Americans to work in sundown towns. After all, one way to keep out African Americans is to refuse to employ them; independent sundown towns have often followed that route. Nick Khan hired an African American to work at his motel in Paragould, in northeast Arkansas, in 1982. He was warned not to do it but defied the warning.[37] The 2000 census showed 31 African Americans in Paragould, among more than 22,000 people, but white residents I spoke with in 2002 knew of no independent black households.[38] I asked Khan why so few black adults lived in Paragould. "They don't get jobs," was his reply. Himself a Pakistani American, he added, "Nobody would hire *us*. We are only here because we own the property." I told Khan about the remarks of a woman who went to her high school reunion at Paragould High School in 1997 after living out of state for four decades. She saw that the town was still all-white in 1997, as it had been 40 years before, and asked how this could be. "Oh, we have a committee that takes care of that," she was told. "They don't *need* a committee," Khan replied. "If black people come in, they will find that they're not welcome here. No one will hire them."[39]

When employers defy community sentiment and do hire African Americans, they then face a form of secondary boycott. During the summer of 1982, for example, the Shell station in Goshen, Indiana, hired a young black woman, the adopted daughter of a white Goshen couple. Within a month, business dropped off so precipitously that she had to be let go. Even owning the property may not suffice: in the 1970s, a black couple bought a gas station in Breese, a sundown town in southwestern Illinois. "I never heard of anyone harrassing or threatening them, people just didn't buy gas there," explained Stephen Crow, a 1976 graduate of Breese High School. So of course they had to leave. Nick Khan survived in Paragould only because his clientele came from outside the town.[40]

In Medford, a sundown town in southwestern Oregon, whites used another ploy, unwillingness to sell. In 1963, they refused to let an African American family buy groceries, according to former Medford resident Elice Swanson. "They moved out of the valley in about 6 months." Dyanna McCarty told of an incident she saw herself, when she was in seventh grade in Arcola, a central Illinois town of 2,700, in 1978. There had been talk in town that a new family was moving in. "They had two small kids (this news excited me, new babysitting opportunities) and the husband worked in Mattoon," she wrote.

> Later in the week I was in the school office . . . when I saw a black woman at the secretary's desk. She looked angry. I overheard that her children could not get registered for school until all their records got transferred. I also overheard lots of conversation regarding not knowing what happened to the records and blaming the mail service, etc. It didn't dawn on me what was happening until a few days later, after school at my grandfather's shop, which was located across the side alley from the Bi-Rite Grocery store. The same woman I had seen in the office at school pulled up to the Bi-Rite and got out of her car with her two kids. She went to the front door and there was a *closed* sign on it and the doors were locked. She looked around, as I did, because the parking lot was full; people inside looked to be shopping. I met her gaze and in a brief instant, I had an epiphany. The light bulb was so bright, I thought I was blinded. I was so angry. I took her across the alley and she met my grandpa; they talked in hushed tones while I played with the kids. I overheard them talking about where she could get some things, he offered her gas, he had his own above ground tank, and he gave her the names and locations of some Amish friends of his that could supply her with milk, eggs, meat, etc.
>
> They were there one day and a couple of weeks later they were gone. I don't blame them for leaving in the middle of the night. . . . Business slowed at my grandfather's shop for awhile, but it picked back up with time; he was the only auto body shop in [town].[41]

It was a good thing her grandfather's position was secure, because whites who befriended black newcomers often found themselves ostracized, socially and economically. In her remarkable memoir, *The Education of a WASP,* Lois Mark Stalvey tells how her white neighbors in suburban Omaha in the early 1960s broke off friendships with her and ultimately got her husband fired, simply because she tried to help a black couple buy a home in their all-white neighborhood. They moved to Philadelphia.[42]

Many white liberals in sundown towns and suburbs worry about social ostracism, so their anti-racism never gets voiced beyond the confines of home. Here is an example from Cullman, a sundown town in northern Alabama. "The first time I remember seeing a Confederate flag (flying on a car in Birmingham), I asked what it was, and Mother told it was waved by troublemakers who believed in being hateful to colored people," wrote a Cullman native about her childhood.

> During the Civil War centennial celebrations when my friends' parents dressed up and went to balls, my parents informed us that the Southern side had nothing to be proud of. In 1963 Mother insisted that we watch the March on Washington on television and kept saying, "This is history. This is history." . . . At the same time, my parents made it clear that my sister and I were not to repeat their most liberal sentiments to just anyone: "There are some things we just don't talk about outside the home."

Virginia Cowan writes of living with her mother-in-law for three months in Barnsdall, Oklahoma, in 1952:

> On the outskirts of town, I saw a big white sign with black letters that said, "Nigger, don't let the sun set on your black ass in this town." I couldn't believe it. . . . I stayed in Barnsdall three months. I never saw a black, ever. When they were talked about, it was always "those niggers" or "those uppity niggers." I cringed every time I heard that word. If someone I knew used it, I just walked away. Mom had asked me please not to make waves. She had to live there, after I left. So, I kept my mouth shut.[43]

Many residents of sundown towns expressed displeasure with their town's anti-black policies when they talked with me. Their disapproval seemed sincere, but they never mentioned voicing such sentiments to their fellow townspeople. They seem to feel they have performed as citizens if they disapprove privately, especially if they move away. One result is that everyone thinks the silent majority in their town favors continued exclusion, since no one speaks up. Edmund Burke famously said, "The only thing necessary for the triumph of evil is for good men to do nothing." Even today, especially in sundown suburbs, many whites are still afraid of being put down by other whites as "nigger lovers" (though elite suburbanites may not use the term itself), so their anti-racist impulses get immobilized. They do nothing. Their quiescence helps explain why sundown towns and suburbs usually stay all-white for decades.

Harassing Invited Guests

Even invited visitors—musicians, athletic teams, or houseguests of private citizens—have been attacked or threatened in sundown towns. African American musicians have often run afoul of sundown rules, partly because their job usually entails working after dark. When students at the University of Oklahoma invited a black band to play for a dance in 1922, residents of Norman left no doubt that the city's sundown rule applied on campus as well. Here is the account in an African American newspaper:

> A gang of ruffians have disgraced this city again in an attempt to maintain the vicious reputation of the city not to let Negroes stay in the municipality after sundown. For many years Norman has had signs and inscriptions stuck around in prominent places which read: "Nigger, don't let the sun go down on you in this berg." Saturday night, when Singie Smith's Orchestra of Fort Worth, Texas, attempted to play in the dance hall where they were employed by the students of the University, a mob of outlaws stormed the hall and practically wrecked it.
>
> A mob of approximately 500 surrounded the dance hall soon after the dance started and began to throw bricks. They were armed with clubs, guns, and some carried ropes. There was talk of lynching the Negroes, and it was said that several automobile loads of persons went to the city park to prepare for the hanging, telling the rest to bring the "niggers." Sheriff W. H. Newblock quickly gathered in all available deputies and deputized nearly 100 students of the U of Oklahoma, in order to protect the musicians.
>
> The orchestra was taken to the interurban station and sent to Oklahoma City when the mob grew in strength and it became evident that there would soon be trouble. Fights occurred between the mob and students who formed a bodyguard while the Negroes were escorted to the station.
>
> Negroes are occasionally seen on the streets of Norman in the daytime, but

the "rule" that they leave at night is strictly enforced. Several other Oklahoma towns have similar customs.

Several prominent businessmen were seen in the mob here Saturday night.[44]

Henry Louis Gates Jr. tells of an incident in about 1960, similar in a way to the "prank" in Rogers, Arkansas. In Oakland, county seat of Garrett, the county at the western tip of Maryland, whites threatened an African American jazz man, Les Clifford:

Mr. Les was "up Oakland," a town full of crackers and rednecks, if ever there was one, located on Deep Creek Lake, 25 or so miles from Piedmont. They hated niggers up Oakland. . . . NIGGERS READ AND RUN, Daddy claimed a sign there said. AND IF YOU CAN'T READ, RUN ANYWAY.

Anyway, Mr. Les was up at The Barn, a redneck hangout, flirting with all the white women, gyrating and spinning those sinuous tones, making that saxophone into a snake, a long, shiny, golden snake. A keg of beer apiece for these rednecks and a couple of hours of Les's snake working on their minds and their girlfriends' imaginations was all it had taken. Let's lynch that nigger, someone finally shouted. And so they did—or tried to, at least. Somebody called the state cops, and they busted down the door just about the time they were going to kick the table out from under Mr. Les and leave him dangling from the big central rafter. They would have given his horn back afterward, they said. To his family, they said.

As in Rogers, the men may not really have planned to kill Clifford; Gates's father, Henry Louis Gates Sr., thought "they were just scaring him." But as in Rogers, the incident was not entirely in jest. According to Gates Sr., Clifford had been dating a white woman: "That's what it was all about." The mock hanging was meant to frighten Clifford from the community to stop the relationship.[45]

Even when audiences loved their performances, musicians and athletes faced the problem of where to spend the night. This difficulty repeatedly beset barnstorming black baseball teams and the two famous black basketball teams, the Harlem Globetrotters and the Harlem Magicians, whenever they played in sundown towns. The town baseball team of El Dorado Springs, a sundown town in western Missouri, invited a black Kansas City team to play them, but the guests were then denied food and lodging. One man made an accommodation: Dr. L. T. Dunaway locked the team in his second-floor office "and some citizens took food to them," according to local historian Jean Swaim. African American workers paving U.S. 54 through El Dorado Springs in the 1940s "also had to spend their nights locked in that office." Swaim does not say whether they were locked in to prevent them from being at large in the town after sundown or to preclude violence against them by local white residents for that offense. Robinson is a small city in southeast Illinois whose main claim to fame is the invention of the Heath Bar. Mary Jo Hubbard, who grew up in Robinson in the 1950s and '60s, remembers

> an incident that took place in the early to mid '60s that involved a visiting high school basketball team that was not allowed to stay in the hotel and were put up in the local jail overnight while the basketball tournament was going on. I remember my parents being horrified at the time that children spent the night in the jail . . . but it did happen. That should tell you something about the town.[46]

Even the great contralto Marian Anderson repeatedly had trouble finding a place to sleep. When she sang at Princeton University in 1937, Princeton's only hotel refused her, as noted in the previous chapter, so Albert Einstein invited her to stay with him; "the two remained friends for life," according to a 2002 exhibit on Einstein at the American Museum of Natural History. In February 1958, Anderson had the same problem in Goshen, Indiana, when she sang at Goshen College, and had to stay the night in Elkhart, ten miles away, because the Goshen Hotel would not allow a black person to stay there. When Anderson sang in Appleton, Wisconsin, she had to sleep in Neenah or Menasha.[47] Actually, hotels in sundown towns like Goshen and Appleton did not differ from hotels in non-sundown towns like Princeton; between 1890 and about 1960, *most* hotels in America would not let African Americans stay the night.[48] But sundown towns posed additional complications. They had, of course, no African American hotels or other facilities. Hence *no* hotel would have housed Marian Anderson or any other African American. And because there were no African American residents, no black private homes existed to house stranded travelers in an emergency. Finally, Goshen and Appleton would not *allow* an African American to spend the night. That is the difference between Princeton and Goshen: Goshen was a sundown town, while Princeton was not. Hence no Einstein stepped forward in Goshen or Appleton. A professor who might volunteer to host Anderson in Goshen would endanger the singer as well as his or her own family.[49]

Scottsdale, Arizona, illustrated the difference in 1959. Twelve years after Jackie Robinson integrated the major leagues, the Boston Red Sox recruited their first African American player (they were the last team to do so). When Pumpsie Green joined the team for spring training camp in Scottsdale that spring, he was not housed in the hotel with the rest of the team, nor anywhere else in Scottsdale. The Red Sox claimed all the hotels were full with tourists, so there was no room for one more player, who just happened to be Green! The real reason was Scottsdale: "Blacks could not live there after dark, and so he was sent seventeen miles away to live in Phoenix," according to Howard Bryant, author of *Shut Out: A Story of Race and Baseball in Boston.*[50]

When residents of sundown towns did step forward to house African American visitors, they often found the experience unnerving. In 1969, a choir from Southern Baptist College performed in Harrison, Arkansas. "It had a black member," according to the wife of a couple I spoke with in Harrison in 2002. "We put her up, but we worried lest our house get blown up." Grey Gundaker, who now teaches American studies at William and Mary, went to junior high school in Manitowoc, Wisconsin, a sundown town on Lake Michigan, between 1962 and 1964. He remembers one occasion when the policy was violated at a stable where he worked after school. "When an African American man who drove a horse van came through town and needed a place to stay, the owner of the stable, Larry Bowlin, put him up. . . . Larry told us kids not to tell, that it would be very dangerous for his friend if he were caught." Left unsaid: it would also be dangerous for Bowlin and his family.[51]

White residents tried to avoid triggering a town's sundown sensibility. In 1982, a young woman was planning her wedding in Pinckneyville, Illinois, where she had grown up, a sundown town 60 miles southeast of St. Louis. "I asked a dear college friend, who was also a long-time friend of my husband's, to be an usher. When going over lists with my mother, she said, 'Who's this Roy?' " The bride-to-be reminded her mother of a photo of her and Roy, who was African American. "She turned six shades of white and said, 'You don't actually think he'll come, do you?' I dug in my heels and swore that if he wasn't welcomed, I'd elope. . . . I did give in somewhat, though: I agreed to move my 6:30 wedding to 6:00 PM so there'd be plenty of daylight while he was in town."[52]

Occasional acts of violence greeted visitors and hosts in these situations, showing that Bowlin's fear and the bride's rescheduling were justified. In September 1946, for example, a white army officer allowed a black army officer to stay overnight in his home in West Lawn in southwest Chicago, according to reporter Steve Bogira. "The two had served together in the war, and the black officer was visiting from out of town. Word got out in the neighborhood, and soon a mob was stoning the home, smashing windows, and yelling, 'Lynch the nigger lover.' " Chicago was not a sundown town, of course, but West Lawn was a sundown neighborhood.[53]

The Importance of the City Limits

Carnival, circus, and railroad workers—who carry their accommodations with them—make plain the difference between sundown towns and towns with no sundown policy but whose hotels were white-only. Sundown towns told black people not to spend the night even when no hotel was involved. Little towns such as Niantic and Villa Grove in central Illinois forced African American railroad workers to move their work cars beyond the town limits at night. A retired miner who has lived his entire life in Zeigler, in southern Illinois, said in 2002, "Nigra [sic] employees would be working with the carnivals, and they had to leave [Zeigler] by sundown." Having spent time in Zeigler, I suspect they didn't leave, because all the surrounding towns are also sundown towns that would have been no better. Probably they simply hid in their carnival vehicles for the night, but they probably moved them beyond the city limits.[54]

To be sure, some rural areas have also been closed to African Americans. In his 1908 classic *Following the Color Line,* Ray Stannard Baker wrote, "A farmer who lives within a few miles north of Indianapolis told me of a meeting held only a short time ago by 35 farmers in his neighborhood, in which an agreement was passed to hire no Negroes, nor to permit Negroes to live anywhere in the region." Later in this chapter we will learn of the lynching of a white farm owner near Lamb, Illinois, who would not dismiss his black farm employee. Much less violent measures were employed at least as recently as 2001 to ensure that rural land is not sold to an African American.[55]

More often, the rules have been looser beyond the city limits. In 1925 in Price, Utah, for example, a white mob twice overpowered the sheriff and hanged Robert Marshall, an African American accused of murdering a white deputy, Marshall being not quite dead after the first hanging. In the aftermath, Price became a sundown town. Four years later, another African American, Howard Browne Sr., was able to settle with his family outside Price, but Price itself, in Browne's words, "was off-limits to blacks." In the 1940s and '50s in Colorado, migrant Mexican beet-field workers were housed in adobe colonies or "colonias" outside of towns, according to a survey of Colorado race relations by the University of Colorado Latino/a Research and Policy Center. After the season, when the colonias closed, some had to winter in Denver slums, unable to live inside the city limits of the towns where they had worked.[56]

For a while in the 1930s, an African American man was allowed to live at the Perry County Fairgrounds at the edge of Pinckneyville, taking care of the horses. Greenup, Illinois, in Cumberland County, some 40 miles west of Terre Haute, Indiana, had a similar policy. Indeed, a longtime resident said that the Cumberland County Fairgrounds was deliberately left out of Greenup's incorporated boundaries because African Americans sometimes stayed there. That way African Americans going to the fair, caring for livestock, or working for the ride operators could stay at the fairgrounds without violating the town's sundown ordinance. An exception was likewise made for two men at the Clark County Fairgrounds in Martinsville, fifteen miles east, in the 1950s. As a former resident wrote, "The rule was, 'Better not catch 'em here after dark—oh, except for Russell and Rabbit.' " Martinsville was nicer than the Chicago suburb Arlington, according to labor historian Mel Dubofsky: "As I recall, Arlington, Illinois was one of your 'sundown towns' into the 1960s. Blacks could work at the track but they could not appear on city streets after dark nor sleep anywhere but at the stables."[57]

In about 1952, the high school band director at LaSalle-Peru was coordinating the visit of the university band of a Big Ten school, probably the University of Michigan. As Chapter 1 told, LaSalle and Peru are adjoining sundown towns on the Illinois River in northern Illinois. To save costs, he planned to have his band members house the visiting university students. Then he got advance publicity for their concert, including a photograph of the band, and realized several of its members were African American. What to do? According to my source, a student at the time, "he feared being in violation of the unwritten but well-acknowledged sundown rule." His prudent solution: he went to a band member who lived outside LaSalle-Peru but in the school district, and asked him to host the African American band members. "This worked out all right, and I don't recall any fracas or community uprising."[58]

Perhaps the most remarkable example of the power of the city line—and yet it was subtle, even invisible until pointed out—was at Elizabethtown College in Pennsylvania in the late 1940s, probably continuing into the '50s. According to a 1950 graduate of the college, to house returning servicemen after World War II, Elizabethtown College put up a barracks-like "dormitory." One end of the long building extended across the city line, so to abide by Elizabethtown's sundown rule, the college required its black students to live in that end of the barracks. The students then crossed over into Elizabethtown within their own dormitory and exited on campus to attend class. In 1948 or 1949, a black gospel quartet performed at the college and had to be put up for the night. As in LaSalle-Peru, a farmer outside the town provided the hospitality.[59]

In sundown counties, the county line plays the role of the city limits. Often, especially in the Cumberlands and Appalachia, it boasted the usual sundown signs. A 1906 report in the *Charlotte Observer* tells what happened when a telephone trunk line was put through Madison County, a sundown county[60] in western North Carolina:

> Negroes were employed on the works and the company building the line was put in some inconvenience by the citizens of Madison refusing to allow the Negroes to stay in the county over night. The Negro laborers were forced to go beyond the Madison county line to spend their nights.[61]

The power of the city limits can be seen still more graphically in suburbia. Often the jurisdictional line between city and suburb is not even visible on the landscape, yet these lines frequently result in an all-white suburb on one side, a majority-black neighborhood just across the street. (Portfolio 30 shows one such line in Maryland.) Driving along Eight Mile Road—the boundary between overwhelming black Detroit and sundown suburb Warren—shows visually that social class is not responsible for suburban segregation, because the houses look the same on both sides.

Something artificial and additional, obviously tied to the invisible line between city and suburb, has kept African Americans on one side in Detroit, whites on the other in Warren. When town boundaries also form racial divides, that shows the extent to which public policies have maintained all-white suburbs.[62]

Zoning

Suburban incorporation gave suburbs power over zoning, which in turn conferred "unprecedented power to control development," according to historian David Freund, which then played a key role in keeping suburbs white. Originally meant to keep out disamenities such as polluting industries, zoning became a tool to keep out the "wrong kind of people." After such decisions as

Lee Sing and *Buchanan v. Warley* (described in Chapter 4) made it more difficult to exclude blacks openly, suburban town governments soon saw that "regular" zoning might accomplish the same result, at least on a class basis. Beginning as early as 1900 and continuing "for many years," sociologist Gary Orfield notes, "suburban governments used their zoning authority to exclude African Americans." It was no accident that Edina became the first town in Minnesota to set in place a comprehensive zoning ordinance, Edina being the premier sundown suburb of Minneapolis–St. Paul. Cities like Edina banned mobile homes, public housing, subsidized housing, housing for the elderly, and apartments—and thus the kind of people who would live in such housing.[63]

In the New York metropolitan area in the mid-1970s, more than 99% of all undeveloped land zoned for residential use was restricted to single-family housing. The next step was to impose minimum acreage requirements for single-family homes. During the 1960s, more than 150 New Jersey suburbs increased their minimum lot sizes. In Connecticut, in 1978, more than 70% of all residentially zoned land carried a one-acre minimum lot size. Greenwich, an upper-class suburb of New York City, had a four-acre minimum. Much of St. Louis County surrounding St. Louis has a three-acre minimum. Given the cost of land in metropolitan areas, such large-lot zoning keeps out inexpensive homes and the people who might buy them. To make doubly sure, elite suburbs require new houses to be larger than a certain number of square feet or cost more than a certain amount. These economic measures could not keep out affluent African Americans, but the reputation they fostered for community elitism did.[64]

Incorporation also let local officials decide if their communities would participate in subsidized or public housing. "Most suburbs never created local housing authorities," according to Michael Danielson, so they never got public housing. Some highly populated suburban counties did create public housing authorities but neglected to build any, he further points out. "DuPage County Housing Authority [just west of Chicago] was established in 1942, but had yet to construct a single unit 30 years later." St. Louis County, which surrounds St. Louis on three sides, had 50 units of public housing in 1970 for a population of 956,000, while St. Louis city had 10,000 units for a population of 622,000. Even suburbs that *do* accept public housing often limit it to the elderly or require prior residence in the suburb for at least a year.[65]

Race, not the market, usually underlies suburban vetoes of public housing and subsidized housing. After a developer tried to build subsidized housing in Parma, a sundown suburb of Cleveland, voters in 1971 overwhelmingly endorsed a proposal requiring public approval for any subsidized housing project. Other Cleveland suburbs followed suit. "Racial fears were prominent in the controversy," Danielson reports. In 1970, Parma had just 50 African Americans in a total population of 100,216, and "one official announced that he did 'not want Negroes in the City of Parma.' " From coast to coast, sundown suburbs of all social classes have voted down public housing. And not just public housing—any housing that African Americans might likely inhabit. After Ford opened a huge assembly plant in Mahwah, New Jersey, for example, the town refused to let the United Auto Workers build subsidized housing there, so thousands of workers, many of them African American, had to commute every day from Newark.[66]

Farley and Frey explain how sundown suburbs have used their independent "zoning laws, school system, and police" to maintain racial purity:

> Zoning ordinances were changed and variances granted or denied to prevent construction that might be open to blacks. Public schools hired white teachers, administrators, and coaches. As a result, in most Midwestern and Eastern metropolitan areas, white families who wished to leave a racially changing city could choose from a variety of suburbs knowing their neighbors would be white and that their children would attend segregated schools.

Circularities get built in. Some working-class or multiclass sundown suburbs have passed ordinances requiring teachers, firefighters, police officers, and other city workers to live within their corporate limits. Thus they can be assured that all their employees will be white. Their schools, police departments, and other offices then present all-white facades to any black would-be newcomers. In turn, African Americans are ineligible to be hired for future openings, since they would first have to move in to be considered. This is subtler than an open prohibition: race does not get used as a criterion for hiring or for residence, yet the suburb stays white.[67]

When all else fails and a black family actually manages to acquire a house in a sundown community, incorporation confers the right to take it for the "public good." No matter if the black family doesn't want to sell, even for an above-market price. For many decades, independent towns and sundown suburbs alike have used this power of eminent domain to force the sale, condemning the land for a public purpose such as a park or school playground.

For instance, in Deerfield, a sundown suburb fifteen miles northwest of Chicago, the Progress Development Corporation bought two tracts of land in
1959 and planned to build integrated housing. An Episcopal minister told his
congregation about it, which, according to Ian McMahan, "was as if a bomb
had exploded in the quiet town of Deerfield." First the city invented trivial
building violations to stop the work. Then an organization called the North
Shore Residents' Association polled Deerfield residents and found they were
eight to one against letting blacks in. Finally, Deerfield decided to keep out the
development by designating the tracts as parks; that proposal passed in a referendum in late 1959 but "only" by a two-to-one margin, with an astonishing
95% of all eligible voters casting ballots. Progress Development took Deerfield to court, accusing the city of coming up with the parks as subterfuges to
stay all-white, but McMahan says Deerfield prevailed, at least as of 1962, and
he must be right, because 40 years later, of 18,420 residents, only 61 were
African American.[68]

Defended Neighborhoods

Officials of sundown suburbs also have subtler weapons at their disposal in
their fight to keep their communities white. Their jobs have two main compo-
nents—providing public services and keeping out undesirables—according
to research in the 1960s summarized by Danielson. Sometimes the two conflict, and when they do, "residents of upper- and middle-class suburbs in the
Philadelphia area ranked maintenance of their community's social characteristics—defined in terms of keeping out 'undesirables' and maintaining the
'quality' of residents—as a more important objective for local government
than . . . the provision of public services." At the "behest" of the wealthy, as
Rosalyn Baxandall and Elizabeth Ewen put it in their study of suburban Long
Island, "officials in Nassau County allowed all public roads to fall into disre-
pair. Moreover, private estate roads were built like mazes—winding and deliberately confusing. Most of the North and South Shore beaches were marked
CLOSED with large private property signs, and were guarded as well." Baumgartner found that residents of "Hampton," her pseudonym for a New York
City suburb, "would rather bear the inconvenience of narrow and congested
streets on a day-by-day basis than make it easier for the inhabitants of New
York City to reach the town." Even street signs are in short supply in Darien,
Connecticut, making it hard to find one's way around that elite sundown suburb. Darien doesn't really *want* a lot of visitors, a resident pointed out, and
keeping Darien confusing for strangers might deter criminals—perhaps a

veiled reference to African Americans. Some Darien residential streets are even posted "Private." [69]

Many sundown suburbs thus exemplify what urban sociologists call "defended neighborhoods." Sidewalks and bike paths are rare and do not connect to those in other communities inhabited by residents of lower social and racial status. Some white suburbs of San Francisco opted out of the Bay Area Rapid Transit system, fearing it might encourage African Americans to move in. Some white suburbs and neighborhoods in and around Washington, D.C., similarly showed no interest in that area's Metro rapid transit. Many sundown suburbs choose not to provide other public amenities that might draw outsiders. If by accident of geography or history they already have such facilities, they usually make access difficult for outsiders. Thus suburbs may admit only residents to beaches. Parks, tennis courts, and playgrounds may be few or located on minor roads where visitors will be unlikely to find them. Rather than set aside large areas for parks, private lawns take on a park-like appearance. Some of these towns come to exemplify what economist John Kenneth Galbraith famously called "public squalor and private affluence." According to Frederique Krupa, writing in 1993, San Marino, an elite suburb of Los Angeles, "closes its parks on weekends to make sure the neighboring Asian and Latin communities are excluded," thus keeping out everyone, even its own residents. [70]

Policies and Ordinances

For years, the public policies and restrictions of suburbs have carried a purposeful racial tinge and have been selectively enforced. Their racial aspect was evident to Bob Johnson and his family in southern California in 1960:

> We lived in Sunland near Glendale. We took the kids to the Verdugo Plunge [swimming pool] in Glendale. There was a sign that said only for residents of Glendale. We are white and did not want to go back home, so we paid our money and they did not ask for our drivers license or identification. I was puzzled how they monitored whether or not I was from Glendale. Then I realized that was a way to keep blacks out since no blacks lived in Glendale.

A Detroit suburbanite had a similar experience in the Dearborn area in about 1985: "Dearborn passed a city ordinance that only city residents could use its parks—*i.e.* whites only. I visited my aunt and uncle who lived there and was never asked for any ID to prove I was a resident, but the local papers had several stories about African Americans who were asked for ID and then removed from the parks."[71]

White suburbs still pass all sorts of ordinances to discourage nonwhite visitors and residents. Highland Park, Texas, has been a leader in criminalizing ordinary behavior. It may have more "No" signs per capita than any other city in the nation. The Dallas suburb brags about being a city of parks, but it does not want outsiders to use them. Lakeside Park is its largest park and continues into Dallas; Highland Park has made it illegal to eat lunch in its portion of Lakeside. Too much litter, said city officials, but the *Dallas Morning News* suspected that an aversion to the possibility of African American picnickers underlay the ordinance. Highland Park also prohibits swimming, wading, climbing trees, drinking alcohol, sleeping, "protractedly lounging," and sitting on railings or "any other property in a park which . . . is not designated or customarily used for such purposes." Outsiders cannot play tennis; reservations are for residents only, and it is illegal to play without one.[72] In 1982, the suburb made headlines for ticketing thirteen joggers, ten of whom were nonresidents, for jogging on city streets; this offense cost a $15 fine or a night in jail. It made fishing without a city permit against the law and charged $5 per year for a fishing permit. Highland Park police have also repeatedly arrested African Americans and Mexican Americans for being "drunk in car." The latter is "a non-existent crime," according to reporter Jane Wolfe. The fishing permit is legal nonsense too, because a Texas fishing license, "which costs $4.50 a year for state residents, entitles the holder to fish free of charge in any body of public water in Texas," as reporter Doug Swanson noted. "And the creeks and lakes of Highland Park, [game warden Billy] Walker said, are public."[73]

Every department of sundown suburbs has been used to enforce these policies and to maintain their communities' desired reputation of being unfriendly to minorities. Police in Cicero, Illinois, told African American would-be residents they could not move their own furniture into Cicero without a permit. The school system played its part too. In 1981, when Christopher Phillips began as a new teacher in the Cicero Public Schools, his introduction to the community came at the district's faculty assembly as the fall semester began. "The superintendent stood at the podium before all the district's teachers and the first words he spoke were, 'There are no blacks in the Cicero Public Schools, and there will be none as long as I am superintendent.' He received wild applause."[74]

Dearborn's longtime mayor Orville Hubbard used the city's police and fire departments and even its sanitation department to harass black newcomers until they fled the city. African Americans who tried to move in found their gas turned off and their garbage uncollected, by city policy. According to David Good, Hubbard's biographer, Hubbard told a reporter that "as far as he was concerned, it was against the law for Negroes to live in his suburb." In 1956, Hubbard said to an Alabama journalist, "They can't get in here. We watch it. Every time we hear of a Negro moving in—for instance, we had one last year—we respond quicker than you do to a fire." Good tells that Dearborn police officers and firefighters made wake-up visits to the new black family's house every hour or so through the night in response to alleged trouble calls. Recall sociologist Karl Taeuber's finding that whites in the Detroit metropolitan area in 1970 were five times more likely than African Americans, even controlling for differences in income, to live in the suburbs. Certainly these actions by Dearborn's city government help to explain why.[75]

Dearborn was an extraordinary case because its mayor was so outspoken, but Good cautions us not to see Hubbard as unique: "In a sense, Orville Hubbard's view was no different from that in any of a dozen or more other segregated suburbs that ringed the city of Detroit—or in hundreds of other such communities scattered across the country."[76]

Restrictive Covenants

The U.S. Supreme Court found openly anti-black ordinances unconstitutional in 1917 in *Buchanan v. Warley,* but sundown towns and suburbs nevertheless acted as if they had the power to be formally all-white until at least 1960; informally some communities have never given up this idea. The federal government was hardly likely to enforce *Buchanan v. Warley* until after World War II; on the contrary, it was busily creating all-white suburbs itself until then. After 1917, most sundown suburbs resorted to restrictive covenants. Covenants were usually private, part of the deed one signed when buying from the developer. Like the Great Retreat, restrictive covenants first targeted Chinese Americans in the West, originating in California in the 1890s, and then spread to the East, where Jews and blacks were targeted for exclusion. The United States Supreme Court unanimously declined to interfere with restrictive covenants in *Corrigan v. Buckley,* a 1926 case originating in Washington, D.C. The Court reasoned that restrictive covenants were agreements between private citizens, hence were OK, whereas ordinances were passed by governments.[77]

Covenants weren't really private, though, because many suburban governments would not approve new developments without them. Nor would the Federal Housing Administration (FHA) insure loans without them. Many communities proceeded to encumber every square inch of their residential land with restrictive covenants, agreement to which became part of the purchase of the property. Thus covenants worked just as well as ordinances to make entire towns all-white. This practice was particularly common in California. In February 1929, for example, the Palos Verdes Homes Association in Palos Verdes Estates, California, published a booklet, "Palos Verdes Protective Restrictions," including this language: "No person not of the white race (except servants and students) shall use or occupy any part of the property." That phrasing was unusual; almost never were students exempt from the restriction. Here is a more typical covenant, from a suburb in Montgomery County, Maryland, built shortly after World War II:

> No persons of any race other than the Caucasian race shall use or occupy any lot or any building, except that this covenant shall not prevent occupancy by a domestic servant of a different race domiciled with an owner or a tenant.[78]

Across the United States, suburbs and white residential districts in cities now hastened to adopt restrictive covenants. According to sociologist Douglas Massey, the Chicago Real Estate Board started using them in 1919. By 1940, more than 80% of the Chicago area was covered by covenants, according to the NAACP. Actually, the proportion of the Chicago suburbs that were covered by covenants was much higher than 80%, because the remaining 20% included those neighborhoods in the city where African Americans already lived. Across the United States, exclusionary covenants were the rule rather than the exception.[79]

In 1948, in *Shelley v. Kraemer,* the U.S. Supreme Court ruled that no court could *enforce* a racial covenant. Although it didn't make voluntary covenants illegal, *Shelley v. Kraemer* nevertheless began to make a difference. In the late 1940s, civic leaders and realtors in South Pasadena, California, tried to blanket the entire city with restrictive covenants. "When pressed about the status of African Americans, Mexican Americans, and Asian Americans," historian Charlotte Brooks writes, "they announced that such people could work in the town, as long as they left by dusk." According to Brooks, "The covenant campaign eventually failed, due to the publicity it received and the *Shelley v. Kraemer* decision." *Shelley v. Kraemer* implied for the first time (since the neglected 1917 decision) that there might be something wrong or illegal about racial exclusion.[80]

Real Estate Agents as the Front Line of Defense

After the Supreme Court emasculated racial covenants, realtors became the front line of defense, keeping suburbs white. According to James Hecht, realtors had conceived of restrictive covenants and popularized them in the first place. After 1948, despite *Shelley v. Kraemer,* realtors could still simply say with impunity, "We don't sell to blacks." Indeed, in 1948 the Washington, D.C., Real Estate Board Code of Ethics adopted the following statement: "No property in a white section should ever be sold, rented, advertised, or offered to colored people." In St. Louis in that year, realtors zoned the entire metropolitan area into "white" and "black" neighborhoods and forbade any realtor "under pain of expulsion to sell property in the white zone to a Negro," as one realtor explained to Dorothy Newman. Even as late as 1957, a teaching manual for Realtors put out by the National Association of Real Estate Boards counseled against introducing "undesirable influences" into a block. Included among these undesirable influences were bootleggers, gangsters, or "a colored man of means who was giving his children a college education and thought they were entitled to live among whites."[81]

These real estate practices had a long history. In 1913, the National Association of Real Estate Boards (now the National Association of Realtors) instructed its members, according to urban historian Stephen Meyer, "not to contribute to residential race mixing." In 1924, the same year that the United States passed the Immigration Restriction Act, Realtors added to their Code of Ethics Article 34, which stated:

> A Realtor should never be instrumental in introducing into a neighborhood a character of property or occupancy, members of any race or nationality, or any individuals whose presence will clearly be detrimental to property values in that neighborhood.

That African Americans (and sometimes Jews) had this effect was an article of faith. "Through this code," Hecht writes, "America's Realtors became committed to segregated neighborhoods.[82] Even when a homeowner was willing to sell to a Negro, the Realtor was prohibited from being a party to such a transaction."[83]

Usually realtors were surprisingly open about refusing to sell to blacks (see Portfolio 28.) In 1944 in Salt Lake City, Utah, for example, Carlos Kimball chaired a "Non-White Housing Control Committee." According to an article in the *Pittsburgh Courier,* he got "most Salt Lake real estate dealers" to sign pledges "to restrict non-whites from white communities." Kimball pointed out that these pledges were "in accordance with the National Association of Real Estate Boards' code of ethics which forbids the sale of property to anyone who might 'lower community standards.' " Kimball then sent a circular about the policy to "Negro leaders" in the Salt Lake City area.[84]

For two decades after *Shelley v. Kraemer*, African Americans routinely encountered open race-based exclusion and could do nothing about it. Most whites thought it was proper to exclude blacks, and exclusion was legal. Consequently African Americans had no available remedy. Consider this complaint, sent to the Connecticut Civil Rights Commission in 1955:

> A building firm has been advertising houses for quite some time with a minimum down payment for veterans. Today, my wife and I went out to see about the purchase of one of these houses. When we talked to the man the first thing he told us was that an agreement had been made that they would sell only to white people. . . . I have tried for months to find some kind of improved living conditions. I have answered hundreds of ads for apartments but the moment they find I am a Negro, the answers given are "Filled," "The neighbors object," or someone else might.

The commission's files reveal its totally ineffective response:

> A representative called at the construction company named in this letter. They were building 208 homes. A partner in the business said their only interest was in selling the homes as fast as they could be constructed. He felt that if it were known that a Negro family had purchased a house it might be more difficult to sell to white purchasers.

The commission could do nothing because "the development has received no subsidy from any public agency and consequently does not come within the purview of the Public Accommodations Act. The complainant was advised to this effect." Thus seven years after the Supreme Court ruled restrictive covenants unenforceable, this couple had no recourse for housing segregation even in "liberal" Connecticut.[85]

Since real estate agents depend on other agents to find buyers for their listings, keeping realtors in line usually proved easy. In 1961 the Greenwich, Connecticut, Real Estate Board criticized one of its members, Olive Braden, for selling to Jews. So she sent a memo to her staff: "From this date on, when anyone telephones us in answer to an ad in any newspaper and their name is, or appears to be Jewish, do not meet them anywhere!" In a suburb of Houston, according to Benjamin Epstein and Arnold Foster, "a builder and a real estate agent who joined in selling a home to a Jewish family were punished severely. The builder was not permitted to build any more homes in that village; the agent was refused property listings in the area."[86]

Sometimes real estate agents in sundown towns have screened out the "wrong kind" of Gentile *whites*. An interesting incident in Martinsville, Indiana, in about 1995, shows an agent unhappy with her would-be clients. Jonathan Welch had a new job in Franklin; his wife, Amy, worked in Greencastle. Martinsville lies in between, so they shopped there for a home. In Amy Welch's words:

> We spent an evening driving around the village, which seemed very nice, and found a beautiful house that we decided to call on. I made arrangements with the real-estate lady to view the house; Jon unfortunately couldn't come with. The house seemed nice, as was the agent. . . . When the tour was complete, she told me I was more than welcome to call her with any questions or concerns and gave me her business card. When I took out my wallet to put away her card, my picture fold fell out onto the bar and opened up to a portrait of some very good friends—good friends who happen to be engaged and Japanese and African American. She looked at the photo, put her finger on the very corner of the picture and turned it slowly toward her, like it could jump up and bite her if she made any sudden movements! Anyway, she said to me: "Oh, you associate with those kind of people?" . . . I turned her business card around to her in the same manner and said, "Yup." And left.

Obviously, the realtor felt that for Martinsville to stay all-white required not only keeping out blacks, but also vigilance as to the type of whites one allows in.[87]

Other Elements of the "System"

Realtors were only part of the system that kept African Americans out of sundown suburbs. Bankers played key roles. In the mid-1950s, the Detroit Urban League reported conversations with various bankers. One said he would loan to blacks regardless of where they bought, but another wouldn't deal with African Americans, period. A third "would not make the first Negro loan in a white area." Another banker tried "to substantiate this position by contending that it is not good common sense to make one friend and alienate eighteen friends, even though the one is a sound credit risk." The FHA sided with the majority. In most cities, no banker like the first even existed.

FHA approval is often required for a bank loan, and Chapter 5 explained how racist were its national policies. In Detroit, according to Thomas Sugrue, author of *Origins of the Urban Crisis,* federal appraisers working for the Home Owners Loan Corporation, predecessor to the FHA, gave a D to "every Detroit neighborhood with even a tiny African American population" and colored it red on their maps. The FHA inherited these maps and the tradition of redlining, nationally as well as in Detroit. Should a potential buyer somehow surmount the credit hurdle, every subsequent step of the homebuying process requires cooperation with someone—invariably someone white in a sundown suburb. The home has to be inspected or appraised, a title search must be completed and the title insured, and so forth. Each of these steps proved difficult or impossible for black would-be homebuyers.[88]

The Grosse Pointe System

Realtors in Grosse Pointe, Michigan, also screened whites, but in a cruder manner. They developed a "point system" (no pun intended) for keeping out undesirables. When the system became public knowledge in 1960, a furor of publicity erupted, including stories in the *New York Times* and *Time* magazine. Don and Mary Hunt, author of several guides to Michigan, supply a useful summary:

> For years into the 1950s, prospective Grosse Pointe home buyers were excluded by the Grosse Pointe Realtors' infamous point system. Prospective buyers were assigned points to qualify for the privilege of living here. A maximum score was 100, with 50 points the minimum for ethnically inoffensive applicants [WASPs]. But Poles had to score 55 points, Greeks 65, Italians, 75, and Jews 85. The private detectives hired to fill out the reports didn't even bother to rate African Americans or Asian Americans. The questions included:
> 1. Is their way of living typically American?
> 2. Appearances—swarthy, slightly swarthy, or not at all?
> 3. Accents—pronounced, medium, slight, not at all?
> 4. Dress—neat, sloppy, flashy, or conservative?

Realtors relied on private investigators who interviewed neighbors of would-be newcomers. Although Jews could allegedly gain entry, they had to be pretty special. Dr. J. B. Rosenbaum was "only half-Jewish" and his wife was a Gentile. Moreover, his mother was a direct descendant of Carter Braxton, a signer of the Declaration of Independence, and Rosenbaum had invented an artificial heart and had received several academic awards in recognition of this achievement. Grosse Pointe rejected him.[89]

The Grosse Pointe Brokers Association threatened to expel any member who didn't use the point system. This was a meaningful threat, because without cooperation from other realtors, representing buyers and sellers, they could no longer do business in the community. And association members backed up the threat with action, expelling at least two members for selling to ineligible buyers under the point system before 1960. One had sold to Italian Americans, the other to a doctor who had remarried and whose new wife had not been screened. No member had dared sell to an African American.[90]

The 1960 furor seemed to lead to action. In May 1960, Michigan's attorney general and the state's commissioner of corporation securities ordered Grosse Pointe to abandon the point system within 30 days. The minister of a Grosse Pointe church stated, "Jesus Christ could never qualify for residence in Grosse Pointe," which was true, of course, he being Jewish and probably swarthy to boot. "It's very unfortunate that the word 'swarthy' ever was used," said the secretary of the Grosse Pointe Brokers Association, still defending the point system. "In our definition, the word 'swarthy' doesn't always mean what it says. Applied to Jews, it would mean how much like a Jew does he look. This relates to his features, rather than just coloring." After hearings on Grosse Pointe, the commissioner of corporation securities, Lawrence Gubow, issued an administrative regulation known as Rule 9, barring realtors from discriminating on the basis of race, religion, or national origin.

Ultimately, however, the publicity resulted in no change. According to Norman C. Thomas, who wrote the standard work on the subject, "Reaction to Rule 9 was swift and vigorous." Officials of the Grosse Pointe Property Owners Association "launched a movement to write into the Michigan constitution an unqualified right of a property owner to refuse to sell or rent 'to any person whatsoever.' " The state legislature then passed a law specifically repealing Rule 9, but the Democratic governor vetoed it. Finally, in 1962 the Michigan Supreme Court unanimously killed Rule 9. It was too much policy making by administrative fiat, the court said, intruding into the powers of the legislature. Grosse Pointe realtors went back to business as usual with fair-skinned whites only.[91]

As implied by the intervention of the Grosse Pointe Property Owners Association, realtors were not the only problem. In 1969, nine years after the scandal over the point system, some residents in Grosse Pointe Farms, one of the five related towns known collectively as Grosse Pointe, tried to get their community to agree with the principle of open housing, which had been endorsed by Congress and the Supreme Court just the year before. Calling themselves the Committee on Open Housing, they proposed an ordinance that levied civil penalties against discrimination in housing on the basis of race, sex, age, or national origin. "It was the showdown for Grosse Pointe on integration," according to Kathy Cosseboom, author of a book on race relations in Grosse Pointe. The Real Estate Board and the Grosse Pointe Property Owners Association opposed it. The ordinance went down to defeat, 2,271 to 1,596, with half of all registered voters going to the polls, high for such a referendum.[92]

Despite these attitudes, in July 1966, the first African American family moved into Grosse Pointe. They had not been able to buy directly through a realtor, and they met with some hostility as well as some welcome from residents. Two months after they moved in, whites placed gravestones on their front lawn. Nevertheless, another black family moved in. The next year, however, both families moved out of the region. In March 1968, shortly before his death, Martin Luther King Jr. spoke at Grosse Pointe High School; he was repeatedly interrupted by hecklers. In 1990, Grosse Pointe had just twelve African American households, most of them live-in domestic couples, according to political scientist Andrew Hacker.[93]

The publicity does allow us to see how exclusion worked in one elite suburb. Otherwise, Grosse Pointe was hardly exceptional. According to Cosseboom, similar crises over sundown policies took place in nearby Birmingham and Bloomfield Hills. Within 10 miles of Detroit lie perhaps 40 more sundown suburbs, including Grosse Ile and Wyandotte—some elite, some middle-class, some working-class, some multiclass.[94]

Picking on Children

An additional factor keeping African American families out of all-white counties and towns was the matter of schooling for their children. Just raising the question would be likely to provoke a hostile response from whites in a sundown jurisdiction. In states that practiced de jure segregation—Delaware, Maryland, West Virginia, Kentucky, Missouri, Arkansas, Texas, Arizona, and parts of Indiana, Illinois, Kansas, Nebraska, New Jersey, New Mexico, Ohio, Pennsylvania, and Oklahoma, as well as the traditional South—white officials in sundown towns sometimes encouraged threats or violence against a black

ENFORCEMENT   265

family to avoid the expense of setting up a new black school for them. In Duncan, Arizona, for example, the signs at the edge of town after World War II "included the usual 'Welcome' and 'Goodbye,' but also, 'Nigger, Don't Let The Sun Go Down On You Here,' " according to Betty Toomes, who lived in Duncan at the time. In 1949, "a Mormon farmer who needed a large number of hands on his 100-acre cotton field" hired the Earl and Corinne Randolph family and provided them with a house. They became "the first colored family ever to live there." Toomes accompanied Corinne Randolph to see the principal of the Consolidated Duncan Schools to get their children enrolled. He promised her an answer the next day. The answer came that very night: after midnight the Randolphs were "awakened by shots and the sounds of horses' hoofs very close to their house which was very isolated; it was probably a half mile from the highway and there were no other houses around it." Frightened, the family huddled "until the shooting and the shouting and the galloping stopped. Then they looked out of the window and they saw three crosses burning." They refused to give in, however, and eventually the Greenlea County Public Schools set up a "colored school" just for the Randolph children.[95]

Obviously children are a weak spot; parents cannot be with them at all times to protect them from harm. In northern states where children were not legally segregated by race, white parents and teachers often looked even less kindly on black faces in their previously all-white classrooms. In the early 1960s, Floyd Patterson, heavyweight champion of the world, tried to move into Scarsdale, a suburb of New York City. According to historian James Grossman, his son was beaten up and the family was hounded out of town. A black girl in high school in Oak Lawn, outside Chicago, "got spit upon and lasted just two weeks" in the fall of 1974, according to a woman who lived in Oak Lawn at the time. In about 1975, Dale Leftridge was transferred to Fremont, Nebraska, a sundown town near Omaha, as a manager on the Chicago and North Western Railroad. Within weeks he requested a transfer to Minneapolis, according to historian Eric Arnesen: "What put a 'dagger' in his heart was the cold treatment his young daughter received from other children." In 1982, into Corbin, Kentucky, moved an African American family whose son signed up to play football, according to Robby Heason's documentary *Trouble Behind.* He practiced with the football team, and "most of the kids were pulling for it," but his mother received death threats for her son if he were ever to play in a varsity game, so they left. In Perryville, Arkansas, in about 1987, "in first grade, our teacher told us not to play with the one black child on the playground," according to a woman who grew up in that sundown town near Little Rock. "We didn't. She left." [96]

Nothing physical happened to the only African American student in West Lawn in southwest Chicago. Although legally part of Chicago, West Lawn is almost a sizable suburb unto itself, including Midway Airport and the largest indoor mall in Chicago. In 1986, Steve Bogira wrote an extensive story on West Lawn and environs. Several residents told him that West Lawn wasn't really a sundown part of Chicago. "They referred to 'that colored mailman and his wife'—a reclusive black couple who, they said, had been living there for years. . . . No one knew how they got there or anything else about them." Bogira met with the couple, Fred and Mary Clark, and learned that they had raised their daughter there. She was the only African American student in her elementary school. Bogira then interviewed West Lawn resident Alexis Leslie, who went to school with the Clarks' daughter.

> "I felt bad for her—she seemed so lonely," Leslie says. "And I imagine a lot of other kids felt bad for her too. But it never occurred for us to actually be friends with her or even to talk to her—because to do so would put us in the same position she was in. There was also some apprehension, with the belief system we had, about the kind of person she was—was she someone you actually *wanted* to be friends with? Because she was black. I often felt bad later, because I didn't have the moral stamina to actually talk to her."

Imagine going through elementary school without a single conversation with a fellow student! Still, the greater sorrow today may be Leslie's.[97]

Often teachers have encouraged students to isolate the one or two black children who ventured into a sundown town or suburb. Once in a while, this backfired. A Pinckneyville, Illinois, resident told how a high school gym teacher in the 1980s tried to get his students to shun Quincy, the one black child in the school:

> He asked his class, "Are any of you friends with Quincy?" My son said, "I am." "Take a lap." Then he asked again. My son's friend said, "I am." "Take *two* laps." Eventually every boy in the class volunteered.

She was going to complain to the principal, "but my son asked me not to: 'Mom, we won.' " More often, whites maintained a united front, and the "intruders" left. In the early 1990s, for instance, an African American family tried to move into Berwyn, a sundown suburb just west of Chicago. The *Wall Street Journal* wrote a piece about how Berwyn had changed and how, despite minor aggravations, the family would stay. A week later the family left, James Rosenbaum at nearby Northwestern University wrote, because "they couldn't stand the harassment, especially against the kids." A resident of Ozark, Arkansas, recalled, "We used to have some blacks here, and we got rid of them." As a junior high school student in 1995, she saw two African American children get beaten up by white students as they got off their school bus on the first day of school in the fall. "They didn't even get to school." The family soon moved. A former police officer in Winston County, Alabama, much of which may yet be a sundown county, told me, "In 1996 [whites] held a meeting to try to kick the one black child out of the school in Addison." He believed that the child stayed in school, but imagine the social conditions under which s/he attended.[98]

How One Town Stayed White Down the Years

Wyandotte, Michigan, illustrates the intimidation, violence, and even murder that towns and suburbs have used to enforce their sundown policy. Indeed, because Wyandotte began as an independent town but then became a suburb of Detroit, it shows how the same methods were used in both environments. Its public library has preserved a file of newspaper clippings, letters, and other material collected by Edwina DeWindt in 1945[99] that reveal the history of race relations in that city.

Ironically, Wyandotte's first non-Indian settler may have been John Stewart, "a free man of color and a Methodist" missionary to the Indians, who arrived at Wyandotte, an Indian village, in 1816. Despite this multiracial start, the last Wyandotte Indians were pushed out of Michigan in 1843, and Wyandotte also excluded African Americans some time before the Civil War, much earlier than most sundown towns. According to an October 1898 story in the *Wyandotte Herald,* "So far as *The Herald* remembers, [Wyandotte] has never had any permanent colored population." Table 2 shows Wyandotte's population by race, from the U.S. census. Its numbers look like those from many other towns and suburbs: as Wyandotte grew from 2,731 in 1870 to 41,061 a century later, its African American population stayed minuscule, 0 in 1870 and 18, or 0.04%, in 1970. Along the years, the numbers fluctuated slightly, as the table shows.[100]

Table 2. Population by Race, Wyandotte, Michigan, 1870–2000

YEAR	TOTAL POP.	BLACK POP.	% BLACK
1870	2,731	0	0%
1890	3,817	0	0%
1910	8,287	2	0.02%
1930	28,368	9	0.03%
1950	36,846	16	0.04%
1970	41,061	18	0.04%
1990	30,938	73	0.23%
2000	28,006	146	0.52%

"Wyandotte History; Negro" allows us to see the drama beneath those numbers. To maintain such racial "purity," Wyandotte has long resorted to violence and the threat of violence. In 1868, "a colored wood chopper" moved into town:

> He was a quiet, peaceable fellow who on his trips downtown had been reviled by rude boys. . . . One day a boy was foolish enough to strike him, upon which the worm turned and gave his assaulter a trouncing. The old spirit was aroused again; threats were made that the old darky should be driven out of town, and steps were taken to organize for that purpose, but . . . the authorities took a firm stand. . . . Twenty special constables were sworn in . . . and the trouble was over.

This 1868 response by "the authorities" was much better than African Americans would get in Wyandotte later in the century. Nevertheless, by 1870, the woodcutter was gone and Wyandotte had returned to a black population of zero.[101]

In the early 1870s, "a colored barber opened a tonsorial parlor in the block between Kim and Oak streets." A mob riddled the barbershop with bullets and ran the barber out of town. Shortly thereafter, a white mob stormed a little steamer that had landed in Wyandotte with a black deckhand on board and beat him nearly unconscious. In 1881 and again in 1888, whites threatened and expelled black hotel workers from Wyandotte, and in 1890, Wyandotte again had no African Americans among its 3,817 residents. In 1907, four young white men accosted African American William Anderson at the West Wyandotte train station. They "asked him if he was going to work in the shipyard, and although he gave a negative answer," they gave him "a severe beating" and robbed him of $9.25. The authorities did nothing in response to any of these incidents.[102]

Often Wyandotte whites had only to threaten violence. In the words of the Wyandotte file, "the policy popularly pursued to enforce the 'tacit legislation' (no Negroes in Wyandotte) is to approach the 'stray' Negro and abruptly warn him that a welcome mat is not at the gates of the city. This quiet reminder hastens the Negro's footsteps with no further action." But by 1916, mere threats must not have worked, because a few African Americans again lived in Wyandotte. In late August of that year occurred the worst riot in Wyandotte's history. According to a story subheaded "Race Riot Monday Night" in the *Herald,* whites bombarded a black boardinghouse, smashed its doors and windows, drove out all African Americans, and killed one. "Colored People Driven from Town," announced the *Herald.* "Most of the Negroes left town Monday night or Tuesday morning."[103]

A year later, a few African Americans were back in Wyandotte, working at Detroit Brass. This led to another expulsion. DeWindt quotes a newspaper account:

> The Negro flare-up in 1917 developed from a strike at the Detroit Brass Co.,
> the only industry to hire Negroes. Near the factory were boarding houses and
> there were loose immoral relations between white and black. The city officials
> did nothing to stop it. The long festering indignation broke out in mob action.

DeWindt then notes that immoral behavior by African Americans was not the real issue, only an excuse. By 1930, 9 African Americans called Wyandotte home, among 28,368 residents, but 7 were female, and all 9 were probably live-in maids and gardeners. As far as I could determine, Wyandotte condoned no independent black households in the 1920s or 1930s.[104]

In the 1940s, police arrested or warned African Americans for "loitering suspiciously in the business district" or being in the park, and white children stoned African American children in front of Roosevelt High School. In about 1952, a black family moved into Wyandotte with tragic results, according to Kristina Baumli, who grew up in Wyandotte in that era and is now a professor at the University of Pennsylvania:

> After several weeks of hazings and warnings and escalating threats, [they] were
> killed and found floating in the Detroit River. My family couldn't give me more
> details. I asked if they thought this was true, or just a rumor—and they said that
> were pretty sure it was true, if not well investigated by the police.

More recently, Baumli reports, Elizabeth Park in Wyandotte has been a racial battleground, "where, I'm told, vigilantes enforced the sundown laws extra-legally. I believe the extent of it was just beating people up if they strayed after dark—my impression is that they beat everyone including women and kids."[105]

Over the years, then, African Americans repeatedly tried to settle in Wyandotte, only to be repulsed repeatedly. In the 1980s, Wyandotte caved in as a rigid sundown town, but its reputation lingers, and in 2000 it still was only 0.5% black.

Violence

Similar series of incidents underlie the zeroes or single digits under "Negro population" in the census, decade after decade, of other all-white towns and suburbs across the United States. Over the years, African Americans have even tried to move into towns with ferocious reputations, such as Syracuse, Ohio: according to a 1905 newspaper report, "two attempts have been made by Negro families to settle in the town, but both families were summarily driven out." When all else fails, after ordinances and covenants were decreed illegal, when steering, discriminatory lending, and the like have not sufficed, when an African American family is not deterred by a community's reputation—when they actually buy and move in—then residents of sundown towns and suburbs have repeatedly fallen back on violence and threat of violence to keep their communities white.[106]

Often the house has been the target. Residents of many sundown towns described incidents involving the destruction of homes newly purchased and occupied by African Americans. Here is a typical account, by a woman who grew up in Brownsburg, Indiana, a few miles west of Indianapolis. She had a conversation with her mother about sundown towns in November 2002 and brought up the topic of sundown signs. Her mother replied, "If you want to know if Brownsburg had them, they did."

> I then asked her about the black family I remembered. My memory was of ru-mors spreading around my school that they had been chased out by fire. (I thought it was crosses burning or something of that nature.) She said when I was around eleven, a black family moved in and their house burned to the ground.[107]

Sometimes the person was the target. If sundown towns have often mis-treated transient visitors such as athletic teams and jazz bands, the person of color who comes into a sundown town with the intent to live there has faced more serious consequences. Residents of town after town regaled me with stories of African Americans who had been killed or injured for the offense of moving in or simply setting foot in them. More stories of violence to maintain sundown towns and suburbs have come to my attention than I can possibly recount here; I have posted some at uvm.edu/~jloewen/sundown. In one way, all the stories are alike: whites use bad behavior to drive out black would-be residents. Often these stories become active elements of the reputations in ongoing sundown towns and suburbs. In LaSalle-Peru, there is a story about a black family that "moved into town, and shortly after the father was found drowned in the Illinois [River]," according to a woman whose parents grew up there. An African American family moved into Oneida, Tennessee, in 1925, according to Scott County historian Esther Sanderson, "but dynamite was dropped on their house and they were severely injured. They soon left and no others ever came in." Writing in 1958, she concluded, "There is not a colored family living in Scott County at the present time." Chapter 7 told that many sundown towns have "hanging trees" that they point out to visitors. Residents of Pinckneyville tell stories of African Americans hanged in at least *three* different places. Even if apocryphal, stories such as these intimidate black would-be newcomers.[108]

Residents of sundown towns who hired or befriended African Americans sometimes found that their membership in the white community did not protect them from violent reprisal. In Marlow, Oklahoma, in 1923, a prominent hotel owner was killed because he refused to get rid of his African American employee. "Marlow's 'Unwritten Law' Against Race Causes Two Deaths," headlined the *Pittsburgh Courier*. "Violation of Ban by Owner of Hotel Leads to Shooting." Here is its account:

> Marlow's unwritten law, exemplified by prominent public signs bearing the command: "Negro, don't let the sun go down on you here," caused the death Monday night of A. W. Berch, prominent hotel owner, and the fatal wounding of Robert Jernigan, the first colored man who stayed here more than a day in years.
>
> They were victims of a mob of more than fifteen men, who went to the hotel where Jernigan had been employed three days ago as a porter and shot them down when Berch attempted to persuade them to desist from their threat to lynch the man.
>
> Marlow, one of the several towns in Oklahoma which has not allowed our people to settle in their vicinity for years, has abided by the custom of permitting no members of the race to remain there after nightfall.

Last Saturday Berch brought Robert Jernigan here to serve as a porter in his hotel. A few hours later he received an anonymous communication ordering him to dismiss the porter at once and drive him from the city.

Berch ignored the letter.

The mob went to the hotel early Monday evening, its members calling loudly for the man and announcing their intention of hanging him on the spot.

The hotel proprietor, with Jernigan at his side, hurried into the lobby to intercede, but was shot dead before he could speak. Jernigan also fell, mortally wounded.

Their assailants then fled.

Mrs. Berch, who witnessed the shooting, said she thought she recognized the man who killed her husband, but authorities Tuesday said they had no clews as to the identity of members of the mob. They were not masked.

Berch's daughter Almarion also witnessed the shooting, at the age of two. She confirmed in 2004 what the last paragraph implies: that nothing was done about the crimes.[109]

As far as I have been able to learn, nothing was done about the 1922 lynching of J. T. Douglas in Hardin County in southeastern Illinois, either. Also unlike most victims of lynching in America, Douglas was white, a landowner, and prominent in the community. Unlike most (though not all) victims, he was not accused of a serious crime such as murder or rape. His offense? He broke the sundown "law" of that part of Hardin County by letting an African American live on his farm. According to the nearby Golconda *Herald-Enterprise*:

FARMER SHOT TO DEATH NEAR LAMB, HARDIN CO.
WAS ATTEMPTING TO PROTECT
COLORED MAN WHO LIVED
AS TENANT ON FARM

One of the most brutal murders that was ever committed in Southern Illinois was the shooting to death of J. T. Douglas, a prominent farmer residing near Lamb, in Hardin county, Thursday night shortly after midnight.

J. H. Douglas, this city, reports that his uncle had a colored hired man living on his farm and that some people of the locality had protested against him keeping the fellow and had warned him that trouble would result if he was not sent away. The murdered man did not heed the warning and his hired man stayed on.

Thursday night about midnight, a mob, composed of parties unknown, went to the house of the colored man and began shooting into the house. Mr. Douglas, from his home about a quarter of a mile away, heard the shooting and hastened to the scene. Just as he was about to enter the house, after calling to the Negro, he was shot dead.

The murder has caused great excitement and indignation in Hardin county, and every effort will be made to find out who composed the mob and did the shooting. Several are suspected and arrests no doubt will soon follow.

I could not find news stories of any arrests.[110]

White suburbs have largely avoided being tagged with the reputations for unsavory behavior that plague independent sundown towns. As we have seen, suburbs have used a variety of subtler methods to achieve all-white status, including clauses in their founding documents, unwritten policies of their developers, formal acts by suburban governments, restrictive covenants embedded in deeds, realtor steering, and redlining by lenders or insurers. Many suburbs seem too genteel to resort to violence and intimidation. This aura may be undeserved, however. Some suburbanites who would never attend a Klan meeting contacted their nearest klavern in time of need. As Stetson Kennedy, who famously infiltrated the KKK in the 1940s, put it, "The Klan has long served as an unofficial police force for maintaining racial zoning." When the William and Daisy Myers family moved into Levittown, Pennsylvania, in 1957, crosses burned throughout Levittown. Whites painted "KKK" on a neighbor's house because members of the family who lived there had not joined the mob. Leaders of the "Levittown Betterment Committee" contacted the Klan and other hate groups to get help in driving the Myerses out. Nearly 100 Levittowners signed to form a local klavern.[111]

Most suburbs have not relied on outsiders. When African American families managed to move into formerly all-white neighborhoods despite all the preventive measures taken by the suburbs, residents themselves typically resorted to shunning, threats of violence, and violence itself. In fact, violence in sundown suburbs and neighborhoods has been, if anything, even more widespread than the attacks on blacks in independent sundown towns. The Great Migration of African Americans from the South to northern cities, beginning around 1915 and continuing into the 1960s, struck many white suburbanites as a threatened "invasion" of their neighborhoods and led to, in Meyer's words, "thousands of small acts of terrorism" by whites determined to keep the newcomers out. Between 1917 and 1921, for example, whites firebombed the homes of 58 African American families that tried to move into white neighborhoods on the South Side of Chicago. "Rather than cresting in the

1920s," Meyer concluded, "the most vicious and extensive violence occur-
ring in the North during the two decades following World War II." In Chicago
during just the first two years after World War II, whites bombed 167 homes
bought or rented by African Americans in white neighborhoods, "killing four
persons, permanently crippling eight, and injuring scores of others," Stetson
Kennedy summarized.[112]

Some of the most severe and most important violence occurred in the
West Lawn neighborhood of Chicago. In 1946, an African American couple,
Theodore and Ida Turner, tried to occupy an apartment in Airport Homes,
temporary apartments that the Chicago Housing Authority was building for
veterans near Midway Airport. A mob of West Lawn residents drove them
out, along with two other African American families and a Jewish couple that
had befriended them. "No black ever again attempted to move into Airport
Homes," wrote Steve Bogira. Indeed, as historian Arnold Hirsch put it, "Chicago Housing Authority policy was made in the streets." Thirty-five years
later, West Lawn and adjacent communities were still more than 99.9% white,
containing 113,000 whites and 111 blacks in the 1980 census.[113]

Restrictive covenants kept African Americans out of most white suburbs
until well after World War II. A new wave of violence struck after their legal demise. "We must refuse to sell to colored people whether the covenants are
valid or invalid," shouted a leader of the Woodlawn Property Owners, trying
to keep a Chicago neighborhood all-white in October 1953. "If the colored
people were convinced that life in Woodlawn would be unbearable, they
would not want to come in." That was in a sundown neighborhood in an interracial city. In sundown suburbs, it was often worse. After Oak Park, Illinois,
failed to keep out Percy Julian's family, as described in "Sundown Suburbs,"
his home "suffered both bomb and arson attacks in 1950 and 1951," in the
words of Arnold Hirsch. Whites in nearby Cicero have repeatedly used violence to repel African American would-be residents. "The first Negro family
to enter the middle-class Chicago suburb of Deerfield," according to housing
expert James Hecht, "moved out of their rented apartment after windows
were broken and excrement was smeared on the front walls of the house."[114]

By no means have the Chicago suburbs been unique. Meyer tells of the
campaign whites in the Los Angeles suburb of Maywood mounted in 1942 to
force out two African American families. "Keep Maywood White" was the
headline in the *Maywood-Bell Southwest Herald*. In nearby Fontana, where
African Americans could only live outside the city limits on a floodplain,
whites firebombed the O'Day Short family when they bought a house in
town, killing Mr. and Mrs. Short and their young children in December 1945.

No one was ever convicted of the bombing, and Fontana remained all-white into the 1960s. On the opposite coast, whites in Oceanside, Long Island, threw a bomb through the dining room window of one of its few black-owned homes in 1967. This made an impact: the owner put his home up for sale, and as of 2000, Oceanside still had just 184 African Americans among its 33,000 residents.[115]

Violence to keep communities all-white may have peaked in the 1980s. In 1985 and 1986, the Klanwatch Project counted 45 cases of arson or cross burning and "hundreds of acts of vandalism, intimidation, and other incidents" aimed at "members of minority groups who had moved into mostly white areas." In 1989 alone, Klanwatch listed 130 cases, and that was surely an underestimate, since the Chicago Commission on Human Rights recorded an average of 100 racial hate crimes each year between 1985 and 1990 in neighborhoods undergoing "racial transition" just in that city.[116]

Developing a Reputation

The best way to stay all-white, many communities concluded, was to behave with such outrageous hostility to African Americans who happened by or tried to move in that a reputation for vicious white supremacy circulated among African Americans for many miles around. Historian Emma Lou Thornbrough told that sundown towns built anti-black reputations in Indiana during the Nadir. By 1900, for example, Leavenworth, "the county seat of Crawford County, had the reputation of being the most 'anti-Negro' town on the Ohio River. Captains of riverboats were said to discipline African American crewmen by threatening to put them off the boat at Leavenworth. By 1900 there was only one Negro resident in Crawford County." Today, African Americans as far away as Florida and California know and spread the reputation of Pekin, a sundown town in central Illinois. Achieving a similar notoriety is the rationale for the otherwise irrational refusal of gas stations in some sundown towns to sell gasoline to African Americans. After all, most motorists do have enough gas to get to the next town, and they will carry with them the message that Pana, Martinsville, and other towns that had this policy are to be avoided at all costs.[117]

Often the first thing said to an African American in a sundown town was to ask if he knew the reputation of the town. Even "pet Negroes," as local whites sometimes referred to them, were in trouble as soon as they ventured beyond the specific town or part of town where they were known. Aaron "Rock" Van Winkle, "born a slave" and "owned by Peter Van Winkle," whose

son-in-law was a state senator from Rogers, Arkansas, was "in Rogers on business," according to an article in the 1904 *Rogers Democrat*. "In a joking way
one of our citizens said to him: 'See here, Rock, you know that sundown don't
want to find a Negro in Rogers.' " The newspaper went on to relate the quip
with which "the old Negro" reproached the white man. Nevertheless, the
white man's statement, while perhaps said "in a joking way," was also flatly
true. Both he and Van Winkle would have known that it was not to be challenged directly and that saying it was a warning, the first step in enforcement.[118]

Some places have built national reputations as sundown towns. From east
to west, these would include Darien, Connecticut; the Levittowns in New
York and Pennsylvania; Forsyth County, Georgia; Cuyahoga Falls and Parma,
Ohio; Dearborn, Grosse Pointe, Warren, and Wyandotte, Michigan; Elwood,
Huntington, and Martinsville, Indiana; Cicero, Pekin, Pana, and Franklin and
Williamson counties, Illinois; Cullman, Alabama; the Ozarks as a region;
Idaho, statewide; Vidor and Santa Fe, Texas; and several suburbs of Los An-
geles.[119] Especially in the African American community, these reputations en-
dure. "This colored person in Florida knew of Pana, Illinois, and its
reputation," a woman who grew up in Pana related, "and that astonished me."
Virginia Yearwood, a native of Pierce City, Missouri, reported that African
Americans with whom she worked in the 1970s in California knew about
Pierce City's anti-black policy.[120]

Reputations are even more important within metropolitan areas. A 1992
Detroit area survey showed that 89% of white respondents and 92% of blacks
thought that residents of suburban Dearborn "would be upset" if a black family moved in. As a result, only 37% of African Americans rated Dearborn a
"desirable" place to live, compared to 66% of white respondents. Of the black
respondents who ranked Dearborn "undesirable," 78% cited the racial prejudice of its residents as their reason. Many residents of sundown suburbs such
as Dearborn are happy that African Americans consider their town undesirable. Then less enforcement is required to keep it white. Moreover, a reputation as overwhelmingly white is part of a suburb's claim to social status. At the
same time, residents of Dearborn don't want their city's reputation to get out
of hand. While they are proud to be from an all-white community, at the same
time they know enough to be ashamed. To put this another way, many whites
want their town or suburb to have a certain notoriety in the African American
community for unfriendly police and unwelcoming residents, so long as this
can be accomplished without giving the town a black eye, as it were, in the
white community.[121]

Sometimes reputations can get out of hand. Tamaroa, a town of about 800 people in southern Illinois, excluded African Americans perhaps around 1900. I did not find anyone who claimed to know how or when. But every person I talked with from Tamaroa or near Tamaroa knew that the town had become infamous as "the rock throwers" some time later. A member of the historical society in nearby Pinckneyville, also a sundown town, told how African Americans from the nearby interracial town of Du Quoin occasionally walked along the railroad tracks to go north. As they passed through Tamaroa, white youths would throw rocks at them. On one occasion the stoning got out of hand and they killed a man. A woman who grew up in Tamaroa, now living in a senior center in Du Quoin, confirmed this account: "They stoned one to death." She was indignant at her town's resulting notoriety: "People all around call us 'rock throwers,' but that was so long ago!" The Pinckneyville historian suggested that Tamaroa's reputation didn't rest on that one incident: another African American tried to run through on the railroad right-of-way but was grabbed and castrated, and a third was hung. Asked how he knew about these incidents,[122] he replied, "Several residents of Tamaroa told me those stories. One man told me he witnessed the hanging. They took him down and burned him on a brush pile."[123]

In a sense Tamaroa's notoriety is unwarranted, however, because the town does not differ from hundreds of other sundown towns. Indeed, the generic nickname for slingshot across the United States in the first half of the twentieth century was "nigger shooter."[124] Moreover, white reactions to this day to an African American in a "white neighborhood" anywhere in America often include fear and hostility. In the 1970 feature film *Watermelon Man,* African American director Melvin Van Peebles depicted a comical example: police in a white suburb respond to phone calls from homeowners frightened by African American actor Godfrey Cambridge, a white suburbanite who has suddenly turned black during the previous night. Cambridge is merely jogging the same route he did the day before, when he was white. As David Harris noted more recently, jogging through white neighborhoods remains problematic, not only in the movies, but also in real suburbia.[125]

The 1964 Civil Rights Act Made Little Difference

Some of these problems might have eased with passage of the 1964 Civil Rights Act, but that legislation was aimed at the South and was not enforced in sundown towns, most of which are not in the South. Thus the 1964 law left all-white towns and suburbs largely untouched. Many towns simply did not obey it for decades. "We were not allowed to serve any colored after sundown," said a woman who had been a waiter in the mid-1970s in Arcola, Illinois. "A white man came in and said, 'I have my buddy in the truck. Will you serve him?' He then served the friend at the booth, getting the stuff from me at the counter." Telling this in 2002, the woman was proud that she let that happen, in violation of the rules.[126]

In 1974, Dale Leftridge, one of the first African Americans allowed to become a railroad engineer in the United States, took trains to South Pekin, Illinois. Ten years after the Civil Rights Act outlawed racial discrimination in public accommodations, the Chicago & North Western Railroad had to post a security guard from the train at the motel, "because the townspeople didn't want blacks in their town," in Leftridge's words. Two years later, a black social worker from the state office in Madison had to stay at a smaller motel outside of Sheboygan, Wisconsin. She couldn't stay at the main hotel within the city, according to June Rosland, then also a social worker in Wisconsin. "And she had an MSW [Master's of Social Work]!"[127]

Nick Khan in Paragould said that when he bought his motel in 1982, no motels in town let African Americans spend the night. Paragould had been a sundown town since 1908, when its 40 black families were ordered to leave at gunpoint. The restaurant across the road locked the door on two black Union Pacific Rail Road workers staying with him in 1983 when they walked over and tried to eat there. Police came and accused the African Americans of trying to break in, according to Khan. "The white boys in the restaurant were cracking up over it. The black guys were so scared." After that, "they never used to go out. If I'm outside, they'll come out, sit in the chairs. But if they go downtown, they'll get arrested!" So they bought takeout fried chicken at Kentucky Fried Chicken and ate it in their rooms.[128]

How are these things possible, so many years after the Civil Rights Act? Enforcement of the law, which should have depended on the federal government, in reality depended on African Americans. Black pioneers tested restaurants and motels across the South, sat wherever they wanted on buses, and sometimes got beaten or killed for their trouble, forcing the government to act. Having no black children, sundown towns had no black students to desegrate their schools after 1954. Having no black populations, these towns had no African Americans to test their public accommodations after 1964. Members of the St. Louis chapter of SNCC, the Student Nonviolent Coordinating Committee, responsible for so many southern sit-ins, did announce to the media that they were going to test restaurants and motels in Williamson County, Illinois, shortly after passage of the act. Almost every community in

Williamson County and adjoining Franklin County was a sundown town then, including Benton, Carterville, Christopher, Herrin, Johnston City, Mulkeytown, Royalton, Sesser, West Frankfort, and Zeigler. The Williamson County sheriff talked with all the motel owners and restaurant owners and told them they had two choices, according to Jim Clayton: "Either they could accommodate them, and they'd all go back to St. Louis, or they could refuse, and all hell would break loose." They complied. Afterward they put their signs back up—"White Only" or "Management Reserves the Right to Refuse Service to Anyone"—and Williamson and Franklin counties disobeyed the law for another two decades.[129]

Today many sundown towns exhibit a pattern exactly opposite to that found in the classic pre-1954 segregated southern city (and many northern ones). Back then, black travelers usually could neither stay in the city's hotels and motels nor eat in its major restaurants, but African Americans were allowed to live in the city, albeit on the "wrong side of the tracks." Today, most motels and restaurants in sundown towns serve African Americans without a second thought, but blacks still cannot live within the city limits.

Throughout the expulsions, the prohibitions, the shunning, and all the other acts that sundown towns have used to stay all-white, all the while an individual "pet" black, such as Aaron Van Winkle in Arkansas—sometimes an entire household—has often been allowed to stay. The next chapter tells of these anomalies—African Americans permitted to live, usually without much difficulty, in towns and counties that nevertheless designated themselves "sundown."

10

Exceptions to the Sundown Rule

During my life I have heard oral history of at least two instances in Missouri where one or a few ex-slaves (or their descendants) were allowed to remain in a county or town, but any visiting blacks were quickly informed that they were "not to let the sun set on them." It is as if there were an unspoken feeling of "these are our blacks and they are okay, but other blacks are unwelcome and dangerous strangers."

—Laurel Boeckman, reference librarian,
State Historical Society of Missouri, 2002[1]

TOWNS THAT TOOK GREAT PAINS to define themselves as sundown towns have nevertheless often allowed an exception or two. Within their otherwise all-white populations, occasionally an African American person or even household was at least tolerated and sometimes celebrated. When Pana, Illinois, for example, forced out its African American population in 1899, whites did not force the black barber and his family to leave. He had an exclusively white clientele and many acquaintances—even friends—in the white community, and no one had a complaint about *him*. Pana did post sundown signs at its corporate limits, signs that remained up at least until 1960, and permitted no other African Americans to move in, so it definitely became a sundown town. Other towns have let in more temporary intruders: flood refugees, soldiers during wartime, college students, and visiting interracial athletic teams and their fans.[2]

What experiences do these exceptions have, in towns that by definition do not allow them to be there? What are their lives like? What difference—if any—do they make?

African American Servants

Many African Americans in sundown towns were or are servants. In a way, they don't violate the sundown rule, because they don't live on their own. Huntington, Indiana, is so anti-black that two residents reported in 2002 that its police still stop any African Americans driving through and warn them "to get out of town—now." Yet a black couple lived in Huntington in the 1920s and 1930s. They were servants in the household of William Schacht, owner of a rubber factory and one of the richest people in town. She was the family's maid and cook, he their handyman. "They lived in the Schacht house, but their movements were circumscribed. They couldn't go downtown—a few blocks away—without problems," according to a man who grew up in the town in those decades. "They spent most of the time indoors." And they had no children, so there were no African American children in the schools. At this same time, after the 1919 riot in which whites drove out the African American population of Marion, Ohio, home of president-to-be Warren G. Harding, "local lore has it that there was one black family left in Marion after the riot," writes Harding scholar Phillip Payne, "and that the woman and her family remained because she had been the Hardings' maid." Also, her husband was the barber, so he knew, serviced, and in a limited sense was friends with upper-class whites.[3]

In the suburbs, these live-in exceptions were common. Laura Hobson's novel about anti-Semitism in Darien, Connecticut, in the 1940s, *Gentleman's Agreement,* pointed out the town's practice of not letting Jews or African Americans live there. Meanwhile, when she wrote, Darien had about 150 African Americans, mostly female—live-in maids, nannies, gardeners, and the like. Similarly, Kenilworth, Illinois, the richest suburb of Chicago, had a population that was 4.3% African American in 1930, all live-in servants. On the West Coast, Beverly Hills, a famed affluent suburb of Los Angeles, had 397 African Americans in 1920. Almost 300 were female; the imbalance implies that at least 200 were live-in maids and nannies. In fact, probably every African American was a maid, gardener, or other live-in servant, because the total of 397 included just four children, all girls who probably assisted their mothers or were older teenagers working on their own. This sexual imbalance then worsened: by 1960, Beverly Hills had 649 African Americans, of whom 554 were females.[4]

Often these exceptions were codified into law. In 1912, Virginia passed a law providing for all-white and all-black neighborhoods or towns: "It shall be unlawful for any colored person, not then residing in a district so defined and designated as a white district, or who is not a member of a family then therein residing, to move into and occupy as a residence any building or portion thereof in such white district," and vice versa. The act immediately went on to make the exception: "Nothing herein contained shall preclude persons of either race employed as servants by persons of the other race from residing upon the premises of which such employer is the owner or occupier." After the Supreme Court invalidated such laws in 1917, suburbs switched to restrictive covenants to keep out African Americans. Typically those covenants similarly exempted servants, as did this succinct example from Chicago suburb Villa Park: "Said premises shall not be conveyed or leased to, or occupied by, any person who is not a Caucasian, except servants." Examples in my collection range from California to Minnesota to Vermont to Florida.[5]

When entire suburbs made it their policy for all neighborhoods to be covered by these covenants, they became sundown towns. After World War II, for example, South Pasadena, California, did so, according to this 1947 newspaper report:

> The city of S. Pasadena, California, provides an example of the extreme to which the trend toward restrictive racial and religious covenants can go. In South Pasadena restrictive covenants, denying persons not of the Caucasian race the right to live within its municipal boundaries, are a matter of official policy. The city administration has been charged with promoting the program under which the entire city will be blanketed with restrictive agreements. South Pasadena is to be completely "white." Of course, persons not of Caucasian ancestry will not be completely barred from residence in South Pasadena. The restrictive covenants specify that non-Caucasians may reside in the city as servants, caretakers, and in similar menial work. Non-Caucasians may work in the city in other capacities, but they must be outside its limits by nightfall.

Again, live-in servants did not and could not constitute real exceptions, because they could not live within the city limits on their own. Often their children could not live there at all; maids and gardeners with children sent them to live with relatives. Sometimes, as in Texas's Park Cities, the suburban school district or the maid's employer paid for her children to attend schools in the central city. Sundown suburbs thus ensured that the only African Americans their white children would meet were servants in positions of inferiority.[6]

Like the Schacht servants in Huntington, live-in servants have often had to practice invisibility. There were African American maids in Johnston City, in southern Illinois, in the 1920s, but "they weren't allowed out of doors after dark," according to Jim Clayton, a *Washington Post* reporter who grew up there. A former resident of nearby Herrin spoke to historian Paul Angle around 1950:

> Some Herrin families do keep hired Negro help in their homes overnight. I had a "Clarissa" who lived with me for four years. The old feeling of "being out of the city limits by dark" was still with her, however. She didn't like to answer my door after the evening meal and usually stayed right in her room. She never appeared on the streets after dark.

Angle's informant seems to locate her maid's "feeling" within the employee, but town policy was to blame. Her acts were prudent and would be appropriate in Herrin for several more decades. A member of the Batesville Historical Society told of "a prominent family" in that southeastern Indiana town "who employed black maids, chefs, chauffeurs for business functions. Those employees were told to never be on the streets at night." Their housekeeper, who worked for them on a more permanent basis, "would only go outdoors to attend the earliest [morning] Mass at the local Catholic church." [7]

As in independent sundown towns, servants in sundown suburbs have also had to watch the sun. In the late 1940s, for example, Lois Johnson, who lived in Glendale, a suburb of Los Angeles, would see maids running to the bus stop "so they would not be caught there after dark." In 1940, among 81,992 residents, Glendale had 68 African Americans, three to one female, surely the ratio of maids to gardeners and chauffeurs; they included just two individuals under 21 years old, both likely maids in their late teens. Probably all 68 were live-in servants, who apparently had no more freedom to poke their heads out of doors after sundown than black servants in Huntington or Herrin. Even more constricted were the lives of servants in Wyandotte, Michigan, the sundown suburb near Detroit, who stayed indoors day and night. Writing in about 1945, Mable Bishop Gilmer told of "a high class type of Negroes, descendants of slaves of George Washington, and so-named Washington." They were the servants she knew as a child in the wealthy Bishop family. "These Negroes sensing the Wyandotte attitude never left the house to enter the streets but sent the Bishop children on errands for their personal needs." [8]

Sometimes African American servants even got in trouble while on their employer's property. In 1948, a graduate student from Panama and his wife came to Norman, Oklahoma, home of the University of Oklahoma, accompanied by their black Panamanian maid. According to a student at the university at the time:

One evening at sundown the maid was hanging clothes out on the line. Apparently someone reported her to the police, because they came and arrested her and took her to the station. She was frightened because she could not speak English and did not know why she was picked up. Her employer . . . got the maid released and, I believe, got the university administration to talk to the police so the maid would be safe from police harassment.[9]

Surely no one in modern America, outside of prison, has lived more restricted or more fearful lives than these lonely live-in African American servants in intentionally all-white communities. Over time, however, live-in maids, gardeners, and other domestic help became less crucial to the lifestyle of even the rich and famous and certainly of the middle class. Gas, oil, and electric heat eliminated the need to stoke the coal furnace, washers and dryers decreased the work on wash day, and gardening and landscaping got redefined as a hobby rather than a chore, at least in the middle class. We see this change in Darien, for example, which showed 161 African Americans in the 1940 census, 112 in 1960, and just 75 in 1990, always three-quarters female because maids and nannies outnumber butlers and gardeners. Similarly, by 1960, the proportion of African American servants in Kenilworth—4.3% in 1930—had fallen to 1.3%, and in 2000, 0.2%—just 4 individuals. Grosse Pointe, Michigan, had 140 African Americans in 1940, 36 in 1960, and just 11 by 1980. These statistics reflect the decline in live-in servants in America, not increased white supremacy in Darien, Kenilworth, or Grosse Pointe.

Hotel Workers

Sundown towns often allowed hotel workers after dark. Such porters, waiters, maids, and others don't exactly violate the sundown rule because they don't live in a residential neighborhood. In the 1930s and '40s and possibly later, an African American lived in the basement of the Pacific House hotel in Effingham, Illinois. He made a living driving a team of horses hitched to a coach, supplying rides from the railroad depot to the Pacific House and elsewhere. A man who lived in Miami Beach in the late 1940s and early '50s, tells that Miami Beach was a sundown town then but made exceptions "for hotel maids and bus boys and Sarah Vaughan!" Like Darien and Beverly Hills, Miami Beach's African American population was more than three-quarters female and included almost no children. Bill Alley of the Southern Oregon Historical Society tells of one African American man in the 1920s, George Washington Maddox, in Medford, which was otherwise a sundown town. Maddox, a dwarf, shined shoes at the Medford Hotel. In southern Pennsylvania, "for decades Ephrata had but a single black resident—George Harris, a barber, who first came to town as a seasonal employee of the grand Mountain Springs Hotel summer resort in or around 1848," according to Cynthia Marquet of the local historical society. "He moved here permanently in 1882 and remained until his death in 1904." Marquet adds, "After Harris died no black persons . . . lived in Ephrata for decades." In 1960, Ephrata had 7,688 people and no African Americans. I must note that Marquet goes on to add, "In my 18 years at the Historical Society, I have never encountered any suggestion that their presence was forbidden." However, three residents of nearby communities tell that the Ku Klux Klan recruits in Ephrata and holds an annual march there and that they hear that African American families usually move out[10] soon after moving into the town.[11]

Like servants, the lives of these hotel workers could be remarkably constricted. Indiana writer William Wilson told of his aunt and uncle who ran The Tavern, a hotel in New Harmony, Indiana, in the 1920s, and of "Aunt Minnie's Lizzie, . . . the only Negro permitted to live in the town. She had a room in the hotel and never went out on the street, day or night. . . . She must have had a great deal of what we used to call 'inner resources.' Certainly she was a finer person than the group of intolerant white people in the town who made it necessary for her to stay indoors."[12]

Some white communities would not abide African Americans even as household servants or hotel workers. When a horse breeder from Kentucky who had bought a farm in Washington County, Indiana, in 1888, brought a black stable hand to care for his horses, there was so much excitement that the stable hand had to be sent back to Kentucky. Five years later, a visitor from Louisville who brought a black cook was forced to send her away because of threats of violence. A wealthy visitor to Utica, Indiana, had a hard time securing permission to bring his carriage driver into the town, because no African Americans were allowed within the city limits. A newspaper in Springdale, Arkansas, itself a sundown town, told of an event in nearby Rogers in 1894: "A hotel in Rogers employs a colored boy to wait on the tables and one night recently some person posted a notice on the gate post warning the proprietor to discharge the boy or steps would be taken to rid the town of his presence. The notice was signed 'citizens.' " Apparently the "boy" left. The River Park Hotel in Wyandotte, Michigan, had African American waiters in 1880 and 1881 "who sang beautifully," according to a newspaper account, but apparently were later expelled. Seven years later, the manager of the hotel arrived with "a retinue of colored servants," but whites in Wyandotte expelled them too. In

1880, three African Americans—two barbers and a cook—came to Bluffton, Indiana, the cook to work in a local hotel. Historian Emma Lou Thornbrough writes that all three "received written notices that they must leave, and the proprietor of the hotel who employed the cook, as well as the sheriff of the county, received warnings to get rid of the Negroes." They did.[13]

Refugees, Soldiers, Students, and Other Transients

Even large numbers of African Americans have sometimes been allowed in sundown towns when they were clearly temporary and when human kindness overrode the sundown rule. Johnston City, Illinois, provided an example during the 1937 flood of the Mississippi River. As its town history recounts:

> On January 20 we received word that some 200 [flood refugees] were to be brought here from around Mounds and Mound City. Eventually this number grew to 287, and these homeless people were housed in the Miner's Hall, the Baptist Tabernacle, [and abandoned stores] ... About half the refugees brought here were colored, and although the town had the reputation of never permitting a black to remain overnight here, they were welcomed with courtesy and kindness in 1937.

Of course, the gesture was easier because the refugees were never perceived as possible residents; from the start, whites understood their sojourn was to be only temporary. "When the danger of flooding had passed, the black people were transferred to Wolf Lake," the account concludes, "the white refugees to Anna."[14]

During World War II, Camp Ellis in west-central Illinois had some African American troops. According to a local lawyer, "Lewiston—an all-white community—opened its restaurants, taverns, theaters, and other public places to African-American servicemen." Lachlan Crissey, the local state's attorney at the time, wrote, "The attitude adopted by most of the people there was, 'Well, they're soldiers, the same as our boys, and if they are shot they bleed and die the same way.' Therefore, the Negro soldiers are free to enter the restaurants, stores, taverns, picture shows, and other public places." Other sundown towns around Lewistown were not so hospitable; as Crissey went on to say, "This was the exception, and not the rule." Again, everyone in Lewistown knew that the soldiers were never going to stay there permanently.[15]

Many towns that would never let them stay in houses permitted African

American and African college and prep-school students to live on campus. Again, it helped that townspeople knew the students were only temporary. In the 1960s, missionaries of the United Brethren Church in Christ recruited students from Sierra Leone to attend Huntington College in Huntington, Indiana, the college for that denomination. The town let the Africans live on campus; indeed, they could even get haircuts in town, while African American students could not. Pretty much the same thing happened at Bethany College in Lindsborg, Kansas, a sundown town founded by "conservative and lily-white Swedes in 1869," in the words of reporter Matt Moline, except at Bethany the Africans were from Kenya rather than Sierra Leone and were Lutheran rather than Brethren. Similarly, African students attended Chapman College in Orange, California, in the 1960s, according to history professor Harold Forsythe, one of the first African Americans to attend Chapman. They were perhaps among the first blacks allowed to spend the night and told Forsythe, "It was a tough town in which to live." [16]

Darien, Connecticut, has no college, but beginning in the early 1980s, its public high school let a few African American girls, mostly from Harlem, attend under the aegis of A Better Chance (ABC), a program that sends minority teenagers to prep schools and affluent suburban high schools to prepare them to enter elite colleges. To avoid the long commute from New York City, the girls live in a group home in Darien, but again, whites know there is no chance that they might stay after they graduate from high school.

Most sundown towns were not hospitable even to transients. The response of Elco, in southern Illinois, to majority-white but interracial religious meetings was typical. In 1923, William Sowders, founder of the Gospel Assembly Churches, established a camp meeting at Elco. He continued to lead religious revivals there for eighteen years, but Elco residents were upset because Sowders allowed people of all races to attend these meetings. In 1941, World War II and local opposition caused him to abandon the Elco camp meeting. [17]

Having a Protector

Now we move to the "real" exceptions: African Americans who lived on their own in towns that did not allow African Americans to live on their own. Some sundown towns made exceptions not just for live-in domestics, hotel workers, and students, but for an actual independent African American household or two. This pattern was more common in the nontraditional South—Appalachia, Texas, and the like—than in the North or West. In areas where slavery had existed before 1865, elderly black couples made use of the "faithful slave" stereotype, so beloved of whites seeking to defend the "peculiar institution" in their minds, to persist in otherwise all-white communities. Often they became locally famous and were remembered decades later with affection.

When whites drove out African Americans from all or parts of six counties southwest of Fort Worth, Texas, in 1886, for example, they made exceptions for a handful of old ex-slaves in Hamilton County, including "Uncle Alec" Gentry and "Aunt Mourn" Gentry, both about 80 years old. "When released from slavery, they were taken to Hamilton County by their former master and given a patch of ground and log cabin. They have lived there ever since," in the words of the Hamilton's centennial county history, *Parade of Progress*. Portfolio 19 shows "Uncle Alec," bent over obsequiously. Even in northern communities with no tradition of slavery, aged ex-slaves were sometimes the only African Americans allowed to stay when towns went sundown. According to local historian Terry Keller, when Anna, Illinois, drove out its African Americans in 1909, they exempted "one old lady who had been a slave." In the quote at the head of this chapter, Laurel Boeckman makes clear the exceptional position of individuals such as these. Many counties and towns in Appalachia, Arkansas, Texas, and the Midwest show a slowly diminishing number of African Americans between 1890 and 1930 because they did not allow new blacks in, and their "Uncle Alecs" and "Aunt Mourns" gradually died or left.[18]

Even though they lived independently, ex-slaves who remained in sundown towns typically had white protectors—often their ex-owners. Protection was important. "Doc" Pitts, the only African American in Beaver Dam, Wisconsin, was the trusted servant and groom of Judge Silas Lamoreaux, President Cleveland's general land commissioner. When the judge returned home to Beaver Dam, he brought Pitts with him to care for his horses. Initially he existed under the protection of Beaver Dam's leading citizen, but after the death of his employer, Beaver Dam allowed Pitts to remain. A town history published about 1941 referred to Pitts as "the town's black." After Pitts's death, Beaver Dam had no black resident. When whites in Corbin, Kentucky, drove out their African Americans in 1919, they missed "Nigger Dennis," "the Mershons' 'man,' " according to historian Hank Everman, referring to one of the wealthier families in town. During the 1919 riot, "the Mershons and Dr. Siler hid him for several days while other blacks fled Corbin." Dennis stayed on, and so did "the beloved 'Aunt Emma' Woods," in Everman's phrase, "a fine cook, laundress, and cleaning lady," and possibly Dennis's mother. In 1930, whites tried to lynch three African Americans in Ste.

Genevieve, in the Bootheel of Missouri. Frustrated by state troopers, the whites turned their wrath on the entire black population. The only African Americans to stay were the extended family of the custodian of the Catholic Church, who was shielded by the priest.[19]

Even with defenders, some sundown towns were too dangerous. During the 1886 eviction of African Americans from the counties southwest of Fort Worth, Matt Fleming, who owned a butcher shop in Comanche County, "offered the services of his shotgun and himself to protect his two colored employees . . . if they wanted to stay," according to Comanche County historian Billy Bob Lightfoot. They left anyway, " 'to keep you from getting into trouble, Mr. Fleming.' " Of course, the employees may also have mistrusted their chances for survival with only one protector against the wrath of the community. "One of the town's doctors refused to have his Negro maid driven from her home," continues Lightfoot, "but a visit from the mob made the girl [*sic*] insist that she be allowed to go to Dublin. The doctor finally gave in and drove the girl across the line himself." [20]

Other Survival Tactics

Some African Americans managed to survive without a protector. Sometimes maintaining a low profile worked as a survival stratagem for African Americans who lived independently. After the 1908 race riot in Springfield, Illinois, when small towns all around Springfield were expelling their African Americans, residents of Pleasant Plains made an exception, ordering all blacks out, except for one elderly couple who were "old and law abiding." When Ambrose Roan, probably the only African American man in Porter County, Indiana, died in 1911 at the age of 66, the *Chesterton Tribune* called him "a hard working, peaceful man, of quiet, unassuming ways." The tiny town of Hazel Dell, Illinois, a few miles south of Greenup, had an African American blacksmith. According to a Greenup resident. "He simply disappeared at sundown and you never saw him again until morning." The fact that his occupation was simultaneously useful and archaic, thus not a threat to most whites, probably helped ensure his safety.[21]

Living in such nonresidential places as above a downtown business worked for some African American individuals, although not for families. Huntington, Indiana, would never let African Americans live independently in a neighborhood, but it allowed an elderly African American man to live downtown, in an otherwise abandoned upstairs room above a store. He was called "Rags" and made a living by washing windows in the downtown area.

"He, too, was tolerated but watched," according to an elderly Huntington native.[22]

Overt identification with the white community was another survival tactic. Such blacks became "Tonto figures"—taking pains to associate with the "white side," differentiated from the hordes of blacks outside of the city limits. White workers in Austin, Minnesota, repeatedly expelled African Americans, and Austin became a sundown town, but like many others, it allowed one African American to stay—the shoeshine "boy." Union member John Winkols tells about him:

> And I'll tell you a good one: so one time we had Frank—I forget his last name—
> he was shining shoes in the barbershop and then afterwards he bell-hopped for
> the bus in town here, and everybody liked him. . . . He'd never go in the pack-
> ing house because he knew he couldn't, he didn't *want* to go there.
>
> So one day I was walking along . . . and here came a couple of niggers, and
> they stood there by the bridge facing the packing house, and . . . [Frank] says,
> "Y'know, John," he says, "when the damn niggers start comin' into this town,
> I'm gonna get the hell outta here." And he was *black!* He was black! *He* didn't
> want them to come into town either. . . . But we never had no trouble with
> Frank at all.

Indeed, they didn't; Frank knew with which side of the color line he had to identify if he was to remain in Austin.[23]

Often the one African American in town becomes a celebrity, in a perverse sort of way. Everyone "knows" that person, including their harmless eccentricities. Piety is good, as is always having cookies ready for neighboring children or going by a nickname—but not voting, wanting to work at jobs where whites also work, or attending civic meetings. African Americans who played this part well became genuinely liked by whites. Kathleen Blee, author of *Women of the Klan,* collected a good example from an Indiana woman in the 1980s: "We didn't hate the niggers. We had the Wills family that lived right here in [this] township. And they were like pet coons to us. I went to school with them." Often they got known by nicknames, such as "Snowball" for the only African American in West Bend, Wisconsin, or "Nigger Slim" for the father of the only black family in Salem, Illinois.[24]

Sometimes whites make a big deal out of the only African American in town. After the person's death, everyone turns out for the funeral. Decades after death, such a person may get warm retrospective articles in the local newspaper. "If there is any one character that everyone hears about sooner or later in connection with West Bend it is 'Snowball,' " wrote Dorothy Williams in a 1980 town history. "Snowball," or Elmer Lynden, was "a young Negro [*sic*] about 25 years old" who was killed by two police officers, allegedly while resisting arrest, in 1924. In 1936 the *Chesterton Tribune* in Chesterton, Indiana, ran a story, "Only Colored Couple," about the death of Ambrose Roan 24 years earlier:

> The story goes that when Ambrose Roan found his eternity the present Congregational church choir showed its respect and love for their "Uncle Tom" by singing a number of his beloved hymns. Mrs. Roan was so much moved by this act of courtesy that she invited the entire group of singers for a good Negro cooked chicken dinner.[25]

Staying out of the File Folder

The exceptions would need all the publicity they could get, because their position was always precarious. To become widely and affectionately known, they usually displayed strong but innocuous personalities, the opposite of the low-profile approach favored by the Hazel Dell blacksmith. Often they dressed exceptionally well or exceptionally badly. Usually they allowed and even encouraged whites to call them "nigger." Sometimes they played a clownish role. Whites in Arab, a sundown town in the hills of north Alabama, let an African American live in a nearby hamlet, according to a local expert who has lived in Arab since 1927. "There was one in the Roof community; they called him 'Rabbit,' 'Nigger Rabbit.' Everybody liked him." He lived there until he died. These lone African Americans had *better* be liked by all, because if one person doesn't, even if one person merely doesn't know who they are, they may be in danger. Indeed, he blamed the anti-black nature of Arab on "one guy, really, a chiropractor," an extreme white supremacist whom no one opposed. All it takes is one white person willing to attack, because it is hard for other whites to come to the defense of the person of color. Whites who do may risk being called "nigger lovers" and accused of the opposite of racial patriotism.[26]

What the exception to the sundown rule tries to achieve is a nonthreatening individuality. Newspaper stories in the 1920s repeatedly featured George Washington Maddox for his full name and for being probably the only dwarf as well as the only African American in Medford, Oregon. Casey, population about 2,500, in eastern Illinois, was a sundown town complete with a sign at its city limits saying something like "Nigger, Don't Let the Sun Shine on Your

Back in Casey," according to nearby resident Carolyn Stephens, but for many years whites exempted their nurse-midwife. Elizabeth Davis was locally famous as "Nigger Liz, the best midwife in Clark County" and the only African American allowed to live in Casey (see Portfolio 20). Eventually she grew old and died there in 1963.[27]

I call this the "file folder phenomenon." Upon first encounter with a person different from ourselves, we all tend to place him or her in a file folder: "woman," "teenager," "lesbian," "black," and so on. Elizabeth Davis needed to be filed as "Nigger Liz, the midwife." She could not afford to be a little-known member of her race, because then she would be filed as "black" first, which would never do, not in a sundown county. George Washington Maddox needed his full name—and his nonthreatening status as a dwarf—in order to live peacefully in Medford. Similarly, the sole African American allowed to remain in Harrison, Arkansas, after its 1909 race riot "insisted that her name was Alecta Caledonia Melvina Smith," which shows her as a strong character, but she also let whites call her "Aunt Vine," which played along with the inferior status connoted by *uncle* and *auntie* as applied to older African Americans.[28]

In a fine book on race relations during the Nadir period in Monroe, Michigan, an interracial city, James DeVries describes the file folder phenomenon:

> In their daily interactions with Negroes, the racist perceptions of Monroe's citizens were brought into play. The framework of the childlike Negro was raised to consciousness whenever African Americans who were not personally known appeared on city streets. Indeed, Negroes who arrived in Monroe in the early 20th century found that their presence was carefully noted.

One of Kathleen Blee's interviewees, a white Indiana woman, provides an example of file folder thinking. She agreed that it might have been all right if a local restaurant served food to a local African American in a back room: "I don't think . . . anybody would have thought anything about it. I certainly wouldn't have of our local Negroes. But, not a strange Negro. You get several of them together and they become niggers. Individually they're fine people." To avoid being pigeonholed into this imperiled outgroup, blacks in sundown towns have struggled to establish themselves as individuals.[29]

The Suburban File Folder

Surviving as the exception in a sundown town is always fraught with peril, be-cause at any point one might be accosted by whites who see one as "a nigger" rather than a specific person. One must then hope that other whites who know one as an individual will come to the rescue. In suburbia this rarely hap-pened: there it is too hard for an African American to create and maintain celebrity as an individual. Suburbs have less community—less "gemein-schaft," as sociologists say. There is less "talk" about neighbors and other townspeople, who aren't known as well, and families move in and out even more rapidly than in independent towns. So it is harder for all the residents to learn that a given African American family is OK, that they are the allowed ex-ception.

Alice Thompson, a longtime resident of Brea, California, a sundown sub-urb of Los Angeles, told in 1982 of one man who almost made it:

> There were no Negroes in Brea; they were not allowed. We had a shoeshine man who we called Neff, and he always spoke to all the kids and everything. He had a little cigar store in front of the barbershop; another man ran a little cigar counter and he [Neff] had the shoeshine place. But at six o'clock, some people say ten but I believe it was six, the bus came through and he left for Fullerton. Fullerton has always had more colored people. He was an awful nice old man, but Brea just would not allow them to be here and I don't know how they stopped them.
>   [Who are they?]
>   I don't know, I would say, maybe, the Ku-Klux Klan.[30]

Fred and Mary Clark did succeed in staying in West Lawn, the sundown neighborhood of Chicago where they were the only black household. Indeed, the Clarks were no interlopers. They had lived in West Lawn since 1893, be-fore there *was* a West Lawn. Nevertheless, newcomers to West Lawn had to learn that their existence was tolerated, or the Clarks were in trouble. "Even now that the Clarks are older," wrote reporter Steve Bogira in 1986, "they have to worry about the reaction of whites—especially young ones—to their presence."

> "Walking down the street is not a pleasant ordeal . . . ," Fred says. "School kids will come and throw stones." . . . The Clarks don't even sit on the porch—they mainly stay inside the house, where they're out of the way of white animosity. Mostly out of the way, that is—they still have rocks and bricks tossed through

their windows periodically, still find racist graffiti scribbled on their garage at times. Several years ago, after all of their front windows, upstairs and downstairs, had been smashed with rocks one night, the Clarks put the house up for sale. "When people would come to look at it and they found a black was here - they'd move on," Mary says. "So it wasn't no way of selling it."

Many decades ago, when West Lawn had more gemeinschaft, white neighbors helped guard the house when whites attacked African Americans throughout Chicago during the 1919 race riot. Gradually "the old-timers moved out, and the new neighbors seemed less comfortable with the Clarks." As an adult, Fred Clark "has been chased through the neighborhood several times, had rocks thrown at him, but his docile attitude has kept him from serious harm."[31]

Exceptions That Embody the Rule

Even transient African Americans, by the sheer fact of their existence, can prompt some change for the better. Bus passengers might find themselves in Cullman, Alabama, a rest stop on U.S. 31, the main route from Nashville to Birmingham and points south. During the segregation era, according to a woman who grew up in Cullman, African Americans

> would step off in Cullman to look for restrooms only to be turned back, and mothers could be heard explaining to their crying children that they would have to wait until farther down the road. Mother never told us that without a catch in her voice. By the time I can remember, a bus station had been built that had a set of facilities for each race—the only place in Cullman that did, to the best of my knowledge.

Those "colored" restrooms brought Cullman partway into the era of "mere" segregation (although African Americans still could not eat or sleep in the town) and therefore marked an advance compared to total exclusion.[32]

Similarly, the solitary black household allowed as the exception in a sundown town can humanize that community to a degree. At least whites have made a distinction among African Americans, even if only to separate out one or two Tonto figures from the otherwise backward horde. And their presence—and that of their children—does "desegregate" some of the institutions in town, such as the public schools and the library, even if only nominally. But I wouldn't want to claim too much for this process. Allowing one

African American person or household has rarely led to a difference in a sundown town's policy or alleviated the racism that defends and rationalizes that policy.

On the contrary: publicizing the African American as an exception reminds the community that this is the *only* African American allowed in the area, thus ironically reinforcing the sundown rule. Even Greenwood, Indiana, for example, a town whose hostility toward African Americans was legendary, had its one African American household as an exception. In the words of Joycelyn Landrum-Brown, an African American who grew up nearby, "The whites in that town 'just loved' that black family," and "they did not come to any harm."[33]

The Austin, Minnesota, story shows another ideological payoff that allowing one household to stay when all others are driven out can have for whites, as they can claim not to be racist: "We're not against all African Americans, after all—look at Frank!" More accurately, whites can claim to be *appropriately* racist. The problem lies with those *other* African Americans—"the damn niggers." Even Frank—"and he was *black*"—agrees. Thus instead of allowing their positive feelings about George Washington Maddox or Elizabeth Davis to prompt some questioning of their exclusionary policies, whites in Medford, Oregon, and Casey, Illinois, merely emphasized how exceptional these individuals were. In turn, this allowed whites to affirm once more how inferior *other* African Americans were, in their eyes. In about 1950, whites in Marshall, Illinois, a sundown town just east of Casey, even declared their exception, "Squab" Wilson, the barber, to be "an honorary white man." Afraid of losing this honor—and perhaps his white clientele and his permission to live in Marshall—Wilson refused to cut the hair of a black writer living temporarily at the nearby Handy Writers Colony, until novelist James Jones threatened him with a boycott.[34]

Interaction with people such as "Frank" or Wilson provides residents of sundown towns with no meaningful experience with African Americans, because such individuals take care not to reveal opinions or characteristics different from those of the white majority. Unfortunately, unless they enlist in the armed forces, most residents of sundown towns never get to know African Americans, except superficially in athletic contests and from television. The impact of the exclusion of African Americans on the residents of these towns—and on white Americans in general—will be the subject of the next chapter.

PART V

Effects of Sundown Towns

11

The Effect of Sundown Towns on Whites

And I said "nigger," and my mother corrected me: "When we're in *this* town you must call them 'Negroes.' "
> —"Susan Penny" of Oblong, Illinois, telling of her
> childhood trip to Terre Haute, Indiana, c. 1978 [1]

WHAT DIFFERENCE DO SUNDOWN TOWNS and suburbs make? In particular, what effect do they have on their inhabitants? Is growing up in an intentionally all-white town unlike growing up in an integrated town? Sociologist William J. Wilson uses "social isolation" as an explanation (in part) for the social pathology of the black ghetto. Here we explore the social pathology of the *white* ghetto, if you will, caused by its comparable social isolation. We will see that residents of sundown towns do become more racist toward African Americans and also more prejudiced toward gays and other minorities. Sundown towns also collect white racists from the outside world who are attracted by the towns' lack of diversity.

White Seems Right

My research shows that residents of sundown towns and suburbs are much more racist toward African Americans than are residents of interracial towns, and also more prejudiced toward gays and other minorities. But do sundown communities collect white supremacists or create them? The question is important. If sundown towns merely collected racists, they might be doing American society a service by sequestering bigots away from the rest of us. Sundown towns do collect white racists from the outside world who are attracted by their lack of diversity. Unfortunately, they also create racists. Living in an all-white community leads many residents to defend living in an all-white community.

These generalizations do not describe everyone in a sundown town, suburb, or neighborhood.[2] Many young adults leave sundown communities precisely to experience greater diversity and escape the stifling atmosphere of conformity that many of these places foster. Indeed, if they want to be successful, young people almost have to leave independent sundown towns, because these towns impart a worldview that limits their horizons. Children of elite sundown suburbs, on the other hand, are likely to move into positions of corporate and political leadership in years to come. This makes their constricted upbringing a problem for us all, because sundown communities inculcate a distinctive form of obtuse thinking about American society—I have elsewhere called it "soclexia"[3]—that incorporates remarkable ethnocentrism as well as NIMBY (Not In My Back Yard) politics.

The first and mildest effect on one's thinking that results from living in a sundown town is the sense that it is perfectly normal to live in an all-white community. Even towns that went sundown by violently expelling their African Americans quickly come to seem all-white "naturally." Billy Bob Lightfoot, historian of Comanche County, Texas, caught this sense when describing the aftermath of that county's expulsion of its black residents in 1886: "Almost immediately it seemed as though there had never been a Negro in Comanche County, and within a month the only reminder . . . was a sign on the public well in De Leon: 'Nigger, don't let the sun go down on you in this town.' "[4] "Almost immediately," whites do not really notice that the town is *not* normal and that an initial incident, in this case a violent expulsion, and a subsequent series of enforcement measures, some violent, were required to achieve and maintain this abnormal result.[5]

Decades later, it is even easier to take a town's whiteness for granted. Not everyone moves to sundown towns to avoid African Americans, after all. Many whites locate in them without even knowing they are sundown towns. Once they have moved in, residents are still less likely to reflect upon the racial composition of their new community. The sun rises in the east and sets in the west, the children go to school, the adults to work, and all seems as it should be. All-white town governments, churches, choral groups, audiences, and even school athletic teams come to appear perfectly normal. African Americans come to seem unusual—abnormal—except maybe on television.

Children who grow up in sundown towns find it especially easy to develop the sense that it is normal, even proper, to grow up in a place where everyone looks like you, racially, and that blacks are *not* the same and not really proper. But newcomers, too, rarely challenge the whiteness of their newly chosen communities. Instead, they tend to take on the culture, including the political ideology and patterns of race relations, into which they move. Carl Withers studied a small Missouri sundown town, Wheatland, in 1940. "New settlers still come in, a dozen or two a year in the whole county," he wrote. "Those who stay become in remarkably short time 'just like everybody else here,' in speech, dress, mannerisms, attitudes, and general way of life. Most of those who are unable to adjust to the community's mores soon sell out and move away." Jacob Holdt, a Dane whose exposé on race relations in the United States, *American Pictures,* was briefly famous in the 1980s, describes Danes' accommodation to racism in the United States: "I have met Danish Americans who were red-hot Social Democrats back in Denmark, but in the course of just five years had been transformed into the worst reactionaries."[6]

Withers's finding—that newcomers become just like everybody else— holds especially true for new arrivals to sundown suburbs. As *Newsweek* put it in 1957, during the peak rush to suburbia: "When a city dweller packs up and moves his family to the suburbs, he usually acquires a mortgage, a power lawn mower, and a backyard grill. Often although a lifelong Democrat, he also starts voting Republican." Sometimes families even change their party membership before they move, a pattern sociologists call anticipatory socialization. The same adjustment seems to take place regarding race relations, which explains why sundown towns that were quite small before suburbanization usually stay all-white after suburbanization, even though nine-tenths of their populations may now be new arrivals. Sundown acorns produce white oak trees. Socialization to suburbia thus increases the level of racism in metropolitan areas, as people move from multiracial cities to all-white suburbs.[7]

White Privilege

Once living in an all-white town seems normal, residents come to think of it as a *right*. Going against this right seems wrong. As we saw in the "Enforcement" chapter, a person of color who strays into an all-white town looks out of place, even outrageous. A white person who claims that this is not how a town should be can similarly sound out of place, even outrageous.

In 1987, Oprah Winfrey, broadcasting from Forsyth County, Georgia, then a sundown county, explored this mentality:

Winfrey: You don't believe that people of other races have the right to live here?

Unidentified Audience Member #2: They have the right to live wherever they want to, but we have the right to choose if we want a white community also. That's why we moved here.

This viewpoint is hardly confined to places as "extreme" as Forsyth County, which expelled its African Americans en masse in 1912. "White people have a right to keep blacks out of their neighborhoods if they want to, and blacks should respect that right" was one of the opinion statements presented to people by the National Opinion Research Center repeatedly in the 1970s, and in 1976, a representative year, 40% of whites across the nation agreed with the item. Of course, many of them lived in all-white suburbs and neighborhoods. Striking is Audience Member #2's "we/they" terminology. White privilege necessarily involves the creation of a black "they"—a racial outgroup. Thus sundown towns increase white racism because they provoke whites to think of a black person not as an individual but as an African American first. The file folder phenomenon rules uncontested.[8]

In 1958, sociologist Herbert Blumer published an important article, "Race Prejudice as a Sense of Group Position," pointing out "that race prejudice exists basically in a sense of group position rather than in a set of feelings." Blumer pointed out that viewing prejudice as feelings "overlooks and obscures the fact that race prejudice is fundamentally a matter of relationship between racial groups." While feelings are definitely involved, prejudice presupposes "that racially prejudiced individuals think of themselves as belonging to a given racial group." It also presupposes that they have an image of the "other" group, against whom they are prejudiced. Blumer went on to identify four feelings that are involved, of which "the third feeling, the sense of proprietary claim, is of crucial importance." "Proprietary claim," of course—the "right" to exclude—is precisely what sundown towns are all about.[9]

This new proprietary claim helps explain why sundown towns usually stayed all-white for so long: once whites have concocted the "privilege" of living in an all-white community, they are then loath to give up this "right." Indeed, what we might call "racial patriotism" keeps them from giving it up. Note the contradiction between the two rights invoked by Winfrey's Audience Member #2: "They" have "the right to live wherever they want," but "we" have "the right to choose if we want a white community." How do "we" exercise that right? Obviously by infringing "their" right to live wherever they want.

A white friend unwittingly displayed this same contradiction upon first learning of my research topic: "I just can't understand why people would *want* to live where they're not wanted!" This statement seems reasonable and I tried to answer it reasonably, but it presumes that African Americans can be expected to assess whether whites want them and should comport themselves accordingly. When "we" (nonblacks) buy a house, we do not assess whether our neighbors will like us. We rarely even meet them before moving in, and if we do, we only meet those right next door. We *presume* we will be accepted or at least tolerated. We also presume the privilege of living wherever we want. My friend's comment does not afford African Americans the same right and instead makes "them" the problem: "they" are wrong to intrude.

Racist Symbols and Mascots

This book is a history of exclusion, yet the excluded are ever-present. They persist in the form of stereotypes and constructions in the minds of those who keep them out. From the Nadir until very recently, sundown town residents have been even more likely than other whites to impersonate African Americans in theatrical productions and revues. After whites in Corbin, Kentucky, drove out all African Americans on Halloween in 1919, May Minstrel Festival with "black-faced comedians" became perhaps its most popular annual event during the 1920s. In Royal Oak, a sundown suburb of Detroit, the Lions Club put on minstrel shows from 1948 to 1968. White residents in blackface performed minstrel shows in all-white towns in Wisconsin, Illinois, and Vermont into the 1970s. Even today, residents of sundown towns are much more likely than in interracial towns to display such atavisms as black "coach boys" or Confederate flags in front of their houses.[10] Students in all-white towns in several states have caused disruptions by wearing Confederate flags, T-shirts, and jackets to school. Such incidents also take place in interracial schools, of course, but much less often, because there they will not go unopposed by other students. Perhaps more worrisome, in some all-white towns, such as Deer Park in eastern Washington, students cause *no* disruption by wearing or displaying Confederate flags, according to recent Deer Park graduates. "You cannot wear all one color—so as to be Goths, etc. But you *can* have Confederate flags on your locker!"[11]

An in-your-face example of white privilege is the use of racial slurs to name athletic teams, a common practice in sundown towns. For several decades Pekin High School in central Illinois called its athletic teams "Chinks" ("Chinklets" for the girls). It was supposed to be funny, referring to the town, named for Peking (Beijing), China; the teams' previous nickname had been "Celestials." When Pekin won the state basketball tournament in 1964 and 1967, the resulting publicity prompted an outcry from outraged Chinese Americans. In 1974, Kung Lee Wang, president of the Organization of Chinese Americans, twice flew to Pekin from his Maryland home. He denounced the name as "a racist slur," met with the mayor, school superintendent, and principals, and addressed the student council. The students then voted 85%

to 15% to stick with "Chinks," and the board of education echoed that decision the following spring. Pekin retained "Chinks" until 1980, when a new school superintendent demanded a change, apparently as a condition of his employment. The change then provoked a student walkout that lasted several days. Unfortunately, the school changed its nickname to "Dragons," which also conjures not only China but also leaders of the Ku Klux Klan.[12] That connotation was not lost in Pekin, which was notorious as a statewide Klan headquarters in the 1920s. Indeed, the Klan owned the *Pekin Times* for a while and ran sections of official Klan philosophy as editorials; today a Klan leader still lives and recruits in Pekin.[13]

"Redskins" is a more common slur used as nickname, chosen by at least three all-white high schools in Illinois and several others in other states. To be sure, naming teams with racial slurs is hardly limited to sundown towns, as the Washington Redskins prove. Nevertheless, without attempting the exhausting task of analyzing the mascots of all U.S. high schools against the racial composition of their student bodies, my impression is that all-white high schools are more likely to adopt racially derogatory nicknames and mascots and less likely to change them when challenged. Many people of color and their allies hate this practice and have protested it, not only to the owners of the Washington NFL team but also in small towns such as Sullivan, Illinois. The typical response from sundown towns—and from supporters of the Washington team—is to deny that they mean anything racist by the nicknames and to say that if people choose to interpret them differently, that's their problem. As Pekin graduate Dianna Adams wrote about the Chinks, "I always thought that it was a compliment to those who chose to take it otherwise."[14]

Names such as "Chinks" and "Redskins" imply that whites are dominant and can use racial slurs anytime they want. Too few Chinese Americans lived in Pekin—and their position was too tenuous—to protest. Similarly, American Indians are less than 1% of the population, and the protesters who appear at every home Redskins football game in D.C. are even fewer, so "we" can do whatever we want.[15] The same sense of privilege holds for displaying a Confederate flag or black coach boy. In interracial towns, whether from fear that such a symbol (or the house behind it) might get vandalized or from a sincere desire not to offend people of color, whites are less likely to flaunt such items.

Athletic Contests in Sundown Towns

In many small towns, high school athletic contests are portentous. Usually a basketball or football game draws more people than any other event of the week; often the game then becomes the main topic of conversation during the next week. The contests are important symbolically as well. Unfortunately, racist mascots are only part of the problem of white misbehavior when players and fans from interracial schools visit sundown towns. Such visits take place under a double cloud of "otherness."

A town already forms an in-group vis-à-vis the next town. In high school athletic contests, this antagonism usually has a lighthearted cast. Cheers like "Smash the Tigers!" aren't meant literally, of course. But when a town is all-white on purpose, the sense of being the racial in-group as well lends a special edge to the contest. A black graduate of Manual, Peoria's most interracial high school, said that when her alma mater plays Pekin, downstate Illinois's largest sundown town, "something racial is definitely going on." A 2001 white graduate of Manual agreed: "There is a special atmosphere when Manual plays Pekin. Lots is at stake. Whole buses of students go, to protect the team." On occasion the team has needed protection; in 1975, for example, according to Randy Whitman, a Manual student at the time, as the team was leaving Pekin "bottles, bricks, and all other kind of debris start pelting the bus." Fans of interracial high school teams near other sundown towns say the same thing: they take a busload of people "to protect their team" in what they surmise is likely to be a hostile environment. Administrators and coaches from interracial schools caution their fans and team members to stay in groups and exhibit extreme decorum when they play schools in sundown towns.[16]

Supporting the cheerleaders become an issue too, especially if they "cheer black." Blacks and whites tend to engage in two quite different styles of cheerleading, each of which can appear laughable to the other. In overwhelmingly white environments, black cheerleaders can face ridicule, even without the racist catcalls that sometimes emanate from fans in a sundown town. When Meadowbrook High School, a majority-white but integrated school southwest of Richmond, Virginia, played Colonial Heights, known informally as "Colonial Whites," the Meadowbrook cheerleading coach recruited extra chaperones to accompany them to help students deal with the racism they routinely experienced there.[17]

Interracial towns and teams need not include a high proportion of African Americans to draw the ire of fans and players in sundown towns. Cleveland, Oklahoma, has a big football rivalry with Hominy, the next town north. According to a 1985 graduate of Hominy High School, that "game was always well attended, even when both teams stank. The story I heard was that the racial difference between Cleveland and Hominy was so great that Cleveland used to call their rivals the 'Hominy Coons.' " In 1990, Hominy had 76

African Americans among 2,342 residents, just 3%, but that looked very black from the vantage point of Cleveland, which had just 8 African Americans—and no black households—among its 3,156 residents, or 0.2%. In a sundown town, emphasizing even the few blacks among an opponent's student body or team can provide a unifying rhetoric for the in-group.[18]

Fans in sundown towns commonly use racial slurs. Across America, coaches and principals from interracial high schools caution their players and fans not to react. They know that racial slurs have often led to more serious altercations. In the 1960s, all-white Cedar Cliff High School in Lemoyne, Pennsylvania, across the river from Harrisburg, played football against Harrisburg's majority-black John Harris High School. According to a high school teacher in the area, "riots occurred every time the game was on the 'White Shore.' " Clearly, more than good-natured rivalries are involved. Fans in some sundown towns seem affronted that African Americans dare to play in their town. Kaye Collins attended Rabun Gap Nacoochee High School, in the northeast corner of Georgia, in 1972–73. "We had a black basketball player on our team, and threats were made against him when we played in Towns County. That was the first time I heard that black people shouldn't be in Towns County after dark." The death threats were made days before the game, but according to Collins, "nothing happened. Our team trounced them!" In the 1990s, whites burned crosses in Dale, Indiana, when a majority-black team from Evansville played there, a high school teacher from the area reported. An African American member of the Danville, Kentucky, football team remembered repeated outrageous fan behavior at Corbin, Kentucky, in the early 1970s. "They would cut the bus tires and the car tires, especially if we were winning." Corbin is the scene of the only film ever made about a sundown town, Robby Heason's documentary *Trouble Behind*. In it, an African American former football player in a nearby town says in 1990,

> We went in there to play; we were scared to death. . . . When we'd come out we'd get "rocked"—they'd throw rocks at your buses, they'd throw big cinderblocks. We had a couple of times where they would throw through the complete windshield. . . . And we had to drive back one night, this is when I was a sophomore, and this is a basketball game, and they crashed the whole front window and we had to drive home without it.

Later in the documentary, Heason films the school superintendent in Corbin saying, "It's a good place to rear our children."[19]

It isn't just fans who misbehave. Often players and even officials act up as well. Cairo, an interracial town at the southern tip of Illinois, played for the regional basketball championship in Anna in 1987. The Cairo Pilots, all black except their coach and one player, led by fifteen points at the half. Thereafter, "every call seemed to favor the hometown Wildcats of Anna-Jonesboro," according to two *Washington Post* reporters at the game. Referees called 24 fouls on Cairo and just 8 on Anna-Jonesboro. Late in the game, a Cairo player struck back after being elbowed by an Anna guard, and a near-riot ensued. "We go through this all the time," said Bill Chumbler, the Cairo coach. "There are no black referees down here, and we know that if it's close near the end, they're going to take it away from us." [20]

Interracial schools have to take measures to shield their black teammates and cheerleaders from harm in some sundown towns. Football and basketball teams in interracial high schools in Evansville—in southwestern Indiana— have a tradition of playing away-games at Jasper, Indiana, "earlier in the day than usual," according to a man who practice-taught in Evansville in 2001. "The reason: it was still commonly understood that for the safety of the student athletes of color and their parents, the team needed to be out of Jasper before dark or as close to it as possible." A 1995 graduate of interracial Carbondale High School in southern Illinois said their wrestling coach warned them to protect their African American players on and off the mat when competing at West Frankfort, a sundown town 20 miles northeast. Athletes in Sullivan, Missouri, were so racist that some coaches chose not to risk letting their African American players play, according to a nearby resident:

> Some local context: It was only about 9 years ago that the sign outside of the town of Sullivan, Missouri, (a stronghold of the KKK in Missouri, and about 30 miles from where I live) was removed. It stated simply "Nigger, don't let the sun set on you in Sullivan." I have friends who live there who have told me of things that they have seen themselves there. My daughter married a man who was born and raised there and has told us that the town fathers, bank president, mayor, and other officials are all known to be members and leaders of the local [KKK] chapter. When my son was in high school and played football, the black kids were always benched when they played in Sullivan. It was not out of discrimination against them, but to protect them from injury. Over the years the coach had too many black players hurt there, and hurt in ways that couldn't be proven were intentional, but appeared to be so. He felt he couldn't risk it any more. The parents went along. [21]

This tradition of racism at athletic contests also besets sundown suburbs, where it has sometimes drawn coverage from major city daily newspapers. The *New York Times* ran a story on Connecticut's 1999 state championship football game between Darien, a sundown suburb, and Weaver High School in north Hartford, where the majority of students are black and Hispanic. "After Game, Aftertaste of Racial Slurs Lingers" was the headline. Weaver won, 69 to 26. "In the hearts of many Weaver players, however, the sweetness of victory mingled with the sting of racism," according to the *Times.* "As the game wore on and the score became more lopsided, members of the Weaver team, all of whom are black or Hispanic, said they heard a number of crude racial epithets hurled at them by Darien's all-white team." Players from Darien, one of the richest suburbs of New York City, also hurled class insults after a Weaver touchdown: "It's O.K. In five years, you'll be working for me." Some Darien players charged that Weaver players had also used racial slurs, and the teams did get together for a constructive session at Weaver later. If the Darien team had included black players, it is unlikely that its white players would have used *nigger,* and if Darien were integrated on social class lines, it would be equally unthinkable that some team members would taunt opposing players for being poor.[22]

Racist language and behavior by athletes and fans begin as early as middle school in some sundown towns.[23] Some situations have grown so tense that interracial middle schools have canceled all future games with sundown schools. Usually this bad behavior takes place at the school in the sundown town. Less often do sundown fans yell racial slurs when they are the visitors, in the minority. Occasionally students in interracial schools engage in belligerent behavior at their home games, aimed at the all-white outsiders. Darla Craft wrote of being a cheerleader of all-white Herrin Junior High School in southern Illinois in 1969–70. "We had a basketball game in Mt. Vernon, where there was racial unrest. As we left the game, we were jumped by a group of African-American girls. I ran, so I wasn't hurt, but a couple of the girls were pretty banged up." Around that time, according to a graduate of Pinckneyville High School, a few miles northwest, "the two or three times we played football or basketball against Sparta or Du Quoin [nearby interracial towns] every year [there] were always melees bordering on race riots. I recall hearing of one game at Sparta at which all of our buses' windows were broken out, and riot police were called in from Carbondale to settle things down." I remember this period of militance in black culture between 1969 and about 1972, but the danger of what might be called "white racial paranoia" also lurks. The Sparta-Pinckneyville fracas may not have been exactly a race riot, considering that Sparta was at the time just 15% black. Surely white Sparta students had to have participated. Perhaps it was primarily an interscholastic melee with racial overtones.[24]

The Talk in Sundown Towns

The foregoing account of bad behavior at athletic contests in sundown towns is not the whole story. Many sundown towns have repeatedly hosted interracial teams and their fans without incident. However, that's partly because the visitors choose to overlook the verbal racism they encounter. Even when on their best behavior, many residents of sundown towns routinely say "nigger." Indeed, another privilege all-white towns confer on their inhabitants is the license to say anything they want about people of color. Perhaps the first thing noticed by visitors to independent sundown towns is their overt verbal racism. During my thirteen years of public schooling in interracial Decatur, Illinois, ending in 1960, I never once heard the word *nigger* in school, on the playground, or said by one of my peers anywhere. But in sundown towns all around Decatur and all across America, the word was in common parlance then and remains the term of choice today. One of the most profound effects of sundown towns is on white rhetoric—on how people in them talk, especially on how they talk about race and about black people.

In 2001, I had a pleasant conversation with a 70-year-old white woman in Sheridan, Arkansas. A year or so earlier, the first African American family to move into Sheridan since blacks were evicted four decades earlier joined her church, Landmark Baptist, the town's most prominent. She favored their membership and said: "Our pastor, I have to hand it to him. He was young, but he knew what to do. He counseled with the nigger family, so then the niggers knew what they were getting into, and it all worked out." This woman did not mean *nigger* maliciously; she seemed happy that the family stayed. She was just thoughtlessly using the term she had heard and used all her life. Her sundown town, fifty years behind the times, encouraged that lack of thought. Many sundown town residents are oblivious to other signs of progress in race relations. In 1993, half the class in Highland High School, a sundown town in Illinois east of St. Louis, thought interracial marriage was still illegal, according to a woman who graduated that year.[25]

One of the chief ways that white Americans have progressed in racial conduct in the fifty years since the 1954 Supreme Court school desegregation decision is in their rhetoric. Words may be shallow, the change may only lie on the surface, but surfaces do matter. People typically relate to each other on the surface, after all. Surface surely matters to African Americans, who take deep offense at whites' use of *nigger*. For that matter, civilized rhetoric is a first step toward civilized behavior. The Civil Rights Movement initiated half a century of conflict and change that has proven difficult but humanizing. Sundown towns have deliberately sidestepped this adventure in healing, through which we are still working our way. Sheridan itself went sundown in 1954, in direct response to *Brown*.

Not just in speech, but also on paper, sundown town residents offend. While they don't write *nigger,* authors typically use *Negro*—often uncapitalized—or the still more ancient *colored people,* even in works intended as serious history and written as late as the 1980s and 1990s. The rest of America left these terms behind decades ago in favor of *black* and *African American.* Writers in independent sundown towns simply haven't bothered to keep up with this progression. When they quote the occasional African American permitted to live in their town as exceptions, often they use dialect. Ralph Rea, for example, historian of Boone County, Arkansas, quotes Alecta Smith, allowed to remain after the expulsions of 1905 and 1909: "Aunt Vine often said that she was 'the best niggah evah bawn, cuz all de rest was run off.' " Of course, just about all Americans pronounce *'cause* "cuz." "Cuz" is correct. But no one writes *cuz* when a white person uses *'cause.* Moreover, whites and blacks from a given part of Arkansas pronounce *ever, born,* and most other words about the same. To put Smith's words in dialect is simply to otherize her, to make her speech different from and inferior to whites' use of language. By even the narrowest definition it is racist, for it treats one group differently and worse than another when they pronounce the same word identically. Such dialect was also antique, even back in 1955.[26]

It is striking when well-meaning whites say *nigger* as a matter of course. More often, whites in sundown towns do not mean well. In 1966, when Gordon Wright and his family moved into Grosse Pointe, Michigan, the first African American family to do so, they endured months of the slur. Adults yelled, "Nigger, go back down South." The Kiwanis Club bus taking children to a park during the summer slowed at the Wright residence so the kids could lean out and yell the epithet. When school started in the fall, the safety patrol boys called the Wright children "niggers" on their way to school.[27]

Kathy Spillman grew up in North Tonawanda, a sundown town near Buffalo, New York, in the 1970s and '80s. "The *nicest* word I learned was *colored. Nigger* was the typical term," she told me. "I learned to hold my breath when blacks walked by, because I was taught they smell bad." Roger Horowitz, now at the Hagley Museum in Delaware, lived in Marquette Park, a sundown neighborhood in Chicago, where "there was and is the casual assumption in bars that you can tell 'nigger jokes.' " Two thousand miles southwest, in Indian Wells, California, Richard Williams and his famous tennis-star daughters Venus and Serena experienced *nigger* at the Pacific Life Open in March, 2001, after Venus pulled out of the tournament with knee tendinitis, conceding her match to Serena. "Accusations surfaced that their father, Richard, was fixing his daughters' matches and that the sisters didn't want to play each other," according to an account in *USA Today*. "In Serena's final match two days later against [Kim] Clijsters, the charged-up crowd unleashed its wrath on her, booing Serena's every move." According to Richard Williams, "When Venus and I were walking down the stairs to our seats, people kept calling me 'nigger.' " [28]

Sundown Humor

It isn't just *nigger*, of course. In Pinckneyville, the sundown town in southwestern Illinois, "one of the town's beloved teachers, Doc Thomas, used to openly make racial slurs in the classroom," according to Ron Slater, who graduated from Pinckneyville High School in 1966. "An example of a Doc Thomas comment that sticks in my mind was as follows: 'Well, boys and girls, we have a track meet with Sparta this Friday. Don't think we have to worry though, as it is supposed to be cold, and you know those jungle bunnies don't run so well when it is cold.' " Such a wisecrack, coming casually from the person in charge, can make quite an impact on a classroom. Certainly no defense of African Americans, no opposition to such witticisms, will likely be attempted by a student. [29]

Sundown town rhetoric descends to its lowest point when speakers try to be funny. A recent graduate of Darien High School, the elite Connecticut suburb of New York City, noted that Darien's whiteness "allowed for the kids to joke and to maintain racist stereotypes. A lot of my friends came in with racist jokes, and you never had to worry about it." Many racial jokes considered funny in sundown towns are simply wretched. Consider this quip, told to Ray Elliott when he was teaching in the public schools of Robinson, Illinois, a sundown town near Terre Haute, Indiana, in the mid-1980s. On Martin Luther King Jr. Day, he walked into a restaurant and saw some friends. One said to him, "If they would've killed four more of the sons of bitches, you could've had the whole week off, Elliott!" Real hatred slinks below the surface of that "joke," the same attitude toward King that Linda Dudek remembers from one of her best friends in second grade in Berwyn, Illinois, a sundown suburb just west of Chicago: "That nigger had it coming," the little girl said the day after Martin Luther King Jr. was assassinated, and Dudek continues, "That was pretty much the attitude that prevailed at my grammar school." [30]

Labor historian Ramelle MaCoy remembers this joke, taught by his civics teacher in an all-white high school, about a black hobo who got off a freight train in an Alabama town unaware of the "N——, Don't Let The Sun Set on You Here" signs at the town lines. A gang of whites beat him soundly before asking, "If we let you go will you catch the next train out of here?" "If you let me go I'll catch that one I got off of!"

Telling such a joke in a sundown town classroom lends it a special relevance, an edge. The teller assumes, almost always correctly, that no one will object, and sharing such jokes bonds teller and audience into a racial in-group. Of course, one does not need to be in a sundown town to hear such jokes; almost any all-white environment will do.[31]

On one occasion I found that *I* had told a side-splitting joke in a sundown town. I was telling a volunteer in the Grant County Museum in Sheridan, Arkansas, about sundown towns in other states and mentioned what the name of the sundown town in southern Illinois, Anna, is said to stand for: "Ain't No Niggers Allowed." He laughed uproariously. People from multiracial towns, including white people, don't think it's funny.[32]

"In *This* Town You Must Call Them 'Negroes' "

An incident from New Market, a sundown town in southwestern Iowa, shows that whites do know to behave better in interracial situations. In about 1986, African American John Baskerville went to a high school play there. In Baskerville's words:

> One of the characters was the black maid of the murder victim who found the body, so she had to testify. When the young girl acting as the black maid appeared on stage, we were all shocked. . . . The young white girl appeared in BLACKFACE! She had very black make-up with white lips and bugged-out eyes and dressed like Hattie McDaniel in *Gone With the Wind*, head scarf and all. . . . After the play, the young girl who played the part tried to hide from us. . . . She was so embarrassed because she knew that it was inappropriate and hadn't expected us there.[33]

Sundown town residents also know that *nigger* is an offensive term. I asked "Susan Penny," who grew up in Oblong, a sundown town in southeastern Illinois, in the 1970s and 1980s, "Did you hear the word *nigger* when you were growing up?" "Are you kidding?" she replied.

> I never knew they were called anything *but* "niggers"! I must have been seven years old, and my mother drove us to Terre Haute, my brother and me. And my

brother and I were in awe because there were two things that we had never seen
in Oblong: black people and nuns! And I said "nigger," and my mother corrected me, "When we're in *this* town you must call them 'Negroes.' "

The admonition shows that Penny's mother knew full well that African Americans do not appreciate the term; for that matter, she probably knew that some
white people in interracial towns don't like it either. So she knew to correct
her children's verbal behavior "in *this* town," Terre Haute, where it might
earn them disapproval. She also knew that nobody cared in Oblong, so she
did not bother to correct their word usage in Oblong. This is a vivid example
of a privilege white towns confer on their residents: unlike other Americans,
they need not think twice about the terms they use to refer to other groups or
the jokes they tell about them. Similarly, the suburbanites in Indian Wells
know that *nigger* is offensive. They also know they can get away with it at an almost all-white tennis venue in an almost all-white town.[34] In the 2000 census
Indian Wells had just 15 African Americans among its 3,816 residents.[35]

Some high school students from sundown towns imagine somehow that
even in interracial situations in the big city, they can behave as they do at
home, where they enjoy the privilege of living in a world of white rhetoric.
They behave with a paradoxical combination of inappropriate, even dangerous arrogance and inappropriate, even fearful timidity. First they dread going
into an interracial restaurant; then they feel they can get away with saying *nigger* in it. Roger Karns, who has taught social studies in several all-white towns
in northern Indiana and also coaches swimming, supplied a rich and complex
account of the rhetoric that high school students from these towns exhibit
when they get to their big city—Fort Wayne, South Bend, Elkhart, or Indianapolis:

> Students ask questions like, "Will we get mugged?" "That black (or as fre-
> quently, 'colored') guy has on a red t-shirt, is he in a gang?" Or, taking swimmers
> into a McDonald's, "I saw a black guy, is this neighborhood safe?" "Is that guy a
> rapper?" And just generalized stupid behavior, fake ghetto accents, caricatur-
> ized walks and behavior. I am still surprised that I need to tell these kids that the
> term "colored" is considered offensive. And several years ago, I had to tell kids
> specifically that "nigger" was never acceptable. After twenty years of teaching
> and coaching, I discovered that if I didn't remind them of that before we went to
> a "big" city, that they would use those kinds of terms and use them loudly. Or
> they would ask an African-American what gang they were in. Or just point and
> laugh out the bus window.[36]

Of course, students like these already know *nigger* is offensive. They just imagine such rules don't apply to them because they come from a sundown town. Some of their antics are mainly performed for the benefit of their fellow white students. As they make fun or ask insensitive questions of a member of the black outgroup, the students confirm their membership in their white ingroup. Karns explains how the demographic makeup of his students' hometown contributes to their rude and racist behavior:

> I think that growing up in an all white community is detrimental for the white kids. I believe that that kind of upbringing allows people to think of minorities as an "other." It allows you to suspend your normal respect for people. Some of these kids don't see a person walking down the street, they see what amounts to a character. They would never consider being so disrespectful to someone, they just haven't thought about what they are doing as disrespectful because they are seeing a unique "other" and not just the guy down the street.

Here Karns supplies a perfect example and analysis of the "file folder phenomenon." His students react to the African Americans they meet not as people, but as examples of a type. His students are not necessarily bad people, even though they behave badly. In a sense their words and acts are shallow. But their surface racism allows white supremacy to fester and makes it harder for a humane response to come forth the next time race is on the table. As Karns concludes: "Growing up in an all white town has a profound impact on those who grow up there. . . . I believe that the lack of diversity is damaging to all." [37]

"We're Not Prejudiced"

These Indiana young people would doubtless deny that they meant anything mean by their comments and antics. Denial is a peculiar characteristic of the talk in sundown towns. When criticized for their racist jokes or use of *nigger,* residents typically deny they are racist. In the early 1990s, football players in Hemet, California, a rapidly growing sundown exurb of Los Angeles, routinely called African Americans on opposing teams "niggers." Scott Bailey, the Hemet quarterback, admitted some of his teammates had aimed the slur at opponents, but "they did not intend it as a racial slur." In Bailey's words, "I don't think anybody who does say it means anything by it." A black football player from Ramona, one of Hemet's opponents, observed, "I just think, you know, there aren't that many black people out there [in the Hemet area], so they think saying that stuff is OK."[38]

Many residents of sundown towns not only deny that their humor is racist, they also deny that their communities' anti-black acts are racist, even as they agree that those acts make it impossible for African Americans to live there safely. A former resident of an Illinois sundown town characterized her former neighbors: "They don't have anything against colored people, they just don't want them to spend the night." Surely there is a certain tension between the two halves of that sentence. "I'm not a racist, but . . . ," a resident of Villa Grove, Illinois, said, prefacing a long story of how in 1990, when he was a senior in Villa Grove High School, he "and 45 or 50 of my buddies" gathered in their pickup trucks at the city limits to head off a carload of African Americans and Latinos from Decatur. They had come intending to date Villa Grove girls, one of whom made the mistake of bragging about it at school. "We beat the shit out of them," he concluded triumphantly, and the episode surely ensured Villa Grove's sundown reputation for another decade or two.[39]

How do residents of sundown towns accomplish the rhetorical feat of admitting they beat up blacks and keep them out while denying they are racist? Only the tiniest proportion of whites are willing to admit to being racist. Typically whites define racism to be almost an empty category, so "we" are not guilty of it. Self-proclaimed white supremacist David Duke saying "I hate niggers" is a case of racism. Almost nothing else passes muster.

This rhetoric of denial is timeless. Here is an example from the *Gentry Journal-Advance*, an Arkansas newspaper, in 1906:

> With a population of 1,000 Gentry has not a solitary Negro inhabitant. We are not prejudiced against the colored man, but we feel that we can get along better without his presence, and are therefore glad to have him remain in some other town or locality. There are plenty of white men here to do the work, ordinarily, and a Negro population under the present conditions, would not only be superfluous, but an annoyance and a nuisance. We are certainly thankful that the dusky denizens have always given our town the go by.

The editor characterizes African Americans as a group as "an annoyance and a nuisance," avoids words such as *people* or *citizens* in favor of "dusky denizens," and clearly favors an indefinite continuation of Gentry's sundown policies. Yet "we are not prejudiced."[40]

A corollary of denial is the curious fact that residents of sundown towns believe they have no problem with racism or race relations. In sharp contrast, people in interracial towns know they do. In Decatur, for example, 33.4% of adults surveyed in about 1985 ranked "racial difficulties" as "the most pressing social problem in Decatur"—well *before* Decatur made national headlines in 1999, when its school system expelled seven African Americans for fighting in the stands during a football game. Few residents of Pana, a sundown town thiry miles south, would rank race relations as their "most pressing social problem." Neither would residents of most sundown suburbs. Nationally, as reported in the 2001 book *Race and Place*, whites living in overwhelmingly white communities perceive the least discrimination against blacks, while whites in majority-black neighborhoods perceived the most. Ironically, then, recognition of "racial difficulties" is a sign of racial progress, and race relations are in fact much more problematic in Pana or sundown suburbs than in Decatur, the latter's moment of notoriety in 1999 notwithstanding. It is true that white children in Pana have no problem getting along with African Americans, since they never encounter them. Nevertheless, as they go through life, these children may encounter some race relations problems that Decatur's white children do not.[41]

The Paradox of Exclusivity

Denial is especially common in suburbia. Residents of elite suburbs are much less likely than residents of independent towns (or working-class suburbs) to admit that their communities keep out African Americans, or did until recently. Their particular need for deniability arises from what we might call the "paradox of exclusivity." We have seen how in metropolitan areas, neighborhoods are ranked more prestigious to the degree that they exclude African Americans, people in the working and lower middle classes, and, in the past, Jews. Such exclusivity connotes social status, even "good breeding." For this reason, white suburbs have usually done little to combat segregation. Instead, they have fostered it. At the same time, exclusivity also suggests prejudice, racism— *"bad* breeding"—even to the elite themselves. As early as 1976, 88% of white Americans agreed with the statement "Black people have a right to live wherever they can afford to," and educated people agreed even more strongly, so residents of sundown suburbs know that they must not admit they live in a place that keeps or kept blacks out.[42]

The ethical paradox is this: on one hand, to live in an exclusive area is good, connoting positive things about oneself and one's family. On the other hand, to exclude is bad, implying negative things about oneself and one's fam-

ily. How do affluent white residents of sundown suburbs deal with this paradox of exclusivity? They don't want to deny that their suburb is exclusive, because exclusivity proves to themselves and others that they are successful and
know how and where to live. But they do want to deny that they are all white
on purpose. So they develop a motivated blindness to the workings of social
structure: soclexia. The talk in sundown suburbs prompts residents to be bad
sociologists and bad historians. Suburban rhetoric has so mystified the exclusion that created sundown suburbs that many suburbanites now sincerely
view residential segregation as nothing but the "natural" outgrowth of countless decisions by individual families.

William H. Whyte Jr. wrote *The Organization Man* in 1956, a study of executives based on fieldwork in Park Forest, a sundown suburb of Chicago. He
noted that several years before he did his research, Park Forest suffered "an
acrid controversy over the possible admission of Negroes."

> For a small group, admission of Negroes would be fulfillment of personal social
> ideals; for another, many of whom had just left Chicago wards which had been
> "taken over," it was the return of a threat left behind.

Most residents, he noted, whom he called "the moderates," were in the middle, and these were "perhaps most sorely vexed." This majority was

> against admission too, but though no Negroes ever did move in, the damage was
> done. The issue had been brought up, and the sheer fact that one had to talk
> about it made it impossible to maintain unblemished the ideal egalitarianism so
> cherished.

In short, most residents of the suburb wanted it to stay sundown[43] but desired
deniability.[44]

In his famous 1944 book about race relations, *An American Dilemma,*
Gunnar Myrdal saw this: "Trying to defend their behavior to others, *people
will twist and mutilate their beliefs of how social reality actually is*" (his italics). Residents deny their town's history of discrimination and its ongoing
sundown apparatus because they want to credit themselves with success, not
blame themselves for prejudice and discrimination. "Yes, we live in an elegant,
affluent, white [but this last goes unstated] area, with lovely amenities and low
crime," people might say. "All of that says good things about us. But anyone
could live here if they wanted to and had the means. It's not our fault; it's to
our credit. America is a meritocracy." That others do not live here merely says

bad things about them, at least implicitly. As Robert Terry put it in *For Whites Only*, commenting on residential segregation in the Detroit area in the 1970s: "Who has ever heard a Northerner admit he did something because he was a racist? Our propensity for moral justification does not permit it. Rather, our racism is couched in quasi-moral terms which command social respectability and accrue social acceptance to us." Just as many white southerners used to believe the legal separation of the races in southern society was natural, many white northerners still seem to believe the geographic separation of the races in northern metropolitan areas is natural.[45]

When the racial composition of their community is so overwhelmingly nonblack that accident cannot plausibly be invoked, residents often blame African Americans for not moving in, saying that blacks "prefer their own." In 2002, I asked a realtor in Kenilworth why no African American family lived in that elite Chicago suburb, to his knowledge. "Birds of a feather flock together," he replied. "People are happier with their own kind." I had noticed his Armenian-sounding last name, so I asked him, "Do you live with other Armenians?" "No," he replied, "but the first generation did. The second generation moved out, lived with other people." I didn't bother to point out that most African Americans are now at least tenth-generation Americans and fourth-generation Chicagoans, much longer than most Armenians.

A resident of an overwhelmingly white neighborhood near a golf club in south Tulsa told me of a black doctor who moved there. He had to move back to north Tulsa, she said, because "his [black] patients rose up in protest." Chapter 8 told how Patrick Clark, curator of the Andrew County (Missouri) Museum, denied that his own county or nearby counties had any history of excluding African Americans. Clark went on to write, "Incidentally, the only community in the state we are familiar with being associated with one racial make-up is/was near St. Louis, Missouri; an all Black community, Kinloch, Missouri"—a small town some 300 miles away. Other whites have echoed Clark's thinking, invoking Boley; Harlem; Mound Bayou, Mississippi; or the South Side ghetto of Chicago.

Some whites go on to hold that the existence of black towns legitimizes the racist policies of white sundown towns. But most black towns and townships never excluded whites.[46] Neither did black neighborhoods. As Myrdal put it in 1944, most mixed residential areas in America "are cases of whites living in 'Negro areas' and not of Negroes living in 'white areas,' " where they would not have been allowed. Even Harlem has never been close to all-black. In 1990, Kinloch had seventeen whites in five white households. Today, although some African Americans do seek majority-black environments, most still prefer diverse neighborhoods with white and black (and other) residents. To a much greater degree, it is *white* Americans who seek "to be with their own kind." To locate the problem in the supposedly free choices of the minority group is soclexic, even though it may be comforting to whites.[47]

Elite suburbanites also avoid responsibility for the racial composition of their community by claiming that African Americans don't have the wherewithal to move there. "It's an economic thing." "They can't afford it here." In America it's considered perfectly all right to exclude on the basis of social class; indeed, an element of the American dream itself is to separate oneself and one's family from the teeming masses. Grouping houses by social class is still a de rigueur principle of real estate. I hope that earlier chapters have laid to rest the claim that income differences explain sundown suburbs. They don't.

It is a small step from blaming African Americans for not having the income to move in to a sundown suburb to blaming them for not having the personal characteristics—IQ, for example—to earn that income. Many residents of elite sundown suburbs take that step. Obviously, to believe that America is a sorting machine based on ability—and African Americans have less ability—eliminates any guilt about living in a community that keeps them out. This explains why *The Bell Curve*, the 1994 book that argued that differences in income by class and race result from differences in intelligence, was so popular in elite sundown suburbs. It located the problem in "them," the outgroups, just as the eugenicists used to do. Precisely because it blames the victim, the resulting ideology is more dangerous than the overt racism of independent sundown towns. Residents of elite sundown suburbs are free to infer that African Americans are inferior, which explains their absence. Residents of such independent sundown towns as Anna or Sheridan can't say that. They *know* their town has kept blacks out.[48]

Claiming that ability results purely from individual achievement rather than one's place in the social structure is also a pleasant way to interpret the high SAT scores earned by one's children and their equally privileged friends in an elite community. Of course, affluent parents really know better. When making decisions about their own children's futures, the rich know that ability is largely socially created, which is why they invest in *Sesame Street Magazine* for their toddler, computer camp for their eight-year-old, and the *Princeton Review* for their eleventh grader facing the SAT. They may get furious when a school principal tries to jettison tracking or their own child does not get into an advanced placement class. They go to great lengths—private schools, hiring "college coaches," and so on—to give their children a leg up in

college admission. Thus when it comes to their own children, they are struc-
tural sociologists who see positive individual outcomes as the result of expenditures and programs.

However, their awareness of suburban advantages, which they employ to
justify why they moved there in the first place, disappears when the time
comes to discuss the outcome of the college admission process. Now elite
whites no longer brag about or even perceive the benefits of class and racial
segregation. Instead, they now "explain" the positive results of these advantages, such as high SAT scores, as stemming from their child's individual intelligence and ability. Suddenly they now assert that aptitude inheres in
individuals and the SAT measures aptitude.[49] Again, to believe that America
sorts people based on ability—and one's child happens to be among the most
able—is more satisfying than to admit that living in a sundown suburb
amounts to a deliberate choice to stack the deck. Such Social Darwinism is
not only soclexic but dangerous to democracy.

Misled by these rationalizations, rich white segregated children usually
do not understand the processes in their own metropolitan areas that conferred advantages upon them, based on their race and social class. They made
it, so why can't everyone? In *Privileged Ones,* Robert Coles interviewed a
male high school student in a sundown suburb of Boston who exemplified
this soclexic thinking: "My father says it'll always be like that; there are people
who are prejudiced against anyone who has tried to work hard and make some
money, and prejudiced in favor of the people who don't care if they work or
not, so long as they collect welfare." In my 63 years in America I have yet to
meet a single person "prejudiced in favor of the people who don't care if they
work or not," and I suspect neither this boy nor his father have either. But
such stereotypes are satisfying, for they imply that as soon as African Americans really apply themselves, our racial problems will be fixed. "We," on the
other hand, are not responsible, so there's nothing we can do about it. Knowing no poor people or people of color firsthand, residents of elite sundown
suburbs are particularly susceptible to stereotypes to explain the visible differences among neighborhoods.[50]

Racial Stereotypes in Sundown Towns

During the past 25 years, while teaching race relations to thousands of white
people and discussing the subject with thousands more, I have found that
white Americans expound about the alleged character and characteristics of
African Americans in inverse proportion to their contact and experience with

them. Isolation and ignorance aren't the only reasons why residents of sundown towns and suburbs are so ready to believe and pass on the worst stereotypes about African Americans, however. They also have a need for denial.

The idea that living in an all-white community leads residents to defend living in an all-white community exemplifies the well-established psychological principle of cognitive dissonance. No one likes to think of himself or herself as a bad person, argued Leon Festinger, who established this principle. People who live in sundown towns believe in the golden rule—or say they do—just like people who live in interracial towns. No one would want to be treated the way sundown towns treat African Americans. On the other hand, it is hard for someone living in an all-white town to define that choice of residence as "wrong" or that policy as "bad for our country." Doing so might entail moving, or taking a risk in trying to change the town's practices. It is much easier to rationalize one's actions by changing one's opinions and beliefs to make what one has done seem right.

What could make living in an all-white town right? The old idea that African Americans constitute the problem, of course. In 1914, Thomas Bailey, a professor in Mississippi, told what is wrong with that line of thinking: "The real problem is not the Negro, but the white man's attitude toward the Negro." Sundown towns only made white attitudes worse. Having driven out or kept out African Americans (or perhaps Chinese Americans or Jewish Americans), their residents then became *more* racist and more likely to believe the worst about the excluded group(s).[51]

That's why the talk in sundown towns brims with amazing stereotypes about African Americans, put forth confidently as reality by European Americans who have never had an honest conversation with an African American in their lives. The ideology intrinsic to sundown towns—that African Americans (or Jews, Chinese Americans, or another group) are the problem—prompts their residents to believe and pass on all kinds of negative generalizations as fact. They are the problem because *they* choose segregation—even though "they" don't, as we have seen. Or they are the problem owing to their criminality—confirmed by the stereotype—misbehavior that "we" avoid by excluding or moving away from them.

Of course, such stereotypes are hardly limited to sundown towns. Summarizing a nationwide 1991 poll, Lynne Duke found that a majority of whites believed that "blacks and Hispanics are likely to prefer welfare to hard work and tend to be lazier than whites, more prone to violence, less intelligent, and less patriotic." Even worse, in sundown towns and suburbs, statements such as these usually evoke no open disagreement at all. Because most listeners in sundown towns have never lived near African Americans, they have no experiential foundation from which to question the negative generalities that they hear voiced. So the stereotypes usually go unchallenged: blacks are less intelligent, lazier, and lack drive, and that's why they haven't built successful careers.[52]

Actually, most African Americans, like most other Americans, are reasonably industrious people who are quietly trying to have a satisfying life and pass on a bit of a start to their children. But many residents of sundown towns and suburbs simply don't believe that. Many also misunderstand basic economics and believe, for example, that African Americans don't pay property taxes when they rent rather than own their homes, not understanding that landlords pay property taxes from the rents they collect. Nor do most whites realize that Social Security acts as a vast transfer program from blacks to whites, because African Americans' life expectancy is so much shorter than that of whites.

Negative generalizations about African Americans are at least as common in sundown suburbs as in independent sundown towns, even though residents of sundown suburbs may have African American friends at work. In a corollary to the "file folder mentality" Chapter 10 described, such individuals are accepted as exceptions, leaving the negative generalizations about the mass of African Americans unscathed. Many residents of these suburbs, especially working- and middle-class suburbs, have fled from city neighborhoods that they believed were about to "turn black." Those who flee such neighborhoods carry white-flight stories with them like a pestilence. Parents think they did the right thing by fleeing the city and its crime and problems, problems they see as inextricably bound up with race. When their children ask them why they moved, they respond with the negative stereotypes, thus passing them on to the next generation. Contact with a nice black co-worker makes no difference. A 1985 study of white voters in Michigan found that residents of blue-collar sundown suburbs of Detroit expressed "a profound distaste for blacks, a sentiment that pervades almost everything they think about government and politics." Many also scapegoated African Americans:

> Blacks constitute the explanation for their vulnerability and for almost everything that has gone wrong in their lives; not being black is what constitutes being middle-class; not living with blacks is what makes a neighborhood a decent place to live.[53]

A librarian in Oak Lawn, a sundown suburb southwest of Chicago, remarked that Oak Lawn residents welcome Hispanics, because "they don't know what they will bring with them. Many know what blacks will bring with them." Many suburbanites left neighborhoods in Chicago when African Americans moved in, she explained, and those areas are now black. They "don't want to have to do that again"; therefore they don't let African Americans in. I asked her, "What would blacks bring with them?" "Crime," she replied immediately. That answer is a textbook example of prejudgment and overgeneralization—in a word, prejudice—from a woman who denied any racial animus herself. We were then joined by a male reference librarian; ironically, both complained about the "Colombian gangs" that now operated in Oak Lawn. Whether African American newcomers would have formed gangs we'll never know, but the fact remains that neither librarian saw any contradiction in justifying excluding African Americans owing to crime while admitting Hispanics despite crime. Since Oak Lawn did not keep out Hispanics, cognitive dissonance did not move them to focus on Hispanic crime. It is *black* crime that really concerned them. At the top end of the status spectrum, residents of Grosse Pointe, Michigan, reacted identically, blocking African Americans while mounting no protest when members of the Mafia, booted out of Canada for criminal behavior, moved in.[54]

Whites often engage in white flight despite evidence right before their eyes that their rationale for leaving makes no sense. Matteson, Illinois, an upper-middle-class suburb south of Chicago, went from 12% black in 1980 to nearly 60% black by 2000. "The blacks moving in are professionals," according to Leonard Steinhorn, co-author of *By the Color of Our Skin*. As a result, the town's median income rose by 73% in the 1980s. "Crime has not increased, schools have maintained the same standards, and home prices continue to rise—if anything, the community is wealthier with its new black residents." Nevertheless, Matteson's whites continue to leave, saying that they "simply want a nice place to raise their kids." As Frederick Douglass put it, back in 1860, such behavior is characteristic of "prejudice, always blind to what it never wishes to see, and quick to perceive all it wishes."[55]

Imagining the "Black Menace"

Sometimes the stereotypes whites form about African Americans create real apprehension in sundown towns. Most residents of these towns see communities outside their city limits as much "blacker" than they are, which frightens them. "Cobden is half black," a local history buff in Dongola, Illinois, a sundown town twelve miles south of Cobden, said in 2003. Actually, Cobden has

16 African Americans among 1,116 residents, or 1.4%. The high school secretary of a sundown town in northeastern Arkansas told me that Oxford, Mississippi, is majority-black, and she worried about it while there; actually, Oxford has 2,463 African Americans among 11,654 residents, about 20%. "We're thinking of going to the Arkansas State Fair this year," she also said, "and a friend told us to take a pistol. It's in a black neighborhood." I told her I'd been to the fairgrounds in Little Rock and never heard of folks having to shoot their way in or out. She didn't laugh. She was considering her friend's advice quite seriously.[56]

In 1994, anthropologist Jane Adams found that a peculiar anxiety gripped residents of Anna, in southern Illinois, about nearby Carbondale, long after student riots at Southern Illinois University and a Black Panther shootout with police there in 1970. "Many people in the area still avoid Carbondale and are afraid to go through the town at night." This fear had no rational basis: student rioters and Black Panthers are long gone, and the campus has been quiet for decades. The fear is partly racial, for African Americans are not gone; Carbondale in 1994 was 20% black, which looks very black from the vantage point of all-white Anna. Thus where one lives affects how one perceives.[57]

When dealing with towns that actually *have* black majorities, fears in sundown towns can become absurd enough to merit the label "paranoia." When West Side High School in Greers Ferry, Arkansas, a sundown town according to a nearby resident, plays Cotton Plant, a majority-black high school to the southeast, the team and buses get escorted by state troopers. When West Side hosts Cotton Plant, according to a recent West Side graduate, administrators warn their students "not to leave jewelry or other valuables in your lockers! Leave them with your parents!" Yet Cotton Plant players are surely already nervous playing in a sundown town and would hardly be likely to wander the halls of an unfamiliar high school scoping out student lockers. A former resident of Herrin, a sundown town in southern Illinois, relates that Herrin natives still warn each other, "Don't go to Colp," a nearby black-majority township, even during the daytime. Residents of independent sundown towns expressed particular anxiety about visiting Atlanta, Detroit, or Washington, D.C., three cities they know have black majorities.[58]

Not just small-town residents, but also some elite white suburbanites seem enfeebled rather than emboldened by their privileged isolated communities and wind up reluctant to go to cultural events or restaurants in central cities. A professor at Western Michigan University reported the reaction of her relatives from Naperville, an elite suburb southwest of Chicago, after going with her to a Jewel Supermarket in Kalamazoo, Michigan: "Oh, how can you go there? Aren't you afraid of being mugged?" The store's interracial clientele made them apprehensive—in broad daylight in Kalamazoo! Imagine their fear of Chicago! Undergraduates at the University of Illinois–Chicago tell that their friends from such suburbs as Naperville went to Iowa or the University of Illinois–Champaign; "they're afraid of Chicago," and not just of those neighborhoods that are in fact dangerous. High school students from sundown suburbs of New York City are similarly wary of Manhattan. "When we rode the subway," said Andy Cavalier about his Darien, Connecticut, school friends, "they would ride wide-eyed, thinking they'd be mugged at any moment." Diane Hershberger, taking high school students from suburban Johnson County to an art exhibit in Kansas City, overheard them saying in worried tones, "I've never been downtown before."[59]

Young people absorb this posture toward the outside world from their parents and other adults in the community, of course. Karns supplied an example:

> My recent Cleveland trip was interesting in that it was two swimmers and their fathers. . . . One father was pretty uncomfortable in general. He made several comments about Cleveland being dangerous because of its racial make-up. We were looking for a reasonably priced place to eat . . . and it took awhile. At one stop, he said 'maybe we should find an area with some more white faces,' attached to some comment about safety. I was surprised because this is one of the gentlest, most accepting men I know, and he allowed himself to fall prey to that kind of thinking. I pass this on, not to belittle him but because I think it illustrates the kind of thinking that is created in small all-white communities.[60]

Residents of sundown towns have long feared black-majority towns. According to historian Norman Crockett, author of *The Black Towns,* citizens of Paden and Okemah, sundown towns in eastern Oklahoma, worried they were in danger while in Boley, a neighboring black town. This anxiety escalated to full-blown panic one warm June night in 1911. A month before, a white mob from Okemah had hanged Laura Nelson and her son, African American farmers living near Boley, from the steel bridge that spanned the North Canadian River (see Portfolio 11.) As customary in such matters, the grand jury investigating the lynchings somehow could not determine who was responsible. Now, in the words of Okemah resident W. L. Payne, townspeople "watched movements of the lawless Negro element," fearing retaliation from Boley. On June 23, according to Payne, "a white 'stool pigeon' informed the sheriff of

Okfuskee County that the Negroes were planning to sack and burn Okemah that night. No mercy was to be shown women and children." Terror and confusion reigned within Okemah. Payne tells what happened next:

> Citizens came from every section of the town with firearms. Ammunition dealers soon sold their entire stock of firearms and ammunition. An armed cordon of men was placed around Okemah at the edge of town and all approaches were guarded. Strategic locations within the city limits were soon fortified. Mobilization officers ordered all street lights cut off to prevent the enemy from observing the movements of the town's brave defenders. The light plant engineer was to signal the attack by blowing the whistle. . . . As both young and old scrambled for safety . . . mothers and children often became separated in the mad rush for safety. Hysterical mothers were screaming for their children and pleading for assistance.

The alarm lasted all night, but in the end, Payne concludes, "while Okemah citizens were preparing for war, their colored foes were at home preparing for a good night's rest, which prevented the loss of blood on both sides." But Payne does not draw the obvious lesson: that white fears were silly. Sixty years later, a similar rumor prompted a similar vigil in Anna, Illinois. "Most of the store owners spent the night in their stores with their guns loaded," according to a woman who grew up there. African Americans in Cairo, 30 miles south, were boycotting its stores, and a rumor flew around Anna one weekend "that the blacks (by the way, no one called them blacks—they were always referred to as 'niggers') were going to come up to Anna and cause trouble." All that happened was that "a few blacks came into town to shop—which was not uncommon—and they went home as usual."[61]

Perhaps a bad conscience of sorts (Freud would call it projection) helped motivate the Okemah panic. Similarly, after whites in Maryville, Missouri, lynched Raymond Gunn in 1931 and threatened the rest of Maryville's small black community, a rumor swept through town that 2,000 African Americans from Kansas City, almost 100 miles south, augmented by reinforcements from Omaha, Nebraska, almost 100 miles northwest, were coming to invade Maryville to avenge the lynching. According to a white minister,

> Every [white] man in town was armed, and on the streets. We were sure we were going to have to protect ourselves in blood. The sheriff deputized numerous men to help with the defense. The streets were crowded all night.

The sheriff sought help from other counties, and plans were made to block the oncoming Nebraska horde at the Missouri River bridge. Of course, no attack ever materialized.[62]

Over the years, when African Americans *have* rioted, even if they are miles away, white paranoia in sundown towns has often reached a fever pitch. Karns grew up in Huntington, former vice president Dan Quayle's hometown, a sundown town in northern Indiana:

> My father owned a sporting goods store and among other things he sold guns. During the race riots of the '60s, particularly following King's assassination, he would get phone calls warning him of black "motorcycle gangs" on their way to Huntington from Ft. Wayne to attack the all-white town as well as his business to steal the guns. No attack ever came but it illustrates the paranoia. I remember two or three such incidents.

Huntington is 30 miles from Fort Wayne, hardly a suburb. Glendale, California, is a suburb of Los Angeles, but it lies "about an hour's drive" from Watts, according to a woman who attended high school in Glendale in the mid-1960s. One day, playing tennis after school, she was "shocked to see what appeared to be an incredibly large contingen[t] of National Reserve soldiers! There were tanks, tents, trucks and a lot of soldiers." City officials of this sundown suburb had called out the National Guard to protect Glendale during the Watts riot—from what, they never specified. Officials of Grosse Pointe, Grosse Ile, Dearborn, and other communities took similarly extraordinary precautions in their sundown suburbs during periods of racial unrest in Detroit. Having no African Americans in town, knowing none, having friends who also know no African Americans and live there partly so they cannot—these conditions foster a "we/they" mentality that can escalate to a sense of being besieged, even though no one is at the gates. Even in calm times and notwithstanding their privilege, many residents of elite sundown suburbs seem to feel beleaguered.[63]

Cognitive Dissonance in Martinsville, Indiana

Recent events in Martinsville, Indiana, provide an eerie example of cognitive dissonance at work. Martinsville is a city of 12,000 located 50 miles south of Indianapolis. In 1890, the town had 53 African Americans; by 1930 it had just 4. Martinsville was a Ku Klux Klan hotbed in the 1920s, but so was most of Indiana. In the late 1950s, Martinsville High School played basketball against Crispus Attucks, Indianapolis's de jure segregated black high school, without incident. By 1967, however, when Martinsville played Rushville in football and Rushville's star running back was African American Larry Davis, Martinsville fans were yelling, "Get that nigger!" Then, on September 16, 1968, someone stabbed Carol Jenkins, a 21-year-old African American from Rushville, to death with a screwdriver as she walked along Morgan Street trying to sell encyclopedias door-to-door. It was her first evening in the city, so she knew no one; thus no one had any conceivable personal motive for killing her. At about 7:30 PM, she had gone to a house briefly, seeking refuge from a car with two white men in it who had been shouting at her. So most people (correctly) assumed the motive to be rage at Jenkins as a black person for being in the city after dark.[64]

In the aftermath of the murder, NAACP leaders and reporters from outside the town levied criticism at the city's police department, alleging lack of interest in solving the crime. Martinsville residents responded by appearing to define the situation as "us" against "them," "them" being outsiders and nonwhites. The community seemed to close ranks behind the murderer and refused to turn him in, whoever he was. "The town became a clam," said an Indianapolis newspaper reporter.[65]

Now Martinsville came to see itself not just as a sundown town—it already defined itself as that—but as a community that united in silence to protect the murderer of a black woman who had innocently violated its sundown taboo. To justify this behavior required still more extreme racism, which in turn prompted additional racist behaviors and thus festered further. During the years after Jenkins's murder, gas stations in Martinsville repeatedly refused to sell gasoline to African American customers, at least as late as 1986. Not only the murder but also actions such as these gave Martinsville a particularly scary reputation among African Americans. According to Professor Alan Boehm, who attended Indiana University in the 1970s, Indianapolis's large black middle-class population got the state to build a bypass around Martinsville, "because they did not want their children put in harm's way when they drove between home and the university."[66]

In the 1990s, fans and students in Martinsville intensified their harassment of visiting athletic teams that had black players. In 1998, that tradition won Martinsville an article, "Martinsville's Sad Season," in *Sports Illustrated*: "On January 23, as Bloomington High North's racially mixed team got off the bus upon arriving for a game at Martinsville, about a dozen Martinsville students greeted the visitors with a barrage of racial epithets." Students shouted things like "Here come the darkies." The *Sports Illustrated* account continues:

> During the junior varsity game several Bloomington players were bitten by Martinsville players. During the varsity game a member of Martinsville's all-white team elbowed a black North player in the stomach so fiercely that the player began vomiting. As he was doubled over on the sidelines, a fan yelled, "That nigger's spitting on the floor! Get his ass off the floor." According to a report that Bloomington North filed with the Indiana High School Athletics Association, epithets like "baboon" and threats such as "You're not safe in this town" continued after the game, which Martinsville won 69–66. "It wasn't just nasty," says one Bloomington North fan, an adult who was in attendance, "it was downright scary."

Martinsville was sanctioned: it could not host a conference game in any sport for a year. "This wasn't the first time that charges of racist behavior were leveled against one of Martinsville's teams," the story made clear. "In the last year at least two high schools in central Indiana have dropped the Artesians from their schedules after games were marred by brawls and racial slurs. School administrators in Martinsville . . . were unwilling to discuss the incident or its aftermath." [67]

Ironically, it turned out that no one from Martinsville murdered Carol Jenkins. On May 8, 2002, police arrested Kenneth Richmond, a 70-year-old who had never lived in Martinsville, based on the eyewitness account of his daughter, who sat in his car and watched while he did it when she was seven years old. Although many people inside as well as outside Martinsville believed its residents had been sheltering the murderer these 34 years, in fact no one in the town had known who did it. No matter: cognitive dissonance kicked in anyway. Again, if situations are defined as real, they are real in their consequences. Because everyone *thought* the community had closed ranks in defense of the murderer, additional acts of racism in the aftermath seemed all the more appropriate. Today, having intensified its racism for more than three decades in defense of its imagined refusal to turn over the murderer, Martinsville is finding it hard to reverse course. Recently some residents have tried to move the city toward better race relations, so far with mixed results. They organized meetings on race relations, hold an annual dinner, and hired a consultant to help Martinsville get beyond its past. At the same time, Martinsville's assistant police chief spoke out against gays, Hindus, and Buddhists after the terrorist attacks of September 11, 2001, and won a standing ovation at a subsequent city council meeting. And the Council of Conservative Citizens, descendant of the notorious White Citizens Council, has more members in Martinsville than the diversity organization.[68]

Stereotyping Other Groups

As Martinsville's assistant police chief demonstrated, residents of sundown towns often do not confine their generalizations and stereotypes to African Americans, although blacks have usually been viewed as the most menacing. Sundown towns are more likely than other communities to oppose additional "theys"—other racial groups, gays and lesbians, unusual religious groups, hippies, and Americans who look different or think or act unconventionally. At East High School in Appleton, Wisconsin, for example, formerly a sundown town vis-à-vis African Americans, conflicts between Hmong Americans and whites were a daily occurrence at the school in 1999, according to reporter John Lee.[69] Quoting a student source, Lee wrote, "Usually it begins with a group of white students taunting an Asian student or his friends with epithets, or pushing them into lockers. He said the white youths 'pick on anybody that's different or anybody who hangs around them.' " Meanwhile, at nearby North High School, incidents occurred between white students and Mexican Americans. On the day after white students had defaced a Mexican flag at North, white students came to school "wearing Confederate Battle Flag symbols hanging from pockets on shirts and on car antennas," according to reporter Kathy Nufer. They already owned these symbols, giving the conflict a white supremacy tinge.[70]

Residents of several sundown towns have told me that their towns also harass homosexuals. Springdale, Arkansas, made news in 1998 when every candidate for mayor, speaking before members of the Christian Coalition, attacked the "Human Dignity resolution" passed in nearby interracial Fayetteville. One mayoral candidate even proposed posting "No Fags in Springdale" signs at the city limits, reminiscent of the sundown signs that Springdale used to sport about blacks. Of course, many interracial small towns also manifest hostility toward gays and lesbians.[71] Such hostility shows itself more easily in sundown towns, however, with their heritage of inhospitality toward an entire outgroup. On the other hand, not every sundown town is as anti-gay as Springdale. Gays live safely if semi-closeted in Cullman, a sundown town in northern Alabama, for instance, and some more or less came out in June 2000 via a story in *The Advocate,* "the national gay & lesbian newsmagazine." Conversely, some racially integrated towns and neighborhoods, including New

Hope, Pennsylvania, outside Philadelphia, and Mt. Rainier, Maryland, outside Washington, take quiet pride in welcoming even "out" gays.[72]

Regarding religious "deviants," we might first recall that the Ku Klux Klan in the 1920s was anti-Catholic and anti-Semitic as well as anti-black. And of course most elite sundown suburbs also kept out Jews until well after World War II; some also barred Catholics. In Santa Fe, Texas, a sundown town, Phillip Nevelow, the town's only Jewish student, said in 2000 that schoolmates had subjected him to two years of anti-Semitic harassment, including threats to hang him, and police charged three students with making "terroristic threats." Santa Fe's "reputation for being 'white only,' " in the words of Shelly Kelly, archivist at the University of Houston, surely contributed to the "climate of intolerance" with which his parents charged the school district.[73]

Other sundown towns attacked leftists and labor leaders. A decade after Harrison, Arkansas, expelled its African Americans, its large Ku Klux Klan chapter targeted striking railroad workers and in 1923 hanged one striker from a railroad bridge, herded the rest together, and escorted them to the Missouri line. The result was a sundown town so far as organized labor was concerned. The same thing happened in Bisbee, Arizona, known as a "white man's camp" after it expelled its Chinese miners. On July 12, 1917, Bisbee expelled more than a thousand striking miners, members of the Industrial Workers of the World ("Wobblies"). Across America, working-class whites today complain about getting stopped and harassed by police in elite white suburbs.[74]

Some sundown towns give a hard time even to white heterosexuals if they seem "different." Based on bad experiences in Marlow, Oklahoma, poet Jodey Bateman generalized: "I think the stories of attempts at exclusion of hippies and hitch hikers would make another 'sundown town' book. . . . From this I believe that the 'sundown town' syndrome in very small towns is not just racism but a fear of all outsiders who don't seem respectable enough." A web post makes the same point about another Oklahoma town:

> I am from a small town of 3,500, Stilwell, Oklahoma. I could not wait to get out of that place. The grape vine is as brutal as they get. I find in towns with no cultural diversity there is a cruelty toward folks that are different. . . . For the longest time there was a sign outside of town that read "Don't Let The Sun Set On Your Black Ass."[75]

When a town goes sundown, the exclusionary mind-set stays for a long time and festers and generalizes. Whites in sundown towns speak authoritatively not only about African Americans, but also about leftists, Muslims, poor whites, union members, or welfare mothers—based on little or no firsthand experience with members of the class. Surely African Americans, Chinese Americans, Jewish Americans, Seventh Day Adventists, gay Americans, lesbian Americans, hippie Americans, poor Americans, and mildly nonconforming Americans cannot all be "the problem." Hence being unwelcoming to every one of those groups obviously cannot fix the problem.

Abraham Lincoln understood the threat to our democracy posed by antiblack prejudice and the likelihood that this sentiment would metastasize to attack other groups. In 1855 he wrote a letter to his lifelong friend Josh Speed, a clause of which has become famous:

> As a nation, we began by declaring that "all men are created equal." We now practically read it "all men are created equal, except Negroes." When the Know-Nothings get control, it will read "all men are created equal, except Negroes, and foreigners, and Catholics." When it comes to this I should prefer emigrating to some country where they make no pretence of loving liberty—to Russia, for instance, where despotism can be taken pure, and without the base alloy of hypocrisy.[76]

Surely Lincoln was right. Surely exclusion itself—not African Americans, not all these other groups—was and remains the problem. Readers might consider if *they* would feel comfortable in a typical sundown town—in Appleton, Wisconsin, say, before it cracked, or Stilwell, Oklahoma. The answer for nonwhites is obvious, but whites too can be at risk if they say the wrong thing, bring home a partner of the opposite sex who is of the wrong race, or *horribile dictu,* bring home a partner of the right race but the same sex. Even if they avoid these transgressions, would whites feel comfortable raising children in a sundown town where the only thing worse than having children who just don't fit in might be having children who *do*?

Inculcating Prejudice in the Next Generation

Cognitive dissonance also helps explain how young whites wind up racist as they mature. Racism is not genetic, of course. Sundown towns help to maintain it. Many sundown towns chose American history textbooks that paid little attention to African Americans and Native Americans for as long as they could. They also preferred the old "Dick and Jane" readers in which all the

characters were white. In the early 1970s, when textbooks became more multicultural, the head of the Follette Publishing Company observed, "The day of
the all-white textbooks is just about over. The big publishers won't fool with
them any more, and all-white towns like Cicero, Illinois, just won't be able to
get them in the future."[77]

Despite the efforts of adults, childhood is not a straitjacket, and it is certainly possible for a white child to grow up in a sundown town and not become racist, or to transcend that racism through later life experiences and
education. John Wooden, the famous UCLA basketball coach, grew up in notorious Martinsville, yet coached such famous African American basketball
players as Kareem Abdul-Jabbar and Sidney Wicks. Presidential candidate
Wendell Willkie opposed racism after he left Elwood, his Indiana sundown
town (although he never did anything about it while he lived there). Nevertheless, teachers who try to convert white young people in sundown towns to an
anti-racist position fight an uphill battle, at best succeeding one student at a
time. All the while, when whites do not go to school with blacks and do not
live with blacks—and everyone in town knows this results from whites'
choices and policies—it is hard for children to conclude that blacks are OK.
Logically, they may infer quite the opposite.

Sometimes having been a sundown town can poison the atmosphere even
after a school goes majority nonwhite. In 1991, Pam Sturgeon, who is Anglo
and was president of the school board in Hawthorne, California, another Los
Angeles suburb, said, "When I went to Hawthorne High, Hawthorne was a
sundown town. All blacks had to be out of town by sundown or be in jail." By
1991, Hawthorne High was majority black and Hispanic, with considerable
conflict between those groups. The teaching staff was still largely Anglo, including many holdovers from its all-white days, and some of them contributed
to the problem by refusing to teach works by such authors as Richard Wright
and Maya Angelou. Sturgeon referred to the sundown legacy: "A lot of adults
in my age group are fighting that bigotry within themselves."[78]

These considerations are perhaps clear for the classic independent sundown town like Martinsville or Sheridan. But if it is unhealthy to bring up
children in such obviously racist environments, is it somehow healthier to
raise them in sundown suburbs like Hawthorne before it desegregated, or
worse yet, in such elite sundown suburbs as San Marino? There the social
structure implies that it is correct to distance oneself not only from African
Americans, but also from the white lower, working, and middle classes. Can
that be good for children to learn? Yet every year thousands of white parents
move *to* rather than *from* sundown suburbs, and they do so "for the children."

It would be far better to raise children in towns that do not declare in their very demography that "white is right."

To some white parents, all this is obvious. A new homeowner in a former sundown county outside Atlanta said that many houses in her community were going up for sale "because the community is becoming more racially mixed and the white people are moving further south. The funny part is that I have been wanting to move because I can't stand the thought of my future children growing up around such racism and narrowmindedness. So I suppose their moving is making my life easier." [79]

Independent Sundown Towns Limit the Horizons of Their Children

Independent sundown towns have another effect on their residents that has nothing to do with race, at least not directly: they narrow the horizons of children who come of age within them. It is an axiom of American small-town life that "youth goes elsewhere to become somebody." Young people in independent sundown towns typically hold ambivalent feelings toward the outside world. Some decorate their bedrooms with posters of Michael Jordan (formerly) or Serena Williams (currently) or even a black rapper if they feel rebellious. They are very aware that the outside world differs from their circumscribed little world; indeed, like their parents, high school and college students from all-white towns and suburbs exaggerate the differences and routinely estimate that the population of the United States is 20 to 50% black.[80] So they are wary of the outside world and not sure they want to venture out there.[81]

For the most part, most high school graduates in independent sundown towns don't venture far. One of the first things I noticed in conversations with young people in these towns was their circumscribed aspirations. "Basically, they didn't go anywhere," a woman from Anna, Illinois, said about graduates from Anna-Jonesboro High School. Bill Donahue followed the high school students from Nickerson, a sundown town in central Kansas, when they took their class trip to Washington, D.C., in 2002. "There were a few Nickerson kids who yearned for a broader existence," he reported. "For many students, though, the Washington trip would be . . . a first and last hurrah." He talked with their teacher, Gary McCown, who said "with sad resignation" that he didn't expect much worldly ambitions from students in Nickerson. "They look at what their parents do and what's offered around Nickerson—mostly service jobs—and they think, 'It's not a bad life. It's pleasant. You can walk into the grocery store and be greeted by people you know.' "[82]

When students from Pana High School, in central Illinois, do go on to college, "it's mostly to Eastern or to the community college in Mattoon," according to a former Pana resident. Eastern Illinois University, formerly Eastern Illinois State Teachers College, is located in Charleston, 50 miles east of Pana and almost as white. Mattoon is closer still. Although the University of Illinois, a world-famous institution, is only about an hour from Pana, few students make the drive even to check it out, and fewer still enroll; school personnel cannot recall any who chose the Chicago campus of the university. Students who venture out of state don't venture far either, and afterward, most return to Pana. "They like the small-town life," a recent high school graduate explained. It isn't just preference for the known, however, but also fear of the unknown. "My sister is actually frightened," said a woman who years ago moved to much larger—and interracial—Decatur. "Frightened of cities, frightened of anything she's not familiar with." Such fear marks many small-town residents, but in sundown towns the fear of African Americans looms foremost. Young adults in Pana granted me a certain respect upon learning that I grew up in Decatur: "It's pretty rough over there, isn't it?" Actually, it isn't—they just *think* it is, believing Decatur to be heavily black.[83]

When high school graduates from independent sundown towns do break out, it can be scary for them. Chantel Scherer, a 1988 graduate of Sullivan High School in central Illinois, put it this way:

> I remember growing up in Sullivan where ALL outsiders were made to feel unwelcome. . . . I love where I grew up, but yes, this unrealistic living situation had its implications when those of us who lived there grew up and moved away. I remember being afraid of all the different people when I was 17 and a freshman at college. There were over 30,000 students representing a huge variety of people.[84]

Many people have told how coming from a sundown town made it awkward when they tried to play a role in the larger society. For example, a recent graduate of Granite City High School in southwest Illinois said that his teachers would warn students before field trips to St. Louis, "Don't tell people you're from Granite City, and for God's sake don't tell people you're from an all-white high school!" Of course, such an admonition could only make them *less* at ease in St. Louis, and their resulting parade of emotions—shame, fear, self-consciousness, discomfort—may provide additional reasons not to venture out next time.[85]

The apprehension of residents of independent sundown towns about the outside world often prompts them to inflate their town beyond reason, perhaps to convince themselves they aren't missing much and made the right choice. "They think they're in the middle of the world," my Decatur informant said, characterizing her Pana relatives. "They don't know how small and how backward they are." Deep down, this ethnocentrism is defensive and carries with it an element of soclexia. Deep down, residents of independent sundown towns know they do *not* live at the center of the universe. Their put-downs of the outside world are only a flimsy shield against that knowledge. Here is an obvious example, from someone using the identity Goneaviking, posted to the online discussion site alt.flame.niggers in May 2001:

> Do you want some pictures of niggers hanged in the town square or what, like Fouke, Arkansas, for the "Nigger Don't Let The Sun Set On Your Ass" [sign] in that town? . . . Lots of loggers and farmers down there richer than any nigger in the USA. 80 acres of pine 50 years old = 1,000,000 dollars. 23,000,000 niggers = pure shit.

In fact, Oprah Winfrey by herself probably has more net worth than all 814 residents of Fouke combined. In some part of his or her mind, Goneaviking surely knows that.[86]

Young people who do break out of the cocoon get derided for it by those back home. A student at the University of Illinois, Chicago, told how her friends back in her sundown hometown asked her, "Why would you go there?" She pointed out that Chicago was world-famous for architecture and music, among other things, but that persuaded no one. Friends of another student were more blunt: "Do you know what you're getting yourself into? There's colored people down there!" "Why would you want to live in Washington, D.C.?" inquired hometown friends of Kathy Spillman, from Tonawanda, a sundown town near Buffalo. They seem to have no idea, Spillman noted, that the Smithsonian museums, concerts at the Kennedy Center, theater all over town, and restaurants featuring cuisines from around the world might actually interest someone. Spillman has no patience when these queries cross the line into overt racism. "People from Tonawanda ask me, 'How do you live with all those niggers down there?' I reply, 'I like having sex with them!' "[87]

Many parents in independent sundown towns are content to have their children stay close to home. "They don't seek opportunities to go to cultural events," Susan Penny said about residents of Oblong, Illinois. "They don't leave town except to go to sporting events." They don't expose their children to different milieux on vacations, instead choosing places such as Branson, Missouri, where the entertainment will be familiar and the audiences white. According to Penny, they don't even try ethnic foods.[88]

Elite Sundown Suburbs Limit Their Children in Other Ways

Young people in working-class sundown suburbs behave much like their compatriots in independent sundown towns. They stay close to home, unless service in the armed forces breaks through to enlarge their horizons, racially and occupationally. Young people in elite suburbs such as Beverly Hills, California; Edina, Minnesota; and Darien, Connecticut, display behavior that is both much the same and much different compared to that of their counterparts in independent towns and working-class suburbs. These young people have grown up with a sense of entitlement. The world is their oyster, and they intend to harvest its pearls. Their parents, especially their fathers, mostly don't work in town but in corporate headquarters in the central city or suburban office parks. Their jobs take them across the country or across the world. Their frequent-flier miles take their families for vacations across the country or around the world. Parochial they aren't.

Yet parochial they are. Families like these can go to Bali and never meet a Balinese family, because they stay in the Sanur Beach Hyatt. Like the residents of Pana or Tonawanda, young people from elite sundown suburbs cannot conceive that another place might be superior to their own hometowns; unlike the residents of Pana or Tonawanda, they are not secretly defensive about that. They are truly ethnocentric, which makes it hard for them to learn from other races and cultures. There is also evidence from social psychology that students who discuss issues in multiracial classes "display higher levels of complex thought" and are thus better prepared for college.[89]

The residential segregation by occupation that marks elite sundown suburbs limits their offspring in another way: it enhances social distance. Since most of the people who work in these suburbs cannot afford to live in them—not just the maids and gardeners but also the teachers and police officers—these adults are not really available to children growing up there as any kind of positive role models. Many children in elite suburbs end up not only ignorant of such human activities as carpentry but subtly disdainful of them. They never encounter people in the working class on a plane of social equality. This limits their own occupational horizons and prompts them to feel that they have failed if they don't make it into an elite white-collar occupation.[90]

Sundown Towns Collect Racists

Thus far we have discussed effects sundown towns and suburbs have on people who live in them. Yet these communities not only create racists, but also attract whites who already believe in white supremacy. Ever since they began advertising themselves pridefully as all-white in the early 1900s, sundown towns have attracted people who want to live in all-white communities. Families have moved to Marlow, Oklahoma, "because there were no blacks in the schools there"; to Bishop in southeastern California, from Los Angeles, "because they don't want to deal with 'those people' anymore"; and to Cullman, Alabama, from Birmingham, "to avoid integration." Kelly Burroughs, a 1988 graduate of Havana High School in western Illinois, wrote in 2002:

> I lived in Havana all my life and knew of no [African Americans] that lived there, and yes the rumor that you heard was a wide known fact amongst the community, that niggers were not welcome to purchase or live in our town. As to that holding true today I don't know, I no longer live there, but if you find out please let me know so I can move back.

Burroughs went on to explain, "I would like to see more all white communities. . . . Would I like to live in an all white community, hell yes."[91]

Once racist whites congregate in sundown suburbs or towns, they tend to keep them all-white. Newcomers usually join in happily. As noted previously, a series of violent incidents by whites kept African Americans out of Wyandotte, Michigan, an independent sundown town that was becoming a suburb of Detroit around World War I. The largest single expulsion took place in the late summer of 1916. City assessor F. W. Liddle blamed that riot partly "on the influx of Detroiters who feeling the penetration of Negroes in Detroit sought Wyandotte real estate on the basis of their past knowledge of the [anti] Negro attitude in Wyandotte."[92]

Retirees are free to choose new communities in which to live, unencumbered by the need to commute to work. Often they select towns because they are all-white. One of the selling points for retiring to the Missouri and Arkansas Ozarks has long been their racial composition. A 1972 survey of residents of Mountain Home, Arkansas, found that many were retirees from northern cities, especially Chicago, and chose Mountain Home partly because it was all-white. According to a 1980 article on Polk County, Arkansas, "It is not an uncommon experience in Polk County to hear a newcomer remark that he chose to move here because of 'low taxes and no niggers.' " A store manager in the late 1990s in the Rogers, Arkansas, mall confirmed: "It was not uncommon for folks moving down here from the Chicago area to retire to openly remark that one attraction of the Rogers area was that there were no blacks." A resident of Pana, Illinois, told that white Chicagoans also move there to retire, knowing its anti-black tradition, and have "radically racist ideas."[93]

Florida is of course the nation's premier retirement destination, and northern newcomers—not just retirees—deserve much of the "credit" for that state's extraordinary residential segregation. Carl Fisher, founder of Miami Beach, exemplified those outsiders. According to historian Alan Raucher, Fisher "was appalled by Jim Crow practices in Florida, but he excluded from his developments both blacks and the 'wrong class' of Jews." The influx of northern retirees after World War II hardly opened communities in Florida to African Americans. On the contrary, Florida wound up with the highest levels of residential segregation in America. Recall D, the Index of Dissimilarity, which can vary from 0 (perfect integration) to 100 (complete apartheid). By 1960, Daytona Beach, Fort Lauderdale, Jacksonville, Lakeland, Miami, Orlando, St. Petersburg, and West Palm Beach each had a D greater than 96, close to total apartheid. Scoring 98.1, Fort Lauderdale was the most segregated city in the nation. In contrast, Pensacola and Tampa—Florida cities that were not primarily destinations for northern retirees—scored closer to the southern average of "only" 90.9.[94]

Racist Organizations Favor Sundown Towns

Sundown towns provided fertile recruiting fields for the Ku Klux Klan in the 1920s and still do today. This might seem absurd: why would whites living in places that face no possible "threat" from other races mobilize to protect white supremacy? Again, cognitive dissonance supplies the explanation: living in all-white towns encourages people to support organizations advocating that kind of social structure. Whitley County, Indiana, had about 100 African Americans in 1880 but just 4 by 1920. In 1923, a Ku Klux Klan leader spoke at a large rally in the county seat: "I want to put all the Catholics, Jews, and Negroes on a raft in the middle of the ocean and then sink the raft." According to Kathleen Blee, author of *Women of the Klan*, "the crowd applauded wildly." In overwhelmingly white towns across America in the 1920s, the Klan held parades and rallies that drew the largest single gatherings these towns have had to this day.[95] (Portfolio 22 shows an example.)[96]

Down through the years, Klan leaders have often located in sundown towns. In Indiana in 1923, the Ku Klux Klan attempted to purchase Valparaiso University in Valparaiso, a sundown town, to be its official college. The Klan never came up with the money to complete the deal, however.[97] Edwin DeBarr, leader of the Oklahoma Klan, made his home in Norman, another sundown town, where he headed the School of Pharmacy at the University of Oklahoma and was the university's first vice president. A headquarters of the Illinois KKK was Pekin, also a sundown town. Today's Ku Klux Klan, much less centralized than the 1920s version, has one headquarters in Harrison, Arkansas, "up in the Ozark Mountains," in the words of *The Economist,* "a part of Arkansas from which blacks vanished almost entirely in the early 1900s, and to which few have returned." For a time another Klan center was in Ross, Ohio, a distant suburb of Cincinnati; the first African American family moved into Ross only around 2000. Other KKK groups have set up shop in sundown towns in Pennsylvania, Michigan, Texas, and other states.[98]

Over the years, many other white supremacist organizations and leaders have also sought the supportive environments of sundown towns. In Aurora, Missouri, in 1911, Wilbur Phelps founded *The Menace,* an anti-Catholic newspaper that had a circulation of 1,000,000 by 1914. Father Coughlin, the notorious radio anti-Semite of the 1930s and '40s, broadcast from Royal Oak, a sundown suburb of Detroit. His followers smashed windows of Jewish shops in New York City in the early 1940s, emulating the Nazis' notorious Kristallnacht. Gerald L. K. Smith, a right-wing extremist and radio evangelist in the 1930s and 1940s, devoted his magazine, *The Cross and the Flag,* to exposing the workings of an alleged "international Jewish conspiracy." When he ran for president on the ticket of the Christian Nationalist Party in 1948, his platform included deporting African Americans from the country. After meeting opposition when trying to locate in the Los Angeles area, Smith moved his headquarters to Eureka Springs, Arkansas, partly because it was all-white.[99] Smith died in 1976, but a passion play and the statue "Christ of the Ozarks," both sparked by Smith, live on in Eureka Springs. Robert Welch, founder of the far-right John Birch Society, charged that an international Communist conspiracy was behind the 1954 Supreme Court decision that called for schools to be desegregated. The Birch Society has had headquarters in Belmont, Massachusetts; San Marino, California; and Appleton, Wisconsin. All were sundown towns, I believe,[100] and San Marino also kept out Jews.[101]

Today many right-wing racist groups still find havens in sundown towns and counties. The "Intelligence Report" put out by the Southern Poverty Law Center is the most complete national list of extreme right-wing and racist organizations. Groups on that list are disproportionately headquartered in sundown towns or frequently recruit in them.[102] The Southern Illinois Patriot's

League, for example, is in Benton, Illinois. East Peoria is home to Matt Hale, head of the World Church of the Creator, a white supremacist religion that inspired a follower to go on a 1999 shooting rampage in Illinois and Indiana against people of color that ended with three dead and several others wounded. Even when headquartered in larger interracial cities, such organizations repeatedly meet, march, and recruit in overwhelmingly white towns such as Parma, Ohio; Elwood, Indiana; and Simi Valley, California. Richard Barrett runs his Nationalist Movement from his home in Jackson, Mississippi, but held rallies in Forsyth County, Georgia, on Martin Luther King Jr.'s birthday in 1987 and again in 1997. He noted gleefully, "The Census lists zero point zero zero percent of the population of the all-American county as African," and called it "Fortress Forsyth." [103]

Many residents in all-white or nearly all-white counties and towns disapprove of white supremacist groups. Nevertheless, the style of rhetoric that we have seen is customary in communities with a sundown legacy confers upon these groups a form of legitimacy. As David Zimmermann said, discussing the KKK chapter in Harrison, Arkansas, "Maybe the Klan is here because it's comfortable here." Thom Robb directs the national Knights of the Ku Klux Klan, pastors a Baptist church, and publishes *The Crusader,* a Klan magazine, in Zinc, a tiny suburb of Harrison. He agreed in 2003: "I moved to Boone County in 1972 from Tucson, Arizona, to raise my child in an area that reflects traditional American cultural values." In 2002, a leader of Aryan Nations announced that his organization was moving to Potter County, in north-central Pennsylvania, precisely because it is so white. Even when located in isolated small towns, these hate groups often have considerable influence through music, literature, and word of mouth with white young people, especially prisoners, throughout the United States. Thus not only do sundown towns and suburbs affect how their own residents think and behave, they also affect the larger society. [104]

The impact of sundown towns and suburbs is not limited to whites. The next chapter asks the opposite question: what is their impact on African Americans who *don't* live in them? Sundown towns and suburbs are based on the premise that African Americans must be kept out because they are likely to be problems. When that ideology reaches African Americans—as it inevitably does—the result is not happy.

12

The Effect of Sundown Towns on Blacks

We had realized years ago, to our sorrow, that the housing market, above all else, stands as a symbol of racial inequality.

—Daisy Myers, pioneering black resident of
Levittown, Pennsylvania, writing in 1960 [1]

IN CONVERSATION WITH EACH OTHER, many African Americans believe that when racial privilege is at stake, Caucasians (the term often used) are to be feared. "Whites will stop at nothing," a sociologist friend said to me. I thought he was overstating his case, but the actions whites have taken to maintain sundown towns and suburbs support his position.

We have seen that the deepening racism of the Nadir—exemplified by its progeny, sundown towns and suburbs—not only affected where African Americans might live but also how, by sapping their morale. Through the years, sundown towns and suburbs have influenced the thinking, modified the travel behavior, and limited the opportunities of African Americans who never even set foot in them. The ordinances, restrictive covenants, acts of private violence, police harassment, white flight, NIMBY zoning, and other mechanisms used to maintain sundown towns have also contributed, we will see, to a certain wariness in African American culture, leading to a persistence of caution that in turn helps maintain sundown towns today.

In metropolitan areas, sundown suburbs in turn gave rise to overwhelmingly black inner-city neighborhoods and a handful of majority-black suburbs. This residential segregation continues to take a toll on many African Americans in the present, making it harder for them to achieve the cultural capital and make the social connections that lead to upward mobility. The ideology that drives sundown towns and suburbs—that blacks are problems to be avoided—also hurts African Americans psychologically, especially when they internalize the low expectations that result from it.

Feeling Ill at Ease

Especially during the Nadir, travel was difficult and often unsafe for African Americans, and not just in the South. Older African Americans can still recall how trips had to be meticulously planned to reach places with restrooms or overnight accommodations in a timely manner. A resident of Rochester, Indiana, recalled that a black chauffeur died in his car in about 1940 because he was not allowed to stay in a local hotel. He had rented a room for the little white boy he was chauffeuring but was not allowed in himself, and he either froze or was asphyxiated by exhaust fumes. Much more common was "mere" humiliation. Until well after the passage of the 1964 Civil Rights Act, which outlawed segregation in public accommodations such as restaurants and motels, African Americans coped by compiling guidebooks of places that would not harm or embarrass them (Portfolio 26). Families also assembled their own lists and shared them with friends.[2]

Or they stayed home. Speaking of her childhood in the 1950s, an African American woman said, "We didn't *go* on trips. My father absolutely refused to take a vacation. Part of that was because he worried about being terrorized on the road." "Terrorized" is an appropriate word choice, because segregation and especially sundown towns rest ultimately on the threat of terror. Her family lived in Mattoon in central Illinois, surrounded by sundown towns. Not only do these communities tell African Americans that many white people consider them so despicable that they must be barred en masse, they also serve as a reminder that we do not really live under the rule of law where black people are concerned.[3]

Although any stop for gas, food, or lodging might prove humiliating to the black traveler, sundown towns posed the worst hazards. In other towns, even if hotels and restaurants refused to serve African Americans, they could secure shelter within the black community. Sundown towns had no black community, of course. Worse still, black travelers were acutely aware that they stuck out in these all-white towns, not only as unusual but also as illegitimate and unwanted. Allison Blakely, professor of African American studies at Boston University, recalls that in the mid-1960s, "blacks were afraid to drive through Grants Pass or Medford" in southwestern Oregon. "A black friend of mine put a loaded pistol on the front seat of his car when he drove through those towns." To this day, some African Americans are very aware of sundown towns and their reputations, even in distant states.[4]

Even benign experiences in sundown towns made impacts that lasted for decades. Joycelyn Landrum-Brown, a psychologist at the University of Illinois–

Urbana, grew up in Indianapolis. She wrote about a trip she made with her parents to Greenwood, ten miles south of Indianapolis, in about 1960:

> If you will recall, my parents had gone to Greenwood to pick up a puppy from one of my mother's co-workers who lived there. I overheard the grownups talking about how we had to get out of town because black people were not allowed in town after dark. I remember being terrified sitting in the back seat of our car holding my new puppy as we drove from Greenwood to Indianapolis. I believe this memory is behind my fear of driving rural highways and traveling through small rural towns (particularly in Indiana).

Olen Cole interviewed an elderly African American who as a young worker in the Civilian Conservation Corps in the 1930s rode through Taft, California. "As we entered the city a sign read, 'Read nigger and run; if you can't read—run anyway. Nigger don't let the sun go down on you in Taft,' " he told Cole in about 1995. "The importance of this experience is that it remained vivid in [his] memory," Cole notes. "Many years later he is still able to remember the entire wording on the sign."[5]

Sundown town reputations remain vivid and current in African American culture. A 70-year-old black professional woman in an interracial town in central Illinois put it this way in 2002: "You did not stop *anywhere*. There was a lot of fear. There still is. I had to go down to Effingham [a notorious nearby sundown town] recently to observe . . . and I was not happy about it." Many older African Americans are still reluctant even to enter sundown towns. The former CCC worker went on to tell Olen Cole, "Even today when I visit Fresno, I make it a point to bypass Taft." An African American professor at Southern Arkansas University related that as of 2001, "blacks don't stop when they pass through Sheridan," the town 30 miles south of Little Rock that got rid of its African American population in 1954. A resident of Paxton, a sundown town north of Champaign, Illinois, said in 2000, "I invited a black man who wouldn't drive into Paxton for Sunday dinner. He'd come [only] if I drove him." An elderly African American woman living in central Missouri avoids the entire southwestern corner of that state. She is very aware that after whites in Springfield, the prime city of the Ozark Mountains, lynched three African Americans on Easter Sunday, 1906, "all the blacks left out of that area," as she put it. Neosho, Stockton, Warsaw, Bolivar, and other Ozark towns are almost devoid of African Americans, who fled the entire region, she said; even today, those are "not places where *I* would feel comfortable going."[6]

Particularly within their own metropolitan area, African Americans know well which suburbs do not welcome them. Only 9% of African Americans in the Detroit area in the late 1990s said they thought Dearborn, the sundown suburb just west of Detroit, would welcome a black family moving in, while 86% said the family would not be welcome. In a 2002 article in the *Detroit News* titled "Invisible Boundaries Created Dividing Line Between Black, White Suburbs," David Riddle, a Wayne State University history professor, explained that the violent anti-black events of the 1970s in the sundown suburb of Warren still affected that city's image three decades later: "When a municipality acquires a reputation like that, I think it's self-sustaining." A professor of African American studies at Bradley University in Peoria told why he would not consider moving to nearby Morton: "Clearly what I've read about the area influences me. Based on what you know, you don't feel comfortable raising your family there, and exposing your children to those influences."[7]

Writing about "mere" segregation on the fiftieth anniversary of *Brown v. Board of Education,* Colbert King, who is African American, agreed with the decision's language:

> To separate [children] from others of similar age and qualifications solely because of their race generates a feeling of inferiority as to their status in the community that may affect their hearts and minds in a way unlikely ever to be undone.

"It does affect you, as a child, and later as a grown man," King wrote, "in ways 'unlikely ever to be undone.' There is a wariness you can't shake." Historically, the still more hurtful existence of sundown towns and suburbs made many African Americans justifiably fearful, less apt to explore new experiences and locales. Even today, many African Americans do *not* feel that the world is their oyster, ready to be explored and enjoyed. And why should they? It would give anyone pause to realize that merely being in a town after dark can be a life-threatening offense. This worry about acceptance, this feeling ill at ease, is the opposite of "white privilege"—that sense of security felt by upper- and middle-class whites that they will *never* be challenged as out of place.[8]

Black Avoidance Helps Maintain Sundown Towns

Today, residents of all-white towns and suburbs often blame African Americans for being overly cautious. A longtime resident of Arab, Alabama, thinks so. After telling how whites used to keep African Americans out of Arab even during the day, he assured me in 2002, "It'd be different now." Of course, blaming blacks for not moving in serves as a handy excuse for whites who do not want to acknowledge that their town ever had a policy to keep them out. However, sometimes whites have a point. Certainly African American sociologist Orlando Patterson thinks they do: "Persisting segregation is partly—and for most middle-class Afro-Americans, largely—a voluntary phenomenon." In response to the Civil Rights Movement, whites lost some of their sense of privilege, especially in the South. No longer do most whites assume they are entitled to exclude African Americans. On public opinion polls, fewer and fewer whites agree with such items as "Blacks should not push into areas where it is known they are not wanted." Ironically, however, in the black community pessimism about white attitudes has grown. In 1968, 47% of African Americans felt whites wanted to see blacks "get a better break," 31% thought them indifferent, and 22% thought whites wanted to "keep blacks down." By 1992, just 22% of African Americans believed whites wanted to see them get a better break, 52% thought them indifferent, and 26% felt whites wanted to keep them down. Such pessimism is hardly conducive to social action.[9]

Most black families merely follow the line of least resistance. In 2001, reporter David Mendell spoke with 66-year-old Willie Buchanan, who bought a house in "Blackfish Bay," as wags call the majority-black neighborhood near Whitefish Bay, an overwhelmingly white suburb north of Milwaukee. Buchanan "said he moved where he felt most comfortable," according to Mendell. "You like to live around people who you feel want to be your neighbor," said Buchanan. "I don't think prejudice is as bad as it used to be. But it's still around, so I just decided to move here."[10]

Such thinking is understandable. Law professor Sheryll Cashin calls it "integration exhaustion." As actor Sidney Poitier put it, explaining why the Poitier family moved to Mt. Vernon, an interracial suburb of New York City, after having problems trying to buy a house in West Los Angeles: "Our children are established in a multi-racial community in Mount Vernon. They attend multi-racial schools. . . . We don't want to barter that kind of atmosphere for something that is hostile." Ruby Dee, another black actor who with her husband, Ossie Davis, chose an already integrated neighborhood in New Rochelle, New York, offered a similar explanation: "I want to be friends with my neighbors. I don't want to be tolerated, on my best behavior, always seeking my neighbor's approval. . . . I admire the pioneers who risk so much in the process of integration, but I cannot break that ice." Reasonably enough, many African American families want to live near neighbors who will accept them, and the best way to find whites like that is in neighborhoods where they already live near African American families.[11]

Choosing this line of least resistance may not lead to the best results for the family in the long run, however. African Americans moving into those neighborhoods that are known to be open to them often wind up in areas with higher tax rates and lower tax bases than whiter suburbs. Eventually these economic realities take their toll, and families find that their homes did not appreciate as fast as those in whiter suburbs. Cashin points to a host of more serious social problems that arise after suburbs go majority black. Certainly following the line of least resistance does not lead to the best results for the metropolitan area. When black families move to an interracial suburb that everyone knows is open—indeed, that is likely to go all black—they only contribute to the sundown suburb problem.[12]

Nevertheless, calling African American complicity in residential segregation "voluntary" overstates the case. According to sociologist Gary Orfield, speaking in 2000, African Americans do still believe in the integrated American dream: 99% favor desegregation, and 59% favor busing if needed to get there. Worry about sundown reactions deters many. In Detroit, Reynolds Farley and others pointed out, only 31% of African Americans said they would be "willing to be the African American pioneer on an all-white block" in 1992, compared to 38% in 1976. But sociologist John Logan stresses, "Black preferences are strongly affected by beliefs about whites' attitudes and behavior," so "their reluctance to live in a predominantly white neighborhood is due to their belief that whites would react negatively." Reputations are important. In Arab, for instance, the 2000 census showed just a single black household among 7,139 total population. "Why so few?" I asked a longtime resident. He referred to the violent exclusion of the past: "That happened a long time ago, and it's still in their [blacks'] minds."[13]

Before smiling at the old ex-CCC worker who still avoids Taft six decades after he learned it was sundown, we might note that Taft also did not change for decades. According to Ronald McGriff, chair of social sciences at the nearby College of the Sequoias, "as recent as the 1980s, [residents of Taft] trashed a black home (with paint and graffiti) and [the family] was told to 'get out of town.' " Before making light of the black man who would come for Sunday dinner in Paxton only if his white host drove him, whites might remember that one can never be sure when one's car might break down. Before blaming African Americans for not moving into Arab, we must note that Arab boasted a sign, "Nigger, Don't Let The Sun Set On Your Black Ass in Arab, Alabama," until the early 1990s, according to Benjamin Johnson, a former University of

Alabama student—hardly "a long time ago." I must confess that I felt unsafe and uneasy when I first started doing this research in such notorious sundown towns as Alba, Texas, and Cicero, Illinois. I worried lest "they" discover my liberal attitudes, before I fully understood that my white skin made me safely part of the in-group.[14]

David Grann, a *New Republic* journalist visiting Vidor, Texas, in 1998, made light of African Americans' continued concern about that town: "Several blacks in the surrounding area told me they still don't stop there for gas at night, even though the hand-painted sign on Main Street saying 'Nigger, Don't Let the Sun Set on You in Vidor' was taken down some 30 years ago." He obviously thought African Americans were overdoing their prudence. But if one doesn't know for sure, one is putting oneself and one's family at risk. African Americans have a legitimate right to fear violent consequences, as well as such lesser repercussions as shunning, if they move into a sundown community. Moreover, just five years before Grann's visit, racial slurs, shunning, refusals to hire, and death threats drove four black households from Vidor's public housing complex, leaving the town again all-white by design. This book is replete with examples of vicious white retribution visited upon unsuspecting African Americans who didn't know enough to be wary of sundown towns and might have survived had they been more prudent. Today, most sundown towns and suburbs would react more placidly than Vidor back in 1993, but some residents might not be welcoming. As an elderly African American in a neighboring town said in 2002, explaining why there are no African Americans in Nashville, Illinois, "If people are inhospitable to you, you leave."[15]

Still, African Americans can overdo their caution into their own form of racial paranoia. Sometimes African Americans take a certain pleasure in overstating the danger: "look what those white folks have done *now*!" There is a streak of gallows humor in black rhetoric that takes mordant satisfaction in seizing on, retelling, and even exaggerating examples of racist white behavior. Patterson writes that African Americans perceive whites as "technically clever, yes; powerful, well armed, and prolific, to be sure; but without an ounce of basic human decency." Despite all the wretched acts by whites recounted in this book, that is too strong. Such thinking only exaggerates the extent and importance of white racism and invites African Americans to show too much caution. The African American woman who "was not happy about" having to go to Effingham, Illinois, in broad daylight in 2002 showed this paranoia, just like the white suburbanite from Naperville who frets about going to a concert in Chicago's Loop. In both cases, a self-fulfilling prophecy sets in: nothing bad happens to the person who avoids places dominated by the other race, and that happy fact legitimizes the avoidance, leaving intact the belief that the opposite race still poses a threat.[16]

Psychological Costs of Sundown Towns

No other group, not even Native Americans, has been so disparaged by the very structure of American society. No other group has been labeled a pariah people—literally to be kept outside the gates of our sundown towns and suburbs. As Daisy Myers put it in 1960, "The housing market, above all else, stands as a symbol of racial inequality." Just as sundown towns drained the morale of African Americans during the Nadir, so sundown suburbs, especially elite suburbs, still contribute to demoralization in black neighborhoods elsewhere in the metropolitan area.[17]

Arna Bontemps and Jack Conroy observed about Watts, the African American ghetto that exploded into violence in Los Angeles in 1965: "A crushing weight fell on the spirit of the neighborhood when it learned that it was hemmed in, that prejudice and malice had thrown a wall around it." On the other side of the country, Irwin Quintyne moved in 1961 to North Amityville, one of the "black townships" that adjoin sundown suburbs on Long Island. He remembered in 2003 how "other growing Long Island communities, Levittown in particular, made it clear that they didn't want blacks." The message hammered home to black suburbanites by their neighboring all-white community is "We do not care who you are or what you have done; so far as *this* town is concerned, you are a nigger and unfit for human companionship." Partly as a result of this message, North Amityville; Kinloch, Missouri; and several other black townships lost morale and came to house drug markets and problem families.[18]

Successful African Americans may be particularly upset by these slights, because their peers, elite whites, are the least likely of all white Americans to accept African Americans into their neighborhoods and organizations. As Ellis Cose famously raged:

> I have done everything I was supposed to do. I have stayed out of trouble with the law, gone to the right schools, and worked myself nearly to death. *What more do they want?* Why in God's name won't they accept me as a full human being?[19]

It *is* frustrating: even voicing the hurt can hurt, because it can seem as if affluent African Americans are only whining because white people won't be their friends. A similar misinterpretation gets applied to school desegregation: "What is it about black people? Do they *need* white children next to them to learn successfully?" But that was not Cose's point in 1993, nor was it the point of *Brown v. Board of Education* in 1954. As the Supreme Court pointed out in decisions flowing from *Brown,* whites are the lawmaking group in America. When they segregated the schools, it was part of a program of white supremacy that declared blacks inferior. That is why segregated schools were *inherently* unequal, as the *Brown* decision stated: the enforced racial separation itself both presupposed and signified black inferiority.

Every time black ingress into a previously white neighborhood prompts white egress to more distant sundown suburbs, all African Americans in the metropolitan area are invited to remember that they are still so despised by our mainstream culture that whites feel they must flee them en masse. Black poet Langston Hughes mused on this matter in 1949 in "Restrictive Covenants," which said in part:

> When I move
> Into a neighborhood
> Folks fly.
> Even every foreigner
> That can move, moves.
> Why?

Cose goes to the heart of the matter: residential exclusion (and the school segregation it purchases) strikes at blacks' worth *as full human beings.* That's why it festers. That's why black respondents on Long Island were significantly less satisfied with their lives than whites with significantly lower incomes, in a 1990 study reported by Cose.[20]

After experiencing some of Chicago's sundown neighborhoods and sundown suburbs firsthand in 1965, Martin Luther King Jr. observed, "Segregation has wreaked havoc with the Negro. . . . Only a Negro can understand the social leprosy that segregation inflicts upon him. Every confrontation with restriction is another emotional battle in a never-ending war." "Social leprosy" is an evocative term for the pariah status that sundown towns and suburbs enforce upon African Americans, inexact only in that leprosy can now be cured.[21]

Countee Cullen's poem "Incident," written in the 1920s, suggests the sting that African Americans can internalize from racial slights:

Once riding in old Baltimore,
Heart-filled, head-filled with glee,
I saw a Baltimorean
Keep looking straight at me.

Now I was eight and very small,
And he was no whit bigger,
And so I smiled, but he poked out
His tongue, and called me, "Nigger."

I saw the whole of Baltimore
From May until December;
Of all the things that happened there
That's all that I remember.

Such behavior wasn't limited to an eight-year-old white boy in Baltimore in 1911. As we have seen, residents of sundown towns persist in expressing racial slights and taunts. Young black adults have supplied many examples of being called "nigger" and worse in these towns in the last ten years, such as this experience by a high school athlete in Pekin, in central Illinois, in 1999:

In track, I was the Conference Champion in the 3200 meters and in cross-country I was Conference and Sectional Champion. One occurrence that I would never forget about running cross-country is when I had a meet in Pekin, Illinois. While running along the course, someone riding alone in a car shouted out the word "Nigger." This was my first time experiencing racism. Through-out my years of living [in Peoria], I had never been in the act of racism. Till this day I can remember this occurrence very visually. This event made me aware that racism does still exist in the '90s.

And till this day the memory sears.[22]

Internalizing Low Expectations

Since the 1970s, the research literature in social science and education has stressed that the expectations teachers and others have of children—and ulti-mately the expectations children have of themselves—make a key difference to their performance in school (and later life), and expectations vary by race (and class and sometimes gender). If teachers think of African American children as less intelligent, they will expect less from them. Soon they get less from them. After a while African American children may start expecting less from themselves. The generalizations that are intrinsic to sundown towns and suburbs—that African Americans must be kept out because they are problematic people who are likely to be intellectually inferior, if not criminal—pervade our general culture. Sociologists Dale Harvey and Gerald Slatin demonstrated how teachers have internalized these expectations. They showed photographs of children to teachers and found them all too willing to predict different levels of school performance based solely on snapshots. "White children were more often expected to succeed and black children more often expected to fail," they summarized.[23]

Unfortunately, these lower expectations can become self-fulfilling prophecies for some members of the oppressed group. African Americans in segregated environments can find it hard to break out of this cycle of lower expectations and inferior self-worth. De facto segregation is no kinder to the excluded minority than the old de jure segregation that the Supreme Court threw out as unconstitutional in 1954; besides, as this book has shown, sundown towns are all-white by policy and official actions, not just de facto. All-black schools often do not and sometimes cannot convince black children they are fully equipped, genetically and intellectually, to challenge the white world. Since the raison d'être for segregated schooling was (and is) to keep an allegedly inferior group from "contaminating" and slowing the progress of white students, it can be hard for teachers in black schools to convince their charges that they are fully equal and ready to take on all comers. "Segregation promotes the devaluation of black life even among blacks, and can lead to self-hatred," wrote psychiatrist Alvin Poussaint in 2002. In this respect teachers in segregated black schools face the same uphill battle faced by teachers in segregated white schools in sundown suburbs who are trying to convince their charges that blacks are fully equal.[24]

All the while, the act of living in sundown neighborhoods and attending all-white schools communicates to everyone in the society that whites are superior. So does the higher prestige accorded to whiter suburbs. The ideology underlying sundown communities relies on stereotypes about African Americans, stereotypes that unfortunately reach African Americans. Claude Steele and his associates at Stanford show that these stereotypes can then "dramatically depress" the performance of African American students on the SAT and similar tests, a phenomenon Steele calls "stereotype threat." In subtle experiments, Steele has created stereotype threats for white students that depress their performance, and the same for women as a group, and so forth. Thus books such as *The Bell Curve*, which claims African Americans have lower intelligence genetically, in turn help to maintain precisely the lower test scores that they claim to "explain," by maintaining the stereotype that African Americans are inferior.[25]

All this is why Malcolm X famously said, "A segregated school system produces children who, when they graduate, graduate with crippled minds." Black parents try to convince their children that they are valuable human beings, but it's not easy when society devalues them. It's also hard to answer such logical questions as "Why are we in the ghetto?" "Why do whites move away?" As an eight-year-old black child said to Jacob Holdt, commenting on this white antagonism: "We must have done *something* wrong!" And lo, the old "blacks as problem" ideology, expressed so clearly in the origin myths of sundown towns, surfaces miles away in the minds and mouths of the victims.[26]

Excluding African Americans from Cultural Capital

Residential segregation makes it easier to give African Americans inferior educations, health care, and other public services. Study after study has shown how expenditures per pupil are higher in suburban schools than in inner cities, even though everyone knows that suburban pupils have many advantages—from their own computers to a higher proportion of two-parent households—that make them easier to teach. Kati Haycock of the Education Trust notes the incongruity: "We take the kids who are most dependent on their teachers for academic learning and assign them teachers with the weakest academic base." Residential segregation not only makes this systematic disadvantaging possible, it makes it desirable, even prestigious, in the eyes of white suburbanites.[27]

Confining most African Americans to the opposite of sundown suburbs—majority-black, inner-city neighborhoods—also restricts their access to what Patterson calls cultural capital: "those learned patterns of mutual trust, insider knowledge about how things really work, encounter rituals, and social sensibilities that constitute the language of power and success." Sundown suburbs shut blacks out from coming into contact with these patterns of the dominant culture,[28] at least before college. This cultural segregation shows up even in something as basic as patterns of speech: many African Americans sound identifiably "black" on the telephone. Their accent and voice timbre are "different." The difference is not racial; Chinese Americans I knew in Mississippi in the 1960s either spoke "Southern white English" (more than half), "Southern black English" (a few), or Chinese-accented En -

glish (many persons older than 40). Historian Barbara J. Fields points out that there is no such thing as "black English" in England, where West Indian immigrants' children learn the English of their class and region. But in America, as a consequence of the Great Retreat, "black English" intensified.[29]

In turn, not coming into contact with patterns of the dominant culture is one reason why African Americans (and to a degree Hispanics and Native Americans) average much lower scores than European Americans on college entrance exams such as the SAT. The SAT and related tests suffer from racial and class (and some gender) bias. This unfairness is in addition to such problems as the far greater access white students have to coaching classes and personal tutors. It derives from the statistical methods the Educational Testing Service, the administrator of the SAT, uses to select items to be included on the tests.[30] Until this bias is eliminated, African Americans need exposure to the vocabulary and thoughtways of white suburbanites to do well on standardized tests. Sundown suburbs prevent that by keeping black children away from high-scoring white children, as well as from the amenities that help them score high.

Research in Chicago by James Rosenbaum and others confirms Patterson's general point. The Chicago Housing Authority (CHA), burned by the white resistance to African Americans who tried to live in Airport Homes after World War II, changed its policies to comply with sundown suburbs and neighborhoods. It built public housing for blacks in black neighborhoods and public housing for whites in white neighborhoods. As a result, CHA was sued for racial segregation in what became known as the Gautreaux litigation. In 1969, federal judge Richard Austin ordered CHA to locate public housing for blacks in predominantly white neighborhoods scattered throughout the city. Eventually, the relief was ordered to extend to the white suburbs as well.[31] The result, getting under way in 1976, located more than 5,000 families in more than 100 predominantly white communities in Cook County and five suburban counties.

Rosenbaum took advantage of the marvelous natural experiment provided by this order. He compared families that happened to get selected for housing in white neighborhoods with families that applied but were not selected. He found that being exposed to new surroundings had transforming effects on the families placed in white neighborhoods: 95% of their children graduated from high school and 54% went on to college. (Both of these rates were higher than for European Americans nationally.) Black parents in suburbia were also much more likely than parents in inner cities to find work in the suburbs. Rosenbaum concluded that residential segregation was itself the problem, promoting hopelessness and keeping poor black families from con-necting with the larger society.[32]

Even apparently unrelated social problems such as crime and school dropout rates turn out to be related to residential segregation, according to re-search by Wayne State University professor George Galster. He analyzed the segregation level and various quality of life indicators across U.S. cities, based on the 1990 census. Looking at Detroit, America's most segregated metropol-itan area, he concluded that if its segregation level were cut in half, "the me-dian income of black families would rise 24%; the black homicide rate would fall 30%; the black high school dropout rate would fall 75%; and the black poverty rate would fall 17%." The Galster and Gautreaux research shows that blaming the pathological conditions of ghetto neighborhoods on their inhab-itants gets causation at least partly backward.[33]

Excluding African Americans from Social Connections

Gautreaux also worked for an additional reason: social connections. Follow-ing a 1973 article by Mark Granovetter, "The Strength of Weak Ties," sociol-ogists have come to see that Americans connect with the larger society in important ways through casual and seemingly unimportant relations. A whole new career might result from a tip from a friend's older sister's boyfriend. "Again and again," wrote sociologist Deirdre Royster in 2003, "the white men I spoke with described opportunities that had landed in their laps, not as the result of outstanding achievements or personal characteristics, but rather as the result of the assistance of older white neighbors, brothers, family friends." The trouble is, these networks are segregated, so important information never reaches black America.[34]

Sundown suburbanites know only whites, by definition, except perhaps a few work contacts. Thus sundown suburbs contribute to economic inequality by race. In the Milwaukee metropolitan area, for instance, often listed as America's second most segregated, African Americans "earn just 49 cents for every dollar that whites earn, far below the national average of 64 cents to the dollar," according to reporter Stephanie Simon. Overwhelmingly white sub-urbs, with which Milwaukee abounds, play a large role in maintaining this in-equality. Similarly, urban studies professor Carolyn Adams found that occupational segregation is worse in the Philadelphia suburbs than in the city itself and blames residential segregation, because networks in inner-city neighborhoods stay within the " 'hood." Even affluent African Americans who live in majority-black suburbs face this limitation.[35]

Darien, Connecticut, nicely illustrates the concentration of opportunity in the casual networks of elite sundown suburbs. Teenagers there have so many summer job offers, as well as other prospects, that they have no interest in working at Darien's McDonald's. Nearby suburbs are almost as elite. So the restaurant hires a private bus from East Harlem, an hour away, filled with teenagers and adults who feel fortunate to work at McDonald's. There they have no meaningful interaction with Darien residents at the take-out window, so they make no connections that might lead to upward mobility.[36]

Because suburbs have become increasingly important economically and culturally, excluding African Americans from suburbs increasingly keeps them out of the centers of American corporate, civic, and cultural life. Many manufacturing jobs have long been located in sundown suburbs such as Dearborn, Michigan, and Brea, California. As whites left the city, they took still more of America's jobs to the suburbs with them. Geographer Charles Christian studied this process in the Chicago metropolitan area, where many jobs moved to the suburbs. Generally, the jobs went to the suburbs with the smallest black populations; in the two suburbs that gained the most jobs, Franklin Park and Des Plaines, "there appears to be no black population." This trend accelerated in the last two decades, during which not only factories but also corporate headquarters have been moving to the suburbs.[37]

Reviewing *Urban Inequality,* a recent comparative urban research study, Anne Shlay summarized, "It is better to be black in Atlanta than in Detroit." Atlanta does not have many of the sundown suburbs, like Grosse Pointe and Wyandotte, that have long cursed Detroit. This makes it easier for African Americans to amass cultural capital and make social connections in Atlanta. Atlanta attaches less stigma to blackness, and upward and geographic mobility is easier there.[38]

William J. Wilson sees this exodus of jobs to the suburbs as the biggest single cause of inner-city hopelessness, which in turn leads to drugs, gangs, and the breakdown of the black family. It also removes from inner-city neighborhoods connections with people who have jobs. Remaining residents face yet another burden: unequal commuting. Most commutes are now suburb to suburb rather than suburb to inner city, and African Americans have the longest commutes to work of any racial/ethnic group.[39]

Our society then stigmatizes the entire racial group identified with the resulting concentration of hopelessness, not only those members of it who live in the ghetto. Meanwhile, the racial group that forced the concentrating—whites—does not get stigmatized as a group. Instead, whiteness gets valorized owing to its identification with elegant elite sundown suburbs. This unequal burden of stigma versus honor is one more social cost blacks bear, derived from sundown towns.

We know how to end these social costs. The Gautreaux families, simply by dint of living in white suburbia, were able to make connections that led to educational and occupational opportunity. That they did so well, even though mostly headed by single mothers on welfare, shows the power of racial and economic integration. Conversely, the much worse educational and occupational outcomes of those *not* selected to participate shows the debilitating influence of segregation, hence ultimately of sundown suburbs, on African Americans in the inner city. The achievements of the Gautreaux families augur that the quick eradication of sundown towns would foster the development not only of whites who are less racist, but also of blacks who are more successful.

The next chapter shows that sundown towns also have bad effects on America as a whole and especially on our metropolitan areas. The more sundown suburbs a metropolitan area has, the lower the vitality of its inner city and perhaps of the entire area.

13

The Effect of Sundown Towns
on the Social System

Our standard of decency in expenditure, as in other ends of emulation, is set by the usage of those next above us in reputability; until, in this way, especially in any community where class distinctions are somewhat vague, all canons of reputability and decency, and all standards of consumption, are traced back by insensible gradations to the usages and habits of thought of the highest social and pecuniary class—the wealthy leisure class.

—Thorstein Veblen, *The Theory of the Leisure Class,* 1899 [1]

NOT ONLY DO SUNDOWN TOWNS and suburbs hurt African Americans and warp white Americans, they also have negative consequences for the social system as a whole. Metropolitan areas in particular are social systems, complexly interlinked. Just as a power surge can cascade through an electrical grid, an overconcentration of whites in one neighborhood can cause difficulties elsewhere in the social system.

Sundown Suburbs Can Hurt Entire Metropolitan Areas

Racial exclusion can decrease opportunity for everyone in a metropolitan area if it makes that area less attractive to newcomers. Detroit was the nation's most segregated metropolitan area in 2000. [2] Historically Detroit has been burdened with some of the nation's most notorious sundown suburbs. Without a doubt, this hypersegregation has hurt the city of Detroit itself. Housing prices within the city reflect Detroit's dismal economic position: its median home cost just $25,600 in 1990, dead last among America's 77 cities with 200,000 or more people. In comparison, the median home in Boston cost $161,400, in Los Angeles $244,500. Detroit also ranked 73rd of 77 in median income. [3]

Homes in Detroit are also worth much less than suburban homes: in 1999, the median Detroit home was valued at $63,400, less than half the median value elsewhere in the metropolitan area. Homes in Boston, in contrast, were worth only slightly less than homes outside Boston, while the median home in Los Angeles was worth more than homes outside Los Angeles. Since the 1950s, Detroit has lost half its population. George Lin, who styles himself an "urban explorer," calls it "the most tragic case of urban abandonment in the United States." Famous for abandoned homes, Detroit also boasts abandoned office buildings, factories, warehouses, and hotels, including several skyscrapers.[4]

While there is no doubt that sundown suburbs have hurt the city of Detroit, they may not have hurt the outlying parts of its metropolitan area. Taken as a whole, the Detroit metropolitan area is among the nation's most prosperous; in 1997, metropolitan Detroit families averaged $56,000 in income, well above New York City ($49,500) or Los Angeles ($47,600). Moreover, a metropolitan area's growth or decline rests on many causes, from the rise and fall of specific industries and even companies to the historic location of hospitals or universities. Still, there is evidence that Detroit's hypersegregation, with sundown suburbs clustered around a central city that in 2000 was 82% black, hurts its prospects as a metropolitan area. Certainly many people in Detroit think so. "Segregation Keeps Businesses, Professionals from Locating to Detroit Area," headlined the *Detroit News* in 2002. The article cited "business officials" as saying, "For a firm evenly split between Detroit and another city as the possible home of its new headquarters, the distasteful aroma of segregation could be a deciding factor." Metropolitan Detroit, not just the city, shrank in population between 1970 and 1998 by 3%, while the United States grew by 32%. Corporate leaders in St. Louis, Cleveland, and other hypersegregated metropolitan areas have voiced similar worries. The three cities that continued to lose the most population in the first three years of the new millennium were Detroit, Cincinnati, and St. Louis, all among our most segregated.[5]

Many whites in hypersegregated cities like Detroit have thrown in the towel on their central city. As Leah Samuel put it, describing the debate in the Detroit Theater Organ Society (DTOS) over whether to move their huge Wurlitzer pipe organ from the Senate Theater in downtown Detroit, "relocating Detroit institutions to the suburbs is a well-established tradition." Dick Leichtamer, president of the society, blames declining attendance on "the part of town that it's in." Former president George Orbits agreed: "The people just do not want to come to Detroit." But Samuel points out, "Despite the fears of crime that they cite as a reason for the move, DTOS board members admit that they don't recall any serious negative incidents involving concertgoers."

It isn't specific fear of crime that drives the exodus so much as a sense that leaving is the right thing to do. But whether a metropolitan area can draw conventions and tourists with nothing to do in its core city remains to be seen.[6]

Sundown Towns Stifle Creativity

In addition to discouraging new people, hypersegregation may also discourage new ideas. Urban theorist Jane Jacobs has long held that the mix of peoples and cultures found in successful cities prompts creativity. An interesting study by sociologist William Whyte shows that sundown suburbs may discourage out-of-the-box thinking. By the 1970s, some executives had grown weary of the long commutes with which they had saddled themselves so they could raise their families in elite sundown suburbs. Rather than move their families back to the city, they moved their corporate headquarters out to the suburbs. Whyte studied 38 companies that left New York City in the 1970s and '80s, allegedly "to better [the] quality-of-life needs of their employees." Actually, they moved close to the homes of their CEOs, cutting their average commute to eight miles; 31 moved to the Greenwich-Stamford, Connecticut, area. These are not sundown towns, but adjacent Darien was, and Greenwich and Stamford have extensive formerly sundown neighborhoods that are also highly segregated on the basis of social class. Whyte then compared those 38 companies to 36 randomly chosen comparable companies that stayed in New York City. Judged by stock price, the standard way to measure how well a company is doing, the suburbanized companies showed less than half the stock appreciation of the companies that chose to remain in the city.[7]

Evidence from Tacoma, Washington, suggests that cities with a racial mix may be more hospitable to new ideas. Today Tacoma has an enormous inferiority complex compared to the metropolitan juggernaut to its north, Seattle. Some commentators, including journalist Charles Mudede, tie Tacoma's relative lack of progress to its sundown policies vis-à-vis Chinese Americans in 1885:

> Tacoma's officials . . . helped force most of the city's Chinese community onto a train headed for Portland. Tacoma faced national embarrassment because of the incident, and its backward way of settling racial disputes became known as "The Tacoma Method." It has yet to recover from this humiliating recognition: recently, the *Tacoma News Tribune* published an article titled "Tacoma faces up to its darkest hour," which posits that Tacoma might have turned out differently had it not booted out its Chinese population.

The *News Tribune* laments the missing Chinese Americans and their ideas, pointing out that to this day Tacoma remains the only city on the West Coast with no large Chinese American population. In addition, the restrictive mind-set established when Tacoma's expulsion of Chinese immigrants was allowed to stand was not conducive to new ideas and new peoples.[8]

Independent sundown towns also hurt their own futures by being closed to new ideas. Nick Khan of Paragould, Arkansas, said nearby interracial Jonesboro is growing much more than Paragould. "If this thing [racism] goes out of here, Paragould will grow rapidly." "To this day, it's a very stuck-in-the-past town," said a 1983 high school graduate of Red Bud, Illinois, a sundown town near St. Louis. "Any time the community is presented with opportunities to provide tax incentives or otherwise bring something new in, the council votes it down." There are exceptions. Some sundown towns do better than others. Murray Bishoff, who lives in Pierce City, Missouri, and works in nearby Monett, thinks Pierce City, which drove out its African Americans in 1901 and has been sundown ever since, has been hurt by its sundown policy. Meanwhile, Monett, which drove out its blacks in 1894 and has been equally white since, is doing better. In 1999, Monett's per capita income was nearly 40% higher than Pierce City's, although still below average for the state. Effingham, an important rail and interstate highway junction in central Illinois, is a printing center and boasts a big new Krispy Kreme doughnut factory, although its per capita income remains below average for Illinois. Effingham and Monett may be exceptions, but on the whole, I think Khan is right. Some industries are reluctant to move to all-white communities because their non-white managers cannot easily find places to live. Even the white managers of these firms increasingly consider such towns backward and unappealing.[9]

Some residents feel that a limited future is not too high a price to pay for the joys of living in an all-white town. While doing a community study of a southern Illinois sundown town in 1958, Herman Lantz and J. S. McCrary elicited this comment from a white barber:

> I don't think that they would let any Negroes live here today, even if a new industry came in and said they would settle here if they could hire Negroes. I don't think that we would let them. That is, as bad as we need industry, if it meant bringing in Negroes, we would not want it. We don't allow any Negroes here now.

In 2002, a genealogist reported the same sentiment from a neighbor in nearby West Frankfort: "Some folks say we've got to let the blacks in, if we want to have progress. Well, we're *not* going to do it!" Such insular people are unlikely to seek new ideas or recruit new companies. They understand that racism interferes with their ability to enjoy the outside world, but given their fears about that world and especially about its African Americans, they do not want to invite that world into their sundown sanctuary.[10]

Research suggests that gay men are also important members of what Richard Florida calls "the creative class"—those who come up with or welcome new ideas and help drive an area economically.[11] Metropolitan areas with the most sundown suburbs also show the lowest tolerance for homosexuality and have the lowest concentrations of "out" gays and lesbians, according to Gary Gates of the Urban Institute. He lists Buffalo, Cleveland, Detroit, Milwaukee, and Pittsburgh as examples. Recently, some cities—including Detroit—have recognized the important role that gay residents can play in helping to revive problematic inner-city neighborhoods, and now welcome them.[12]

The distancing from African Americans embodied by all-white suburbs intensifies another urban problem: sprawl, the tendency for cities to become more spread out and less dense. Sprawl can decrease creativity and quality of life throughout the metropolitan area by making it harder for people to get together for all the human activities—from think tanks to complex commercial transactions to opera—that cities make possible in the first place. Asked in 2000, "What is the most important problem facing the community where you live?" 18% of Americans replied sprawl and traffic, tied for first with crime and violence. Moreover, unlike crime, sprawl is increasing. Some hypersegregated metropolitan areas like Detroit and Cleveland are growing larger geographically while actually losing population.[13]

Sundown Suburbs Make Integrated Neighborhoods Hard to Achieve

In most northern metropolitan areas, the key race relations issue, generating the most anguish and the most headlines, has long been the black ghetto and its expanding edge. Conflict at this "frontier" provoked the great Chicago race riot back in 1919 and hundreds of clashes since, in Chicago and elsewhere. This boundary is still where white resistance is most apparent, where blockbusting and white flight take place, where whites sometimes riot. News stories from the inner city are also usually full of conflict: gang or school violence, disputes between black residents and Asian or Jewish store owners, or charges of police brutality. Our media naturally go where the action is. Like journalists, most social scientists have directed their attention to the inner city, trying to figure out what to do about its indisputable social pathologies, and to the line of demarcation between the ghetto and the adjacent frontline suburb, refining such concepts as "tipping point theory" to predict when whites will flee and blockbusting will succeed.

All this seems reasonable enough, on the surface. Many—not all—inner-city neighborhoods do manifest social problems, and white flight from working-class sundown suburbs closer to the expanding black ghetto does confirm white racism. But there is more to it. The engine that drives "front-line" suburbs to go overwhelmingly black lies neither in those suburbs nor in the expanding black ghetto, but across town—in the elite sundown suburb. Concentrating on where the problems appear can cause journalists and social scientists alike to overlook the seat of the problem. It is hard for interracial suburbs to retain whites when overwhelmingly white suburbs offer more prestige. Indeed, residents of elite sundown suburbs often put down interracial suburbs precisely because they are interracial. Like residents of independent sundown towns, sundown suburbanites also exaggerate how black an interracial suburb is. Carole Goodwin found that as soon as a few blacks moved into Oak Park, an interracial frontline suburb just west of Chicago, people in more distant sundown suburbs perceived it to be half-black. They further "knew" it would go all-black.[14] Believing this prediction legitimized their own decision to locate in sundown suburbs nowhere near a black or interracial neighborhood.[15]

The resistance to integration in these placid all-white elite suburbs, often miles away from the frontline suburb, drives the entire blockbusting process. Interviewed by a Detroit newspaper in 1955, a working-class homeowner in an interracial suburb understood this all too well: "It gets so tiresome being asked all the time to sell your house. I bet they don't call out in Grosse Pointe or Bloomfield Hills or Palmer Park all the time asking those people if they want to sell." She was complaining about real estate agents who solicited whites to sell and then steered black would-be buyers into these "changing neighborhoods," rather than to all-white suburbs.[16]

Even without steering, African Americans know they may not be welcome and will not feel welcome in places such as Grosse Pointe. Understandably, they therefore prefer interracial suburbs to all-white ones, so they move to recently desegregated towns. Meanwhile, European Americans know they will be welcome and feel welcome in sundown suburbs; indeed, some choose them precisely because they are so white. Others move there to get real amenities—fine schools, nice parks, good city services, safety, and aesthetic values—but the biggest single draw of sundown suburbs is status. Housing segregated along race and class lines still signifies social power and success. As families prosper, they both display and purchase their status by moving to a more prestigious and exclusive neighborhood, and the whiter the suburb, the higher its status. In that sense, *most* families move to elite sundown suburbs because they are so white. We have seen that upper-class suburbs such as Darien, Connecticut; Tuxedo Park, New York; Kenilworth, Illinois; Edina, Minnesota; and Beverly Hills, California, were founded as white (and usually WASP) enclaves. Each is the richest and most prestigious suburb of its metropolitan area, or close to it. Kenilworth, for example, was Chicago's wealthiest suburb in 1990 and the sixth richest town in the United States, according to historian Michael Ebner. Other towns ultimately compare themselves to these elite white suburbs. The value of living in all-white suburbs thus filters down from the upper class to all other (white) classes.[17]

In the quote at the head of this chapter, Thorstein Veblen famously explained how the upper class typically influences all Americans' values. Tuxedo Park offers literal confirmation of Veblen's analysis, for it was the epitome of taste, as defined by resident Emily Post and yes, the source of the dinner jacket that bears its name. Post was the daughter of architect Bruce Price, who designed the town. From 1920 to at least 1975, she set the standard of good behavior for the entire United States, with her book *Etiquette,* daily newspaper column on good taste, and weekly radio show.[18] So long as towns such as Tuxedo Park bestow the highest status and are so very WASP, neighborhoods that are less WASP and less affluent cannot afford to welcome African Americans—or sometimes even Jews or Hispanics—without further reducing their own social status. Thus the existence and prestige of these places in turn makes it harder for interracial suburbs to stay interracial. Even many families who don't want to avoid African Americans do want to move to "better" suburbs, which means whiter suburbs.[19]

Sundown Suburbs Cause White Flight

Why would white home buyers flee an interracial area, especially one where African Americans made up only 1% of the population? Careful research by Ingrid Gould Ellen shows how sundown suburbs cause white flight elsewhere in the metropolitan area. She points out that it isn't merely racism that fuels this flight, but also three predictions by white suburbanites. First, whites "know" that when African Americans move in, property values go down. And in fact, they have a point: the same home in an elite sundown suburb is usually worth more than in the inner city. But there is more to it. Excluding African Americans from sundown suburbs creates pent-up housing demand in black neighborhoods, so blacks will likely outbid whites when one former sundown suburb opens up. Back in 1917 in *Buchanan v. Warley,* the Supreme Court saw that white property owners would be damaged if they could not sell to all, rather than only to whites. This is another reason—on the demand side, having nothing to do with white flight—why a former sundown suburb may quickly go majority-black.[20]

Ellen invites us to answer this question: when African Americans move into a formerly sundown suburb, who is more likely to move first—renters or owners? The obvious answer would be renters; it is much easier for renters to move, being more transient and usually less wedded to their communities. If avoidance of African Americans were the primary motivation for white flight, renters would leave first. In fact, owners usually move first. Ellen suggests that renters, having no investment at stake, feel less need to leave.[21] So it isn't just living near African Americans that bothers many white suburbanites; it is also concern for property values.

In the past, a fleeing family, "knowing" that property values are going down because blacks are moving in, often sold to a real estate speculator for less than market value, the agent having said, "It's all you can hope for now." Speculators had two advantages over regular buyers: they often offered cash, and they were white. Cash was important, because the selling family needed it for the down payment on their new house in the sundown suburb to which they were moving. Also, until recently many lending institutions would not grant mortgages to black families in still-white areas, so the middleman's role was essential. Second, the sellers saved face with their former neighbors by selling to a white. In one study in Chicago, 24 of 29 parcels that were sold between 1953 and 1961 were sold through speculators and purchased by black families on installment contracts.[22] Property values did not go down, especially not at first. On the contrary, usually the speculator *raised* the price substantially and then sold the home to a black family willing to pay more for a residence in one of the few "white" neighborhoods where blacks could buy. The average markup among the 24 Chicago parcels was 73%! Luigi Laurenti compared twenty interracial neighborhoods and nineteen all-white neighborhoods in seven cities from 1943 to 1955. He concluded, "The entry of nonwhites was much more often associated with price improvement or stability than with price weakening." Thus even though the first of Ellen's three predictions—that when African Americans move in, property values go down—isn't accurate, the fleeing white family never learned that part of the story. Instead, it "knew" that black newcomers lower property values and carried that prediction to its new community.[23]

Ellen's second prediction is that whites "know" that communities go all-black once a few African Americans enter. So they flee. It is the prophecy, not the actual racial composition of a town or neighborhood in the present—nor simple avoidance of African Americans—that prompts the exodus. Of course, it becomes a self-fulfilling prophecy because whites who believe it leave. Sundown suburbs are particularly likely to go overwhelmingly black once they crack and admit their first African American family. In the Cleveland metropolitan area in the 1980s, for instance, George Galster found that among census tracts starting with the same black percentage back in 1970, those predicted to have stronger "segregationist sentiments" lost much more of their white populations. Their own ideology supplies the reason. To those European American residents of sundown suburbs who believe it is correct to live in all-white towns, when even a handful of African American families move in, their town no longer seems defensible.[24]

Bellwood, Illinois, illustrates the process. Until 1968, Bellwood had been a sundown suburb west of Chicago. Then its first African American family moved in. By 1970, 1.1% of Bellwood's total population of 22,096 was black. At this point, the dam burst: by 1980 Bellwood was more than one-third black. Bellwood tried to stop the flood, restricting realtor solicitation and banning "For Sale" signs. Bellwood tried to end realtor steering by sending black and white would-be home buyers to see if African Americans got shown homes in "changing neighborhoods" while European Americans got shown homes in securely white suburbs. The suburb tried to market its homes to white home buyers and counsel blacks about available homes in nearby all-white suburbs. Bellwood even took its case before the United States Supreme Court and won the ability to sue realtors who steer, but it did no good—in fact, the case only further publicized to African Americans throughout the Chicago metropolitan area that Bellwood was now open to them. By 2000, Bellwood was 82% African American.[25]

Sometimes whites start to flee a town or neighborhood before the percentage of African Americans reaches even 1%. "Lily White Lynwood," for instance, as it was called, a sundown suburb of Los Angeles, had just 9 African Americans in 1960, and 89 "others," among 31,614 residents. All 9 were female; surely all were maids in white households. By 1970, 160 African Americans lived in Lynwood among 42,387 whites and 806 others, less than 0.4%, a tiny crack in the dike, but enough: ten years later, almost 15,000 blacks lived in Lynwood.[26] Now Mexicans and Mexican Americans also flooded in, and by 2000, fewer than 1,500 non-Hispanic whites still lived in Lynwood.

Sundown Suburbs Put Their Problems Elsewhere

We have seen that sundown suburbs behave as defended neighborhoods. Once they get into the NIMBY mind-set, they try to keep out *any* problem or "problem group," pawning off their own social problems on central cities and multiracial, multiclass inner suburbs. Consider those members of society who are dramatically downwardly mobile—some alcoholics and drug addicts; some Down syndrome children; most criminals; people unhinged and impoverished by divorce; many schizophrenics; elderly people whose illness and incapacity have exhausted their resources and their relatives; employees fired when an industry downsizes and no one wants their skills. Every social class—even the most affluent—generates some of these people. Elite sundown suburbs offer no facilities to house, treat, or comfort such people—no halfway houses for the mentally ill or ex-criminals, no residential drug treatment facilities, no public housing, often not even assisted-living complexes for the elderly or persons with disabilities. This is no accident. Elite white suburbanites don't want such facilities in their neighborhoods and have the prestige, money, and knowledge to make their objections count. "Without such homes, people with mental illnesses often wind up homeless, especially in wealthy areas," according to an AP article telling how an elite white neighborhood in Greenwich, Connecticut, blocked a halfway house for years.[27]

When sundown suburbanites do become homeless, they simply have to leave. Most sundown suburbs do not allow homeless people to spend the night on their streets, and of course they provide no shelters for them. "In suburban jurisdictions," said Nan Roman, of the National Alliance to End Homelessness, in 2000, "there is no sense that these are our people." Community leaders worry that if their suburb provides services, that will only bring more homeless people to their town because no other suburb does. The result, nationally, is that cities provide 49% of all homeless assistance programs, suburbs 19%, and rural areas 32%. Yet suburbs have more people than cities and rural areas combined. Less affluent inner suburbs and central cities must cope with the downwardly mobile people that more affluent sundown suburbs produce, as well as with their own. These social problems burden cities twice. First, cities provide some of the halfway houses, shelters, and other social services. Second, cities can tax neither their own agencies nor the nonprofit institutions that provide those services, even though they use police, fire protection, streets, and other city services.[28]

Black and interracial neighborhoods end up with most of the other "disamenities" in metropolitan areas, too, such as trash "transfer stations" (in former times these were "dumps"); impound lots for abandoned and illegally parked cars; storage lots for street cleaners, buses, and other city vehicles; public housing projects; and maintenance yards for street repair supplies. Zoning protects affluent white neighborhoods from these problems, which generate truck traffic, odors, and noise. Private disamenities, such as polluting industries, can make black and interracial areas still worse, while most sundown suburbs have the clout to keep them out. One result, according to survey data, is that African Americans are almost twice as likely as whites to rate their neighborhood "poor." Probably they're right! Foretelling that interracial neighborhoods will go downhill, compared to sundown neighborhoods, is the third prediction by whites that Ellen believes accounts for white flight. Again, whites don't have to be racist to want to avoid such neighborhoods.[29]

Suburban Hitchhikers

Not only disamenities but also amenities can burden cities and older multiracial suburbs. Such amenities as universities, museums, cathedrals, churches, parks, arts organizations, concert halls, and nonprofit hospitals are located in central cities but are used by people from the suburbs, including the sundown suburbs. Indeed, some amenities, such as private colleges and universities, are used *mostly* by suburbanites. These institutions do not pay property taxes.[30] Their users, too, pay no taxes to the city, except sales tax on incidental purchases. Yet cities provide services—police, streets, fire protection—to these amenities and their users. In some cities, as much as a third of the potential tax base is exempt from taxes, compared to as little as 3% in many suburbs. In some metropolitan areas, this has been an issue for a long time. In 1943, for example, Dallas Mayor J. W. Rodgers pointed out that "well-heeled" residents of the Park Cities, the two sundown "suburbs" entirely surrounded by Dallas, relied more than most Dallas residents on Love Field, the Dallas airport. They "needed to assume their rightful burden in its upkeep and administration," in the words of Dallas historian Darwin Payne. The *Dallas News* called the Park Cities " 'suburban hitchhikers' using Dallas's facilities free of charge."[31]

The use of city services by suburban visitors wouldn't be so bad if it were a two-way street, but it's not. City residents do not use suburban facilities equally and often are not allowed to. We have seen how sundown suburbs often barricade their amenities against outsiders or make them hard to find. No sign points to the beach in Darien, for example, and a visitor who does manage to find it encounters signs marking it "Private." A sentry checks even cyclists and pedestrians for beach stickers that only Darien residents can get.

Even basketball courts are amenities worth keeping African Americans away from in Ohio, according to a man who grew up in the sundown suburbs of Cincinnati: "Saint Bernard and Elmwood Place were two of a number of all-white towns in the Millcreek Valley area of Cincinnati when I was growing up. Just a few years ago, the parks and basketball hoops still bore signs saying that the facilities were for the use of St. Bernard residents only." [32]

One response might be, "What's wrong with that? Don't Darien taxpayers pay to keep that beach clean? Doesn't St. Bernard maintain those basketball courts?" But Darien residents would be furious if New York City kept them out of Central Park. Ohio suburbanites would protest if Cincinnati kept them away from its beautiful new Riverfront Park. Residents of sundown suburbs consider it their right to make use of the facilities of the central city. They do not reciprocate.

In yet another way, elite sundown suburbs fail to pay their way: their zoning, lot requirements, and other restrictions force their maids, supermarket clerks, police officers, and even teachers to live elsewhere. These people simply cannot afford to live in the affluent suburbs where they work. These suburbs have never allowed public housing, and they impose minimum lot and zoning restrictions that make private housing too costly. Thus the property taxes paid by affluent whites in elite sundown suburbs do not help pay for the city services their employees use. Instead, less affluent and less white towns house them and try to educate their children, without the benefit of the tax base their employers' homes and businesses would provide.

A few suburbs have done better in providing public housing, including Summit, New Jersey; Palo Alto, California; and Prince Georges County, Maryland. But again, it's hard for a suburb to do this as long as it's the only one; it may wind up majority-black and labeled a social problem. In the Washington metropolitan area, Prince Georges County was one of the few suburbs that allowed FHA-subsidized apartments; as a result, it wound up with nearly all of them, as of the mid-1970s. By 2000, the county was about 64% African American. [33]

Better Services, Lower Taxes

In his famous book *An American Dilemma,* written as World War II wound down, Gunnar Myrdal noted that residential segregation has been a key factor accounting for the subordinate status of African Americans. Separating people geographically makes it much easier to provide better city services to some than to others, to give some children better schooling than others, and indeed to label some people better than others. In Roosevelt, the black township on Long Island, "as tax money dried up, the schools withered," as *Washington Post* reporter Michael Powell put it. Across the United States, Jianping Shen concluded in 2003, schools with 50% or more minority enrollment had the highest rate of teachers teaching outside their field, the highest rate of inexperienced teachers and teachers with temporary certification, and the highest teacher attrition. Money is not the only issue. Professors in some schools of education routinely try to place their best graduates in elite suburban school districts, partly because they boast better working conditions and higher salaries, but also because they are more prestigious; hence the placements reflect credit back upon the graduate school. "The best teachers should be in the best schools"—this attitude permeates the field. "Most teachers consider it a promotion to move from poor to middle-class schools," Kahlenberg notes, "and the best teachers usually transfer out of low-income schools at the first opportunity." Again, the whites in Ingrid Ellen's research are often right to associate predominantly black neighborhoods with poor schools—even if it's not African Americans' fault.[34]

Often, the better schools and nicer amenities that suburbs offer come bundled with *lower* taxes. The reason is simple: elite suburbs often have "five times as much taxable property per capita as the poorest suburbs," according to social scientist Michael Danielson. In 1990, Philadelphia had the highest tax burden in its metropolitan area, yet brought in less money per pupil than elite suburbs with much lower tax rates. Black townships suffer from this problem even worse than cities. Roosevelt, for example, has a student population that was "99.7% black and Latino in 2002," according to Powell. "They attend decrepit schools and read tattered textbooks." Yet, "to support these failing schools, homeowners here pay the highest property tax rates on Long Island, as their 1½-square-mile town has no commercial tax base to speak of. Far wealthier and far whiter towns border Roosevelt to the north and east."[35]

Companies frequently leave interracial areas to get lower taxes. Often, sundown suburbs wind up with an area's best taxable draws. In 1956, for example, Edina, Minnesota, got Southdale shopping center, still a potent commercial site. On Long Island, what Powell calls "the massive and successful Roosevelt Field shopping malls" were built just five miles north of Roosevelt, "with the help of county subsidies and zoning regulations. From the point of view of Roosevelt, however, the malls might as well have been in Des Moines, because tax revenue is not shared across town lines." The result was catastrophic for the black township. "As Roosevelt Field thrived, stores died in Roosevelt itself," further shrinking Roosevelt's taxable property base.[36]

Sundown Communities and the Political System

Finally, sundown towns influence their residents' politics. With this discussion we return to the effects of these towns on whites with which the chapter began, but now in the context of their impact on our political system as a whole. The racial exclusiveness of sundown suburbs helped move the Republican Party away from the equal-rights creed of Lincoln, which had lingered in vestigial form as late as 1960. Most independent sundown towns started out Democratic, but beginning in 1964, voters defected for racial reasons—first to Alabama governor George Wallace and then to Richard Nixon and subsequent Republicans. Anecdotal evidence and some statistical analyses suggest that in 1964, in his first presidential campaign, Wallace carried most sundown towns in the Indiana Democratic primary, for example, while winning 35% of the white vote statewide. He did even better in the Wisconsin primary, winning more than 40% of the white vote. His only issue—and he was clear about it—was President Lyndon Johnson's use of the federal bureaucracy to improve race relations. For Wallace to do so well as an awkward, angry southern white in his first try for national office made a striking comment about midwestern white voters and their desire for continued white supremacy.[37]

In the 1964 general election, the two parties again began to articulate consistently different racial programs, for the first time since 1890. Democrats after Johnson would be identified with civil rights, and Republicans after Goldwater would be identified with resistance to civil rights. In 1968, Richard Nixon followed an explicit "southern strategy," appealing to white southerners upset about black claims to equality and dismissing black voters. Nixon called for "law and order," condemned civil rights (and student) protests, and said he favored neither integrationists nor segregationists. He appointed four Supreme Court justices thought to be soft on desegregation, ordered the Justice Department to oppose immediate desegregation in 1969 in *Alexander v. Holmes,* and sent a bill to Congress to outlaw busing for desegregation.

Nixon's southern strategy also turned out to be a winning strategy in sundown suburbs and independent sundown towns. After 1964, most sundown towns and suburbs voted Republican or, in 1968 and 1972, for Wallace. Before 1964, Owosso, a sundown town between Lansing and Flint, Michigan, had usually voted Republican, but not for racial reasons, the two parties not being clearly different in racial policies. That year, however, it went for Democrat Lyndon Johnson, "an exception and a mistake, according to everyone interviewed here" by a *New York Times* reporter in 1968. In 1968, Owosso switched to George Wallace. "A lot of people like what he has to say about handling riots and aggressive law enforcement," said a local Republican leader. The reporter saw through this rhetoric, noting, "Such talk seems ironic in a town where the most pressing law-and-order problem is teen-agers' hot-rodding past the pizza house on Friday and Saturday nights." The real issue was that "Owosso has no Negroes, has never had any, and, according to many private opinions, does not want any." After 1968, Owosso voted Republican.[38]

Owosso was hardly alone. Bill Outis grew up in Sandoval, Illinois, which he thinks was a sundown town, moved to Ramsey in 1962, another sundown town, and now lives in Pana, a third. In 1968, he recalled, Sandoval and Ramsey high school students held straw votes for president. About half voted for Nixon, the Republican and eventual winner, half for Wallace, and *one student* in each high school chose Hubert Humphrey, the Democrat nominee. Dearborn, Michigan, held a huge rally for Wallace in May 1972, and Wallace went on to win a stunning victory in Michigan's 1972 Democratic primary. Across the North, Wallace frequently spoke in sundown towns, where he knew he could count on positive crowds. Kathy Spillman reports on her hometown in upstate New York: "George Wallace was so popular in North Tonawanda. And this was a Democratic union town!"[39]

With his "southern strategy," Richard Nixon headed off Wallace in 1968. Once in office, Nixon stated that denying housing to people because of their race was wrong, but it was equally wrong for towns to have integrated housing "imposed from Washington by bureaucratic fiat." The next successful Republican candidate, Ronald Reagan, deliberately chose a citadel of white supremacy—the Neshoba County Fair in Mississippi—as the kickoff site for his presidential campaign, where he declared his support for "states' rights," code words signaling that the federal government should leave local jurisdictions alone to handle the "race problem" as they see fit. George W. Bush understands the rhetoric in sundown suburbs, having chosen one (Highland Park, Texas) as home for his family. As a result of such leadership, Republicans have carried most sundown towns since 1968, sometimes achieving startling unanimity. For example, Donahue noted that every single student from Nickerson, Kansas, that he met during their field trip to Washington in 2002 was sympathetic to the Republican Party. Of course, those groups that usually vote most Democratic—African Americans and Jewish Americans—simply aren't represented in sundown towns. So the "southern strategy" turned out to be a "southern and sundown town strategy," especially effective in sundown suburbs. Macomb County, for example, the next county north of Detroit, voted overwhelmingly for Wallace in the 1972 Democratic primary. Wooed by Nixon, many of these voters then became "Reagan Democrats" and now are plain Republicans. The biggest single reason, according to housing attorney Alexander Polikoff, was anxiety about "blacks trapped in ghettos trying to penetrate white neighborhoods." [40]

Republicans do especially well in sundown suburbs owing not only to their racial ideology, but also to their NIMBY principles and small-government philosophy. [41] But these principles too have a racial tinge and tie in with the soclexia that results from living in sundown towns and suburbs. In *Chain Reaction,* their analysis of the GOP's appeal to racism from 1964 to 1990, Thomas and Mary Edsall pointed to Republicans' use of the stereotype that whites work and succeed, while blacks don't work, hence don't succeed. As former Nixon aide John Ehrlichman put it, Republicans win in the suburbs partly because they present positions on crime, education, and housing in such a way that a voter could "avoid admitting to himself that he was attracted by a racist appeal." [42]

Sundown suburbs are politically independent and usually quash efforts at metropolitan government. Their school systems are separate and usually oppose metro-wide desegregation. They resist mightily what they view as intrusions by people or governments from the larger metropolitan area or the state. In New Jersey, trying to comply with a New Jersey supreme court decision mandating equal educational opportunity, the legislature passed the Quality Education Act, and Governor Jim Florio proposed higher taxes on families earning more than $100,000 to pay for it. Suburbanites responded by voting out of office many of the politicians who supported the equalization bill, including Florio, whom they replaced with Republican Christine Todd Whitman. [43]

The Edsalls point out that the principle of self-interest explains what otherwise might seem to be an ideological contradiction: sundown suburbanites usually try to minimize expenditures by the state and federal governments, but locally they favor "increased suburban and county expenditures, guaranteeing the highest possible return to themselves on their tax dollars." The Edsalls cite Gwinnett County, Georgia, as an example. Gwinnett, east of Atlanta, is "one of the fastest growing suburban jurisdictions in the nation, heavily Republican (75.5% for Bush [senior]), affluent, and white (96.6%)." Its residents "have been willing to tax and spend on their own behalf as liberally as any Democrats." Such within-county expenditures increase the inequality between white suburbs and interracial cities. They also do nothing to redress or pay for the ways that Gwinnett residents use and rely upon Atlanta and its public services.[44]

Meanwhile, white suburbs favor "policies of fiscal conservatism at the federal level." Interestingly, despite enjoying more than half a century of federal intervention on behalf of whites in suburbia—FHA and Veterans Administration (VA) loan guarantees, FHA and VA policies that shut out blacks, highway subsidies, and all the rest—residents feel they achieved home ownership in their all-white suburb entirely on their own. Since 1968, whenever African Americans have mobilized to try to get the federal government to act on *their* behalf, suburban Republicans have rejected the idea: "We've done so much for them already." Many white suburbanites identified attempts of the federal government to be fair about housing, such as the 1968 housing act, with the Democratic Party, and considered them outrageous examples of "special interests" and "federal intervention in local affairs."

Today the most important national impact of sundown towns and suburbs is through their influence on the Republican Party. The Edsalls conclude, "The suburban vote is becoming the core of the Republican base." Since elected officials from safe districts develop seniority, suburban Republicans dominate committees in the House of Representatives and in state legislatures when Republicans control those bodies. They also wield much power over their party in most states.[45]

Where Is "the Problem"?

Most people, looking around their metropolitan area, perceive inner-city African American neighborhoods as "the problem." It then follows all too easily that African Americans themselves can get perceived as the source of the problem. Residents of affluent sundown suburbs rarely see such newly black elite suburbs as Country Club Hills, south of Chicago, or Mitchellville, east of Washington, D.C., but problematic inner-city and inner-suburban neighborhoods are on their commute to the city's center. So whites generalize: blacks can't do anything right, can't even keep up their own neighborhoods. All African Americans get tarred by the obvious social problems of the inner city. For that matter, some ghetto residents themselves buy into the notion that they are the problem and behave accordingly.

Focusing on African Americans and overlooking the impact of sundown suburbs on the social system as "the problem" is understandable. When I visit central cities and sundown suburbs, the former look problematic to me too.

As I drove with friends in the late 1990s through an overwhelmingly white elite section of Lower Merion, just outside Philadelphia, for example, no problems seemed evident. The streets were in good repair, the houses were in perfect condition, the landscaping was gorgeous. White racism was nowhere visible. A few miles west, in the Ardmore part of Lower Merion, problems struck our eyes, sometimes our noses, or even our buttocks, transmitted by the suspension of our car. Ardmore is an interracial neighborhood; most of the people visible walking on the streets, playing on the sidewalks, or washing their cars are African Americans. Ardmore has been saddled with most of Lower Merion's disamenities, such as halfway houses and maintenance yards, perhaps because its residents are not as politically connected or socially powerful as families in the rich white neighborhood.

The affluent white and interracial working-class parts of Lower Merion are part of the same political jurisdiction, so the unfairness in clumping most of Lower Merion's disamenities in one area is clear. It is not quite so obvious how the pleasures of a lovely spring day in Kenilworth, say, are the flip side of the problems in distressed neighborhoods just eight miles away in Chicago. Since affluent sundown suburbs are not politically connected to nearby inner-city neighborhoods, the system of white supremacy that makes them so much nicer is not obvious. Most people automatically problematize the ghetto. The problems in black neighborhoods look like black problems.

It takes an exercise of the sociological imagination to problematize the sundown suburb. As one drives west from downtown on Chicago Avenue toward Oak Park, the adjacent suburb, the problems of the Near Northwest neighborhood in Chicago are plain. Oak Park then presents its own problem: can it stay interracial, having gone from 0.2% African American in 1970 to 22.4% in 2000? The source of both problems lies not on Chicago Avenue in either city, however, but elsewhere—in neighborhoods miles away that look great, such as Kenilworth, which in 2000 had not one black household among its 2,494 total population. Once one knows its manifestations, white supremacy is visible in Kenilworth, the sundown suburb, and in Near Northwest Chicago, and it is inferable in Oak Park as well. Lovely white enclaves such as Kenilworth withdraw resources disproportionately from the city. They encourage the people who run our corporations, many of whom live in them, not to see race as their problem. The prestige of these suburbs invites governmental officials to respond more rapidly to concerns of their residents, who are likely to be viewed as more important people than black inner-city inhabitants. And they make interracial suburbs such as Oak Park difficult to keep as interracial oases.

Are these problems of metropolitan areas getting worse or better? Is our nation getting over sundown towns, or do they continue unabated into the 21st century? What effect is America's increasing racial and ethnic complexity having on sundown towns and suburbs? These are the questions the next chapter will address.

PART VI

The Present and Future of Sundown Towns

14

Sundown Towns Today

In 1968, the Kerner Commission . . . warned that the United States was in danger of splitting into "two societies, one black, one white—separate and unequal." Over thirty years later, that danger seems to have been realized. The dream of a residentially integrated society has been laid to rest by the phenomenon of white flight from the cities and a marked unwillingness of whites to live in neighborhoods with significant numbers of those of another race.

—Donald Deskins Jr. and Christopher Bettinger,
"Black and White Spaces in Selected Metropolitan Areas," 2002[1]

DURING THE LAST FEW YEARS while I have been doing the research for this book, many people have asked, after learning that hundreds or thousands of sundown towns and suburbs dot the map of the United States, "Still? Surely it's not like that today?" It is a good question—so good that it's hard to answer, because it is hard to know for sure whether a town remains sundown as of the present moment. But those who ask the question usually mean it rhetorically and assume the answer to be "Of course not."

Unfortunately, many towns are still locked into the exclusionary policies of the past, and this chapter will begin by looking at a few of them. We will then see that some social scientists conclude that America as a social system is moving toward more intense residential segregation; such innovations as neighborhood associations and gated communities support that judgment.

Discouraging as those trends are, I take a more optimistic view. Sundown towns have been on the defensive since the start of the Civil Rights Movement, which prompted the zeitgeist to move back toward what it had been before the Nadir of race relations set in. We will see that 1968 may be as important a date in changing the spirit of race relations in America in a positive direction as 1890 was in a negative direction. Since 1968, residential prohibitions against Jews, Asians, Native Americans, and Hispanics have mostly disappeared.

Even regarding African Americans, the sundown signs and formal policies have come down everywhere. Many towns and suburbs relaxed their exclusionary policies in the 1980s and 1990s, and we will probe why. In the end, whether we are moving toward more or less racial exclusion will be left for you to assess.

The Persistence of Sundown Towns

It's easy to empathize with those who assume that sundown towns cannot still be "like that today." That they still might be interferes with our sense of progress and our claim to live under law. And progress has been made. As recently as the 1990s, some sundown towns still flaunted their condition with signs saying "Don't Let The Sun Go Down On You in __," according to credible reports from Arab, Alabama; Marlowe, Oklahoma; and Sullivan, Missouri; in 1998, a related text was posted in White County, Indiana. By 2005, I knew of no town so reckless, although two small towns in Tennessee still displayed black mules painted near their city limits (see Portfolio 8).[2]

But was this apparent progress real? Are sundown policies no longer enforced? Consider the experience of Clarence Moore, a pioneering archaeologist in the Lower Mississippi Valley. In 1910, mostly using black workers, he excavated American Indian sites on Little River, which parallels the Mississippi a few miles northwest of Memphis. Dan and Phyllis Morse, who reissued Moore's classic work in 1998, state in their preface that Moore "dared not proceed beyond Lepanto, Arkansas, on Little River because blacks were not tolerated there. Race relations remain strained in that region." That's a polite way of saying what my research in the area confirms: almost a century later, African Americans *still* do not and probably cannot live in much of the northeastern corner of Arkansas or the western half of the Bootheel of Missouri. Nor is this area unique.[3]

Many decades ago, some Americans were shocked that towns and counties openly kept out people of color. During World War II, Malcolm Ross of the federal Fair Employment Practices Commission learned about Calhoun County, the sundown county 65 miles southwest of Springfield, Illinois. He was outraged, calling the county "an earthly paradise for those who hate Negro Americans. But can the rest of America remain indifferent to their 'self-determination?' " Ross obviously meant the question rhetorically. Surely he would have been dismayed to learn that sixty years later, the 2000 census would record not one black household in Calhoun County.[4]

Similarly, in 1952 Paul Angle wrote in *Bloody Williamson*, his famous history of Ku Klux Klan and other violence in southern Illinois, "Even today, in several Williamson County towns . . . no Negro is permitted to remain overnight." More than half a century later, in several towns in Williamson County and adjacent Franklin County, no African American is yet permitted to live.[5] Zeigler, for example, had no black householder in 2000, and when I asked the town librarian in 2002 if she thought Zeigler had stopped being a sundown town, she replied, "I wish it would change, but I don't see it changing here." According to Deidre Meadows, who graduated from Johnston City High School in 1990, "When I was a sophomore in high school, we had a black family move in town for about a month. They were driven out by hate crimes." The 2000 census showed not one African American family among 3,557 residents in Johnston City. Speaking in 2002 of a third sundown town, Sesser, which also had no black household in the 2000 census, an African American in nearby Du Quoin said, "You would have some problems if you went there, right now." Angle's phrase "even today" connotes his sense that sundown towns were an anachronistic relic from our past in 1952. I wonder what he would think to learn that such practices were still allowed in 2005.[6]

Corbin, a sundown town in the Kentucky Cumberlands, had not relented as of 1990. In his 1991 movie on the community, *Trouble Behind,* Robby Heason asked a young white man if it would be a good thing for blacks to move into Corbin. "Black people should not live here," he replied. "They never have, and they shouldn't." He did not know that African Americans *had* lived in Corbin until whites drove them out at gunpoint in 1919, and his attitude surely boded ill should a black family try to move in. As of 2000, almost none had; Corbin's 7,742 people included just 6 African Americans; adjacent North Corbin had just 1 African American among 1,662 inhabitants. Around 1990, McDonald's brought in an African American to manage a new restaurant, but he and his family left before it even opened, reportedly after a cross was burned in his yard.[7]

Although the public accommodations section of the 1964 Civil Rights Act did not get enforced in most sundown towns for at least ten years after its passage, since the 1980s, most restaurants and hotels in sundown towns have complied with the law and do now provide food and lodging to transients. Now African Americans can eat in restaurants and sleep in motels in otherwise all-white towns. Buying or renting residential property in neighborhoods is quite another matter.

Even public accommodations can still be a problem in out-of-the-way sundown towns. Speaking of the western half of the Bootheel, in rural southeastern Missouri, Frank Nickell, director of the Center for Regional History, wrote in 2002, "Many restaurants, motels, cemeteries, etc., remain off-limits to African-Americans." In some sundown towns, African Americans may get served successfully but must endure glares from white customers while they eat. Whites in Erwin, Tennessee, drove African Americans from Unicoi County in 1918. Rebecca Tolley-Stokes, archivist at East Tennessee State University, wrote about a recent incident involving Erwin:

> Several years ago I was friends with a woman who worked at a convenience store just off the interstate [in Johnston City, twelve miles north of Erwin]. I was visiting with her one evening when a black couple stopped there for gas and to inquire about a hotel room for the night in the next town, Erwin. Jennifer told them that they would have trouble getting a room if they just showed up. Additionally, she told them that she would call and make the reservation for them because if the owner spoke to someone who she/he thought was black, the owner would tell the caller that their rooms were all booked up.

In Erwin, motel operators apparently still wanted to discriminate, but not enough to cause an altercation. Erwin still had no black households as of 2000, and according to Tolley-Stokes, "all the blacks in the area have been warned within their own communities to steer clear of Erwin." In a few other towns, an altercation seems likely if an African American tries to stay after dark. In 1995, Christy Thompson of Cedar Key, Florida, said about African American tourists, "I saw a couple of 'em not long ago, a black man and woman riding bicycles down by the pier, but I guarantee they didn't spend the night. They've *all* been told there's only one way in and one way out and you better be out before dark." That was 1995. What about 2004? Cedar Key had no black households in the 2000 census.[8]

Even after the turn of the millennium, there were also still towns that African Americans believed were not safe simply to pass through. "Never walk in Greenwood [Arkansas] or you will die," an African American college student said, dead seriously, to a group of other students and me at the University of the Ozarks in 2002. The 2000 census listed 17 African Americans in Greenwood, however, including two households, so perhaps his information was out of date. A black undergraduate at the University of Illinois–Chicago told in September 2001 of Beecher, a white suburb of Chicago, "Blacks need to have enough gas to get through." Certainly they would not want to have to purchase fuel from the Beecher gas station called Knute's Kountry Korner, whose three *K*'s are no accident, according to the student.

Beecher's reputation in the black community may be warranted; in the 2000 census, the town had 1,993 people, including not one African American.[9]

Oral history in and around New Palestine, Indiana, suggests that African Americans do well to be wary of it. If they can help it, African Americans "don't drive through New Palestine," according to a former New Palestine resident, who has friends in the community. A black woman moved to New Palestine "somewhere between 1992 and 1995 and lasted two days." A former teacher tells that there is oral history still current in the school system that the KKK donated land for the New Palestine High School, "with the stipulation the mascot was to be a dragon." A professor at DePauw University confirmed that New Palestine's athletic teams had been the Redbirds; "in the 1920s, when the KKK craze hit, they became the Dragons." School officials contest this and claim "Dragons" is a coincidence. Still, the 2000 census lists New Palestine with no African Americans at all, and to be the first African American family to move into New Palestine would require courage. And what do we make of the comment that the manager of a gas station in Mt. Sterling, Ohio, made in 1991 to an African American woman, then 30 years old, when she stopped for directions: "Girl, you don't know what danger you're in"? Was he being helpful? Trying to steer her away from trouble? Or himself trying to intimidate her? Or just being "funny"? Prudently, she did not do the research required to find out, but Mt. Sterling had no black family in it at the time.[10]

The Present Moment

I cannot know if every town I describe as sundown in the past is still sundown as of 2005. Indeed, I do not think that every town I describe as sundown even in the recent past is still sundown today. The foregoing anecdotes don't prove that African Americans *cannot* live in Zeigler, Erwin, Cedar Key, Beecher, New Palestine, Mt. Sterling, and other such places, even though the 2000 census does not show a single black family in any of those towns. Proving continuing exclusion to the present moment is difficult,[11] and by its nature the proof must be anecdotal.

We shall consider several examples, beginning with Anna, Illinois. The 2000 census listed 89 blacks among Anna's 5,136 total population. Anna also had 14 Asians, 49 Mexican Americans, 24 other Latinos, 13 American Indians, and a few persons listing more than one race. At first glance, Anna seems no longer to be a sundown town. But Anna's 89 African Americans may all reside at the state mental hospital. The 2000 census lists just one family with a black householder in Anna, with just two people, and we cannot be sure they are both black.[12] In 2002, neither the Anna newspaper editor nor the reference librarian could think of a single black family in Anna or in adjacent Jonesboro. "Oh no, there are no black people in Anna today," a farmer near Anna said in 2004. Is Anna still sundown? A prudent answer would be yes, at least until there is evidence to the contrary, given that the phrase "Ain't No Niggers Allowed" is still current in and around the town. But I do not know for sure.[13]

Has Villa Grove changed—the town in central Illinois that sounded a siren at 6 PM every evening to tell African Americans to be gone? In about 1999, Villa Grove stopped sounding its siren. I had hoped it stopped the practice because residents became ashamed of why it was first put in place, no longer cared to explain its origin to their children or guests, and had reconsidered their sundown policy. No, I learned, it stopped owing to complaints about the noise from residents living near the water tower, on which the siren was located (see Portfolio 9). On the other hand, in 2000 Villa Grove had 8 African Americans among its 2,553 residents, in two households. Perhaps Villa Grove now accepts black families, perhaps not. Certainly many African Americans in nearby Champaign-Urbana still avoid driving through or stopping in the town.

It isn't always clear, even to a town's own residents, whether African Americans can live there in peace. A state trooper told of his hometown, Chandler, Indiana, near Evansville. It had been a sundown town complete with sign. Around 1971, a black family moved in, to be greeted by a burning cross in their front yard; "they were run off." Two years later, a second family tried, and they were not molested; years later their children graduated successfully from the high school. So Chandler seemed to have opened up. But Ronald Willis, who pastored the Methodist Church in Chandler from 2001 to 2004, painted a gloomier portrait. In the fall of 2001, a black family moved into a house across the street from the church, and Willis heard "words of hatred, violence, and intolerance" from members of his own congregation as they dropped off their children for preschool. "Within a few days the family moved." Willis went on to tell of inhumane acts that he witnessed as late as 2003. The 2000 census credited Chandler with three black households, but their situation seems precarious.[14]

What about Martinsville, Illinois, a sundown town near Terre Haute, Indiana? In 2002, I asked an attorney who grew up in Martinsville, "What would happen if a black family moved into Martinsville today?" "I really don't know," he replied. "It's hard to imagine that there'd be a violent reaction, and yet, it wouldn't surprise me." As of 2002, none had tried, although two black men had worked for Marathon Oil Company in Martinsville around 1990 and had not been run out.[15]

Consider this claim about Fouke, in southwest Arkansas, made by "goneaviking" at the discussion site alt.flame.niggers: "As of 2 PM May 23 2001, it is still nigger free, no niggers bus in, and urine head would piss in his pants if he stopped in that town." I don't think "goneaviking" lives in Fouke, but some citizens of Fouke may share this attitude toward African Americans. Smokey Crabtree, who does live in Fouke, confirmed in 2001, "As of this date there are no colored people living within miles of Fouke, so the attention getter, the means to shake the little town up isn't 'the Russians are coming,' it's 'someone is importing colored people into town.' " The census found two elderly African Americans among Fouke's 814 residents in 2000, but no household, and I believe "goneaviking" and Crabtree. At the least, they show that considerable animus exists in and about Fouke toward the idea of black residents.[16]

It's pretty clear that North Judson, in northern Indiana, has not given in. A history teacher from that area said in 2001 that a black family moved there in the late 1990s but left within a week, owing to harassment. The 2000 census showed just 1 African American—a child—in the town of 1,675 people. And Elwood, in central Indiana, definitely has not. "Elwood is by reputation still off-limits," a black former police officer in nearby Marion reported in 2002, and the 2000 census confirmed his judgment, finding no African Americans in Elwood's 9,455 population. There is no way such a large town could show such a complete absence without continuing enforcement. According to a teacher in a nearby town, in recent years Elwood has hosted[17] a Ku Klux Klan headquarters and an annual KKK parade.[18]

The 2000 census

In the 2000 census, Scott County, west of Springfield, Illinois, had not one black household. Stark County, northwest of Peoria, had just one. Mason County, between Peoria and Springfield, where oral history says the sheriff used to tell black newcomers to move on, had not a single black family. It is unlikely that entire counties, located near sizable interracial cities, could show such a dearth of African Americans without continuing enforcement. On the other hand, sometimes the census can falsely indicate that a town or county is still sundown, if African Americans have moved in since it was taken. Steeleville, Illinois, 60 miles southeast of St. Louis, had 2,077 people in 2000, with no African Americans. But according to a librarian at the Steeleville Library, since 2001 "about a dozen Mexicans and three or four colored" moved to Steeleville to work at a new plant. So Steeleville may no longer be a sundown town.[19]

When the census shows an influx of African Americans, it can also be inaccurate to conclude that a former sundown town now admits blacks. As we saw in earlier chapters, the 2000 census includes African Americans in institutions, live-in servants, and plain errors, and is already five years out of date. For Pinckneyville, Illinois, near Steeleville, the 2000 census shows 1,331 blacks among 5,464 residents, but that includes the inmates, mostly African American, of a large state prison. The census lists five households with a black householder, but two longtime residents I talked with agreed that only one African American couple lived in the town. That couple had lived in town for some 25 years and raised children there. One of my conversation partners asked the other his view of them. "They're harmless," he replied. After he left, she said that his comment shocked her. "You see what an insult that is? Would you like that to be said about you? This man is intelligent, he's very well-spoken, he sat behind me at a funeral and so I know he has a beautiful singing voice. 'Harmless!' " She was disappointed in her friend. I pointed out that his comment was typical sundown town rhetoric—if whites judge a given African American harmless, then she or he can stay—and she agreed. Such a judgment exempts *that* family, while implying that whites still reserve the right to bar blacks who have *not* proven themselves "harmless." A black resident of nearby Du Quoin said that Pinckneyville's one black couple was joined by another in 2000 (just in time for the census), but the landlord wouldn't renew their lease, probably owing to pressure from his white neighbors, so the couple moved to Du Quoin. Thus we cannot simply list Pinckneyville as no longer sundown owing to the 2000 census. Research today is required. In August 2004, a woman who grew up in Pinckneyville wrote: "I was just home this past weekend for a funeral, and while the 'official' anti-black rules may no longer be in effect, the talk and the attitudes sure are."[20]

There is no substitute for firsthand research. Such information, up-to-date at least as of 2002, suggests that Windsor, a small town of 1,100 people in central Illinois, has not changed its anti-black policy. The 2000 census found no African Americans in Windsor, and a businessman who runs a bookstore in nearby Mattoon told a story that explains why:

Just this past summer [2002] a customer came in [from Windsor] and related to me that she was babysitting for a friend's half-black grandchild. Within a few days of beginning to watch the child she was threatened, a cross was burnt in her yard, and her own children were threatened. She said she had filed a police report but didn't know if that even made it to a public record. She didn't seem to think that the officer taking the report cared. One of the gentlemen attending our church grew up in Windsor, and as we reminisced one evening he shared that blacks were definitely not welcome.[21]

It seems reasonable to use the present tense as of this writing: African Americans *cannot* live in Windsor, as well as most of the other towns described above. But again, that was 2002. Before coming to a conclusion about a specific town as of *this* moment, do your own research.

Sundown Exurbs

Not only do many sundown towns remain all-white, but whites are still forming new ones and converting independent sundown towns to sundown suburbs by fleeing to them from newly desegregating inner suburbs. One way to find these new sundown places is by studying what the census calls CDPs—census designated places. These are unincorporated areas that nevertheless contain substantial residential populations, often more than 2,500. Many are new developments that have not yet incorporated and probably will do so by the next census. Many are distant suburbs—"exurbs"—that exemplify urban sprawl. Other CDPs have remained unincorporated for decades because residents are content to have counties supply their schooling, policing, and other services.

CDPs vary from census to census, so I mostly omitted them from my analysis, having my hands more than full with my already impossible effort to learn something about the past of every all-white incorporated town larger than 1,000. I couldn't help notice, however, that CDPs seemed much more likely to be all-white in 1990 and 2000 than did incorporated places. This trend is discouraging, because it means we are growing new sundown exurbs just as many of our older sundown suburbs are finally giving up their restrictive policies.

Sundown exurbs often breathe new vitality into independent sundown towns that otherwise might become smaller and more obsolete. I anticipated finding such exurbs in metropolitan areas, and I was not disappointed. Independent sundown towns in northwestern Indiana, for example, are filling with whites fleeing sundown suburbs of Chicago as they become interracial. But I had not anticipated finding sundown exurbs around smaller cities with much smaller black populations. In central Illinois, whites depart Peoria for

Morton and Metamora. They leave Springfield for Sherman and Ashland. Little sundown towns such as Farmer City, Mahomet, St. Joseph, and Villa Grove have become havens for whites who commute to work in Champaign-Urbana.

White flight from majority-black large cities such as Birmingham or Detroit to sundown suburbs is not news, but flight from smaller cities such as Champaign-Urbana is a new phenomenon, partly because such cities are not very black. Nevertheless, race is definitely a factor in many people's decision to subject themselves to such commutes. A Champaign-Urbana resident emphasized, "People leave Champaign-Urbana and move out to Farmer City, St. Joe, and so forth, *to* live in an all-white town." In 2000, Champaign was just 15.6% black and Urbana 14.3%, so five-sixths of their residents were non-black. Surprised that whites would find living in such a majority uncomfortable, I asked, *"In order* to live in an all-white town?" "Yes," she replied, and several residents of Mahomet and Monticello agreed. In 2000, Mahomet had 7 African Americans among 4,877 people (0.1%), Monticello 4 among 5,138 (0.1%), St. Joseph 3 among 2,912 (0.1%), and for the purists, Farmer City had 0 among 2,055.[22]

Similarly, whites fleeing the African American population of Decatur (19.5%) move to places such as Maroa (0.2%), Niantic (0.0%), and Pana (0.1%), 30 miles south. Consider this conversation I had in 2001 with a spokeswoman for Pana:

> [Why do you like Pana?]
> Because it's quiet. We don't have any—[Breaks off]
> We don't have—[Breaks off]
> Well, it's quiet.
> [You say the schools are good. Are they better than Decatur's?]
> Yes . . . We don't have much of a racial mix here. So we don't have some of the problems they have. Our kids feel real safe here. There's no police in the schools. Well, there's one, but he comes in and goes out. It's just real quiet here.

Her satisfaction with Pana partly owes to its "racial mix": 4 blacks among 4,514 people, including no black household and no children of school age. Even though Decatur is just one-fifth black, Pana residents are very aware and wary of its African American population. When Jesse Jackson came to Decatur in 1999 to garner publicity for several African Americans expelled from high school for fighting in the stands during a football game, residents of Pana expressed intense satisfaction about their isolation from that kind of fray. As one resident said, "If Jesse Jackson did stuff again in Decatur, you'd hear 'nigger' all over McDonald's in Pana."[23]

The lengths some whites go to avoid African Americans is surprising. The seat of Forsyth County is 40 miles from Atlanta. In 2002, a newcomer relayed that when her family moved to the Atlanta area, "our realtor told us that if we did not like 'blacks' then Forsyth was the perfect place for us." Despite the distance, Forsyth County evolved from independent sundown county to sundown suburb before finally desegregating in the late 1990s. Oak Grove, Missouri, has become a bedroom community for people working in Independence and even Kansas City who seek an all-white environment, even though it lies more than 40 miles east of Kansas City. Whites commute to Birmingham, Alabama, from all-white Cullman, 50 miles away. Whites leave Los Angeles for Bishop, California, 300 miles away, because Los Angeles is "too black," although this is a relocation, not a commute. In their search for stable white neighborhoods, some white families have moved across the country, leaving the suburbs of large multiracial metropolitan areas for smaller and less multiracial areas.[24]

Surely the white-flight prize goes to those who flee Joplin, Missouri. A librarian in the Joplin Public Library told of her neighbor who moved from Joplin to Webb City around 1985, because "his daughter was about to enter the seventh grade and he didn't want her to go to school with blacks at that age." The librarian stayed in touch during the relocation process and reported:

> At one point [the mother] told me she had found the perfect house for their family, only it was on the wrong side of the street. The line between Joplin and Webb City was that street, and the house she liked was on the Joplin side, so she couldn't consider it. Eventually they found a house in Webb City.

Webb City adjoins Joplin, as the story implies, but the move amazes because Joplin itself was just 2% black. Webb City, on the other hand, had just 1 African American among its 7,500 residents, and that person was not of school age.[25]

White flight to sundown exurbs is a national problem. Forsyth County more than doubled in the 1990s, making it the second fastest-growing county in the country. While Forsyth is no longer flatly closed to African Americans, for every new black resident 100 new whites move in. Many of the other fast-growing counties share similar demographics, including Delaware County,

2.6% black, outside Columbus, Ohio; Pike County, Pennsylvania, 3.3% black, outside New York City; and Douglas County, 0.7% black, near Denver. The racial motivation behind this sprawl is clear, at least to Atlanta sociologist Robert Bullard: "That's not where people of color are." [26]

Neighborhood Associations

In addition to sundown exurbs, another innovation threatens to maintain sundown suburbs, morphed into a new form: suburbs hypersegregated by social class. I first noticed this alarming development in 1999, driving past large subdivisions north of Dallas. On one side, for as far as I could see, were "Exclusive Homes from $279,000 to $299,000." On the other, again stretching to the horizon, were "Exclusive Homes from $299,000 to $339,000," or thereabouts. The authors of *Suburban Nation* decry this trend: "For the first time we are now experiencing ruthless segregation by minute gradations of income." If a lot owner tries to build a $200,000 house in a $350,000 development, "the homeowners' association will immediately sue." [27]

As they did with separation from African Americans, realtors and developers tout class-based segregation as prudent investment strategy. In a 2001 syndicated article, Ellen Martin advised home buyers not to ignore the "financial advantages" of "a prestigious address and a fancy ZIP code." She quoted Leo Berard, "charter president" of the National Association of Exclusive Buyer Agents: "You're almost always better off trading down on the amenities of a home if the payoff is getting into a classy neighborhood." Then the home is more likely to appreciate in value. [28]

Such thinking may be prudent for the individual investor, but the result on the societal level is a dramatic increase in the separation of the rich from the poor, and even from the only slightly less rich. In 1970, as this new economic segregation got under way based on these minute differences in house price, Kenneth Jackson noted that the median household income in cities was 80% of that in suburbs. Just thirteen years later, it had sunk to 72%. According to economist Richard Muth, writing around 1980, the median income in American cities rose at about 8% per mile as one moved away from the central business district. By ten miles away, income doubled. The United States already has more economic inequality than any other industrialized nation; now we are winding up with greater geographic separation between the classes.

Homeowners associations maintain the barriers once residents have moved in. The resulting isolation has unfortunate consequences for the rich, the poor, and the country, just as the previous chapters showed the unfortunate repercussions of sundown towns upon whites, blacks, and the social system. Children of the rich don't learn working-class skills or develop respect for working-class people, because every nearby family inhabits the same occupational niche as their parents. Poor children, meanwhile, end up with little knowledge of the occupations of the affluent and how to enter them. Separating everyone by class also has negative effects for continuity, because over time families need different kinds of housing. They may begin with an apartment, relocate to a starter home, move up to a three-bedroom ranch, then require a larger house to accommodate the birth of twins or the decline of a parent. Reduced economic circumstances or an empty nest may dictate a smaller home, followed by a condominium when they become senior citizens. If each move requires relocation to another area because each neighborhood—or even the entire suburb—is limited to a given income level and house size, towns may find it difficult to maintain a sense of community.[29]

Homeowners associations are multiplying nationwide. By 2000, 42,000,000 Americans lived in neighborhoods governed by these associations. Especially in the fast-growing suburbs of the South and West, almost all new homes now come with a homeowners association attached. Above all else, these associations aim to protect property values. One result is a plethora of rules.[30] Sometimes these rules are eerily reminiscent of an earlier time, such as the common requirement that "all pickup trucks must be out by sundown." These days, neighborhood associations never mention race, but in earlier times they were quite frank about it. One of the first neighborhood associations, the University District Property Owners' Association near Los Angeles, was established in 1922 as the Anti-African Housing Association.[31]

Gated Communities

A related development is the gated community, all of whose units are usually priced within a narrow range. According to author Robert Kaplan, gated communities came to the United States from South America, particularly Brazil. In 1985, gated communities were rare, but by 1997, more than 3,000,000 American households lived behind walls. Mary Snyder, a city planning professor, estimates that eight out of ten new developments in the United States are gated. Gated communities are particularly prevalent on Long Island and in California. Entire towns have gone gated in Florida, Illinois, and California.[32]

Gated communities epitomize defended neighborhoods, providing *no* amenities, not even streets, that are open to the public. Their walls and fences keep the public away from streets, sidewalks, playgrounds, parks, beaches, and even rivers and trails—resources that normally would be shared by all the citizens of a metropolitan area. The rationale for all this exclusion is allegedly relief from crime, and some communities do offer that. But often the security is largely illusory:[33] the gatehouses in many gated communities are never staffed.[34]

In fact, status and marketability, rather than security, usually drive gating. Often the gating is only symbolic and the gates never close. A development in an elite suburb northeast of Columbus, Ohio, went gated more than a decade after its initial opening. According to a student who had spent most of his life in the community, it had five unsold houses; after it went gated, they sold quickly. Before the gates, no crime had bedeviled the area; the increased security served no real purpose other than increased status and salability. According to a real estate salesman in suburban Maryland. "Any upscale community now would have to be gated. That's what makes it upscale."[35]

We have seen how whites have often used the occasion of retirement to relocate to sundown towns. Today the tradition of retiring to white enclaves continues, often gated and built around private beaches, golf courses, marinas, or all three. They may provide community, because purchase of a house or town house includes use of a clubhouse, restaurant, sports facilities, and other amenities. Whether residents also connect to any larger, more diverse community is dubious. Certainly such old-fashioned aspects of community as Girl Scout cookie sellers, trick-or-treaters, and political canvassers are forbidden. While not quite racially segregated, these new towns and developments advertise themselves as "exclusive" and are often overwhelmingly white, although race goes unmentioned. A friend who stayed in a gated community in Sarasota, Florida, in 2002 reported that she saw no black residents. Conversely, all the workers were people of color, "but they had to be out by nightfall, along with their pickups." Blakely and Snyder likewise encountered almost no nonwhites while interviewing in gated communities.[36]

End of the Nadir

Offsetting such negative developments has been a massive shift in the zeitgeist, the spirit of the times, achieved by the Civil Rights Movement, beginning in 1954. The Civil Rights Movement did not take place in a vacuum, of course. Just as race relations worsened after 1890 in the context of national and even international ideological developments, so did the improvements in race relations after World War II. We identified the three *i*'s—Indian wars, immigrants, and imperialism—as underlying causes of the worsening of race relations during the Nadir. Three factors also help explain why the racism of the Nadir began to erode after 1940.

First came the Great Migration. While the move of African Americans from the South to northern cities further inflamed the racism of some white northerners, it also created black voting blocs in northern cities. The Great Retreat further concentrated African Americans from scattered towns across the North into a few large cities. Soon a few African Americans were back in Congress, elected from those cities. African Americans also won seats in state legislatures and on city councils. Although whites continued to dominate the powerful positions of mayor and governor, they now took care not to alienate urban black voters with overtly racist rhetoric. Moreover, this moderation in rhetoric affected both parties, because from 1912 through 1962, neither party could take black votes for granted.

A second crack in the wall of white supremacy came from abroad: the imperialist sun began to set. Emboldened by the erosion of certainty in the European vision prompted by World Wars I and II, conquered nations—India, the Philippines, Indonesia, and later most of Africa—won their independence. Now the United States faced a new international environment: we had to relate to self-governing countries of color around the world. After World War II, engaged in a struggle with the USSR for world supremacy, the United States had no desire to antagonize these newly independent nonwhite nations by behaving badly toward our own citizens of color. On the positive side, seeing African leaders such as Haile Selassie of Ethiopia and Kwame Nkrumah of Ghana on the world stage made it easier for white Americans to understand that African Americans had done and could achieve important things.

Third and most important was the role played by World War II. Germany gave white supremacy a bad name. It is always in victors' interests to demonize the vanquished, but the Nazis made this task easy. Americans saw in the German death camps the logical end result of eugenics and apartheid, and it appalled us. As we sought to differentiate ourselves from Hitler's discredited racial policies, our own overt racism now made us uneasy. Swedish social scientist Gunnar Myrdal called this conflict our "American dilemma" and predicted in 1944, "Equality is slowly winning." [37]

World War II made a new rhetoric available to those who wanted to treat nonwhites as equal citizens. In Redwood City, 22 miles south of San Francisco, the newly built home of John J. Walker, black war veteran, was burned in December 1946, "after he had received threats to move out," according to a news story in *Pacific Citizen*. The couple planned to rebuild. Perhaps in reaction, some realtors suggested making the entire San Mateo peninsula, perhaps even including San Francisco itself, a sundown area. On July 11, 1947, Harry Carskadon, an agent in nearby Atherton, proposed that the peninsula was "not a proper place" for "Negroes, Chinese, and other racial minorities" and urged exclusive "white occupancy in the region." Other realtors were only slightly more tolerant: "Several members of the realty board felt the only way to handle the minority problem was to set aside acreage and subdivide it for minority groups with schools, business districts, etc.," according to the *Pacific Citizen.* But Emmit Dollarhyde, president of the Santa Clara County NAACP, called this "native fascist racism." He maintained that "Negro and other minority war veterans" who "risked their lives to protect our country from foreign fascism" deserved better. Carskadon's proposal was shelved, and by 1950 Redwood City had 410 African Americans among its 25,544 residents.[38]

The anti-Nazi ideology opened more sundown suburbs to Jews than to African Americans. Probably *Gentleman's Agreement,* Elia Kazan's 1948 Academy Award–winning movie exposing Darien, Connecticut, as an anti-Jewish sundown town, would not have been made except in the postwar anti-Nazi era.[39] To be sure, Darien did not immediately open to Jews. Four decades later, a realtor still cautioned that if a Jewish client asked him about Darien, "Would I be comfortable there?" he would caution her, "No. Don't even look. The brokers will be nice and you can buy a house. But can you enjoy the amenities? Can you join the club?" I suspect he would answer the same in 2005. Many other sundown suburbs did welcome Jews, however.[40]

The Civil Rights Movement

Those three factors underlay the legal challenge to segregation and the ensuing Civil Rights Movement. In turn, the Civil Rights Movement, coupled with the legal campaigns that civil rights lawyers waged against segregated schools and other institutions, began to open sundown towns and suburbs to African Americans. Of course, the movement and the lawsuits mostly took place in the South, where independent sundown towns were few, but they did lead to the quick desegregation of most southern sundown suburbs.

The Civil Rights Movement rarely addressed northern sundown towns and suburbs directly, and when it did, such as Martin Luther King Jr.'s 1966 march for open housing in Cicero, Illinois, it usually failed. Still, the movement's success in the South did help to undercut the rationale for sundown towns in the North. White northerners were jolted by the televised images of black young people peacefully picketing and sitting in and getting beaten or jailed in the process. These images made clear that white misbehavior—not alleged black inferiority—was the source of America's racial problem. Now that African Americans were no longer seen as the problem, white students and faculty pressured their colleges and universities to participate in the solution by recruiting and admitting black students. Now welcoming African Americans was the thing to do in college, while just the opposite still held in the sundown suburbs and neighborhoods from which so many college students had come.

The Civil Rights Movement took actions that exposed some of America's racial contradictions, which helped President Lyndon Johnson, leaders of Congress, and Earl Warren and other Supreme Court justices mobilize the power of the federal government to oppose racial segregation. However, the government did little about housing, because whites were most opposed to residential desegregation. A 1961 poll by the Connecticut Civil Rights Commission shows this in an allegedly liberal New England state. The commission's survey of Connecticut residents, "Attitudes Toward Specific Areas of Racial Integration," found that 95% of whites "favored" or "would accept" racial integration in public schools, 86% in parks and recreational areas, and 76% in hotels. But only 28% favored integration in "private residential neighborhoods," while another 29% would accept it; a plurality, 37%, opposed such integration. Opposition to residential integration was higher than to any other form of integration except "[private] parties." Ironically, Connecticut, like many northern states, had supposedly outlawed racial discrimination in housing decades earlier, although its open-housing law was not enforced. The commission concluded drily, "Opposition to integration in both public and private housing is greater than might be expected in view of the fact that such discrimination has been illegal for years."[41]

1968 as Turning Point

While the foregoing factors and the Civil Rights Movement did begin to erode the ideological foundation of sundown towns, such communities kept forming, especially in the suburbs, probably reaching their peak number in 1968. Three critical events took place in that year that began to weaken sundown towns directly. First, Dr. Martin Luther King Jr. was assassinated by a white racist in Memphis.[42] As some Democrats embraced President Lincoln in his martyrdom, so some formerly recalcitrant whites now mourned King and, to a degree, accepted his cause. Second, and in reaction to King's murder, Congress passed Title VIII of the Civil Rights Act of 1968, the Fair Housing Act. Even though enforcement has been spotty, by its very existence this law clearly put the federal government on the side of prohibiting rather than promoting racial discrimination in housing. Third, the Supreme Court held in *Jones v. Mayer* that an 1866 civil rights law bars discrimination in the rental and sale of property.

Sociologist Karl Taeuber summarized the positive results of these changes:

> Most federal housing programs did strengthen their anti-discrimination policies and practices during the 1970s. The Department of Justice filed and won court cases and settlements against state and local housing agencies and private real estate companies. Many state and municipal fair housing agencies were provided some tools for effective enforcement. There was a proliferation of private fair housing groups and neighborhood efforts to foster and preserve racially mixed neighborhoods.[43]

Then, as commonly happens, public opinion shifted in the wake of public policy. The National Opinion Research Center (NORC) asked Americans to agree or disagree with the statement "White people have a right to keep blacks out of their neighborhoods if they want to, and blacks should respect that right." In 1968, only 43% disagreed, but four years later, 63% did. Even in the Detroit metropolitan area—the most segregated in America—the proportion of whites agreeing with the NORC statement fell from 60% in 1964 to 20% in 1990. Thus, since 1968, whites who argue for sundown towns and suburbs have been on the defensive. Indeed, the proportion of whites openly in favor of racial segregation of neighborhoods declined nationally to just 15% by 1994.[44]

These responses must be taken with a large grain of salt. There is a huge gap between what people say when asked by strangers and what they do.[45] Depending on the situation, the proportion of whites who discriminate against people of color is often much higher than the proportion who admit they do. Still, it is an important first step that many closet white supremacists are now unwilling to be white supremacist when asked.

After 1968, Sundown Towns Began to Desegregate

The Civil Rights Movement wound down around 1970, leaving sundown towns and suburbs largely untouched in the North. But wheels had been set in motion. Developments in American popular culture comprised another force for change. Beginning with Elvis Presley in the 1950s, American popular music grew increasingly interracial. So have most sports, many television shows, and some movies, beginning with 1961's *A Raisin in the Sun,* which specifically treated sundown neighborhoods. In the 1970s, white teenagers put up posters of such African Americans as Diana Ross and Jimi Hendrix in their bedrooms. In the 1980s, it was Bill Cosby and Alice Walker, among others. In the 1990s, Michael Jackson, Michael Jordan, and Denzel Washington were popular, and in the new millennium, Venus and Serena Williams, Tiger Woods, and an endless succession of hip-hop stars were in fashion.[46] Nor can the influence of Oprah Winfrey be discounted: it is harder to keep African Americans out of your town when you keep inviting them into your living room via television.

In 1972, the National Association of Realtors finally adopted a pro-fair-housing position. The federal Home Mortgage Disclosure Act of 1975 required banks to release data on their lending patterns, making it possible to see if they were redlining. In 1977, redlining was officially outlawed by the Community Reinvestment Act, which requires banks to lend money throughout the regions they serve, including poor neighborhoods (without taking undue risks). Although the federal government showed less concern about segregated housing in the Reagan-Bush years (1981–93), the 1988 Fair Housing Amendments Act strengthened the enforcement of open housing laws and increased the punitive damages that plaintiffs could win for proving housing discrimination. White residents still resorted to violence to keep out blacks, but increasingly in the 1980s and '90s, the perpetrators got arrested. All this made a difference: in the 1990s, the number of African Americans concentrated in all-black census tracts declined dramatically.[47]

Proponents of integration have also won additional legal victories striking down some of the ordinances that suburbs have used to keep out undesirables. Brenden Leydon sued Greenwich, Connecticut, after a guard kept him from jogging on Greenwich Point, a 147-acre park with a beach on Long Island Sound. Greenwich allowed nonresidents to walk on its beaches only if they paid a $6 fee and were accompanied by a Greenwich resident. In 2000, the Connecticut Appellate Court said the ordinance "violates a public trust doctrine that says municipalities hold parks on behalf of all citizens." In the

late 1990s, a similar challenge invalidated Dearborn's ordinance that only residents could use its parks. In 2003, nearby Grosse Pointe lost the tax exempt
status of its parks when a judge ruled that they were not "open to the public
generally." Several other sundown suburbs faced comparable legal challenges
as of 2004.[48]

Hispanics and Asians Prompt Change

Today, Hispanics and Asians live throughout the United States, not just in the
West. In the 2000 census, Hispanics and "Others" outnumbered African
Americans by 20% in America's 100 largest metropolitan areas, and while the
West has America's most diverse population, other sections have become surprisingly multicultural as well. Hispanics will soon outnumber African Americans in the Midwest. Asians now are the largest nonwhite group in many
towns in the upper Midwest.

Even during the depths of the Nadir, most sundown towns did not keep
out Mexican Americans. Except in the West, most did not bar Asian Americans. As a result, nationally, Hispanics or Asians with third-grade educations
are more likely to live among whites than is an African American with a Ph.D.
today. Historically, even sundown suburbs such as Cicero and Berwyn, Illinois, long notorious for their hostility to African Americans, allowed Mexican
Americans as residents. By the 2000 census, Cicero's 85,616 population was
almost 80% Hispanic, and Berwyn's was almost 40% and rising.

Today, not only Mexican Americans but Mexican nationals, right off the
truck that brought them to work for a chicken processing factory in a little
Arkansas Ozarks town or a broom corn factory in Arcola, Illinois, are immediately allowed to live in those sundown towns and have their children attend
school. Most can speak no English and may also have had little schooling in
Spanish in Mexico. Some are unfamiliar with such basics of modern life as a
supermarket, laundromat, or library. Asian Americans—even Hmongs and
Khmers with little English and very different cultural backgrounds—have
found even readier acceptance. As Ricardo Herrera put it, speaking of California in 2000, "For the purposes of suburban migration 'out and up' from
Los Angeles, in certain complex ways Asian Americans and Latinos have been
treated as 'non-black' in contradistinction to being treated as 'non-white.' "
Although they have much less in common with white Americans than do
black Americans, these immigrants are admitted by towns and suburbs that
continue to keep out African American families who have lived in this country,
worshiped Jesus Christ, and spoken English for ten generations.[49]

However, once sundown towns admit Hispanics and Asian Americans, to admit African Americans may seem tolerable, rather than a catastrophe to be mobilized against.[50] The rush of Latino and Asian Americans into Cicero and Berwyn finally loosened the prohibitions against African Americans, and both suburbs now have black householders, including homeowners. In 2000, Cicero had 956 African Americans in 275 households; 54 own their homes; Berwyn had 588 African Americans in 221 black households; 81 own. This is a transformation: such numbers would have been inconceivable in 1981, when the school superintendent bragged that there would be no blacks in the Cicero Public Schools "as long as I am superintendent" and was wildly applauded.[51]

Ironically, some of the more racist whites have been leaving Cicero and Berwyn because the suburbs have grown "too Mexican" for them. For decades, Cicero had required firefighters and police officers to live within the city, partly to avoid hiring African Americans. Since African Americans were kept out of town, they couldn't be hired, and since no African Americans worked in the police and fire departments, it was easy to mobilize those departments to keep blacks out of town. Now Cicero's firefighters are trying to eliminate the residency requirement, supposedly to encourage African Americans living elsewhere to apply. "But critics suspect another motive," according to reporter Danielle Gordon: "White workers want the freedom to escape . . . [Cicero's] fast-growing Latino population." The irony that racist whites are arguing for a rule change that may lead to the hiring of nonwhites is not lost on African Americans, who have suffered decades of humiliation in Cicero and Berwyn.[52]

In Dearborn, Michigan, thousands of Arab Americans moved in while African Americans were kept out. The statue of Orville Hubbard, mayor of Dearborn from 1942 to 1978, was one of the 100 historic sites treated in my last book, *Lies Across America*. I poked fun at its accompanying historical marker—"He made Dearborn known for punctual trash collection"—and pointed out that Hubbard actually made Dearborn notorious for being a sundown suburb. In 2000, Dearborn's director of public information wrote me to complain about the entry: "We are proud to be home to more than 70 nationalities, including African-Americans, Arab-Americans, and Hispanics in addition to people from Western and Eastern Europe." Dearborn also makes this point on its web site. In the 2000 census, Dearborn had 1,275 African Americans, more than 1% of its nearly 100,000 total population, a sea change from twenty years earlier. Surely Dearborn's Arab Americans and Hispanics helped make this possible, if only by contributing to a new rhetoric. To brag about Dearborn's diversity is not compatible with keeping out African Americans.[53]

Recent research by Nancy Denton suggests that this complexity helps to desegregate formerly all-white neighborhoods across the nation. Whites do not often flee neighborhoods that become 50% nonwhite *if* those nonwhites include substantial numbers of Asian Americans and Hispanics as well as African Americans, and the number of census tracts with all four groups has soared. Nationally, residential segregation against African Americans decreased most in metropolitan areas where Asians and Latinos were most prevalent.[54]

Even in small independent towns across the Midwest, including sundown towns, Mexicans and Mexican Americans now do much of the work. In 2000, Arcola, Illinois, for example, was 20% Mexican, mostly employed by its broom corn factories. Beardstown, Illinois, west of Springfield, also had about 20% Mexicans, mostly employed by Excel, a meatpacker. Both were sundown towns, and Arcola may still be, but Beardstown has changed. Wyatt Sager, a lifelong resident, welcomes the change: "We would never have heard Mexican music 10 years ago. Now it is commonplace to hear different ethnic music. Beardstown has a much greater world scope now than it did 10 years ago." Immigrants from Senegal followed the Mexicans to Excel, and Beardstown now has eleven black households among its 5,766 residents. But Arcola shows that it is too early to tell: perhaps Mexican Americans and Asian Americans will become "honorary whites," leaving African Americans again shut out.[55] A realtor in Barry County, a sundown county in the Missouri Ozarks, leaned in this direction in remarks made in 1994:

> Blacks are so different that I just can't stand them. I can't help it, I hate them. My Doberman pinscher, Lady, used to terrorize Blacks. I really enjoyed that. I can tolerate Mexicans—I even have some Mexicans working for me—but I just can't tolerate Blacks.[56]

The Process of Change

In the last decade of the twentieth century and the first decade of the new millennium, even in the absence of Asians or Hispanics, many formerly sundown communities caved in peacefully and no longer keep out African Americans. A composite depiction of the process goes something like this: a white couple or two with adopted biracial children moved to town and enrolled their school-age children, thus desegregating the school system. Then a young white woman, daughter of longtime residents, left for the big city, had an affair with a young African American man, and returned home with her biracial child to live in the town. Eventually the child's father joined them. White residents did nothing to him, partly because he wasn't exactly an outsider, with his family connections. An African American couple moved in perhaps a year later . . . and lo, the town was no longer sundown.

Even towns that have not yet accepted a black household often do include adopted biracial children of white parents or children of interracial couples. "We see more and more interracial families," said a librarian in Cullman, Alabama. Most are young white women with interracial children, divorced, with no father living in town. This pattern is so common that I came to believe it happens on purpose. It may be too strong to suggest that some white teenage girls, disgusted at the hypocrisy shown by their parents and sundown community on race relations, deliberately set out to get pregnant by an African American male. Certainly they do set out to experience what their narrow-minded towns have told them is forbidden fruit.[57]

The children have mixed experiences. "I hope it will get better and I think it has some," reported a resident of Piggott, Arkansas, a sundown town near the Missouri Bootheel. "We have two black children in our church now with a white mother, who grew up in this community. She married while in college. They were accepted pretty well up until teen age. I know it has been hard on them." Often the dating age poses a problem. In 1992, the one African American student in Benton High School in Illinois, a girl in the junior class, accepted an invitation from a white football player to the junior/senior prom. "And that was it," in the words of a teacher in the school. "She was ostracized by the students from then on." She stuck it out for the rest of the school year and her family then moved. In these cases, the students never achieved full individuality in white eyes but remained merely representatives of a problematic race.[58]

Things were a little better in Comanche, Texas. In 2000, after an absence of more than a century, Comanche again had African American children in school: Talila Harlmon and her brother. "I do things by myself a lot," said Talila.

> I feel like I have to try harder to fit in. That's why I keep my hair braided and long, to look like the other girls. . . . The other girls, they go out to get their hair done—but I can't go, because the hairstylists here can't do my hair. I wish there were more black kids. I'd have someone to relate to in history class, when they're talking about the slaves or Martin Luther King. If I were at a school with

black kids, I could go to their house, they could come to mine. With a bunch of kids' parents here, the white girls can't date Hispanics or blacks. It bothers me. Some people aren't like that. I went to the prom with a white boy whose parents didn't mind. But sometimes kids in our school will be having a party, and if I find out and say why wasn't I invited, you could tell that they really want to invite me but they can't.

Thus Talila went to her prom and was not ostracized for it. Still, she gets lonely. "But my mom takes me places, and we go do stuff. My mom tells me it's just life, you just have to deal with it." [59]

Students Can Make a Difference

Whites in several sundown towns in Arkansas, Illinois, and Wisconsin report that even one or two African American high school students can help to humanize a community. Some residents use their existence as grounds to stop defining their towns as sundown towns. When this is done as a first step toward welcoming African American families, it is a positive step. Interaction with the one or two African American or mixed-race children can help white students learn to treat nonwhites with respect. Maybe Talila Harlmon had that effect in Texas.

In the 1990s in Sheridan, Arkansas, not long after white football fans were screaming, "Get the nigger," as told in Chapter 4, Sheridan High School got its first African American student. He lived outside Sheridan; for several more years, Sheridan still did not allow African Americans to be in town after dark. Regardless, "they made a mascot of him, loved him to death," my source reported. "Of course, *some* didn't." Being "a mascot" in Sheridan continues the pattern of the "pet Negro" who often played an ultra-humble or clown role in previous decades. But sometimes whites accept the lone African Americans as people, not mascots or Tontos or other "representatives of their race." They get known as individuals and beat the file folder phenomenon. Often they find themselves particularly well liked, partly because some white students are consciously doing what they can to break through their cocoon of isolation and prejudice and join the larger interracial world. [60]

Students have sometimes prompted the collapse of a town's racist policies. ABC students, mostly African American, came into Appleton in the early 1970s. Hayden Knight, born in Trinidad and raised in Brooklyn, remembers when he arrived in Appleton as a high school student in 1973: "Appleton knew about the Green Bay Packers and that was it." [61] He went on to add, "It was quite a shock. Appleton was small-minded at that time. We ABC kids helped them get through that." In 1960, exactly one African American lived in Appleton, a sundown city of almost 50,000 people. Twenty years later, 47 did, but most were students at Lawrence University or the ABC program. But in the 1980s, Appleton finally relented: the 1990 census found 163 African Americans among 65,695 residents, and by no means were they all students. Knight ended up returning to Cedarburg, Wisconsin, where he coaches soccer in the high school and helps to diversify another formerly all-white town.[62]

On the other hand, sometimes lone black students have made little difference. In 1974 James Lockhart spent his senior year in Highland Park High School, a Dallas sundown suburb, the first African American student. Whites called him "nigger," ripped his pants, and stole his books. Afterward, Lockhart recalled, "At first a lot of people rejected me. But later, as they got to know me better, they accepted me. They said I'd scared them because they'd never been around blacks." His parents viewed the harassment as the work of "no more than five students." Nevertheless, Highland Park, former home to both President George W. Bush and Vice President Richard Cheney, did not really desegregate until May 2003. In that month, the first African American family bought a house in the suburb. James Ragland, columnist for the *Dallas Morning News,* commented:

> I find it hard to believe that no black person ever has owned a home in Highland Park, an exclusive suburb often referred to as "the bubble."
> No black CEO. No black athlete. No black entertainer. No black entrepreneur. No black lawyer or doctor.
> No one?
> "As far as we know, that's true," said Tom Boone, editor of *Park Cities People.*

Thus so far as Highland Park knows, it was a sundown suburb until 2003.[63] Unless the new black family gets driven out by hateful incidents, which I doubt will happen, and if additional African American households join them, then Highland Park has finally cracked.[64]

Athletics Can Prompt Change

Athletics can provide a bridge. In town after sundown town, principals and teachers say that their lone black student fits in if s/he could play ball. In Duncan, Arizona, in 1950, athletics even provided a bridge across racially separate schools. Earl Randolph Jr. was kept out of Duncan High School and confined to a "school" devised just for himself and his siblings, but he was allowed to play on Duncan's athletic teams. Partly owing to his prowess, according to Duncan resident Betty Toomes, "they were unbeatable." The next year, the family moved to nearby Clifton, Duncan's traditional rival, and "Duncan was very sorry to see them go." Earl Randolph Jr. went on to become a multisport varsity athlete at Arizona State University.[65]

Not only does the individual black student find acceptance through athletics, but the high school and even the town modifies its definition of the ingroup. When all-white athletic teams become interracial, even if they remain mostly white, gradually the rhetoric changes: no longer do team members or fans indulge in the racial slurs of their sundown past. No longer do they throw rocks at the team buses of visiting interracial squads. Overtly racist comments and behaviors cannot be performed by interracial teams, because the African Americans on the team would not allow it. Indeed, white students on an interracial team would never yell "nigger" at an opposing player in the first place. It would never occur to them to "otherize" their opponents on *racial* grounds, since doing so would otherize some of their own players. Of course, interracial teams and fans can still otherize opponents in other ways: parody their fight songs, disrupt their cheers, call opposing linemen "sissies," and so forth. But they don't use racial slurs or think in racial terms. Such rhetoric would create an ingroup—whites—that would be divisive and inappropriate on an interracial team in an interracial town.

Within interracial schools, athletics are a unifier, say principals across the land. Cairo, Illinois, has had a difficult racial history, verging on open warfare in the early 1970s.[66] Even in that milieu, Cairo's athletic teams brought some students together. According to Bruce Brinkmeyer, the white quarterback at the time, "We were just trying to play ball, and when you see a black teammate out there sweating and working just like you, you don't see him as different." By 1987, thanks to racial bias from a neighboring sundown town, athletics was bringing some racial harmony to the entire city. After unfair officiating at a basketball game in Anna that year, whites and blacks in Cairo were outraged together.[67] As Cairo's white school superintendent, Ed Armstrong, put it:

> This time it was obvious even to some people who might not be as objective in
> their racial attitudes as they should be, that the team was mistreated. It was obvious why. There's an awful lot of racial hatred involved. The whites in Cairo
> see that, and they know it's not fair. Their team, a black team, was suffering unfairly.[68]

Hate rhetoric directed toward Mexican American basketball players performed the same unifying service in Beardstown in 2003. About 20 fans of nearby Brown County High School, a sundown county, showed up wearing sombreros and yelling "We want tacos" at the Beardstown team. According to Beardstown senior Tomas Alvarez, "People were mad. They really care about the image of Beardstown. That wasn't just against an ethnic group. It was against the whole town." [69]

Letting in a mere handful of African Americans may not always do the trick, as shown by Hemet, southeast of Los Angeles. As reporter Bill Jennings put it in 1992, "Hemet was pretty well a sundown town, meaning blacks could work over here during the day but they had better head for Perris or wherever at dusk." In 1989, Hemet had about 23 African Americans among its 25,000 residents, less than 0.1%. Three were on the Hemet High School football team, 6% of its 50-man roster. Still, Hemet's white players continued their long tradition of taunting African Americans on opposing teams as "niggers." Having three black teammates did not suffice to humanize Hemet's rhetoric, and the three apparently said little about the matter. By 2000, 1,500 African Americans lived in Hemet, 2.6% of the total population. No more reports of race-baiting at its athletic contests made the press. [70]

Colleges Can Prompt Change

African American college students have usually made less impact on sundown towns. They stay on campus and are seen as transients, so they don't challenge or ameliorate the sundown rule. All too often, neither do their institutions, which have more often been a captive of their town rather than a point of leverage to change it. The University of Oklahoma was a large state university in the relatively small sundown town of Norman, but the university itself kept out African American students until after a court order in 1949. According to George Callcott, university historian, the University of Maryland made no attempt to change the exclusionary policy of University Park, Maryland, which prohibited Jews as well as African Americans: "The University administration was very conservative and wouldn't have *wanted* to touch it." Likewise, to the best of my knowledge, throughout the years down to 1968, Lawrence University made no attempt to change Appleton, Wisconsin; North Central College made no impact in Naperville, Illinois; Eastern New Mexico University made none in Portales, New Mexico; and several colleges never tried to desegregate their sundown suburbs of Los Angeles. [71]

In a few towns colleges did promote tolerance. Regarding Jews, the University of California made a difference in La Jolla, in southern California. La Jolla had a "gentleman's agreement" to keep out Jews and African Americans from the 1920s through about 1959. Most and probably all residential areas were covered by covenants limiting owners and tenants to "the Caucasian race," interpreted to exclude Jews. After *Shelley v. Kraemer* made covenants unenforceable, La Jolla relied on realtors to discourage Jewish would-be buyers. "Every Jewish person I know was given the runaround," explained the wife of a Jewish scientist hired by the Scripps Institution of Oceanography, part of the University of California system, regarding their failed attempt to buy a house in La Jolla in 1947. In the 1950s, the California university system wanted to locate a major new campus in La Jolla. The man in charge of the process, Roger Revelle, felt, "You can't have a university without having Jewish professors." Clark Kerr, president of the University of California system, agreed. In 1958, Revelle made "a more or less famous speech," as he put it later, to the Real Estate Brokers Association in which he said, "You've got to make up your mind. You're either going to have a university or you're going to have an anti-Semitic covenant. You can't have both." Even faced with this ultimatum, most realtors still wouldn't comply, but their unanimity was broken: two agents—Jim Becker and Joseph Klatt—refused to exclude Jews in the 1960s, and the University of California at San Diego came into being. Becker died in 1981; at least as late as 1996, Jews in La Jolla still "remember[ed] his stand against the La Jolla real estate brokers," according to historian Mary Ellen Stratthaus. In the late 1960s, when many colleges began to recruit African American students, they—along with progressive white students and professors—pushed their institutions to make a difference in their communities. For example, the next chapter tells how faculty members at Valparaiso University led a private campaign in 1969 that desegregated their sundown town in northwestern Indiana.[72]

The South

Responding to all of these factors, some sundown towns across the United States have given up their exclusionary policies. We shall begin our quick tour in the South, which has progressed furthest in doing away with sundown towns, owing to the influence of the Civil Rights Movement. The traditional South had the fewest sundown towns to begin with; there, sundown towns were mostly limited to newer suburbs that developed mostly after World War II. These suburbs stayed all-white only for two to three decades and began to desegregate as early as the 1970s. Most suburbs of Southern cities desegregated before the 1990s.

Chamblee, Georgia, is an example. By 1970 it had become a sundown suburb; its 9,127 residents included just 1 black woman, probably a maid. Then, during the 1980s, Chamblee not only desegregated, it became cosmopolitan, even international. By 1990, among 7,668 residents were 1,482 African Americans and 1,108 others, mostly Asians and Asian Americans. By the 2000 census, two-thirds of Chamblee's 9,838 residents were born outside the United States.[73]

International immigrants were not required to achieve the integration of southern suburbs. Pearl, a suburb of Jackson, Mississippi, exemplifies the more usual process. Like Chamblee and many other formerly rural southern towns, as Pearl suburbanized, it got rid of its African American residents. By 1970, Pearl had 9,623 residents, including just 10 African Americans, disproportionately female, probably live-in servants. But Pearl's life span as a sundown suburb was brief, because in January 1970, public schools throughout Mississippi were fully desegregated by federal court order. Now most white neighborhoods and suburbs in the state, including Pearl, opened rather suddenly to African American residents.

It wasn't that thousands of white Mississippians suddenly realized they should let African Americans live next door to them, although some did come to that conclusion. Rather, the policy of racism and resistance that the state and city had followed from 1890 to 1970 had failed, at least so far as the schools were concerned. The whites who ran the public schools had done everything they knew to do to keep them segregated; the result was they were now fully desegregated. This unanticipated outcome removed the wind from the sails of those whites who had previously been determined to avoid residential desegregation. Gordon Morgan's survey of white attitudes in Mountain Home, a sundown town in the Arkansas Ozarks, caught this sense of inevitability. Most of his respondents expected that African Americans "*will* move in, in about five years."[74] To be sure, whites could still flee a neighborhood when a black family entered, just as they could enroll their own children in a private school. But they had lost faith in their ability to keep blacks out of their neighborhood, having failed to keep them out of their white public schools. By 1980, Pearl had 2,341 African Americans among its now nearly 21,000 residents. The same thing happened in other sundown suburbs across Mississippi[75] and the South.[76]

Some progress also took place a little later in the nontraditional South, where sundown towns and counties abounded. At least half of the independent sundown towns in the nontraditional South stopped excluding African Americans in the 1990s or since the 2000 census. Consider Arkansas. During the Nadir, whites expelled African Americans from many places in the Ozarks, as well as from other towns and counties in the northwestern half of Arkansas, most recently from Sheridan in 1954. By 1960, six Arkansas counties had no African Americans at all (Baxter, Fulton, Polk, Searcy, Sharp, and Stone), seven more had one to three, and another county had just six. I suspect all fourteen were sundown counties and have confirmed eight.

By 1990, census figures showed little change, but in the 1990s, many of these counties seem to have relaxed their restrictions. The 2000 census showed that every Arkansas county had at least ten African Americans except Searcy, with three, and Stone, with nine. Some counties showed considerable change. Benton County, which grew from 97,499 people in 1990 to 153,406 in 2000—fueled by growth at Wal-Mart's corporate headquarters—included 629 African Americans in that new larger population. African Americans were only 0.4% of the total in 2000, and the black increase amounted to fewer than one person in every 100 newcomers. Nevertheless, African Americans have reasserted their right to live in Benton County. The same holds for Sharp County, farther east in the Ozarks: 84 African Americans lived there in 2000, in 24 households.

Six Arkansas counties still teetered on the verge of being all-white, with only one or two black households in 2000. All lay in the Ozarks: Searcy and Stone, of course, and Fulton, Izard, Marion, and Newton.[77] Otherwise, counties in the rest of Arkansas—although not every town—seem willing to tolerate African American residents. The public schools of Sheridan, Arkansas, for example, desegregated around 1992, when students from two small nearby interracial communities were included in the new consolidated high school. In about 1995, the first black family moved back into Sheridan, and in the late 1990s they were joined by three more families—slow progress, but progress nevertheless. A few Appalachian counties in Virginia, North Carolina, Tennessee, and Kentucky may still keep out African Americans—including Erwin, as we have seen—but some of these places also cracked in the 1990s.[78]

The West

Most sundown towns and suburbs in the Far West cracked before 2000. These communities did not have residents who experienced and lost the battle for formal school segregation, but they shared with southern suburbs continued growth in the period 1970–2000. In addition, the West became increasingly multiracial, with continuing immigration of Hispanics and Asians. The West boasted most of the towns noted in earlier chapters as closed to Mexicans and Mexican Americans, Asians and Asian Americans, and Native Americans. But by 1970, most of these communities were open to nonblack minorities. Then they opened to African Americans as well.

The West's new multiethnic suburbs are very different from its old sundown suburbs. Journalist William Booth summed up research by Hans Johnson and others at the Public Policy Institute of California:

> The fastest-growing suburbs, with lots of new, relatively affordable tract housing—the kind of places whites used to fly to—became some of the most ethnically and racially diverse neighborhoods in the state during the 1990s. Ozzie and Harriet now live beside Soon Yoo and Mercedes Guerrero.

Asian and Latin Americans have been much less likely than European Americans to bar African Americans from their neighborhoods.[79]

With upward mobility, however, the anti-racist idealism of these groups may decrease over time, like that of white ethnic groups. Research by Camille Zubrinsky Charles suggests this is happening. She found that when asked to draw their "ideal multi-ethnic neighborhood," Latinos, especially those from Central America, and Asian Americans were *more* likely than whites to draw them containing *no* African Americans.[80]

Nevertheless, William Clark found much less segregation against African Americans in southern California in 2002, especially against rich African Americans:

> The change in the status of blacks is particularly striking. As late as 1970, rich and poor blacks were equally likely to be segregated from white households, but today in Southern California, high-income black households live in highly integrated neighborhoods. Families with incomes less than $10,000 had an Index of Dissimilarity close to 90—highly segregated[81]—while D for those with earnings above $60,000 = 40, reasonably integrated.

Some rich suburbs were still overwhelmingly white. Elite Indian Wells had only five black households. But most suburbs of San Francisco and Los Angeles had at least 150 African Americans and may be moving toward "postracial" identities. Statewide, using the term *segregated* for census tracts that are

> 80% monoracial, only 25% of California neighborhoods were segregated in 2000, down from 43% in 1990.[82]

Most independent sundown towns in the West are also giving up their policy of racial exclusion. A swath of towns in southwestern Oregon were sundown towns, according to oral history and other sources, including Eugene, Umpqua, Grants Pass, Klamath Falls, Medford, and others. In 2000, Grants Pass had 76 African Americans, Klamath Falls, 96, and Medford, 313, leaving their restrictive pasts behind. Eugene had 1,729, and most were not students at the University of Oregon. Another sundown town, Tillamook, on the coast due west of Portland, had just 7 blacks among its 4,352 residents and no households, so we cannot be sure it has given in.[83] But most towns in the Far West have. Kennewick, Washington, which had a sundown sign in the 1940s, had 579 African Americans in 2000. Oregon City, where the KKK drove out the only black citizen in 1923, had no African Americans at all as late as 1980; ten years later it boasted eight families. Taft, California, which like Kennewick formerly had a sundown sign, showed five black households in the 2000 census, at least a beginning.[84]

The Midwest

News from the Midwest is not so encouraging. I estimate that about half of Illinois's sundown towns have changed. To calculate this estimate, I examined 2000 census data for the 167 Illinois communities that I had confirmed as sundown towns as of mid-2004.[85] Of these, 59, or almost 40%, were no longer "all white." To that total, I added a few towns that had no black households as of 2000 but have opened up since then, such as Steeleville, based on the information that at least two African American families recently moved in without opposition.

I tried to be positive, so I included Vandalia, for example, the state capital for a time in the nineteenth century. In 1960, it had 5,537 residents, of whom not one was African American. In 1962, when Joseph Lyford wrote *The Talk in Vandalia,* the town was openly sundown. He quotes one minister saying ruefully,

> We call our town the land of Lincoln, but the hotels won't rent a room to a Negro, and no Negro can buy property or rent a home in Vandalia. There is an old saying that people in Vandalia are glad to help a Negro as long as he keeps on going right out of town.

Vandalia was still sundown as of the late 1990s. A college professor who grew up there wrote:

> Sometime in the mid-90s, a black couple moved to Vandalia. . . . The neighbors of this black couple at first were outraged. I heard the couple referred to as "those people," as in "What are those people doing in our town?" As the neighbors got to know the couple, though, they learned they were really nice people, and then everyone quieted down. After a year or so, the couple moved away. I'm not sure why, but I heard that the wife never felt comfortable in Vandalia. I certainly can't blame her.

By 2000 Vandalia's numbers had swelled to 6,975, including 1,047 African Americans. Had Vandalia had a change of heart or policy? Not exactly; the 2000 census counted inmates at the nearby Vandalia Correctional Center as part of the population of the city. But also around 1995, ironically, the Ku Klux Klan brought about some improvement. My source continues:

> Vandalia was the site of a big KKK rally also sometime in the mid-90s. . . . The rally did have a positive effect on the town in a way, as several churches and groups banded together to hold candlelight vigils to protest the KKK. Many people in Vandalia came forward arguing that racism is not acceptable. Things have gotten better in Vandalia since then. We now have a handful of black families who seem to live and work in the town with no trouble. I don't hear as many racist comments.

Despite Vandalia's amelioration, however, the professor wanted to remain anonymous, and the 2000 census showed only five African Americans in just two households, not counting its huge prison population. Thus Vandalia may still be a sundown town, but I think it has given up that distinction, since the professor indicated "a handful" of families moved in since 2000.[86]

As elsewhere, suburbs showed the most improvement. A disproportionate share of the 59 Illinois towns that opened by 2000 were suburbs. Granite City, a suburb of St. Louis, is an example. According to a man who grew up in Granite City and whose father lived there from 1919 to 1997:

> Blacks who worked in Granite City (mainly in the steel mills) had to walk directly to the streetcar line to catch the first streetcar out of the city. There was one exception: a janitor who worked for Ratz Drug Store on 19th and State

Street. He was known as "Peg" because of his peg leg and was allowed to sleep in the basement of the building.

Around 1980 Granite City relented; by 1990 69 African Americans lived among its 32,862 residents, and the 2000 census showed 622. An administrator at Manchester College in Indiana said in 1997 that students from Granite City "are very racist" and have to be worked with closely if they become dormitory counselors. Maybe ten years from now, that will no longer be necessary, for in 2002 as I drove around the town, I saw interracial groups of children walking home from school and using the library together.[87]

Other Illinois towns, from Anna through Zeigler alphabetically, do not allow as much optimism. Of course, still other Illinois towns may now welcome African Americans, but none has recently knocked at their gates. So I would estimate that more than 40%—and probably at least half—of Illinois's former sundown towns no longer keep out African Americans. If at least 50% of Illinois's sundown communities had abandoned their sundown policies, then across the Midwest, my impression is that at least two-thirds have caved in, because some other states seem more progressive than Illinois. In Wisconsin, for example, a higher proportion of sundown towns seem to have lowered their barriers during the 1980s and especially the '90s. Some places even welcomed them. Fond du Lac, which had had 178 African Americans in the nineteenth century before the Great Retreat, had just 12 in 1970, but 112 in 1990 and 767 by 2000. West Bend had only 31 in 1990, but that included a deputy sheriff, showing considerable acceptance. To be sure, not every Wisconsin sundown town now accepts African Americans. In 1990, eleven Milwaukee suburbs were "violating agreements that they take steps to promote fair housing," according to the Milwaukee County public works director. Milwaukee's suburbs averaged just 2% black in 2000, while Milwaukee was 37% black. The Milwaukee metropolitan area remains the second most segregated in the United States, after Detroit, owing mostly to suburban exclusion.[88]

Many Indiana communities dropped their sundown policies in the 1990s. Portfolio 25 shows the 1970 census for 34 Indiana towns of 1,000 to 2,500 population. Of the eight communities I confirmed as sundown towns in 1970, only one has broken for sure, Zionsville, with 29 African Americans among its now 8,775 residents. Nevertheless, where there had been 26 communities with no African Americans at all, by 2000 there were just 3. There had been no towns with more than one black household, so all 34 might have had sundown policies, with one household or individual—like Granite City's "Peg"—allowed as an exception.[89] Now ten had two or more households.

Among larger towns, Chesterton, in northern Indiana, had only 9 African Americans out of 9,124 people in 1990 and a long history of keeping blacks out. But by 2000, it had thirteen black households, including that of its postmaster, who retired and continues to live there. Clearly Chesterton stopped excluding African Americans around 1990. Valparaiso, a few miles south, admitted them earlier. Merrillville, a suburb of Gary, is now 23% African American. The Northwest Indiana Quality of Life Council recently gave the region a poor rating for its race relations, but at least Chesterton, Valparaiso, and Merrillville have moved beyond exclusion.[90]

Many towns elsewhere in the Midwest have also begun to let in African American residents. Is Warren, Michigan, just north of Detroit, open? As early as 1990, it appeared to have cracked, having 1,047 African Americans among 144,864 total population. That was the year that John and Cynthia Newell and their young son moved to Warren. Because they were African American, they had a rough time. Skinheads burned a cross on the lawn of their rented home. According to "The Cost of Segregation," a 2002 *Detroit News* story:

> In the two years the Newells lived on Campbell near Nine Mile, they were accosted by teen-agers who told them to "go back to Africa" and stuffed their mailbox with "White Power" stickers. "I had a white friend that I lost my friendship with because they kept calling her 'nigger lover' whenever we walked to the store," Cynthia Newell said. "They threw eggs at her when she was with me. All of the neighbors weren't racist. Some of them wanted to socialize. But they couldn't because they were afraid for their safety."

Warren was touch-and-go for a while, but by 2000, Warren had 3,697 African Americans, less than 3% but clearly a black presence.[91]

Whether Owosso, Michigan, is still a sundown town is less clear. In 2000, Owosso had 27 black residents, but that included "kids from Africa in the Bible College," in the words of local historian Helen Harrelson. In 1942 Owosso had allowed African Americans traveling by bus to be in the bus station but no farther. In 2002, when a member of the Owosso High School class of '42 asked a hotel clerk at his sixtieth reunion, "Are Negroes allowed to leave the bus station?" she considered the question absurd. However, the same year, asked if Owosso was still a sundown town, Harrelson replied, "It hasn't really changed yet. Sure, they let in one or two, if they behave themselves. I doubt if there are any black kids in the [public] schools." The 2000 census did show children of school age, among eight households with black house-holders; I think Harrelson was overly pessimistic.[92]

Ohio seems to have made more progress. It had no county in 2000 with fewer than about 40 African Americans. Waverly, which stoned and drove out its sole African American resident decades ago, had 51; nearby Piketon, which likewise drove out its lone black resident, had 21. The cities of Parma and Cuyahoga Falls, which had achieved national notoriety for keeping out African Americans, had almost 1,000 each.

Sundown Suburbs and Neighborhoods

Because social scientists have computed the Index of Dissimilarity for metropolitan areas throughout the period studied by this book, D is useful to assess change in sundown neighborhoods and suburbs over time.[93] From 1860 to 1960, the index increased until the average northern city had a D of 85.6; southern cities averaged 91.9—close to the total apartheid denoted by D = 100. After about 1968, D finally started to decline. Black suburbanization then grew during the 1970s and 1980s, although much of the increase went to a few black suburbs. The average D for all metropolitan areas with large black populations was 69 in 1980 and 64 in 1990. The number of hypersegregated cities (D > 85) decreased from 14 to 4 during the '80s, while the number showing only moderate segregation (D < 55) increased from 29 to 55.[94]

Residential segregation declined further in the 1990s. By 2000, some midsize cities in the South and West boasted D's as low as 40 to 45—low enough to suggest that residential segregation was drawing to a close there. The largest changes took place in the South, owing partly to desegregated countywide school systems. In such metropolitan areas, moving to whiter suburbs does not secure a whiter school district, eliminating one reason for such moves.

Older cities in the Midwest and Northeast—exactly the areas most plagued by sundown suburbs—showed the smallest decreases. Between 1968 and 1980, when the proportion of black students in overwhelmingly minority schools (90–100%) was falling in the rest of the nation, in the Northeast it actually rose 6% to almost half, higher than any other region. In Milwaukee, jeers and flying bricks met black marchers in the 1960s when they crossed the bridge over the Menomonee River to the white neighborhoods on the other side. In 2000, an astonishing 96% of all African Americans in the Milwaukee metropolitan area still lived within Milwaukee itself. David Mendell pointed to the role sundown suburbs played in contributing to this statistic:

In Milwaukee, many middle-class blacks have settled in mostly black city neighborhoods on the north side. That trend follows a history of racial inequity in the Milwaukee area. Until the civil rights era, some suburbs enforced laws that forbade blacks to buy homes in their communities or to walk the streets after 10 PM

For the Milwaukee metropolitan area, D was 83 in 1990 and 82 in 2000. This means 82% of all African Americans in the Milwaukee area would have to move to white neighborhoods for Milwaukee to achieve a uniform racial mix. Moreover, at its current rate of improvement, it will take four hundred years for the level of segregation in Milwaukee to resemble such southern metropolitan areas as Greenville, South Carolina, or Raleigh-Durham, North Carolina, today. Detroit, Philadelphia, and some other "rustbelt" metropolitan areas showed equally minuscule declines.[95]

Even around Detroit, however, most suburbs have admitted a few African Americans. Patti Becker, who has mapped Detroit for decades, calls this "honest integration" to distinguish it from the expanding black ghetto of Detroit, now spilling over into suburbs. Despite this progress, segregated neighborhoods remain the rule, especially in the East and Midwest. In 1995, Maggie Jorgensen, a longtime advocate of integration in Shaker Heights, Ohio, one of the few integrated suburbs in the Midwest, said, "It's still a battle to convince [white] people that it's OK to live in an integrated community." Ingrid Ellen, taking an optimistic view, began her 2000 book, *Sharing America's Neighborhoods,* with the claim "Racially mixed neighborhoods are no longer as rare or as unstable as people tend to think. Nearly one-fifth of all neighborhoods in the United States were racially mixed in 1990."[96] But this is hardly an impressive rebuttal of what "people tend to think," since more than 80% of all neighborhoods were *not* racially mixed, according to her.[97]

Some elite suburbs have given in, if at all, only barely. Kenilworth, for example, the elite Chicago suburb, admitted an African American family in the mid-1960s, but that didn't go so well. A woman who graduated from high school in Kenilworth in 1971 wrote,

I clearly remember when the first black family moved in around 1964. They were very nice and both parents were professionals. I was in seventh grade. Some boys from my class actually stuck a large wooden cross in the family's lawn and burned it. Even during those times I was shocked at the prejudice.

That family stayed for more than a decade but eventually left, and by 2002, no African American households existed in Kenilworth. Tuxedo Park, New York, America's first gated community, had at most one black or interracial family in the 2000 census. The four municipalities that made up Chevy Chase, Maryland, next to Washington, D.C., had just six families with at least one African American householder; their 19 people comprised 0.3% of Chevy Chase's population.[98] On the other hand, Edina, the upper-class sundown suburb west of Minneapolis, had 546 African Americans among 47,425 total population, more than 1%. Beverly Hills and Palos Verdes Estates, elite suburbs of Los Angeles, were also open: Beverly Hills had about 500 African Americans, almost 2% of its population, while Palos Verdes Estates had 132, almost 1%.[99]

Perhaps the best summary is to say that progress has been real but uneven.[100] Metropolitan areas in the Midwest and Northeast have maintained "almost an iron curtain," in sociologist John Logan's phrase, dividing black neighborhoods from white. Most suburbs in the South and West have torn this curtain down.[101]

One Step Forward, One Back?

It would be wrong to end our analysis of the present on this optimistic note. Clouds loom. Despite the symbolic importance of the 1968 law, in 1993 law professor John Boger gave a pessimistic summary of its impact: "By most accounts, the Fair Housing Act has been a disappointing failure." Nancy Denton agrees, finding that "hypersegregation persists and often is worsening" in most metropolitan areas.[102]

If the positive zeitgeist of the Reconstruction and post-Reconstruction years in the North was undone by the view of African Americans as "the problem" during the Nadir, then the changes wrought by the Civil Rights Movement are endangered by the fact that many whites see African Americans as "the problem" today. Even if many white Americans no longer think that sundown towns and suburbs are appropriate ways to deal with that "problem," most people still do not turn first to history and social structure to explain why African Americans have less wealth, lower test scores, and are concentrated in inner cities and a few suburbs. Refurbished as "the ghetto as problem," this rhetoric remains alive and well and is both the result of unequal race relations in America and the cause of further inequality.[103] The solution still seems to be flight to outlying communities that are, if not quite sundown, preponderantly white and affluent. Thus "the ghetto as problem" continues to legitimize overwhelmingly white suburbs and neighborhoods in the eyes of many non-black residents.[104]

To be sure, many former sundown towns and suburbs now include a handful of African American families. Although this marks an important first step toward real integration, the danger of soclexia lurks close behind. Just as living in an all-white community once seemed "natural," now token desegregation quickly comes to seem natural. To paraphrase Billy Bob Lightfoot, quoted about Comanche County, Texas, as a sundown county, almost immediately it seems as though there had always been a few African Americans in Grosse Pointe, Edina, or Beverly Hills. Now these elite suburbs may develop an ideology that endangers further progress. Their new demography now allows their white residents to claim they never were racist—"it's class." In other words, token residential desegregation can prompt whites to forget that their town or suburb flatly kept out African Americans for decades. Without this memory, how can whites understand why there are so few African Americans there now?

I can explain this best by analogy. In the 1990s, many former "segregation academies," founded in the South around 1970 when public schools massively desegregated, relaxed their whites-only policies. Jackson Preparatory Academy in Mississippi now proclaims this goal on its web site: "To achieve the broader educational goal of preparing students to participate in the world community, Prep is committed to diversity in race, color, and national origin in the student body, faculty, and programs." Its student body looks integrated to whites, now that African Americans are no longer shut out entirely. White students may not remember that "Prep" was founded for whites only, to avoid contact with African Americans, but the black community remembers, making many black students reluctant to apply. White students can infer that it is "natural" for a school to be less than 5% black, but it isn't, not in central Mississippi. Even worse, they may conclude that the shortage of black students results from differences in merit, with African Americans being less able on standardized tests.[105]

We have seen how residents often interpret the continued overwhelmingly white population of sundown suburbs as the result of economic differences and individual housing decisions, including those made by black families. Even worse, suburban whiteness can get laid at the eugenics doorstep: whites can blame African Americans for being too stupid or lazy to be successful enough to live in their elite all-white town. Token desegregation makes these interpretations easier to believe, because now nonblacks can point to a handful of black families to "prove" that "we have nothing to do with the overwhelming whiteness of our suburb." Such "explanations" only compound the problem, because whites can infer that racism is over, the metropolitan area and the nation are fair regarding race, and African Americans are responsible for whatever racial inequalities remain. Between 2000 and 2005, arguments such as these have intensified in America, not just in discussions about residential segregation but about affirmative action and many other policy areas. That is why it is so important to know the history of sundown towns and suburbs—to give this cheery optimism the lie.

Perhaps the most prestigious suburban mix at present is 1% African American—just enough to avoid the charge of sundown policies but not enough "to be a problem," not enough to pull down school test scores or perpetrate much crime. That old "African Americans as the problem" line of thought comes through once again. Thus in the 1990s, Forsyth County was the fastest-growing county in Georgia and the second-fastest in the United States, according to the census, partly because it was so white, yet no longer sundown.[106]

Unfortunately, 1% is not black enough to prompt a town or county to face that its schools and other institutions are still white in culture, rather than American in culture. Maybe elite suburbs will go just this black and no further, since elite suburbs seem to get what they want. I doubt it, however, because when a town is only 99% nonblack, rather than 100% nonblack, it is harder to mobilize the white violence, police harassment, and other tools required to keep out additional black newcomers.

One Future: Increasing Exclusion

Keeping out people who do not live the way "we" live is an increasingly common response to America's increasing gap between the affluent and the working class, not to mention the poor. Some analysts consider São Paulo, Brazil, a city of 18,000,000, an augury of future urban life in our country. São Paulo is "populated by the fantastically wealthy and the severely poor with little in between," to quote *Washington Post* reporter Anthony Faiola, writing in 2002. And São Paulo illustrates where gated communities and microscopic economic segregation may be taking us. Faiola told of life in Alphaville, "a walled city where the privileged live behind electrified fences patrolled by a private army of 1,100." Affluent residents "whisk to and from their well-guarded homes to work, business meetings, afternoons of shopping, even church," via helicopter. The city boasts 240 helipads, compared to 10 in New York City. "Brazil has one of the most marked disparities of wealth in the world," continued Faiola, "with the richest 10 percent of the population controlling more than 50 percent of the wealth." While this sentence may be correct,[107] it is embarrassing that Faiola did not seem to know that in the United States, the richest 10 percent of the population controls more than 66 percent of the wealth.[108]

Certainly, residential exclusion is still the norm within the United States. The census took what it calls the American Housing Survey (AHS) in 1993 (and earlier years), including 680 subsamples called kernel clusters. Within these clusters, the AHS begins with one respondent and then asks the same questions of up to fifteen others in residences nearest the respondent. According to sociologist Samantha Friedman, in 1993 about 80% of all whites lived in all-white clusters.[109] The only reason this book doesn't treat 80% of American cities and towns is that larger municipalities escape getting listed because they have black neighborhoods as well as white neighborhoods. Especially in the East and Midwest, most white neighborhoods remain overwhelmingly white, but overwhelmingly black neighborhoods elsewhere in these cities deflect them from being classed as sundown. Sundown neighborhoods persist today partly because our social system, a captive of its history, still builds in residential segregation in many ways. Business principles in the three key industries related to where Americans live—development, banking, and real estate—continue to encourage the new forms of residential exclusion described above.[110]

Another Future: Decreasing Exclusion

As I took my leave of John Peters, the black retiree with whom I talked in Du Quoin in 2002, a biracial town in southern Illinois, a retired white neighbor dropped in unannounced, to chat and maybe go somewhere with Peters. After spending so many days in towns and suburbs where casual interaction simply could not take place across racial lines, I'm afraid I stared at the two of them. Racially integrated towns and neighborhoods are becoming more common and more stable, however. Soon, I believe, they will no longer be viewed as unusual. At least, I believe it when I'm in my "glass half full" frame of mind.

At the same time, many sundown towns and suburbs have not caved in. In one sundown town, the reference librarian, sympathetic to my research, warned me twice in 2002 to "be careful who you talk with." She wasn't kidding; she was concerned for me, and I am white. I also recall my last conversation in Arcola, Illinois, also in the library. I was talking with the librarian and her mother about Arcola's remarkable history of exclusion and asked if it was still a sundown town. In the 2000 census, Arcola had one household with an African American householder, a family of three, but neither woman knew of such a household. One said, and the other concurred, "There was a black family here ten or fifteen years ago, but they moved on." They didn't know if the family was forced out, but they agreed Arcola was a sundown town. Just then a young man, maybe eighteen years old, walked in. His ears perked up as soon as he heard "black family," and he stopped, shocked. "Blacks in Arcola?" he asked intently. "Where? Who?" We hastened to assure him that we were just talking about things in the past. Was he just curious? Or fixing to act? I could not tell.

Nationally, research popularized around the 50th anniversary of *Brown v. Board* in 2004 shows that many African American students attend class in metropolitan areas whose schools are now more segregated by race than they were ten or twenty years ago. Perhaps the most accurate assessment of the state of sundown towns at present would be to leave it up in the air. Everywhere I went in sundown towns and suburbs, I met some people who would like their community to move beyond its restrictive policy. On the other hand, a gap between attitudes and behavior remains. Many whites endorse the principle of desegregation while living in white areas and are privately uncomfortable with the thought of African Americans moving in. Therefore they do not act on their principles, which allows those who do—the excluders—to carry the day.[111]

Living in a place where not everyone looks alike and not everyone votes alike is surely good for the mind as well as the children. Also, since people usually defend their choice of place to live, living where not everyone looks alike pushes residents to defend living where not everyone looks alike, thus making them less racist in their attitudes. Scenes like the interracial friendship I witnessed in Du Quoin do take place all across the country, and if they don't in your neighborhood, the next chapter suggests possible steps to take. Indeed, the question before us now is: What can we do to end sundown towns and suburbs in our lifetime? What can we get our institutions to do, and what can we do ourselves?

15

The Remedy:
Integrated Neighborhoods and Towns

And now a child
Can understand,
This is the law
Of all the land,
All the land.
—Three Dog Night, "Black and White,"
1972 song about school integration

WE HAVE SEEN that sundown towns and neighborhoods have bad effects on whites, blacks, and our social system as a whole. Surely we want to stop all this. So how do we get there? How do we desegregate sundown towns and suburbs, racially and maybe even economically?

This final chapter is a call to action on four fronts: investigation, litigation, institutional policy changes, and personal choice. At the end, I add my plea for a Residents' Rights Act that could be passed by state or federal governments to make it in the interest of sundown towns to change their policies immediately. I must add that I submit these remedies humbly.[1] I am sure that lawyers, community activists, and other experts will find them wanting.

Bringing the History of Sundown Towns into the Open Is a First Step

To end our segregated neighborhoods and towns requires a leap of the imagination: Americans have to understand that white racism is still a problem in the United States. This isn't always easy. Most white Americans do not see racism as a problem in their neighborhood. We need to know about sundown towns to know what to *do* about them.

During the Nadir, and even to the 1960s in most places, sundown towns were not at all shy about their policies. Nothing could be more blatant, after all, than a sign stating "Nigger, Don't Let the Sun Go Down on You in __," or a brochure advertising "No Negroes" as a selling point of a suburban neighborhood. So it is encouraging that few sundown towns and suburbs today, even those whose sundown policies remain in force, admit that they keep out African Americans. Hypocrisy is to be encouraged as a first step toward humane behavior. When residents claim that their community is all-white by accident or blame African Americans for not moving in, at least they no longer openly brag that the town is anti-black. No longer do whites feel it is OK to advertise their racism. Since 1968, when overt discrimination became illegal, they know to keep it hidden.

On the other hand, this secrecy helps racism endure. "The truth will make us free," goes an important verse of the anthem of the Civil Rights Movement, "We Shall Overcome." Surely it is right: surely one reason we are not free of sundown towns is that the causes of residential segregation have been obscured. In 2002, the Pew Research Center surveyed attitudes about housing and race. Surprisingly, they found that only 50% of Americans "had heard that 'neighborhoods are still mostly racially segregated.' " [2] And as late as November of that year, a professor could routinely e-mail a web discussion list in history, in an attempt to begin a discussion of what he called "the problems of mandating desegregation," this assumption: "Residential segregation is the result of individual, rather than government actions." Had he known about the violent expulsions that gave rise to so many independent sundown towns, condoned by local governments, or the blatant acts of public policy (and also violent resistance) that led to sundown suburbs, he simply could not have written such a sentence. [3]

Awareness of unfairness undercuts unfairness. People who perceive that the social system discriminates against racial minorities are more likely to support policies to reduce that discrimination. Racists know this. That's why denial of racism is a time-honored tactic. During the lawsuit to integrate the University of Mississippi, the State of Mississippi actually claimed in 1962 that Ole Miss was not segregated; no African Americans "happened" to go there. Therefore the school had not rejected African American James Meredith owing to race! Amazingly, the trial judge bought this claim, but John Minor Wisdom, speaking for the Federal Court of Appeals, held it to be "nevernever land" and proclaimed, "What everybody knows the court must know." Similarly, if we wish to mobilize lawyers, judges, local institutions, and families to do something about sundown towns, we must make them realize what the residents of these towns already understand. If everyone in Anna knows that the letters of the town's name stand for "Ain't No Niggers Allowed," then "the court must know," and so must we all. These policies need to be exposed, "hidden in plain view" no longer.[4]

Concealment has been especially vital in the suburbs. The system of racial status that sundown suburbs embody needs mystification to work. Remember the paradox of exclusivity: living in an exclusive area is good, connoting positive things about one's family, but participating in exclusion is bad, connoting "lower-class" prejudices. Therefore white families achieve status by living in elite sundown suburbs only so long as the racial policy of those suburbs remains hidden. Exposing the unsavory historical roots of sundown towns and suburbs can help to decrease the status that most Americans confer upon elite white communities and undercut the policies that still keep them that way. Elite suburban racism is particularly vulnerable, because no one can defend a suburb's all-white racial composition as right without appearing "lower-class." Thus the paradox of exclusivity provides a point of leverage for opening suburban communities to African American residents.

In many communities, then, more research is the first order of the day. Indeed, in some towns, time is running out. Doing oral history on the period 1890 to 1940, the peak years for creating sundown towns, is becoming difficult, because people who came of age even toward the end of it are now nearing their 90s. Children may not learn the local history that their parents and grandparents know. At my web site are suggestions as to how to proceed. Professional historians and sociologists can do much of this research, but so can local historians, "mere" residents, even middle-school students.[5] My hope is that this beginning will inspire researchers in each state to identify more of these towns, tell how they came to be sundown, how they preserved their racial exclusivity, and hopefully how they are changing.[6] The race relations history of any neighborhood or town deserves to be investigated if its population has long been overwhelmingly white. Of course it is possible that no African Americans ever happened to go there, but it is more likely that formal or informal policies of exclusion maintained the whiteness of the place.

Most states have historical marker programs that now incorporate advisory committees, including professional historians, that must approve the text of any new marker for accuracy before it goes up. After completing the research required to convince such a panel, the next step, with the assistance of church groups, civic organizations, or the local historical society, is to propose an accurate marker telling your town's history of exclusion and offering to fund and erect it.[7] Even if opposition mobilizes to block the marker, the resulting uproar itself will end the secrecy.

Truth and Reconciliation

Once we know what happened, we can start to reconcile. Publicizing a town's racist actions can bring shame upon the community, but recalling and admitting them is the first step in redressing them. In every sundown town live potential allies—people who care about justice and welcome the truth. As a white man said in Corbin, Kentucky, on camera in 1990, "Forgetting just continues the wrong." "Recovering sundown towns" (or wider metropolitan areas or states) might set up truth and reconciliation commissions modeled after South Africa's to reveal the important historical facts that underlie their continuing whiteness, reconcile with African Americans in nearby communities, and thus set in motion a new more welcoming atmosphere.[8]

The next step after learning and publicizing the truth is an apology, preferably by an official of the sundown town itself. In 2003, Bob Reynolds, mayor of Harrison, Arkansas, which has been all-white ever since it drove out its African Americans in race riots in 1905 and 1909, met with other community leaders to draw up a collective statement addressing the problem. It says in part, "The perception that hangs over our city is the result of two factors: one, unique evils resulting from past events, and two, the silence of the general population toward those events of 1905 and 1909." The group, "United Christian Leaders," is trying to change Harrison, and it knows that truth is the starting place. "98 years is long enough to be silent," said Wayne Kelly, one of the group's members. George Holcomb, a retiree who is also a reporter for the *Harrison Daily Times,* supports a grand jury investigation into the race riots: "Get the records, study them, give the people an account of what happened. Who lost property, what they owned, who had it stolen from them and who ended up with it."[9]

In some towns, as Holcomb's comment implies, truth and reconciliation logically leads to reparations. This book has mentioned many towns and counties whose African American residents were driven out at gunpoint between 1890 and 1954. I spent a morning walking around the former black neighborhood in Pinckneyville, Illinois, for instance. It was a haunting experience. I photographed houses, including one that formerly was the black school (Portfolio 4), and talked with residents, all of them white, of course. Today whites call the area "the Black Hills," by which they do *not* imply a similarity to a Sioux sacred site in South Dakota. In about 1928, whites drove African Americans from Pinckneyville. "They strung one black up, at the square," a cemetery worker told me as he showed me around the black section of the town cemetery, which has only two stones but perhaps twenty graves, he said.[10]

What about the home pictured in Portfolio 3, burned by whites as they drove African Americans from Pierce City, Missouri? All 200 African Americans in Pierce City ran for their lives at 2 a.m. on August 19, 1901. Almost certainly the family that owned this house got no compensation for its destruction and probably never even felt safe enough to return to try to sell the burned-out hulk and the land. Do their heirs have a claim? Virginia Yearwood grew up in one of the houses that was not destroyed. She wrote, "As a result [of the riot], a number of very nice homes with views had been standing empty for a very long time. My Uncle Emil bought one of these nice homes (nice for that time) which had been formerly occupied by blacks. . . . It must have been really tragic as all the houses were abandoned for a long time, some with belongings still in them." Did Uncle Emil pay for the home? Surely he did not pay the owners.[11]

What of the owners of the black private school in Eldorado, Illinois—Eldorado Normal and Industrial Institute—who were stoned in 1902, "and the principal, Jefferson D. Alston, his wife, and pupils were compelled to leave for fear of mob violence," in the words of the *Indianapolis Freeman*? Governor Richard Yates of Illinois said they would get protection, but that never happened, and all African Americans in Eldorado fled to nearby Metropolis to save their lives. Did they get a fair price for their property? Certainly it was a distress sale. As Gordon Morgan, whose monograph *Black Hillbillies of the Arkansas Ozarks* is the pioneering treatment of the disappearance of African Americans from that region, asked in 1973, "To what extent are those counties legally liable for allowing the forcing of blacks out, under duress, without assuring that they or their descendants were adequately compensated for loss of life, property, or opportunities?"[12]

We are not talking ancient history. In 2004, I talked with Almarion Hollingsworth, whose father, A. W. Birch, owned the hotel in Marlow, Oklahoma, a sundown town, refused to fire his black porter, and was shot by a mob that then killed the porter. She has lived 81 of her 83 years without a father. Does she have a claim? What of the porter's children? What about Cleveland Bowen, who was 3 years old when whites in Forsyth County, Georgia, "told us we had to be out by sundown," according to testimony taken in 1987, when he was 78?

We left that same night. It was kind of rainy. I slept. I was only about three years old, but everybody was so scared and everything, I remember it. We came off and left cotton and corn in the field and two mules and two cows standing in the yard. My daddy said he picked just two bales of cotton and sold 'em and the rest was left in the field. I heard my Daddy say he was just one payment from having paid for the farm. We had 40 acres. My daddy—it hurt him so bad, he cried like a whupped child. We rented a farm out here, and my daddy never did get it together to buy another farm.[13]

And what about the black children of Vienna, Illinois, driven from their homes in a firestorm in 1954 and now in their fifties? What about the lost opportunities of all the people driven out in all the expulsions described in this book—opportunities to make a living in the towns from which they were "cleansed"? Most of them were employed, after all. What about the possibilities African Americans lose out on today, growing up in central city neighborhoods surrounded by poor people and rusting factories, while whites in sundown suburbs grow up surrounded by resources and opportunities?

Legal Remedies

There are precedents for reparations. After the 1885 murder and expulsion of Chinese coal miners in Rock Springs, Wyoming, the United States paid survivors and heirs $150,000. Springfield, Illinois, did pay damages to black citizens whose property was destroyed in the 1908 riot; indeed, the city had to issue bonds to pay all the claims. More famously, the United States paid $20,000 to every Japanese American who had been placed in a concentration camp during World War II. More recently, North Carolina made modest reparations to people its Eugenics Board ordered sterilized between 1929 and 1974. On one occasion, a state paid monetary reparations to African Americans to compensate them for losing their homes and employment as the result of violent expulsion. In 1994, Florida paid nine survivors of the 1923 Rosewood massacre—in which whites destroyed an entire black town, leaving a sundown town nearby—$150,000 each. A state commission recommended that Oklahoma follow suit in 2001, to compensate survivors and heirs of blacks attacked in the 1921 riot when whites tried to make Tulsa a sundown city, killing somewhere between 30 and 300 African Americans in the process. But Oklahoma and Tulsa seem to lack the political and moral backbone to emulate Florida, even though a similar breakdown of the state and city function of maintaining order made the riot possible. Having failed to get

Oklahoma to pass a reparations bill, attorneys have launched a lawsuit in federal court.[14]

Nevertheless, Rosewood remains a useful precedent for reparations, particularly since it resulted in at least one sundown town, Cedar Key. So does what happened in West Frankfort, Illinois. Whites drove Sicilians and African Americans from that southern Illinois city on August 5 and 6, 1920. Many of the Sicilians returned to live in West Frankfort within the week, but African Americans have not returned in any number to this day. Some Sicilians then brought suit for damages, and a U.S. federal court eventually awarded them more than $11,000 (the equivalent of more than $100,000 in 2005). African Americans won nothing, having no chance to obtain justice from a town that had just expelled them. According to a newspaper account, "They have sent back a representative to settle their bills and wind up all affairs of the colored race in this city."[15]

The case for reparations resulting from the many violent expulsions that led to sundown towns avoids most of the issues that are brought up by opponents of reparations for slavery. We do know or can learn who specifically was injured in each expulsion. Some victims and many heirs are still alive. Also, slavery was not illegal, while the expulsions of the Nadir were, yet federal, state, and city governments refused to provide African Americans with the equal protection of the laws guaranteed them under the Fourteenth Amendment to the Constitution. In 1863, the federal government punished the whites from Anna, Illinois, who had expelled African Americans from Union County—and that was *before* passage of the Fourteenth Amendment. But from 1890 to 1968, the federal government rarely if ever interfered with a sundown town. It showed no interest in prosecuting the whites who expelled African Americans from Anna in 1909, for example. State and local governments were often equally lax. As David Zimmermann put it, writing about the 1905 and 1909 race riots that drove African Americans from Harrison, "Diligent research has failed to reveal any records of actions taken by law enforcement officers or any other local officials to protect Harrison's African American community at any time preceding, during, or after the attacks." Thus not only the perpetrators but also local and state governments share responsibility for repairing the damages caused by the expulsions and the sundown towns that resulted.[16]

Legal actions can remedy other governmental actions and inactions that have helped sundown towns last so long. As we have seen, beginning in the 1930s, the federal government *required* neighborhoods to be all-white for participation in mortgage and housing programs, and it even built several sundown towns itself. State governments were also complicit bystanders that ignored or facilitated actions that created sundown towns and counties. Most local governments of sundown towns and counties worked actively to keep their jurisdictions all-white; some still do. Governmental complicity yesterday can provide openings for judicial intervention today. The previous chapter gave examples of lawsuits that have succeeded against sundown towns and their exclusive ways. The 1977 Seventh Circuit decision known as "Arlington Heights II" held that plaintiffs do not have to prove that town officials had a conscious intent to keep out minorities; it is enough to show that their policies had that effect. Of course, since sundown towns and suburbs have oral traditions of intent as well as effect, sound historical research can make lawsuits against them very winnable.[17]

State courts hold promise, too, because many states already have useful open housing laws on their books, some dating to the Reconstruction era.[18] The Mount Laurel judgment in New Jersey and the New Castle case in New York, as summarized by historian Kenneth Jackson, require suburbs "to accept a 'fair share' of the disadvantaged populations in their areas and to make 'an affirmative effort to provide housing for lower-income groups.' " In 1999, "an affordable housing developer" sued Bluffdale, "an all-white suburb of 4,500 people south of Salt Lake City, Utah, for what they contend is a discriminatory zoning scheme that will continue to exclude racial and ethnic minorities and people with disabilities," according to the National Low Income Housing Coalition. Apparently the plaintiff succeeded in winning new policies from Bluffdale. And in 2000, a federal district court found that Sunnyvale, Texas, a suburb of Dallas, had long engaged in what the court concluded was "discriminatory zoning."[19] The judge's opinion includes a careful and useful review of federal law in these cases and notes that "the Fair Housing Act prohibits not only direct discrimination but practices with racially discouraging effects."[20]

These decisions offer important precedents, because many sundown suburbs have used zoning, minimum lot size, and related polices to keep out African Americans. If such cases as Sunnyvale can be won without specific evidence of exclusionary practices, then testimony about these practices should make successful legal actions against sundown towns and suburbs still easier. That these practices originated decades ago does not render them moot, for once a policy is in effect, the burden shifts to the community to show that its policy has changed. Many sundown towns have done nothing to publicize or implement a new policy, which is why they continue to be all-white. Now that suburbs have become more populous and more important economically than inner cities or small towns and rural areas, it is critical that they shake off their sundown origins.

Undoing *Milliken v. Bradley*

Unfortunately, one legal decision constitutes a dangerous precedent. The previous chapter told how school desegregation decisions in southern states helped lead communities there toward residential desegregation. This same process had begun to desegregate northern metropolitan areas too, until halted by the U.S. Supreme Court in 1974. In *Milliken v. Bradley,* the Court "largely freed white suburban districts from any legal obligation to participate in metropolitan desegregation efforts," as Jack Balkin put it, writing in 2001. African Americans in Detroit had recognized that the Detroit public schools were going overwhelmingly black, so they sought desegregation with white populations in the suburbs. Of course, the white schools of Dearborn, Warren, and other suburbs did not admit to being white as a matter of law or public policy—de jure. They merely served the children who lived within their district boundaries, and those children just "happened" to be all white—de facto.[21]

The *Milliken* opinion awarded primacy to suburban school district boundaries. Supreme Court Justice Potter Stewart cast the deciding vote, denying African American students' request for integration with suburban schools. We have seen how most white Americans came to view residential segregation as natural, rather than resulting from governmental policies. Like them, Stewart claimed to be baffled about the causes of residential and school segregation:

> It is this essential fact of a predominantly Negro school population in Detroit—caused by unknown and perhaps unknowable factors such as immigration, birth rates, economic changes, or cumulative acts of private racial fears—that accounts for the "growing core of Negro schools," a "core" that has grown to include virtually the entire city.[22]

The factors behind all-white suburbs *are* knowable, of course. "Immigration, birth rates, and economic changes" do *not* explain why thousands of workers built cars in Dearborn and Warren, but the black ones all lived in Detroit or Inkster while the white ones lived where they worked. "Private racial fears" do play a role, but not merely because they motivate thousands of private decisions by individual white and black families. These private racial fears result in part from a panoply of private *and public* policies that have been responsible for making and keeping suburbs white. Indeed, sundown towns show that no clear distinction can be maintained between de jure and de facto segregation. For decades, as we have seen, government officials were decisively involved in keeping Dearborn white, for example. Previous chapters told of the repeated attempts by African Americans to live in Wyandotte and the repeated private acts of violence by Wyandotte residents and formal acts by its city government to keep them out. A similar list of violent and nonviolent actions performed or condoned by city governments has interfered with the free choices of African Americans to live in Grosse Ile, Grosse Pointe, and other suburbs in the Detroit area. When the perpetrators of violence go unpunished, the government is again involved, albeit one step removed from the actual acts against black would-be residents.

Evidently little of this information about Detroit's sundown suburbs— including the explicit actions over the years taken by their governments to stay all-white—was considered by the Supreme Court.[23] In the absence of this information, five of the nine justices held, as Potter Stewart put it, "the mere fact of different racial compositions in contiguous districts does not itself imply or constitute a violation." Therefore they said that residential segregation was not open to remedy by litigation. In turn, school segregation resulting from residential segregation was also not open to remedy. Absurdly, so long as a sundown suburb avoided segregating its handful of black students into a majority-black school, the judges held that it was operating lawfully. Thus because Dearborn, Grosse Ile, the Grosse Pointes, Warren, Wyandotte, and others had been so racist as to exclude African Americans almost totally, in 1974 their school systems were declared not racially segregated.

Looking back three decades later, the importance of *Milliken* is obvious. This ruling largely ended the efforts of federal courts to desegregate school systems in the North, following the promise of *Brown*. Today we can see that not only was this decision bad sociology, it also amounted to a tragedy for Detroit and the nation. In effect, it told whites that if they didn't want to live in a majority-black neighborhood, have their children attend an overwhelmingly black school, and suffer the lower prestige and other disadvantages that such schools and neighborhoods entail, they had better move to a sundown suburb. At the same time, the decision signaled suburbs that they could continue to be all-white, so long as they did not openly say they were. The consequences were further white abandonment of Detroit (and some other central cities), continued resistance to African American newcomers in the suburbs, and further mystification of the sundown process.[24]

In *Milliken*, the majority stated, "It must first be shown that there has been a constitutional violation within one district that produces a significant segregative effect in another district."[25] Perhaps a new case can be brought against those Detroit suburbs that remain overwhelmingly white today, fully revealing the links between past public policies in sundown suburbs and residential segregation, and then making the obvious connection between that residential segregation and today's overwhelmingly black schools in Detroit.[26]

Local Institutions Can End Sundown Towns

Litigation is not the only avenue to change racist policies. People connected with institutions—governments, corporations, school systems—can get them to act to undo sundown towns. Here are some specific steps, starting with the gentlest and moving to the harshest. Every sundown town or county should announce officially that it intends to become more diverse and should set up a human relations commission to accomplish that end. The town should then send a letter to every real estate agent in its area informing them that housing in the town is open without regard to race, requiring them to state their intent to show, rent, and sell property to all, and inviting them to contact the human relations commission in case of any problem. Schools and city departments should also state their intent to welcome and hire nonwhite employees to overcome their town's history of exclusion and should drop any requirement that prospective employees must live within their boundaries before employment.[27] As with historical markers, if a jurisdiction refused a request from citizens to do or say these things, the resulting publicity would be valuable in itself.

Of course, talk is cheap. Many sundown towns have already subscribed to anti-discrimination statements and keep on discriminating.[28] Nevertheless, such statements are a first step. Moreover, the presence of a human relations commission counterbalances the "bad apples" that otherwise can seem to speak for a sundown town while the majority does nothing. It sends a signal that some whites, at least, will oppose acts of hostility toward a black would-be resident, and it provides people of color with a place to report threats or other problems.[29]

Fayetteville and Jacksonville, North Carolina, which are among the least segregated cities in the United States, show what leaders of local institutions can do—in this case the local commanders of the United States armed forces. Fayetteville is near Fort Bragg. After the 1964 Civil Rights Act pointed the way, Army leadership helped open Fayetteville's golf courses, bars, and other public facilities. Camp Lejeune, a Marine Corps base, made a similar difference in Jacksonville.[30] Because the armed forces realizes that its men and women live or spend time in nearby communities, for decades it has made relationships with nearby communities, including race relations, part of the evaluation process for base commanders. To be sure, some commanders treat this requirement merely as a bureaucratic nuisance. Nevertheless, it helps, and every government agency—state and federal—needs to make these concerns part of the job definitions of those who run its local offices. After all, government offices and agencies exist in almost every sundown town. Imagine what might happen if each of them tried seriously to end their town's exclusionary policies![31]

Governments in metropolitan areas or state governments can also equalize the amount of money spent on students in different school districts, so students enjoy something approaching equal educational opportunity. In most states, the way we pay for public K–12 education, as well as other local public services, pits suburb against suburb across a metropolitan area. This competition makes it in no suburb's interest to provide or even allow affordable housing. Equalizing tax dollars across the state or across municipalities in a metropolitan area solves this problem.[32] Although elite sundown suburbs often oppose such tax equity, courts have found unequal property-tax-based school finance systems unconstitutional in twenty-one states, and other states have taken steps toward more equality without the spur of lawsuits. Whites move to sundown suburbs for four main reasons: to achieve status, avoid African Americans, enjoy amenities such as better parks and nicer neighborhoods, and provide better schools for their children—and not necessarily in that order. Fiscal equalizing can remove the last two as incentives luring whites to move to white suburbs.[33]

Schools can adopt other policies that promote school and neighborhood integration. In some districts—Denver and Louisville, for example—previously all-white or all-black neighborhoods can get neighborhood schools back, with no busing, if they desegregate residentially. This provides an incentive for residents of sundown neighborhoods to let African Americans move in, so their own children won't have to be bused out. Some school systems, including Wake County, North Carolina (Raleigh), and LaCrosse, Wisconsin, take care to make each of their schools diverse in social class, as well as race.[34]

School districts can also take steps to end "test flight." In today's metropolitan real estate markets, lofty school test scores have become a sought-after commodity. One reason why parents move to the suburbs is to get good schools, and an easy—if shallow—way to compare schools is by standardized test scores. In Massachusetts, for example, according to a 2000 report, "school districts that score badly on the MCAS [that state's standardized test] are likely to have houses for sale as parents try to move their kids to schools with better scores." The trouble is, high scores on standardized tests correlate with race (white and Asian) and class (affluent) at least as well as with good teaching. Elsewhere I have presented some of the reasons why African Americans, Native Americans, and Hispanics score lower on these tests.[35] Given these gaps, it is in suburbs' interest to keep out these groups so their schools will look better as measured by the test scores, so their homes will be worth more.[36]

School districts should disaggregate scores by race, income category, and academic program. Disaggregating allows everyone to face the statistics openly. Many white parents will not move into a school district that they think will disadvantage their children. Yet white students in an interracial district may score as well as white students in an elite sundown suburb, so they are *not* being disadvantaged—but that fact cannot be inferred from overall school means that include black students.[37] Similarly, college-oriented parents will not move into a school district if they think its students are likely to score poorly on college entrance exams. Yet some economically diverse high schools prepare their college-bound students at least as well as elite sundown high schools, where almost everyone is college-bound, but their success cannot be inferred from overall school averages that include non-college-bound students.[38]

Institutions of higher learning can also help to desegregate sundown towns and suburbs by admitting students without giving so much credit to the stacked deck that elite suburbs provide. This means jettisoning standardized tests such as the SAT and ACT or factoring into account their built-in racial and class biases, as well as the various aids that elite suburban children use to score higher on them.[39] It also means returning to straight high school grade-point averages rather than something called "uncapped GPAs," which artificially raise the grades students get when they take advanced placement (AP) courses. Enhancing grades in AP courses results in striking geographic unfairness: the *average* uncapped GPA for suburban students admitted to the University of California at Berkeley in 1999 was at least 4.33, for example, when an A equals 4.0. Meanwhile, the valedictorian of an inner-city high school with a straight A average but no AP courses earned "only" a 4.0 and was not even competitive—and all because of where the student lived.[40]

Corporations can also do much to undo sundown towns and suburbs. Many companies are already becoming good citizens regarding race relations. Some got the message the hard way, after bad racial practices brought them notoriety. Once a company has been doing a good job hiring and promoting people of color, it naturally becomes more concerned about the race relations of the communities where it is located. Now it has African American managers who want to live in hospitable and pleasant towns, and white executives who want to keep those managers happy. The Quaker Oats Company required Danville, in central Illinois, to pass an open-housing ordinance as a condition of locating a plant there, for example, and Danville isn't even a sundown town; we can infer that Quaker Oats would never locate in a town that it knew excluded blacks. And not just Quaker; Earl Woodard, executive director of the Chamber of Commerce in Martinsville, Indiana, notorious for its sundown policy, complained in 1989 that owing to "its bad image," Martinsville "hasn't nabbed a single one" of the industrial facilities that "rained down on central Indiana" in the 1980s.[41]

White Families Can Dismantle Sundown Towns

Those of us not a part of any large corporation or other institution and without much governmental influence—what can we do? Surely every American has a stake in remedying sundown towns and suburbs. White people created sundown towns, and whites—and "others"—can dismantle them.

People who live in an overwhelmingly white community can move. After they realize that choices by white families to live in white neighborhoods aggregate to form a social problem that then affects an entire metropolitan area, some whites refuse to live in a place that is part of the problem rather than part of the solution.[42] When they move to an interracial neighborhood, often they help it get better schools, parks, and all the other accoutrements that make a successful community.

Moving into an interracial or majority-black community can seem intimidating for whites from sundown towns who have never known African American friends and neighbors. It needn't be. Sociologist Karyn Lucy found the best race relations in majority-black suburbs. Whites who moved into these suburbs after they were already substantially black "get along [particularly] well with their neighbors and are involved in neighborhood activities." My experience confirms her findings.[43] Whites do not have to be so bold as to move to predominantly black neighborhoods, however. Almost every metropolitan area contains at least one majority-white suburb that is struggling to stay interracial against the pressures deriving from sundown suburbs. Moving there not only provides such suburbs with incoming white families that help them stay integrated, it can also deter white flight by families who already live there.[44]

People who don't live in sundown neighborhoods can challenge the "paradox of exclusivity" described in Chapter 11. Asking "Why?" with quiet astonishment when acquaintances announce that they are thinking of moving to a town or suburb known to be overwhelmingly white invites people to explain their decision—suddenly no longer obvious—to live in such places and may make them think. So do questions such as "But don't you hate to send your children to such an overwhelmingly white school system?" put to residents of such towns. Such conversations begin to reverse the status hierarchy that confers prestige on residents of all-white or overwhelmingly white communities, in turn, decreasing their hold on the popular definition of "the nice part of town." This challenging of racial exclusion is beginning to happen: as early as 1992, the authors of *Detroit Divided* noticed that some whites in the Detroit area rated Dearborn—renowned for its sundown policies—undesirable because they did not want racist neighbors. Suddenly where one is "supposed to" live isn't so clear. Decreasing the prestige of all-white neighborhoods and towns helps all parts of the metropolitan area become more open and attractive to all races and social classes.[45]

Whites who don't want to move from their overwhelmingly white communities can instead move their towns toward diversity and justice. White residents can persuade their school system that it cannot be competent without a seriously interracial faculty. Nor can a police department be fair—or perceived as fair—while being all-white. They can persuade their zoning board that these new teachers, police officers, etc., need to be able to live in the community where they teach, so affordable housing must become a priority. They can represent the excluded, who by definition cannot represent themselves because they have been kept out. They can even bring them in: in 1969, residents of Valparaiso, in northern Indiana, brought families from Chicago public housing projects to new homes in Valparaiso. The residents made the mistake of revealing their plan before finalizing their first home purchase, and a white supremacist stepped in to buy the house at a higher price. Eventually, however, they relocated Barbara Frazier-Cotton and her children, and later another family, to Valparaiso. At first, telephoned threats and cars slowly driving by were terrifying. Frazier-Cotton tells of "sleeping with the lights and television on to dissuade would-be intruders." Valparaiso University students set up patrols outside the house at night, and white couples sometimes slept in the home to provide support. Despite the opposition, Frazier-Cotton stuck it out for ten years, during which she earned a bachelor's degree from Valparaiso and her six children got a start that helped each of them build middle-class careers. Valparaiso was a tough case. If a few white liberals could crack it in the 1970s, surely most sundown towns and suburbs can be overcome today.[46]

Sometimes old-fashioned protests help. Demonstrators, mostly from Atlanta and mostly African American, marched in Forsyth County, Georgia, in early 1987, continuing into the 1990s. Five residents of Forsyth County marched with the group on the first day, and more thereafter. Racist groups such as Richard Barrett's Nationalist Movement held counterdemonstrations, not understanding that *all* publicity about sundown behavior helps bring about change. Oprah Winfrey gave coverage to the issue on two occasions. By the late 1990s, Forsyth County had several hundred black residents, while sundown counties to its north,[47] such as Towns County, without the benefit of demonstrations or publicity, did not.[48]

White families have standing to bring cases on their own behalf against realtors, city officials, and others responsible for their town's all-white makeup. Quoting Justice William O. Douglas for a unanimous Supreme Court in *Traficante v. Met Life et al.*, tenants in a California apartment house whose manager kept out African Americans "had lost the social benefits of living in an integrated community; . . . [and] had suffered embarrassment and economic damage in social, business, and professional activities from being 'stigmatized' as residents of a 'white ghetto.' " This 1972 case and others decided more recently provide useful precedents for white families to act to force sundown towns to reverse course and announce that they have done so.[49]

African American Challenges to Sundown Towns

Even well-meaning whites cannot desegregate a sundown town without the help of black households. This book hopes to spur action to end sundown towns, suburbs, and neighborhoods, and some of that action can be taken only by African Americans. I believe a black family, backed by an alert civil rights attorney if necessary, can now buy a home in most of America's persisting sundown towns. Some towns would still meet them with a freeze-out or violence, but black families have increasingly found welcoming neighbors.

Admittedly, moving into a sundown town differs from any other civil rights action. Unlike the marcher or sit-in participant of years past, the black family moving into a sundown town eats and sleeps on the picket line, and risks all its members, including babies, toddlers, and elderly. "There is a terrible isolation that surrounds the lone black family in a hostile white neighborhood," pointed out Dorothy Newman, an expert on segregated housing, in the 1970s. Even today, for African Americans to move into a town that has not had any African Americans for decades violates the norm, and sociologists know that norm violators usually get sanctioned. So blacks are right to be cautious. Families do not seek to be pioneers in civil rights; they simply want a nice place to live. Even absent any hostility from whites, there are logistical problems in moving to a sundown town: "Where can we go to get our hair styled? Where will we go to church? Will we find friends?" An African American who lives in Peoria suggested a major reason why black families don't desegregate the many sundown towns and suburbs around that city: "Black kids raise a fit about being the only black kids in the high school." [50]

African Americans have a legacy of heroes who have gone before to inspire them. One I knew personally: Medgar Evers, selfless leader of the Mississippi Civil Rights Movement. Evers's vision of the America of the future did not encompass allowing sundown suburbs to remain all-white. In her memoir of him, his widow, Myrlie, makes this clear:

> One of Medgar's greatest pleasures during those summers in Chicago was the chance to explore the suburbs. Whenever he could, he would borrow a car and drive out of the city to wander up one street and down another looking at houses. He had a dream of the sort of house he hoped someday to live in, the kind of street and neighborhood and town where he might raise a family, and the white suburbs of Chicago seemed to him right out of that dream. He would spend whole days just driving slowly through the suburbs of Chicago's North Shore, looking at the beautiful houses and wishing. Years later, when we were in Chicago together, he took me on these drives and by that time he had picked out specific houses that came closest to his dream.

One of the suburbs Evers drove through four decades ago was Kenilworth. Although one black family did live there in the 1960s and '70s, today Kenilworth still awaits its pioneer. So do many others. [51]

Black efforts *have* changed sundown towns. In town after town, African Americans have braved appalling conditions, sometimes bringing along friends and family members for backup, usually persevering in the long run and winning the right to live in the former sundown town in peace. Sociologist

George Henderson became the first black homeowner in Norman, Oklahoma, when he joined the faculty of the University of Oklahoma in 1967. In his memoirs, Henderson wrote, "Garbage was thrown on our lawn, a couple of car windows were broken, and we received obscene phone calls." In an interview with the student newspaper 35 years later, he recalled, "I feared for my family, but I was willing to die trying to make a difference. I had to come to terms with the fact I might be killed, but I believe that anything worth living for should be worth dying for." Henderson's fears were not exaggerated, for residents of Norman had engaged in repeated acts of real or threatened violence toward African Americans over the years. Indeed, historian Bill Savage, who came to the University of Oklahoma the year before Henderson, was shown a big tree on a hill in Norman by a man who said his father took him there just ten years earlier, in 1957 or '58, and pointed to a black man hanging from it, "the last black man to violate the sundown rule in Norman."[52]

Sundown suburbs can be equally threatening. In 1957, William and Daisy Myers were the first African Americans to move into Levittown, Pennsylvania, built as a sundown suburb after World War II. They faced telephoned death threats, a mob milling across the street, and burning crosses on neighboring lawns. Daisy Myers, wife and mother of the family, kept a journal during the ordeal. She makes vivid the possible costs they anticipated:

> We thought we should take the three children to York, Pennsylvania [to stay with their grandparents], but because Lynda was so young we decided to keep her with us. I felt that she would be too much of a burden on Bill's family, with a formula to prepare and the other attention an infant requires. I remember saying to Bill that if we were killed in the house, Lynda would be too young to know. At least we would have the boys to carry on.[53]

Despite the initial tension, usually the enterprise ends happily. A lawyer who left the black ghetto of San Francisco for a white neighborhood was struck "that for the first time I was friendly with my immediate neighbors. They have the same interests we do." In his 1970 book about housing desegregation, James Hecht summarized, "When a Negro family moves into a white area there are problems which few whites appreciate, but these problems usually are far less than the blacks anticipated." He traced records of some 500 black families who had moved into previously all-white neighborhoods in the Buffalo, New York, area since 1964. "None are known to have moved back to the ghetto," he reported. "About fifty of these families, including most of those who experienced unpleasant incidents, were interviewed in

some depth. All were glad they had made the move. All would do it again."
Hecht was able to generalize these results beyond Buffalo:

> Most of the families who moved found something else they had not anticipated,
> a warm welcome by some of their new neighbors. Fair housing groups through-
> out the nation report that black families moving into white neighborhoods usu-
> ally had more friendly calls of welcome than did white families who moved into
> the same neighborhoods.

The Gautreaux program in Chicago likewise proves that whites *do* accept
African American neighbors, even low-income ones.[54]

Victor Ward started the process of change in Cherokee, Oklahoma, during the summer of 1977. A young petroleum engineer newly minted by Mari-
etta College in Ohio, Ward landed a job with Conoco, and they assigned him
to Cherokee. "I arrived at the beginning of the summer and started to look for
a place to live. I started with my work associates, and then asked around. And
they sent me from one person to the next and I got 'No, that's not available,'
and 'Sorry, that's been rented.' " Ward ended up "in a shack, really, at the edge
of town, didn't even have electricity." Then he got a breakthrough: a woman
who had earlier turned him down phoned him at the Conoco office. She said
she had talked with her pastor about it. Ward repeated her words to him: "I'm
thinking, if I'd sent my son to some other town, I would hope they wouldn't
treat him the way the people of Cherokee have treated you." So she rented to
Ward, who became the first African American to live in previously sundown
Cherokee, at least the first in decades. His co-workers socialized with him
after work and invited him to their homes, and he had a fine summer. That he
came in under the aegis of Conoco surely helped, but so did Ward's positive
outlook. "I think at the end of the day, I kind of won the town." The census
showed Cherokee with no African Americans in 1950, 1960, and 1970, but
five in 1980, after Ward's breakthrough. Cherokee may need another Ward,
however, because in 1990 it was back to its former all-white status, and in
2000 it had but two African Americans, and no black households.[55]

Often blacks do "win the town." Henderson is now a treasured senior
member of the faculty and community in Norman. Although it took decades,
Levittown now honors the Myerses: in December 1999, Bristol Township
mayor Sam Fenton invited Daisy Myers to Levittown (her husband had died
in 1987) and offered her a public apology. Levittown named a blue spruce tree
in front of the municipal building "Miss Daisy" and uses it as the township

Christmas tree. There can be no doubt that white residents now fully accept the right of African Americans to live in both Norman and Levittown.[56]

Sometimes it takes two attempts. After the first family is forced out from a town, the racists who rebuffed them may be surprised to receive mixed messages, even condemnation, from other residents, so they don't mount another attack when another family tries, a year or so later.

Passing a Residents' Rights Act

All the solutions suggested thus far may not suffice to remedy the tougher cases, whether these turn out to be independent towns like Anna or elite suburbs like Kenilworth. Indeed, the remedies America has tried thus far are reminiscent of the "freedom of choice" phase of school desegregation (1955–69). Just as policies in that discredited era placed the burden of desegregating our nation's schools on individual black children, so our attempts at desegregating our nation's neighborhoods have placed the burden on individual black families. But our nation has a *national interest* in desegregating white communities.

What is needed is a law—a Residents' Rights Act—that makes it in an entire town's interest to welcome African Americans. This proposed remedy embodies the conclusion reached by Zane Miller, who wrote a history of Forest Park, Ohio, established as a sundown suburb of Cincinnati in the 1950s. He noted that African Americans first began to move into Forest Park during 1967, and by 1970, 470 lived in "larger Forest Park." This was more than enough to make Forest Park a frontline suburb, and by 2000 its population was 56% black. Miller understood the key role played by Cincinnati's all-white suburbs in Forest Park's transformation and realized that the only way to achieve stable racial desegregation in metropolitan areas is by attacking sundown suburbs.

> What Forest Park . . . needed was a national and metropolitan policy which would . . . open up the wedges of overwhelmingly white suburbs on the metropolitan area's western and eastern flanks. . . . Until that happened, the pattern of metropolitan ghettoization within scattered political jurisdictions would persist.[57]

Sociologist Herbert Gans, who studied New Jersey's Levittown (now called Willingboro), came up with a similar recommendation: "If all communities must integrate, no one can expect to live in all-white communities." So did William Levitt himself, whose company built more sundown suburbs than any other. Levitt knew that sundown suburbs were bad for America. Nevertheless, he continued to build them. "Only when all builders are forced to sell on a fair basis, he reasoned, would any of them be able to 'afford' an end to discrimination," according to housing expert Dorothy Newman. Otherwise, if Levitt didn't keep African Americans out, he'd be the only developer that didn't, so all the blacks would flood into his towns. When members of CORE demonstrated at his sundown development in Belair, Maryland, Levitt called on President John F. Kennedy to put some real teeth into his ineffectual order opposing discrimination in housing, to force all suburbs to end discrimination. Kennedy did not respond, and Levitt took no steps on his own to desegregate the communities he built.[58]

Ironically, the evolution of Levitt's development in New Jersey shows that Levitt had a point. The three Levittowns developed very differently. The first black family moved into Levittown, Pennsylvania, in 1957; the town wasn't very welcoming and by 2000 was still only 2.4% black. "Not a single one of the Long Island Levittown's 82,000 residents was black" in 1960, according to Kenneth Jackson, and by 2000 only 266 were, just 0.5% of 53,067 residents, a clear reflection of its racist heritage. The third Levittown, now Willingboro, New Jersey, had a very different history. In 1958, William Levitt announced that he would not sell any of its homes to African Americans. New Jersey's governor ordered an investigation; U.S. Senator Clifford Case requested that the FHA refuse to insure mortgages in Levittown; and two African Americans who were turned away from the development sued Levitt in state court. Levitt took the case to the New Jersey Supreme Court, claiming his houses were a private matter, but the court held that the involvement of the FHA and other agencies made them publicly assisted, and Levitt was forced to desegregate Willingboro. Eventually, agents began to steer African Americans *toward* Willingboro, which by 1980 was 38% black. Willingboro residents struggled to stay interracial in the midst of overwhelmingly white competitors; one step was to ban "For Sale" signs, to slow white flight. But the U.S. Supreme Court struck down the ban, finding that the town failed to establish that it was necessary to maintain integration. In 2000, Willingboro does remain integrated, being 61% black, but some commentators dismiss it as "black" or "80% black," which may be a self-fulfilling description. Thus Willingboro may wind up proving Levitt's (and Gans's and Miller's) larger contention: that it is hard for one suburb to stay interracial while others stay all-white. Willingboro also shows that government action—in this case by a governor, senator, and court—is the surest way to cause change.[59]

To be effective, a law must be written to preclude a town from merely *claiming* that it welcomes all newcomers without regard to race. After all, since 1968, towns don't admit they are all-white on purpose, realtors don't admit they steer, bankers don't admit they redline, police deny racial profiling, and in many places, neighbors deny they threaten or shun. Proving that officials of a town or suburb keep out African American residents today can thus be difficult, just as in the early 1960s no southern registrar would admit that would-be voters had to be white to register, even though their majority-black county might have thousands of white and only a handful of black registered voters. Therefore I suggest a Residents' Rights Act parallel to the registration clause of the Voting Rights Act of 1965 (extended and strengthened in 1982). This law provides that in counties with an unusual disparity between the percentage of the black and white electorates registered to vote, the Department of Justice can send in federal examiners, once complaints have been received from ten individuals who were rebuffed when trying to register. Similarly, a blatant disparity between the percentage of a town's population that is African American compared to the proportion in the metropolitan area (the entire state for independent sundown towns) will trigger sanctions under the Residents' Rights Act[60]—*when coupled with at least two valid complaints from families who were rebuffed when trying to buy or rent a home in the community and a careful showing that it was a sundown town.*[61] Proving that a community was a sundown town is doable if it was one, even if gathering candid admissions of continuing discriminatory behavior in the present is not. Because sundown policies are typically self-maintaining, it is appropriate to shift the burden to the community to show that it has changed them.

The Residents' Rights Act in Operation

Congress or a state could pass a Residents' Rights Act.[62] If Congress acted, the required complaints would go to the Department of Housing and Urban Development, which would have the power to hear complaints of recent discrimination and collect evidence on whether the town has a sundown past. The first consequence for towns that trigger the Residents' Rights Act will be federal housing examiners, parallel to the elections examiners of the Voting Rights Act. These examiners will investigate complaints, provide community relations services to the town, and meet with town officials, real estate agents, schools, and representatives of churches and other organizations to try to create an atmosphere more hospitable to African Americans or others claiming to have been excluded. The examiners can require local officials to proclaim that their town is open to all, set up a human relations commission, and order all real estate agents licensed to sell property in the town to state their intent to show, rent, and sell property without regard to race. The examiners will also be empowered to sit in on meetings between agents and African American would-be renters or purchasers.

Real estate agents may not be the problem, or at least not the whole problem, so housing examiners may not lead to real progress. In that event, the examiners will have the power to penalize the town. What sanctions are appropriate? Everyone from city officials to bankers to police to nearby neighbors may play a role in making it hard for African Americans to move to sundown towns and suburbs. So sanctions must make it in all these actors' interest to open up. The Clean Air Act offers a useful parallel. Under its provisions, if a city's air quality falls below a certain minimum, no more tax dollars can be spent on highways and development until it cleans up its air. Similarly, under the Residents' Rights Act, no more tax dollars can be spent on discretionary programs in a sundown town or suburb until it cleans up its segregation. Tax money that assists innocent people, such as for disaster relief, aid to disabled children, and the like, will still flow. Ongoing expenditures will not be affected. But the town will be shut out from seeking new funds for sewage facilities, police training, and 1,001 other programs. After all, every dollar of federal or state tax money spent in a sundown community is a dollar spent only on white Americans, yet collected from all Americans.

There are precedents for this. In 1947, under the auspices of the American Heritage Foundation, the United States government and America's railroads sent a "Freedom Train" around the country, carrying original copies of the Declaration of Independence and other important documents. This joint public-private venture proved very successful, drawing some 3,500,000 visitors in 322 cities. Columnist Drew Pearson helped instigate the effort. When Pearson learned that the train was scheduled to stop at Glendale, California, knowing that Glendale was a sundown town, "on his national radio broadcast he stated that the train would not stop in Glendale because Negroes could not stay there after dark," according to Bob Johnson, who remembers the broadcast.[63] The train also bypassed Birmingham, Alabama, after city officials there refused to let African Americans visit it except during hours specifically set aside for them. Langston Hughes wrote a poem about the Freedom Train, including the line "Everybody's got a right to board the Freedom Train." In its refusal to visit segregated Birmingham and sundown Glendale, the Freedom Train indeed lived up to its name.[64]

The chief federal judge for southern Illinois wants to deny Benton federal tax dollars today because it is a sundown town. His district, the Southern District of Illinois, epitomizes the sundown problem in America. The United States District Court holds court in two cities there: East St. Louis, 97.7% black, and Benton, 99.5% white. Judge G. Patrick Murphy is trying to keep a new $70,000,000 federal courthouse from being built in Benton. "I think it is fundamentally wrong to send the resources of the federal government, particularly in regard to the court system, to a community that is not diverse and is not enthusiastic about letting our employees participate fully in community life," said Murphy in October 2002. The mayor of Benton, Patricia Bauer, made her position clear: "We are a very small community, and I don't apologize[65] for Benton's racial makeup." [66]

Murphy is not the only official concerned about sundown towns. An attorney in Monticello, Illinois, said that his central Illinois sundown town had similar "trouble getting federal funding" for a county courthouse project, because they had no nonwhite workers. In 1982, a class action lawsuit filed on behalf of African Americans alleged widespread deliberate housing discrimination throughout East Texas. In response to the complaint, U.S. District Court judge William Wayne Justice ordered desegregation of public housing in towns throughout East Texas. Several, including Vidor and Alba, were sundown towns, so of course their public housing projects were all-white; *every* public expenditure in those towns was reserved for whites. In 1992, Vidor gained national notoriety when several black households moved into a public housing project, became the town's first African American residents, and were all driven out by Ku Klux Klan demonstrations, racial slurs, and threats.[67]

Making sundown towns ineligible for federal or state funds may not suffice, especially in affluent communities. Some school districts and institutions of higher education similarly turned their back on funds for education, loans for dormitories, and the like, choosing to stay segregated. If needed, a simpler sanction will come into play, making use of the income tax code: denial of the federal home mortgage interest deduction. This deduction has long been one of the important ways our tax code favors middle- and higher-income Americans, allowing homeowners to deduct the largest single component of their housing outlay, while renters get no such break. The rationale for this deduction is our national interest in encouraging home ownership. Surely America has no national interest in encouraging home ownership in sundown towns, however. So it should grant no exemption for mortgage interest payments by homeowners who choose to live in such communities.[68]

Denial of the mortgage interest exemption has additional benefits that should make it attractive to lawmakers. It costs nothing and commits the federal government to no massive new program of housing construction; on the contrary, it brings in revenue. Second, we have seen that because all-white suburbs have more prestige, typically they enjoy higher housing values.[69] Removal of the interest exemption will make such property less valuable, offsetting this gain from sundown policies.[70] Third, it allows for local control. A sundown town or suburb can opt to stay all-white. Alternatively, it can desegregate any way it wants, from developing low-cost housing to recruiting African American families to buy existing homes. Best of all, eliminating the mortgage interest exemption avoids problematizing "the poor black family," for whom perpetual government assistance seems required. Instead, the Residents' Rights Act recognizes segregated white communities as the problem and makes it in their residents' interest to stop their problematic behavior.

Indeed, all a town has to do to end or avoid these sanctions is to publicize that it is now open to all, take the steps suggested by federal housing examiners, and admit a few African American residents. As soon as its population no longer displays the blatant racial disparity that triggered suspicion in the first place, it will be off the list. For example, Grosse Pointe will need to become about 2.3% black, 1.5% higher than its 2000 proportion, 0.8%. Since it had 5,670 people in 2000, this requires it to welcome 85 more African Americans—an easy task, since neighboring Detroit has 775,000 African Americans and is more than 82% black. Independent sundown towns such as Arcola might find it harder. Arcola would need about 38 more African Americans to reach 1.54% black, one-tenth as black as Illinois statewide. It could (and should) recruit them, perhaps from larger nearby towns such as Decatur and Champaign—after all, it now draws white flight from those towns. If it finds this problematic, then after recruiting two or three families, thus moving beyond the sundown town threshold, it could ask the examiners to be removed from the sanction list, so long as they concur that the town has ended its discriminatory practices. The Residents' Rights Act requires not integration but an end to exclusion. It merely uses demography as evidence that exclusion has ceased. Recovering sundown towns can submit other evidence showing they have ended their restrictive policies and thus avoid any penalty.

At present, instead of penalizing sundown towns, governments reward them. For the last quarter of the twentieth century, sundown towns in southern Illinois, for example, got *more* than their share of federal expenditures. During that era, Kenneth Gray, representative in Congress for the region, earned the nickname "Prince of Pork" for all the federal money he brought to his hometown, West Frankfort, all-white since it drove out its African Americans in 1920, and to nearby sundown towns. Independent sundown towns often languish economically: their leaders don't seek new ideas or new companies, so employment plummets. Instead of withdrawing state and federal aid from these towns, governments award them prisons and juvenile detention centers to give their economies a boost. To penologists, places such as Chehalis, Washington; Clarinda, Iowa; Izard County, Arkansas; Pollock, Louisiana; Brown County, Dwight, Pinckneyville, Vandalia, Vienna, and other locations in Illinois; Perry County, Indiana; Wayne County and various other white valleys in Pennsylvania; the Adirondack counties of New York; Garrett County, Maryland; and other places with overwhelmingly white populations[71] seem to be ideal. In a circular process, prisons then put more people into sparsely settled, overwhelmingly white districts—people who cannot vote—magnifying the clout of their representatives in state legislatures.[72]

Governments also often honor sundown towns. At their city limits, sometimes right where the infamous sundown signs used to be, now stand congratulatory signs toasting the towns with such designations as "Governor's Hometown Award," "Illinois Main Street Community," "Illinois Certified City," "Michigan Educational Excellence Award," "U.S. Dept. of Education Exemplary School," and the like. Surely no sundown town deserves these awards. The Illinois Main Street program, for example, run by the lieutenant governor's office, has to do mostly with revitalizing downtowns. Among its guidelines are "Demonstrate broad-based private- and public-sector support for downtown revitalization" and "Develop vision and mission statements." Surely "broad-based support" should include support from people other than whites. Surely a town should have a vision of itself as a multiracial community, moved beyond its petty prejudices. Surely Main Streets that a state recognizes as exemplary should be streets that people of color can feel comfortable strolling down. Owosso, Michigan, won the 2000 Michigan Educational Excellence Award, but Owosso High School cannot help but impart racism, along with chemistry, algebra, and its other subjects, owing to its historically intentional racial makeup. Mariemont, Ohio, boasts a plaque saying "U.S. Dept. of Education Exemplary School," but an all-white school can hardly be exemplary. Surely citizens should demand that civic and educational competitions like these establish standards of racial tolerance that communities must meet before they can receive these awards.

Integrated Neighborhoods and Towns Are Possible

The Residents' Rights Act would have aided integration in Southfield, Michigan, which, according to *Detroit Divided,* had "the distinction of being the only prosperous Detroit suburb with a large and growing black population: 29% in 1990." Precisely because it had this "distinction," by 2000 Southfield was 56% black. In the absence of policies that would open up overwhelmingly white suburbs, towns such as Southfield are likely to become overwhelmingly nonwhite.[73]

The recent past offers hope for an end to racial exclusion, however. The previous chapter showed that at least half of our sundown towns and suburbs have probably given way. Surely we can desegregate the last half. Some tough towns have cracked. Residents of Valley Stream on Long Island intimidated realtors and black clients in the 1980s. Nevertheless, by 1990, it had 149 African Americans among its 33,946 residents, and in 2000, 2,714 African Americans called Valley Stream home. Even Martinsville, Indiana, whose sundown notoriety was confirmed by new episodes of hateful behavior in the 1990s, may have given in. The 2000 census showed two African American households, and reports indicate that one or two other families have since moved in.

Entire suburbs have resisted "tipping point" theory, which predicts that once African Americans reach a certain proportion—often said to be 15%—whites will flee. Park Forest, Illinois, shows how. Its leaders made a conscious decision to stop being a sundown town in 1961. Ted Hipple, who lived in Park Forest at the time, described the process:

> Blacks were moving from Chicago to the suburbs, and some looked at housing in Park Forest. Leo [Jacobson] and others in the government, to avoid any possible clustering of the black families and any resulting blockbusting consequences, were instrumental in allocating them to various parts of town, well separated from each other, with prior notification of the neighbors that a black family would be moving in.

As of 2000, Park Forest was still stably integrated, with 9,247 African Americans in a total population of 23,462. Another Chicago suburb, Oak Park, employed a similar strategy. In the early 1970s, Oak Park "began to experience substantial black in-migration," according to Carole Goodwin, who wrote *The Oak Park Strategy* about its methods for staying interracial. Oak Park garnered national renown as an integrated suburb after giving up its sundown status. "In 1977," Goodwin wrote, "Oak Park could not confidently be called a racially stable, integrated community." But by 2000, Oak Park could be, having 11,788 African American residents among more than 52,000 total population, about 22%. White demand for houses continues to be strong; Oak Park led all suburban zip codes in housing appreciation over the period 1998–2003.[74]

In the last twenty years, whites have sometimes moved *into* majority-black neighborhoods.[75] When this happens, liberals often cry gentrification, but the resulting class and racial mix usually lasts for many years, to the betterment of municipal services and the city's tax base. Tipping point theory cannot explain gentrification. Nor can it explain Mt. Rainier, Maryland, a working-class suburb of Washington, D.C., that was 56% black in 1990, 62% in 2000, and probably 59% in 2005. "The experiment of living together," said one white newcomer in 2003, "as opposed to being polarized as black or white or Latino, makes those labels break down and leaves a whole lot more room for finding common ground."[76]

Once a town eases its restrictive policies, all kinds of interesting people may move in. Among the families that seek to live in multiracial towns are multiracial families. D'Vera Cohn visited meetings of the Interracial Family Circle, a Washington, D.C., area group, in 2002. "The pros and cons of different neighborhoods are constant topics of conversation," she wrote. She quoted the group's president, Nancy Leigh Knox: "People want to be where it's diverse. Everyone talks about it as being the primary criterion." Knox and her husband are white but have two black adopted sons. "We want our children to live where there are lots of different kinds of people," Knox said. It turns out lots of people are like Knox, and not just members of interracial families. A librarian in Decatur, my central Illinois hometown, spoke with pride of his interracial neighborhood in the West End, which had been a sundown neighborhood when I grew up in it. "And there's a gay couple on the block, and no one thinks anything about it!" Because of whites who want to live in tolerant places, towns such as Mt. Rainier and Oak Park and interracial neighborhoods within cities not only survive but develop cachet. Other towns and neighborhoods may not be as well known for being integrated, especially those that are working- and lower-middle-class, but they endure, decade after decade, providing African Americans and European Americans (and Asian Americans, Hispanics, and Native Americans) with unheralded places to live that are stably 10% to 80% black.[77]

The goal is worth pursuing, partly because living in an integrated environment causes each racial group to define "we" nonracially. Interracial contact itself thus usually becomes a humanizing process. Here is an example from Baltimore, back in about 1947, in the words of a white housewife, 37 years old, the mother of three children:

> When a colored family moved next door to us I was horrified. I just couldn't see why they wanted to live where white people lived. I wanted my husband to move right away. We have lived here for fifteen years and we own our home. I would never let our children play with the children next door, or even talk with them. But in spite of all I told them about colored people, they still talked with them. One day my youngest boy came in the house with a ball that he said the little colored boy next door had given him. I was mad and made him give it back. My child was hurt, and it seemed that I was both cruel and unfair to him. After several weeks it suddenly occurred to me that those people weren't bothering me at all. They were polite and always spoke to us. Their children were—well—just children. My husband and Mr. W __ soon began to talk to each other over the back fence, and Mrs. W __ and I also began to exchange greetings. The children run back and forth to both houses. We do favors for each other just as other neighbors do. They're no different now from any of my other neighbors.

That is only one woman's opinion, of course, but other researchers made a systematic comparison of the attitudes of white residents of two integrated public housing projects and two white-only projects. Attitudes in the integrated projects were much more favorable toward people of different races.[78]

In suburbs like Oak Park and Mt. Rainier, whose residents made a decision to stay integrated, white residents have perforce made black friends. As Emilie Barnett of Shaker Heights, Ohio, put it, "Because there was a need to do this, we came to know people intimately. It was the only way we could get past race."[79]

Desegregating independent sundown towns benefits their residents, especially their children, by lessening their unease about the interracial outside world, thus expanding their options for college, vacations, and places to live and work. Children in elite sundown suburbs already have lots of options, but desegregation can likewise help them decrease their stereotypes about other races and be more comfortable in interracial milieux. Research by Orfield shows that most students in desegregated schools hold positive views about their experience. More than 90% of a sample of high school juniors in Louisville, Kentucky, for example, say they are comfortable working with stu-

dents of another race. Whites and blacks also feel they can discuss racial issues across racial lines. Adults benefit too. In her Philadelphia-area research,
Carolyn Adams found that "the most liberal racial attitudes were observed
among whites living in neighborhoods that were racially integrated—defined
as those in which at least 5% of the local population was black."[80] Merely en-
countering African Americans as neighbors, PTA members, and so on can
improve white rhetoric, because social and political discussions are impoverished by the absence of African Americans. We have seen that sundown towns
both collect and create racists, while integrated towns both collect and create
anti-racists. Just as cognitive dissonance makes whites more racist when they
live in a sundown town, which they must justify, so it makes whites less racist,
even anti-racist, when they live in a multiracial town, which they must justify.
Ideology and attitudes thus flow from social structure, with profound consequences for the next generation. For readers wanting a personal rationale for
living an integrated lifestyle, this is one.[81]

Moving Toward an Integrated America

America should not *have* white neighborhoods or black neighborhoods. It
should have just neighborhoods. People who live in interracial neighborhoods and towns have taken an important stand in favor of better race relations. Integration is no panacea, but there is no substitute. There seems to be
no stable resting point between slavery—which, though stable in a way, required constant vigilance—and fully equal democracy. Since we have not yet
attained fully equal democracy, race relations remains unstable, fluid, a source
of continuing contention in our society. In this situation, those who act for
racial justice are also helping to build social stability—maybe even the
"beloved community" yearned for in the Civil Rights Movement. Integrated
towns and suburbs are a necessary first step to integrated hearts and minds.
Until we solve the problem of sundown neighborhoods and towns, we do not
have a chance of solving America's race problem.

It all seems to be taking a very long time. As the last chapter noted, "Ain't
No Niggers Allowed" Anna—the town with which this book began—still may
not allow African Americans to live within its city limits. Surely its continued
existence as a sundown town—and that of all the other sundown towns and
suburbs that still have not changed—tells us it is taking far too long.

The remedies suggested here—especially the Residents' Rights Act—
remove the all-important badge of governmental approval or at least government neutrality from sundown towns and suburbs. In "Black and White,"

their 1972 hit song about school integration, the rock group Three Dog Night showed that they understood the importance of government action. After the federal government finally enforced school desegregation in the South, they sang, "Now a child can understand / This is the law of all the land / *All* the land." But was it? School desegregation was the law only in the South. In the North, after *Milliken,* sundown suburbs maintained school segregation by excluding African Americans from their neighborhoods.

> So now the child remains confused.
> Blacks passing through may be abused.
> What is the law of all the land?
> Do sundown policies still stand?

Or might we yet, as Three Dog Night put it, "learn together to read and write"? Then indeed, as they go on to sing, "The whole world looks upon the sight / A beautiful sight."[82]

Appendix A
Methodological Notes on Table 1

General notes

Several states, including Minnesota, the Dakotas, and notably Texas, had counties with as few as 3 to 999 residents, especially in 1890. Table 1 excludes them; such tiny populations should not be given equal weight as datapoints compared to counties with 5,000 or 50,000 people. Moreover, there is little reason to believe that African Americans were shut out if none appear in a county with a mere handful of inhabitants. Leaving out such counties also accords with my general omission of hamlets smaller than 1,000.

The second column under each date, counties with "<10 bl.," includes counties listed in the first column, counties with "0 bl." This is appropriate: any county with no African Americans obviously also has fewer than ten. Thus the columns "<10 bl." convey correct information without requiring addition from another column.

Why does Table 1 omit Alaska and Hawaii?

I omitted Alaska and Hawaii because they were not states during the Nadir and have had quite different racial histories since. Both are complexly multiracial, with Native American and Inuit populations in Alaska, and Native Hawaiian, Japanese, Chinese, and Filipino Americans, and others in Hawaii. Perhaps enterprising readers can investigate whether whites created sundown neighborhoods, suburbs, or towns in those states.

Minnesota's mixed pattern

Minnesota showed more counties in 1890 with no blacks, but more in 1930 with just a few blacks; however, in 1890 its counties had much lower total populations. Nine had fewer than 5,000, compared to just one in 1930. Their average population, excluding the counties containing Minnesota's three major cities—Duluth, Minneapolis, and St. Paul—was 18,502 in 1930, 50% more than the 1890 average of 12,102. Since their total populations were up, Minnesota counties should have had more African Americans in 1930. Instead, by 1930, seven of every eight black Minnesotans lived in Minneapolis–St. Paul, compared to less than one-third of whites, thus confirming a retreat to the city.

States with no counties in either year with fewer than ten blacks

Having only three counties, Delaware could not show any trend using county analysis. Neither could Rhode Island with five, although blacks did lose ground in three of Rhode Island's five counties and showed a sizable population increase only in Providence. In Connecticut, only three counties showed increases in African American population, comparing 1930 to 1890: Fairfield County near New York City, Hartford, and New Haven. These are Connecticut's most urban counties, and whites moved to them too, but whites also moved to other counties such as Middlesex, Windham, Litchfield, and New London. Blacks did not. The same pattern held in Massachusetts, New Jersey, and New York. By 1930, New York held many sundown towns and suburbs but at most one sundown county.

As a former slave state, every Maryland county had at least 1,000 African Americans in 1890, except one, Garrett, the farthest west, which had 185. By 1930, Garrett had gone overwhelmingly white, with only 24 African Americans (and just 4 by 1940). Although Garrett thus didn't quite make the cut by 1930, I have confirmed that it became and remained a sundown county. Moreover, although Maryland has no other sundown counties, it has many sundown suburbs that developed after 1890. So Maryland is no exception either.

States with only slightly greater numbers of counties with zero or fewer than ten blacks in 1930

Some of the trends in Table 1 seem inconsequential, but they are not when the huge increases in black population in Northern states are considered. Between 1890 and 1930 the black population of Pennsylvania, for example, increased almost fourfold, so for the state to show "only" a slight increase in the number of counties with few or no African Americans actually offers spectacular corroboration of the Great Retreat. The same point holds for West Virginia. Kansas had the same number of counties with no African Americans in 1930 that it had in 1890, but by the latter year its overall black population had increased by 72%. Meanwhile, the number of its counties with fewer than ten blacks actually increased. Similarly, no county in Ohio was all-white in 1890, compared to just one in 1930; one county had fewer than ten blacks in 1890, compared to just two 40 years later. Underlying this modest trend, however, are statistics like these: 13.6% of Ohio's black population lived in small cities (2,400 to 10,000) in 1860, a proportion that rose to 18.7% by 1890. Then by 1930, that proportion fell to a mere 5.0%—dramatic evidence of the Great Retreat, verified by numerous examples of confirmed sundown towns. Nevada's retreat was modest, but the state had only 242 African Americans in 1890 and possessed no large city to retreat to by 1930, Las Vegas being still in swaddling clothes.[1]

Confirmation by Jack Blocker

Historian Jack Blocker showed the Great Retreat in the Midwest with a different statistical method. Studying communities in Ohio, Indiana, and Illinois, he found an inverse correlation or no correlation between the black population in 1860 and its growth by 1890. In other words, African Americans dispersed in those decades; they did not move primarily to places where blacks already lived. But after 1890 the correlations turned positive in Indiana and Ohio, and after 1910 in Illinois, as African Americans concentrated in fewer locations. As Blocker put it, after about 1890, "dispersion, the pattern of the previous 30 years, was replaced by concentration."[2]

Do more counties introduce a bias?

Some states, mostly in the West, had considerably more counties by 1930, which might seem to make it easier to have more counties with no or few African Americans. Actually, the increased number of counties did not introduce a bias, because the populations of these states increased proportionately much more than their number of counties.

Consider Idaho, for example, which had only 18 counties in 1890 and had 44 by 1930. In 1890 its counties averaged fewer than 5,000 in total population. In 1930, its counties average more than 10,000. Based on total population, the average county had more than twice as great a chance to attract African Americans in 1930. Yet they did not. Only one Idaho county in 1890 had no African Americans; in 1930, fourteen counties had none. Only eight counties in 1890 had 1–9 African Americans; by 1930, nineteen counties had 1–9. Again, bear in mind that the 1930 counties averaged more than twice as many people, even though most were now smaller in area. Each is therefore a legitimate datapoint. Population, not geographic area, is the important variable. We are not testing whether a given array of square miles would draw black residents; rather, the assumption is that African Americans, unencumbered by prohibitions, would go where other populations go.

Appendix B
How to Confirm Sundown Towns

A sundown town is "all white" on purpose. To confirm, we must first show that it is "all white." We are only interested in exclusion, not "mere" segregation. However, the exclusion need not be total—that's why "all white" is in quotation marks. Chapter 10 tells how a town may have driven out its blacks, even posted the traditional sundown town signs, yet allowed one family to remain. Larger cities have even allowed more than one, in a way. Cicero, Illinois, for example, when burning out a would-be black apartment renter, had some 40 African Americans in town—probably servants in white households; inmates of such institutions as jails, hospitals, and colleges; or renters in large apartment houses not really located in residential neighborhoods and hence below the radar of whites. Since Cicero defined itself as all white and took steps to keep out the next black would-be household, it certainly qualifies.

Then we must find information confirming that the community kept blacks (or other groups) out (*if* it did!), either through the use of restrictive covenants throughout the town, violence or threats, bad behavior by white individuals, an ordinance, realtor steering, bank redlining, or other formal or informal policies.

In the past, many sundown towns kept out other groups, such as Mexicans, Asian Americans, Jews, and so on. Today most sundown towns have accepted all but African Americans. Between 1970 and today, many towns have stopped excluding altogether, yet it's still important to confirm them in the past. They may suffer from second-generation sundown town problems. Besides, residents should know of such an important aspect of their town's history.

Census Research

A first step, then, is to look up the census of population by race in various years. A website at the University of Virginia, fisher.lib.virginia.edu/census/, provides the racial proportions of every county from 1790 through 1960.

Data at census.gov provide the population by race of every town in the country with more than a few hundred inhabitants for 1990, 2000, and 2010 and will in subsequent censuses. Incorporated is information as to age and sex in the black population and number of households with black adult householders. This information helps us avoid misattributing residential status to African Americans living in institutions such as colleges or prisons or within white households as servants. For 1860 to 1980, the racial composition of your town will be in the printed bound volumes of the census, probably at your local library and certainly at your nearest university library. Get the actual census figures, decade after decade. They are also online at census .gov/prod/www/abs/decennial/index.htm. However, in some years breakdowns by race are provided only for towns larger than 2,500 and in one decade only for towns larger than 4,000. For smaller towns, count the number of African Americans listed in the "manuscript census," for 1940 and prior decades (except 1890, most of which was destroyed by fire). This is the raw data of the census, usually one line per person, with address, occupation, and, important for our purpose, race. It is on the web at various sites, such as your state historical society or library. Ancestry.com has it all. Large libraries and genealogical collections also have it on microfilm. Even small libraries will often have it for their state. It's actually fun to skim.

Sharp drops in black population are of course suspicious. Low numbers of blacks, decade after decade, are also suspicious, especially if African Americans are hardly absent from nearby towns and counties or if the town's total population is increasing.

Local Histories, Newspapers

Then, go to the local libraries (in person) and read (skim) any local history books, such as centennial histories and county histories. Usually the local library has a local history room (or local history shelf, in small libraries). Probably you will find nothing about blacks, but sometimes there are surprises. If there are notes on file from the WPA Federal Writers Project (c.1935–40), skim those. Also, see if there are vertical files (newspaper clippings) on "blacks," "Negroes," "segregation," "Ku Klux Klan," or other related topics. Sometimes libraries have transferred these to microfilm.

Then scan local newspapers for the decade between two adjacent censuses that show a sharp decline in black population, to see if they describe any actions whites took to cause the decline. Sometimes the nearest newspaper *outside* the town in question will be more forthcoming.

Oral History

Then ask the librarian in charge of the local history collection if s/he knows anything about the absence of blacks. Has she or he ever heard it might have been on purpose? Does she or he know of any stories (oral history) about anything bad that happened to a black family that tried to move into the town in the 1920s, 1970s, or any other decade? Ease into that topic gently, maybe by asking what the town's major employers used to be. Eventually ask, "Have you ever heard that [name of town] used to keep out blacks?" Maybe mention that some nearby towns (by name) used to keep out blacks, and follow by asking if *this* community had the same policy. If she or he says yes, then ask how she or he heard it, from whom, about when (year), and so on. Follow up by asking the librarian, "Who knows the most about the history of the town?" Every town has its expert. Then interview that person(s). Ask them too, "Who else should I talk with?" Is there a genealogical society? If so, attend its next meeting, after talking with its leader.

Oral history is fine, so long as it is solid. Thus, if a person says, "Blacks were not allowed . . ." follow up by asking, "How do you know that?" Also, seek details: "Did you ever hear of any family that moved in, then left?" and so on. Visit local nursing homes and places where seniors live or hang out (community center, SRO hotel). Old folks love to hold forth on the long-ago past. Also talk with retired realtors, minority group members in nearby towns, and other likely sources. Take good notes, including "quote notes" (with ") when you actually capture phrases verbatim.

Repeat the interview process with the city clerk and the head of the local historical society. Bear in mind, however, particularly with a local history society, that interviews rarely work unless you are there in person. Usually these folks don't want to say anything bad about their town if they can help it. In person, however, they don't want to lie. And of course, you flatter them by telling them (correctly) that they are the expert on the town's history. In general, e-mailing does not work, not on such a ticklish subject. It only sets off respondents' alarms, and they reply carefully if at all. Leaving phone messages is only slightly better. Talk with people, face to face if possible, on the phone if face to face is not possible.

Do also seek written sources, such as some ordinance about keeping out blacks (or another group). The ordinance, however, may merely be a motion passed in a city council meeting on a Tuesday evening in 1911, perhaps not even noted in the minutes of that meeting, and impossible to find now. Land records can also help. The sale of the black church or a house owned by a black resident (from the manuscript census) can provide an approximate date for the departure of the black community. You may be able to find the same name of the departed family in a nearby town in the next manuscript census, see if they're still there in 1940, and then see if you can locate descendants to interview today.

Always we must recall that a community's overwhelming whiteness *might* be an accident, that perhaps no African Americans ever happened to go there. We cannot classify an "all-white" town as a "sundown town" unless we have evidence about its racial policies, formal or informal. Moreover, one must use common sense and historical and sociological knowledge in this work. Lemhi County, in northern Idaho, all white in 1930, appears less suspicious than Garrett County, in western Maryland, which had 24 African Americans in that year, because 13 other Idaho counties also had no African Americans, while other Maryland counties all had more than 1,000. But then, a historian whose parents were born and raised in Lemhi County wrote that, according to her relatives, "Black people were 'run off' in some distant past." Meanwhile, several sources, including Henry Louis Gates Jr., confirmed that Garrett was a sundown county. So suspicion is appropriate in both cases, and additional sources have solidly confirmed Garrett.

Happy hunting; we await your results!

Notes

PREFACE TO THE 2018 EDITION

1. The interactive map of sundown towns at my website, sundown.tougaloo.edu/content
    .php?file=sundowntowns-whitemap.html, includes many towns that I learned about after
    the book came out. If you know towns I should list but don't, towns I do list but shouldn't,
    or additional details about towns I do list, please tell me: jloewen@uvm.edu.
2. The census must be used carefully, to avoid conflating institutional residents with house-
    holds. Pekin, a city in central Illinois mentioned later in this preface, illustrates this problem.
    In 1970, not one African American lived in Pekin, and not by chance. The 2000 Census
    showed 863 African Americans, a dramatic increase since 1990. Most were male, aged 18 to
    44, however—prisoners. The residential population showed just five households with a
    black householder, having a total population of only sixteen, some of whom may have been
    white. So Pekin was still a sundown town in 2000.
3. In 2015, the polling site *FiveThirtyEight* summarized years of survey research on the ques-
    tion of white attitudes toward blacks by the General Social Survey. They found about
    27 percent of whites still said "a homeowner should be allowed to refuse to sell to a potential
    buyer based on race." In 1980, 66 percent agreed, and in 2000, the number who agreed was
    40 percent. (Anna Maria Barry-Jester, "Attitudes Toward Racism and Inequality Are Shift-
    ing," fivethirtyeight.com, 6/23/2015, fivethirtyeight.com/features/attitudes-toward-racism
    -and-inequality-are-shifting/.)
4. Ed Pilkington, "From the Green Book to Facebook, How Black People Still Need to Outwit
    Racists in Rural America," *The Guardian*, 2/11/2018, theguardian.com/world/2018/feb
    /11/green-book-facebook-black-motorists-racist-america-road-trip-pitstops-safe.
5. Comment on Pete VanBaalen: "When Words Still Hurt," *Greensburg Daily News*,
    7/22/2006, greensburgdailynews.com/opinion/columns/pete-vanbaalen-when-words-still
    -hurt/article_26ecda88-d5ea-5ec7-9379-b8ee47aecdfa.html.

    Greensburg does show a willingness to discuss its racial past in "Greensburg, Indiana,"
    its entry on Wikipedia (3/2018), en.wikipedia.org/wiki/Greensburg,_Indiana.
6. Rex W. Huppke, "Letter Brings Controversy in Ind. Town," AP, 11/7/2001; Stephen Stueb-
    ner, "In Hate's Wake: Extremists Undermine a Small Town's Efforts to Overcome a Legacy
    of Racism," Southern Poverty Law Center *Intelligence Report* #107 (Fall 2002),
    splcenter.org/get-informed/intelligence-report/browse-all-issues/2002/fall/in-hates-wake.
7. In addition, 29 households had householders "of more than one race," but it is hard to know
    what that means. Some may be Latinos, others Asians married to whites, but they may in-
    clude black/white interracial couples.

8. Jon Webb, "Indiana Still Has a Racism Problem," *Courier & Press*, courierpress.com
    /story/opinion/columnists/jon-webb/2017/11/07/webb-indiana-still-has-racism-problem
    /827560001/.

9. "Justice Department Announces Findings of Two Civil Rights Investigations in Ferguson,
    Missouri," Washington, DC: U.S. Dept. of Justice, 3/4/2015, justice.gov/opa/pr/justice
    -department-announces-findings-two-civil-rights-investigations-ferguson-missouri.

10. Eugene P. Ericksen and Joseph B. Kadane, "Estimating the Population in a Census Year
    1980 and Beyond," *Journal of the American Statistical Association* 80: 389 (1985), 9–109,
    tandfonline.com/doi/abs/10.1080/01621459.1985.10477140.

11. "The Educational Value of 'News,'" *The State* (Columbia, SC), 12/5/1905.

12. "Indicts Six More on Riot Charges," *Chicago Tribune*, 8/22/1908.

13. William English Walling, "The Race War in the North," *Independent*, 529–34 (9/3/1908),
    reprinted in Jonathan Birnbaum and Clarence Taylor, eds., *Civil Rights Since 1787* (New
    York: NYU Press, 2000); Allen Grimshaw, ed., *A Social History of Racial Violence* (New
    York: Routledge, 2009); Arthur and Lila Weinberg, eds., *The Muckrakers* (Urbana: Univer-
    sity of Illinois Press, 2001 [1961]); Roberta Senechal, *The Sociogenesis of a Race Riot*
    (Urbana: University of Illinois Press, 1990); and the first edition of this book.

14. Why the 2000 U.S. Census shows no African Americans in Buffalo, Illinois, I cannot say,
    since I have been in at least one home owned by a black homeowner. Perhaps he is included
    in the seven persons of "two or more races"; certainly his children should be, since his wife
    is white.

15. The Indianapolis chapter of the NAACP eventually got Honda to extend its hiring radius to
    65 miles. Of course, that is only a band-aid over the larger problem: that Honda chose to lo-
    cate hundreds of new jobs 50 miles away from black residences, guaranteeing an over-
    whelmingly white workforce. Some in the industry speculate that Honda does such things
    from simple racial prejudice; others suggest that Honda management thinks African Ameri-
    cans are likely to be pro-union.

16. See Loewen, "Mitch Daniels: Friend or Foe to Academic Freedom?" *History News Network*,
    1/20/2013, historynewsnetwork.org/blog/150218, for sources. Cf. Loewen, "'Confronting'
    Mitch Daniels at Purdue," *History News Network*, 11/3/2013, historynewsnetwork.org
    /blog/153195.

17. Loewen, "Honda's All-American Sundown Town," *History News Network*, 7/9/2006,
    historynewsnetwork.org/article/27821.

18. Mike Leonard, "Is Honda Pick an 'Outstanding Community of White People'?" *Bloomington
    Herald-Times*, 7/6/2006, heraldtimesonline.com/stories/2006/07/11/news.0711?HT?A7
    _PJR58138.sto; Pete VanBaalen: "When Words Still Hurt" and comments, *Greensburg
    Daily News*, 7/22/2006, greensburgdailynews.com/opinion/columns/pete-vanbaalen-when
    -words-still-hurt/article_26ecda88-d5ea-5ec7-9379-b8ee47aecdfa.html; cf. Roger Bybee,
    "Indiana's Civics Lesson from Honda," 11/1/2008, Z-Net, zcomm.org/znetarticle/indianas
    -civics-lesson-from-honda-by-roger-bybee/.

19. Michael N. Danielson, *The Politics of Exclusion* (New York: Columbia University Press,
    1976), 146.

20. Of course, he began by recruiting allies who can also justly take credit for the outcome. See
    "Goshen, Indiana, Pledges to Transcend Its Sundown Town Past," at my website, sundown
    .tougaloo.edu/sundowntowns.php.

21. See "La Crosse, Wisconsin, Pledges to Transcend Its Sundown Town Past," sundown
    .tougaloo.edu/sundowntowns.php.

22. Murray Bishoff, interview, 9/2002, e-mail, 10/2006; Jefferson Strait, "'May Community Be Restored,'" *New Leader*, 8/16/2001. The councilman later became fire chief in a Kansas town, according to Bishoff, "New Mayor Takes Over in Pierce City," *Monett Times*, 4/14/2010, monett-times.com/story/1626562.html.

23. sundown.tougaloo.edu/content.php?file=sundowntowns-howto.html.

24. sundown.tougaloo.edu/content.php?file=sundowntowns-whitemap.html.

CHAPTER 1: THE IMPORTANCE OF SUNDOWN TOWNS

1. "All-white" will be defined below.

2. Mere neighborhoods won't do, although occasionally I do briefly discuss sundown neighborhoods, especially when they are very large.

3. Such communities forced me to ease my definition of "all-white town" to include places with as many as nine African Americans, since a single household might easily include six or seven. Nonhousehold blacks, such as prison inmates, live-in servants, and interracial children adopted by white parents, also do not violate sundown town rules that forbid African American households, so they should be excluded from census totals. See the longer discussion in Chapter 8. From here on I will stop using quotation marks around "all-white" or "white town," but they are implied.

4. I give 1970 populations because in that year, most sundown towns and suburbs had not changed and definitely still maintained sundown policies.

5. John M. Goering, "Introduction," in John M. Goering, ed., *Housing Desegregation and Federal Policy* (Chapel Hill: University of North Carolina Press, 1986), 10; Michael N. Danielson, *The Politics of Exclusion* (NY: Columbia University Press, 1976), 223.

6. The total includes 50 towns smaller than 1,000 whose racial histories I learned.

7. I would like to thank the Newberry Library for an Arthur Weinberg fellowship early in my research. Their staff proved very helpful even though their extensive collection of local histories, for reasons discussed in Chapter 8, did not. I also want to thank the University of Illinois, Chicago, especially Anthony Martin and his student advisors, and the University of Illinois, Urbana, especially Unit One/Allen Hall, for extending month-long residences, access to students and colleagues, and use of their libraries. The Library of Congress, the Catholic University library, and the census at the University of Maryland were also helpful, as was David Andrew Timko when he was at the Census Bureau library. David Cline was a fun and helpful intern.

8. My web site, uvm.edu/~jloewen/sundown, contains a bibliography on sundown towns. The topic is at least mentioned in Ray Stannard Baker, *Following the Color Line* (New York: Harper Torchbook, 1964 [1908]); V. Jacque Voegeli, *Free But Not Equal* (Chicago: University of Chicago Press, 1967); Frank U. Quillen, *The Color Line in Ohio* (Ann Arbor: Wahr, 1913); David Gerber, *Black Ohio and the Color Line* (Urbana: University of Illinois Press, 1976); Emma Thornbrough, *The Negro in Indiana* (Indianapolis: IN Hist. Bureau, 1957); Howard Chudacoff, *Mobile Americans: Residential and Social Mobility in Omaha* (New York: Oxford University Press, 1971); James DeVries, *Race and Kinship in a Midwestern Town* (Urbana: University of Illinois Press, 1984); Roberta Senechal, *The Sociogenesis of a Race Riot* (Urbana: University of Illinois Press, 1990); and unpublished papers by Jack Blocker Jr. on Illinois, Indiana, and Ohio. A few sources treat individual sundown towns; they are footnoted in later chapters and listed at my web site.

9. Malcolm Brown and John Webb (WPA), *Seven Stranded Coal Towns* (Washington, D.C.:

GPO, 1941); John Coggeshall, "Carbon-Copy Towns? The Regionalization of Ethnic Folklife in Southern Illinois's Egypt," in Barbara Allen and Thomas J. Schlereth, eds., *Sense of Place* (Lexington: University Press of Kentucky, 1990), 103–19; C. S. Stein, *Toward New Towns for America* (Boston: MIT Press, 1966); Lewis Atherton, *Main Street on the Middle Border* (Bloomington: Indiana University Press, 1954).

10. James Danky, e-mail, 6/2002.

11. To be sure, whites still occasionally kill African Americans because they are black, the most notorious recent incident being the 1998 murder of James Byrd Jr. in Jasper, Texas, who was dragged to death behind a pickup truck, but these incidents are not lynchings. A lynching is a public murder, and the dominant forces in the community are usually in league with the perpetrators. Byrd's death was "merely" a hate crime and a homicide.

12. Historians debated Woodward's thesis and persuaded him to recognize that he had overstated it, but 1890–1920 or so is now recognized as a crucial formative period for the "new South."

13. C. Vann Woodward, *The Strange Career of Jim Crow* (New York: Oxford University Press 1975 [1955]); Edwin Yoder Jr., "The People, Yes," *Washington Post Book World*, 6/15/2003, 6.

14. The most important national treatment of this backlash is Rayford W. Logan's *The Negro in American Life and Thought: The Nadir*, reprinted as *The Betrayal of the Negro* (New York: Macmillan Collier, 1965 [1954]), although it too focused on the South. George Sinkler's *The Racial Attitudes of American Presidents* (Garden City, NJ: Doubleday, 1971) includes some treatment of the North. Leon Litwack's pioneering work *North of Slavery* (Chicago: University of Chicago Press, 1961) treats the antebellum North, while his later books, *Been in the Storm So Long* (New York: Knopf, 1979) and *Trouble in Mind: Black Southerners in the Age of Jim Crow* (New York: Knopf, 1998), as the subtitle of the latter suggests, concentrate on the traditional South. Local works are cited in note 8 above and in later chapters.

15. Woodward, ibid., xiii.

16. Du Quoin resident, 9/2002; Tim Wise, *White Like Me* (New York: Soft Skull Press, 2005), 17.

17. Edwina M. DeWindt, "Wyandotte History; Negro" (Wyandotte, MI: typescript, 1945, in Bacon Library, Wyandotte), 12, citing *Wyandotte Herald*, 10/7/1898.

18. DeWindt, "Wyandotte History; Negro," 4.

19. Vienna city employee, 2/2004, confirmed by two other residents; —, "Three Negro Homes Burned Here Monday," *Vienna Times*, 9/9/1954.

20. William Gremley, "Social Control in Cicero," in Allen Grimshaw, *Racial Violence in the U.S.* (Chicago: Aldine, 1969), 170–83; Stephen G. Meyer, *As Long as They Don't Move Next Door* (Lanham, MD: Rowman & Littlefield, 2000), 118.

21. Peter M. Bergman and Mort N. Bergman, *The Chronological History of the Negro in America* (New York: Mentor, 1969), 527; David Lewis, *King* (Urbana: University of Illinois Press, 1978), 321; Norbert Blei, *Neighborhood* (Peoria: Ellis Press, 1987), 29.

22. The term "ethnic cleansing" grew popular in the 1990s to describe what happened as Yugoslavia broke apart. From areas under Serb control, Muslims and Croatians fled, were expelled, sometimes even murdered; pretty much the same happened to Serbs and Muslims in areas under Croatian control; and so forth. The term does not mean "mass murder"; most victims fled but did not perish.

23. My web site, uvm.edu/~jloewen/sundown, lists some of these riots.

24. Since sundown towns are rare in the traditional South, I excluded Wilson, Carter, Clinton, and Gore.

25. Cedar County had 37 African American residents in 1890; just 2 remained by 1930. West Branch has a substantial Quaker population, however, and initial research unearthed no oral tradition of sundown practices in the town.

26. Even in 2000, Johnson City, Texas, had not 1 black resident among its 1,191 total population; in *Master of the Senate* (New York: Knopf, 2002), Robert A. Caro implies but does not quite state that they were not allowed.

27. Cheney traveled to Wyoming to register to vote shortly before the 2000 nominating convention to avoid conflict with the Twelfth Amendment, which prohibits electing a president and vice president from the same state.

28. McKinley, Bryan, Teddy Roosevelt, Harding, Willkie, Dewey, Truman, LBJ, and George W. Bush grew up or lived in confirmed or probable sundown towns (TR and LBJ are "probable"). Parker, Taft, Hughes, Davis, Cox, Smith, FDR, Landon, Eisenhower, Stevenson, JFK, Goldwater, McGovern, Ford, Reagan, Bush I, Dukakis, and Dole grew up in towns that probably did allow African Americans. I haven't confirmed or disconfirmed the towns identified with Coolidge, Hoover, Nixon, Humphrey, and Mondale.

29. William D. Jenkins, *Steel Valley Klan* (Kent: Kent State University Press, 1990), 65; Ed Hayes, e-mail to Salem High School bulletin board, Classmates.com, 11/2002; Phillip Payne, e-mail, 10/2002; Morris Milgram, "South Has Little to Fear from Truman of Missouri, *Pittsburgh Courier*, 10/2/1944; David Mark, "Carpetbagging's Greatest Hits," *Washington Post*, 8/15/2004.

30. Since 2002, most Krispy Kreme mix has been made in a new factory in Effingham.

31. Catherine Jurca, *White Diaspora* (Princeton: Princeton University Press, 2001), 42.

32. For a discussion of race in *Gone with the Wind* see Loewen, "Teaching Race Relations Through Feature Films," *Teaching Sociology* 19 (1/91): 82–83, reprinted in Diana Papademas, *Visual Sociology* (Washington, D.C.: ASA, 1994).

33. Chapter 8 discusses three Hollywood films that set sundown towns in the traditional South, where they rarely existed in real life.

34. Kathy Orr, "West Lawn: From Marsh to Thriving Neighborhood," West Lawn Chamber of Commerce, westlawncc.org, 1/2004; Steve Bogira, "Hate, Chicago Style" *Chicago Reader*, 12/5/86.

35. Colp resident, 9/2002.

36. Pennsylvania teacher, e-mail, 8/2002.

37. In 2000, Naperville was 3.0% African American, Edina 1.2%, and Darien 0.4%. Thus all three may have passed beyond being sundown suburbs, although since the totals include nonhousehold blacks, Darien may not have. Please note my repeated cautions against concluding that a sundown town or suburb remains sundown as of the date you read about it.

38. Meyer, *As Long as They Don't Move Next Door*, 1.

39. Doing otherwise would have entangled my prose in a mass of adjectives like "formerly," "continuing," or perhaps "recovering" sundown towns. In turn, such judgments would have led to countless errors, because I could not know if a practice confirmed in the past continues in the present.

40. James Pool, *Hitler and His Secret Partners* (New York: Pocket Books, 1997), 117; Jewish Virtual Library, us-israel.org/jsource/Holocaust/kristallnacht.html, 11/2003.

41. Anna editor, 10/2002; Anna librarian, 10/2002; Union County farmer, 1/2004.

42. Newman, ibid; Robert Park, *Human Communities: The City and Human Ecology* (New York: Free Press, 1952), 14.

43. Untitled story about Anna, *Carbondale (Ill.) Free Press,* 11/13/1909; John Baker, post at his web site at cougartown.com, 3/2001; Deborah Morse-Kahn, *Edina: Chapters in the City History* (Edina: City of Edina, 1998), 94–95; Edina resident, 1963; Don Cox, "Linguistic Expert Says Ancient Indian Languages Are Dying," *Reno Gazette-Journal,* 1/2/2002, sfgate.com/cgi-bin/article.cgi?file=/news/archive/2002/01/02/state1722EST7955. DTL; William H. Jacobsen Jr., 8/23/2003.

CHAPTER 2: THE NADIR

1. Leola Bergmann, "The Negro in Iowa," *Iowa Journal of History and Politics,* 1969 [1948], 44–45.

2. Robert Green, Laura L. Becker, and Robert E. Coviello, *The American Tradition* (Columbus: Merrill, 1984), 754.

3. Rayford W. Logan, who first employed "Nadir of race relations" as a term (so far as I know), used "1877–1901" in the subtitle of his 1954 book, *The Negro in American Life and Thought: The Nadir,* but his book actually treats 1877–1921, to the end of the Wilson administration. Although I use (and defend) somewhat different dates (1890–1930s), my thinking has been greatly influenced by Logan's fine work, reprinted as *The Betrayal of the Negro* (New York: Macmillan Collier, 1965 [1954]).

4. In 1859, Arkansas passed a law requiring all free Negroes to leave the state by January 1, 1860. Any free blacks who remained after the deadline could be sold into slavery. But this law never applied to slaves and was more a reaction to fear of slave revolts, said to be instigated by free blacks, than an attempt to create an all-white state.

5. Quoted in James M. McPherson, *Battle Cry of Freedom* (New York: Oxford University Press, 1988), vi.

6. Shepherd W. McKinley, reviewing Heather Cox Richardson's *The Death of Reconstruction* on H-South, h-net.org/~south/, 5/16/2002, citing xiii–xiv.

7. See Robert Dykstra, *Bright Radical Star* (Ames: Iowa State University Press, 1997).

8. In reality, Native Americans would not be included until 1924.

9. Sally Albertz, "Fond du Lac's Black Community and Their Church, 1865–1943," in Clarence B. Davis, *Source of the Lake* (Fond du Lac, WI: Action Printing, 2002), 34–35.

10. During the Civil War and Reconstruction, expulsions happened in other states too, of course, again mostly in Democratic areas. For example, 187 African Americans lived in Washington County, Indiana, 20 miles northwest of Louisville, Kentucky, before the Civil War. By 1870, just 18 remained, and a county history published in 1916 stated, "Washington County has for several decades boasted that no colored man or woman lived within her borders." Willie Harlen, president of the Washington County Historical Society, credits the expulsion to the Knights of the Golden Circle, a secret organization of Copperhead Democrats in northern states that also provided something of a model for the Ku Klux Klan. Cf. Emma Lou Thornbrough, *The Negro in Indiana* (Indianapolis: Indiana Historical Bureau, 1957), 225; Harlen, e-mail, 10/2002.

11. *Chesterton Tribune,* 7/24/1903; Darrel Dexter, *A House Divided: Union County, Illinois* (Anna: Reppert, 1994), 75; V. Jacque Voegeli, *Free but Not Equal* (Chicago: University of Chicago Press, 1967), 89.

12. Many soldiers had *not* died for this purpose, to be sure, but solely to hold the nation to-

gether. I know that, and Lincoln knew it. See Chapter 6 of James Loewen, *Lies My Teacher Told Me* (New York: New Press, 1995) for a more nuanced treatment of this issue. But increasingly as the war went on, that *is* why they died, and Lincoln's saying so helped make it true.

13. Lerone Bennett, *Black Power U.S.A.: The Human Side of Reconstruction* (Baltimore: Penguin, 1969), 11.

14. I intend "Ku Klux Klan" as a synecdoche for all the groups—Red Shirts, Knights of the White Carnelia, and plain Democrats—who used violence and intimidation to end interracial governments in the South.

15. *History of Lower Scioto Valley* (Chicago: Interstate, 1884), 737; Jeanne Blackburn, e-mail, 11/2003.

16. James Loewen, *Lies Across America* (New York: New Press, 1999), 394–404, summarizes the collapse of Republican anti-racism after 1890.

17. The proportion also takes immigration into account.

18. See Carey McWilliams, *A Mask for Privilege* (New Brunswick: Transaction Books, 1999 [1948]), 14.

19. Philip A. Klinkner and R. M. Smith, *The Unsteady March* (Chicago: University of Chicago Press, 1999), 96.

20. Of course, one did not have to be Republican to dream of wealth. But tycoons such as J. P. Morgan and John D. Rockefeller were Republican, almost without exception. Democrats were more likely to deride such wealth as excessive and at base crooked, rather than a sign of merit.

21. Arkansas librarian, 9/2002; Douglas opinion, *Jones v. Alfred H. Mayer Co,* 392 U.S. 409, 445–47 (1968), also quoted in Joe R. Feagin, *Racist America* (New York: Routledge, 2000), 25.

22. After 1896, if not before, schools became segregated statewide in Delaware, Maryland, West Virginia, Kentucky, Missouri, Arkansas, Oklahoma, Texas, and Arizona, as well as much of Ohio, Indiana, Illinois, Kansas, and California. Of course, the South already had segregated schools.

23. Donald Grant, *The Anti-Lynching Movement* (San Francisco: R & E, 1975), 66–67.

24. Ray Stannard Baker, "The Color Line in the North," *American Magazine* 65 (1908), in Otto Olsen, ed., *The Negro Question: From Slavery to Caste, 1863–1910* (New York: Pitman, 1971), 268; Quillen, *The Color Line in Ohio,* 120; Loewen, *Lies Across America,* 400.

25. Historian John Weaver, e-mail to H-Net Ohio History list, 1/2003.

26. Bergmann, "The Negro in Iowa," 44–45.

27. Michael L. Cooper, *Playing America's Game* (New York: Lodestar, 1993), 10; Gordon Morgan, "Emancipation Bowl," Department of Sociology, University of Arkansas, Fayetteville, n.d.

28. "The Passing of Colored Firemen in Chicago," Chicago *Defender,* 3/11/1911; Lester C. Lamon, *Black Tennesseans, 1900–1930* (Knoxville: University of Tennessee Press, 1977), 141.

29. Ralph R. Rea, *Boone County and Its People* (Van Buren, AR: Press-Argus, 1955), 121; Fon Louise Gordon, *Caste and Class: The Black Experience in Arkansas, 1880–1920* (Athens: University of Georgia Press, 1995), 45.

30. Jacqueline Froelich and David Zimmermann, "Total Eclipse: The Destruction of the African American Community of Harrison, Arkansas, in 1905 and 1909," *Arkansas Historical Quarterly* 58, 2 (1999): 141–42; Zimmermann quoted in Laurinda Joenks, "Roughness of Citizens Blamed on Lean Times," *The Morning News,* 5/7/2000.

31. Joenks, "Roughness of Citizens."
32. Frederick Douglass pointed this out at the time, in 1895: "The American people have fallen in with the bad idea that this is a Negro problem, a question of the character of the Negro, and not a question of the nation." Quoted in Kevin Gaines, *Uplifting the Race* (Chapel Hill: University of North Carolina Press, 1996), 67.
33. See Baker, "The Color Line in the North," 266.
34. Heather Cox Richardson, *The Death of Reconstruction* (Cambridge: Harvard University Press, 2001), xiii–xiv, 119, 224; McKinley, review of same on H-South, h-net.org/~south/, 5/16/2002.
35. Morgan, "Emancipation Bowl."
36. Actually, only South Carolina's ever had a black majority.
37. Since some textbook authors still made such claims as late as the 1970s, many readers may have encountered this biased interpretation of Reconstruction in high school as fact. For correction, refer to any modern treatment of the period, such as Bennett, *Black Power, U.S.A.,* or Eric Foner, *Reconstruction* (New York: Harper & Row, 1988).
38. Albert Bushnell Hart, *Essentials of American History* (New York: American Book Co., 1905), 504; W. E. B. DuBois, *Black Reconstruction* (Cleveland: World Meridian, 1964 [1935]), 722; Loewen, *Lies Across America,* 39, 164–93.
39. Carl Wittke, *Tambo and Bones* (Westport, CT: Greenwood, 1968 [1930]), 93; Joseph Boskin, *Sambo* (New York: Oxford University Press, 1986), 85; James Weldon Johnson, *Black Manhattan* (New York: Knopf, 1930), 93; James DeVries, *Race and Kinship in a Midwestern Town* (Urbana: University of Illinois Press, 1984), 51.
40. Loewen, "Teaching Race Relations Through Feature Films," *Teaching Sociology* 19 (1991): 82; Adrian Turner, *A Celebration of* Gone with the Wind (New York: W. H. Smith, 1992), 166, citing *Variety.*
41. Richard Weiss, "Racism in the Era of Industrialization," in Gary Nash and Richard Weiss, eds., *The Great Fear* (New York: Holt, Rinehart, & Winston, 1970), 136; Andrew R. Heinze, "Jews and American Popular Psychology," *Journal of American History* 88, 3 (2001): 959–60; Dinesh D'Souza, *The End of Racism* (New York: Free Press, 1995), 118.
42. John Higham, *Strangers in the Land* (New Brunswick: Rutgers University Press, 1955), 265; Gordon A. Craig, "The X-Files," *New York Review of Books,* 4/12/2001, 57.
43. The last of the latter was Carleton Coon, whose *The Origin of Races,* published in 1962 (New York: Knopf), claimed that *Homo sapiens* evolved five different times, blacks last. Its poor reception by anthropologists, followed by evidence from archaeology and paelontology that mankind evolved once, and in Africa, finally put an end to such pseudoscience.
44. Logan, *The Betrayal of the Negro,* 360–70; Nancy J. Weiss, "Wilson Draws the Color Line," in Arthur Mann, ed., *The Progressive Era* (Hinsdale, IL: Dryden, 1975), 144; Harvey Wasserman, *America Born and Reborn* (New York: Macmillan, 1983), 131.
45. W. E. B. DuBois, *The Seventh Son* (New York: Random House, 1971), 2:594.
46. Richard Delgado and Jean Stefancic, *Home-Grown Racism* (Boulder: University of Colorado Latino/a Research & Policy Center, 1999), 30, 44, 74.
47. Willis D. Weatherford and Charles S. Johnson, *Race Relations* (Boston: D. C. Heath, 1934), 314; Lorenzo J. Greene, Gary Kremer, and Antonio Holland, *Missouri's Black Heritage* (Columbia: University of Missouri Press, 1993), 151; Bergman and Bergman, *The Chronological History of the Negro in America,* 458.
48. Greene, Kremer, and Holland, *Missouri's Black Heritage,* 151; Walter E. Williams, *The State Against Blacks* (New York: McGraw-Hill, 1982), Chapter 8.

49. The First Lady and Interior Secretary Harold Ickes made some important symbolic gestures, such as allowing Marian Anderson to sing at the Lincoln Memorial in 1939.

CHAPTER 3: THE GREAT RETREAT

1. Emma Lou Thornbrough, *The Negro in Indiana* (Indianapolis: Indiana Historical Bureau, 1957), 224.

2. I define the "traditional South" as Virginia, North Carolina, South Carolina, Georgia, Florida, Alabama, Tennessee, Mississippi, and Louisiana—states historically dominated by slavery. Note 63 in this chapter defends this definition.

3. Admittedly, some towns in the Midwest went sundown vis-à-vis African Americans earlier, during the Civil War, and some even before it, but most towns in that region and elsewhere did so later.

4. Unlike most southern Illinois towns, Cairo never tried to get rid of its black population. It simply had too many blacks. Also, some whites in and around Cairo adhered to traditional southern race relations, using African Americans as cotton pickers, maids, janitors, railroad labor, etc., and would have opposed any expulsion. Map 1 shows this area of traditional southern race relations in Illinois.

5. *Cairo Bulletin* quoted in *Marion Daily Republican,* 8/12/1920.

6. Historian Jeri L. Reed, e-mail, 6/2002; *Guide and Directory for the City of Rogers* (Benton County, 1907), 4; "Siloam Springs, Arkansas," brochure in collection of Siloam Springs Museum; Michael Birdwell, e-mail, 5/2002; *Terry County Herald,* 3/27/1908; Betty Dawn Hamilton, e-mail, 7/2002; Eulalia N. Wells, *Blazing the Way* (Blanket, TX: author, 1942), 77.

7. *Owosso and Shiawassee County Directory, 1936* (Owosso: Owosso Chamber of Commerce, 1936); David M. Chalmers, *Hooded Americanism* (New York: Franklin Watts, 1976 [1965]), 165; David M. P. Freund, "Making It Home," Ph.D. dissertation, University of Michigan, 1999, 225.

8. "Come see Woodson" ad from Dale Steiner.

9. There was a wave of anti-Chinese activity just before the Civil War, including expulsions from many mining camps and small towns in 1858–59. See Stanford Lyman, *Chinese Americans* (New York: Random House, 1974), 60.

10. Craig Storti, *Incident at Bitter Creek* (Ames: Iowa State University Press, 1991), 112–15, 118, 125, 159–60; Bill Bryson, *Made in America* (New York: Morrow, 1994), 127; Grant K. Anderson, "Deadwood's Chinatown," in Arif Dirlik, ed., *Chinese on the American Frontier* (Lanham, MD: Rowman & Littlefield, 2001), 423; Ed Marston, "Truth-telling Needs a Home in the West," *High Country News,* 9/25/2000; "Files Found in Oregon Detail Massacre of Chinese," *New York Times,* 8/20/1995; Brigham Madsen, *Corinne: The Gentile Capital of Utah* (Salt Lake City: Utah State Historical Society, 1980), 252.

11. Florence C. Lister and Robert H. Lister, "Chinese Sojourners in Territorial Prescott," in Dirlik, ed., *Chinese on the American Frontier,* 55; Kathy Hodges, e-mail, 6/2002; Li-hua Yu, "Chinese Immigrants in Idaho," Ph.D. dissertation, Bowling Green State University, 1991, Chapter 7; Priscilla Wegars, e-mail, 8/2003, summarizing her "The History and Archaeology of the Chinese in Northern Idaho, 1880 Through 1910," Ph.D. dissertation, University of Idaho, 1991.

12. Jean Pfaelzer, paper presented to the American Studies Association, Washington, DC, 2001; Pfaelzer, "A Proposal for *Driven Out: Ethnic Cleansing and Resistance,*" n.d., 4, 10; Visalia

oral history via Gilbert Gia, e-mail, 9/2002; Keith Easthouse, "The Chinese Expulsion—Looking Back on a Dark Episode," *North Coast Journal Weekly*, 2/27/2003, northcoast journal.com/022703/cover0227.html, 2/2004; Kevin Hearle, e-mails, 9/2002, 5/2004, quoting Diann Marsh, *Santa Ana: An Illustrated History* (San Diego: Heritage, 1994), 95–96; cf. Pfaelzer, *Driven Out* (New York: Random House, forthcoming).

13. Lynwood Carranco, "Chinese Expulsion from Humboldt County," in Roger Daniels, ed., *Anti-Chinese Violence in North America* (New York: Arno Press, 1978), 332–39.

14. The *Humboldt Times* overstated its case: several other towns kept out Chinese Americans in 1937. Also, apparently not all Chinese Americans were expelled from Orleans, an inland mining hamlet barely in Humboldt County.

15. Easthouse, "The Chinese Expulsion"; Carranco, "Chinese Expulsion from Humboldt County."

16. Joseph A. Dacus, *Annals of the Great Strike* (New York: Arno Press, 1969 [1877]; Online Encyclopedia of Seattle and King County History, historylink.org, 3/2003.

17. A few places drove out their blacks well before 1890.

18. Cf. Jack S. Blocker Jr., "Choice and Circumstance," Organization of American Historians, Toronto, 4/1999, 2–3.

19. Ibid.; Loewen, *The Mississippi Chinese* (Prospect Heights, IL: Waveland, 1988).

20. I did not study Alaska or Hawaii and did very little research on Montana and the Dakotas.

21. I used 1930 statistics in Table 1 to avoid contamination from the Great Depression. I didn't want readers to imagine that African Americans may have retreated to the cities for economic reasons. Using 1930 avoids this issue, because the Crash happened on October 24, 1929, only months before enumerators fanned out to take the 1930 census, and it had prompted little population movement by that time. (For the record, the Great Depression actually prompted some migration *from* big cities back to subsistence farming in the South.)

22. Columns with < 10 African Americans include those with none.

23. I define the "traditional" South as Virginia, North Carolina, South Carolina, Georgia, Florida, Alabama, Tennessee, Mississippi, and Louisiana. A later section in this chapter explains why the table includes Arkansas and Texas. The Appendix tells why Table 1 omits Alaska and Hawaii, describes idiosyncrasies in some states, and discusses other methodological issues underlying the table. Arizona, New Mexico, and Oklahoma were not states in 1890; I substituted data from 1910, the first census after statehood.

24. Minnesota had more counties in 1890 with no blacks, but more in 1930 with just a few blacks.

25. The Appendix also comments on other states whose counties showed only slight trends. It also summarizes recent work by historian Jack Blocker Jr. that reinforces the conclusions presented here.

26. Additional causes included a farm depression in the South, harm done to cotton by the boll weevil in 1915–16, and the South's continuing denial of civil rights to African Americans.

27. Beloit (WI) *News*, 8/25/1916, quoted in C. K. Doreski, *Writing America Black: Race Rhetoric in the Public Sphere* (New York: Cambridge University Press, 1998), 31–32.

28. T. J. Woofter Jr., *Negro Problems in Cities* (New York: Harper & Row, 1969 [1928]), 28–31, quotes from 31.

29. My web site lists confirmed counties in all states.

30. I don't believe the detail that he literally met them at the line, but I do believe that the sheriff enforced the sundown policy.

31. Malcolm Ross, *All Manner of Men* (New York: Reynal & Hitchcock, 1948), 66; 83-year-old Mason County resident, 4/2000; Carol Speakman, 9/2002.

32. This figure is approximate. I may have overlooked a town or two that exceeded 1,000 in 1970 but not in adjoining censuses; I omitted some usually unincorporated places the census tags as CDPs, or "census designated places."

33. All suspected and confirmed sundown towns are listed at uvm.edu/~jloewen/sundown. Another researcher might come up with slightly different numbers, because I included smaller towns that people brought to my attention as sundown towns and did not include a few small towns that reached 1,000 people only in recent censuses. Other reasons to exclude an occasional town were judgment calls and my own exhaustion. I also excluded CDPs unless I knew them to be considered towns by residents of the area.

34. These communities are listed at uvm.edu/~jloewen/sundown. The exception was Newton. Confirmed towns form a scattered subset of all suspect towns, clustered near locations where I had speaking engagements, knew someone, or otherwise had connections. In addition, I contacted all 56 suspected sundown towns on Map 1. The proportion of confirmed sundown towns among those 56 was very similar to that among my scattered subset, so I don't believe any important error resulted from my nonrandom sampling.

35. I often use 1970 figures because most sundown towns were still all-white on purpose in that year. To be sure, some still are, but many relaxed their policy in the 1970s or thereafter, especially towns that grew rapidly. Using 1970 figures is conservative in that it underestimates the size of the cities today.

36. My process of information gathering was not perfectly random: when I invited audience members to share with me information about sundown towns, for example, people from overwhelmingly white towns that were *not* sundown towns would not be likely to speak, having nothing to impart. But I also made efforts to learn about *all* towns on Map 1, for example, and the proportion of confirmed sundown towns that I uncovered from that quest was no different than that obtained from volunteered sources.

37. Actually, we shall compute confidence limits for our estimate of 99.5% of 278 unknown towns, or 277 probable towns.

38. To find the standard error of the difference of two percentages, first we calculate each standard error separately. Beginning with the 194 towns on which we have information, the formula is $s_{p1} = \sqrt{pq/n}$, where n = the number of towns for which we have data (194), p = the proportion that were sundown (.995), and q = (1 - p) or .005. This standard error = .005 or 0.5%.

   We also need to compute the standard error of the percentage of sundown towns among the 228 towns for which we have no information. Since we don't know this percentage, we can assume just 90% will be, lower than the most likely estimate; such a conservative assumption provides a larger-than-likely standard error, which results in a more conservative overall estimate. Using the same formula, we substitute: n = 228, p = .9, and q = .1. This standard error = .020 or about 2%.

   We then combine these two standard errors, using the formula $s_{(p1-p2)} = \sqrt{s^2_{p1} + s^2_{p2}}$, to find the standard error of the difference of two percentages, which = .0205 or 2.05%.

39. Statistical tables tell us that 99 times out of 100, a range that is ÷2.58 standard errors from our best estimate will include the actual percentage. 2.58 x .0205 = .053 or 5.3%.

40. This correction is not normally computed, is unlikely to drop the lower limit as low as 90%, and is at least partly offset by the conservatively calculated standard error described in note 38.

41. Three previous authors have estimated the extent of sundown towns in Illinois. Their

estimates are in basic accord with mine. "Illinois: Mecca of the Migrant Mob," originally published in 1923 by the well-known black sociologist Charles S. Johnson, tells of "Granite City, where [Negroes] by ordinance may not live within the city limits . . . and 200 other towns where they may not live at all." Johnson's short essay does not list these towns. My number of likely suspects, 474, is larger than Johnson's, perhaps because when he wrote in 1923, some towns were still in the process of expelling their African Americans or resolving that none were to be admitted. Also, he may not have included towns smaller than 2,500, and he did not try to research the entire state. Sociologist Roberta Senechal quotes Johnson's sentence with approval in her fine study of the 1908 race riot in Springfield, Illinois. Writing of towns "that forbade blacks to cross the city limits or remain after dark," historian John Keiser compiled "a list of some 52 Illinois cities in which such unwritten 'ordinances' were said to exist by the local citizens," and he did not claim to have researched the subject exhaustively. One other book, *Land Between the Rivers,* a 1973 coffee-table book by three professors at Southern Illinois University, briefly acknowledges that sundown towns were widespread in that section of the state: "Many Southern Illinois towns solved the problem simply by refusing to allow blacks within the town boundaries between sunset and sunup." Such candor is rare; also worth noting is these authors' nonchalant use—well after the Civil Rights Movement—of the rhetoric that African Americans are "the problem" and keeping them out "solved the problem." See Charles S. Johnson, "Illinois: Mecca of the Migrant Mob," reprinted in Tom Lutz and Susanna Ashton, eds., *These "Colored" United States: African American Essays from the 1920s* (New Brunswick: Rutgers University Press, 1996), 109; Roberta Senechal, *The Sociogenesis of a Race Riot* (Urbana: University of Illinois Press, 1990), 129; John Keiser, "Black Strikebreakers and Racism in Illinois, 1865–1900" (*Journal of the Illinois State Historical Society* 65 (1972), 314; and C. William Horrell, Henry D. Piper, and John Voigt, *Land Between the Rivers* (Carbondale: Southern Illinois University Press, 1973), 163.

42. Of course, the smaller the community, the more likely that the absence of African Americans is not due to a policy of exclusion.

43. I know I missed sundown towns in this way, because two—Dwight and Vienna—came to my attention during my research.

44. Copperheads were pro-South Democrats, so called by pro-Union Republicans.

45. *Magnificent Whistle Stop: The 100-Year Story of Mendota, Illinois* (Mendota: Mendota Centennial Committee, 1953), 332; *Tribune* quoted in Ronald L. Lewis, *Black Coal Miners in America* (Lexington: University Press of Kentucky, 1987), 85; Tom Trengove, e-mail, 9/2002; male undergraduate, University of Illinois–Chicago, 9/2001.

46. Administrative secretary, University of Illinois, 2/2001.

47. Paul M. Angle, *Bloody Williamson* (New York: Knopf, 1952), 98, 110–15; Carl Planinc, 9/2002.

48. Senechal, *The Sociogenesis of a Race Riot,* 129.

49. Two other writers estimated impressionistically the extent of sundown towns in Indiana. Emma Lou Thornbrough's 1957 comment is reproduced at the head of the chapter. Kathleen Blee, author of the 1991 book *Women of the Klan* (Berkeley: University of California Press, 1991), 78, cited Leibowitz as the authority for this sentence: "Sundown laws that prohibited blacks from remaining in town after sunset were enforced, though often unwritten, in nearly every small town in Indiana."

50. Irving Leibowitz, *My Indiana* (Englewood Cliffs: Prentice-Hall, 1964), 208.

51. Frances L. Peacock, "The Opposite of Fear Is Love: An Interview with George Sawyer," *Quaker Life,* 3/2002, fum.org/QL/issues/0203/index.htm, 6/2002.

52. These 229 include 212 towns larger than 1,000 in population that were overwhelmingly white in census after census, as well as 17 hamlets with fewer than 1,000 residents that oral and/or written historical sources confirmed as having sundown policies. This number is smaller than in Illinois because Indiana has fewer towns, being a smaller state with a smaller population.

53. These communities are listed at uvm.edu/~jloewen/sundown. The number of confirmed sundown towns in Indiana is smaller than in Illinois because I spent less time researching Indiana.

54. The 1970 census is the next after Leibowitz's 1964 claim. It also allows thirteen years for possible desegregation after Thornbrough's 1957 statement and follows the 1954 *Brown v. Board of Education* school desegregation decision by sixteen years.

55. See uvm.edu/~jloewen/sundown for a list of confirmed Indiana sundown towns with evidence.

56. Leibowitz, *My Indiana,* 208; Mike Haas, "You Betcha," post to alt.discrimination, 2/18/2002.

57. The 126 towns, 9 confirmed, and 10 suspects are listed at uvm.edu/~jloewen/sundown. I omitted towns smaller than 2,500 for two reasons: out of respect for Wisconsin's small statewide black population—just under 3% in 1970, less than half Indiana's—and because I knew I would not have time to investigate any of Wisconsin's smaller towns on site.

   There is some circularity in allowing a state's small overall black population, which is depressed partly by its towns' sundown policies, to "excuse" the overwhelming whiteness of its towns. If *all* Wisconsin towns kept out African Americans, then the statewide proportion would be 0%, and I would have to infer that *no* towns were sundown! This may be a larger problem in Idaho and Oregon, the latter owing in part to its law flatly excluding blacks, passed in 1849.

58. These populations are approximate, rounded for the period 1970–2000.

59. Former Sheboygan resident, 10/2002; Grey Gundaker, e-mail, 7/2002.

60. The exception was Doc Pitts, whose story Chapter 10 will tell.

61. Moira Meltzer-Cohen, e-mail, 9/2002.

62. Priscilla Wegars, "Entrepreneurs and 'Wage Slaves': Their Relationship to Anti-Chinese Racism in Northern Idaho's Mining Labor Market, 1880–1910," in Marcel van der Linden and Jan Lucassen, eds., *Racism and the Labour Market* (Bern: Peter Lang, 1995), 471–72; Jim Kershner, "Segregation in Spokane," *Columbia* 14, 4 (2000–01), wshs.org/columbia/0400-a2.htm, 3/2003.

63. Those nine states, along with Arkansas and Texas, seceded to form the Confederacy, of course. Table 1 includes Arkansas and Texas because they had large areas that, like West Virginia, opposed both secession and slavery. The northwestern half of Arkansas supplied many recruits for the United States Army after U.S. forces broke the Confederacy's hold on it. The Confederacy had to occupy much of north Texas, owing to Unionist sentiments there. Early in the twentieth century, Texas became more western than southern. Arkansas and Texas were also the only former Confederate states to desegregate their state universities in the immediate aftermath of *Brown*.

   Table 1 also includes three other states—Maryland, Kentucky, and Missouri—that had substantial areas that were traditionally southern. These states did not secede and, on balance, included more areas that were not traditionally southern.

64. Thornbrough, *The Negro in Indiana*, 225.
65. I have not confirmed Belmont as a sundown town but think it was. In 1980, it had 1,420 people including 1 African American. By 2000 it had 11. Burnsville barely reached 1,000 population in 2000. A handful of even smaller Mississippi communities may be sundown hamlets, listed at uvm.edu/~jloewen/sundown. I have confirmed one, Mize, population about 300, southeast of Jackson. Mize is the "capital" of Sullivan's Hollow, a rural area known for past outlawry, including intimidation of African Americans. The fact that Mize is widely known as "No-Nigger Mize" and Sullivan's Hollow is notorious for the practice implies that sundown towns are unusual enough in the traditional South that even such a small one is remarked about.
66. Putting a practice in the past—"Alabama *had* two sundown counties"—might imply that both counties now admit African Americans, which I don't know to be true. At the same time, putting the practice in the present might imply that they still keep blacks out today—which I also don't know for sure. Here as elsewhere (unless context implies otherwise), using *has* means that a town or county kept African Americans (or other groups) out for decades and not that it necessarily does so now. Chapter 14 treats this problem of verb tense at greater length.
67. These counties and towns are listed at uvm.edu/~jloewen/sundown.
68. "Threat Against W. Va. Families Is Laid to Klan," *Pittsburgh Courier*, 10/27/1923.
69. I deliberately echo the title of Harry Caudill's well-known 1963 book about the region's depressed economic conditions, which unfortunately contains no mention that the region expelled most of its African Americans four or five decades earlier and kept them from returning.
70. This was the school where Martin Luther King Jr. was photographed and the result enlarged and plastered on billboards across the South with the caption "Martin Luther King at Communist Training School." Neither Horton nor Highlander was Communist.
71. George Brosi, 6/1999; Esther S. Sanderson, *County Scott and Its Mountain Folk* (Nashville: Williams Printing, 1958), 186; John Egerton, *Shades of Gray* (Baton Rouge: Louisiana State University Press, 1991), 69; Charles Martin, e-mail, 6/2000; cf. "Scottsboro Trial Moved Fifty Miles," *New York Times*, 3/8/1933, 14.
72. William Pickens, "Arkansas—A Study in Suppression," *The Messenger* 5 (1923), reprinted in Tom Lutz and Susanna Ashton, eds., *These "Colored" United States: African American Essays from the 1920s* (New Brunswick: Rutgers University Press, 1996), 35; Milton Rafferty, *The Ozarks* (Fayetteville: University of Arkansas Press, 2001), 60; use of *Negro* in 2001 is antiquated.
73. Gordan D. Morgan, *Black Hillbillies of the Arkansas Ozarks* (Fayetteville: University of Arizona Department of Sociology, 1973 typescript), 60.
74. William H. Jacobsen Jr., 8/2003; Don Cox, "Linguistic Expert Says Ancient Indian Languages Are Dying," *Reno Gazette-Journal*, 1/2/2002, sfgate.com/cgi-bin/article.cgi?file=/news/archive/2002/01/02/state1722EST7955.DTL, 8/2003; Loren B. Chan, "The Chinese in Nevada," in Arif Dirlik, ed., *Chinese on the American Frontier* (Lanham, MD: Rowman & Littlefield, 2001), 96–97. Elmer Rusco, *"Good Time Coming?" Black Nevadans in the 19th Century* (Westport, CT: Greenwood, 1975), 207.
75. "Tale of Two Cities," *Pacific Citizen*, 1/4/1947; Fred S. Rolater, e-mail, 6/2002.
76. MariaElena Raymond, e-mail, 9/02; Margaret Marsh, *Suburban Lives* (New Brunswick: Rutgers University Press, 1990), 172; Richard Delgado and Jean Stefancic, *Home-Grown Racism* (Boulder: University of Colorado Latino/a Research & Policy Center, 1999), 30, 44, 74.

77. *Bellingham Souvenir Police Album,* photocopy, no date, 11; —, "The Hindus Have Left Us," *Bellingham Herald,* 9/6?/1907; cf. —, "Hindus Hounded from City," *Bellingham Herald,* 9/5/1907.
78. These include North Fond du Lac, Neenah, Menasha, Kimberly, Little Chute, Kaukauna, and Green Bay.
79. Michael Dougan, *Arkansas Odyssey* (Little Rock: Rose Publishing, 1994), 317; "An Elco Man Says Feeling Is Strong Against Negroes," *Cairo Bulletin,* 2/19/1924; "Attempt Is Made to Dynamite Cauble Home," *Cairo Bulletin,* 3/4/1924; "No Reason for Sending Troops to Elco, Opinion," *Cairo Bulletin,* 3/7/1924; Scott Peeples, "Building Diversity Awareness Day," Appleton, WI, 4/8/2003, 2, paraphrasing Bob Lowe; Andrew Kirchmeier, 4/2002; Jack Tichenor, 2/2004.
80. Carey McWilliams, *A Mask for Privilege* (New Brunswick: Transaction, 1999 [1948]), 6–7; Michael Powell, "Separate and Unequal in Roosevelt, Long Island," *Washington Post,* 4/21/2002.
81. William Stock, "Nigger Sam," *Urban Hiker,* 37, urbanhiker.net/archive/febstories/UH-02_03(stock).pdf, 6/2003; Elizabeth C. Baxter, 5/2003, and e-mail, 5/2003.
82. When capitalized, *Realtor* is a trademark of the National Association of Realtors (formerly the National Association of Real Estate Boards). The NAR has long tried unsuccessfully to get journalists to capitalize *realtor* when referring to an NAR member and use *real estate agent* otherwise. Currently the NAR campaigns to get its own members to use *REALTOR* in all capital letters with a trademark symbol attached. This book uses *realtor* as synonymous with the unwieldy *real estate agent.* Often, as here, I do not know whether the agent was a member of the NAR or NAREB. I use *Realtor* only when membership in the national or local association is part of the story.
83. "Housing: How High the Barriers," *ADL Bulletin* 16, 1 (1959), 2; former Delray Beach resident, 8/2000; Mary Ellen Stratthaus, "Flaw in the Jewel: Housing Discrimination Against Jews in La Jolla, California," *American Jewish History* 84, 3 (1996): 194; Leonard Valdez, e-mail, 4/2003.
84. Charles T. Clotfelter concurs: "The 1970 census marked a high-water mark for the residential segregation of blacks." See his *After Brown* (Princeton: Princeton University Press, 2004), 80.
85. Portfolio 25 and Map 1 (page 63) demonstrate this point for Indiana and Southern Illinois.
86. As noted in Chapters 1 and 14, "can be confirmed" does not imply that the discrimination necessarily continues to the present.
87. The exact number depends on the size of what is referred to as a "town."
88. Baker meant not that African Americans were excluding others, but that ghettoes were becoming exclusively black as "other classes of people" left.
89. Howard Chudacoff, *Mobile Americans: Residential and Social Mobility in Omaha* (New York: Oxford University Press, 1971), 127; Ray Stannard Baker, "The Color Line in the North," *American Magazine* 65 (1908), in Otto Olsen, ed., *The Negro Question: From Slavery to Caste, 1863–1910* (New York: Pitman, 1971), 268.
90. D is particularly useful because it is not affected by the overall proportion of African Americans in the metropolitan area, and because it has intuitive clarity. D works for two groups at a time, here blacks and nonblacks.
91. Reynolds Farley and William H. Frey, "Changes in the Segregation of Whites from Blacks During the 1980s," *American Sociological Review* 59, 1 (1994): 24.
92. In fact, segregation was even worse than that, especially in the North. At any given moment,

northern metropolitan areas looked more integrated than they really were, owing to the Great Migration, which continued at least to 1968. This influx of African Americans from the South led to blockbusting, in turn creating "transitional" or "changing" neighborhoods. Such neighborhoods are temporarily desegregated and artificially reduce D. After factoring out changing neighborhoods, Ds in both regions would rise, but especially in the North. Perhaps 94 would be a reasonable estimate for the average D in both regions, controlling for transitional neighborhoods.

93. James Loewen and Charles Sallis, eds., *Mississippi: Conflict and Change* (New York: Pantheon, 1980), 177, 186–87; Art T. Burton, "Gunfight at Boley, Oklahoma," on Bennie J. McRae Jr.'s "Lest We Forget" web site, coax.net/people/lwf/gunfight.htm, 5/2003; William E. Bittle and Gilbert Geis, *The Longest Way Home* (Detroit: Wayne State University Press, 1964), 37.

94. These were not the first black homes to be blown up in Okemah. The nearby *Paden Press* observed on 3/16/1905, "Once the darkey was not allowed to have his habitat in the town [Okemah] and he was discouraged by high explosives."

95. Norman Crockett, *The Black Towns* (Lawrence: Regents Press of Kansas, 1979), 92; W. L. Payne, "Okemah's Night of Terror," in Hazel Ruby McMahan, ed., *Stories of Early Oklahoma,* on Rootsweb, rootsweb.com/pub/usgenweb/ok/okfuskee/history/town/oknite01 .txt; "Terrific Blast Rocks Town From Slumber Saturday," *Okemah Daily Leader* 4/23/ 1908, on Rootsweb, rootsweb.com/~okokfusk/cities.htm, 5/2003.

96. Okmulgee Historical Society, *History of Okmulgee County, Oklahoma* (Tulsa: History Enterprises, 1985), 166–68.

97. Bittle and Geis, *The Longest Way Home,* 37.

98. William E. Bittle and Gilbert Geis, "Racial Self Fulfillment and the Rise of an All-Negro Community in Oklahoma," in August Meier and Elliott Rudwick, eds., *The Making of Black America II* (New York: Atheneum, 1969), 116–21.

99. Sometimes whites—especially "river rats" in floodplains—live in similar settlements, but with a key difference: residents of black townships outside sundown towns are not *allowed* to live elsewhere.

100. Oakley V. Glenn, untitled manuscript (summary of events leading to a Eugene Human Rights Commission), (Eugene: Commission on Human Rights Office, n.d.), 3.

101. Clarence D. Stephenson, "Indiana Area Blacks Battle for Civil Rights," *Indiana Gazette,* 6/8/1985, and *175th Anniversary History of Indiana County* (Indiana: A.D. Halldin, 1979), 2:770–74, citing Dorothy Lydic et al., "Negro Progress in Indiana County," WPA manuscript, 1938, and Ralph Stone, "A Social Picture of Chevy Chase," Indiana (PA) State College (now Indiana University of Pennsylvania), 1960, 2–5.

102. Cullman librarian, e-mail, 3/2002; former Cullman resident, e-mail, 5/2002; Helen Bass Williams, manuscript fragment, "History of Negroes in Southern Illinois," n.d., in possession of Mary O'Hara; Noel Hall, 9/2002; untitled clipping in J. A. Gordon, comp., *"Days Beyond Recall,"* vol. 2, reprints from *Warsaw Bulletin,* in Carthage (IL) Museum collection.

103. Brentwood, Central Islip, Flanders, Freeport, Gordon Heights, Hempstead, New Cassel, North Amityville, North Bay Shore, North Bellport, Roosevelt, and Uniondale.

104. Examples include North Brentwood, Maryland, outside Washington, D.C., and Kinloch, Missouri, outside of St. Louis. Unlike townships, North Brentwood incorporated in 1924 and is proud today to claim the title of "oldest incorporated black town in Maryland."

105. Vivian S. Toy, "Stuck in Last Place," *New York Times,* 5/4/2003; Leonard Blumberg and

Michael Lalli, "Little Ghettoes: A Study of Negroes in the Suburbs," *Phylon* 27 (1966): 125; Andrew Wiese, *Places of Their Own* (Chicago: University of Chicago Press, 2004), 6, 17, 21; Harold M. Rose, *Black Suburbanization* (Cambridge: Ballinger, 1976), 29.

106. According to historian Lee Buchsbaum (e-mail, 3/2003), its prostitutes, all of whom were black, "could only be patronized by white customers. Black men were not even allowed in the building, day or night." The sheriff never challenged the arrangement, so long as he was paid off.

107. After the 1933 repeal of Prohibition nationally, it continued for many decades in some counties and the entire state of Oklahoma. So did white purchases of alcohol in black townships in those places.

108. Buchsbaum, e-mail, 3/2003; Jane Adams, e-mail, 6/2003; Stone, "A Social Picture of Chevy Chase," 7; Dean E. Murphy, "This Land Is Made, Finally, for Chinese Settlers," *New York Times,* 6/29/2003.

109. "Denver Closing Door of Hope Against Americans," Chicago *Defender,* 4/9/1910.

110. Chudacoff, *Mobile Americans,* 156.

111. Ibid.; original has "ethic group" in error.

CHAPTER 4: HOW SUNDOWN TOWNS WERE CREATED

1. Cf. "Decatur, Indiana, Is Suffering from a Bad Attack of 'Negrophobia,' " *Indianapolis Freeman,* 6/14/1902.

2. Jean Nipps Swaim, "Black History in Cedar County, Missouri," in *Black Families of the Ozarks,* Bulletin 45 (Springfield, MO: Greene County Archives, n.d.), 2:534.

3. Swaim doubts that any specific event took place, but I think it did, because the black population decline was so precipitous and the ensuing sundown ideology so strong.

4. Swaim, "Black History in Cedar County," 535; Cedar County historian, 10/2002. Swaim, 10/2002, does not know why blacks evacuated the county and thinks some merely relocated to Humansville, across the line in Polk County. Possibly, but Polk County also showed a drastic decline in black population shortly thereafter.

5. In most of the riots Horowitz describes, mass murder competed with forced relocation as an outcome; in almost all of the riots I have uncovered, forced relocation was the preferred outcome and killings were few and in the service of that goal. Exceptions include Rock Springs, Wyoming (1885); Rosewood, Florida (1923); and possibly Zeigler, Illinois (1905), and Mindenmines, Missouri (unknown date).

6. Donald Horowitz, *The Deadly Ethnic Riot* (Berkeley: University of California Press, 2001), 1–2.

7. Patrick Huber, "Race Riots and Black Exodus in the Missouri Ozarks, 1894–1905," Ozark Cultural Celebration, Harrison, AR, 9/2002, 7.

8. Straight-line 1908 projection based on 1900 and 1910 total populations; 1908 total percentage increase then applied to 1900 African American population.

9. Roberta Senechal, *The Sociogenesis of a Race Riot* (Urbana: University of Illinois Press, 1990), 135.

10. National outrage over this riot helped spark the formation of the NAACP the next year.

11. Nancy C. Curtis, *Black Heritage Sites: The North* (New York: New Press, 1996), 59; officer quoted in Allen C. Guelzo, *Abraham Lincoln, Redeemer President* (Grand Rapids: Eerdmans, 1999), 452; Philip A. Klinkner and R. M. Smith, *The Unsteady March* (Chicago: University of Chicago Press, 1999), 106–7.

12. Cf. ustrek.org/odyssey/semester2/013101/013101beckyriot1.html, 11/3/2002, based on Senechal, *The Sociogenesis of a Race Riot;* Klinkner and Smith, *The Unsteady March.*

13. Taylorville had a small African American population and did not go sundown, although new African Americans, especially refugees from Springfield, may have been kept out.

14. *Illinois State Register* quoted in Senechal, *The Sociogenesis of a Race Riot,* 129, 191; "Indicts Six More on Riot Charges," *Chicago Tribune,* 8/22/1908, also quoted in William English Walling, "The Race War in the North," *Independent,* 9/3/1908, 529–34; Michelle Cook, interviews, 2001, 2018; Lester C. Lamon, *Black Tennesseans,* 1900–1930 (Knoxville: University of Tennessee Press, 1977), 134.

15. See Chapter 6 for a fuller account of Spring Valley.

16. Carterville had already been sundown when this expulsion of strikebreakers took place.

17. Otto H. Olsen, *The Negro Question: From Slavery to Caste, 1863–1910* (New York: Pitman, 1971), xxi; "Negroes Have Always Avoided Beardstown," unidentified Beardstown newspaper clipping, 1929, via S. Lynn Walter; Malcolm Ross, *All Manner of Men* (New York: Reynal & Hitchcock, 1948), 51; Felix Armfield, "Fire on the Prairies," *Journal of Illinois History* 3, 3 (2000): 191; Victor Hicken, "The Virden and Pana Mine Wars of 1898," *Illinois State Historical Society Journal* 52, 2 (1959): 265–78; Millie Meyerholtz, *When Hatred and Fear Ruled* (Pana, IL: Pana News, 2001); Paul M. Angle, *Bloody Williamson* (New York: Knopf, 1952), 99–109; "Race War in Illinois," *New York Times,* 6/17/1902; "The Eldorado, Illinois Affair," *Indianapolis Freeman,* 7/19/1902; Senechal, *The Sociogenesis of a Race Riot,* 129–30; untitled article datelined "Anna, Ill., Nov. 13," *Carbondale Free Press,* 11/13/1909; Winifred M. Henson, "History of Franklin County, Illinois," M.A. thesis, Colorado State College of Education, 1942, 143; Pinckneyville native and homeowner, 9/2002, Pinckneyville motel owner, 9/2002, and warranty deed record, Edwards Addition Block 5 Lot 11, sale by Colored Free Will Baptist Church to Riley J. Boyd, 8/29/1928; "Lynch Law in Lacon," *Lacon Journal,* 11/10/1898; for Zeigler controversy see Ruby B. Goodwin, *It's Good To Be Black* (Garden City, NY: Doubleday, 1953), 174–75, Angle, *Bloody Williamson,* 128–31, Allan Patton, *In the Shadow of the Tipple: Zeigler, Illinois* (Zeigler: author, 1994), 34–38, Bob Proctor, 9/2002, and Noel Hall, 9/2002.

18. Again, according to Murray Bishoff, they got the wrong man.

19. Murray Bishoff, "Monett's Darkest Hour: The Lynching of June 28, 1894," *Monett Times,* 6/27–28/1994; Connie Farrow, " 'The Anger and the Hatred Ends,' " *News-Leader,* 8/18/2001.

20. Bishoff, "Monett's Darkest Hour"; Huber, "Race Riots and Black Exodus in the Missouri Ozarks, 1894–1905," 10.

21. Tom W. Dillard, "Madness with a Past: An Overview of Race Violence in Arkansas History," Arkansas Black History Online, cals.lib.ar.us/butlercenter/abho/bib/MADNESS.pdf, 2003, 7; Gordon D. Morgan, "Black Hillbillies of the Arkansas Ozarks," Department of Sociology, University of Arkansas, Fayetteville, 1973, 60.

22. My web site has a page collecting information on expulsion riots across the nation.

23. The departure of a major employer, such as a railroad, might affect most African American families at once. In that event, however, *some* blacks who worked for other employers—in domestic service, etc.—would remain, and whites would not develop a tradition that they prohibited African Americans from staying the night.

24. Frank U. Quillen, *The Color Line in Ohio* (Ann Arbor, MI: Wahr, 1913), 166.

25. James Allen et al., *Without Sanctuary* (Santa Fe: Twin Palms, 2000), shows lynching postcards and other souvenir photos.

26. "The Lynching of 'Nigger Pete,' " *Mena Star,* 2/16/1986; "The Real Polk County," *The Looking Glass* (Hatfield, AR), 1/1980, 16; Inez Lane, "Down Back Roads," *The Looking Glass,* 5/1977, 24; "Those Warning Notices," *Mena Star* 7/21/1897; "The Mayor Gives Good Advice," *Mena Star,* 8/17/1898; Shirley Manning, e-mail, 9/2002.

27. James B. Jones Jr., "A Chronological List of Lynchings in Tennessee, 1866–1946," Southern History Net, southernhistory.net, 3/2002; Stewart E. Tolnay and E. M. Beck, *A Festival of Violence* (Urbana: University of Illinois Press, 1995), 219; "Lynch Law in Lacon," *Lacon Journal,* 11/10/1898; Jack S. Blocker Jr., "Choice and Circumstance," Organization of American Historians, Toronto, 4/1999, Table 5.

28. *Burlington* (VT) *Free Press,* 6/1/1925.

29. Henson, *History of Franklin County, Illinois,* 151; Sally Albertz, e-mail, 5/2002.

30. Howard Goodman, "Bigotry: Oregon's Sad History," *Salem Statesman Journal, Oregon Territory* magazine, 2/8/1981, G3-5.

31. Lynwood Carranco, "The Chinese in Humboldt County, California: A Study in Prejudice," *Journal of the West,* January 1973, 334.

32. All sundown towns with evidence of ordinances are listed at my web site, uvm.edu/~jloewen/sundown. Information from readers confirming or disconfirming these towns can be e-mailed to me through that site.

33. Donald M. Royer, "Indiana's 'Sundown Ordinances' in Nineteen Indiana Towns and Cities" (Indianapolis: Indiana Civil Rights Commission, 1965), photocopy in the Indiana University Library, Bloomington; Olen Cole Jr., *The African-American Experience in the Civilian Conservation Corps* (Gainesville: University Press of Florida, 1999), 57.

34. Chapter 8 tells why I think these towns probably did pass such ordinances and describes the difficulty of locating them today.

35. Monticello lawyer, 10/2002; former De Land trustee, 10/2002; De Land official, 10/2002.

36. Jon L. Craig et al., eds., *Ordinance Law Annotations* (Colorado Springs: Shepard's/McGraw-Hill, 1990 [1969]), 433; cf. John T. Noonan, opinion in *Ho v. SFUSD,* 9715926, 6/4/1998, at Findlaw, laws.lp.findlaw.com/9th/9715926.html.

37. This was the amendment, you will recall, that was passed to guarantee equal rights to all Americans without regard to race. By 1917, the Court had effectively gutted it so far as its utility for improving the rights of African Americans.

38. Charles S. Johnson, *Negro Housing* (New York: Negro Universities Press, 1969 [1932]), 36–40; Susan D. Carle, "Race, Class, and Legal Ethics in the Early NAACP (1910–1920)," *Law and History Review* 20, 1 (2002), historycooperative.org/journals/lhr/20.1/carle.html, 8/2004; T. J. Woofter Jr., *Negro Problems in Cities* (New York: Harper & Row, 1969 [1928]), 71; Peter M. Bergman and Mort N. Bergman, *The Chronological History of the Negro in America* (New York: Mentor, 1969), 367, 380; *Buchanan v. Warley,* 245 U.S. 60.

39. Actually, scores of "exclusively white" towns dotted the North and West by 1915, some much larger than North Chattanooga, but people in North Chattanooga were oriented toward southern cities and towns, where sundown policies were rare.

40. J. Voigt, "Segregation for Suburb," *Chattanooga Daily Times,* 11/10/1915; "North Chattanooga Is Exclusively White Now," 12/22/1915, on Southern History web site, southernhistory.net/index.cfm?FuseAction=DisplayArticleContent&Art_ID=8933, 5/2003.

41. Indianapolis, for example, passed a residential zoning ordinance in 1926.

42. W. A. Low and V. A. Clift, eds., *Encyclopedia of Black America* (New York: McGraw-Hill, 1981), 446.

43. Vincent Jaster, "Education in Brea," interviewed by Cynthia Churney, California State University–Fullerton, Oral History #1720, 4/10–24/1982, 40.

44. Although Arthurdale had no African Americans until at least 1990, I do not know for sure that it was set up on a white-only basis.

45. Decatur, IL, resident, 20/2001; Martinsville native, 10/2002.

46. Emma Lou Thornbrough, edited and with final chapter by Lana Ruegamer, *Indiana Blacks in the Twentieth Century* (Bloomington: Indiana University Press, 2000), 2–3; Thornbrough, *The Negro in Indiana* (Indianapolis: Indiana Historical Bureau, 1957), 225–26; former resident of Crawford County, e-mail, 9/2002.

47. Hank Roth, "Who Is Hank Roth?" pnews.org/bio/5bio.shtml, 6/2003.

48. My web site lists these towns, along with others to be added as information comes in.

49. Willie Harlen, letter, 10/18/2002; David Roediger, e-mail, 8/2003.

50. Jim Clayton, e-mail, 11/2002; Judy Tonges, e-mail, 9/2002.

51. Niles resident, e-mail, 11/2002.

52. Lorenzo J. Greene, Gary Kremer, and Antonio Holland, *Missouri's Black Heritage* (Columbia: University of Missouri Press, 1993), 107, 147.

53. Stephen Vincent studied two small African American communities in east-central Indiana that went into a similar decline, and for the same reasons. He concluded, "The special bond shared by these [black] families and their surrounding white neighbors was loosened if not altogether undone in the late nineteenth century." Stephen A. Vincent, *Southern Seed, Northern Soil* (Bloomington: Indiana University Press, 1999), 127.

54. Robert Azug and Stephen Maizlish, eds., *New Perspectives on Race and Slavery in America* (Lexington: University Press of Kentucky, 1986), 118–21, 125; Robert C. Nesbit, *History of Wisconsin,* vol. III: *Urbanization and Industrialization, 1873–1893* (Madison: Wisconsin Historical Society, 1985), 437–38. Nesbit dates the community to 1848, but in 1860 only 10 blacks lived in the whole of Grant County, compared to 98 by 1870.

55. Edwina M. DeWindt, "Wyandotte History; Negro," typescript, 1945, in Bacon Library, Wyandotte, MI, 20–21; southern Illinois woman, 10/2002.

56. "Mass Meeting, Bell City, Mo. Resolutions," from Frank Nickell, Center for Regional History, Southeastern Missouri State University.

57. DeWindt, "Wyandotte History; Negro," 2.

58. *Chesterton Tribune,* 1/26/1922; Edward H. Sebesta, e-mail, 7/2002.

59. Dorothy K. Newman et al., *Protest, Politics, and Prosperity* (New York: Pantheon, 1978), 144.

60. Deborah Morse-Kahn, *Edina: Chapters in the City History* (Edina: City of Edina, 1998), iii, 56–59.

61. Ibid., 56–59, 61, 94–95; Joyce Repya, 9/1999.

62. Chamblee native, 3/2003; former mayor, 3/2003.

63. Kathryn P. Nelson, *Recent Suburbanization of Blacks* (Washington, DC: HUD Office of Economic Affairs, 1979), 13.

64. Thomas L. Philpott, *The Slum and the Ghetto* (New York: Oxford University Press, 1978), 154.

65. Patrick M. McMullen, "Gated Communities," entry for *Encyclopedia of Chicago,* draft, 10/17/2000; Albert F. Winslow, *Tuxedo Park* (Tuxedo Park: Tuxedo Park Historical Society, 1992), 64–66.

66. Richland and Norris were not exactly suburbs but new communities near huge new military-industrial entities. The developers of Park Forest felt pressured by the FHA to set up

their city for whites only. The original plan for Boulder City, Nevada, was also influenced by Howard's ideas, but that plan was never carried out. Also, one restauranteur defied the federal czar of Boulder City and hired a black cook.

67. Edward J. Blakely and Mary Gail Snyder, *Fortress America* (Washington, DC: Brookings, 1997), 19; Cynthia Mills Richter, "Integrating the Suburban Dream: Shaker Heights, Ohio," Ph.D. dissertation, University of Minnesota, 1999, 19; Allan Hepburn, review of Catherine Jurca's *White Diaspora, Journal of American History* 89, 4 (2003), 1572; "Blacks in Greenbelt," otal.umd.edu/~vg/mssp96/ms12/expla.html, 10/2002; Zane Miller, *Suburb* (Knoxville: University of Tennessee Press, 1981), 128; campus.murraystate.edu/academic/faculty/Bill.Mulligan/Kyv.htm, 9/2003; Mike Davis, *City of Quartz* (London: Verso, 1990), 161–67; Robert Parker, "Robert Parker Discusses Afro-Americans in Boulder City," interview with Dennis McBride, 11/9/1986, Banyan Library web site, banyan .library.unlv.edu/cgi-bin/htmldesc.exe?CISOROOT=/Hoover_Dam&CISOPTR=56& CISOMODE=1, 11/2004; Dennis McBride, "The Boulder City Dictator," *Las Vegas Review-Journal,* lst100.com/part1/ely.html, 11/2004.

68. John H. Denton quoted by Michael N. Danielson, *The Politics of Exclusion* (New York: Columbia University Press, 1976), 31; Frank Harold Wilson, *Footsteps from North Brentwood* (North Brentwood, MD: Historical Society, 1997), 8; Darwin Payne, *Big D* (Dallas: Three Forks Press, 1994), 216–17.

69. Larry McClellan, "Phoenix," entry for *Encyclopedia of Chicago,* draft, 10/1/1999.

70. Sheridan natives, about 65 and 75 years old, in Grant County Museum, 10/2001; Jean Bancroft, post to AAPS Online Forum, aaps.forums.practicenotes.com/forums/Thread.cfm? CFID=946732&CFTOKEN=65413367&&Thread_ID6881&mc=4, 10/15/2003. Note that Searcy the town is quite different from Searcy County, a sundown county in the Ozarks, and is not in Searcy County.

71. De Land official, 10/2002.

CHAPTER 5: SUNDOWN SUBURBS

1. Supplied by Joyce Repya, associate planner for Edina, 9/1999.

2. "A Northern City 'Sitting on Lid' of Racial Trouble," *US News & World Report,* 5/11/1956, 38–40; David L. Good, *Orvie: The Dictator of Dearborn* (Detroit: Wayne State University Press, 1989), 40–41, 264, 386–87; Reynolds Farley, Sheldon Danziger, and Harry Holzer, *Detroit Divided* (New York: Russell Sage, 2000), 154–55; August Meier and Elliott Rudwick, *Black Detroit and the Rise of the UAW* (New York: Oxford University Press, 1979), 12.

3. Andrew Wiese, *Places of Their Own* (Chicago: University of Chicago Press, 2004), 49.

4. Kenneth T. Jackson, *Crabgrass Frontier* (New York: Oxford University Press, 1985), 283–84; M. P. Baumgartner, *The Moral Order of a Suburb* (New York: Oxford University Press, 1988), 6; Thomas Byrne Edsall and Mary D. Edsall, *Chain Reaction* (New York: Norton, 1992), 229, 231.

5. John Palen, *The Suburbs* (New York: McGraw-Hill, 1995), xiii, 3–7; Lizabeth Cohen, *A Consumers' Republic* (New York: Knopf, 2003), 255.

6. Moving to the suburbs was hardly the obvious path to "the good life." From Johannesburg to Lima to Jakarta, suburbs are inconvenient places where poor people live who must travel miles to the central city to work or attend cultural events. In nineteenth-century America, elegant rowhouse districts such as Boston's Beacon Hill were what American families wanted as they grew more affluent.

7. Larry Peterson, e-mail, 3/2004.

8. Ford quoted in Jackson, *Crabgrass Frontier,* 75.

9. Jackson, *Crabgrass Frontier,* 149–50, 272–73.

10. Ellen James Martin, "Set Some Priorities When Buying in a Classy Community," Universal Press Syndicate, in *Chicago Tribune,* 9/14/2001.

11. Thomas Pettigrew, "Attitudes on Race and Housing," in Amos Hawley and Vincent Rock, eds., *Segregation in Residential Areas* (Washington, DC: National Academy of Sciences, 1973), 38; Andrew Hacker, "Sociology and Ideology," in Max Black, ed., *The Social Theories of Talcott Parsons* (Englewood Cliffs, NJ: Prentice-Hall, 1961), 289; Stephen G. Meyer, *As Long as They Don't Move Next Door* (Lanham, MD: Rowman & Littlefield, 2000), 1.

12. Other similar suburbs include Stamford, Connecticut; Montclair and Orange, New Jersey; New Rochelle and Mt. Vernon, New York; Coral Gables, Florida; Webster Groves, Missouri, and Pasadena, California.

13. Jackson, *Crabgrass Frontier,* 100–1, 241.

14. Bernard Nelson, *The Fourteenth Amendment and the Negro Since 1920* (New York: Russell & Russell, 1946), 23–24; Colleen Kilner, *Joseph Sears and His Kenilworth* (Kenilworth: Kenilworth Historical Society, 1990), 138, 143, her italics.

15. Newlands, senator from Nevada, honed his racism as a leader of anti-Chinese sentiment there. In 1909, he wrote "Race tolerance . . . means race amalgamation, and this is undesirable" and argued that the United States "should prevent the immigration of all people other than those of the white race." Quoted in Loren B. Chan, "The Chinese in Nevada," in Arif Dirlik, ed., *Chinese on the American Frontier* (Lanham, MD: Rowman & Littlefield, 2001), 88–89.

16. Not all of those 18 may have been black; some may be nonblacks in an interracial family. In all, Chevy Chase had 42 African Americans, but that total includes live-in maids and gardeners. The census also showed 20 mixed-race persons who listed "black" or "African American" among their component identities, hard to classify, since the census does not reveal how they identified. Some may be mixed-race children adopted by white couples. I summed the four entities that collectively make up Chevy Chase: Chevy Chase (town), Chevy Chase Section Three, Chevy Chase Section Five, and Chevy Chase Village.

17. Marc Fisher, "Chevy Chase, 1916: For Everyman, a New Lot in Life," *Washington Post,* 2/15/1999; washingtonpost.com/wp-srv/local/2000/chevychase0215.htm, 1/2003.

18. Fisher, "Chevy Chase, 1916."

19. Mt. Auburn Cemetery web site, mountauburn.org/history.htm, 8, 2004.

20. Unlike sundown suburbs, sundown cemeteries rarely forced out existing black "residents."

21. "Denial by Cemetery Company of Burial Space for Colored Person, Held Not to Be Violation of a Civil Right," 258 IL 36, in Illinois State Archives.

22. David Charles Sloane, *The Last Great Necessity* (Baltimore: Johns Hopkins University Press, 1995), 188, 268.

23. Kilner, *Joseph Sears and His Kenilworth;* Michael Ebner, *Creating Chicago's North Shore* (Chicago: University of Chicago Press, 1988), 230, 314; Harry Rubenstein, 9/2000; "Housing: How High the Barriers," *ADL Bulletin* 16, 1 (1959): 2.

24. The Ku Klux Klan did target Jews and Catholics verbally in independent sundown towns in the mid-1920s, but rarely did they actually drive them out or keep them out.

25. Grosse Pointe did not completely bar Jews but required them to amass more points on Grosse Pointe's notorious "point system" than any other permitted group. See pages 262–64.

26. I don't think many whites really believed Jews were genetically less intelligent. The attacks on Jews, whether by Nazis in Europe or by real estate developers in the United States, were more subtle than those on African Americans. Jews were considered "crafty" rather than intelligent—a distinction wholly in the mind of the beholder.

27. Some are listed at uvm.edu/~jloewen/sundown.

28. We shall see in the next chapter that this perception has some validity.

29. Laura Z. Hobson, *Gentleman's Agreement* (New York: Simon & Schuster, 1947); "Housing Discrimination Against Jews," *ADL Reports* 2, 5 (1959), 41; Graham Hutton, *Midwest at Noon* (Chicago: University of Chicago Press, 1946), 48; Mary Ellen Stratthaus, "Flaw in the Jewel: Housing Discrimination Against Jews in La Jolla, California," *American Jewish History* 84, 3 (1996): 190.

30. *Memorandum on Specific Methods for Promoting Good Will Among Racial Groups in Illinois* (Illinois Interracial Commission, 1943), #4, 2; Jackson, *Crabgrass Frontier,* 241; Levitt & Sons, ad taken out after murder of Martin Luther King Jr., 4/1968, in exhibit, "Levittown," Pennsylvania State Museum, Harrisburg, 11/2002; Geoffrey Mohan writing in *Newsday,* quoted by Kevin Schultz, e-mail, 6/2002.

31. Donald Cunnigen, "Myrdal, Park, and Second Generation African American Sociologists," in Bruce Hare, ed., *2001 Race Odyssey* (Syracuse: Syracuse University Press, 2002), 42; Arnold Hirsch, *Making the Second Ghetto* (Cambridge: Cambridge University Press, 1983), 63; James Hecht, *Because It Is Right* (Boston: Little, Brown, 1970), 8.

32. Thomas Sugrue, *Origins of the Urban Crisis* (Princeton: Princeton University Press, 1996), 43; Jack Star, "Negro in the Suburbs," *Look,* 5/16/1967; Brian Berry et al., *Chicago* (Cambridge: Ballinger, 1976), 30; Troy Duster, "The 'Morphing' Properties of Whitness," in Birgit Rasmussen et al., eds., *The Making and Unmaking of Whiteness* (Durham: Duke University Press, 2001), 119; Mike Davis, *City of Quartz* (London: Verso, 1990), 167.

33. Abrams quoted by Jackson, *Crabgrass Frontier,* 214, cf. 208, 213, 229–43; Lawrence J. Vale, *From the Puritans to the Projects* (Cambridge: Harvard University Press, 2000), 169–70; Lockwood quoted in Newman, *Protest, Politics, and Prosperity,* 163.

34. W. A. Low and V. A. Clift, eds., *Encyclopedia of Black America* (New York: McGraw-Hill, 1981), 449; "Outline of Protective Covenants for Mayfair Park," supplied by Elise Guyette, 4/2003.

35. Palen, *The Suburbs,* 58; Cohen, *A Consumers' Republic,* 196; Nancy A. Denton, "Segregation and Discrimination in Housing," in Rachel Bratt, Chester Hartman, and Michael E. Stone, eds., reader on housing (Philadelphia: Temple University Press, forthcoming), ms. pp. 23–24; cf. Thomas W. Hanchett, "The Other 'Subsidized Housing,'" in John Bauman et al., *From Tenements to the Taylor Homes* (University Park, PA: Penn State University Press, 2000), 166.

36. Low and Clift, eds., *Encyclopedia of Black America,* 451–52.

37. The first and fourth chapters of *Because It Is Right* by James Hecht bring to life the process by which white suburbs ignored 1968 and stayed overwhelmingly white through the 1970s (and some to this day), with examples of African Americans who could not buy even though they were doctors, lawyers, or famous professional athletes.

38. Douglas Massey, talk at the Fund for an Open Society (OPEN), Philadelphia, 12/2000; Michael N. Danielson, *The Politics of Exclusion* (New York: Columbia University Press, 1976), 12; David M. P. Freund, *Colored Property,* 15, typescript, 2001; cf. Hecht, *Because It Is Right,* chapters 1 and 4.

39. Western shore native, e-mail, 11/2002; state worker, 9/2002.

40. Margery Turner et al., *All Other Things Being Equal* (Washington, DC: Urban Institute, 2002), executive summary, i-v; Shanna Smith, in panel discussion, "A Foot in the Door? New Evidence on Housing Discrimination," Urban Institute, Washington, DC, 2/4/2003.

41. Jackson, *Crabgrass Frontier,* 283. By 1990, most of Baltimore's sundown suburbs had relented, and the proportion of African Americans in Baltimore and Baltimore County (not quite the same as the metropolitan area) who lived in Baltimore County was 16.4%; by 2000, it was 26.6%.

42. For a list, see uvm.edu/~jloewen/sundown/.

43. Harold M. Rose, *Black Suburbanization* (Cambridge: Ballinger, 1976), 5, 7, 9, 29, 31, 47–48, 84, 158.

44. Michael Powell, "Separate and Unequal in Roosevelt, Long Island," *Washington Post,* 4/21/2002; Joe T. Darden, "African American Residential Segregation," in Robert D. Bullard et al., *Residential Apartheid* (Los Angeles: UCLA Center for Afro-American Studies, 1994), 88–89.

45. Camilo Jose Vergara, *American Ruins* (New York: Monacelli, 1999), 92; Danielson, *The Politics of Exclusion,* 8–9; Arthur Hayes, "Managed Integration," *Black Enterprise,* 7/1982, 44; Meyer, *As Long as They Don't Move Next Door,* 217.

46. Jeff R. Crump, "Producing and Enforcing the Geography of Hate," in Colin Flint, ed., *Spaces of Hate* (New York: Routledge, 2003), 227.

CHAPTER 6: UNDERLYING CAUSES

1. John C. Boger, "Toward Ending Residential Segregation: A Fair Share Proposal for the Next Reconstruction," *North Carolina Law Review* 71 (1993): 1576.

2. My web site, uvm.edu/~jloewen/sundown, lists these towns.

3. Therefore I use "all-white" to refer to towns that admit Asian, Native, and Mexican Americans, while barring African Americans.

4. John Ogbu, *Minority Education and Caste* (New York: Academic Press, 1978).

5. Jews and Mexicans *are* "white," of course, by the definitions of 2005. Jews weren't exactly, between 1900 and about 1950, and Mexicans weren't exactly, between 1930 and about 1970. Later chapters comment on this issue.

6. "His Flight to Save Prisoner," *Carbondale Daily Free Press,* 11/13/1909; Darrel Dexter, *A House Divided: Union County, Illinois* (Anna: Reppert, 1994), 73–75.

7. Dexter, *House Divided,* 75.

8. Jerry Poling, *A Summer Up North* (Madison: University of Wisconsin Press, 2002), 10.

9. Forrest C. Pogue Public History Institute web site, campus.murraystate.edu/academic/faculty/Bill.Mulligan/Kyv.htm, 10/2004; Robert Parker, "Robert Parker Discusses Afro-Americans in Boulder City," interview with Dennis McBride, 11/9/1986, Banyan Library web site, banyan.library.unlv.edu/cgi-bin/htmldesc.exe?CISOROOT=/Hoover_Dam& CISOPTR=56&CISOMODE=1, 11/2004; "A Northern City 'Sitting on Lid' of Racial Trouble," *US News & World Report,* 5/11/1956, 38–40; Michigan Advisory Committee on Civil Rights, *Civil Rights and the Housing and Community Development Act of 1974, v. I: Livonia* (Washington, D.C.: U.S. Commission on Civil Rights, 1975), 6; George Hunter, "Booming City Has Home to Fit Every Need, Price Range," *Detroit News,* 2/2/97.

10. Chairman, Illinois Inter-Racial Commission, 11/19/1943, minutes in Illinois State Archives.

11. Sociologist Gordon Morgan suggests that African Americans left some Ozark counties in

the early decades of the twentieth century because they lacked the critical mass necessary to maintain community. This is an aspect of social isolation and at first blush seems reasonable. In *The Mississippi Chinese* (Cambridge, MA: Harvard University Press, 1971), I myself wrote, "There will come a time of 'critical mass,' when a Chinese community in any sense of the word will prove unmaintainable," and went on to predict a rapid drop in the population of Chinese Americans in the Mississippi Delta. The prediction came true after 1975. But the Chinese case was different: economic and educational upward mobility led to geographic mobility for their children, while at the same time, the end of racial segregation in Mississippi eliminated the peculiar niche for Chinese Americans as a middleman minority, leaving no particular reason for new immigrants to enter the Delta.

To be sure, when the African American population falls below a minimum, it becomes difficult to date or marry another African American or support a black church. Until Missouri's schools desegregated (well after 1954), fifteen African American children were required before a school district had to provide a "colored school," and eight of high-school age before it had to provide a high school. In the absence of a school for their children, some parents will certainly move. Morgan's hypothesis doubtless explains why some African Americans left, especially families with children seeking marriage mates. He believes it explains Huntsville, Arkansas, which had 15 blacks in 1940 and just 1 in 1950, and it may.

Critical mass also helps explain the departure of most of the remaining African Americans from Maryville, Missouri, after the 1931 lynching described in Chapter 7. Most blacks fled immediately, and enrollment at the "colored school" fell from sixteen students to six. Two years later it closed entirely, causing the black population of Nodaway County to decline still further. But the root cause of Nodaway as a sundown county remains the lynching and subsequent threats to the black community, not critical mass. (See Patrick Huber and Gary Kremer, "A Death in the Heartland," presented at Missouri Conference on History, St. Louis, 3/1994, 10.) Similarly, critical mass theory does not explain why black newcomers no longer entered counties across America after 1890, as they had earlier. If numbers alone could explain why a group leaves an area, then no new group would ever enter unless they could do so en masse.

12. Andrew Wiese, *Places of Their Own* (Chicago: University of Chicago Press, 2004), 19, 145.

13. Boger, "Toward Ending Residential Segregation," 1576.

14. I simplify. Affluent whites also choose elite suburbs for other reasons, such as better schooling, as later chapters acknowledge, but again "better" often implicitly involves separation from people seen as problems—usually those of lower caste and class position.

15. Michael N. Danielson, *The Politics of Exclusion* (NY: Columbia University Press, 1976), 9–10; Frederick M. Wirt et. al., *On the City's Rim* (Lexington, MA: D.C. Heath, 1972), 43, citing research by John Kain and Joseph Persky.

16. Karl Taeuber, "Racial Segregation: The Persisting Dilemma," *The Annals* 422 (11/1975), 91.

17. "A Northern City 'Sitting on Lid' of Racial Trouble," 38–40; Michigan Advisory Committee on Civil Rights, *Civil Rights and the Housing and Community Development Act of 1974, v. I: Livonia* (Washington, D.C.: U.S. Commission on Civil Rights, 1975), 6; George Hunter, "Booming City Has Home to Fit Every Need, Price Range," *Detroit News*, 2/2/97.

18. Albert Hermalin and Reynolds Farley quoted in Dorothy K. Newman et. al., *Protest, Politics, and Prosperity* (New York: Pantheon, 1978), 143; Farley, Sheldon Danziger, and Harry J. Holzer, *Detroit Divided* (New York: Russell Sage, 2000), 165.

19. *Worth* supplied four other lists of 50 towns each, covering the richest 250 towns in all.
20. Bobbie Gossage, "The Best Address," *Worth* 11, 4 (5/2002), 59; Ellen Revelle Eckis, interviewed 2/1996 by Mary Ellen Stratthaus, "Flaw in the Jewel: Housing Discrimination against Jews in La Jolla, California," *American Jewish History*, 84, 3 (1996), 219, n.1.
21. Garrett County historian, 5/2002.
22. Texas A&M professor, 9/99; woman from Buffalo, 7/2002.
23. Inadvertently, this argument assumes that African Americans are much better at economic prognostication than whites, who seem not to have the common sense to avoid these backwaters. It also implies that their all-white status is not worth correcting: either it results from blacks' rational choice or, if white residents do forbid their entrance, African Americans do well to avoid these towns anyway.
24. Stephan Thernstrom and Abigail Thernstrom, *America in Black and White* (New York: Simon & Schuster, 1997).
25. Nicole Etcheson, *The Emerging Midwest* (Indianapolis: Indiana University Press, 1996), 97.
26. Contrast Robert Gerling: *Highland: An Illinois Swiss Community in the American Civil War* (Highland, IL: Highland Historical Society, 1978), 21, for example, with *The History of Peoria County* (Chicago: Johnson & Co., 1880), 360, 409, 418.
27. Princeton, another Republican town, is near but not on the Illinois River or it would also be an exception.
28. Dexter, *House Divided*, 73–75; *Combined History of Shelby and Moultrie Counties, Illinois* (Philadelphia: Brink, McDonough, 1881), 31; I. J. Martin, *Notes on the History of Moultrie County and Sullivan, Illinois* (Sullivan: R. Eden Martin, 1990), 29; Jacque Neal, e-mail, 10/2001; Moultrie County teacher at Illinois Council for the Social Studies, 9/2002.
29. S. M. Lipset, *Political Man* (Garden City, NY: Doubleday Anchor, 1963 [1960]), 374–83.
30. Western Virginia, of course, succeeded.
31. Esther S. Sanderson, *County Scott and Its Mountain Folk* (Nashville: Williams Printing, 1958), 187.
32. Michael W. Fitzgerald, *The Union League Movement in the Deep South* (Baton Rouge: Louisiana State University Press, 1989), 17–18; David K. Shipler, *A Country of Strangers* (New York: Knopf, 1997), 108; Cullman librarian, e-mail, 7/2002; Steve Hicks, 6/2002; Haleyville librarian, 6/2002.
33. Melissa Sue Brewer, "Historical Context: Sundowning in Myakka City," typescript, Myakka City, 2002, 1; Ralph R. Rea, *Boone County and Its People* (Van Buren, AR: Press-Argus, 1955), 53; several other county histories.
34. Mark Lause, e-mails, 6/2002, citing *History of Franklin, Jefferson, Washington, Crawford, and Gasconade Counties, Missouri* (Chicago, 1888); Art Draper, e-mail, 7/2002.
35. Bob Neymeyer, e-mail, 5/2002.
36. Lancaster resident, 8/2004.
37. Political scientist Larry Peterson suggests that Italian Americans also lacked social power to keep blacks out. He further notes that Jews fled "racially changing neighborhoods as fast as, if not faster than, other whites" (Peterson, e-mail, 3/2004).
38. Jan Reiff, 9/2001; T. J. Woofter Jr., *Negro Problems in Cities* (New York: Harper & Row, 1969 [1928]), 39; Hillel Levine and Lawrence Harmon, *The Death of an American Jewish Community* (New York: Free Press, 1992), 6; Thomas Sugrue, *Origins of the Urban*

Crisis (Princeton: Princeton University Press, 1996), 243–44; Charles Bright, e-mail, 4/2004.

39. Noel Ignatiev, *How the Irish Became White* (New York: Routledge, 1995), 112, and quoting John Finch, "an English Owenite who traveled the United States in 1843," 97.

40. Carl Weinberg tells of the beginning of this white ethnic solidarity, vis-à-vis blacks, in the aftermath of the successful United Mine Workers strike at Virden, Illinois, in 1898. See "The Battle of Virden, the UMWA, and the Challenge of Solidarity," in Rosemary Feurer, ed., *Remember Virden, 1898* (Chicago: Illinois Humanities Council, n.d.), 7–8.

41. Yes, I know *Norwegians* dominate Lake Wobegone, which is precisely why they tell Swedish jokes on occasion.

42. Granite City Public Library, *75th Year Celebration of the City of Granite City, Illinois* (Granite City: n.p., 1971), 24; Matthew Jacobson, *Whiteness of a Different Color* (Cambridge: Harvard University Press, 1998).

43. Peter Baldwin, "Italians in Middletown, 1893–1932," B.A. thesis, Wesleyan University, 1984, 18–19; David Roediger, 8/2003.

44. Ronald L. Lewis, *Black Coal Miners in America* (Lexington: University Press of Kentucky, 1987), 81.

45. Some Greek Americans never returned to Zeigler, however, and the town still has fewer than it did before the expulsion.

46. John Higham, *Strangers in the Land* (New Brunswick: Rutgers University Press, 1955), 264; *Marion Daily Republican*, 8/13/1920, 1; Williamson County genealogist, 9/2002; Winifred M. Henson, "History of Franklin County, Illinois," M.A. thesis, Colorado State College of Education, 1942, 143; retired Zeigler miner, 9/2002.

47. Sometimes they played this role wittingly, having no loyalty to a labor union that had kept them out, and sometimes unwittingly, having been lied to by company recruiters, lured in from hundreds of miles away, and now unable to leave owing to company coercion and lack of funds.

48. See conflicting reports in Caroline Waldron, " 'Lynch-law Must Go!' " *Journal of American Ethnic History*, Fall 2000, 50–74; Felix Armfield, "Fire on the Prairies," *Journal of Illinois History* 3, 3 (2000): 188–97; Arna Bontemps and Jack Conroy, *Anyplace but Here* (New York: Hill & Wang, 1966 [1945]), 143; and various newspaper articles.

49. Millie Meyerholtz, *When Hatred and Fear Ruled . . . Pana, Illinois* (Pana, IL: Pana News, 2001), 1; citing Eleanor Burhorn, *Strike of Coal Miners at Pana, Illinois—1898–99*, 7, 12–13; Victor Hicken, "The Virden and Pana Mine Wars of 1898," *Illinois State Historical Society Journal* 52, 2 (1959), 274.

50. Meyerholtz, *When Hatred and Fear Ruled*, 8, 17, 21, 25–26, 33; Lewis, *Black Coal Miners in America*, 92–93.

51. Marvin L. Van Gilder, *The Story of Barton County* (Lamar, MO: Reiley, 1972), 20; staff member, Missouri Southern State College, 4/2001.

52. Paul M. Angle, *Bloody Williamson* (New York: Knopf, 1952), 120–25; Patton, *In the Shadow of the Tipple*, 30–32.

53. Angle wrote contemporaneously with Goodwin but should have known of her as a source because of her prominence in the black community.

54. It isn't always clear, especially in the oral tradition, which disaster was which, or who—by race and ethnicity—was blown up when. Historian Paul Angle claims most of the dead were Hungarians; others think most of the casualties were African Americans. Historians also disagree with each other and with the oral tradition as to the causes of the disasters, without explaining

adequately the basis for their positions. At the time, the mine management thought the strikers blew up the strikebreakers, and a coroner's jury agreed. On the other hand, an inquiry by the state called it an accident and blamed it on gas buildup, and Angle and Patton agree.

55. Angle, *Bloody Williamson*, 126–30; Patton, *In the Shadow of the Tipple*, 34–36; Ruby B. Goodwin, *It's Good to Be Black* (Garden City, NY: Doubleday, 1953), 174–75.

56. Of course, it has always been easier for the white industrialist or mine operator to be more tolerant on race than for white workers. It's in the capitalist's immediate interest to hire anyone who will work for lower wages. African Americans have long constituted a reserve army of unemployed and underemployed labor, often willing to work at lower pay than whites. Sometimes capitalists hired African Americans for this reason and worked them alongside whites in the same jobs for lower pay, which of course had a chilling effect on white workers' efforts to win higher wages. It's also in owners' interests to hire people who will work when others won't, during a strike. Capitalists often found it easy to engage African Americans as strikebreakers. Blacks had little solidarity with white workers and their unions, since those same unions had shut them out of skilled jobs and restricted union membership to whites only. Hiring the best person for the job regardless of color also fits with the capitalist ethos and with the shards of anti-racist idealism that sometimes remained from the broken vessel of Republican abolitionism. Most important, after African Americans have been hired, the capitalist remains above his black employees—as well as his white employees—in social status, whereas the white worker is not above a black co-worker. Thus when the workplace integrates, the white worker is asked to give up white supremacy, while the capitalist is not.

57. Since these industries were among the few that employed African Americans, such occupational exclusion may have helped to cause the Great Retreat to the cities. But African Americans were no more likely to find jobs in these occupations in cities. I am also not persuaded that the rise of unions suffices to explain all-white towns and counties, because African Americans in such nonunion fields as domestics, barbers, janitors, haulers, and farmworkers also left.

58. Peterson, e-mail, 3/2004; Marc Karson and Ronald Radosh, "The AFL and the Negro Worker, 1894–1949," in Julius Jacobson, ed., *The Negro and the American Labor Movement* (Garden City, NY: Doubleday Anchor, 1968), 157–58.

CHAPTER 7: CATALYSTS AND ORIGIN MYTHS

1. *Chesterton Tribune*, 7/24/1903.
2. The census did find five individual African Americans, but black householders are the more important test of sundown policies.
3. Emma Lou Thornbrough, *The Negro in Indiana* (Indianapolis: Indiana Historical Bureau, 1957), 226–27; Steve Byers, e-mail, 6/2002; history teacher, 4/2002.
4. *The Worker*, 7/26/1903, quoted in Philip Foner and Ronald Lewis, eds., *The Black Worker from 1900 to 1919* (Philadelphia: Temple University Press, 1980), 198; Andrew Kirchmeier, 4/2002.
5. Ruby B. Goodwin, *It's Good to Be Black* (Garden City, NY: Doubleday, 1953); "Gentleman of Color Elected Alderman," *Herrin News*, 4/25/1918, 4.
6. Paul M. Angle, *Bloody Williamson* (New York: Knopf, 1952), 97–109; Herbert Gutman, "The Negro and the UMW," in Julius Jacobson, *The Negro and the American Labor Movement* (Garden City, NY: Doubleday Anchor, 1968), 49.

7. Nebraska Writers' Project, *The Negroes of Nebraska* (Omaha: Urban League, 1940), 10; Philip Jenkins, e-mail, 8/2002; Gutman, "The Negro and the UMW," 99.

8. This "local legend" was still extant in 2002, when I interviewed residents of Zeigler.

9. Allan Patton, *In the Shadow of the Tipple: Zeigler, Illinois* (Zeigler: author, 1994), 28.

10. Cf. Willis D. Weatherford and Charles S. Johnson, *Race Relations* (Boston: D. C. Heath, 1934), 59; Ralph E. Luker, *The Social Gospel in Black and White* (Chapel Hill: University of North Carolina Press, 1991), 237; Mark Odintz, "Slocum, Texas," in *Handbook of Texas Online,* tsha.utexas.edu/handbook/online/articles/view/SS/hls57.html, 2003; Sitton and Conrad, *Nameless Towns,* 108–9.

11. Thornbrough, *The Negro in Indiana,* 225.

12. Ferguson quoted in Roberta Senechal, *The Sociogenesis of a Race Riot* (Urbana: University of Illinois Press, 1990), 136; Deepak Madala, Jennifer Jordan, and August Appleton, "Prominent Resident Killed," library.thinkquest.org/2986/Killed.html, 8/2002.

13. Perhaps they were only trying to get a key. Accounts differ.

14. One black barber, Alex Johnson, was allowed back, a pattern we shall encounter frequently.

15. "KKK in Owosso," *Owosso Press,* 10/11/1871; Helen Harrelson, 10/15/2002.

16. John Womack, "Blacks, The First Year[s] in Oklahoma," typescript, Norman, 1982, 4–7.

17. Bianca White, "The History/Ocoee: Legacy of the Election Day Massacre," iml.jou.ufl .edu/projects/Fall01/white/2ocoee1.html, 12/2002; Evan Bennett, e-mail, 2/1998; Edwin Reuter, *The American Race Problem* (New York: Crowell, 1927), 418; cf. Maxine Jones, "The African-American Experience in Twentieth-Century Florida," in Michael Gannon, ed., *The New History of Florida* (Gainesville: University Press of Florida, 1996).

18. "Drive Out Race After Bloody Tilt," *Chicago Defender,* 9/24/1921; Afi O. Scruggs, e-mail, 9/2002.

19. Male Sheridan native, about 65 years of age, and female native, about 75, 10/2001; professor, Southern Arkansas University, 10/2001.

20. C. K. Bullard quoted in Dorothy Brown, "The Encircled Schools: Park Cities and Wilmington," *Dallas Times Herald,* 11/30/1975; Charles Martin, e-mail, 7/2002.

21. Womack, "Blacks, The First Year[s] in Oklahoma," 22–24.

22. My web site, uvm.edu/~jloewen/sundown, lists these counties.

23. Waalkes goes on to note, "I have also heard that Polk County simply pressured black families to send their children to school in Bradley County."

24. Mary Waalkes, e-mail, 7/2002; Esther S. Sanderson, *Scott County, Gem of the Cumberlands* (Huntsville, TN: author, 1974), 72.

25. Judith Joy, "Memorial to a Slain Girl Recalls a Violent Episode in Cairo's History," *Centralia Sentinel,* 1/3/1982, based on 1909 accounts in the *Sentinel.*

26. "His Flight to Save Prisoner," *Carbondale Daily Free Press,* 11/13/1909; Judith Joy, "Memorial to a Slain Girl."

27. "Hang and Burn Negro—White Man Also Lynched," *Carbondale Daily Press,* 11/12/1909.

28. Untitled article datelined "Anna, Ill., Nov. 13," *Carbondale Daily Free Press,* 11/13/1909; Dexter, *House Divided,* 73–75; local historian, 6/10/2003.

29. Donald F. Tingley, *The Structuring of a State: The History of Illinois, 1899 to 1928* (Urbana: University of Illinois Press, 1980), 291–92; James Allen et al., *Without Sanctuary* (Santa Fe: Twin Palms, 2000), #46, 181–84; "In Memory Of Miss Pelley," *Carbondale Free Press,* 11/17/1909.

30. Two were tried and hanged in Cummins, the county seat.

31. Garland C. Bagley, *History of Forsyth County, Georgia, II* (Greenville, SC: Southern Historical Press, 1985), 614.

32. Philip A. Klinkner and R. M. Smith, *The Unsteady March* (Chicago: University of Chicago Press, 1999), 106–7; Pinckneyville motel owner, 9/2002; LaSalle native, 6/2000.

33. Eulalia N. Wells, *Blazing the Way* (Blanket, TX: author, 1942), 159–61.

34. Felix Armfield, "Fire on the Prairies," *Journal of Illinois History* 3, 3 (2000); Arna Bontemps and Jack Conroy, *Anyplace but Here* (New York: Hill & Wang, 1966 [1945]); Edwina M. DeWindt, "Wyandotte History; Negro," typescript, 1945, in Bacon Library, Wyandotte, MI; *Chesterton Tribune,* 7/24/1903.

35. "His Flight to Save Prisoner"; Senechal, *The Sociogenesis of a Race Riot,* 158; Roadside Georgia, Forsyth County, roadsidegeorgia.com/county/forsyth.html, 1/2004; and Dawson County, roadsidegeorgia.com/county/dawson.html, 1/2004.

36. "Hindus Hounded from City," *Bellingham Herald,* 9/5/1907.

37. Bill Kaplin, 4/2002; Kathy Spillman, 12/2000.

38. *Lexington Herald,* 11/1/1919, and Corbin resident, quoted in Robby Heason, *Trouble Behind* (Cicada Films, 1990); Hank Everman, "Corbin, Kentucky: A Socioeconomic Anomaly," Department of History, Eastern Kentucky University, 2002, unpaginated.

39. George C. Wright, *A History of Blacks in Kentucky* 2 (Lexington: Kentucky Historical Society, 1992), 15; Murray Bishoff, 9/2002.

40. Patrick Huber and Gary Kremer, "A Death in the Heartland," paper presented at Missouri Conference on History, St. Louis, 3/1994, 12–13; "The Lynchings," Minnesota Historical Society, collections.mnhs.org/duluthlynchings/web_assets/icon_arrowback.gif, 12/2003.

41. Wells, *Blazing the Way,* 162; Billy Bob Lightfoot, "The Negro Exodus from Comanche County, Texas," *Southwestern Historical Quarterly* 56 (1953): 410–13; John Leffler, "Comanche County," *The Handbook of Texas Online,* 6/2002.

42. I have not found any midwestern ordinances, let alone a chain of dated ordinances that would demonstrate their diffusion. Chapter 8 discusses this problem.

43. "June 12, 1992," Nationalist web site, nationalist.org/docs/law/supreme.html#Top, 1/2004; Andrew H. Myers, "Winter Day in Georgia," typescript, 1997; Oprah Winfrey, "Vintage Oprah: Racial Tension in Georgia," Harpo Productions, Chicago, 2001 (1987), 7.

44. Smokey Crabtree, *Too Close to the Mirror* (Fouke: Days Creek Production, 2001), 186.

45. But then, some towns whose origin myths do not include black strikebreakers also refused to let African Americans work or shop in them during the day.

46. Apparently he did; I use "allegedly" because there was no trial, hence no proof beyond a reasonable doubt.

47. Wells, *Blazing the Way,* 162; Lightfoot, "The Negro Exodus from Comanche County, Texas," 410–13; Leffler, "Comanche County."

48. DeWindt, "Wyandotte History; Negro," 16.

49. "Race War In Illinois" and "Bitter Race War Threatened," *New York Times,* 6/17/1902.

50. Robyn Williams, e-mail, 9/2002; employee of Southern Illinois University who lived in Eldorado for several years in the early 1990s.

51. "Bitter Race War Threatened."

52. Peter M. Bergman and Mort N. Bergman, *The Chronological History of the Negro in America* (New York: Mentor, 1969), 444.

53. Thad Sitton and James H. Conrad, *Nameless Towns: Texas Sawmill Communities, 1880–1942* (Austin: University of Texas Press, 1998), 71–73, 112.

54. John Hay, *The Pike County Ballots* (Boston: Houghton Mifflin, 1912 [1871]), 21–24.

55. Miller is quoted in Martha Biondi, *To Stand and Fight* (Cambridge: Harvard University Press, 2003), 128; cf. 124–32.

56. I believe that Sayles did not live in Boulder City but commuted from Las Vegas, so he did not violate Boulder City as a sundown town.

57. "Robert Parker discusses Afro-Americans in Boulder City," transcript of 11/9/1986 interview, Banyan Library, UNLV, banyan.library.unlv.edu/cgi-bin/htmldesc.exe?CISOROOT= /Hoover_Dam&C ISOPTR=56&CISOMODE=1, 10/2004.

58. Although most Humboldt County sources state—some even brag—that all other Chinese Americans were expelled from the county, apparently some Chinese miners survived in Orleans, a mining hamlet in the remote northeastern corner of the county, sheltered by whites and perhaps using European names. See Philip Sanders and Laura Sanders, "The Quiet Rebellion," *Humboldt Historian*, 1998, cited by Keith Easthouse, "The Chinese Expulsion," *North Coast Journal Weekly*, northcoastjournal.com/022703/cover0227.html, 2/2004.

59. Easthouse, "The Chinese Expulsion"; Lynwood Carranco, "Chinese Expulsion from Humboldt County," in Roger Daniels, ed., *Anti-Chinese Violence in North America* (New York: Arno Press, 1978), 336–37; Laurinda Joenks, "Roughness of Citizens Blamed on Lean Times," *The Morning News*, 5/7/2000.

60. Again, I use "allegedly" because there was no trial.

61. Audree Webb Pratt, "Unicoi County Court: 1876–1918," M.A. thesis, East Tennessee State University, 1960, 27–29; "Erwin Mob Shoots and Burns Body of Negro Who Attacked Girl," *Bristol Herald*, 5/21/1918; "Triple Tragedy at Erwin on Sunday When Negro Runs Wild," *Johnson City Daily*, 5/20/1918; cf. Charles Edward Price Papers, Box 1, Folder 6, "Blacks in Unicoi County, Tennessee," undated, "Blacks: Tom Devert," Hoskins Library, University of Tennessee.

62. Anne Braden, *The Wall Between* (Knoxville: University of Tennessee Press, 1999 [1958]), 137–38, 253, 286.

Chapter 8: Hidden in Plain View

1. Rogers Chamber of Commerce Publicity and Public Relations Committee, "Committee Report," 1/29/1962, in Rogers Historical Museum files.

2. Comment on presentation, 1/2003, via James Onderdonk Jr., e-mail, 2/2003.

3. The squirrels may not be true albinos.

4. Ray Elliott, e-mail, 7/2002, citing conversation with Olney resident; Gregory Dorr, e-mail, 7/2002.

5. Pat Smith, "'Sundown' rebuttal," *Greensburg Daily News*, 8/19/2015, greensburgdaily news.com/opinion/columns/sundown-rebuttal/article_2cbb296c-ce7a-5201-9c49-af08bb 45149c.html, and comments; cf. other Smith articles; John Vanderbur, "Greensburg 1907 riot; Correcting a possible wrong," 4/14/2017, *Daily News*, greensburgdailynews.com /opinion/columns/greensburg-riot-correcting-a-possible-wrong/article_f592a2c2-2119-5b b9-9302-a7c743befbb4.html; "Mayor Ryle" in "Greensburg Sundown Town" thread in "Greensburg Forum," 6/1/2013 (may have been redated), topix.com/forum/city/greensburg -in/T8H2KSCS6NOAURDV0.

6. About a year later, an African American family moved into Sheridan.

7. James Loewen, *Lies Across America* (New York: New Press, 1999), 198–99.

8. Terrie Epstein, "History and Racial Identity in an Urban High School," *AHA Perspectives*,

12/2001, 26; Maya Angelou, *I Know Why the Caged Bird Sings* (New York: Random House, 1969), 47; Tennessee Williams, *Orpheus Descending* (Peter Hall, dir., 1990); William Burroughs, *Naked Lunch* (New York: Grove, 1962 [1959]); Malcolm Ross, *All Manner of Men* (New York: Reynal & Hitchcock, 1948), 66; Jerrold Packard, *American Nightmare, The History of Jim Crow* (New York: St. Martin's, 2002), 108, my italics.

9. *The Fugitive Kind* derives from Tennessee Williams's play *Orpheus Descending*, from which it takes these lines.

10. This would be *Gentleman's Agreement,* Elia Kazan's 1948 movie adaptation of Laura Hobson's novel, a sensitive portrayal of anti-Semitism in Darien, Connecticut, although it makes no mention of Darien's exclusion of African Americans. Also, Lorraine Hansberry's play *A Raisin in the Sun*—about a black family that encounters opposition, rejects a buyout offer, and finally moves into a sundown neighborhood—was filmed.

11. Longtime southern Indiana resident, 10/2002; Evansville cheerleader, 12/2004. Jasper was the site of the 1954 regional tournament fictionally depicted in the movie. Milan, the town on which Hollywood's fictional Hickory was based, was also an all-white town, probably sundown.

12. Marian Anderson, *My Lord, What a Morning* (Madison: University of Wisconsin Press, 1992 [1956]), 239–40, 267–68; "Einstein" exhibit label, American Museum of Natural History, 12/2002; Scott L. Malcomson, *One Drop of Blood* (New York: Farrar, Straus, and Giroux, 2000), 383. Of course, the Civil Rights Movement also targeted the South because conditions were worse there than in much of the North (sundown towns excepted). Most important, the movement was largely born in southern black churches and colleges.

13. *Comprehensive Handbook* to *Indiana in the Civil War: Away from the Battle,* exhibit at Indiana State Museum, 1995–1997, 17.

14. Jack Blocker Jr., "Channeling the Flow," unpublished ms., Ch. 5, "Violence."

15. Roberta Nelson, "Myakka City's Black History a 'Mystery,'" *Tampa Tribune,* 2/26/2001; Melissa Sue Brewer, e-mail, 8/2002. Brewer has confirmed these details with the 1930 manuscript census and other records.

16. Librarian, West Frankfort, IL, 9/2002; *One Hundred Years of Progress: The Centennial History of Anna, Illinois* (Cape Girardeau: Missourian Printing, 1954).

17. *Life Newspapers 35th Anniversary Issue* (Northbrook, IL: Liberty Group, 12/1961), "Cicero . . . the Best Town in America," 139.

18. Baptist minister quoted in Joseph Lyford, *The Talk in Vandalia* (Santa Barbara: Center for the Study of Democratic Institutions, 1962), 93.

19. *The Pekin Centenary 1849–1949* (Pekin: Pekin Chamber of Commerce, 1949), 93–95; Lowell Nye, *Our Town* (Libertyville: Lions Club, 1942), 11; Edna Ferber, *A Peculiar Treasure* (New York: Doubleday, 1939), 57; James Cornelius, 7/2002.

20. Clarence D. Stephenson, *175th Anniversary History of Indiana County* (Indiana, PA: A. D. Halldin, 1978–80), 354, quoting *Indiana County Gazette,* 2/25/1903; cf. Denise Dusza Weber, *Delano's Domain: A History of Warren Delano's Mining Towns of Vintondale, Wehrum and Claghorn,* vol. I, *1789–1930* (Indiana, PA: A. G. Halldin, 1991); Loewen, *Lies Across America,* 408–13.

21. Please tell me of more: jloewen@zoo.uvm.edu.

22. Three cities that tried but failed to expel their African Americans have recently marked those events. Springfield, Missouri, put up a historical marker about its Easter lynchings of 1906. Springfield, Illinois, set up a walking tour denoted by eight historical markers telling of its 1908 race riot. Tulsa, Oklahoma, erected a black granite memorial in its Greenwood section detailing whites' 1921 attempts to drive all African Americans from Tulsa. Because these

cities remained interracial, African American citizens existed to help spur the memorials, and European Americans had not joined hands for decades in support of a sundown policy, so they were more open to telling the truth. Similarly, a state historical marker in Detroit tells accurately of the 1948 court case won by the Orsel McGhee family when their white Detroit neighbors tried to keep them from moving in by invoking "a restrictive covenant forbidding non-white residents," to quote the marker. (The case was merged with *Shelley v. Kraemer,* and the U.S. Supreme Court declared racial covenants unenforceable, as Chapter 9 tells.) Another Michigan marker, erected in 2004, tells of the riot that greeted Dr. Ossian Sweet when he moved into a sundown neighborhood in Detroit in 1925.

23. Pinky Zalkin, e-mail, 11/2002; *Idaho Highway Historical Marker Guide* (Boise: Idaho Transportation Department, 1990), 10; Connie Farrow, " 'The Anger and the Hatred Ends,' " Springfield (MO) *News-Leader,* 8/18/2001.

24. Jacqueline Froelich and David Zimmermann, "Total Eclipse: The Destruction of the African American Community of Harrison, Arkansas, in 1905 and 1909," *Arkansas Historical Quarterly* 58, 2 (1999): 159; Laurinda Joenks, "Roughness of Citizens Blamed on Lean Times," *Springdale* (AR) *Morning News,* 5/7/2000, paraphrasing Zimmermann; Randy Krehbiel, "Answers the Facts Cannot Provide," *Tulsa World,* 6/5/2000.

25. Arnold Hirsch, *Making the Second Ghetto* (Cambridge: Cambridge University Press, 1983), 60–63; Mary Ellen Stratthaus, "Flaw in the Jewel: Housing Discrimination Against Jews in La Jolla, California," *American Jewish History* 84, 3 (1996): 199.

26. The 2000 census showed 8 African Americans among 2,553 people, including two households.

27. Anna editor, 10/2002; Villa Grove editor and secretary, 10/2002.

28. Gordon D. Morgan, "Black Hillbillies of the Arkansas Ozarks," Department of Sociology, University of Arkansas, Fayetteville, 1973, 21; "A Really Good Show," *Rogers Daily News,* 1/25/1962.

29. Rogers Chamber of Commerce Publicity and Public Relations Committee, "Committee Report," 1/29/1962, in Rogers Historical Museum files.

30. Robby Heason, *Trouble Behind* (Cicada Films, 1990).

31. Peter Rachleff, e-mail, 6/2002.

32. John Winkols, interview by Roger Horowitz c. 1990, tape 37 side 2.

33. History teacher, e-mail, c. 6/2002; Hobart native, e-mail, 8/2004; Elin Christianson, e-mail, 9/2002; Moria Meltzer-Cohen, e-mail, 9/2002.

34. No "large band of Negroes" could have existed. The nearest black population was St. Joseph, just 4% black, and two counties away.

35. Patrick Clark, e-mail, 7/2002; Arthur F. Raper, *The Tragedy of Lynching* (New York: Dover, 1970 [1933]), 407, 427–28; cf. MacKinlay Kantor, *Missouri Bittersweet* (New York: Doubleday, 1969), 140–69; Patrick Huber and Gary Kremer, "A Death in the Heartland," presented at Missouri Conference on History, St. Louis, 3/1994, 7; "Maryville Alarmed Over Riot Rumors," *St. Joseph Gazette,* 1/18/1931; cf. John Rachal, "An Oral History with Jan Handke," University of Southern Mississippi Oral History Program, 5/8/1996, lib.usm.edu/~spcol/crda/oh/handketrans.htm, 8/2003; Howard B. Woods, "Lynching Spectre Still in Mo. Town; Maryville Group Cites 'N . . . Free' Community," *St. Louis Argus,* 10/10/1958; Albany native, e-mail, 10/2002.

36. Sylvia J. Smith, "The Island on Williston Road Otherwise Known as Mayfair Park," *Chittenden County Historical Society Bulletin* 36, 4 (2003): 8–9; "Outline of Protective Covenants for Mayfair Park," supplied by Elise Guyette, 4/2003.

37. Tim Long, Great Lakes Regional Conference, National Council for the Social Studies, Indianapolis, 4/2002.

38. My web site, uvm.edu/~jloewen/sundown/, provides an "anti-bibliography" that critiques studies whose authors should have noted that the communities they described were all-white on purpose.

39. William H. Whyte Jr. based *The Organization Man,* his famous 1956 interpretation of suburbia, on fieldwork in Park Forest, and the next chapter quotes from Whyte's account of a controversy over the possible admission of "Negroes," resolved by renewing the community's decision to keep them out. Randall knew Whyte's work. See Whyte, *The Organization Man* (New York: Simon & Schuster, 1956), 311.

40. Karl B. Lohmann, *Cities and Towns of Illinois* (Urbana: University of Illinois Press, 1951); Gregory Randall, *America's Original GI Town: Park Forest, Illinois* (Baltimore: Johns Hopkins University Press, 2000); C. S. Stein, *Toward New Towns for America* (Boston: MIT Press, 1966).

41. Carl Withers, *Plainville, USA* (Westport: Greenwood, 1971 [1945]), 4, n.; Art Gallaher, *Plainville Fifteen Years Later* (NY: Columbia University Press, 1961); Gallaher, "Plainville: The Twice-Studied Town," 285–303 of Arthur Vidich, Joseph Bensman, and Maurice Stein, *Reflections on Community Studies* (New York: Wiley, 1964); James Jacobs, "The Politics of Corrections; Town/Prison Relations as a Determinant of Reform," *Social Service Review 50,* 4 (1976), 623–63; Otto H. Olsen, *The Negro Question: From Slavery to Caste, 1863–1910* (New York: Pitman, 1971), xxi; James R. Grossman, Ann D. Keating, and Janice L. Reiff, eds., *Encyclopedia of Chicago* (Chicago: University of Chicago Press, 2004); Alex Kotlowitz, "How Regular Folks in Berwyn, Ill., Tried to Fight Prejudice," *Wall St. Journal,* 6/3/1992.

42. Merrill Matthews, Jr., "Human Experimentation," *Texas Republic,* 3/1994, 28; Richard Stewart, "Desegregation at Public Housing Ripped by Audit," *Houston Chronicle,* 7/11/1997; Indiana Historical Bureau official, 10/2004.

43. Catherine Jurca, *White Diaspora* (Princeton: Princeton University Press, 2001), 8.

44. At uvm.edu/~jloewen/sundown/, a bibliography lists all books and articles that treat sundown towns significantly. It includes several novels, including three for younger readers. Undoubtedly my literature review has been incomplete, and readers can post suggestions.

45. Frank Kardes and David Sanbonmatsu, "Omission Neglect," *Skeptical Inquirer* 27, 2 (2003): 45.

46. Patrick Huber, "Race Riots and Black Exodus in the Missouri Ozarks, 1894–1905" (Harrison, AR: Ozark Cultural Celebration, 9/2002).

47. I began with the census definition of "city"—larger than 2,500 in total population. Then I discovered towns far smaller than 2,500 that posted signs, passed ordinances, spread the word informally, burned houses, or took other steps to keep out African Americans (and sometimes other groups). So I enlarged my definition of "town" to include places from 1,000 to 2,500. When jurisdictions even smaller than 1,000 came to my attention for excluding African Americans, I included them as well, although I did not try to study these hamlets systematically. (In many states, I have not been able to study towns smaller than 2,500 systematically and have merely taken note of information on them when I obtain it in the course of my research.)

     Such small towns can be important, partly because when they do expand, usually they remain sundown. Malcolm Ross investigated East Alton, Illinois, for example, for the Fair Employment Practices Commission during World War II. The town's industrial patriarch,

F. W. Olin, told him that East Alton had an ordinance dating back to 1895, when a "Negro boy" committed some crime, and men had gone hunting for him with shotguns. He got away, but his angry pursuers reportedly swore that no Negro would ever again set foot in East Alton. Ross noted that during the next fifty years, East Alton had grown from a few families to a sizable town without any Negro ever having stayed the night. During World War II, Olin's munitions plant employed more than 13,000 workers—not one of them African American or Native American. In 1940, shortly before Ross wrote, its population had increased to 4,680, with 1 stray African American. By 1960, East Alton had 7,309 residents but only 4 African Americans, probably none of whom lived in an independent household. It finally cracked in the 1990s.

Larger cities tested my operational definition in a different way. A cutoff of ten proved too low to do justice to large cities widely known to keep out African Americans, such as Cicero. In 1951, as we have seen, the governor had to call out the Illinois National Guard to stop a riot against one African American who had tried (and failed) to move into Cicero. "Of primary significance in understanding the violence," sociologist William Gremley points out, "is the fact that it was widely believed by the residents of the community that no Negroes lived in Cicero." Actually, the U.S. Census in 1950 showed 31 African Americans in the city, but they were apparently live-in servants, biracial adopted children, or individuals living unobtrusively in rental property. Cicero clearly defined itself as a sundown town, no matter what the census said. Indeed, according to a report issued after the 1951 riot, "It is said that no Negroes now live within the limits of Cicero, although one or two families have done so in the past." But "fewer than ten African Americans" would have missed Cicero. So for cities larger than 10,000, I changed my definition for "all-white town" to "less than 0.1% black," decade after decade. For towns smaller than 10,000, "fewer than ten blacks" remained in force.

48. Live-in institutions include prisons, hospitals and long-term care facilities, armed forces bases, and residential colleges and prep schools. Other groups understood to be nonhousehold include railroad track-laying crews, CCC work camps, Job Corps trainees, and construction personnel.

49. John Paul Myrick, e-mail, 3/2002; Richard Todd, "Darien, Connecticut," *New England Monthly*, 3/1986, 43; Gregory Dorr, e-mail, 7/2002.

50. Kotlowitz, "How Regular Folks in Berwyn, Illinois, Tried to Right Prejudice."

51. Morgan, "Black Hillbillies of the Arkansas Ozarks," 152; Jim Clayton, e-mail, 11/2002.

52. Michelle Tate, typescript, 10/2002.

53. Nebraska Writers' Project, *The Negroes of Nebraska* (Omaha: Urban League, 1940), 10; "Inventory of the County Archives," WPA Federal Writers Project, Waverly, 1942, supplied by James L. Murphy, 3/2004; James Emmitt, *Life and Reminiscences* (Chillicothe, OH: Peerless, 1888), 287–89.

54. Colleen Kilner, *Joseph Sears and His Kenilworth* (Kenilworth: Kenilworth Historical Society, 1990), viii, 143, her italics; Paul Wong, e-mail, 8/2003.

55. Derfner successfully sued a small town to change an ordinance that he was able to find in its records, but neither the original ordinance nor the new version ever got into the file of codified ordinances.

It is possible that knowledge of *Buchanan v. Warley* prompted city councils to avoid putting any ordinance in writing, thus making legal attack more difficult, but I doubt it. Not only does no oral history or other evidence support this hypothesis, I have uncovered no concern about such a challenge outside the South. Moreover, southern and border cities continued to enact *Buchanan*-like segregation ordinances for decades, despite their uncon-stitutionality.

56. Armand Derfner, 11/2003.

57. Landis quoted in Ken Burns, *Baseball* (PBS, 1994).

58. Harrisburg (IL) *Daily Register*, 4/5/1923.

59. Clayton Cramer, e-mail, 6/2000.

60. Letter to *New York Times* citing 3/15/1973 story, my italics; John D. Baskerville, e-mail, 7/2003; I eliminated the name of the city councilor because Baskerville was not certain of it.

61. Nationally it is also possible, I suppose, that a plethora of errors of inclusion might convince readers that sundown towns have been more common than in reality they have. Such errors might unnecessarily increase readers' motivation to eliminate sundown policies, sending some readers charging off to fix something that isn't broken. Since so many towns and sub-urbs *have* been unwelcoming to African Americans, however, increasing the cross-racial hospitality of all-white communities, even some that were all-white only by accident, will hardly harm our nation.

62. Pinckneyville native, e-mail, 6/2001.

63. My web site, uvm.edu/~jloewen/sundown, contains a longer discussion of my methods, in-cluding my assessment of sources on three additional towns, and can help you decide if you should trust my judgment.

CHAPTER 9: ENFORCEMENT

1. Michelle Tate, typescript, 10/2002.

2. *Illinois State Register*, 8/17 or 8/18/1908, quoted in Roberta Senechal, *The Sociogenesis of a Race Riot* (Urbana: University of Illinois Press, 1990), 129.

3. Billy Bob Lightfoot, "The Negro Exodus from Comanche County, Texas," *Southwestern Historical Quarterly* 56 (January 1953): 415.

4. "For White Men Only," Fairmont (WV) *Free Press*, 12/7/1905.

5. Ann Hammons, *Wild Bill Sullivan* (Jackson: University Press of Mississippi, 1980), 52; Gregg Andrews, *City of Dust* (Columbia: University of Missouri Press, 1996), 11; probably notes from an interview by Van Ravenswaay, Missouri state supervisor of the WPA Federal Writers Project, with Judge Williams, 11/20/1937, now in folder 1089, Western Historical Manuscript Collection, University of Missouri.

6. Senechal, *The Sociogenesis of a Race Riot*, 130.

7. Comanche County historical society spokesman, 8/2003; Lightfoot, "The Negro Exodus from Comanche County, Texas," 415; Bud Kennedy, "Signs of a Racist Past in the Small Towns of Texas," *Ft. Worth Star Telegram*, 2/17/2002, realcities.com/mld/startelegram/mon/news/columnists/bud_kennedy/archive.htm; Ronald L. Lewis, *Black Coal Miners in America* (Lexington: University Press of Kentucky, 1987), 83–84; "Negroes Killed or Driven Away," *Chicago Tribune*, 8/21/1901.

8. William Pickens, "Arkansas—A Study in Suppression," originally published in *The Messenger 5* (January 1923), reprinted in Tom Lutz and Susanna Ashton, eds., *These "Colored" United States* (New Brunswick: Rutgers University Press, 1996), 35; Arthur F. Raper, *The Tragedy of Lynching* (New York: Dover, 1970 [1933]), 452.

9. "See First Dark Face in County in Many Years," *Chicago Defender*, 4/2/1921; Esther Sanderson, *County Scott and Its Mountain Folk* (Nashville: Williams Printing, 1958), 186.

10. Tate, typescript, 10/2002; David Blair, e-mail via Classmates.com, 3/5/2003; motel clerk, Owosso, 10/2002.

11. Jeanne Blackburn, e-mail, 11/2003.

12. Scotland native, e-mail, 6/2002.

13. "White Men Shoot Up Church Excursioners," *Pittsburgh Courier*, 8/17/1940.

14. Barbara Elliott Carpenter fictionalizes this incident in *Starlight, Starbright . . . ,* a novel for teenagers (Bloomington, IL: 1st Books, 2003), 185–200, including the antipathy that underlay the helpful gesture.

15. Helen Harrelson, 10/2002; former Pinckneyville resident, e-mail, 6/2002; elderly white Harrison couple, 9/2002; Arcola native, e-mail, 1/2003; cf. Barbara Elliott Carpenter, e-mail, 9/2002; several African Americans at Crispus Attucks Museum, Indianapolis, 8/2001.

16. Jean Nipps Swaim, "Black History in Cedar County, Missouri," in *Black Families of the Ozarks,* Bulletin 45 (Springfield, MO: Greene County Archives, n.d.), 2:535; Shirley Manning, e-mail, 9/2002; Carl Jackson, 1/2004.

17. John Keiser, 1/2005; woman at Richland Community College, 10/2001; Thad Sitton and James H. Conrad, *Nameless Towns: Texas Sawmill Communities, 1880–1942* (Austin: University of Texas Press, 1998), 108–9; Millie Meyerholtz, *When Hatred and Fear Ruled . . . Pana, Illinois: The 1898–99 Mine War* (Pana, IL: Pana News, 2001), 34; 1986 Resident Assistant at Indiana University, e-mail, 11/5/2002.

18. James Clayton, e-mail, 11/2002; student from Salem, University of Illinois–Chicago, 10/2002; Melissa Sue Brewer, e-mail, 8/2002; Dwight ambulance volunteer, e-mail, 10/2003; cf. Kenneth Meeks, *Driving While Black* (New York: Broadway, 2000); David A. Harris, *Profiles in Injustice* (New York: New Press, 2002).

19. Mary Pat Baumgartner, *The Moral Order of a Suburb* (New York: Oxford University Press, 1988), 119–20; Gary Kennedy, e-mail, 6/2002.

20. Gregory Dorr, e-mail, 7/2002.

21. Bob Johnson, e-mail, 1/2003; name withheld by request, e-mail, 10/2002.

22. Ibid.

23. Harris, *Profiles in Injustice,* 105.

24. Frank U. Quillen, *The Color Line in Ohio* (Ann Arbor: Wahr, 1913), 161; Wali R. Kharif, e-mail, 9/2002, citing William Hiram Parrish, interview, 12/23/1975, and Walter Maxey, interview, 12/29/1975, in the Folklife Collection, Western Kentucky University; Elvin Light, 6/2002; Herbert Aptheker, remarks at the graveside of Mary Brown, Saratoga, CA, 5/6/2000, and letter, 7/7/2000; Tate, typescript, 10/2002; Wise County, Virginia, native, e-mail, 8/2002; African American Bluefield native, b. 1932, 3/2004.

25. Washabaugh quoted in David M. P. Freund, "Making It Home," Ph.D. dissertation, University of Michigan, 1999, 548; Carole Goodwin, *The Oak Park Strategy* (Chicago: University of Chicago Press, 1979), 98; Baumgartner, *The Moral Order of a Suburb,* 119–20; Diane Hershberger, 11/2000.

26. Al Brophy, 4/2002.

27. "Tricksters Discourage Black Settlers," undated, unidentified newspaper clipping in files of Rogers Historical Museum.

28. "Attorney Is Driven from Court," *Chicago Defender,* 12/24/1921.

29. "Negroes Are Threatened," *Benton Republican,* 7/26/1923.

30. Olen Cole Jr., *The African-American Experience in the Civilian Conservation Corps*

(Gainesville: University Press of Florida, 1999), 19, 30, 57; Shirley Ann Moore, "Getting There, Being There," in Joe W. Trotter Jr., ed., *The Great Migration in Historical Perspective* (Bloomington: Indiana University Press, 1991), 57, 107–11.

31. DeWindt, "Wyandotte History; Negro," 24–26, quoting *Wyandotte Daily News,* 12/4/1935, and *Wyandotte Herald,* 12/6/1935.

32. Truman K. Gibson, Jr., civilian aide to the secretary of war, remarks to Illinois Inter-Racial Commission, 12/19/1943, minutes in Illinois State Archives, 7.

33. Stetson Kennedy, *Jim Crow Guide* (Boca Raton: Florida Atlantic University Press, 1990 [1959]), 80; Emma Lou Thornbrough, *The Negro in Indiana* (Indianapolis: Indiana Historical Bureau, 1957), 226.

34. "Blacks in Greenbelt," summarizing research by W. H. Form, otal.umd.edu/~vg/mssp96/ms12/expla.html, 10/2002; Tate, typescript, 10/2002.

35. Former theater worker, e-mail, 10/2002; Peoria resident, 2/2001.

36. Oak Lawn librarians, 4/1997; University of Illinois–Chicago student, 9/2001; person at Mattoon, 10/2002.

37. Khan let the man live in the motel; after a few months he went back to his hometown.

38. The 2000 census lists nine households with at least one black householder, so Paragould may be moving beyond its sundown status.

39. Jim Clayton, 11/2002; Nick Khan, 9/2002.

40. Female 1983 Goshen College graduate, relayed by Kathryn Reimer, e-mail, 9/2004; Stephen Crow, e-mail via Classmates.com, 11/2004.

41. Elice Swanson, e-mail, 1/2003; Dyanna McCarty, e-mail, 10/2002 (her italics).

42. Lois Mark Stalvey, *The Education of a WASP* (New York: William Morrow, 1970).

43. Cullman native, e-mail, 5/2002; Virginia Cowan, "An Essay," robandjen.net/jen/mom.html, 10/2002.

44. "Norman Mob After Singie Smith Jazz," Norman, OK, 2/5/1922, in *Oklahoma City Black Dispatch,* 2/9/1922, 1, thanks to Al Brophy; "Don't Let the Sun Set on You Here, Understand?" *Chicago Defender,* 2/11/1922.

45. Henry Louis Gates Jr., *Colored People* (New York: Knopf, 1994), 119–20; Henry Louis Gates Sr., 7/2002.

46. Swaim, "Black History in Cedar County, Missouri," 535; Mary Jo Hubbard, e-mail to Class mates.com bulletin board, 12/2002, her ellipses.

47. Ironically, Neenah and Menasha may also have been sundown towns, but at least someone or some hotel in one of them was willing to let her spend the night.

48. In her autobiography, Anderson tells how hotels occasionally housed black celebrities such as herself, even though she could sense they admitted no other African Americans.

49. Marian Anderson, *My Lord, What a Morning* (Madison: University of Wisconsin Press, 1992 [1956]), 239–40, 267–68; "Einstein" exhibit label, American Museum of Natural History, 12/2002; Judy Zimmerman Herr, e-mail, 3/2002; librarian, Appleton, 4/2002.

50. Howard Bryant, *Talk of the Nation,* NPR, 9/26/2002.

51. Elderly couple, Harrison, AR, 9/2002; Grey Gundaker, e-mails, 7/2002.

52. Pinckneyville native, e-mail, 6/2001.

53. Steve Bogira, "Hate, Chicago Style," *Chicago Reader,* 12/5/1986.

54. Zeigler miner, 9/2002.

55. Ray Stannard Baker, *Following the Color Line* (New York: Harper Torchbook, 1964 [1908]), 126.

56. Browne quoted in Shane Johnson, "Read No Evil," *Salt Lake City Weekly,* 9/25/2003,

slweekly.com/editorial/2003/feat_2003-09-25.cfm, 10/2003; Richard Delgado and Jean Stefancic, *Home-Grown Racism* (Boulder: University of Colorado Latino/a Research & Policy Center, 1999), 30, 44, 74.

57. Pinckneyville resident, Greenup resident at Mattoon, 10/2002; Martinsville native, 10/2002; Mel Dubofsky, e-mail, 6/2002.

58. Former resident, LaSalle-Peru, e-mail, 10/2001.

59. Elizabethtown graduate, 8/2004.

60. Actually, although considered a sundown county, Madison County does contain Mars Hill, a small college town that allowed African Americans to live in it.

61. "Where Negroes are Barred," *Charlotte Daily Observer,* 8/18/1906.

62. Dante Chinni, "Along Detroit's Eight Mile Road, a Stark Racial Split," *Christian Science Monitor,* csmonitor.com/2002/1115/p01s02-ussc.html, 11/15/2002.

63. Freund, "Making It Home," 93–95, 120; Orfield quoted in Dennis R. Judd, "The Role of Governmental Policies in Promoting Residential Segregation in the St. Louis Metropolitan Area," *Journal of Negro Education* 66, 3 (1997): 233; Deborah Morse-Kahn, *Edina: Chapters in the City History* (Edina: City of Edina, 1998), 94.

64. Michael N. Danielson, *The Politics of Exclusion* (New York: Columbia University Press, 1976), 53, 59–61; Dorothy K. Newman et al., *Protest, Politics, and Prosperity* (New York: Pantheon, 1978), 159.

65. Danielson, *The Politics of Exclusion,* 93, 102.

66. Kenneth T. Jackson, *Crabgrass Frontier* (New York: Oxford University Press, 1985), 224–25; Danielson, *The Politics of Exclusion,* 40, 100–1.

67. Farley and Frey, "Changes in the Segregation of Whites from Blacks During the 1980s," 26.

68. Ian D. McMahan, *The Negro in White Suburbia* (New York: Freedom of Residence Funds, 1962), 22–24; James Hecht, *Because It Is Right* (Boston: Little, Brown, 1970), 27.

69. Danielson, *The Politics of Exclusion,* 28, citing Oliver P. Williams et al., *Suburban Differences and Metropolitan Policies* (Philadelphia: University of Pennsylvania Press, 1965), 217–19; Rosalyn Baxandall and Elizabeth Ewen, *Picture Windows: How the Suburbs Happened* (New York: Basic Books, 2000), 23–24; Baumgartner, *The Moral Order of a Suburb,* 119–20; former Darien resident, 7/98.

70. Herbert Gans, 1/2001; Frederique Krupa, "Los Angeles: Buying the Concept of Security," Chapter 3 of "Privatization of Public Space," unpaginated, translucency.com/frede/pps.html, 1/2004.

71. Detroit suburbanite, e-mail, 6/2002; Bob Johnson, e-mail, 1/2003.

72. In 1975, two young white students, one law, one medical, committed the crime of "playing tennis without a reservation." Violation carries a $25 fine, but "the court clerk lowered each of their fines to $5," according to reporter Alice Love. Nevertheless, the students "stuck with their decision to pay their debt behind bars." After some publicity, an anonymous source from Southern Methodist University paid their fines, which was a relief to the students because Highland Park also does not let prisoners have books in their cells. See Alice Love, "Students Prefer Jail Stay to $5 Fines," *Dallas Times Herald,* 10/16/1975.

73. Edward H. Sebesta, e-mail, 7/2002; "Picnicking Banned at Highland Park Park," *Dallas Morning News,* 7/2/1989; Debbie K. Solomon, "Jogging to Court," *Dallas Times Herald* 2/25/1982; Doug J. Swanson, "Official Calls HP's Fishing Permit Illegal," *Dallas Times Herald,* 2/23/1980.

74. Camille DeRose, *The Camille DeRose Story* (Chicago: Erle Press, 1953), 169; Christopher Phillips, e-mail, 6/2000.

75. "A Northern City 'Sitting on Lid' of Racial Trouble," 38–40; David L. Good, *Orvie: The Dictator of Dearborn* (Detroit: Wayne State University Press, 1989), 40–41, 264, 386–87.

76. Ibid.; Good, "Orville Hubbard—The Ghost Who Still Haunts Dearborn," *Detroit News,* 1/3/1997, detnews.com/history/hubbard/hu2/98.

77. Reynolds Farley, Sheldon Danziger, and Harry J. Holzer, *Detroit Divided* (New York: Russell Sage, 2000), 148; Nelson, *The Fourteenth Amendment and the Negro Since 1920,* 31; *Corrigan v. Buckley,* 299 Fed 898 (1924) and 271 U.S. 328.

78. Palos Verdes Homes Association: "Palos Verdes Protective Restrictions" (Palos Verdes Estates: n.p., 1929), sent by Paul Wong, e-mail, 7/2003; Maryland restrictive covenant sent by Christopher Lewis, 12/2002.

79. Massey, talk at OPEN, Philadelphia, 12/2000; NAACP estimate in Gunnar Myrdal, *An American Dilemma* (New York: McGraw-Hill, 1964 [1944]), 624; Margaret Marsh, *Suburban Lives* (New Brunswick: Rutgers University Press, 1990), 201.

80. *Shelley v. Kraemer,* 334 U.S. 1, 1948; Charlotte Brooks, e-mail, 9/2002.

81. Hecht, *Because It Is Right,* 51; Kennedy, *Jim Crow Guide,* 75; St. Louis realtor quoted in Newman et al., *Protest, Politics, and Prosperity,* 151; manual quoted in Stephen G. Meyer, *As Long as They Don't Move Next Door* (Lanham, MD: Rowman & Littlefield, 2000), 7; cf. Lorenzo J. Greene, Gary Kremer, and Antonio Holland, *Missouri's Black Heritage* (Columbia: University of Missouri Press, 1993), 164.

82. Hecht capitalizes "Realtor" to refer to members of the National Association of Real Estate Boards, later the National Association of Realtors. Most of my sources, oral or written, were not so precise, and neither is the public at large, so I use the generic *realtor* (uncapitalized) to mean any licensed seller of real estate.

83. Hecht, *Because It Is Right,* 51; Realtors Code of Ethics quoted in Newman, *Protest, Politics, and Prosperity,* 149.

84. "Barred: Non-Whites Restricted from Urban Areas by Salt Lake Realtors," *Pittsburgh Courier,* 5/20/1944.

85. "Typical Cases: Private Housing—Commercial Development," *Connecticut Civil Rights Bulletin* 1, 4 (1955): 3.

86. Benjamin R. Epstein and Arnold Foster, *"Some of My Best Friends . . ."* (New York: Farrar, Straus, and Cudahy, 1962), 117–18, 120.

87. Amy Karelus Welch, e-mail, 10/2001, relayed by Andrew B. Raker.

88. William L. Price, *Factors Influencing and Restraining the Housing Mobility of Negroes in Metropolitan Detroit* (Detroit: Urban League, c. 1955), 10, 14; Thomas Sugrue, *Origins of the Urban Crisis* (Princeton: Princeton University Press, 1996), 44.

89. Don and Mary Hunt, *Hunts' Guide to Southeast Michigan* (Waterloo, MI: Midwestern Guides, 1990), 122; Norman C. Thomas, *Rule 9: Politics, Administration, and Civil Rights* (New York: Random House, 1966), 35–36.

90. Thomas, *Rule 9,* 44–45.

91. "G.P. Gets 30 Days to Ban Point System," *Detroit News,* 5/14/1960; "Klan Standards Prevail in G.P., Rabbi Charges," *Detroit News,* 5/14/1960; Joseph Wolff and Bob Popa, "Special Jewish 'Point' Form Described at G.P. Inquiry," *Detroit News,* 5/3/1960; Thomas, *Rule 9,* 5, 61, 63, 68.

92. Kathy Cosseboom, *Grosse Pointe, Michigan* (East Lansing: Michigan State University Press, 1972), 12–13.

93. Ibid., 9, 11; Andrew Hacker, "Grand Illusion," *New York Review of Books,* 6/11/1998, 28.

94. Cosseboom, *Grosse Pointe, Michigan,* 55.

95. Charles T. Clotfelter, *After Brown* (Princeton: Princeton University Press, 2004), 18–19; Betty Toomes, transcript of interview (Yuma, AZ, 1963: Robert B. Powers, interviewer), sunsite.berkeley.edu:2020/dynaweb/teiproj/oh/warren/powers/@Generic_BookTextView/ 4030, 1/2003.

96. Former Oak Lawn resident, e-mail, 10/2002; Eric Arnesen, *Brotherhoods of Color* (Cambridge: Harvard University Press, 2001), 246; James Grossman, 9/2001; Robby Heason, *Trouble Behind;* female undergraduate, University of the Ozarks, 9/2002.

97. West Lawn Chamber of Commerce, Westlawnncc.org, 1/2003; Steve Bogira, "Hate, Chicago Style."

98. Pinckneyville woman, 9/2002; James Rosenbaum, letter, 11/1996; female undergraduate, University of the Ozarks, 9/2002; Winston County law enforcement officer, 6/02.

99. Apparently material was added to this file as late as the late 1950s.

100. Thelma Marsh, *Moccasin Trails to the Cross,* excerpts, and Squire Grey Eyes, "Farewell to A Beloved Land," Wyandot Nation of Kansas web site, ku.edu/kansas/wn/8/2003; Edwina M. DeWindt, "Wyandotte History; Negro," typescript, 1945, in Bacon Library, Wyandotte, MI, 4.

101. DeWindt, "Wyandotte History; Negro," 12, citing *Wyandotte, Past, Present, and Future 1854–1917,* 17.

102. Ibid., 6, 13, 17.

103. Ibid., 2, 15, citing *Wyandotte Herald,* 8/25/1916.

104. Ibid., 16–17.

105. Ibid., 24–30, quoting *Wyandotte Herald,* 12/6/1935, and *Wyandotte Daily News,* 12/4/1935; Kristina Baumli, e-mail, 6/2000.

106. "For White Men Only," Fairmont, WV, *Free Press,* 12/7/1905.

107. Brownsburg source wishes to remain anonymous, e-mail, 11/2002.

108. LaSalle-Peru native, e-mail, 1/2004; Sanderson, *County Scott and Its Mountain Folk,* 186.

109. "Marlow's 'Unwritten Law' Against Race Causes Two Deaths," *Pittsburgh Courier,* 12/29/1923; Almarion Hollingsworth, 2/2004. The *Courier* misspelled Berch's name, which I corrected. Berch had also organized and circulated a petition requesting an anti-Klan law prohibiting masks, requiring secret organizations to file membership lists, etc., that may have contributed to the enmity against him. See Berch, "Initiative Petition #83," supplied by Hollingsworth, and "Klan Murder Says Wife," in the political tabloid *Jack Walton's Paper,* 1/6/1924.

110. "Farmer Shot to Death Near Lamb, Hardin Co.," *Golconda* (IL) *Herald-Enterprise,* 11/2/1922.

111. Kennedy, *Jim Crow Guide,* 82; J.D. Mullane, "Still a Long Way to Go," *Bucks County Courier Times,* phillyburbs.com/millmag/race.shtml, 7/2002; Daisy Myers, "Breaking Down Barriers," *Pennsylvania Heritage* 28, 3 (2002): 11.

112. Reynolds Farley and William H. Frey, "Changes in the Segregation of Whites from Blacks During the 1980s," *American Sociological Review* 59, 1 (1994): 24–25; Jodi Becker, "Chicago Matters," on Chicago Public Radio, c. 2002; Meyer, *As Long as They Don't Move Next Door,* 6; Kennedy, *Jim Crow Guide,* 82.

113. "For White Men Only," Fairmont (WV) *Free Press,* 12/7/1905; Sanderson, *County Scott and Its Mountain Folk,* 186; Bogira, "Hate, Chicago Style"; Arnold Hirsch, *Making the Second Ghetto* (Cambridge: Cambridge University Press, 1093), 41.

114. Hirsch, *Making the Second Ghetto,* 63; Hecht, *Because It Is Right,* 201, 204–5.

115. Meyer, *As Long as They Don't Move Next Door,* 76–77; Kristina Baumli, e-mail, 8/2001; Baxandall and Ewen, *Picture Windows,* 30.

116. Meyer, *As Long as They Don't Move Next Door,* 219; Kennedy, *Jim Crow Guide,* 82.

117. Thornbrough, *The Negro in Indiana,* 224; Emma Lou Thornbrough, *Indiana Blacks in the Twentieth Century,* edited and with final chapter by Lana Ruegamer (Bloomington: Indiana University Press, 2000), 2–3.

118. Reprinted as "County Press Pays High Tribute to a Former Slave," *Rogers Daily News* (?), 7/1/1950. In a 2001 brochure on "Cultural Diversity in Benton County" the Rogers Historical Museum agrees that the statement was a warning, not just a joke.

119. Idaho statewide may not be more racist than, say, Montana or Oregon, but it has collected several extremist white power groups that have given it that reputation, deserved or not.

120. White woman at Richland Community College, 10/2001; Clayton Cramer, e-mail, 6/2000.

121. Farley, Danziger, and Holzer, *Detroit Divided,* 186–87, 193.

122. I do not have independent confirmation of the local historian's stories, but he seems a thoughtful source to me. Even if exaggerated, the stories show that Tamaroa's reputation for violence toward African Americans is well known.

123. Pinckneyville historian, 9/2002; Du Quoin woman, 9/2002.

124. In the Ozarks, it was "nigger flipper"—yet many Ozarks youth never saw a black person until after they were grown, since most of the region had driven out its African American population.

125. Harris, *Profiles in Injustice,* 102.

126. Woman at Mattoon, 10/2002.

127. Leftridge quoted in Arnesen, *Brotherhoods of Color,* 245; June Rosland, 4/2002.

128. Michael Dougan, *Arkansas Odyssey* (Little Rock: Rose Publishing, 1994), 318; Nick Khan, 9/2002.

129. Jim Clayton, 11/2002.

CHAPTER 10: EXCEPTIONS TO THE SUNDOWN RULE

1. Laurel Boeckman, e-mail, 6/2002.

2. See Millie Meyerholtz, *When Hatred and Fear Ruled* (Pana: Pana News, 2001).

3. Elderly Huntington resident as interviewed and reported by his son and by me, 6/2002; Phillip Payne, e-mail, 11/2002.

4. Michael Ebner, *Creating Chicago's North Shore* (Chicago: University of Chicago Press, 1988), 234; Kenilworth realtor, 10/2002.

5. *Virginia Acts of Assembly,* 330–31; 1947 Villa Park deed, extant in 1963, sent by Donna Marquart, 8/2002.

6. "Tale of Two Cities," *Pacific Citizen,* 1/4/1947.

7. Jim Clayton, 11/2002; Paul M. Angle, *Bloody Williamson* (New York: Knopf, 1952), 98; Batesville Historical Society member, e-mail, 9/2002.

8. Bob Johnson, e-mail, 1/2003; Mable Bishop Gilmer, paragraph in Edwina M. DeWindt, "Wyandotte History; Negro," typescript, 1945, in Bacon Library, Wyandotte, MI, 14.

9. Jodey Bateman, e-mail, 7/2002.

10. Some have not moved out; by 1990 Ephrata had 27 African Americans, including four households, among 12,133 residents.

11. Hilda Feldhake, ed., *Effingham County Illinois, Past and Present* (Effingham: n.p., 1968),

338; former Miami Beach resident, e-mail, 7/2002; "Since You Asked," Medford, OR, *Mail Tribune*, 1998, mailtribune.com/news/dailynws.htm, 2001; Cynthia Marquet, 9/2002; Judy Zimmerman Herr, e-mail, 3/2002; Millersville University student, 3/2002; longtime Pennsylvania resident, e-mail, 4/2002.

12. William E. Wilson, *On the Sunny Side of a One-Way Street* (New York: Norton, 1958), 91, thanks to Wanda L. Griess, letter, 9/2002.

13. Emma Lou Thornbrough, *The Negro in Indiana* (Indianapolis: Indiana Historical Bureau, 1957), 225–27; untitled clipping, *Springdale News*, 7/13/1894, in files of Rogers Historical Museum; DeWindt, "Wyandotte History; Negro," 8, 11.

14. Pearl Roberts, *Glimpses of the Past in Johnston City, Illinois, 1894–1945* (Johnston City: Business & Professional Women's Club, 1977), 123.

15. "Local attorney" quoted in exhibit on Camp Ellis at Dickson Mounds Museum, 2001; Lachlan Crissey, "Racial Minorities in the Operation of County Government," in Illinois Inter-racial Commission, *First Annual Report* (Springfield: State of Illinois, 1945), 32.

16. Roger Karns, e-mail, 9/2002; Matt Moline, e-mail, 6/2002; Harold S. Forsythe, e-mail, 7/2002.

17. Gospel Assembly web site, dmgospelassembly.org/church/aboutus2.html, 12/2003.

18. *Parade of Progress: Hamilton County, 1858–1958* (Hamilton: Hamilton Herald-News, 1958), unpaginated; Terry Keller, 6/10/2003.

19. Moira Meltzer-Cohen, e-mail, 9/2002; Jean Messinger, *A Closer Look at Beaver Dam* (Colorado Springs: Cottonwood Press, 1981); Hank Everman, "Corbin, Kentucky: A Socioeconomic Anomaly," Department of History, Eastern Kentucky University, 2002, unpaginated; Lorenzo J. Greene, Gary Kremer, and Antonio Holland, *Missouri's Black Heritage* (Columbia: University of Missouri Press, 1993), 153; Patrick J. Huber, e-mail, 9/2002.

20. Billy Bob Lightfoot, "The Negro Exodus from Comanche County, Texas," *Southwestern Historical Quarterly* 56 (January 1953): 414.

21. Woman from Greenup at Mattoon, 10/2002; Roberta Senechal, *The Sociogenesis of a Race Riot* (Urbana: University of Illinois Press, 1990), 130; "Death of Ambrose Roan," *Chesterton Tribune*, 11/30/1911.

22. Elderly Huntington native interviewed by his son, e-mail, 6/2002.

23. John Winkols, interview by Roger Horowitz c.1990, in "Pete Winkols Interview," tape 37 side 2, UPWA Oral History Project, State Historical Society of Wisconsin, Madison.

24. Dorothy E. Williams, *The Spirit of West Bend* (Madison: Straus Printing, 1980), 318; Barbara Carpenter, e-mail, 10/2002; Kathleen M. Blee, *Women of the Klan* (Berkeley: University of California Press, 1991), 156, based on oral history, c.1987.

25. Carolyn Stephens, e-mail, 11/2001, recounting conversation with George Hendrick; George Hendrick, Helen Howe, and Don Sackrider, *James Jones and the Handy Writers' Colony* (Carbondale: Southern Illinois University Press, 2001), 121; Williams, *The Spirit of West Bend*, 318; "Only Colored Couple," *Chesterton Tribune*, 8/20/1936, referring to 1/4/1912 story. The 1936 story uses markedly more stereotypical language than the 1912 story quoted earlier, perhaps indicating that Porter County's attitudes toward African Americans had hardened in the decades since the deaths of its only black couple.

26. Long-term Arab resident, 6/2002.

27. Carolyn Stephens, e-mail, 1/2001.

28. Ralph R. Rea, *Boone County and Its People* (Van Buren, AR: Press-Argus, 1955), 141–42.

29. James DeVries, *Race and Kinship in a Midwestern Town* (Urbana: University of Illinois Press, 1984), 58; Blee, *Women of the Klan*, 156. Bear in mind that this interview took place

around 1987, 23 years after the public accommodations section of the 1964 Civil Rights Act became law.

30. Alice J. Thompson, "Changing Social Values in Brea," interviewed by Ann Towner, California State University–Fullerton, Oral History #1726, 4/17/1982, 22.

31. Steve Bogira, "Hate, Chicago Style," *Chicago Reader,* 12/5/1986.

32. Cullman native, e-mail, 5/2002.

33. Joycelyn Landrum-Brown quoting her mother, e-mail, 8/2002.

34. Greenup, Illinois, resident, 6/2000; Martinsville, Illinois, resident, 10/2002; Hendrick, Howe, and Sackrider, *James Jones and the Handy Writers' Colony* 115, 121, 133; Carolyn Stephens, e-mail, 2/2001; Stephens, 9/2002.

CHAPTER 11: THE EFFECT OF SUNDOWN TOWNS ON WHITES

1. Oblong native, 4/2000.

2. Like all-white towns, all-white neighborhoods are usually no accident, and residents of sundown neighborhoods show most of the characteristics of residents of sundown towns and suburbs, especially if the neighborhood is large enough to have its own high school.

3. Loewen, "Soclexia," New England Sociological Society keynote address, 4/1997.

4. Actually, at this time the sign stood at the train station.

5. Lightfoot, "The Negro Exodus from Comanche County, Texas," 415.

6. Carl Withers, *Plainville, USA* (Westport, CT: Greenwood, 1971 [1945]), 6; Jacob Holdt, *American Pictures* (Copenhagen: American Pictures Foundation, 1987?), 16.

7. *Newsweek,* 4/1/1957, 42, quoted in J. John Palen, *The Suburbs* (New York: McGraw-Hill, 1995), 81.

8. Oprah Winfrey, "Vintage Oprah: Racial Tension in Georgia," Harpo Productions, Chicago, 2001 (1987), 4; Howard Schuman, Charlotte Steeh, and Lawrence Bobo, *Racial Attitudes in America* (Cambridge: Harvard University Press, 1985), 60.

9. Herbert Blumer, "Race Prejudice as a Sense of Group Position," *Pacific Sociological Review* 1, 1 (1958): 3–4.

10. Also called "lawn jockeys," these figures stopped being painted black several decades ago, except in sundown towns. Most manufacturers never bothered to change their molds, however, so the now "Caucasian" coach boys still have thick lips and a broad nose but are painted "white." Residents of Beaver Dam, a southern Wisconsin sundown town, invented a new form, "black boys in Green Bay Packers garb," according to former resident Moira Meltzer-Cohen, who sent photos.

11. Hank Everman, "Corbin, Kentucky: A Socioeconomic Anomaly," Department of History, Eastern Kentucky University, 2002, unpaginated; David M. P. Freund, "Making It Home," Ph.D. thesis, University of Michigan, 1999, 409; Moira Meltzer-Cohen, e-mail, 9/2002; University of Washington undergraduates, 2/2002.

12. Teams from New Palestine High School in Indiana had been "Redbirds." In the 1920s, when the KKK craze hit, they too became "Dragons," according to a professor at DePauw University, 10/2001. According to Chris Meno (e-mail, 10/2002), who has family connections in the town, oral tradition in New Palestine and at the high school holds that the Klan donated land for the high school with the stipulation the mascot was to be a dragon. Although New Palestine is less than 10 miles from Indianapolis, it was still all-white in 2000. Meno tells that a black woman moved to New Palestine somewhere between 1992 and 1995 and "lasted two days. Blacks don't even drive through."

13. Rick Baker, "Pekin Students Veto 'Chinks' Name Change," 11/28/1974, clipping in Pekin library, name of newspaper omitted; Rose M. Hasler, *Pekin, Illinois: A Pictorial History* (St. Louis: Bradley, 1998), 42; "KKK Holds Local Recruiting Session," *Pekin Times,* 11/29/1999; Karen McDonald, "KKK Recruiting Local Teen-agers," *Peoria Journal Star,* 11/29/1999.

14. Ted Boyer, letter, *Decatur Herald and Review,* 11/13/2001; Dianna Adams, 10/2000 e-mail to Classmates.com bulletin board.

15. This "we" includes African Americans as well as European Americans, because many Redskin players and fans are black. Native Americans and their supporters launched a legal challenge to the Washington Redskins logo, since it is illegal for the government to grant trademarks for racial slurs. They won initially, were reversed, and are now appealing. If the suit succeeds, the team might change its nickname rather than face competition for T-shirt and souvenir sales.

16. Peoria resident, 2/2001; male undergraduate, University of Illinois–Chicago, 9/2001; Randy Whitman, e-mail via Classmates.com, 6/2004.

17. Circa 1993 Meadowbrook graduate, 12/2002.

18. Hominy, Oklahoma, native, e-mail, 11/2001.

19. Western Shore teacher, e-mail, 11/2002; Kaye Collins, e-mail, 6/2002; social studies teacher, Great Lakes National Council for the Social Sciences (NCSS), 4/2001; Robby Heason, *Trouble Behind* (Cicada Films, 1990).

20. David Marniss and Neil Henry, "Race 'War' in Cairo," *Washington Post,* 3/22/1987.

21. Indiana teacher, e-mail, 10/2004; undergraduate, University of Illinois–Urbana, 4/2000; Missouri resident, e-mail, 6/2000.

22. Paul Zielbauer, "After Game, Aftertaste of Racial Slurs Lingers," *New York Times,* 12/14/1999.

23. My web site, uvm.edu/~jloewen/sundown, provides examples.

24. Darla Craft, email via Classmates.com, 10/2002; Pinckneyville native, e-mail, 6/2001.

25. Longtime Sheridan resident, Grant County Musuem, Sheridan, AR, 10/2001; University of Illinois–Urbana undergraduate from Highland, 10/2002.

26. Ralph R. Rea, *Boone County and Its People* (Van Buren, AR: Press-Argus, 1955), 141–42.

27. Kathy Cosseboom, *Grosse Pointe, Michigan: Race Against Race* (East Lansing: Michigan State University Press, 1972), 52.

28. Kathy Spillman, 12/2000; Roger Horowitz, 9/2000; "Williams Sisters Will Skip Indian Wells Again," *USA Today,* 3/6/2003; "Williams Recounts Racist Taunts," *International Herald Tribune,* 3/27/2001.

29. Ron Slater, e-mail via classmates.com, 10/2002.

30. Ray Elliott, 9/2002; Linda Dudek, e-mail via classmates.com, 8/2002.

31. Ramelle MaCoy, e-mail to Ken Lawrence, 3/2003.

32. Grant County Museum volunteer, 10/2001.

33. John D. Baskerville, e-mail, 7/2003.

34. Actually the Williams family, unlike the usual African American in such a situation, had some resources, notably their own eminence. They have boycotted the Pacific Life Open since 2001. In 2003 the tournament director called the incident "unfortunate" and said "he understands why the Williamses are staying away" but went on to claim "the event will do just fine without them."

35. Oblong native, 4/2000.

36. Roger Karns, e-mail, 5/2002.

37. Ibid.

38. Pete Danko, "Hemet Team Uses Racial Slurs, Rivals Say," *Riverside County Press Enterprise,* 11/19/1989.

39. Villa Grove native, 9/2002.

40. *Gentry Journal-Advance,* reprinted in *Rogers Democrat,* 10/17/1906.

41. Maren A. Stein, "The Agricommercial Tradition," in Daniel J. Elazar, ed., *Cities of the Prairie Revisited* (Lincoln: University of Nebraska Press, 1986), 229; Susan Welch et al., *Race and Place* (Cambridge: Cambridge University Press, 2001), 85–92.

42. Joe T. Darden, "African American Residential Segregation," in Robert D. Bullard et al., *Residential Apartheid* (Los Angeles: UCLA Center for Afro-American Studies, 1994), 82.

43. Five years later, Park Forest stopped excluding blacks.

44. William H. Whyte Jr., *The Organization Man* (New York: Simon & Schuster, 1956), 311.

45. Gunnar Myrdal, *An American Dilemma* (New York: Harper & Row, 1944), lxxiii; Robert Terry, *For Whites Only* (Grand Rapids: Eerdmans, 1970), 41.

46. Colony, Alabama, has long been about one-eighth white, according to a librarian in nearby Cullman. In 1960 whites made up about half of the population in Chevy Chase Heights, Pennsylvania. Of course, to white residents in the nearly all-white neighboring town of Indiana, African Americans seemed in the overwhelming majority. In 1930 Colp, Illinois, had 1,250 residents, including 397 whites. Today it has a white mayor. Nevertheless, a white woman who lived and taught school in Herrin in the 1980s assured me in 2001 that Colp was all-black. Again, believing such a fallacy helped her to rationalize the fact that for decades Herrin was all-white, except for live-in maids. Over the years, whites have made up one-tenth to one-quarter of North Amityville's population, on Long Island, and Hispanics are now about one-eighth. When residents of the sundown towns near Boley charged that Boley made whites leave at sundown, "O. H. Bradley, editor of the *Boley Progress,* insisted that many whites lived near Boley, several shopped there both day and night, and most used it as their P.O.," according to historian Norman Crockett. Crockett does admit that whites were discouraged from buying real estate in Boley and Mound Bayou. Poet Jodey Bateman "was told by a black man from Tatum that up until 1972, whites could not stay overnight there." Tatum is a tiny hamlet of fewer than 200 people in southern Oklahoma; Bateman notes drily, "I don't know if whites ever tried to visit Tatum at night." Certainly neither I nor other whites had any difficulty living in Mound Bayou around 1970. Moreover, when a black community *has* kept out whites, sometimes it did so to avoid white retaliation. Leaders knew that one reason whites allowed their town to exist was because its all-black nature legitimized segregation in white eyes. Hence some "black" towns and townships maintained a low profile about their openness to all. See Patrick Clark, e-mail, 7/2002; Myrdal, *An American Dilemma,* 619; Norman Crockett, *The Black Towns* (Lawrence: Regents Press of Kansas, 1979), 74–75; Jodey Bateman, e-mail, 7/2002.

47. Kenilworth realtor, 10/2002; Tulsa resident, 9/2000.

48. Richard J. Hermstein and Charles Murray, *The Bell Curve* (New York: Free Press, 1994), Chapters 2–16.

49. Some years ago the Educational Testing Service, which once called the SAT the Scholastic Aptitude Test, dropped "Aptitude"; they could not defend the claim that the test measured "aptitude for college work." ETS renamed it the Scholastic Assessment Test, but perhaps due to the obvious redundancy, more recently ETS simply calls it the SAT. This has the added advantage of not drawing attention to the name change; most people still think the acronym means "Scholastic Aptitude Test."

50. Robert Coles, *Privileged Ones* (Boston: Little, Brown, 1977), 259; cf. 296–97.

51. Thomas P. Bailey, *Race Orthodoxy in the South* (New York: Neale, 1914), 41.

52. Lynne Duke, "But Some of My Best Friends Are . . . ," *Washington Post* National Weekly Edition, 1/14/1991.

53. Douglas S. Massey and Nancy A. Denton, *American Apartheid* (Cambridge: Harvard University Press, 1993), 94, citing Stanley B. Greenberg, *Report on Democratic Defection* (Washington, DC: Analysis Group, 1985), 13–18, 28.

54. Oak Lawn librarian, 1997; Cosseboom, *Grosse Pointe*, 56.

55. Leonard Steinhorn, "Is America Integrated?" History News Network, 12/23/2002, hnn.us/articles/1174.html, 5/2004; Frederick Douglass, *Douglass Monthly* 3 (10/1860): 337.

56. Dongola genealogist, 6/2003; Arkansas secretary, 9/2002.

57. Jane Adams, *The Transformation of Rural Life, 1890–1990* (Chapel Hill: University of North Carolina Press, 1994), 227.

58. Darla Craft, e-mail via Classmates.com, 10/2002; undergraduate at University of the Ozarks, 9/2002; Herrin native in Decatur, 9/2001; Donahue, "Wrestling with Democracy," 26.

59. Professor, Western Michigan University, 11/2000; undergraduates, University of Illinois–Chicago, 9/2001; André Cavalier, 7/1998; Diane Hershberger, 11/2000.

60. Karns, e-mail, 5/2002.

61. Norman Crockett, *The Black Towns* (Lawrence: Regents Press of Kansas, 1979), 74; W. L. Payne, "Okemah's Night of Terror," in Hazel Ruby McMahan, ed., *Stories of Early Oklahoma,* on Rootsweb, rootsweb.com/~okokfusk/cities.htm, 5/2003; Anna native, e-mail, 1/2003.

62. Arthur F. Raper, *The Tragedy of Lynching* (New York: Dover, 1970 [1933]), 426.

63. Karns, e-mail, 5/2002; Glendale native, e-mail, 11/2003.

64. Mark Singer, "Who Killed Carol Jenkins?" *New Yorker,* 1/7/2002, 25.

65. Ibid., 26.

66. Ibid.; 1987 Indiana University residence advisor, e-mail, 11/2002; Alan Boehm, e-mail, 6/2002.

67. "Martinsville's Sad Season," *Sports Illustrated,* 2/23/1998, 24.

68. Singer, "Who Killed Carol Jenkins?"; Bill Hewitt, "Slow Justice," *People Weekly* 58, 3, July 15, 2002: 89ff., web3.infotrac.galegroup.com/ . . . , #A88718549, 11/2002; Jeff Herlig, "Dateline Diversity" radio program, 11/1/2002, words-at-work.com/dateline.htm, 1/2003; Stephen Stuebner, "Extremists Undermine a Small Town's Efforts to Overcome a Legacy of Racism," *Intelligence Report* 107 (2002), indianacofcc.org, 12/2003.

69. Hmongs are refugees from highland Laos, many of whom had enlisted to fight on our side during the Vietnam War in both Vietnam and Laos.

70. John Lee, "Three Incidents at HS Connected," *Appleton Post-Crescent,* 10/7/1999; Kathy W. Nufer, "Racial Tensions Mount at North," *Post-Crescent,* 9/24/1999.

71. Matthew Shepard was killed for being gay in Laramie, Wyoming, and Laramie was never a sundown town. African Americans, too, have showed intolerance toward gays.

72. "Anti-Gay Extremism," posted at Yahoo.com News Community Headlines, 7/18/1998, and followup by CWBarton, 7/23/1998; New Hope resident, 4/2001; Mt. Rainier gay/lesbian page, hometown.aol.com/glmr20712/page2.html, 10/2002.

73. Shelly H. Kelly, e-mail, 7/2002; Claudia Kolker, "Santa Fe, Texas: Town Struggles to Outgrow Hate," *San Francisco Chronicle,* 9/11/2000.

74. Brooks Blevins, "The Strike and the Still," *Arkansas Historical Quarterly* 52, 4 (1993): 405–20; Charles C. Alexander, *The Ku Klux Klan in the Southwest* (Lexington: University of Kentucky Press, 1965), 62; Katie Benton-Cohen, e-mail, 8/2003.

75. Jodey Bateman, e-mail, 7/2002; post by cyberella5 at virtualtourist.com/f/p/1489/?r=ae52, 5/2002.

76. Abraham Lincoln, letter to Joshua Speed, 8/24/1855, Abraham Lincoln Online, showcase .netins.net/web/creative/lincoln/speeches/speed.htm, 5/2003.

77. Paul Delaney, "Use of 'Multi-Ethnic Textbooks' Grows," *New York Times*, 6/7/1971.

78. Elaine Woo and Kim Kowsky, "Schools' Racial Mix Boils Over," *Los Angeles Times*, 6/14/1991, via LexisNexis.

79. Forsyth County resident, e-mail, 5/2002.

80. The correct figure is less than 13%.

81. Joseph Amato, review of Richard Davies, *Main Street Blues* (Columbus: Ohio State University Press), in *American Historical Review*, 2/2000, 236–37; student estimates from University of Vermont undergraduates, introductory sociology, 1990–96.

82. Longtime resident of Anna now at Northern Illinois University, 10/2002; Donahue, "Wrestling with Democracy," 27.

83. Native of Pana in Decatur, 10/2001; Pana fast-food workers and other residents, 10/2001.

84. Chantel Scherer, e-mail via Classmates.com, 12/2002.

85. Granite City High School graduate (c.1995) at Ripon College, 4/2002.

86. Oblong native, 4/2000; post by goneaviking to uncensored-news.com/alt.flame.niggers, 5/23/2001.

87. Pana native in Decatur, 10/2001; undergraduates, University of Illinois–Chicago, 9/2001; Kathy Spillman, 12/2000.

88. Oblong native, 4/2000.

89. Anthony L. Antonio et al., "Effects of Racial Diversity on Complex Thinking in College Students," ingenta.com/journals/browse/bpl/psci, summarized in "How Racial Diversity Helps Students to Think," *Chronicle of Higher Education*, e-mail, 8/4/2004.

90. Coles, *Privileged Ones*, 416–18.

91. Oklahoma informant, e-mail, 5/2003; former Bishop resident, e-mail, 8/2002; Cullman native, e-mail, 5/2002; Kelly Burroughs, e-mail via Classmates.com, 11/2002.

92. Edwina M. DeWindt, "Wyandotte History; Negro," typescript, 1945, in Bacon Library, Wyandotte, MI, 22.

93. "The Real Polk County," 1/9(?)/1980; Gordon D. Morgan, "Black Hillbillies of the Arkansas Ozarks," Department of Sociology, University of Arkansas, Fayetteville, 1973, 155–59; wife of store manager, e-mail, 8/2002; Pana resident, 10/2001.

94. Alan Raucher, review of Mark S. Foster, *Castles in the Sand*, in *Journal of American History*, 3/2002, 1574; Mark S. Foster, *Castles in the Sand* (Gainesville: University Press of Florida, 2000), 159–60, 209–10; Karl Taeuber, *Negroes in Cities* (Chicago: Aldine, 1965), 32–37.

95. Among the many overwhelmingly white towns that hosted huge KKK rallies were Milo, Maine; Montpelier, Vermont; Fond du Lac, Wisconsin; Brookston and Valparaiso, Indiana; Fisher and Palestine, Illinois; Grand Saline, Texas; Grants Pass, Oregon; and several suburbs of Los Angeles.

96. Kathleen M. Blee, *Women of the Klan* (Berkeley: University of California Press, 1991), 172.

97. Blee, *Women of the Klan*, 213, believes some clause in the original charter of the university may have prevented the sale. Others hold that the growing split between the national Klan

headquarters in Georgia and the Indiana leadership may have prompted the national organization to withhold the funds.

98. Lance Trusty, "All Talk and No 'Kash,' " *Indiana Magazine of History* 82, 1 (1986): 19, 21; James Loewen, *Lies Across America* (New York: New Press, 1999), 238; "Still Riding, with a Bigger Banner," *The Economist*, 4/8/2000, 29–30; Transylvania University student, 10/2001; Central Michigan University student, 10/2002; Texas A&M staffer, e-mail, 6/2000.

99. There is debate about whether Eureka Springs was a sundown town or whether its African Americans departed voluntarily. However, according to a man who lived in Eureka Springs in the mid-1970s, the town has some oral tradition that after the last African American man "died or left town, his house was burned to the ground and that no blacks had lived in the county since that incident" (former Eureka resident, e-mail, 6/2002).

100. I have not confirmed Belmont, but its demographics were stark. In 1930, for example, among 21,748 people in the suburb lived 16 African Americans, 15 of whom were female. None was younger than the age bracket 15–19; surely the fifteen women were live-in maids and the other one was a live-in butler or gardener.

101. John Higham, *Strangers in the Land* (New Brunswick: Rutgers University Press, 1988), 180; Aviva Kempner, *The Life and Times of Hank Greenberg*, PBS-TV documentary, 4/4004; Michael Tomasky, "New York's Finest," *New York Review of Books*, 2/12/2004, 28; Michael Dougan, *Arkansas Odyssey* (Little Rock: Rose, 1994), 608; former Eureka resident, e-mail, 6/2002; Robert Welch, "A Letter to the South," John Birch Society, jbs.org/visitor/focus/refute/letter_south.htm, 5/2003; Tony Platt, e-mail, 9/2002; Stephen Kercher, review of *Joseph McCarthy: A Modern Tragedy*, exhibit at Outagamie Museum, *Journal of American History*, 12/2002, 1004.

102. Many organizations on the list, like most other organizations, are headquartered in cities that are too large to be uniracial. A disproportionate share are headquartered in the South, which still has many racists but few sundown towns.

103. Southern Poverty Law Center Intelligence Report, splcenter.org/intelligenceproject/ip-index.html, 5/2003; re Simi Valley, see the John Birch Society web site, jbs.org, 4/2003; Nationalist web site, nationalist.org/ATW/1997/feb.html, 10/1998.

104. Zimmermann quoted in Laurinda Joenks, "Roughness of Citizens Blamed on Lean Times," *The Morning News*, 5/7/2000; Robb quoted in Jacqueline Froelich, "A City Confronts Its Ghosts," *Arkansas Democrat-Gazette*, 4/27/2003; Potter County discussed on *All Things Considered*, National Public Radio, 2/15/2002.

CHAPTER 12: THE EFFECT OF SUNDOWN TOWNS ON BLACKS

1. Daisy Myers, "Breaking Down Barriers," *Pennsylvania Heritage* 28, 3 (2002): 12.

2. Shirley Willard, "Black History in Fulton County Since 1920s," Fulton County Historical Society, Rochester, n.d., unpaginated.

3. Middle-aged Mattoon woman, 2/2004.

4. Allison Blakely, e-mail, 9/2002.

5. Joycelyn Landrum-Brown, e-mail, 8/2002; Olen Cole Jr., *The African-American Experience in the Civilian Conservation Corps* (Gainesville: University Press of Florida, 1999), 25.

6. Mattoon woman, 10/2002; Cole, *The African-American Experience;* Paxton resident, 10/2000; Southern Arkansas University professor, 10/2001; Missouri resident, 7/2002.

7. Reynolds Farley, Sheldon Danziger, and Harry Holzer, *Detroit Divided* (New York: Russell

Sage, 2000), 154–55; Gordon Trowbridge and Oralandar Brand-Williams, "Invisible Boundaries Created Dividing Line Between Black, White Suburbs," *Detroit News*, 1/14/2002, detnews.com/2002/homepage/0201/14/index.htm, 1/2002; Bradley professor, 2/2001.

8. Colbert King, "The Kings of Foggy Bottom," *Washington Post Magazine*, 2/1/2004, 20.

9. Elderly Arab resident, 6/2002; Orlando Patterson, *The Ordeal of Integration* (Washington, DC: Civitas/Counterpoint, 1997), 46; Susan Welch et al., *Race and Place* (Cambridge: Cambridge University Press, 2001), 38.

10. David Mendell, "Midwest Housing Divide Is Still Race," *Chicago Tribune*, 6/21/2001, mumford1.dyndns.org/cen2000/newspdf/chicagotribune0621.html, 7/2003.

11. Sheryll Cashin, *The Failures of Integration* (New York: Public Affairs, 2004), 9; Sidney Poitier and Ruby Dee quoted in Andrew Wiese, *Places of Their Own* (Chicago: University of Chicago Press, 2004), 154, 157.

12. Cashin, *The Failures of Integration*, 137–60, 171–75.

13. Gary Orfield, talk at OPEN meeting, Philadelphia, 12/2000; Farley, Danziger, and Holzer, *Detroit Divided*, 204; John R. Logan, review of same in *Contemporary Sociology* 31, 5 (2002), 519; Light, 6/2002.

14. Cole, *The African-American Experience in the Civilian Conservation Corps*, 25; Ronald McGriff, e-mail, 6/2002; Benjamin Johnson, post 8/6/2001, umb.edu/forum/1/AMST203/member/Forums/s-484415211-.html#47101 6211, 12/18/2002.

15. David Grann, "Firestarters," *New Republic*, 7/20/1998, 17; Richard Stewart, "Desegregation at Public Housing Ripped by Audit," *Houston Chronicle*, East Texas Bureau, 7/11/1997; Mimi Swartz, "Vidor in Black and White," *Texas Monthly*, 12/1991, 161; Du Quoin resident, 9/2002.

16. Patterson, *Ordeal of Integration*, 65.

17. Myers, "Breaking Down Barriers," 12.

18. Arna Bontemps and Jack Conroy, *Anyplace but Here* (New York: Hill & Wang, 1966), 9, quoted in Quintard Taylor, *In Search of the Racial Frontier* (New York: Norton, 1998), 301; Vivian S. Toy, "Stuck in Last Place," *New York Times*, 5/4/2003.

19. Ellis Cose, *The Rage of a Privileged Class* (New York: HarperCollins, 1993), 1.

20. Ibid., 39; Langston Hughes, "Restrictive Covenants," in Arnold Rampersad, ed., *The Collected Poems of Langston Hughes* (New York: Vintage, 1994), 361.

21. Martin Luther King Jr., remarks at Palmer House, Chicago, summer 1965, quoted in *How Long? Not Long* (Chicago: Leadership Council for Metropolitan Open Communities, 1986).

22. Student of Joseph Braun's at Illinois State University, 9/1999, e-mailed by Braun, 11/2001.

23. Dale Harvey and Gerald Slatin, "The Relationship Between Child's SES and Teacher Expectations," *Social Forces* 54, 1 (1975): 141. James Loewen, "The Difference Race Makes," in Howard Ball et al., eds., *Multicultural Education* (Hillsdale, NJ: Erlbaum, 1998), 53–55, summarizes some of the expectation literature about race.

24. Poussaint quoted in Gordon Trowbridge and Oralandar Brand-Williams, "The Past: A policy of exclusion," *Detroit News*, 1/14/2002, at mumford1.dyndns.org/cen2000/othersay/detroitnews/Stories/Blacks . . . , 7/2003.

25. See Claude Steele, in Steele, Teresa Perry, and Asa Hilliard III, *Young, Gifted, and Black* (Boston: Beacon, 2004); Steele and Joshua Aronson, "Stereotype Threat and the Intellectual Test Performance of African Americans," *Journal of Personality and Social Psychology* 69 (1995): 797–811; and J. Aronson et al., "When White Men Can't Do Math," *Journal of Experimental Social Psychology* 35 (1999): 29–46.

26. Malcolm X, *Malcolm X Speaks,* quoted in Joseph R. Conlin, *Morrow Book of Quotations in American History* (New York: Morrow, 1984), 327.

27. Kati Haycock, "Passing Grades," *Trust,* summer 2000, 13.

28. Only affirmative action allows an appreciable number of African Americans into America's elite colleges, where this capital is most readily acquired. One reason why affirmative action is necessary leads right back to sundown suburbs: African Americans average much lower than European Americans on standardized tests. The reasons are several, but excluding African Americans residentially is one factor, coupled with test bias on the SAT (and ACT). See James Loewen, "Presentation," "Discussion," and "A Sociological View of Aptitude Tests," in Eileen Rudert, ed., *The Validity of Testing in Education and Employment* (Washington, DC: U.S. Commission on Civil Rights, 1993), 41–45, 58–62, 73–91, and James Loewen, Phyllis Rosser, and John Katzman, "Gender Bias on SAT Items," American Educational Research Association, 4/1988, ERIC ED294915.

29. Patterson, *The Ordeal of Integration,* 9, 20; Barbara J. Fields, "Of Rogues and Geldings," *American Historical Review,* 108 #5 (12/2002), 1401.

30. See Loewen, "Presentation," "Discussion," and "A Sociological View of Aptitude Tests," 41–45, 58–62, 73–91; Loewen, Rosser, and Katzman, "Gender Bias on SAT Items."

31. This relief, placing Section 8 families in white suburbs, resulted from a related lawsuit against HUD.

32. I relied on several articles by Rosenbaum, but the most accessible compilation of these results is in Leonard S. Rubinowitz and James E. Rosenbaum, *Crossing the Class and Color Lines: From Public Housing to White Suburbia* (Chicago: University of Chicago Press, 2000).

33. Galster summarized in Trowbridge and Brand-Williams, "The Past: A Policy of Exclusion."

34. Mark Granovetter, "The Strength of Weak Ties," *American Journal of Sociology* 78 (1973): 1360–80; Deirdre A. Royster, *Race and the Invisible Hand: How White Networks Exclude Black Men from Blue-Collar Jobs* (Berkeley: University of California Press, 2003), 182.

35. Stephanie Simon, "Segregation Still Strong in North," *Los Angeles Times,* 1/19/2003, reprinted in *Holland* (MI) *Sentinel,* 3/30/2003, hollandsentinel.com, 4/2003; Carolyn Adams et al., *Philadelphia: Neighborhoods, Division, and Conflict* (Temple University Press, 1991), 53.

36. Former Darien resident, 8/1999.

37. Charles Christian, "Emerging Patterns of Industrial Activity Within Large Metropolitan Areas," in Gary Gappert and Harold M. Rose, eds., *The Social Economy of Cities* (Beverly Hills: Sage, 1975), 241.

38. Anne B. Shlay, review of Alice O'Connor, Chris Tilly, and Lawrence Bobo, eds., *Urban Inequality,* in *Contemporary Sociology* 31, 5 (2002): 511.

39. William J. Wilson, *When Work Disappears* (New York: Vintage, 1996).

CHAPTER 13: THE EFFECT OF SUNDOWN TOWNS ON THE SOCIAL SYSTEM

1. Thorstein Veblen, *The Theory of the Leisure Class* (New York: NAL/Mentor, 1953 [1899]), 81.

2. This statement is based on its Index of Dissimilarity, D = 85, meaning that 85% of its African Americans would have to move to nonblack areas to achieve a completely neutral distribution of both races.

3. More recent figures, which may not reflect identical methodology, show some narrowing of this gap. According to the *American Housing Survey, 1999,* median owner-occupied housing units in 1999 were valued at $63,400 in the city of Detroit, $168,200 in Boston, and $215,600 in Los Angeles (Census web site, census.gov/prod/2001pubs, 5/2004).

4. John Logan et al., "Ethnic Diversity Grows, Neighborhood Integration Lags Behind," Mumford Center, 12/18/2001, 7, mumford1.dyndns.org/cen2000/WholePop/WPreport/page1.html, 1/2003; Reynolds Farley, Sheldon Danziger, and Harry Holzer, *Detroit Divided* (New York: Russell Sage, 2000), 1–2; *American Housing Survey, 1999,* at U.S. Census, census.gov/prod/2001pubs, 5/2004; Carolyn Crowley, "Urban Explorers, Crawling and Climbing into the Past," *Washington Post,* 12/30/2001.

5. Farley, Danziger, and Holzer, *Detroit Divided;* Francis X. Donnelly, "Region Pays Price for Reputation," *Detroit News,* 1/21/2002, detroitnews/2002/homepage/0201/21/index.htm, 2/2002.

6. Leah Samuel, "Organ Transplant," *Detroit Metro Times,* 9/10/2003.

7. Jane Jacobs, *The Death and Life of Great American Cities* (New York: Vintage, 1961), Chapter 11, and *Cities and the Wealth of Nations* (New York: Vintage, 1985); William Whyte, *City* (New York: Doubleday, 1988), 288; cf. discussion in Andres Duany, Elizabeth Plater-Zyberk, and Jeff Speck, *Suburban Nation* (New York: Farrar, Straus, and Giroux, 2000), 9.

8. Charles Mudede, "How Tacoma Fought Seattle for the Future and Lost," *The Stranger* 9, 47 (2000), thestranger.com/2000-08-10/feature-2.html, 6/2003.

9. Nick Khan, 9/2002; Red Bud native, 2/2004.

10. Herman Lantz and J. S. McCrary, *People of Coal Town* (Carbondale: Southern Illinois University Press, 1971 [1958]), 42; West Frankfort genealogist reported to me, 9/2002.

11. Lesbians more often locate in suburbs, although they do seem to prefer multiracial suburbs, according to Gates. I do not know of research on the relationship of lesbians to creativity and economic development.

12. Gary Gates, "The Demographics of Diversity," Urban Institute, 6/3/2003, also summarizing Richard Florida's findings; Tatsha Robertson, "Finding Hope in Gay Enclaves," *Boston Globe,* 1/15/2003.

13. Pew Center for Civic Journalism, *Straight Talk From Americans—2000,* pewcenter.org/doingcj/research/r_ST2000nat1.html#nation, 6/2003; Haya El Nasser and Paul Overberg, "What You Don't Know About Sprawl," *USA Today,* 2/22/2001.

14. Actually, as of 2000 Oak Park was still just 22% black.

15. Carole Goodwin, *The Oak Park Strategy* (Chicago: University of Chicago Press, 1979), 108–9.

16. Quoted in Thomas Sugrue, *Origins of the Urban Crisis* (Princeton: Princeton University Press, 1996), 196.

17. Michael Ebner, *Creating Chicago's North Shore* (Chicago: University of Chicago Press, 1988), 230, 314.

18. Post died in 1960, but her granddaughter-in-law, Elizabeth Post, brought out the 12th edition of *Etiquette* in 1969.

19. Patrick M. McMullen, "Gated Communities," entry for *Encyclopedia of Chicago,* draft, 10/17/2000; Albert F. Winslow, *Tuxedo Park* (Tuxedo Park: Tuxedo Park Historical Society, 1992).

20. Ingrid Gould Ellen, *Sharing America's Neighborhoods* (Cambridge: Harvard University Press, 2000), 71.

21. Larry Peterson, who has studied housing and race in the Chicago suburbs for four decades,

points out that another reason owners move first is the behavior of realtors. Since they make far more money from sales than rentals, it is in their interest to encourage turnover, so they focus on persuading white homeowners to sell.

22. Installment contracts differ from mortgages in that the buyer builds no legal equity until payments are complete. Missing a single payment can put the buyer in default, leading to the loss of the entire investment and leaving the speculator free to sell the house again.

23. Arnold Hirsch, *Making the Second Ghetto* (Cambridge: Cambridge University Press, 1983), 32; Luigi Laurenti, "Property Values and Neighborhood Integration," in Raymond Mack, ed., *Race, Class, and Power* (New York: American Book Co., 1968), 435.

24. George Galster, "Neighborhood Racial Change, Segregationist Sentiments, and Affirmative Marketing Policies," *Journal of Urban Economics* 27 (1990): 334–61, summarized in Ellen, *Sharing America's Neighborhoods*, 63.

25. Arthur Hayes, "Managed Integration," *Black Enterprise*, 7/1982, 43; Goodwin, *The Oak Park Strategy*, 157–58; cf. Ellen, *Sharing America's Neighborhoods*, 162–63.

26. White flight is not inevitable. Whites are not fleeing Mt. Rainier, Maryland, for example, which was 56% black in 1990 and just 62% black in 2000. In the last twenty years, whites have sometimes moved *into* majority-black neighborhoods, such as parts of Capitol Hill in Washington, D.C., and made them majority-white. Between 1960 and 1970, Kirkwood, a neighborhood in Atlanta, went from being 91% white to 97% black. Then in the 1990s, some whites returned, making Kirkwood 14% white by 2000. Tipping point theory, which holds that whites will not flee until a neighborhood reaches a certain percentage and then will leave, cannot explain gentrification. Nor can it explain Lynwood.

27. Richard Morin, "The Odds of Being Poor," *Washington Post*, 3/23/1999; "Proposed Group Home Sparks Long Legal Battle," Associated Press, 3/16/2002, on Advocacy and Protection for People with Mental Illness web site, geocities.com/ahobbit.geo/group_home .html, 6/2003; "Local Judge Rejects Effort to Stop Group Home in Greenwich," Associated Press, in *Hartford Courant*, 9/9/2002, on Homeless News web site, groups.yahoo .com/group/HomelessNews/message/2094, 6/2003.

28. Mary Otto, "Suburbs Struggle to Help Homeless," *Washington Post*, 12/18/2000.

29. Jonathan Kozol, *Savage Inequalities* (New York: Crown, 1991), 7–9; Ellen, *Sharing America's Neighborhoods*, 4, 118.

30. Some do pay a lesser amount that reimburses a city for some of the services—police, streets, fire protection, etc.

31. Kozol, *Savage Inequalities*, 55; Darwin Payne, *Big D: Triumphs and Troubles* (Dallas: Three Forks Press, 1994), 214.

32. Longtime Cincinnati suburbanite, e-mail, 11/2002.

33. Michael N. Danielson, *The Politics of Exclusion* (New York: Columbia University Press, 1976), 88, 110.

34. Gunnar Myrdal, *An American Dilemma* (New York: McGraw-Hill, 1964 [1944]), 618–22; Jianping Shen, "Have Minority Students Had a Fair Share of Quality Teachers?" *Poverty & Race* 12, 4 (7/2003), 7; Michael Powell, "Separate and Unequal in Roosevelt, Long Island," *Washington Post*, 4/21/2002.

35. Danielson, *The Politics of Exclusion*, 21; Carolyn Adams et al., *Philadelphia: Neighborhoods, Division, and Conflict* (Philadelphia: Temple University Press, 1991), 163; Powell, "Separate and Unequal in Roosevelt, Long Island."

36. Witold Rybczynski, *City Life* (New York: Harper Collins, 1995), 206–7; Powell, "Separate and Unequal."

37. Dan T. Carter, *The Politics of Rage* (New York: Simon & Schuster, 1995), 433; John Gehm, *Bringing it Home* (Chicago: Chicago Review Press, 1984), 193; Janet L. McCoy, "AU Prof: Remember Wallace for Changing U.S. Political Ideology," at auburn.edu/administration/univrel/news/archive/9_98news/9_98wal lace.html, 8/2003; Ken Rudin, "Flunking Out of the Electoral College," *Washington Post,* 10/15/1999, washingtonpost.com/wp-srv/politics/campaigns/junkie/archive/jun kie101599.htm, 8/2003.

38. "Quiet Town in Michigan Has 'a Feeling for Wallace,' "*New York Times,* 9/12/1968.

39. Bill Outis, 10/2001; Reynolds Farley, Sheldon Danziger, and Harry Holzer, *Detroit Divided* (New York: Russell Sage, 2000), 11; Dan T. Carter, *The Politics of Rage* (New York: Simon & Schuster, 1995), 434; Kathy Spillman, 12/2000.

40. Nixon quoted in George Lipsitz, "The Possessive Investment in Whiteness," in Jonathan Birnbaum and Clarence Taylor, eds., *Civil Rights Since 1787* (New York: New York University Press, 2000), 674; Donahue, "Wrestling with Democracy," 18; Sugrue, *Origins of the Urban Crisis,* 266; Alexander Polikoff, "Racial Inequality and the Black Ghetto," *Poverty & Race* 13, 6 (11/2004), 1.

41. To be sure, the Republican administration in 2001–05 hardly shrank the federal government.

42. Thomas Edsall and Mary Edsall, *Chain Reaction* (New York: Norton, 1992), 226, 229; Dan T. Carter, "The Southern Strategy," in Birnbaum and Taylor, eds., *Civil Rights Since 1787,* 738; cf. David M. P. Freund, "Making It Home," Ph.D. dissertation, University of Michigan, 1999.

43. Sheryll Cashin, *The Failures of Integration* (New York: Public Affairs, 2004), 270.

44. Edsall and Edsall, *Chain Reaction,* 228.

45. Ibid., 226, 229.

CHAPTER 14: SUNDOWN TOWNS TODAY

1. Donald Deskins Jr. and Christopher Bettinger, "Black and White Spaces in Selected Metropolitan Areas," in Kate A. Berry and Martha L. Henderson, eds., *Geographical Identities of Ethnic America* (Reno: University of Nevada Press, 2002), 38.

2. Benjamin Johnson, post to umb.edu/forum/1/AMST203/member/Forums/s-484415211 .html#471016211, 8/2001; former Marlowe resident, e-mail, 11/2004; Missouri resident, e-mail, 6/2000; Roger Karns, e-mail, 5/2002; Margaret Alexander Alam, e-mails and photo, 9/2003.

3. Dan F. Morse and Phyllis A. Morse, "Introduction," *The Lower Mississippi Valley Expeditions of Clarence Bloomfield Moore* (Tuscaloosa: University of Alabama Press, 1998), 2.

4. Malcolm Ross, *All Manner of Men* (New York: Reynal & Hitchcock, 1948), 66.

5. Herrin, which was sundown when Angle was there, had 104 African Americans, almost 1% of its population, in 2000.

6. Paul M. Angle, *Bloody Williamson* (New York: Knopf, 1952), 98; Zeigler librarian, 9/2002; Deidre Meadows, e-mail via Classmates.com, 9/2002; Du Quoin resident, 9/2002.

7. Robby Heason, *Trouble Behind* (Cicada Films, 1990).

8. Frank Nickell, e-mail, 6/2002; professor, Taylor University, 6/2004; Rebecca Tolley-Stokes, e-mail, 8/2002; Michael D'Orso, *Like Judgment Day* (New York: Putnam's, 1996), 329.

9. Undergraduate, University of the Ozarks, 9/2002; undergraduate, University of Illinois–Chicago, 9/2001.

10. Chris Meno, e-mail, 10/2002; professor, DePauw University, 10/2001; clerk, National Afro-American Museum at Central State University, 10/2000.

11. If the census shows no black families, that does not prove that African Americans *cannot* live there. Only continuing incidents prove that, and I cannot be up to the moment for every town I've studied. For most communities my information is current only as of 2001–04 or even earlier. Checking each town anew would take years, at the end of which we would be in a new present, no longer up to the moment. Also, in many sundown towns the question simply cannot be resolved, even with up-to-date information, owing to no recent trials. Until another black family (or better, two or three) tests a town by trying to move in, we cannot know for sure if it still keeps out African Americans. We know it did, but we do not know that it does.

12. Listing more than one race was allowed on the 2000 census for the first time. Few (<5%) chose such categories, and usually I omitted them, being unsure how they classed themselves. Neither I nor the census achieved consistency, however. Sometimes I included individuals of both African and European ancestry as "black," and the census apparently includes nonblack family members, as it should, in its table of population in households with one or more black householder. I use the term "black household" to mean "household with one or more black householders." Like the IRS, I required "households" to include more than one person; otherwise I could not distinguish them from unattached individuals.

13. Anna editor and reference librarian, 9/2002; Anna farmer, 1/2004.

14. Illinois state trooper, 1/2004; Ronald Alan Willis, e-mail, 9/2004.

15. Martinsville native, 10/2002.

16. Post by "goneaviking" to uncensored-news.com/alt.flame.niggers, 5/23/2001; Smokey Crabtree, *Too Close to the Mirror* (Fouke: Days Creek Production, 2001), 186.

17. Of course, many residents of Elwood want no part of such events, the KKK marches in many multiracial towns, and "hosting" KKK events costs Elwood money for police overtime. See "The High Price of Policing Hate," 10/28/2002, Anti-Defamation League, adl.org/learn/news/cost_of_hate.asp, 6/2003.

18. North Judson teacher, 4/2001; former Marion, Indiana, policeman, 6/2002; Indiana teacher, e-mail, 6/2000.

19. David Cline, e-mail, 6/2003, confirming conversation with Steeleville librarian, 6/2003.

20. Two Pinckneyville residents, 9/2002; Du Quoin resident, 9/2002; Pinckneyville native, e-mail, 8/2004.

21. Mattoon businessman, e-mail, 10/2002.

22. Champaign-Urbana resident, 2000.

23. Pana spokeswoman, 10/2001; Pana resident, 10/2001.

24. Forsyth County, GA, resident, e-mail, 5/2002; native of Oak Grove, 3/2004; D'Vera Cohn, "1990s Further Reshape Suburbs," *Washington Post,* 5/25/2001.

25. Librarian, Joplin Public Library, 9/2002.

26. Robert Bullard quoted in Jonathan Tilove, "2000 Census Finds America's New Mayberry Is Exurban, and Overwhelmingly White," Newhouse News Service, 2001, newhouse.com/archive/story1a051001.html, 8/2004.

27. Andres Duany, Elizabeth Plater-Zyberk, and Jeff Speck, *Suburban Nation* (New York: Farrar, Straus, and Giroux, 2000), 43.

28. Ellen James Martin, "Set Some Priorities When Buying in a Classy Community," *Chicago Tribune,* 9/14/2001.

29. Kenneth T. Jackson, *Crabgrass Frontier* (New York: Oxford University Press, 1985), 8; Duany, Plater-Zyberk, and Speck, *Suburban Nation,* 44.

30. Common rules include no JetSkis or boats in driveway; no fence, no gazebo, no unapproved lawn furniture; any doghouse must resemble your house and must be hidden from the street by a six-foot fence or greenery. Diane Hershberger of Kansas City told of subdivisions in suburban Johnson County where "you can't leave your garage doors open, you can't work on your cars in your own driveway, you can't hang laundry outside at any time." These restrictions need not be racial. Sociologist Karyn Lacy described a suburb that has gone majority black and has similar rules: "Residents must not allow their grass to grow more than 4 inches tall. (At the same time, they are also precluded from not maintaining grass at all.) Detractors are hit with heavy penalties." Diane Hershberger, 11/2000; Karyn Lacy, "A Part of the Neighborhood," *International Journal of Sociology and Social Policy* 22 (2002): 62.

31. Elizabeth Razzi, "House Rules," *Kiplinger's Magazine,* 9/2000, 87–88; Frederique Krupa, "Los Angeles: Buying the Concept of Security," Chapter 3 of "Privatization of Public Space," unpaginated, translucency.com/frede/pps.html, 1/2004.

32. Kaplan quoted in Anthony Faiola, "Brazil's Elites Fly Above Their Fears: Rich Try to Wall Off Urban Violence," *Washington Post* Foreign Service, 6/1/2002; Edward J. Blakely and Mary Gail Snyder, *Fortress America* (Washington, DC: Brookings, 1997), 2–3, 7, 17, 26.

33. The entry gates at Country Club Estates in New Albany, Ohio, where houses sold in 2000 for $800,000 to $1,200,000, open automatically when a car drives close to them. No sign tells this, so I suppose some would-be thieves might be deterred. Exit gates in most gated communities open automatically.

34. Blakely and Snyder, *Fortress America,* 69.

35. Ibid., 17, 83; Columbus Academy student, 10/2000.

36. Lacy, "A Part of the Neighborhood"; Annemei Curlin, 8/2002; Blakely and Snyder, *Fortress America,* 153–54.

37. Gunnar Myrdal, *An American Dilemma* (New York: Harper & Row, 1944), 9.

38. "Real Estate Operator's Plan for Exclusion of Minorities Condemned by Civic Leaders," *Pacific Citizen,* 7/5/1947.

39. In the late 1940s, most Jewish American leaders chose to downplay the Holocaust, "with an eye to an internal assimilationist goal and an external Cold War agenda," according to Tim Cole, "Representing the Holocaust in America" [reviewing Peter Novick's *The Holocaust in American Life*], *Public Historian* 24, 4 (2002): 128. In the 1960s, according to Novick and Cole, American Jewish leaders made "a U-turn," and by 1990 the Holocaust had become "the iconic event of the twentieth century, for American Jews in particular and Americans more generally." This increased emphasis on the Holocaust, exemplified by the very popular Holocaust Museum near the Mall in Washington, D.C., includes modest attention to our reluctance to accept Jewish refugees during and before World War II, but almost none to the rise of anti-Semitism in America during the Nadir.

40. Richard Todd, "Darien, Connecticut," *New England Monthly,* 3/1986, 43.

41. "Attitudes Toward Specific Areas of Racial Integration," *Connecticut Civil Rights Bulletin* 3, 4 (1961): 2.

42. Yes, the event is disputed. I do think James Earl Ray did it, but I don't believe he acted alone; see James Loewen, *Lies My Teacher Told Me* (New York: New Press, 1995), 224.

43. Karl Taeuber, "Research Issues Concerning Trends in Residential Segregation," University of Wisconsin Center for Demography and Ecology, Madison, Working Paper 83-13, 11/1982, 5.

44. Howard Schuman, Charlotte Steeh, and Lawrence Bobo, *Racial Attitudes in America* (Cambridge: Harvard University Press, 1985), 59–60; Reynolds Farley and William H.

Frey, "Changes in the Segregation of Whites from Blacks During the 1980s," *American Sociological Review* 59, 1 (1994), 27; Orlando Patterson, *The Ordeal of Integration* (Washington, DC: Civitas/Counterpoint, 1997), 61.

45. Commenting on the NORC item, Howard Schuman, Charlotte Steeh, and Lawrence Bobo concur. Evidence indicates that some of the 63% agreed more in the abstract than in the concrete. In 1972, NORC also asked respondents to choose "between two possible laws to vote on. One law says that a homeowner can decide for himself who to sell his house to, even if he prefers not to sell to blacks. The second law says that a homeowner cannot refuse to sell to someone because of their race or color. Which law would you vote for?" Only 34% supported the second alternative. See Schuman, Steeh, and Bobo, *Racial Attitudes in America*, 97.

46. To be sure, much popular culture is youth culture, which makes it partly a matter of the life cycle. One cannot project the life cycle onto society as a whole. When today's white teenagers become parents and reach thirty or forty, they may choose to live in white suburbia. After all, some white parents who moved to sundown towns in the 1980s had venerated African Americans such as Muhammad Ali or Ray Charles in the 1960s.

47. Dorothy K. Newman et al., *Protest, Politics, and Prosperity* (New York: Pantheon, 1978), 141, 152; Stephen G. Meyer, *As Long as They Don't Move Next Door* (Lanham, MD: Rowman & Littlefield, 2000), 220; Paul Jargowsky, "Concentration of Poverty Declines in the 1990s," *Poverty & Race* 12, 4 (7/2003), 1; David Mendell, "Midwest Housing Divide Is Still Race," *Chicago Tribune*, 6/21/2001, at mumford1.dyndns.org/cen2000/newspdf/chicago tribune0621.html, 7/2003.

48. Associated Press, "Ruling Opens Connecticut Beaches," *Washington Post*, 5/11/2000; Deborah Pollard, professor, University of Michigan–Dearborn, e-mail, 7/2002; *Michigan State Tax Commission v. Grosse Pointe*, Michigan Tax Tribunal #284,585, Opinion, 7/16/2003.

49. Ricardo A. Herrera, e-mail, 6/2000.

50. This is reminiscent of the finding that multiethnic towns were less likely than monoethnic towns to exclude blacks between 1890 and 1940.

51. Mendell, "Midwest Housing Divide Is Still Race"; Christopher Phillips, e-mail, 6/2000.

52. Danielle Gordon, "Residency Rules Ignite Race Debate," *Chicago Reporter*, 12/1998, chicagoreporter.com/1999/01-99/tear400.gif, 4/2003.

53. James Loewen, *Lies Across America* (New York: New Press, 1999), 170–72; Michael Bsharah, letter, 7/20/2000; Dearborn Online, dearborn-mi.com, c.10/2002.

54. Leonard Steinhorn, "Is America Integrated?" History News Network, 12/23/2002, hnn.us/articles/1174.html, 5/2004; Nancy A. Denton, "Segregation and Discrimination in Housing" in Rachel Bratt, Chester Hartman, and Michael E. Stone, eds., reader on housing (Philadelphia: Temple University Press, forthcoming), ms. pp. 23–28; Susan Welch et al., *Race and Place* (Cambridge: Cambridge University Press, 2001), 168.

55. This would not be the first time. Between 1920 and 1950 or so, as we have seen, "white" came to incorporate Jews, Italians, and other groups that had been considered separate races. Irish became "white" earlier; Arabs, Pakistanis, and Asian Indians later. Chinese Americans were admitted to "white" public schools in the Mississippi Delta in the 1930s and '40s. Today, "white" may be incorporating most Asian, Pacific, Mexican, and affluent Native Americans. Certainly their acceptance in sundown towns implies as much.

This process offers payoffs for "real" whites. For one, the oft-repeated claim that whites will be a minority by 2040 or 2050 may not come to pass: "white" may simply morph into a broader category by then. Also, whites have often used their acceptance of "honorary whites" to avoid the charge of racism. Sundown town residents are quick to cite their Mexican and Asian Americans to prove that they are not prejudiced, even though they still do exclude African Americans. Admitting Hispanics and Asian Americans may help make these groups more racist over time, as it did Chinese Americans in Mississippi (see Loewen, *The Mississippi Chinese: Between Black and White* [Prospect Heights, IL: Waveland Press, 1988], 93, 195–200).

56. Arcola official, 9/2002; Darrin Burnett, "Cross Burning Fans Flames in Beardstown," Jacksonville (IL) *Journal-Courier*, 8/13/1996; Sager quoted in S. Lynne Walker, "Dealing with Change," *Springfield State Journal-Register*, 11/12/2003; comment by real estate broker at Ozarkopathy web site, ozarkopathy.org, 8/2003 and e-mail, 9/2003.
57. Lisa Coleman, e-mail, 7/2002.
58. Piggott, AR, resident, e-mail, 8/2002; Benton, IL, teacher, 9/2002.
59. "Alone in the Crowd," *New York Times Magazine*, 7/16/2000, 56.
60. Sheridan native at Grant County Museum, 10/2001.
61. Actually, the Green Bay Packers were the next-to-last team in the National Football League to accept a black player, doing so only in 1950, three years after Jackie Robinson. See Larry Names, *The History of the Green Bay Packers*, vol. IV: *The Shameful Years* (Wautoma: Angel Press, 1995), 44.
62. Dan Benson, "Despite Rocky Start, Minorities Call Cedarburg Home," *Milwaukee Journal Sentinel*, 3/14/2001.
63. Ragland noted, "The latest census data in 2000 showed 34 blacks residing in Highland Park, but as far as anyone knows, they're renting." This is another case where the census counts people who are not known to local residents. Perhaps they are live-in servants, adopted children, inmates of penal, educational, or other institutions, or mistakes by census respondents.
64. Dorothy Brown, "The Encircled Schools: Park Cities and Wilmington," *Dallas Times Herald*, 11/30/1975; James Ragland, "New HP Couple Spurs Media Tizzy," *Dallas Morning News*, 6/9/2003; cf. Mark Miller, "At Last," MSNBC News, 6/4/2003, msnbc.com/news/922226, 6/2003.
65. Betty Toomes, transcript of interview (Yuma, AZ, 1963: Robert B. Powers, interviewer), sunsite.berkeley.edu:2020/dynaweb/teiproj/oh/warren/powers/@Generic_BookTextView/4030, 1/2003.
66. White snipers repeatedly shot at the black housing project, forcing residents to douse their lights; blacks in turn fired at the police station and at firemen answering calls. All public officials were white, elected at-large by voters polarized along racial lines; blacks took the city to court, demanding single-member districts so they could win some representation on the city council. See James Loewen, "Report for Land of Lincoln Legal Assistance Foundation in *Kendrick et al. v. Moss et al.*," typescript, Burlington, VT, 1979.
67. Mexican American basketball players played the same unifying role in Beardstown in 2003. About 20 fans of nearby Brown County High School, a sundown county, showed up wearing sombreros and yelling "We want tacos" at the Beardstown team. According to Beardstown senior Tomas Alvarez, "People were mad. They really care about the image of Beardstown. That wasn't just against an ethnic group. It was against the whole town." Quoted in Walker, "Dealing with Change."
68. David Marniss and Neil Henry, "Race 'War' in Cairo," *Washington Post*, 3/22/1987.
69. Alvarez quoted in Walker, "Dealing with Change."

70. Bill Jennings, "Left-hander Finds Many Who Impress," *Riverside Press Enterprise,* 12/11/1992, via LexisNexis; Pete Danko, "Hemet Team Uses Racial Slurs, Rivals Say," *Riverside County Press Enterprise,* 11/19/1989.

71. George Callcott, 5/2004.

72. San Diego Online, sandiego-online.com/retro/janretr1.stm, 3/2003; Mary Ellen Stratthaus, "Flaw in the Jewel: Housing Discrimination Against Jews in La Jolla, California," *American Jewish History* 84, 3 (1996): 189, 193–95, 198, 201–2, 210, 215–16.

73. John Palen, *The Suburbs* (New York: McGraw-Hill, 1995), xiv, 3.

74. Actually, while Mountain Home's population ballooned from 3,936 in 1970 to 9,027 by 1990, its black population decreased from 1 to 0. Not until 2000, when three African American families finally ventured in, did Mountain Home cease being a sundown town. Long before that, the sense that integration was unavoidable played a major role in desegregating sundown suburbs across most of the South.

75. For a brief period after World War II, three other suburbs in Mississippi tried to emulate northern sundown suburbs and became almost all-white: Southaven, a suburb of Memphis, East Tupelo, a former suburb of Tupelo, and D'Iberville, on the Gulf Coast. Each went through a brief period—no more than twenty years—as a sundown suburb, but none is sundown any longer.

76. Gordon D. Morgan, "Black Hillbillies of the Arkansas Ozarks," Department of Sociology, University of Arkansas, Fayetteville, 1973, 155–59.

77. Izard County had actually grown whiter. In 1960, it had 54 African Americans, about evenly divided between males and females, while in 2000 it had 191—but the increase was illusory. The 191 African Americans included just 12 females and 179 males; a state prison accounts for almost all of them.

78. White male resident, Sheridan, about 65 years of age, Grant County Museum, 10/2001.

79. William Booth, "Booming California Suburbs Highly Diverse, Data Show," *Washington Post,* 8/18/2002; cf. Juan O. Sandoval, Hans P. Johnson, and Sonya M. Tafoya, "Who's Your Neighbor," *California Counts* 4, 1 (2002): 5.

80. Camille Zubrinsky Charles, talk, OPEN meeting, Philadelphia, 12/2000.

81. Remember, the higher the D, the greater the segregation, with 100 being complete apartheid.

82. William A. V. Clark, "Residential Segregation Trends," in Abigail Thernstrom and Stephan Thernstrom, eds., *Beyond the Color Line* (Stanford: Hoover Institution, 2002), 86, hoover.stanford.edu/publications/books/fulltext/colorline/83.pdf, 2/2003.

83. Tillamook did have 28 African American residents in 1970, however. I have not studied race relations in Tillamook after 1970.

84. Eric Wetterling, "An Interview with Ernie de la Bretonne," 5/4/1997, "The Tri-Cities," users.owt.com/rpeto/wet/tri-cities.html, 10/2002.

85. The number of confirmed sundown towns later rose to nearly 200.

86. Joseph Lyford, *The Talk in Vandalia* (Santa Barbara: Center for the Study of Democratic Institutions, 1962), 34; professor from Vandalia, 10/2002.

87. Former Granite City resident, e-mail, 10/1999; Manchester College administrator, 11/1997.

88. Stephanie Simon, "Segregation Still Strong in North," *Los Angeles Times,* 1/19/2003, reprinted in *Holland* (MI) *Sentinel,* 3/30/2003, hollandsentinel.com, 4/2003; Daniel P. Henley Jr., "Study Says Suburbs Violate Agreement on Fair Housing," *Milwaukee Journal,* 7/11/1990.

89. One of the 34, Smith Valley, listed as unincorporated in 1970, was no longer a census town.

90. Betty Canright, e-mail, 1/2003; John Gehm, *Bringing It Home* (Chicago: Chicago Review Press, 1984); David Mitchell, "A Struggled Balance of Hope and Fear," *Valparaiso Times,* 6/29/2003.

91. Gordon Trowbridge and Oralandar Brand-Williams, "The Past: A Policy of Exclusion," *Detroit News,* 1/14/2002, at mumford1.dyndns.org/cen2000/othersay/detroitnews/Stories/Blacks . . . , 7/2003.

92. Helen Harrelson, 10/2002.

93. D has no utility *within* a sundown town or suburb, because such towns are monoracial.

94. Taeuber, "Research Issues Concerning Trends in Residential Segregation," 6; Farley and Frey, "Changes in the Segregation of Whites from Blacks During the 1980s," 30.

95. Gary Orfield, *Public School Desegregation in the U.S., 1968–1980* (Washington, DC: Joint Center for Political Studies, 1983), 4; Simon, "Segregation Still Strong in North"; Mendell, "Midwest Housing Divide Is Still Race"; Kathryn P. Nelson, *Recent Suburbanization of Blacks* (Washington, DC: HUD Office of Economic Affairs, 1979), 13; John Logan, "Ethnic Diversity Grows, Neighborhood Integration Lags Behind," Lewis Mumford Center, 12/18/2001, 7, mumford1.dyndns.org/cen2000/WholePop/WPreport/page1.html, 1/2003.

96. Ellen defines "integrated"—which I think she uses as a synonym for "racially mixed"—as 10 to 50% black. This can be problematic for cities such as Washington, D.C., or Jackson, Mississippi, both more than 60% black, or Willingboro, New Jersey, two-thirds black, for in such jurisdictions, neighborhoods that mimic the city appear "segregated." Ironically, only if some neighborhoods are overwhelmingly black will others be white enough to appear "integrated." To be sure, these cities' metropolitan areas are much less than 50% black, and that is the appropriate overall area to analyze. Nevertheless, since I live in a stably integrated 80% black neighborhood, I would be happier if Ellen had widened her definition to include it.

97. Patti Becker, 7/2004; Cynthia Mills Richter, "Integrating the Suburban Dream: Shaker Heights, Ohio," Ph.D. dissertation, University of Minnesota, 1999, 110; Ingrid Gould Ellen, *Sharing America's Neighborhoods* (Cambridge: Harvard University Press, 2000), 1.

98. Chevy Chase, Chevy Chase Village, Section Three, and Section Five. Note that not all nineteen were necessarily black.

99. Kenilworth native, e-mail, 12/2002; Ellen, *Sharing America's Neighborhoods,* 21; Kenilworth realtor, 10/2002.

100. America's seven FDR towns, all sundown from the start, exemplify this unevenness. Greenbelt, Maryland, is now 41% black, while Greenhills, Ohio, is 2.6% black. Richland, Washington, the atomic town, allowed African Americans to live within its city limits in the 1950s; in 1971 it hired a black assistant city manager; and by 2000 it was 1.4% black. Greendale, Wisconsin, is just 0.3% black but does have fifteen different African American households. Boulder City, Nevada (the Hoover Dam town) had eight black households by 1998, but Norris, Tennessee (the TVA town) may still be sundown: in 2000 it had exactly one black couple and a black child. Arthurdale, West Virginia, is very small; in 2000 it had at most two male African American individuals. On Richland, see Bob Carlson, post to The Sandbox #102 (11/1/2000), the.sandbox.tripod.com/BOXarchives/BOX2000-05.htm, 7/2003.

101. Logan quoted in Simon, "Segregation Still Strong in North."

102. John C. Boger, "Toward Ending Residential Segregation: A Fair Share Proposal for the Next Reconstruction," *North Carolina Law Review* 71 (1993): 1583; Nancy Denton, "Are African Americans Still Hypersegregated?" in Robert D. Bullard, et al., eds., *Residential Apartheid* (Los Angeles: UCLA Center for Afro-American Studies, 1994), 62.

103. In this sense, our thinking has not yet returned to the understanding that Republicans had reached when they passed the Civil Rights Amendments around 1868: that slavery and postslavery discrimination, not "the Negro," was the problem.

104. Jargowsky, "Concentration of Poverty Declines in the 1990s," 1.

105. Jackson Preparatory Academy, jacksonprep.edu, 5/2003.

106. Census Bureau statement on Forsyth County at Chamber of Commerce web site, forsythchamber.org/800/community/history.php, 1/2004.

107. Estimates of the proportion of the wealth owned by given proportions of the population differ notoriously from country to country, depending on who did them, using what methodology.

108. Anthony Faiola, "Brazil's Elites Fly Above Their Fears." For U.S. figure, see, inter alia, Donald L. Barlett and James B. Steele, *America: Who Stole the Dream?* (Kansas City: Andrews and McMeel, 1996), 4–5, 8; Foundation for the Mid South, "The Mid South IDA Initiative, Request for Proposals," fndmidsouth.org/PDFs/Grant_Guidelines.pdf, 7/2003, 2; Social Security Network, "Social Security Testimony: Balanced Capitalism," socsec.org/opinions/testimony/leone_capitalism.htm, 7/2003; Institute for Washington's Future, "Precarious Prosperity: Washington's Economy in 1999," forwashington.org/pub/reports/pp-2.php, 2, 7/2003. Interestingly, income is distributed more equally in the United States, where the highest 10% of earners gets 30.5% of the income; in Brazil they get 46.7%. Jon Jeter, "New Generations Face Old Struggles in Brazil," *Washington Post,* 11/13/2003.

109. This is similar to the 80% that Ingrid Ellen calculated.

110. Samantha Friedman, 5/2002.

111. See John Logan, "Choosing Segregation," Lewis Mumford Center, 3/2002, mumford1.dyndns.org/cen2000/SchoolPop/SPReport/page1.html, 1/2003.

CHAPTER 15: THE REMEDY

1. Ending sundown towns and suburbs will not cure all our nation's racial problems; other approaches, such as working to improve minority neighborhoods and schools, make sense too. See, inter alia, Sheryll Cashin's suggestions in the last chapter of *The Failures of Integration* (New York: Public Affairs, 2004).

2. Moreover, almost 30% of their respondents, having been told that neighborhoods are segregated, did *not* agree that this was "a bad thing."

3. Pew Research Center for the People and the Press, people-press.org/cen01rpt.htm, 4/2003; David Herr, e-mail to H-South, 11/2002.

4. Anne B. Shlay, review of Alice O'Connor, Chris Tilly, and Lawrence Bobo, eds., *Urban Inequality,* in *Contemporary Sociology* 31, 5 (2002): 510; *Meredith v. Fair,* 305 F.2d, 344–45.

5. For an example of work on race relations produced by middle-school students, see Bernadette Anand et al., *Keeping the Struggle Alive: Studying Desegregation in Our Town* (New York: Teachers College Press, 2002).

6. I hope this book spawns a genre of "sundown studies," because much remains to be investigated. My web site, uvm.edu/~jloewen/sundown, has a page for posting your findings. It also suggests topics for further research, including studies of the moment-by-moment process by which a town went sundown, the contagion by which many did at once, why white supremacists locate in sundown towns and whether their expectations of support are met, communities that refused to go all-white, what prompted towns to relent, and how they desegregated successfully.

7. States might usefully require an honest historical marker in every sundown town within its borders, telling the origin of its policy, summarizing its population by race over time, and relating incidents that kept it all-white. States might also require towns to include a unit in a middle- or high school history course about their history, including their racial history. Since no black citizens exist to prompt such steps in sundown towns, such a nudge from outside might be in order.

8. Robby Heason, *Trouble Behind* (Cicada Films, 1990).

9. Jacqueline Froelich, "A City Confronts Its Ghosts," *Arkansas Democrat-Gazette,* 4/27/2003.

10. Pinckneyville resident and cemetery worker, 9/2002.

11. Virginia Yarwood with Clayton E. Cramer, *Depression Life: A Memoir of Growing Up in Texas* (manuscript in possession of Cramer, 2002), 6.

12. Murray Bishoff, 9/2002; Bishoff, "The Lynching That Changed Southwest Missouri," part 2, *Monett* (MO) *Times,* 8/15/1991; "The Eldorado, Illinois Affair," *Indianapolis Freeman,* 7/19/1902; "Race War in Illinois," *New York Times,* 6/17/1902; Gordon D. Morgan, "Black Hillbillies of the Arkansas Ozarks," Department of Sociology, University of Arkansas, Fayetteville, 1973, ii, 10.

13. Cleveland Bowen quoted in Morris S. Thompson, "Marchers Descend on County that Progress Forgot," *Washington Post,* 1/24/1987.

14. Roberta Senechal, *The Sociogenesis of a Race Riot* (Urbana: University of Illinois Press, 1990), 182; Sucheng Chan, *Asian Americans* (New York: Simon & Schuster/Twayne, 1991), 50; "N.C. to Aid Sterilization Victims," *Washington Post,* 9/29/2003; Donald E. Skinner, "UUs Lead as Riot Survivors Receive Payments in Tulsa," *UUWorld,* 5/2002, 45; cf. Alfred L. Brophy, *Resurrecting the Dreamland* (New York: Oxford University Press, 2002); Scott Gold, "Judge Weighs Suit on Tulsa's '21 Riot," *L.A. Times,* 2/14/2004, latimes.com/news/nationworld/nation/la-na-riot14feb14,1,3332317.sto ry, 2/2004.

15. Winifred M. Henson, "History of Franklin County, Illinois," M.A. thesis, Colorado State College of Education, 1942, 144; *Marion Daily Republican,* 8/13/1920, 1.

16. Zimmermann quoted in Laurinda Joenks, "Roughness of Citizens Blamed on Lean Times," *Springdale* (AR) *Morning News,* 5/7/2000.

17. *Metro. Hous. Dev. Corp. v. Arlington Hts.,* 558 F.2d 1283 (7th Cir. 1977), *cert. denied,* 434 U.S. 1025 (1978). Cf. *Huntington NAACP v. Huntington,* 844 F.2d 926, 938 (2d Cir.), *aff'd,* 488 U.S. 15 (1988) (per curiam).

18. State courts are also important because the present makeup of the Supreme Court discourages some lawyers from seeking redress there. Ironically, the Fourteenth Amendment to our national constitution, guaranteeing "equal protection" without regard to race, is now used by whites to blunt attempts to redress past discrimination against nonwhites, so state courts may be more hospitable than the Supreme Court to anti-discrimination cases.

19. Of course, Sunnyvale did not zone its residential areas whites-only. But it did engage in a pattern of acts—requiring one-acre (or more) lots throughout the entire town, banning apartments, and refusing to cooperate with nearby towns in accepting government-assisted Section 8 renters—that the court found had "a discriminatory effect on African Americans *and* are motivated by a discriminatory purpose." In the 1990 census, the most recent when the case was decided, Sunnyvale had 16 African Americans among its 2,228 residents, including four households with black householders, so it did not quite qualify as a sundown suburb by my definition, but the court found that "the statistics speak for themselves." 109 F.Supp.2d 533–34.

20. Kenneth T. Jackson, *Crabgrass Frontier* (New York: Oxford University Press, 1985), 301; *South Burlington County NAACP v. Township of Mount Laurel,* 336 A.2d 713 (NJ 1975), "Mount Laurel I"; same, 92 NJ 158, 456 A.2d 390 (1983), "Mount Laurel II"; cf. Osborne Reynolds Jr., *Handbook of Local Government Law* (St. Paul: West, 1982), 371–74, David Kirp, John Dwyer, and Larry Rosenthal, *Our Town* (New Brunswick: Rutgers University Press, 1995), 9, and Lizabeth Cohen, *A Consumers' Republic* (New York: Knopf, 2003), 236–37; *Dews v Bluffdale,* 109 F. Supp. 2d 526; cf. "Litigation and Grassroots Advocacy to Promote Affordable Housing," National Low Income Housing Coalition: The NIMBY Report, 11/2000; nlihc.org, 2/2003; 109 F.Supp.2d 526; cf. "Fiscal Zoning Struck Down in Texas," NIMBY Report, 12/2000, nlihc.org, 2/2003, and Westlaw KeyCite History.

21. Jack Balkin, "Is the 'Brown' Decision Fading to Irrelevance?" *Chronicle of Higher Education,* 11/9/2001, B12.

22. Potter Stewart, concurring opinion, *Milliken I,* 1974, 756, 418 U.S. 717, 94 S.Ct. 3112, 41 L.Ed.2d 1069, n.2.

23. Evidence of racial residential exclusion committed or condoned by suburban governments was in the trial transcript, but the appeals court didn't consider it because the court found that evidence of school segregation policies sufficient to decide the case in favor of the plaintiffs. The Supreme Court reversed that finding but then failed to consider the trial court's evidence on residential exclusion!

24. Reynolds Farley, Sheldon Danziger, and Harry J. Holzer, *Detroit Divided* (New York: Russell Sage, 2000), 40–41.

25. The next sentence continues, "Specifically, it must be shown that racially discriminatory acts of the state or local school districts . . . have been a substantial cause of interdistrict segregation." Surely showing racially discriminatory acts by city governments—facilitated by state laws empowering exclusionary zoning and the like—should suffice. Furthermore, school districts probably participated in keeping out minorities by refusing to hire black teachers and other actions.

26. *Milliken v. Bradley,* 418 U.S. 717, 745 (1974).

27. Requiring such residence afterward is perfectly acceptable.

28. In 1990, for example, Villa Grove, IL, still sounded its siren at 6 PM every evening to warn African Americans to get out of town before dark and had not a single African American resident. Nevertheless, Villa Grove passed an elaborate series of ordinances mandating "Fair Housing": "It is hereby declared to be the policy of the city . . . to assure equal opportunity to all persons to live in decent housing facilities regardless of race, color . . ." These ordinances hardly represented a sea change of public policy; they turn out to be boilerplate paragraphs outlawing discrimination, identical to language passed by Oakland, Illinois—another confirmed sundown town that in 1990 had no African American residents—and probably many other Illinois towns seeking continued federal subsidies for their housing programs.

29. Villa Grove City Council, Ordinance 092490, Section 97.01, Declaration of Policy.

30. Fayetteville also teaches that the United States should pursue policies that decrease the income inequalities and narrow the wealth gap between blacks and whites. Black family income there is higher as a percentage of white family income than in any other North Carolina city, owing to the military. I write as President George W. Bush is asking Congress to repeal the inheritance tax. I do not understand how we can make any pretense to equal opportunity when children of the rich can inherit, untaxed, thousands of times as much as children of the middle class, let alone children of the poor. Since about 1980, the federal government has

taken many steps to increase the wealth gap between poor and rich and between blacks and whites. They have worked; the gap has grown. We need to shrink it.

31. Catherine Lutz, *Homefront* (Boston: Beacon Press, 2001), 110, 125, 129; C. M. Waynick et al., *North Carolina and the Negro* (Raleigh: North Carolina Mayors' Cooperating Commission, 1964), 114–15; Andrew H. Myers, "Black, White, and Olive Drab," Ph.D. dissertation, University of Virginia, Charlottesville, 1998, 424–25; Darrell Fears and Claudia Deane, "Biracial Couples Report Tolerance," *Washington Post,* 7/5/2001.

32. The Minneapolis–St. Paul metropolitan area did this, and not just for school finances but for overall tax dollars. According to Myron Orfield, author of *American Metropolitics,* it then realized an unanticipated benefit: instead of pitting city legislators against suburban legislators against those from outer suburbs, delegates to the state from the metropolitan area now found themselves more unified, even across parties, and were able to develop clout to get assistance for their area from state government. Fiscal equalizing also mitigates some of the shockingly unequal ways we treat children based upon where they happen to live. See Myron Orfield, talk at OPEN meeting, Philadelphia, 12/2000, and his web site, metrore search.org; cf. Jonathan Kozol, *Savage Inequalities* (New York: Crown, 1991).

33. Lizabeth Cohen, *A Consumers' Republic* (New York: Knopf, 2003), 249.

34. Gary Orfield, OPEN, 12/2000; Orfield, "Residential Segregation: What Are the Causes?" *Journal of Negro Education* 66, 3 (1997): 208; Brigid Schulte and Dan Keating, "Choosing Route to Ending Gap Rife with Risk," *Washington Post,* 9/3/2001.

35. See James Loewen, "Presentation," "Discussion," and "A Sociological View of Aptitude Tests," in Eileen Rudert, ed., *The Validity of Testing in Education and Employment* (Washington, DC: U.S. Commission on Civil Rights, 1993), 41–45, 58–62, 73–91; cf. "Analysis" in the same volume, 161; Loewen, Phyllis Rosser, and John Katzman, "Gender Bias on SAT Items," American Educational Research Association, 4/1988, ERIC ED294915.

36. Associated Press story, 12/1/2000, reprinted in "Worldview," *Stay Free!* 18 (n.d.), 8.

37. According to a South Orange/Maplewood, New Jersey, school administrator, disaggregating scores by race persuaded some of his white parents that their kids would not suffer from attending a diverse high school. Only then would they move in.

   Disaggregating scores by race and perhaps class is consistent with the No Child Left Behind Act. The disparities may lead some parents to pressure the school system to develop more effective educational programs for their children. Educators may analyze the tests to see if they accurately measure what students are learning. If some racists or elitists use the results to demean children of color or children of poverty, well, probably they were already doing so.

38. Gary Orfield, OPEN, 12/2000; Orfield, "Residential Segregation," 208; Schulte and Keating, "Choosing Route to Ending Gap Rife with Risk"; Associated Press story, 12/1/2000, reprinted in "Worldview," *Stay Free!* 18 (n.d.), 8.

39. The statistical process used to vet SAT items makes it unlikely that any item disproportionately favorable to African Americans or poor Americans will ever appear on an SAT; it follows that the more students know about suburban white culture, the higher their SAT score is likely to be. Coaching and test-wiseness also favor those in elite sundown suburbs compared to students in multiclass interracial cities.

40. See Loewen, "Preliminary Conclusions on Admissions of Racial/Ethnic Groups at the University of California Berkeley," typescript, Washington, DC, 2000.

41. Michael Danielson, *The Politics of Exclusion* (New York: Columbia University Press, 1976),

146; Earl Woodard as paraphrased by Jeff Swiatek, "Martinsville Tired of Living with Image of Racism, Bigotry," *Indianapolis Star*, 6/25/1989.

42. On their way out of town, nonblacks might sell or rent their home to a black family, thus fixing sundown towns all by themselves. As they leave, they might arm that family with introductions to their best friends, a church, and other organizations that will provide sources of strength as they perform the lonely, even risky work of opening a sundown town for use by all. Organizational allies include the Fund for an Open Society in Philadelphia (opensoc .org, 215-482-OPEN) and the National Fair Housing Alliance, in Washington, DC (nation alfairhousing.org, 202-898-1661).

43. Since 1996, I have lived in a neighborhood in Washington, D.C., that is more than 80% African American. For seven years I lived in majority-black neighborhoods in Tougaloo and Jackson, Mississippi. In all three places I have enjoyed my neighbors and have never been made to feel out of place.

44. Karyn Lacy, "A Part of the Neighborhood," *International Journal of Sociology and Social Policy* 22 (2002): 59–60.

45. Farley, Danziger, and Holzer, *Detroit Divided*, 194.

46. John Gehm, *Bringing It Home* (Chicago: Chicago Review Press, 1984); David Mitchell, "A Struggled Balance of Hope and Fear," *Valparaiso Times*, 6/29/2003.

47. Admittedly, these counties are also farther from Atlanta.

48. Oprah Winfrey, "Vintage Oprah: Racial Tension in Georgia," Harpo Productions, Chicago, 2001 (1987), 13.

49. *Trafficante v. Met Life et al.*, 409 U.S. 205 (1972).

50. Dorothy K. Newman et al., *Protest, Politics, and Prosperity* (New York: Pantheon, 1978), 139; Peoria native, 2/2001.

51. Myrlie B. Evers with William Peters, *For Us, the Living* (Garden City, NY: Doubleday, 1967), 30–31.

52. I think this hanging was apocryphal, at least at so late a date, but the story intimidates anyway. Bill Savage notes via Robert Griswold, e-mail, 6/2002; George Henderson, *Our Souls to Keep* (Yarmouth, ME: Intercultural Press, 1999), 210; Melissa Merideth, "Henderson Sparked Civil Rights Movement at OU," *Oklahoma Daily Online*, 2/18/2002, oudaily .com/vnews/display.v/ART/2002/02/18/3d3c2e102b065?in_archive=1, 6/2003; Bill Savage, 2/26/2004.

53. Daisy Myers, 1957 journal rewritten in 1960 as manuscript, "Sticks and Stones," excerpted as sign in exhibit on Levittown, Pennsylvania State Museum, Harrisburg, 9/2002.

54. Attorney quoted in Andrew Wiese, *Places of Their Own* (Chicago: University of Chicago Press, 2004), 160; James Hecht, *Because It Is Right* (Boston: Little, Brown, 1970), 199, 209–10.

55. Victor Ward, 6/2002.

56. J. D. Mullane, "Exhibit Recalls Clashes in Summer of 1957," *Bucks County Courier Times*, 7/9/2002, phillyburbs.com/couriertimes/levittown50th/0103daisy.htm, 7/2002.

57. Zane Miller, *Suburb* (Knoxville: University of Tennessee Press, 1981), 145, 219.

58. Herbert Gans, *The Levittowners* (New York: Pantheon, 1967), 428; Newman, *Protest, Politics, and Prosperity*, 140; cf. Cynthia Mills Richter, "Integrating the Suburban Dream: Shaker Heights, Ohio," Ph.D. dissertation, University of Minnesota, 1999, 102.

59. Jackson, *Crabgrass Frontier*, 241; Ingrid Gould Ellen, *Sharing America's Neighborhoods* (Cambridge: Harvard University Press, 2000), 162–63; Karen Beck Pooley, "The Other Levittown: Race and Place in Willingboro, New Jersey," The Next American City web site,

americancity.org/Archives/Issue2/pooley_issue2.html, 3/2004; *Linmark Associates v. Willingboro*, 431 U.S. 85 (1977).

60. What defines a blatant disparity under the Residents' Rights Act? I suggest that any town less than one-tenth as black as its state—or any suburb less than one-tenth as black as its metropolitan area—falls under suspicion. (To a degree, this rewards widespread sundown areas. The Ozark Plateau, for example, is so large that it makes up a considerable part of the total populations of Missouri and Arkansas. Thus its whiteness pulls down the statewide proportion of African Americans, especially in Arkansas, making the trigger—one-tenth of that proportion—artificially low. This may be a serious problem in Idaho if it is true, as some claim, that the entire state has been inhospitable to African Americans.) Of course, only blacks in households with an African American householder will count, to avoid including prisoners, maids, live-in caregivers, etc. (The appropriate adjustment would also be made to total population: number in households.) In 2000, Illinois was 15.4% black, so to avoid qualifying, towns must be 1.54% black. In Indiana, the benchmark is 0.87% black.

Obviously all towns having no African Americans at all will immediately qualify, such as Elwood, Indiana, still reportedly off-limits to blacks as of 2002. So will our old favorite Anna, having no more than two people in families with a black householder in 2000. Since their histories immediately confirm them as sundown towns, after two complaints Elwood and Anna will immediately face sanctions. In 2000, Arcola, Illinois, had one qualifying household with 3 people in it among 2,652 residents, or 0.1%. That was far less than the required 1.54%, so Arcola qualifies. Former sundown town Valparaiso, Indiana, on the other hand, now being about 1.6% black, is exempt.

The calculation is similar within metropolitan areas. The Detroit primary metropolitan area was 23.4% black in 2000. Any jurisdiction within that area that was less than one-tenth as black, or less than 2.34% black, will trigger sanctions—if it has been confirmed as having a sundown past—once two complaints have been received. Grosse Pointe's point system and other details of its past confirm the five Grosse Pointe jurisdictions as sundown towns. Statistically, Grosse Pointe itself, 0.8% black in 2000, qualifies, as does Grosse Pointe Farms, 0.6%, Grosse Pointe Shores, 0.6%, and Grosse Pointe Woods, 0.6% black; Grosse Pointe Park, a whopping 2.95% black, is exempt. Many other Detroit suburbs also qualify, such as Grosse Ile at less than 0.4% black, Dearborn at 1.3%, and our old friend Wyandotte, 0.5%, each of which "boasts" a sundown past.

61. I suggest two complaints, rather than the ten required under the Voting Rights Act, because to seek housing with enough tenacity to be rebuffed requires more time and energy than to try to register to vote. Moreover, the reputation set in place by sundown towns' past policies is their first line of defense, chilling many black would-be newcomers before they even try. Finally, the main trigger for the Residents' Rights Act, unlike the Voting Rights Act—in addition to the statistical disparities required by both acts—is the finding of a sundown past.

62. Congress can act under the authority granted by Section 5 of the Fourteenth Amendment. To ensure that the Supreme Court will find it constitutional, Congress needs to show a widespread pattern of intentional past actions by local governments across the United States to keep out African Americans. This book makes such a showing; readers can contribute additional evidence of sundown towns at my web site, uvm.edu/~jloewen/sundown. States can (and should) pass their own versions, tailored to their local conditions, without having to worry quite so much about a judicial challenge.

63. An official at the Museum of America's Freedom Trains said, "I don't know that there was

ever any talk of the Freedom Train stopping in Glendale," but the museum staff hasn't researched the matter, so far as I can tell. Museum official, e-mail, 7/2003.

64. Richard Sommer and Glenn Forley, "The Democratic Monument," paper given at "Commemoration and the City," Savannah, GA, 2/2002; Bob Johnson, e-mail, 1/2003.

65. She should apologize, because she knows full well how Benton has maintained its "racial makeup." Long notorious for not letting African Americans stay after dark, Benton flirted in 1923 with the idea of barring them even during the day. Its citizens have never stopped their tradition of racist behavior. In the mid-1980s, teenage boys hurled eggs and epithets at African Americans driving through Benton after dark. In 1992, students ostracized the only African American girl in Benton High School after she accepted a social invitation from a white boy. In the late 1990s, Benton students put graffiti on the bus from visiting Carbondale High School, a nearby interracial school, according to a 2000 Carbondale graduate, and some Benton basketball players shouted "nigger" at Carbondale's African American players. Residents throughout Franklin and Williamson counties report repeated KKK rallies and cross burnings in Benton within the last five years. In about 1998, according to a Benton High School history teacher, whites burned a cross on the lawn of an elderly Benton resident merely because he had a black physical therapist from another town work on him in his home. Among Benton's 6,880 residents in 2000, the census found only 2 African Americans in a household with a black householder. (It did find 20 blacks, 17 of whom were males, mostly 18–44, undoubtedly temporary residents connected with some institution. Another 13 people listed two races, white and black. Indeed, all of Franklin County, of which Benton is the seat, had just 59 African Americans among nearly 40,000 residents, about 0.1%, and half of those did not live in households with an African American householder.) In 2001 and 2002, several Benton residents said they thought Benton had no black families. Benton shows no indication—including its mayor's posture—that it is over being a sundown town. African American from Colp, 1/2004; undergraduate from Carbondale, University of Illinois, 10/2000; Benton teacher, 9/2002.

66. "Judge Wants Courthouse Built in More Diverse Community," *Coles County Daily Times Courier*, 10/11/2002.

67. Monticello attorney, 2002; Richard Stewart, "Desegregation at Public Housing Ripped by Audit," *Houston Chronicle*, 7/11/1997; Janet Heimlich and Bob Edwards, "Housing Discrimination in Texas," *Federal Document Clearing House*, 7/10/1997, morning edition.

68. Florence Roisman suggested this remedy to me, based on John C. Boger, "Toward Ending Residential Segregation: A Fair Share Proposal for the Next Reconstruction," *North Carolina Law Review* 71 (1993): 1608–14. Boger's proposal is detailed and nuanced; he also suggests taxing the interest on municipal bonds issued by governments found in violation.

69. This is already changing, however, as noted below regarding such suburbs as Oak Park, Illinois.

70. The sanction ignores renters, but renters own no housing, so they have not participated in refusing to sell or rent to African Americans. It also seems to omit families who have no mortgages, hence pay no mortgage interest, but it does actually sanction them by making their homes less attractive to would-be buyers, thus decreasing their resale value.

71. Perhaps penologists may have in mind a "social Alcatraz" theory—like the frigid waters and archetypal sharks around Alcatraz (the sharks are not man-eating, it turns out), the area surrounding these prisons is presumably hostile to black escapees. More likely, the political clout of sundown legislators explains the placement of these prisons in their districts. Such locations may amount to cruel and unusual punishment. In sundown towns, African Amer-

ican prisoners and juveniles have few role models who look like them among guards and administrators. They have little chance to see a black psychologist or medical doctor, learn from a black teacher, meet with a black prison volunteer, or talk with a black college student intern, because there are no African Americans in the community. Family members and friends live miles away, making it hard for prisoners to maintain ties to the outside world. Visitors who do make the trip usually take care to be out of town by nightfall. In sum, locating prisons in sundown towns ensures that prisoners, many of whom are people of color, will be guarded, cared for when ill, counseled, and "rehabilitated" by people who live in towns that prevent African Americans from living within their corporate limits. This is hardly good penology. It also invites sundown town residents to grow more racist. A resident of Vienna described the discourse in that southern Illinois town after Vienna got its prison around 1970: "Since that time, you get constant remarks about black people and how bad they are. Of course, [prisoners] are the only black people they know" (Vienna resident, 2/2004).

72. Susan Luke, "Barbie and Ken, and All Things Presidential," *Washington Post,* 8/10/2003; Mary Otto, "Grasping for a Thread of Hope," *Washington Post,* 9/7/2004.

73. Farley, Danziger, and Holzer, *Detroit Divided,* 180.

74. Don DeMarco, talk at OPEN Conference, Philadelphia, 11/2000; Ted Hipple, e-mail, 10/24/2001; Carole Goodwin, *The Oak Park Strategy* (Chicago: University of Chicago Press, 1979), 1, 53; CNN/*Money* Fiserv CSW report, money.cnn.com, 7/2003.

75. Whites moved into majority-black census tracts on Capitol Hill, in Washington, D.C., and made them majority-white. Between 1960 and 1970, Kirkwood, a neighborhood in Atlanta, went from being 91% white to 97% black. Then in the 1990s, some whites returned, making Kirkwood 14% white by 2000.

76. Lesley Reid and Robert Adelman, "The Double-Edged Sword of Gentrification in Atlanta," *ASA Footnotes* 31, 4 (2003): 8; Mark Knight quoted in Nurith C. Aizenman, "Diversity Puts Vitality into Aging Mt. Rainier," *Washington Post,* 12/30/2003, washingtonpost.com, 1/2004.

77. D'Vera Cohn, "Integrated People, Integrated Places," *Washington Post* 7/29/2002; librarian, Decatur, 10/2002.

78. Baltimore woman quoted in J. W. Dees Jr. and J. S. Hadley, *Jim Crow* (Westport, CT: Negro Universities Press, 1970 [1951]), 159; Eunice and George Grier, "Discrimination in Housing" (New York: Anti-Defamation League of B'nai B'rith, 1960), 34, citing generally Morton Deutsch and Mary Evans Collins, *Interracial Housing* (Minneapolis: University of Minnesota Press, 1951).

79. Barnett quoted in Richter, "Integrating the Suburban Dream: Shaker Heights, Ohio," 48.

80. I must admit that this racial liberalism may also result from the flight of more racist whites from these neighborhoods.

81. Gary Orfield, talk at OPEN, Philadelphia, 12/2000; Carolyn Adams et al., *Philadelphia: Neighborhoods, Division, and Conflict* (Philadelphia: Temple University Press, 1991), 24.

82. Three Dog Night, "Black and White," 1972; the "sundown policies" quatrain is mine, with apologies.

APPENDIX A

1. Jack Blocker Jr., "Contours of African-American Migration in Ohio, 1850–1930" (Cambridge: British Society for Population Studies, 1998), tables 3, 9.

2. Jack Blocker Jr., "Choice and Circumstance," paper presented at Organization of American

Historians meeting 4/1999, 29, 34–35. He did not use the term "Great Retreat." Cf. his "Contours of African-American Migration in Ohio, 1850–1930," 7; "Patterns of African-American Migration in Illinois, 1860–1920" (Edwardsville, IL: Conference on African Americans in Illinois History, 1998), and "Opportunity, Community, and Violence in the Shaping of Indiana's African-American Migration, 1860–1930" (Minneapolis: Conference on Race, Ethnicity, and Migration, 2000).

PORTFOLIO

All notes for this section refer to image numbers.

2. Lynwood Carranco, "Chinese Expulsion from Humboldt County," in Roger Daniels, ed., *Anti-Chinese Violence in North America* (New York: Arno Press, 1978), 336; Joseph F. Endert, "Chinese," *Bulletin of the Del Norte County Historical Society* (3/1978 [1965]), 5–6; "DN Pioneers Load Sons of Flowery Kingdom on Boats," *Del Norte Triplicate* Bicentennial Edition, 1976; Jean Pfaelzer, talk (Washington, D.C.: American Studies Association., 2001); Keith Easthouse, "The Chinese Expulsion: Looking Back on a Dark Episode," *North Coast Journal Weekly*, 2/27/2003, northcoastjournal.com/022703/cover0227.html, 2/2004.

4. "Negroes Killed or Driven Away, *Chicago Tribune*, 8/21/1901; Murray Bishoff, 9/2002.

6. Donald F. Tingley, *The Structuring of a State: The History of Illinois, 1899 to 1928* (Urbana: University of Illinois Press, 1980), 291–92.

7. These towns and counties are listed on my website, uvm.edu/~jloewen/sundown.

9. Jimmy Allen, e-mail, 10/2002; Margaret Alexander Alam, e-mail, 11/04/2003; *Villa Grove News*, 7/4/1976; seven Villa Grove residents.

11. Scott Ellsworth, *Death in a Promised Land* (Baton Rouge: Louisiana University Press, 1982); Alfred L. Brophy, *Reconstructing the Dreamland: The Tulsa Race Riot of 1921* (New York: Oxford University Press, 2002); cf. William F. Pinar, *The Gender of Racial Politics and Violence in America* (New York: Peter Lang, 2001), 1174; Kelly Kurt, "After 75 Years, Tulsa Heals," Burlington *Free Press*, 6/2/96; James Allen, et al., *Without Sanctuary* (Santa Fe: Twin Palms, 2000), #38, 179–80; W. L. Payne, "Okemah's Night of Terror," in Hazel Ruby McMahan, ed., *Stories of Early Oklahoma,* on Rootsweb, rootsweb.com/~okokfusk/cities.htm, 5/2003.

13. "Don't Let The Sun Set On You Here, Understand?" *Chicago Defender*, 2/11/1922; "Norman Mob After Singie Smith Jazz," Norman, OK, 2/5/1922, in *Oklahoma City Black Dispatch*, 2/9/1922; "White Men Shoot Up Church Excursioners," *Pittsburgh Courier*, 8/17/1940.

15. Lin Shi Khan and Tony Perez, *Scottsboro, Alabama: A Story in Linoleum Cuts* (New York: New York University Press, 2001 [1935]), 49; "Scottsboro Trial Moved Fifty Miles," *New York Times*, 3/8/1933.

16. Kurt Vonnegut Jr., *Breakfast of Champions,* (New York: Delacorte, 1973), 245–46; Vonnegut, 3/2005.

18. R. Bruce Shepard, *Deemed Unsuitable* (Toronto: Umbrella Press, 1997), 3.

20. *Parade of Progress: Hamilton County, 1858–1958* (Hamilton: *Hamilton Herald-News*, 1958), unpaginated; Charles Titus, 6/2000; Carolyn Stephens, e-mail, 2/2001.

24. David M. P. Freund, *Making It Home* (Ann Arbor: Univeristy of Michigan Ph.D., 1999), 515; Rick Baker, "Pekin Students Veto 'Chinks' Name Change," 11/28/1974 clipping in

Pekin library, name of newspaper omitted; Jane White, Pekin High School, 1950, post at Classmates.com, 6/1/2000.

28. "The Real Polk County" (Mena: no publication indicated, 1/9?/1980), 16.

30. "A Northern City 'Sitting on Lid' of Racial Trouble," *US News & World Report,* 5/11/1956, 38–40; Denise Thomas, 10/2003.

31. Bill Griffith, "Zippy the Pinhead," *Washington Post,* 6/24/2002

32. Camille DeRose, *The Camille DeRose Story* (Chicago: Erle Press, 1953), 171.

33. Kenneth T. Jackson, *Crabgrass Frontier* (New York: Oxford University Press, 1985), 278; Reginald Pickins quoted in Kurth, "Exclusivity Tax," *Detroit News,* 2/21/2001, detnews.com/2001/homepage/0102/21/index.htm.

34. Edgar Rice Burroughs, "Tarzan," 12/2/1934, in Robert C. Harvey, *Children of the Yellow Kid* (Seattle: University of Washington Press, 1998), 77.

Photography Credits and Permissions

Illustrations were courteously provided by and are used with permission of:

1. Del Norte County Historical Society—Crescent City, California
2. Humboldt County Historical Society—Eureka, California
3. St. Louis Public Library
5. Allen-Littlefield Collection
7. Tubman African American Museum—Macon, Georgia
8. Margaret Alexander Alam
10. Tulsa Historical Society via Alfred L. Brophy
11. Allen-Littlefield Collection
15. Tamiment Library, New York University
16. Kurt Vonnegut
18. Western Historical Manuscript Collection—University of Missouri, Columbia
19. *Hamilton Herald-News*—Hamilton, Texas
20. *Casey Reporter* (Illinois) via Carolyn Stephens
21. Dorothy Ring and Casey Township Library via Carolyn Stephens
24. Pekin Public Library—Pekin, Illinois
27. Shirley Manning
28. Utah State Historical Society, *Beehive History*
31. Bill Griffith
34. United Feature Syndicate

Index

Publishing in the Public Interest

Thank you for reading this book published by The New Press. The New Press is a nonprofit, public interest publisher. New Press books and authors play a crucial role in sparking conversations about the key political and social issues of our day.

We hope you enjoyed this book and that you will stay in touch with The New Press. Here are a few ways to stay up to date with our books, events, and the issues we cover:

- Sign up at www.thenewpress.com/subscribe to receive updates on New Press authors and issues and to be notified about local events
- Like us on Facebook: www.facebook.com/newpressbooks
- Follow us on Twitter: www.twitter.com/thenewpress

Please consider buying New Press books for yourself; for friends and family; or to donate to schools, libraries, community centers, prison libraries, and other organizations involved with the issues our authors write about.

The New Press is a 501(c)(3) nonprofit organization. You can also support our work with a tax-deductible gift by visiting www.thenewpress.com/donate.